# *Praise for*
# MASTERING TRADITIONAL A

CW01498825

"Drawing from Hellenistic, Medieval, and Renaissance au
presents a beautifully written and clearly explained trea̶t̶i̶s̶e̶ ̶a̶b̶o̶u̶t̶ ̶t̶h̶e̶ ̶o̶n̶g̶o̶i̶n̶g̶
development of traditional astrology and its relevance to contemporary practice.
Grounding his approach with chapters on cosmology and astronomy, he adds his own
insightful and generous commentary throughout the text, explaining various ways to
interpret the doctrines and apply them in chart examples. A brilliant first book."
– **DEMETRA GEORGE**, author of *Ancient Astrology in Theory and Practice, volumes* 1 *&* 2

"At last, here is a text that truly gives an astrologer context and meaning to the art. Mychal's
vast knowledge of spiritual and cosmological systems creates a solid philosophical
foundation to underpin his lucid technical explanations of every traditional concept.
The result is the most extraordinary and comprehensive book of instruction in
traditional astrology that has existed in modern times. Not only does it explain the
reason behind each astrological method, it clarifies common misunderstandings,
resolves confusions in ancients texts and corrects the errors time has wrought.

This book doesn't just cover all the foundations of traditional astrology with
unprecedented depth and clarity, it answers all the difficult questions modern students
have such as what to do with modern planets and how to make sense of contradictory
teachings about aspects. It empowers the fledging astrologer to confidently stand on
the firm ground of justifiable, informed judgements.

It is said that every generation needs a new beginner's book so as to receive knowledge
in their own contemporary voice. *Mastering Traditional Astrology* is not merely that
voice for the many who have been drawn back to the art in the twenty-first century, it
is truly a book for the ages."
– **ROD SUSKIN**, author of *Synastry: Understanding the Astrology of Relationships*

"It is exceedingly rare to see the topic of astrology presented within the full context of
its history, esoteric philosophy, and practice. Rarer still is the author who can elucidate
this material with both thoroughness and grace. In this landmark work, Mychal A.
Bryan accomplishes all of this, while also masterfully weaving a story about the real
meaning astrology can bring to our lives."

– **DR. DAVID SHOEMAKER**, clinical psychologist, esoteric teacher, & author of
*Living Thelema*

*For my gods, my ancestors, my students, & the students of my students –*

*both this book & my life are for you.*

*The beginning of wisdom
is the fear of the Lord.*

PROVERBS 9:10

*For Nature is also rooted in God.*

Corpus Hermeticum 3:4

# MASTERING

# TRADITIONAL ASTROLOGY

*Praise for*
# MASTERING TRADITIONAL ASTROLOGY

"*Mastering Traditional Astrology* may well be the most comprehensive book on traditional Western astrology ever written. Mychal's work remediates his own observation "The dumbing down of astrology is a modern convention." If you aspire to become a skilled and genuine practitioner, then this book is for you!

Today's astrological student is well advised to comprehend the roots of their ancient and venerable craft. Mychal A. Bryan's brilliant debut work guides you toward this needful goal. Personally, I was astonished and thrilled by the breadth, depth and clarity of this book, including many helpful illustrations.

The rounded inclusiveness of material is a treat. The reader is guided through ancient mystical paradigms, history, astronomy, plus your traditional reading room techniques - all with the same crystalline precision. Truly, Mychal is one of those few geniuses born to each century who carries the flame of our Western astrological heritage forth through time and generations."
– **JUDITH HILL**, President & Founder of *The Academy for Astrological Medicine*, author of *Medical Astrology: A Guide to Planetary Pathology*

"In *Mastering Traditional Astrology*, Mychal A. Bryan presents a clearly explained compendium of the core ideas and philosophical underpinnings of Western astrology. As if this weren't enough, he also outlines an orderly and systematic approach, informed by his own extensive astrological experience, to learning these concepts and applying them in practice to actual charts. The result is a highly useful text which will be treasured by both students and more advanced practitioners of the art."
– **ANTHONY LOUIS**, author of *Horary Astrology: Plain & Simple*

"I thoroughly enjoyed reading *Mastering Traditional Astrology*, and would recommend this book to all students of astrology. Mychal A. Bryan is a gifted writer, as well as an accomplished astrologer, with a deep knowledge of esoteric doctrines. For me, the uniqueness of his book lies in the fact that he shows how traditional astrology is an integral part of the larger system we know as Western esotericism. To my knowledge no such book has been published to date, and we should applaud the author for undertaking such a herculean task."
– **PETER STOCKINGER**, author of *William Lilly: The Last Magician, Adept & Astrologer*

"The author's passion for astrology is clearly visible and his familiarity with the reference material from traditional sources adds authenticity to his text. *Mastering Traditional Astrology* is an ambitious study of traditional astrology with a comprehensive list of topics and in-depth explanations of various astrological principles."
– **JOY USHER**, author of *A Tiny Universe: Astrology and The Thema Mundi Chart*

# Mastering
# Traditional Astrology

## A Depth of Beginning in the Celestial Art

\*

### Mychal A. Bryan

Oraculos Press

2023

First Edition, Oraculos Press Ltd., 2023
© Mychal A. Bryan 2023

www.oraculosastrology.com

ISBN: 979-8-9881009-5-9

For information, address: hello@oraculosastrology.com

COVER IMAGE: *Josef Bartoň*
CALLIGRAPHY: *Izzy Pludwinski*
COVER DESIGN: *Joseph Uccello | Umamah Nawaz*
AUTHOR PORTRAIT: *Cameron Salvatore*
GRAPHIC DESIGN: *Umamah Nawaz*
INDEX: *Philip Graves*
TYPESETTING: *Umamah Nawaz | George Kirilov | Mychal A. Bryan*

# CONTENTS

i

# PART 3

# PART 4

# LIST OF FIGURES

## CHAPTER 4 – A PRIMER IN ASTROLOGICAL SYMBOLISM

## CHAPTER 5 – ASTRONOMY OF ASTROLOGY

CHAPTER 23 – The Practice of Concrete Astrology

# LIST OF TABLES

CHAPTER 12 – Essential Dignities & Debilities in Practice

CHAPTER 13 – On Reception & Mutual Reception

CHAPTER 14 – Exaltations of the Planets

CHAPTER 15 – Triplicity Rulership

# SYMBOLS AND ABBREVIATIONS USED IN THIS BOOK

### CLASSICAL PLANETS

♄ SATURN (SA)

♃ JUPITER (JU)

♂ MARS (MA)

☉ SUN (SO)*

♀ VENUS (VE)

☿ MERCURY (ME)

☽ MOON (MO)

### MODERN PLANETS

♅ URANUS (UR)

♆ NEPTUNE (NE)

♇ PLUTO (PL)

### CELESTIAL FACTORS

⊕ EARTH (ER)

⊗ PART OF FORTUNE (POF)

☊ NORTH NODE (NN)

☋ SOUTH NODE (SN)

### SIGNS

♈ ARIES (ARI)

♉ TAURUS (TAU)

♊ GEMINI (GEM)

♋ CANCER (CAN)

♌ LEO (LEO)

♍ VIRGO (VIR)

♎ LIBRA (LIB)

♏ SCORPIO (SCO)

♐ SAGITTARIUS (SAG)

♑ CAPRICORN (CAP)

♒ AQUARIUS (AQU)

♓ PISCES (PIS)

### ASPECTS

✶ SEXTILE (60 °)

□ SQUARE (90 °)

△ TRINE (120 °)

☍ OPPOSITION (180 °)

☌ CONJUNCTION (00 °)**

### AUXILIARY ASPECTS

∠ SEMI-SQUARE (45°)

⚼ SESQUIQUADRATE (135°)

|| PARALLEL

# CONTRA-PARALLEL

### ELEMENTS

△ FIRE

△ AIR

▽ WATER

▽ EARTH

### ALCHEMICAL PRINCIPLES

☿ MERCURY

🜍 SULFUR

🜔 SALT

### ABBREVIATIONS

ASC — ASCENDANT

DSC — DESCENDANT

MC — MEDIUM COELI

IC — IMUM COELI

S — STATION

Rx. — RETROGRADE (℞)

SR — STATION RETROGRADE

SD — STATION DIRECT

### NON-ASPECTS

⚺ SEMI-SEXTILE

⚻ QUINCUNX

---

*These abbreviations are taken from the German schools of Uranian Astrology and Cosmobiology.
The German name for the Sun is "Sonne." Thus, the abbreviation for the Sun is SO and not SU.
** The conjunction is included amongst the aspects, even though it is not technically an aspect.

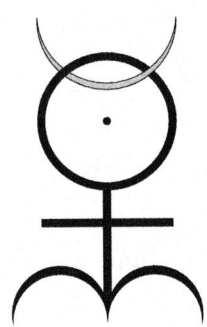

# Acknowledgments

I BECAME A STUDENT OF ASTROLOGY, Tarot, magic, and Jewish mysticism at a very young age. I grew up deeply imbedded in an orthodox Christian environment. My parents, grandparents, and their parents had all been Seventh-day Adventists. No one wore jewelry and women only wore skirts. The outside world ceased to exist on Friday evening, the movie theatre was the invention of the devil himself, and heaven forbid anyone should drink a Coca-Cola, or even harbor a secret craving for anything remotely caffeinated. I went to an Adventist preschool, primary school, high school, and university. Every facet of my education was heavily Bible-based; which means that every step of the way, I got in trouble for my strange interests.

As a child, I've had my books burned. My first semester in university, my Tarot cards and runes were confiscated – thrown into the same locked cabinet with the porn, drugs, and weapons of the other boys on my dorm. I've been baptized and prayed over; and faced expulsion on at least one occasion for "believing the wrong thing." There have been many attempts within my childhood to squash this book out of my heart and soul. *We almost didn't make it.* And yet, in what feels like a lifetime later, I present this book to you as a glorious testament of my love for the wisdom and the magic of the ancient world. Somewhere along the way, I feel my journey has been guided – by powerful hands whose owners I will never know. To the ancestors and old gods who have kept me through all of these experiences, I thank you.

It takes a very special household to see a weird child being weird and to let him be himself. Though my magical interests often clashed with the faith of my family, for the most part I was left alone; to grow and to flourish and to engage in a rigorous self-education in the Western mystery tradition. They even snuck me to the movie theatre on occasion to consort with the devil and the minions of hell. I am grateful that my family gave me the space to be weird enough for long enough so that I could turn my weirdness into a profession.

Thank you to my mother for sending her friends to me to get readings. I sold my first written report to her boss when I was sixteen years old. For my mother, it was more important to have children she could brag about than to have children that were pleasing to the Seventh-day Adventist church. My budding mystical abilities gave her bragging rights. I was a grade A student *and* I could tell the future. Thank you to my father who – after seeing the Israeli psychic Uri Geller bend spoons with his mind – rushed to the kitchen and brought me the thinnest spoon he could find so that I'd have an easy go at it. Almost two decades later, it's still unbent. Thank you to my sister for sharing the love of magic with me when we were young. Thank you to my aunt for allowing me to give paid readings to the patrons of her nail salon when I was only thirteen years old. All of you have inadvertently aided me in becoming the astrologer I am today. And to the grandfather who I never met: thank you for being interested in astronomy and mysticism even though you were a devout Christian. I will never know why. The mystery of who you were will always intrigue me.

The back cover of this book says that it was made "in the classroom for the classroom" and that is very true. This book was made over the course of six years for my students. It would not have been possible without their praise and their criticism. To all the students who have assisted along the way, I thank you.

Thanks to SHANE POWERS who first took on the task of reviewing this book in 2021, long before it was fit to be published. Shane taught me that some things were better heard when whispered, and that other things were better left unsaid. He tactfully bludgeoned the raw bones of this book into a pulp – a humbling experience that I sincerely needed.

Thanks to AILIN LU for making a plan to see this book through to its completion. Thanks to my student, author TRACEY PACELLI, for reading the very rough early manuscript. Thanks to JACK KOVALESKI for also reading the first draft and enjoying the Mychalness and the humor within the work. You made me feel like it was worth reading and writing. Thanks to MARTHA KUEHN who simultaneously reviewed each chapter while being a student in the course this book is based on. Your practical observations and requests were very much appreciated. Thank you for also crafting such a heartfelt Foreword.

Thanks to ANDRÉ DIAS. Even though he had already read this book once, he was still willing to listen to me read it out loud, giving me insightful feedback along the way. You've given me exactly the moral support and honesty I've needed to continue this journey. RAJESHRI BASU met with me during the days and times when André could not. Without the two of you, this book could never have been completed on time. I love you both.

I believe some of the brightest thinkers in Western astrology are: ANTHONY LOUIS, KENNETH BOWSER, RUMEN KOLEV, and GARY CHRISTEN. The four of them reviewed various sections of this book. I could not be more humbled and honored.

My immense gratitude goes out to ANTHONY LOUIS. Tony reviewed this book with jaw-dropping speed in the course of two weeks when both of us were very sick. I thought he had just skimmed through it and had gone to the parts that interested him; but he read every word of 139 pages in the very first night of me sending it. I couldn't pay for someone to do a faster, more incisive job. KENNETH BOWSER similarly was very fast in his review and feedback. After giving me a proper literary thrashing, his follow up e-mail to me said "should I continue?" I said yes. His critical eye made this an even better text. Ironically, he – like Tony – was also sick when he made his revisions. Maybe that's a sign.

GARY CHRISTEN laid out the initial groundwork for the diagrams in the chapter on astronomy. He also gave very helpful feedback regarding how I structured that chapter. Thank you, Gary, for your support.

My deepest gratitude goes out to Grandmaster of Memory KEVIN HORSLEY. Kevin planted the seed of self-publishing within me long before I felt the impulse to write this book. He said, "I uploaded one Word document and I've never had to work another day in my life." Words like that have most certainly contributed to the creation of a book like this. Let's see where this road takes us.

CHRIS BRENNAN – you have my deep gratitude. You are the one who made me feel like I could successfully self-publish, even when people told me it was a crazy idea. Chris talked me through every step of this process. He told me the team I needed to build. He even showed me how much money he was making from book sales as a self-published author. Without that conversation, this project would have gone down a very disappointing path.

I am deeply grateful to DR. BENJAMIN DYKES. Ben took the time to talk me through last minute concerns I had as a self-published author. He also gave his permission for me to use many of the quotes that populate this book from his translations of ancient astrologers.

My gratitude goes out to AARON CHEAK. Aaron helped me form a team consisting of JEZABEL GARCÍA and JOSEPH UCCELLO. Jezabel gave invaluable guidance regarding structure and content, and transformed blocks of dense text into reader-friendly tables. Thank you for your contribution. Joseph designed an extraordinary cover after countless iterations and was willing to follow my vision through to completion. Thank you.

To RICARDO GUEVARA, who laid out the initial designs for the diagrams that populate this book. This was a mammoth task, but you've never left my side. Thank you for your wonderful work.

Two men singlehandedly took this book over its final creative hurdles towards its beautiful completion. GEORGE KIRILOV worked tirelessly with me to make sure that the typesetting was consistent, organized, and perfect. UMAMAH NAWAZ worked for one month with me, seven to fifteen hours each day in order to triple check every diagram and redesign them in a way that met my very high standards. Thank you both for creating a beautiful container for my words and ideas to shine magnificently within the world.

ELIZABETH GOFFE ran my school and managed my clients while I was deep in the trenches of bringing this book to life. The ship of Oraculos would likely have crashed and burned if you weren't at the helm. Thank you for your support.

My absolute gratitude goes to PHILIP GRAVES. Philip was the last person to review this book before it went out for publication. After at least a dozen other people had reviewed it, there were still tiny pernicious typographical errors tucked discretely within blocks of text. Philip reviewed every page and did an extraordinary job at finding them and bringing them to my attention. Philip also created an impeccable index, infinitely more detailed than I could ever have imagined. Philip's devotion to this project has enormously increased the overall value of this book.

Attending dance school in Cuba and studying Iyengar Yoga have taught me how to teach well. In particular, Senior Certified Iyengar Yoga Teacher LOIS STEINBERG trained me from absolutely nothing and turned me into the Certified Iyengar Yoga Teacher I am today. She taught me not just how to be a practitioner, but how to be a technician. Those skills of systematic intelligence have translated into how I teach everything. They have definitely been applied in how I organize the larger curriculum of my astrological teaching and the content of this book. Thank you for your impact on my life.

My calligraphy teacher, world-renowned Hebrew calligrapher and author of *Mastering Hebrew Calligraphy* IZZY PLUDWINSKI listened to my tales of every loss and victory I experienced on the path towards publishing this book. He gave his time and energy to helping me figure out how to successfully self-publish, for which I am eternally grateful. A fun fact about this book is that its original name was *Foundations of Classical Astrology*. After deciding that no one would buy a book with a name as boring as that, I chose to follow Izzy's lead and came up with the name *Mastering Traditional Astrology* instead. Izzy is also responsible for the artwork that can be found on the inner front and back covers of this book. Thank you for blessing my work.

To MEIRA EPSTEIN and LEE LEHMAN, my two greatest traditional astrology influences. You introduced me to the names of the ancient astrologers who I have devoted my life to studying. You taught me how to form opinions from reading primary sources, regardless of the overarching astrological consensus. You showed me how knowing traditional astrology laid the foundation for me to do anything I wanted to do in life astrologically. You taught me that in putting first things first, traditional astrology was the foundation. Thank you, Meira, for also introducing me to Uranian Astrology. I pray to live long enough so that I can one day publish a book on that topic as well.

And finally, to all my astrology mentors and teachers throughout time. I chose to consistently work with you because you epitomize excellence in our field. You represent concrete, real, event-based astrology. You were the template of what it meant for me to practice astrology that can be proven. You taught me how to be the best, because you were the best first: MEIRA EPSTEIN, LEE LEHMAN, GARY CHRISTEN, JUDITH HILL, FAITH MCINERNEY, CHRISTEEN SKINNER, NICOLA SMUTS-ALLSOP, and everyone else who has illuminated my astrological path with your wisdom, your insight, your excitement, and love for astrology. All of us, the Children of Urania, shine brighter because of you.

# FOREWORD

*Welcome to Mastering Traditional Astrology!* This is a book that is designed to introduce you to the world of traditional astrology for the modern age. Mychal A. Bryan presents us with ancient wisdom, filtered through his extensive client experience and distilled for the contemporary student. He provides an approachable and engaging introduction to the basics of traditional astrology.

In my higher education career, I was a long-time college instructor of both psychology and yoga. I taught thousands of students, designed courses and selected and reviewed textbooks. I hired, supervised and evaluated liberal arts instructors when I worked as a college dean for several years. These experiences in academia have given me the ability to recognize high quality teaching and writing when I find it.

I have been a student of Mychal's since June 2022 when I enrolled in his Summer Horary Astrology Intensive. Recently retired, I had been exploring the wild and wide world of astrology on the internet. I found Mychal online when he took part in a panel discussion of astrological forecasts for 2022. His words resonated with me, and I followed up by scheduling a reading with him. The reading was just what I was looking for, and I have been Mychal's student at the Oraculos School of Astrology since then.

Mychal practices concrete, predictive astrology. While rooted in Renaissance astrology, he also weaves in more contemporary concepts from Uranian astrology. This blend of traditional and modern research-based methods creates a potent combination to delineate horoscopes. Mychal is an NCGR Level IV Certified Astrologer who combines teaching, research and client work.

Mychal is an incredible teacher. He combines his vast knowledge of traditional astrology with his personal warmth and love of teaching to create a community of learners. His classes are a crucible of learning where the instruction is rigorous, the pedagogy is sound, the students are a community, and a shared love of astrology brings people together across many differences. The online classes are intimate, and Mychal's obvious caring shines through everything that he does. Mychal's knowledge extends to many areas of esoteric wisdom and the Western mystery traditions, so his classes are sprinkled with gems from alchemy, the tarot and other methods of divination. He is able to apply metaphysical concepts on a concrete level and interpret challenging themes in a manner that is both coherent and compassionate.

Mychal wrote this book to serve as a textbook for beginning students, especially those in his *Foundations of Classical Astrology* program. In *Mastering Traditional Astrology*, he curates and interprets the works of classical astrologers such as Marcus Manilius, Abraham Ibn Ezra, Guido Bonatti, and William Lilly, making this ancient material accessible to the modern astrology student. Mychal teaches with heart, warmth and humor, and he writes with these qualities as well. This book provides an excellent overview of traditional astrology for the beginning student. Full of charts, quotes, tables and examples, it is both approachable and comprehensive. His love of language shines through his writing and shines a light on the ancient texts as well. The result of this is a book that is clear, accessible and rigorous, providing a practical and applied introduction to traditional astrology while integrating the modern planets as well.

By curating and interpreting classical astrological writings, *Mastering Traditional Astrology* makes this material accessible to the modern student. This book gives the beginning student access to invaluable materials without having to wade through challenging translations of primary sources. *Mastering Traditional Astrology* is a book that is focused on practice rather than history. Mychal has sifted through and condensed a vast amount of material, and based on his years of practice has produced a book that distills what the contemporary student needs to know as they prepare to practice astrology. It is a book that is written from the trenches, for the student who wishes to practice concrete, event-based traditional astrology.

*Mastering Traditional Astrology* is constructed as Mychal's classes are constructed: mindfully, analytically, and sequenced so that each new element builds upon what has already been presented. This method of organization allows the student to systematically construct their understanding of traditional astrology in a logical fashion, and the result is solid learning of fundamental astrological frameworks. From basic astronomy to learning how to integrate concepts such as essential dignity and accidental debility, Mychal leads the reader down the path of learning towards becoming a professional astrologer. His well-developed rubrics allow the reader to systematically approach chart delineation in a confident, concrete and orderly manner.

*Mastering Traditional Astrology* is intended to be the first book in a series for the contemporary student. Horary astrology is the focus of the next book, inviting the reader to practice applying the principles of traditional astrology to divine answers to significant questions. Mychal views horary as an appropriate first practice of astrology as it is less personal than natal astrology, allowing the student to grow their skills in a more dispassionate manner than natal astrology allows. Future books will cover the full two-year diploma curriculum at the Oraculos School of Astrology.

I am confident that you will find this book to be an indispensable addition to your astrological library, and a valuable guide to learning concrete predictive astrology.

MARTHA KUEHN
Brainerd, Minnesota
JANUARY 2023

# Preface

## The Purpose of this Book

A NY BOOK CAN TEACH YOU A LITTLE something about astrology. This book will teach you how to be an astrologer. I've dedicated my life to the craftsmanship of good astrology, and I know a thing or two about training students to become excellent practitioners within this field. Don't get me wrong: this is by no means an easy feat. Despite popular belief, astrology is a very difficult subject. You can't learn it in a weekend intensive; and it isn't as simple as memorizing the signs of the zodiac. No newspaper horoscope you've read has ever done it justice, and your best friend's cousin Cindy who gives readings at birthday parties – she more than likely isn't that good. Most people you'll meet in public who say that they, too, are astrologers, can't tell you the difference between the Equator and a flying meatball. There is no single factor that captures your entire story within your birth chart. Regardless of what anyone tells you, unravelling the mysteries of your North Node and Pluto don't even begin to scratch the surface of what makes you a complex human being. Learning how to be a technically proficient astrologer is as difficult as learning to speak a new language. Like learning a foreign language, mastering astrology is as equally rewarding.

Astrology is the method of predicting the impact of celestial forces upon earthly life. More than that, it is a means of understanding how inevitable outcomes are the natural result of the combinations of specific stellar influences. In order to even begin to think in a way that will lead to effective astrology, you need a framework to guide how those thoughts will unfold. You'll need clarity and some level of training – whether that comes solely from trial and error or through the aid of a mentor. You'll need to cultivate the ability to ward off distractions that exist within a chart while in search of specific answers on a specific topic. You'll need to maintain the versatility to modify your interpretation as you pierce deeper still into the heart of the chart. You'll need intuition that has grown out of logic and experience, as well as a firm grasp of the real-world limitations of your astrological practice and abilities. You are not God. Astrology will not grant you infinite wisdom into the machinations of the cosmos. Though all-knowingness will never be yours no matter how good you become at your craft, you will still need to hone the ability to come to a definitive conclusion from a sea of a thousand possibilities. In a nutshell, you'll need to be sharp – sharp in a way that keeps you committed to providing a useful and practical service to people who come to you for help; sharp in a way that keeps pushing you towards growth. To this end, *Mastering Traditional Astrology* is the best place for you to begin this work of astrological refinement and study.

Astrology doesn't suffer from a lack of information. The principal challenge in astrology is that it has *too much* information. This often leads to a certain boundlessness within the practice of an untrained astrologer. They don't know what to say, when to say it, why not to say it, or when they've said enough. On a larger scale, this is reflected in how we teach and write about astrology. Clarity begets clarity. Clear, organized thinking makes for clear, organized astrology.

I created this book to be useful for the beginner student wanting to find a gateway into this field. Its purpose is to provide you with the foundational training you need at the start of your journey to becoming a professional astrologer. This book is not meant to be an exhaustive encyclopedia of every facet of classical astrology. I have taken the liberty to free both you and I of having to wade through countless pages outlining the historical transmission of astrology from the gods to humankind. I have chosen not to engage in the squabbles of who stole what from who – as to whether or not we in the West nicked our entire system from the Indians, or whether they were the ones who borrowed the entire kit and kaboodle from the Greeks. My intention is to help you cultivate a way of thinking that will be vital to how you professionally practice astrology later. Hopefully, you receive this as a kindness.

My training in astrology began at a young age. As a child I was curious about all things mysterious and magical. This led me to study Hermeticism, Qabalah, and the Tarot. It was sheer dumb luck that all of these traditions were based heavily on classical astrology. The desire to "get it right" forced me to give myself a comprehensive mystical education. When my efforts could take me no further, I sought out the best teachers to carry me the rest of the way. Through my years of apprenticeship, self-study, and practice, I have honed a distinct teaching style. My approach to astrological pedagogy has emerged out of my classical training as both a dancer and an Iyengar Yoga teacher.

I've taught astrology to many people – some who began practicing long before I was born – and the feedback I've received has been the same. How I organize the information of my teaching has given them more than the ability to just learn astrology. It has given them the confidence to practice astrology fearlessly and without feelings of personal inadequacy. Astrology, being the inexhaustible system of study that it is, provides many opportunities for both the beginning student and the advanced practitioner to feel inadequate.

Students often study astrology for years – attending every conference, purchasing every book, watching every video – all the while never feeling competent to pick up the mantle of a professional astrology practice. These students have informed me that in all their studies, they still don't know how to take the first steps in reading a chart. They've never been taught a consistently sequential system in order to begin, maintain, and confidently end a reading. Knowing that they technically should have enough knowledge to start a practice, yet still feeling highly incompetent, these students challenge themselves to overcome these genuine doubts by taking on clients. For fear of leaving things out, they have gone on to give lengthy readings, as long as three-hours in some cases. This is a tedious and nebulous performance that neither has a sense of direction nor a center of gravity. It is waste of both words and time that leaves their clients no wiser than before the reading began.

Practicing astrology purely based on intuition, without a larger structure or framework of *how to practice* is an exhausting endeavor, both for the practitioner and their "clients." This common and disorganized approach is often rooted in those students being uncertain about how the various parts of astrology fit together in general. They know they use a zodiac of twelve signs, but they don't know why. They know they prefer tropical to sidereal astrology, but they don't really understand the difference. They know there are four elements, but they also know some people include a fifth element called "spirit" or "aether." They have no idea why a four-element system was chosen for traditional astrology in light of this other option. They may have a strong orientation towards traditional astrology, yet even within that, they may find room for confusion. They see some traditional astrologers using the modern planets of Uranus, Neptune, and Pluto, without understanding why these non-traditional factors would be integrated into a traditional astrological practice at all. At the same time, they see other traditional astrologers vehemently against including anything into their astrological toolkit that wasn't in use two thousand years ago. As a means of filling these deficits within their knowledge, these students seek out answers from sources that have none to give – further muddying the waters of their confusion. The accumulative effect of not knowing why we practice in the way we do, inevitably leads to a deep sense of paralysis and anxiety. Some students have expressed feeling like frauds or as if they are unfit to be astrologers, even while knowing they have done enough study not to feel that way.

At the end of studying with me, students no longer feel ill-equipped to perform a confident act of astrology. The hallmark of their experience of both learning and practicing in this way is *clarity*. I organize the body of my astrological teaching in the same way I would a curriculum for teaching dance or Iyengar Yoga: sequentially, intentionally, and meticulously. I hope to share that same experience with you here.

This book provides questions, exercises, and prompts at the end of each chapter, making it a valuable self-study textbook that can also be used in a larger class setting. At the same time, the text is meant to read as prose. My intention is for students to feel as if they are entering a conversation about astrology as opposed to reading a textbook on the subject. It is my hope that the conversation within this book is one which will inspire students to return to it often throughout their astrological careers.

## CURRICULUM AND APPROACH

I have written this book in the style of a "Book of Reasons" – a classical approach to astrology texts that I appreciate and enjoy. It is my intention to present within this and future publications the entire two-year diploma program that I offer at Oraculos School of Astrology (OSA). This book represents the first two modules of the first semester of that program. What this means is that everything I believe a new student should learn within their first two to three months of studying astrology is written within this book.

There is no shortage of astrology books that exist. Hundreds, if not thousands, have been written with the intention of shedding light on the subject of astrology for the beginner student. In many modern texts we can learn about techniques, ancient astrologers, and different trends within our astrological history. Few authors tackle the wider topic of why things are done the way they are or why the ancients conceived of these principles and practices in the ways they did. This has left a hole within the heart of the revivalist movement in traditional astrology. It has created a generation of traditional and modern astrology practitioners ill-informed about their roots. The renewal of interest in ancient astrology has brought with it a burning desire in people to learn about the subject. This should also lead us in the direction of reclaiming the philosophically elegant cosmology that the ancients left us – one in which astrology naturally makes sense.

This book is that reclamation. In it, I offer my understanding of what the ancients taught. It is my attempt to expand on what they discovered; to continue walking this path by means of their light. This book is a celebration of the very real way in which the wisdom of our ancestors still has the power to amplify our modern experience of living.

As a rule, I believe in the distillation of everything to its fundamental principles. This is because – as a rule – I believe that knowledge must be made simple in order for it to be useful. I have no intention in writing a useless book; one that flaunts my scholarship by sharing things that ultimately have no relevance in the formation of a full-fledged journeyman astrologer. My intention in writing this book is to share the systematic intelligence that is the hallmark of the education I have provided my students for years. Clarity, compassion, and the ability to organize information are the traits of a great astrologer. Compassion demands that this be a simple book so that anyone who picks it up can feel as if their journey to becoming an astrologer is something that someone else cared about deeply. I do care: for the elevation of the standards surrounding how we teach and practice astrology. Most importantly, I care for you, gentle reader, who will blaze the path for the astrology of tomorrow. It is my deepest wish that through reading this book you may fully seize your divine birthright to grow and become wise, and use these timeless teachings to guide others deeply into the heart of wisdom.

Astrology is being called now, like never before, to rise to the occasion of guiding the soul in peril. As in every age, there are those within our field who see this as an opportunity for their advancement. Within every discipline there are charlatans with no true knowledge or ability to guide or lead. There are those who have no practice, who have not received direct teachings, and who have not perspired in the laboratory of constant trial and error in order to truly distill a body of concrete tools and skills *that work*. I have tilled the soil of that selfsame work, and so have the astrological elders with whom I've received a great portion of my training. Everyone who studies directly with me is held accountable to do the same. The world is now demanding more of those who call themselves astrologers. It is demanding depth of knowledge, a clear understanding of core principles, and most of all accuracy in concrete delineation.

The psychological astrology that ushered us into the new millennium has served our practice well. It has aided people in knowing themselves in a deeper way. It has helped them heal. However, it is not sufficient. It does not have the range to truly prove the validity of astrology in concrete ways in our modern world. Its very subjective parameters cannot be tested or verified in the manner that the astrology of the future must inevitably be. It cannot be trusted to bear the burden of proof. The scope of practice of the purely psychologically trained astrologer cannot match the full gamut of the human experience. It cannot truly begin to peel away the layers of concrete events that contribute to a person becoming exactly who they are. Sharper tools and a sharper mind are demanded of the astrologer now being called to stand on the world stage. Ultimately, the world is challenging us to present it with a more accurate and whole astrology.

We are in need of an astrology that respects itself enough to demand more of the people who call themselves astrologers. This new astrology must respect itself enough to demand excellence within the syllabi we teach from. And though we may attain all of this, in the words of nineteenth century astrologer Rupertus Stella "yet it is not sufficient." A constant striving towards mastery must be our goal – a mastery that has the potential to return our craft to its rightful place amongst the arts and sciences of an evolving global culture.

The astrology of tomorrow is an athletic creature. It is one that runs faster, jumps higher, and dives deeper through the use of tools that can provide tangible assistance to the soul in need. It does not deny the importance of soul and psyche. Rather, it shows how they are developed through both our physical and nonphysical engagement with the world around us. It provides commentary on real and tangible events that have occurred within people's lives, not fantastic stories of who they were in previous incarnations. The astrology of tomorrow is an astrology that is, above all, helpful. The astrology of tomorrow is, in a sense, *complete*.

My Guru BKS Iyengar is noted for having said that "a good book is better than a bad teacher." I hope you consider this to be a good book.

With all my love,


MYCHAL A. BRYAN
Jamaica Plain, Massachusetts
NOVEMBER 2022

# INTRODUCTION

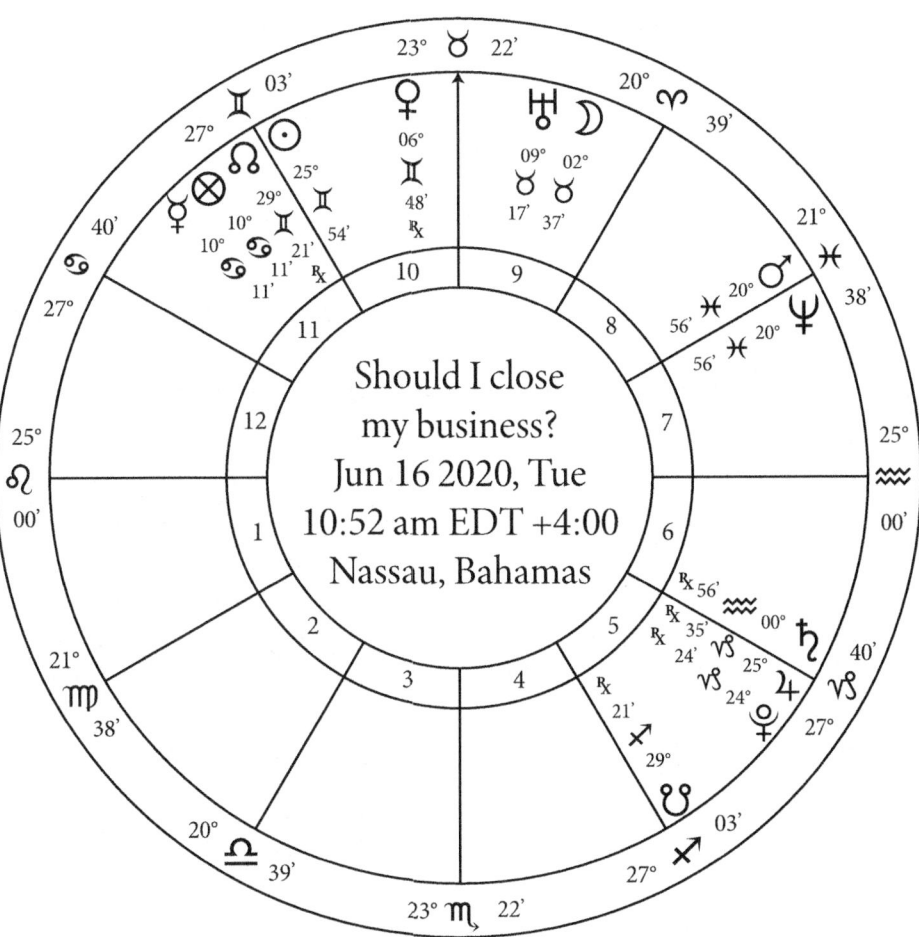

FIGURE 1: *Should I Close My Business ? (horary chart)*

Tᴴɪꜱ ɪꜱ ᴀɴ ᴀꜱᴛʀᴏʟᴏɢɪᴄᴀʟ ᴄʜᴀʀᴛ. A chart is sometimes called a nativity, scheme of heaven, radix, vitasphere, cosmogram, or horoscope. Although more common, "horoscope" isn't really the most appropriate term to describe the chart in its entirety. "Horoscope" is derived from the Greek "hōra" and "sko-pos" meaning "time" and "observer." Within a chart, this only defines the line that separates the first and twelfth house. It is also referred to as the Ascendant (ᴀꜱᴄ). We'll learn more about this later on.

7

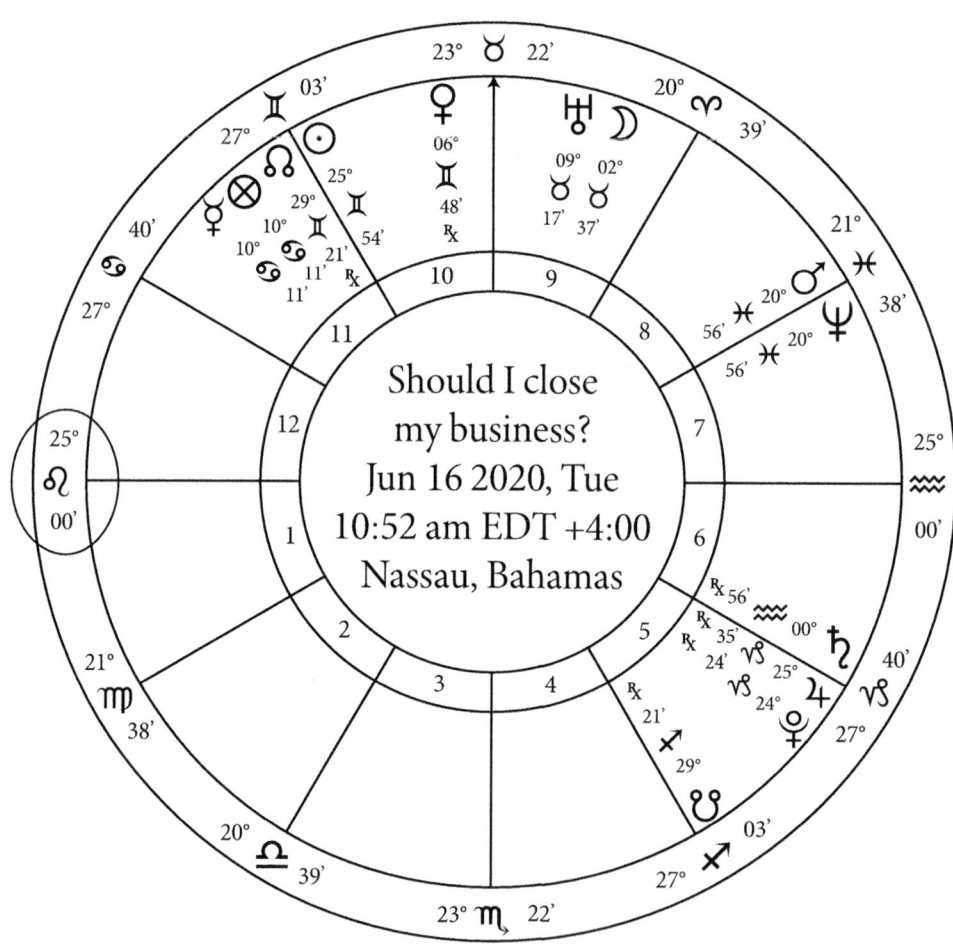

FIGURE 2: *Horoscope or Ascendant*

A chart is a map of the sky for a particular moment in time. It crystallizes what the sky looks like from our perspective on Earth, like a photograph that simultaneously shows the visible sky above and the non-visible sky below us.

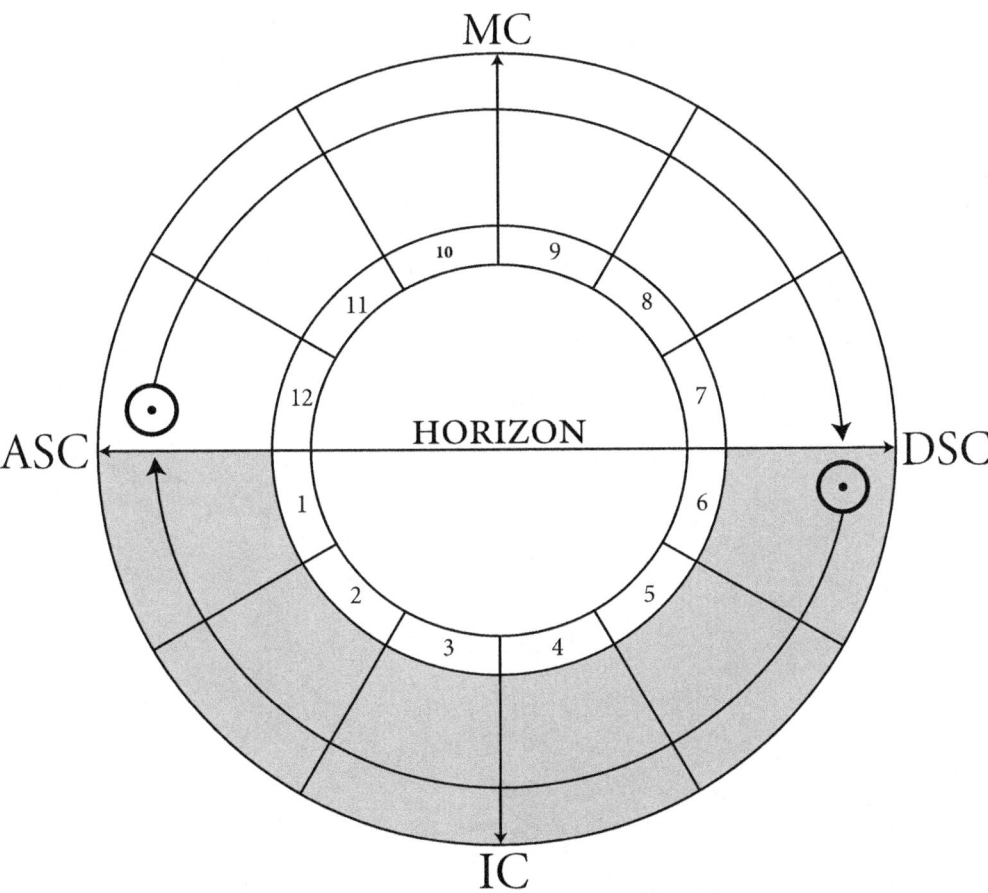

FIGURE 3: *Visible & Non-Visible Sky*

For astrologers, the heavens reflect the destiny of every person, place, or thing born under it. From the astrologer's point of view, a chart drawn for the beginning of an event describes both the unfolding and outcome of that event.

Charts can be drawn for any reason. Here are a few charts that serve very different purposes.

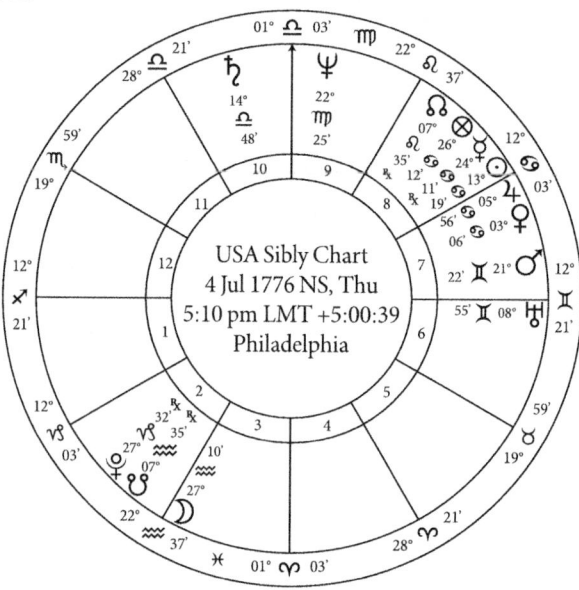

FIGURE 4. *The chart that astrologer Ebenezer Sibly considered to be the birth chart for the USA known as a mundane chart.*

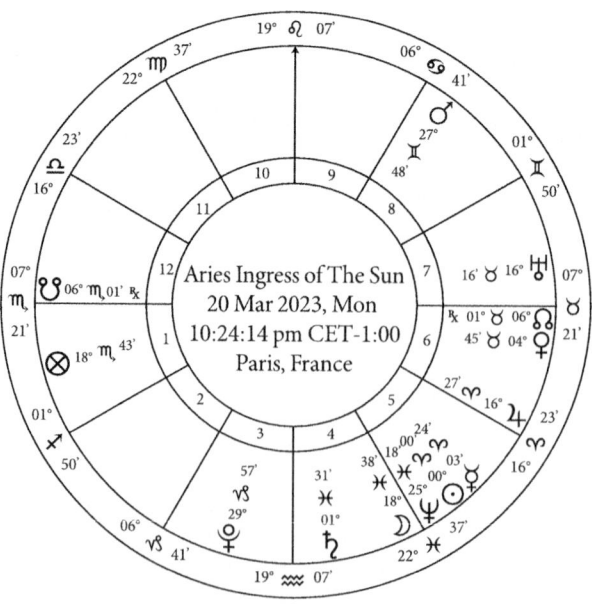

FIGURE 5. *The annual predictive chart for France known as the Aries Ingress chart, erected for the first day of Spring.*

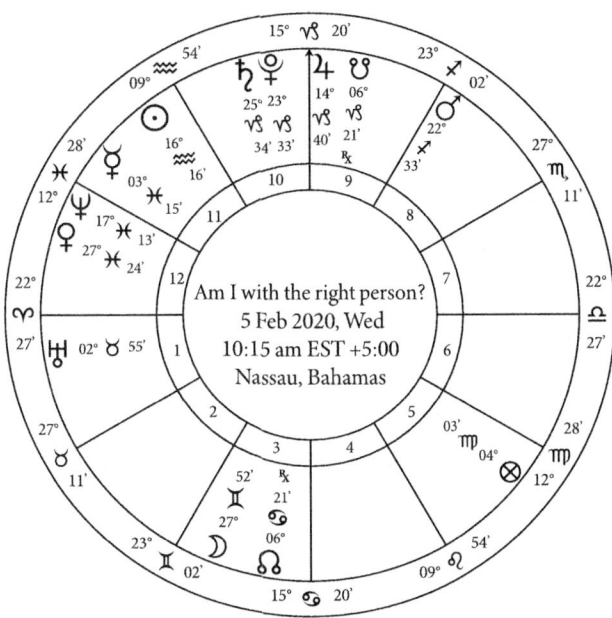

FIGURE 6. *The chart of the question*
*"Am I with the right person?" known as a horary chart.*

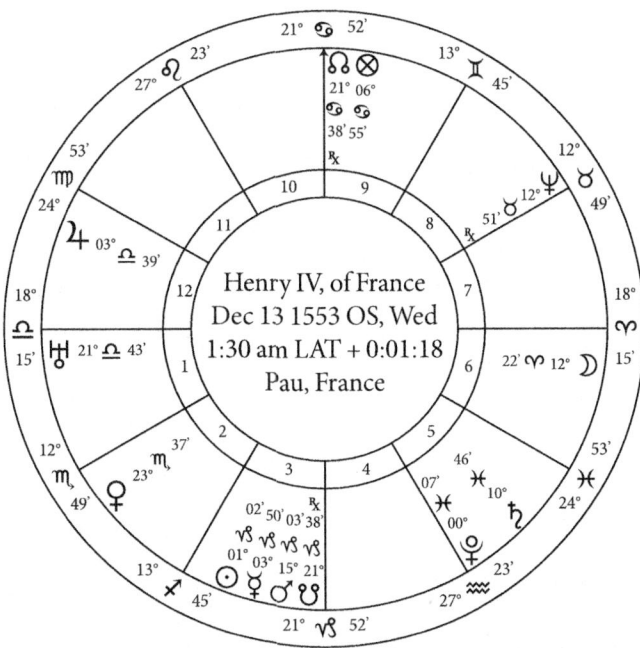

FIGURE 7. *The alleged birth chart of King Henry IV*
*known as a nativity or natal chart.*

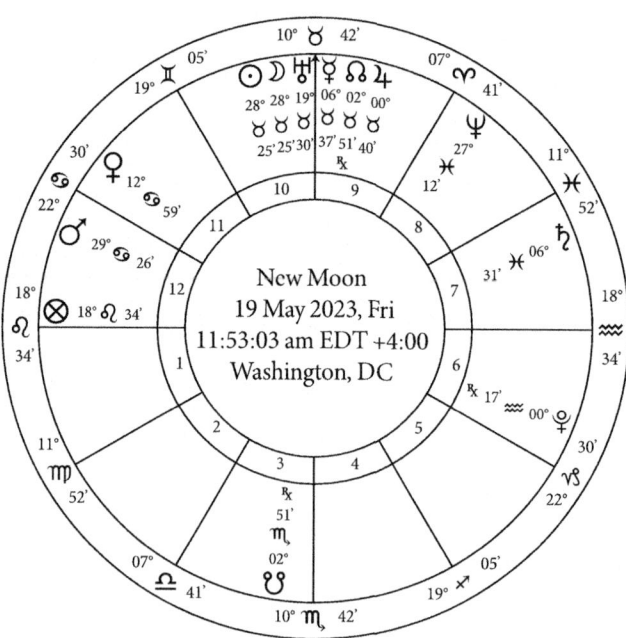

FIGURE 8. *A New Moon chart for Washington, DC known as a lunation chart.*

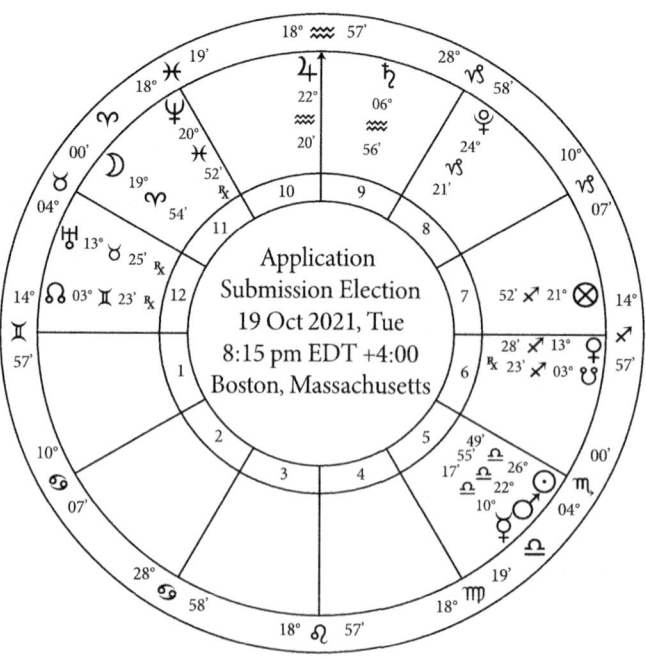

FIGURE 9. *The chart that was chosen for the launch of a creative project, known as an electional chart.*

These charts look very similar. That is because they all include the same components.

1. Each chart has thirteen celestial factors (ten planets, two lunar nodes, and the Part of Fortune).
2. Each of these factors can be found in one or another of the twelve sections of the chart known as the "terrestrial houses."
3. These twelve houses (and the locations of the planets within them) are projected against a backdrop of twelve signs, known as the "zodiac." The signs of the zodiac are referred to as the "celestial houses" in traditional astrology to distinguish them from the twelve terrestrial houses. These twelve signs are also known as the "domiciles" or homes of the planets.

We will explore these factors (planets, houses, and signs) in their respective chapters. The thirteen celestial factors have a constantly changing relationship to the backdrop of the zodiac. The twelve terrestrial houses can vary tremendously in their sizes based on the time and location that a chart is erected. This, combined with the movement of the thirteen celestial factors, makes every chart unique.

Another important point is that houses aren't signs and signs aren't houses. They represent two completely different symbolic systems that each have their own beautiful and philosophically rich reasons for existing. Philosophically speaking, they are quite independent of each other.

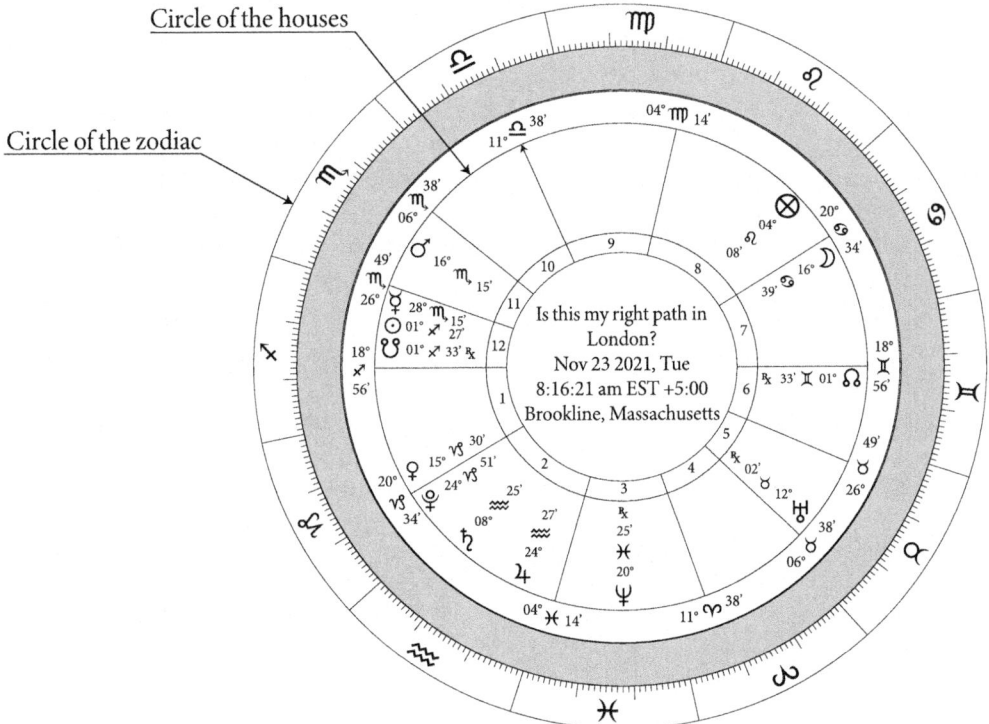

FIGURE 10: *Zodiacal Wheel (outer) vs. Terrestrial Houses (inner)*

We begin our astrological journey here: through looking at charts and gaining a basic understanding of what we are seeing. Admittedly, if this is your first time learning astrology, this may feel like jumping in off the deep end. This is a vital part of the process. The sooner we start seeing charts and getting comfortable with their landscape, the easier our astrological studies will be.

Take another look at our list of charts and study them closely. They've mapped the sky at different times on different dates, from different locations, for different purposes. Each chart has a unique planetary arrangement. The sky above us is constantly changing due to the whirling of the planets. Even if the planets are moving minimally, they are still moving at their individual rates of motion.

Comparing these charts is similar to comparing books of different topics that are written in the same language. One book may be a textbook on the political history of a country. In our chart examples, this would correspond to the mundane chart for the USA. Another book may be a deeply personal story about a woman's struggle with her husband's infidelity. This novel would correspond with our horary chart. Another book may be an autobiography, which is an apt description for the natal chart. Another may be an outline for creating a successful event, which perfectly describes the rationale behind an electional chart. All of these "books" may look the same on the surface. Upon reading them, however, we find that they serve vastly different purposes.

Reading an astrological chart is a bit different from reading a book. When we read a book, we automatically know what that book is about. However, if we were to find ourselves surrounded by a sea of unlabeled astrological charts, we would have no idea what person, place, or thing each chart was meant to describe. In order for us to read a chart, we have to first know what type of chart we are reading. At first glance, each chart may look the same, but we wouldn't read a mundane chart in the same way we would read a natal chart. It would also make no sense for us to try to read an electional chart in the same way we would read a horary. Nothing about the chart itself will tell us what its purpose is unless we know which branch of astrology it corresponds with. Each branch of astrology requires its own investment of time and study. Talking about the future of a country is quite different from talking about the destiny of a person.

The student who is well-versed in the language of all astrology will become far more skillful than the student who only focuses on one of its branches. I believe that astrology has to be understood as a universal subject before specializing in a particular part of it. This is the holistic approach to teaching I offer my students, and it is this approach that I offer you within this book.

# A Technical
# Depth of Beginning

**B**EFORE TAKING THE ASTROLOGICAL PLUNGE, it is important to first lay a technical foundation. After all, astrology is a technical art. This foundation will allow you to understand what you are seeing when you look at a chart. It will also give you the ability to approach the assignments at the end of each chapter in a more confident way.

Here is a chart.

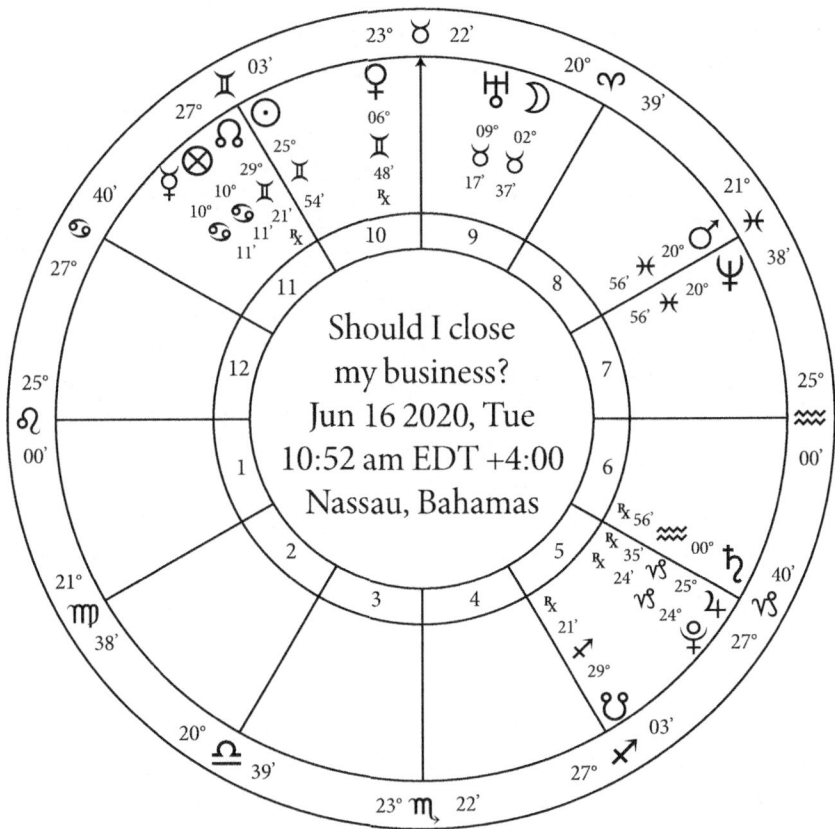

LATITUDE: 25° N 05' LONGITUDE: 077° W 21'
GEOCENTRIC | TROPICAL | REGIOMONTANUS | MEAN NODE

FIGURE 1: *Horary Sample Chart*

Every chart is both time-based and location-based. On the previous page, you saw the information required for casting that chart. Included was the title of the chart, as well as the date, time, and location that chart was erected.

GEOGRAPHICAL LONGITUDE AND LATITUDE

The geographical coordinates allow us to erect the correct chart. Without knowing these coordinates, we would never be able to cast an accurate figure.

25° N 05' refers to the geographical latitude of Nassau, Bahamas. 077° W 21' refers to the geographical longitude of Nassau, Bahamas. On the Earth, circles of geographical latitude will always be measured North or South of the Equator. On the other hand, circles of geographical longitude will always be measured East or West of the prime meridian, also known as the "Greenwich Meridian." The furthest latitudes from the Equator are 90° North at the North Pole and 90° South at the South Pole. The furthest geographical longitude from the prime meridian is called the "antimeridian." It is 180° away from the prime meridian. It passes through parts of Russia, Fiji, and near to the Aleutian Islands of Alaska.

The word "geocentric" refers to the Earth-based perspective from which we see the universe. The alternative to this is the "heliocentric" model, which uses the Sun as the central point of reference for observing the universe. We live on the Earth and not the Sun. Thus, we practice geocentric astrology, even though we know we live in a heliocentric (solar) system. Astrology is meant to help us understand why we are the way we are. However, this can only be accomplished from the perspective of where we are. We are on Earth. Therefore, geocentric astrology gives us an Earth-based commentary on how we are meant to navigate our journey through the world. We'll discuss all of these astronomical considerations in far greater detail later on.

The word "tropical" refers to the type of zodiac we use. We use the tropical zodiac, which is different from the constellational zodiac and the sidereal zodiac. We will discuss these three zodiacs in the chapter on *Astronomy of Astrology*.

"Regiomontanus" refers to the specific house system we use. A house system is how we divide the space around our Earth in order to derive what are known as the "twelve terrestrial houses." These houses help us understand the important areas of life. They also help us understand who we are and how we relate to the material world around us. Regiomontanus isn't the only house system used in astrology, but it is the only house system we will be using consistently within this book.

"Mean Node" refers to the North and South Nodes of the Moon. The Nodes can either be the true nodes or the mean nodes. In general, the nodes move backward through the zodiac. The true nodes tend to wobble a bit in their backward motion. Sometimes they are moving backwards and at other times they are not. The mean nodes, on the other hand, consistently move in a backward direction throughout the zodiac without this "wobble." The mean node is what was used in traditional astrology in the seventeenth century. Therefore, we will use the mean nodes within our work.

Now that we know what the words on the page mean, let's take a look at an actual chart.

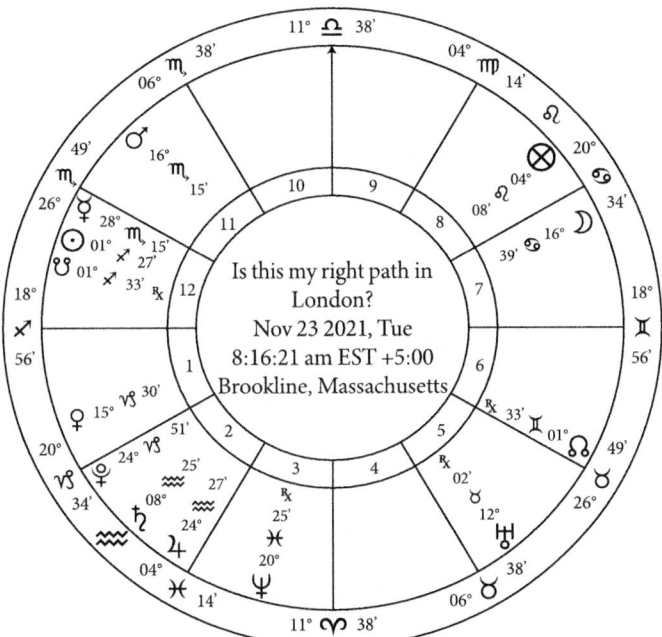

FIGURE 2: *Non-Proportional Houses*

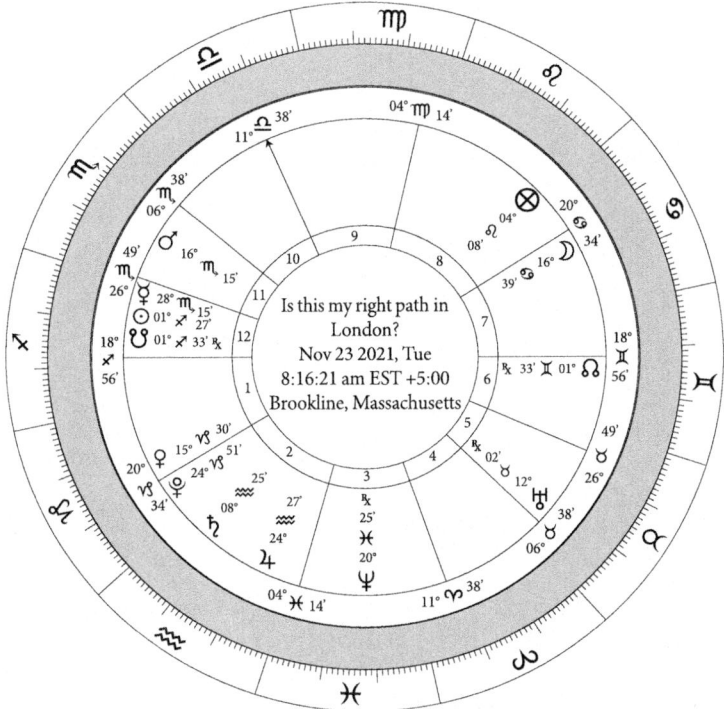

FIGURE 3: *Proportional Houses*

On the previous page is a horary chart presented in two formats. Both charts are divided into twelve sections. These are the twelve terrestrial houses of astrology.

The upper chart is an idealized version of what this chart looks like. I've chosen to make the houses look as if they are all equal in size, when in fact they are not. The lower chart shows the actual proportions of the houses in relation to each other.

The shape of the houses change based on our physical location in relation to the Equator, as well as the time of day. The further North or South a location may be from the Equator, the more bizarre the houses may appear. My personal preference is to see the houses equally spaced as they are depicted in FIGURE 2. However, you should know that choosing to represent the houses in this way does not mean that these are truly equal houses. This is important to bear in mind because there is a house system called the "Equal House" system, in which every house contains 30° of the zodiac. Depicting Regiomontanus houses equally does not make them equal houses.

When we demonstrate the houses with varying sizes, they are called "proportional houses." When we demonstrate Regiomontanus houses in an idealized equal way, they are called "non-proportional houses."

The lines dividing the houses are called "cusps." There is a number that is attached to each house cusp. This number reflects the exact degree and minute of the zodiac that the house cusp crosses.

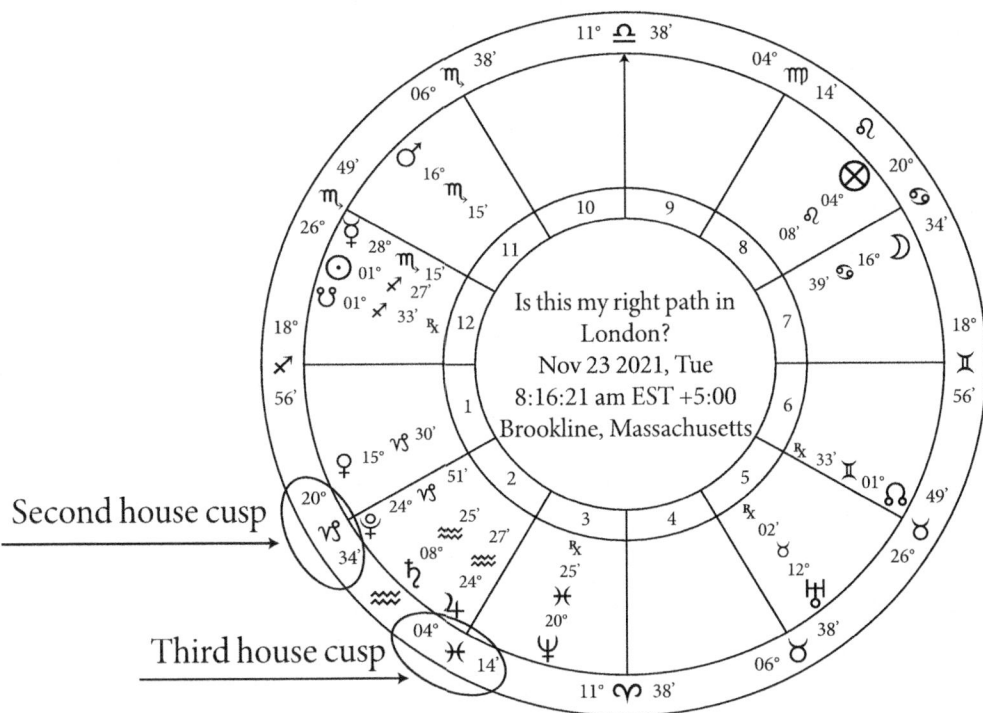

FIGURE 4: *House Cusps*

When we refer to "minutes" we are referring to minutes of space, not minutes of time. Just as we can divide time into hours, minutes and seconds, we divide our measurement within the zodiac into degrees of space, minutes of space, and seconds of space. Since we are trying to measure locations on a round plane, we actually refer to these units of space as degrees of arc, minutes of arc, and seconds of arc. Our charts don't show us seconds of arc, but they do show us degrees and minutes.

TABLE 1: *Seconds, Minutes, & Degrees of Arc*

| SPACE MEASURED | UNIT OF SPACE | EXAMPLE |
|---|---|---|
| 60 SECONDS | ONE MINUTE OF ARC | 15" |
| 60 MINUTES | ONE DEGREE OF ARC | 15' |
| 30 DEGREES | ONE ZODIACAL SIGN | 15° |

In order to read the information on the cusps of the houses, we would start by saying the degree first, then the sign, and then the minute.

TABLE 2: *Sample Chart House Cusps*

| FIRST HOUSE CUSP | 18 DEGREES SAGITTARIUS 56 MINUTES | (18° SAG 56') |
| SECOND HOUSE CUSP | 20 DEGREES CAPRICORN 34 MINUTES | (20° CAP 34') |
| THIRD HOUSE CUSP | 04 DEGREES PISCES 14 MINUTES | (04° PIS 14') |
| FOURTH HOUSE CUSP | 11 DEGREES ARIES 38 MINUTES | (11° ARI 38') |

Notice that the degree of the first house is the same as the degree of the seventh house. The only difference is the sign that is on the cusp of both houses. This is because certain houses oppose each other.

TABLE 3: *Oppositions Between Houses*

| OPPOSITE HOUSES | |
| --- | --- |
| FIRST | SEVENTH |
| SECOND | EIGHTH |
| THIRD | NINTH |
| FOURTH | TENTH |
| FIFTH | ELEVENTH |
| SIXTH | TWELFTH |

Therefore, opposite houses will always carry the same degree, minute, and second of their opposite signs.

TABLE 4: *Oppositions Between Signs*

| OPPOSITE SIGNS | |
| --- | --- |
| ARIES | LIBRA |
| TAURUS | SCORPIO |
| GEMINI | SAGITTARIUS |
| CANCER | CAPRICORN |
| LEO | AQUARIUS |
| VIRGO | PISCES |

You'll notice that in our example chart, neither Aquarius nor Leo is on any of the house cusps. They are "trapped" between the cusps of two houses, and have no house cusp of their own within this chart. This is called "interception." It doesn't happen all the time in every chart, but it happens often enough. This can be based on the time at which we cast a chart. It can also be based on the location where a chart is casted. Locations at extreme North or South latitudes tend to create charts with more extreme interceptions.

If you were asked to say the cusps of the houses, you would say:

✳ "The first house cusp is 18 degrees Sagittarius 56 minutes."
✳ "The second house cusp is 20 degrees Capricorn 34 minutes."
✳ "Aquarius is intercepted in the second house."
✳ The third house cusp is 04 Pisces 14 minutes."

After saying the eighth house cusp, you would also say that Leo is intercepted in the eighth house.

A chart depicts the sky above and below us, as if we were standing in the center of that chart.

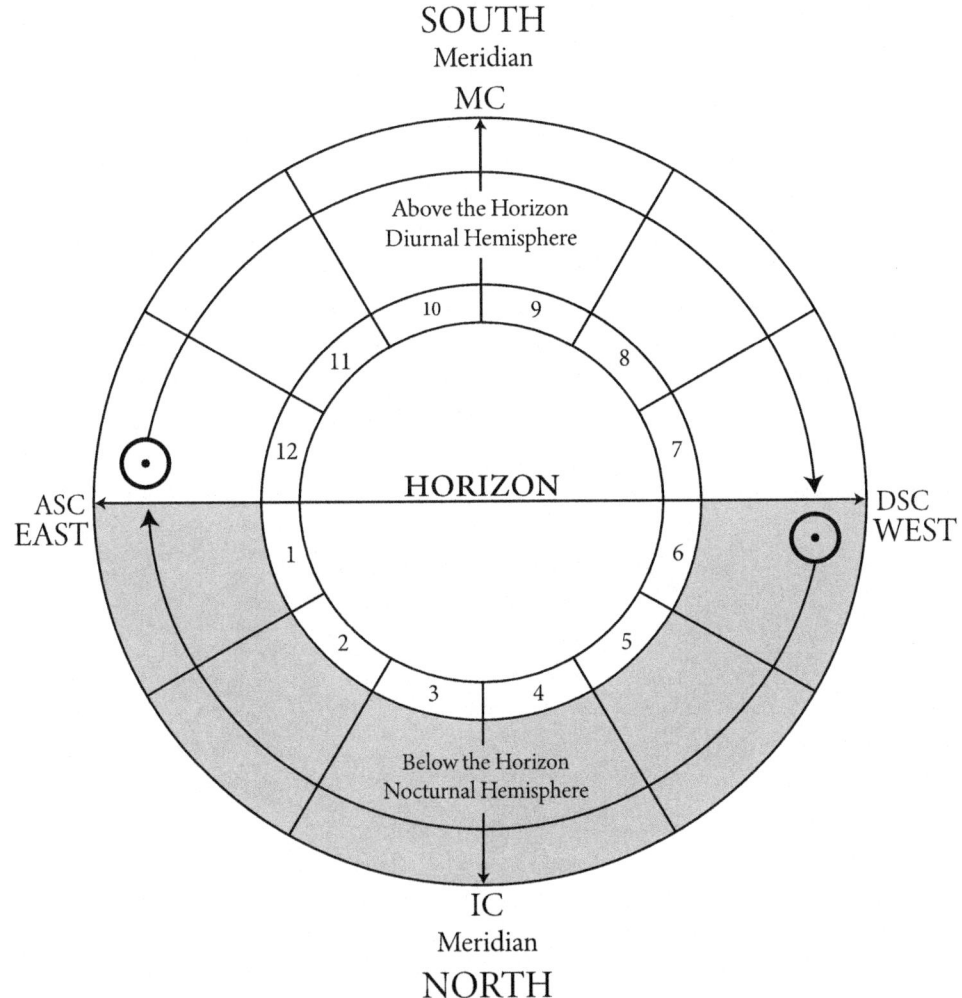

SOUTH
Meridian
MC

Above the Horizon
Diurnal Hemisphere

10    9
11          8
12          7

HORIZON

ASC                    DSC
EAST                   WEST

1           6
2        5
3    4

Below the Horizon
Nocturnal Hemisphere

IC
Meridian
NORTH

FIGURE 5: *Above & Below the Horizon*

The line of the first and seventh house represents our local horizon. Anything that is above the horizon in houses seven through twelve is going to be visible to us in the sky. Anything below the horizon in houses one through six is going to be invisible to us.

In the horary chart below, we can see that the Sun is above the horizon. That means this chart was erected in the daytime.

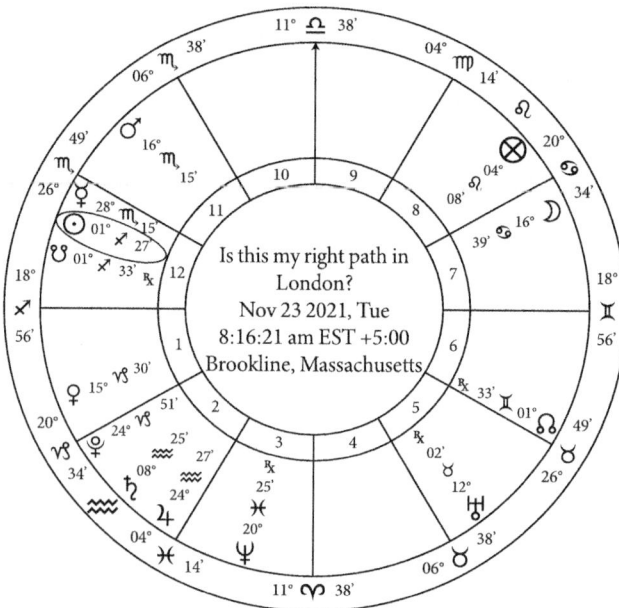

FIGURE 6: *Diurnal Chart*

Compare that to the following Aries Ingress chart, where the Sun is below the horizon. This means the chart was erected in the nighttime.

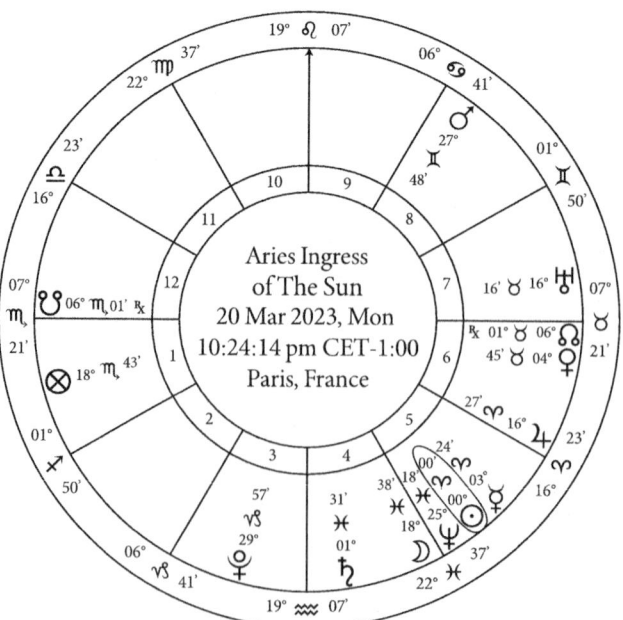

FIGURE 7: *Nocturnal Chart*

If the Sun is above the horizon line – represented by the first and seventh house axis – it is a daytime chart. If the Sun is below the horizon line, it is a nighttime chart. A daytime chart is known as a "diurnal chart." A nighttime chart is known as a "nocturnal chart."

Take a look at the planets within FIGURE 6. We read a planetary position in the same way we read the information on the cusp of a house. The only difference is that we begin by stating which planet we are referring to. Then, we say the degree, sign, and the minute of that planet.

In this chart we find:

TABLE 5: *Planets in Relation to the Horizon*

| | |
|---|---|
| VENUS 15° CAPRICORN 30' | BELOW THE HORIZON |
| PLUTO 24° CAPRICORN 51' | BELOW THE HORIZON |
| SATURN 08° AQUARIUS 25' | BELOW THE HORIZON |
| JUPITER 24° AQUARIUS 27' | BELOW THE HORIZON |

The next planet we see is Neptune at 20° Pisces 25' RX. The "RX." means "retrograde." This means that from Earth, Neptune appears to be moving backward in the zodiac. We would say "Neptune 20 degrees Pisces 25 minutes, retrograde." The only other symbols or letters that will come after the minutes of a planet will be S, SD, or SR.

TABLE 6: *Station, Retrograde, Direct*

| | |
|---|---|
| S | STATION |
| Rx. | RETROGRADE ( ℞ ) |
| SR | STATION RETROGRADE |
| SD | STATION DIRECT |

When a planet stations, it is either about to start moving backward (retrograde) in the zodiac or a planet that was previously moving backward is about to begin moving forward (or direct) in the zodiac.

A direct or forward moving planet stations retrograde when it comes to a standstill before it begins moving retrograde.

A retrograde planet stations direct when it comes to a standstill before it begins moving direct in the zodiac once more.

The Sun and the Moon are called "luminaries." This is because they are the lights which illuminate the sky in the daytime and nighttime, respectively. The luminaries can never turn retrograde. This also means that they can never come to a station as far as their journey through the zodiac is concerned. They can move slower or faster, but they will never be stationed direct or stationed retrograde. The Mean Nodes will always be retrograde. Many programs do not write "SD" or "SR" when a planet stations, and may simply write "S." In this case, you will say that the planet in question has "stationed." If we knew whether it was about to go direct or retrograde, we would say "stationing/stationed direct" or "stationing/stationed retrograde."

If RX., S, SD, or SR follow the minutes of a planet, they must be noted. They represent important information regarding how that planet is functioning within the chart.

## ON EPHEMERIDES

An "ephemeris" is a convenient tool that astrologers use in order to help them know where the planets are on a daily basis. The plural of ephemeris is ephemerides. Most ephemerides will give the location of the planets for a set time. This is commonly either midday or midnight Universal Time. Universal Time is based on the Greenwich Meridian. While an ephemeris is an indispensible tool that every astrologer should own, most astrological computer programs have the ability to generate the exact chart for a given location.

## FIVE-DEGREE RULE

There is one more thing to know about the planets in relation to the houses. A house is strongest at its cusp and weakest in the zone that is near to the house cusp that comes after it. When a planet is within five degrees of the next house cusp and in the same sign as the next house cusp, that planet is considered to be *energetically* in that next house. Even though the body of the planet may be in the previous house, it's power and "loyalty" has already "crossed the border." This is known as the Five Degree Rule.

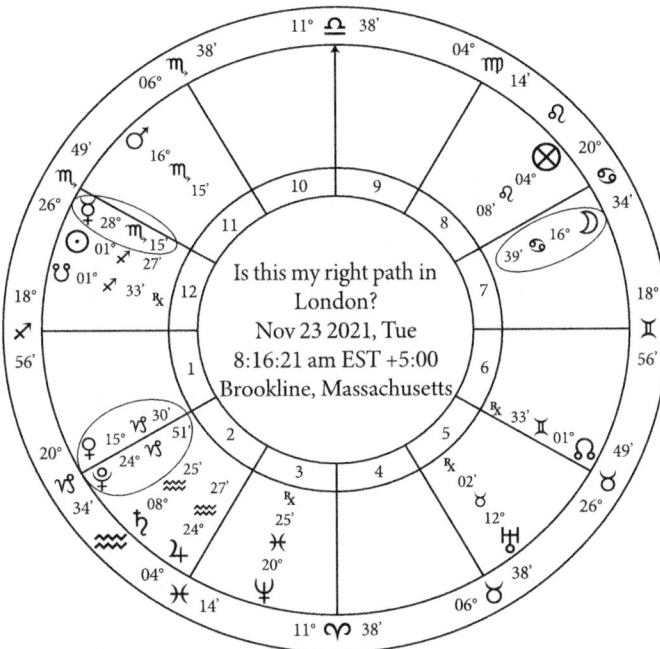

FIGURE 8: *Five Degree Rule*

In this chart, we see Venus at 15° Capricorn 30'. If we add five degrees to fifteen degrees, we get twenty degrees. The second house cusp is 20° Capricorn 34'. Is Venus in the second house or not? In this case, Venus is not in the second house. Even though adding five degrees to Venus puts her that much closer to the second house, it doesn't put her in the second house. Her minutes are less than the minutes of the second house cusp.

If Venus were at 15° Capricorn 35', then by the Five Degree Rule, she would be in the second house. She would be one minute further into the second house than the second house cusp itself. Venus in our example is, therefore, still in the first house. As far as first house planets go, she is weakly in the first house because she is very far removed from the first house cusp. However, she is in the first house nonetheless.

The Moon on the other hand does fit within the five-degree range of the Five Degree Rule insofar as the eighth house cusp is concerned. The Moon is 16° Cancer 39'. The eighth house cusp is 20° Cancer 34'. Though the Moon is bodily in the seventh house, she has given her power over to the eighth house by virtue of the Five Degree Rule. If we add five degrees to the sixteen degrees of the Moon, she would have twenty-one degrees. This would push her beyond the eighth house cusp, thus making her an eighth house planet.

It is important to note that the Five Degree Rule only works in one direction. Planets in the previous house can be pushed into the next house by the Five Degree Rule. However, planets in the next house and conjunct that house cusp cannot be pushed backward into the previous house by the Five Degree Rule. In our example chart, Pluto is in the second house. Adding five degrees to Pluto would only take Pluto further into the second house. We can't subtract degrees from Pluto to pull it into the first house. Mercury is in the twelfth house and conjunct the twelfth house cusp. Adding five degrees to Mercury takes him deeper into the twelfth. We cannot subtract degrees from him to take him into the eleventh house.

I believe the Five Degree Rule specifically applies to planets that have an actual physical body. The Nodes and the Part of Fortune are not planets and they do not have a physical body. I believe this rule shouldn't apply to them. We will learn more about these celestial factors further on within this book. As with everything, practice and experience must pave our way beyond doubt. It is my hope that your practice brings you further insights that allow you to excel far beyond the foundation established here.

## THE BEAUTY OF THE ORDER OF CREATION.

*O that you could grow wings and fly up into the air, and that, poised between earth and heaven, you might see the firmness of the earth, the liquidity of the sea, the course of the rivers and the free flow of the air, the piercing fire, the revolution of the stars, the swiftness of the heavenly movement encircling all these things. What most blessed vision, O son, to behold all that in one moment; the unmoving being moved, the unmanifest being made manifest through what it creates! This is the very order of the universe and this is the beauty of that order.*

—CORPUS HERMETICUM 5:5

# Part 1

*Now is heaven the readier to favour those who search out its secrets, eager to display through a poet's song the riches of the sky. Only in times of peace is there leisure for this task. It is my delight to traverse the very air and spend my life touring the boundless skies, learning of the constellations and the contrary motions of the planets. But this knowledge alone is not enough. A more fervent delight is it to know thoroughly the very heart of the mighty sky, to mark how it controls the birth of all living beings through its signs, and to tell thereof in verse with Apollo tuning my song. The poet must sing to a fixed measure, and the vast celestial sphere rings in his ears besides, scarce allowing even words of prose to be fitted to their proper phrasing.*

—MARCUS MANILIUS

CHAPTER 1 OBJECTIVES

* Provide a sketch of how prehistoric civilizations viewed themselves in relation to the universe.
* Define what astrology is and how it naturally evolved out of the cosmology of the ancients.
* Outline why a geocentric model is most appropriate for traditional Western tropical astrology.
* Discuss how astrology helps us interact with time in a more sacred way.
* Establish astrology as a means of spiritual contemplation and personal development.

# CHAPTER 1

## WHAT IS ASTROLOGY?

*Nous, God, being male and female, beginning as life and light, gave birth, by the Word, to another Nous, the Creator of the world; he, being the god of fire and air, formed seven powers who encompass in their circles the sensory world, and the governance of these powers is called destiny.* –CORPUS HERMETICUM 1:9

For as long as human beings have existed, we have looked to the heavens to find some light on the meaning of life. There has been no civilization of humanity that hasn't sought to frame itself against the Ambient for reasons both inspired and practical. "Ambient" is how Ptolemy referred to the sky in his book the *Tetrabiblos*. Today we consider the word "ambient" to suggest something all-encompassing, both soft and safe. This isn't far from our characterization throughout history of the universe being an overarching maternal force. Even in ancient mythology, where we imagine the universe to be populated by gods and goddesses, the bedrock of existence has always been thought of as a deep oceanic womb. In viewing the cosmos as Mother, we've chosen to view it as a protective shell – containing the full spectrum of life within it.

This "maternalizing" of the Unknown must have been, at first, a survival instinct; a reactionary protection against the notion of our own annihilation in the wild and uncharted void of space. In his book *A History of Astronomy*, author A. Pannekoek tells us that:

> … primitive man had so hard a struggle simply to make his life secure that there was no room for luxury incentives. To maintain himself he had to fight for his existence incessantly against the hostile powers of nature. The struggle for life occupied his thoughts and feelings entirely, and in this struggle he had to acquire such knowledge of the natural phenomena as influenced his life and determined his work; the better he knew them, the more secure his life became.

Pannekoek describes ancient man not as a fool, but as a pragmatist, seeking in every way to build relationships between himself and the natural world that would ensure his continued survival. In the *Astronomica* of Marcus Manilius, we read:

> … but long ages sharpened human wits, the struggle for survival endowed those wretched folk with ingenuity, and the burden of each man's lot forced him to look to himself to better it…

How this prehistoric human would go on to characterize and personalize nature must also have been born out of this primal need.

Man sought to project images familiar to him onto the cosmos as a means of feeling safe. What universal concept could encapsulate this idea of safety better than that of motherhood? Within which other natural or social construct might we find a sense of all-pervading security, justice, and meaning? Who other than the mother can we rest upon, even in the face of catastrophe and mayhem? Antiquity is full of stories of ancient goddesses both terrible and loving; dynamic matriarchs of the universe, complex in every way.

We are told of grieving Isis in search of the scattered remains of her slaughtered beloved; but still willing to gift everlasting life to a sick and dying mortal child. Cerridwen, upon finding herself pregnant after swallowing the seed of her enemy, could not bring herself to kill the newly born babe with the shining brow. We find Demeter plunging the world into a cruel and deadly winter, until she is reunited with her abducted daughter, Persephone. Even in the near destruction of the world, ancient mythology teaches us to have compassion for the goddess in her role as destroyer. The pain she feels – as a mother who has lost her child or as a lover who has been betrayed – is a pain with which we can all deeply sympathize. In sympathizing with the goddess, we ultimately were sympathizing with larger processes and cycles of life within the cosmos. We were inadvertently imbibing our universe with qualities of intention and motivation that corresponded with our own way of responding to life. Through "building the cosmos in our image" we were building the pillars of rationale that supported our sense of being in relationship with the natural world.

The notion of a mother-force giving birth to everything within the universe, naturally led to the idea of the universe being birthed and not created. Upon giving birth, it is a natural instinct for the archetypal mother to care for her offspring. A created universe could all too easily be discarded at the whim of its inventor. Comparatively, creation does not carry the same weight of responsibility and care that birth does. In the fourteenth chapter of the *Bhagavad Gita*, we find Krishna telling Arjuna:

> *The total material substance, called Brahman, is the source of birth, and it is that Brahman that I impregnate, making possible the births of all living beings, O son of Bharata... It should be understood that all species of life, O son of Kuntī, are made possible by birth in this material nature, and that I am the seed-giving father.*

This is not to say that creationist mythology wasn't also a part of some ancient people's understanding of how the universe began. We find a treasury of creation myths occurring within pagan and Abrahamic religious teachings alike. However, the mystical explanation of those myths often describes creation as a process of continuous unfolding; an eternal spiraling outward of worlds from within worlds. The Kabbalah tells us that the creator lovingly carved a hole into the solid darkness of space within which to extend a ray of his infinite light. In that emptiness, he planted the seeds of what would become our material universe. Those seeds emanated outward and downward until they finally gave birth to our physical world. Though complete within itself on a mythological level, modern Kabbalists have viewed this myth as an ancient prototype of the Big Bang Theory.

We find stories such as these replete throughout antiquity. However, these stories only serve as a springboard; an urge for us to look beneath the surface of their outer clothing to find the heart of meaning they carry. In *The Hermetic Tradition*, Julius Evola tells us:

> *In order to make sense of this teaching it is clearly necessary to abandon the idea of the Creation as a historical fact over and done with in the spatial and temporal past. We must conceive of it as functioning in an ongoing state, metaphysical in its own right and therefore beyond space and time, beyond past as well as future, which is more or less that same state that some mystics, even Christian mystics, have called eternal creation.*

Whether they viewed the universe as being birthed from some pre-cosmic womb, or unfolded organically from a singular source, the fact remains clear. The ancients – in order to truly feel at home within the universe – first established that they were blood relatives with that universe by means of their various cosmological myths. To not view the universe at least as a somewhat maternal guardian would be to allow room for the notion of a universe inherently alien and hostile; one that holds us at a distance, and, thus may discard of us at will. The prospect of our disposability when added to the normal survival pressures of ancient life may have posed too much of an existential discomfort for the burgeoning human species to bear. The idea of us living in a caring universe presided over by gods and goddesses was born out of a human necessity to feel loved, chosen, acknowledged, and cherished. Star-based mythology allowed the ancients to create the stories that would serve as the core pillars of belief and comfort within an uncertain world.

This mythic perception of our cosmos created a sense of fellowship and familiarity between our ancestors and the starry heavens above. To them, the planets were not simply cold and distant specters wandering through the night. They were siblings with a familiar rivalry. Sometimes, they were even secret lovers engaged in every manner of inappropriateness. The ancients perceived these stellar giants as men, women, and parents in their own divine right. The sky for the ancients wasn't simply an endless sea of stars stretched across a dark expanse. The ancient sky was heavily *peopled* – teeming with every manner of celestial, yet highly personal, life. It was the home to the gods and our ancestors knew their divine stories. Understanding these stories gave them insight into how the gods dynamically interacted with each other. The better our forefathers understood the relationship of the gods with one another, the more skillfully they could navigate how their stellar influences spilled into our material world. This ability to measure and predict how the cosmic interplay of the stellar gods would concretely impact the world would come to be known as "astrology."

## ASTROLOGY DEFINED

Astrology is the study of the relationship between time, destiny, and the cosmos. Central to our philosophy as astrologers is that time is imprinted upon all of us like a birthmark that tells the story of how our lives will unfold. This story is told using the symbolic language of the stars, signs, and planets. Each of us bears a unique cosmic pattern which outlines our individual destinies. The ability to clearly understand and interpret how time imprints a destiny onto every being within the material world is what makes a good astrologer.

## MINIMUS MUNDUS ELEMENTORUM – TINY WORLD OF ELEMENTS

Millenia of observation led our ancestors to the conclusion that certain heavenly occurrences corresponded with the tides of change that arise within the lives of all living beings. The alterations of the material world were thought to always express one of the four life processes of generation, preservation, corruption, and destruction. These symbolically correspond to the four elements of fire, earth, air, and water; which, for the ancients, were the building blocks of our material universe.

Guido Bonatti was an eminent Italian astrologer who flourished in the thirteenth century CE. In his book *Liber Astronomiae*, he tells us:

> *The elements, in fact, cannot be more or less than four because every elementatum [elemental being] is made up out of the four elements and has in itself the four qualities: hot, dry, cold, and humid [wet]; and the four accidents are characteristics of it: namely, generation, duration or conservation, corruption, and destruction.*

These elements didn't just refer to their physical forms that we perceive through our five senses. Symbolically they refer to how the arrangement of atoms determines whether an object is a solid (earth), liquid (water), gas (air), or plasma (fire). On the level of our humanity, they denote all aspects of our spiritual (fire), mental (air), emotional (water), and physical (earth) life.

TABLE 1: *Elements & Correspondences*

| FIRE | AIR | WATER | EARTH |
|------|------|-----------|----------|
| PLASMA | GAS | LIQUID | SOLID |
| SPIRITUAL | MENTAL | EMOTIONAL | PHYSICAL |

The ancients referred to the planets as "supercelestial," meaning "above the cosmos." These old gods, though residing within the cosmos, were above the chaos and mutability of our material world, since they were composed of something wholly different from the transient elements of Earth. By the Medieval period, it was a firmly established astrological fact that the planets were composed of a fifth, non-material element. Therefore, they were not considered to be corruptible or alterable. However, our Earth – composed wholly of corruptible, unstable, material elements – was thought to be constantly transformed through the whirling motion of the supercelestial planets above. In his *Tetrabiblos*, ancient Greek astrologer Claudius Ptolemy – who flourished in the second century CE – tells us:

> *From these premises it follows not only that all bodies, which may be already compounded, are subjected to the motions of the stars, but also that the impregnation and growth of the seeds from which all bodies proceed, are framed and molded by the quality existing in the Ambient at the time of such impregnation and growth.*

By "compounded" he is referring to the specific mixture of elements each of us have inherited as our unique composition from the sky under which we were born. The state of the heavens at the time of our birth is imprinted upon us as a signature and a promise that we fulfill as our individual destiny in this lifetime. While the movements of the planets reflect changes in our elemental constitution that have psychological, physiological, and physical effects, the core structure of our destiny does not change. The events that impact our character and trajectory in life can only occur within the predetermined sphere of possibility that our destiny allows. The purpose of astrology is to predict the events that unfold throughout our lives within the established framework of predestiny.

"EXPERIENCE BUILT UP THE SCIENCE"

Generation after generation, ancient astrologers handed down their teachings until a reliable observation-based system was formed.

Marcus Manilius was an ancient Roman astrologer and poet who flourished in the first century CE. In his *Astronomica* we read:

> *Embracing long ages in unremitting toil, [the priests] assigned to each period of time its particular events, noting an individual's nativity and the subsequent pattern of his life, the influence of every hour on the laws of fate, and the great differences effected by small moments. After every aspect of the sky had been observed, as the stars returned to their original positions, and each figuration had assigned to it its powers of influence in accordance with the sure cycles of destiny, by repeated practice and with examples pointing the way experience built up the science; and from wide observations discovered that by hidden laws the stars wield sovereign power and that all heaven moves to the eternal spirit of reason and by sure tokens distinguishes the vicissitudes of fate.*

For the ancients, astrology was part and parcel of the sublime harmony that served as the very basis of the cosmos. Manilius writes:

> *Nature adheres to the paths which she herself has made and commits not the errors of inexperience...*

In no part of its fabric was the universe permitted to deviate from its divine uniformity. The edifice of heaven was built and sustained by immutable cosmic law. Within the cosmology of the ancient world, astrology was a natural extension of this principle – an unfolding of one inevitable truth from another more all-encompassing. Our destinies were governed by Nature because Nature governed every operation under her domain. This doctrine of stellar influences that we call astrology served as a guiding light within the heart of our ancestors. It taught them how to organize their lives within a universe governed by law.

Imagine how extraordinary the frontier of astrology must have been! How overwhelming was it for ancient humanity to realize that for every occurrence within this world, there was a correspondent echo of sameness within the cosmos? Their vast records would indicate that this was no great surprise at all. A study of ancient thought proves that our ancestors expected that the relationship between the heavens and the Earth would bear fruit in observable ways. For them, it was a fact of life that the sky of the day would predict the events of the day. Because of their ability to see their lives reflected in the daily tides of celestial change, they set out to enshrine their history and their wisdom upon the star-studded canopy of heaven. They projected themselves onto the cosmos because this act allowed them to navigate life with greater wisdom. However, it is more truthful to say that it was the cosmos that was projecting itself onto them. The heavens were creating humanity in its own image; and humanity was meant to be its reflection. The astrology didn't work because it was some magical creature that had no relation to our existence. The astrology worked because it showed us that we were the reflections of a larger cosmic life.

Astrology is meant to help us measure the impact of invisible cosmic influences on our visible earthly world. Once these influences are brought into our awareness, they can help us better understand our lives. Modern technology allows us to practice astrology with greater ease. Computer programs now perform all the technical tasks and calculations of the practicing astrologer. However, our ancestors had no such technology. Their astrology took them out into the open fields, under the outstretched body of the ancient night-goddess, Nuit, to observe the traveling pinpricks of light across an endless sea of stars. They observed the eternal march of the planets in relation to each other, like a cosmic highway of infinite grandeur. From these combinations of stellar influences juxtaposed against events occurring on Earth, our ancestors derived the initial meanings of what these influences meant. This understanding of the heavens allowed them to gather insight into the secrets of futurity.

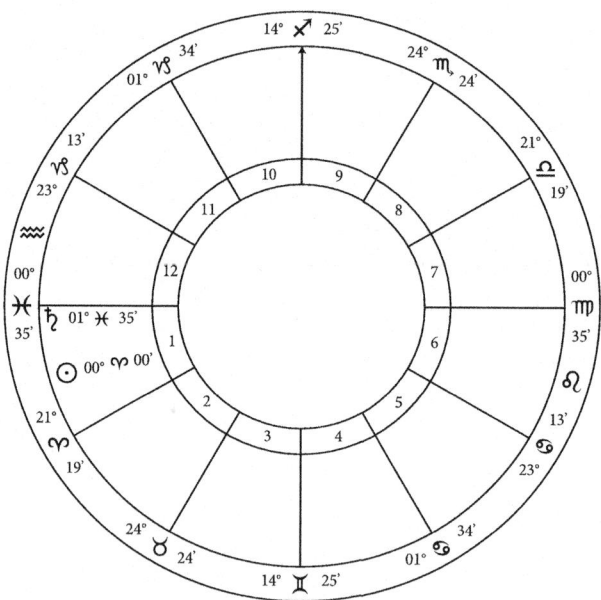

FIGURE 1: *Spring Equinox, Saturn Rising*

After observing and recording for over four thousand years, one would imagine that certain patterns of geocosmic life became evident. Ancient astrologers may have found that when cold and foreboding Saturn was the first stellar body to rise in the East at the Spring Equinox, this symbolized a time of war, a period of famine, or an increase of death within the kingdom.

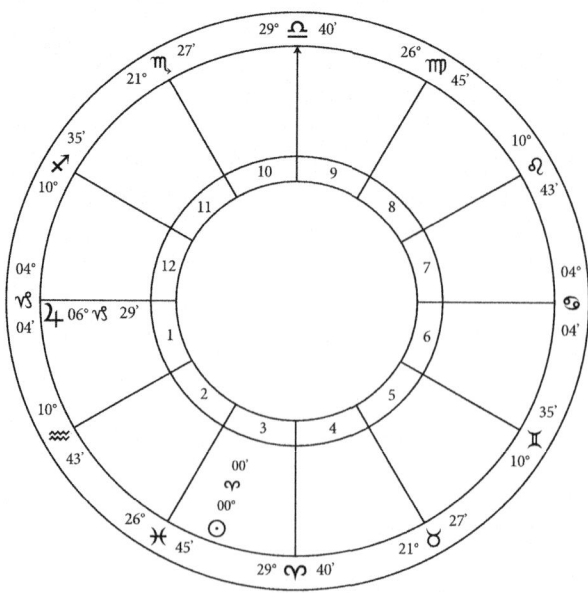

FIGURE 2: *Spring Equinox, Jupiter Rising*

Conversely, crops and livestock may have flourished when Jupiter, the god of plenty, was the first to rise in Saturn's stead. As nondimensional as these observations may seem to us now, it is from these rudiments of prehistoric stargazing that the entire canon of ancient astrology was born.

Chief amongst the achievements of the ancient astrologers was a mastery of time. Pannekoek tells us that:

> Time-reckoning was, apart from navigation, the oldest astronomical practice, out of which science later developed.

Mastering time meant the ancients also gained a certain mastery of the weather. This was a critical ability upon which their survival greatly depended.

Having established a more secure world for themselves, they sought to expand their domain. They began sailing the previously uncharted oceans and probing the infinite depths of the sky. Manilius writes:

> After reason had referred these several [meteorological] happenings to their true causes, it ventured beyond the atmosphere to seek knowledge of the neighbouring vastness of heaven [to] comprehend the sky as a whole; it determined the shapes and names of the signs, and discovered what cycles they experienced according to fixed law, and that all things moved to the will and disposition of heaven, as the constellations by their varied array assign different destinies.

Our ancestors began to observe certain predictable occurrences within the heavens. One of these observations was that planets didn't just do as they pleased based on temper tantrums thrown by fickle gods. They realized that planets moved in very certain cycles. Not only could they predict these cycles for the week or month ahead, but they discovered methods to consistently make accurate astronomical predictions far into the future.

This ability to cast far-reaching predictions about the exact movements of the supercelestial gods shook the very fabric of ancient religion. James Herschel Holden, in his masterful work *A History of Horoscopic Astrology*, writes:

> The acquisition of the ability to predict solar, lunar, and planetary positions, to determine in advance the appearance of the Moon and the occurrences of eclipses caused a change in the way Babylonian Astrologers thought about their art. In the old days a celestial phenomenon was thought to be of divine origin, hence subject to the whim of the gods, but now it was seen that such phenomena followed mathematical rules. There was order in the universe. It may have been established by the gods, but once they had set the celestial machine in motion, they evidently let it run unattended.

No longer was it necessary to offer sacrifices to prevent certain cosmic calamities and stellar events from happening. The fact was that they would consistently happen whether our ancestors sacrificed or not. The mastery of time changed the station of the astrologer from that of religious duty to scientific exploration. Holden tells us:

> *Consequently, the link between astrology and religion gradually dissolved. More and more the astrologer became the practitioner of a technical art.*

## Orienting to the Ancient Worldview

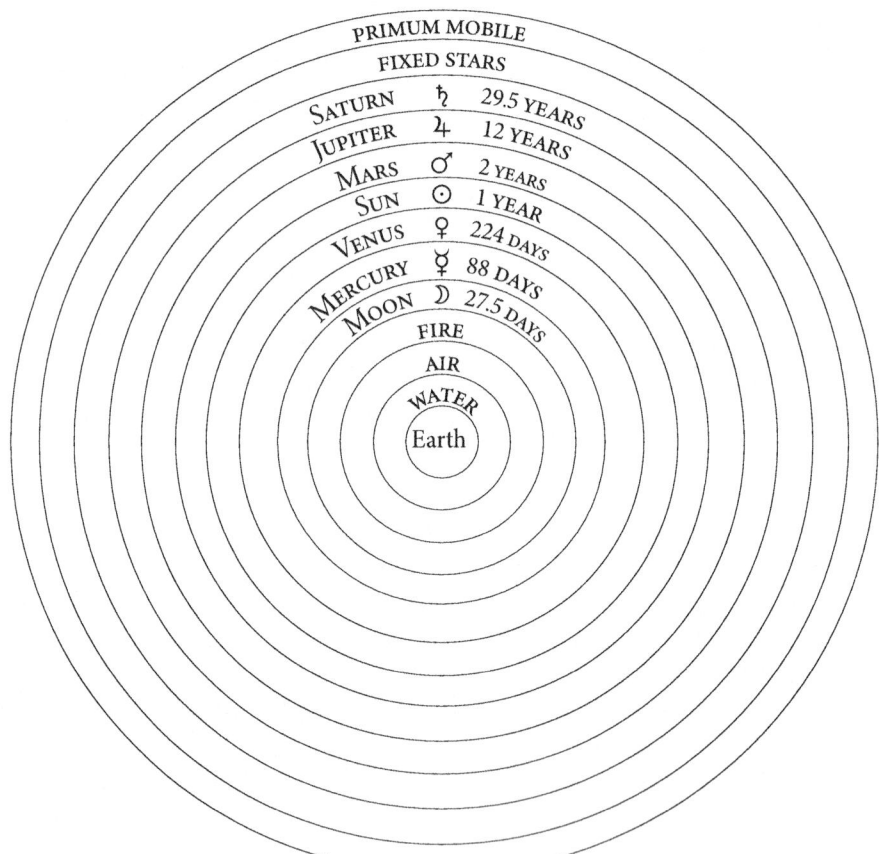

FIGURE 3: *Chaldean Order*

For Ptolemy, the original moving force that set and kept the universe in motion was called the "Primum Mobile" (pree-mum moe-be-lay), or "Prime Mover." This philosophy proliferated throughout the classical world and held sway even into the late Renaissance period. Under the dome of this Prime Mover, there were eight concentric shells. One shell contained the fixed stars. The other seven shells belonged to the seven visible planets. This organization of the cosmos is known as the "Chaldean Order." The Chaldeans were a people who became assimilated into the indigenous population of Babylonia. According to Holden, the Babylonians invented astrology.

The Chaldean Order lists the planets from the furthest to the closest observable planet to Earth: Saturn, Jupiter, Mars, Sun, Venus, Mercury, and Moon. "Planet" is derived from the Greek "planētes asteres," or "wandering stars." Though the ancient Babylonians knew the Sun and the Moon were luminaries and not planets, they – along with many ancient astronomers – treated them as if they were planets for simplicity's sake. Because of the apparent motion of the Sun and the real orbital motion of the Moon, both luminaries were considered to be "wandering stars." The ancients thought that beyond Saturn lay the constellations of the fixed stars, the backdrop against which the planets etched their orbits across the sky. Beyond these fixed stars was yet another shell, filled with a fluidic, crystalline substance. Beyond this crystalline ring of heaven was the domain of the Primum Mobile, which, through its daily motion from East to West, took the entire dome of heaven with it. For the ancients, this Chaldean Order represented the body of the universe. Manilius writes:

> These then are the constellations which decorate the sky with even spread, their fires paneling the ceiling of heaven with various designs. Higher than these there is nothing [that belongs to our material universe], for they are the roof of the universe; they are the limits within which the common abode of nature is content to be held, embracing the sea and lands that lie beneath. They all move on a consistent course, coming into view and setting where heaven ever sinks and, turning, reappears. There exist other stars [the planets], which strive against the contrary movement of the sky and in their swift orbits are poised between heaven and earth: Saturn, Jupiter, Mars, and the Sun, and beneath them Mercury performing its flight between Venus and the Moon.

The orbital shells of the planets increased in diameter the further they were from Earth. The ancients thought this was the reason for the varying rates of planetary speed. No two planets completed one full orbit in the same amount of time. They observed Saturn as the slowest moving planet, making a full revolution around Earth in approximately thirty years, whereas the Moon completed one revolution in approximately twenty-seven and a half days. The Prime Mover maintained all of these cycles in motion. It orchestrated the daily micro-cycle of the rising and setting of the Sun. However, it also was the cause behind the macro-cycle of the larger turning of the wheel of the year and the orbits of the planets with it.

PLANETARY RELATIONSHIPS

This initial setting-in-motion caused the planets to interact with each other in certain angular relationships. These angular relationships came to be called "aspects." Aspects remain at the very heart of an astrologer's toolkit of assessment and interpretation. The planets represent individual universal concepts such as love, hate, happiness, sorrow, fortune, poverty, victory, and defeat. However, when brought into relationship with each other, they form complex ideas that mirror the intricacies of earthly life. Thus, we may find that during a particular period of time Mars has a certain angular relationship with Saturn, while the Sun is having a certain angular relationship to them both.

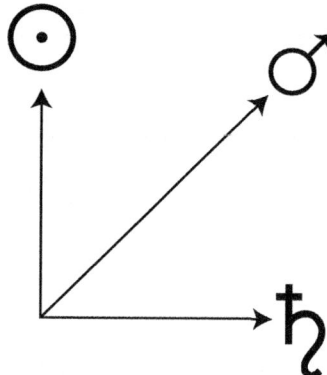

FIGURE 4: *Sun, Mars, & Saturn in Aspect*

This constellation of planetary influence, this "planetary picture" in a sense, holds potent meaning for the correspondent things that are simultaneously occurring on Earth. Author and Uranian astrologer Richard Svehla (1937) writes:

> *The fundamental idea of Astrology is that the planetary constellations exert an influence upon human behavior and all sublunar events... we believe that the underlying idea always was, that the constellations of the planets act as a basic influence, producing certain impulses which are driving springs for practically every manifestation of life on our plane... The astronomical constellations [of the planets] are according to this theory, just the symbols signifying by their momentary relative positions, a certain state of affairs within the Universal Law.*

The horoscope – in the words of Svehla – is the picture of an entity in planetary terms. Moment by moment, the sky changes due to the constant whirling motion of the Prime Mover. With each passing moment the eternal sky is born anew. Within the course of one hour the micro-planetary combinations can change extraordinarily. Imagine, then, the innumerable possibilities that twenty-four hours can bring. Every child that is born, every event that is begun, every war or love that has ever been wrought through time, has occurred under a newly born sky. Thus, our astrology isn't the study of the machinations of an impotent cosmos. Our astrology is the study of a universe in constant evolution, simultaneously pushing us all towards the same.

OUR PERSPECTIVE FROM EARTH

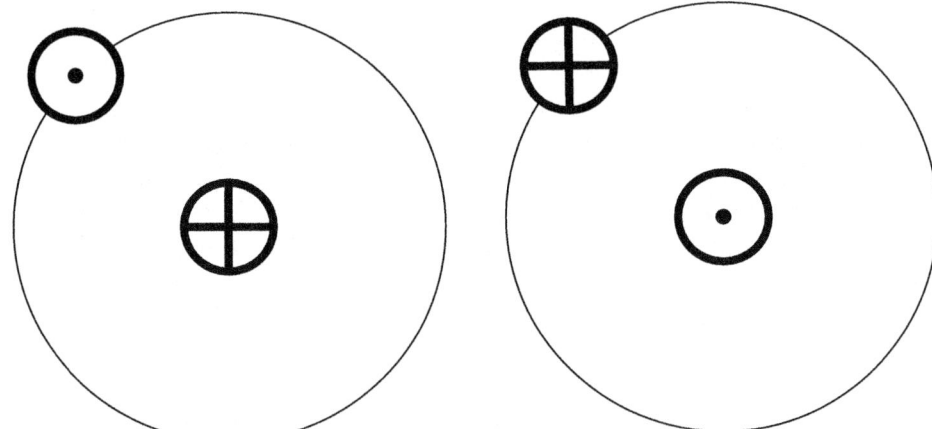

FIGURE 5: *Geocentric Model*          FIGURE 6: *Heliocentric Model*

Geocentrism is a view of the cosmos from Earth as if the Earth were the center of the cosmos. Conversely, heliocentrism is a model of the universe that references the Sun as the center around which the Earth and all the other planets revolve. It is now a well-established scientific fact that we live in a solar system, not an Earth system. However, if we are meant to build an astrological practice that has the ability to reflect our lived experience, it must be built on the foundations of our earthly experience. At their core, our earthly experiences are geocentric.

Our entire life is oriented around the notion of the rising and setting Sun, even though we know this is an optical and spatial illusion. However, the sailor lost at sea doesn't argue with himself at the sight of glorious Helios rising in the East. He doesn't attempt to dissuade his mind against this optical trickery. Instead, he thanks the day and navigates onward, greeting the rising Sun as a familiar guide. Our relationship to the Sun and sky allows us to better orient ourselves on Earth, both spatially and astrologically. Despite its obvious subjectivity, our Earth-based understanding of the cosmos is vital to how we survive and interact with our environment.

In order for astrology to be useful, it must first be relatable. While we cannot relate to the infinite on its own terms, we can relate to it from the vantage point we possess on Earth. Geocentric astrology is extraordinarily valuable. It reflects our personalized experience of the infinite sky. It shows us how that tiny slice of eternity dynamically impacts our lives. Like the sailor, many of us find in astrology the ability to navigate the sea of life. What we experience in an astrological reading is often a familiarity no different than that of the rising and setting Sun. Astrology gives us all the opportunity to feel known.

Everything about the shape of traditional Western astrology is built on this geocentric perspective. This is why two babies born at the same time but in different parts of the world will relate to the cosmic pattern of their birth in entirely different ways. While the pattern remains the same, the areas of life impacted and governed by the planets will be different for each child. Upon writing this passage, I am in a relationship with the sky in Jamaica Plain, Massachusetts that is extraordinarily different from the sky my student is experiencing in Sydney, Australia. The old adage that one man's trash is another man's treasure is applicable here. The sky at 2:00 PM grants a different destiny to the child born on the East Coast than it does to another simultaneously being born at 11:00 AM on the West Coast. The sky that portends wealth for one person most certainly predicts poverty for another. Each of us localizes the cosmos based on where we are on Earth. We all draw down the heavens in an individualized way.

## Reconsidering Our Understanding of Time

Our modern relationship to time flattens our awareness of the significance of the moment. We tend to perceive time as a constant river of unbroken similarity. We move through life unaware of the invisible forces that shape our daily existence. As disconnected from the truth as this perception of reality may be, this, too, is built into the requirements of our survival.

As God tells Moses in Exodus 33:20, "no man shall see me and live," we are reminded that what truly lay on the other side of the veil of our limited perception are the titanic forces of nature. Beyond our frail comprehension are the lords of fate and destiny, both birthing worlds and crushing a universe all at once. We cannot handle being aware of the specialness of every moment, for then every blade of grass would demand reverence; each breath we take would overwhelm us with awe. If the mystery of each moment was constantly made available to our psyche, we would sooner shatter the shell of that psyche before we could truly grasp it all. Eastern civilizations consider this all-knowingness – this awareness of the spiritual undercurrent that exists within everything – as enlightenment. Evola writes:

> In general, the danger is the same anyone runs in seeking the conquest of immortality or enlightenment by contacting the universal force; the one who makes contact must be capable of withstanding overwhelming grandeur.

The "universal force" he is referring to is the unifying intelligence that penetrates deeply into the heart of our material world. It is a vitalizing force that gives every being an organizing principle and purpose. It is an intelligence that allows so many of our vital physiological functions to occur without our conscious effort. Like the absorption of nutrients in the lining of our intestines or the ongoing deterioration and reconstitution of our bodies, we are not meant to be aware of the creative and destructive power of each infinitesimal cross-section of time. A constant perception of the micro-worlds around us would greatly hinder our ability to live in a functional way. Thus, the filtered reality that we perceive "through a glass seen darkly" is the version of the world most practical to our human existence. Evola considers this limitation of perception to be the spiritual burden that accompanies physical embodiment. He writes:

> *...but even underneath this burden, the soul struggles and thinks, though these are not the same kinds of thoughts that it would have if it were detached from the body; instead of energies, it knows only sensations and passions that proceed from the body.*

When pursuing highly spiritual aspirations in life, the limitations of embodiment may seem to be an unnecessary hinderance to soul growth. However, our bodies are a vital safeguard against the volatile cosmic potential that is present in every moment. If the veil of the physical exteriority of the world were to be lifted for only a minute, we would all surely go mad or die from the sheer impact of it all. Perhaps God's warning to Moses was a direct reference to this. Perhaps this is a pure description of what it means to see the face of God: utter and ecstatic annihilation.

While we cannot live in constant awareness of these forces, astrology enables us to analyze them. It teaches us that time is not an abysmal deluge, falling down on us like the flood of ancient Noah. Time is a multitude of moments, each imbued with indescribable cosmic power and intelligence. A unit of time is comparable to one of the trillions of cells within the human body, each containing the kernel seed of the story of a life. In astrology, time is something more profound than the passing of one second to the next. Time is the very flesh and marrow of the gods. It is through time that the gods continue to unfold the destiny of our world. Time is the manifestation of their governance.

From this perspective, time is filled with wells of cosmic information and potential; blueprints of actions and their outcomes. Every moment of time holds captive within itself an unmanifest existence, like a forest of ten thousand trees lying dormant within a single seed. The birth of anything – be it a child or a city – captures one of these cascading particles of celestial time and unfolds it in accordance with the laws of destiny that govern the operations of our world. Therefore, the natal chart truly is "the picture of an entity in planetary terms."

In general, the only time we realize the importance of any moment is when time specifically happens to us through concrete events that bear significant meaning. It is the business of every astrologer to study and understand the generation of these moments in order to aid each individual in discovering light on life. Bonatti writes:

> *The astrologer knows of what kind is every motion of every supercelestial body. If he knows the qualities of motions, he knows what kind of impression they imprint, and of what kind their significations are, and all things which come to be in Earth according to the natural order... therefore, all things which come to be in the present, and which have been hitherto, and which come to pass in the future, can be known by the astrologer...*

The duty of every astrologer is to study the imprint of time upon matter, and how the collective nature of those imprints both sustain and transform our world. Within each horoscope is the frozen, yet living imprint of time upon the individual – the natal promise of the life to come.

Astrology is the study of life in all its multivalence. However, our gazing outward into the infinite beyond shouldn't cause us to forget our central objective in doing so. We practice astrology with the intention of understanding more of who we are at our divine core. Astrology is meant to teach us how to live in harmony – within ourselves and with each other. The *Corpus Hermeticum* tells us:

> *Through their own wonder-working course the [planetary] gods sent forth every soul clothed in flesh, so that men should survey heaven, the paths of the heavenly gods, the works of God and the activity of nature... so men began to live and understand the destiny assigned to them by the circling gods...*

Destiny, fate, and natal promise are interchangeable terms. They represent the law that governs each individual life. To live in accordance with this law is to live in harmony with the universe. The outcome of our astrological studies must inevitably be a return to original harmony; one which allows us to "live and understand" the destiny assigned to us by the lords of fate and the forces of life. Our astrological practice has no value if it cannot help illuminate the path of our return.

## Why Receive an Astrological Consultation

I have often wondered why people come to me to receive a reading of their natal charts, especially when they have worked with astrologers before. After all, how much self-knowledge can a person hope to gain? How would a middle-aged man benefit from a stranger telling him that his mother was emotionally and physically unavailable, and that she herself may have been addicted to tranquilizers as a means of dealing with her own anxiety? What can a person hope to gain from hearing that his youngest brother struggles with finding a sense of direction in life, his oldest brother has lost himself completely in his toxic marriage, and that his oldest brother's wife is someone who the family finds untrustworthy? How many times does someone need to hear that she both looks and acts like her grandfather, which is why her family has always had a very strained relationship with her? These are anecdotes from my client practice. They represent moments when, through only reading the individual chart of a client, I was able to tell the story of not just the client's life, but also the lives of the people closest to them.

What is the value of being told that which you already know to be true about the core event structures that have shaped your life? Why would you pay a considerable fee to learn virtually nothing new about yourself? The answer to these questions is to be found in the gift of remembrance that astrology has to offer.

On the one hand, hearing our story told by a stranger who should know nothing about us at all provides us with a touchstone of genuine magic. Being witnessed and understood as we are without having to explain or justify ourselves can be invaluable, especially if we struggle with vulnerability. It reminds us that the limitations of perception imposed upon us by our experience of the physical world is a lie. It tells us that there is something that bridges the gap between the possible and the impossible in a tangible way. It gives us all a sense of existing in the world as a conscious decision that was made within the mind of God, as opposed to being a random mistake, aimlessly wandering through life. An astrological reading can provide us with the clarity that supports us manifesting our destiny in the highest, most joyful way.

## ASTROLOGY SHOWS US THE MAP

For those of us who have experienced an inordinate amount of suffering within this lifetime, astrology provides distance from the weight of our stories, long enough to realize that we no longer have to be hurt by them. It allows us to explore the possibility of letting the healing process begin. For those of us who have experienced extraordinary success and good fortune as dominant life themes, astrology gives us a means for understanding the celestial structure of our blessedness so that we may further explore the possibilities available to us. For the vast majority who live somewhere in the middle of both fortune and challenge, our natal chart opens for us a "book of reasons." It explains why our lives have developed in the ways that they have, and how we can live in harmony with our soul's truest purpose.

Astrology shows us the map of our life experiences, the people we've evolved into as a result of those experiences, and ultimately the people we may yet become should we continue along our path. We practice astrology throughout the course of our lives because every time we do, we participate in the song of self-remembrance.

Knowing our destiny allows us to better co-create that destiny alongside the governors of time. In the *Corpus Hermeticum*, Hermes Trismegistus explains:

> *... there are these three: firstly, God, Father and the Supreme Good;*
> *secondly, the cosmos; and thirdly, man. God contains the cosmos and*
> *the cosmos contains man. The cosmos is the son of God, man the son*
> *of the cosmos, and as it were, the grandson of God.*

We all carry the imprint of the cosmos within our thoughts, decisions, and actions, as if it were celestial DNA. The planets reside within us as the motive forces that inspire us towards the various events we encounter. While the heights to which we may aspire in life are circumscribed by the parameters of our natal promise, the pathways available to us for expressing that promise are infinite.

Astrology is the most sublime of our earthly contemplative arts. On the wings of this astrology, we endeavor to fly to the edge of the starry stair, and meet the gods where they reside. It is to that end that we study, and that we continue in the unending perfection of our craft. We may live and practice for a thousand lifetimes and still never exhaust the breadth of the knowledge that is held within this discipline. No matter how far down the path of mastery we travel within our practice of astrology, we will forever only be at the threshold of the beginning of wisdom.

CHAPTER 1 QUESTIONS

1. What is astrology?
2. Which ancient state was the birthplace of classical Western astrology?
3. What does the word "planet" mean?
4. List the planets in the Chaldean Order.
5. The Chaldean Order shows the planets from the closest planet to Earth to the farthest. True or False?
6. Why were the Sun and the Moon considered to be planets by the ancients?
7. What is geocentrism?
8. What is heliocentrism?

CHAPTER 2 OBJECTIVES

* Identify the major branches of traditional astrology.
* Learn why all branches of astrology are "question-based."
* Understand where each of these branches fit within the education of an aspiring astrologer.
* Explore some of the technical challenges that exist within practicing client-based astrology without centralizing the natal chart of the client.
* Learn about the sub-categories that exist within natal astrology.
* Learn the importance of non-personal, mundane astrology in an astrologer's overall training.

# CHAPTER 2

## BRANCHES OF
## TRADITIONAL ASTROLOGY

*The multiplicity of first things will not dismay the beginner. It
does not really matter which of several necessities is learnt first.*
–MARGARET C. HONE

TRADITIONAL ASTROLOGY CAN BE divided into four main branches: horary astrology, electional astrology, natal astrology, and mundane astrology. These four branches contain the entire doctrine of classical astrology. What follows is a detailed description of each branch and how they might be organized within the complete education of an astrological student.

### HORARY ASTROLOGY

Horary (ho-RUH-ree) astrology is the divinational branch of astrology. Divination is the art and science of communicating with the divine by means of an established symbolic language. In horary, our established symbolic language is the language of astrology itself. Horary astrology is a way of answering a question that a person has in the moment through interpreting the chart of the moment when that question was asked. In charts such as these, the Ascendant usually represents the "querent" or the person asking the question. "Quesited" refers to the thing that is being asked about.

The quesited will be found in one or more of the twelve astrological houses. For example, the question "Will I make money from this business venture?" will be answered through an analysis of the first house of the querent and the second house which represents the querent's money. The second house will also represent any financial benefit the querent may receive from the business. The business venture itself will be signified by the querent's tenth house of career. Houses within a chart symbolize the various topics of life that a person may ask about. Once we have a solid understanding of what the houses mean, we can confidently determine which houses will be most appropriate for answering a specific question.

All astrology can be thought of as question-based. In electional astrology, we ask about the best time to begin something. In natal astrology, we ask about our overall destiny in life. In mundane astrology, we inquire into global and political events. Within traditional astrology, we believe that all questions that can be asked about any sphere of life fall under the various headings of the twelve terrestrial houses. Whether we are speaking about our personal money or the money of a nation, the second house of the chart will refer generally to finances in the four branches of traditional astrology. Horary astrology is a wonderful training ground for new students to familiarize themselves with how the twelve houses can be used to answer questions that may arise within a consultation.

As far as learning and teaching astrology is concerned, I prefer to teach a general course in the Foundations of Classical Astrology (FOCA) first. After rooting students in a firm foundation of all astrology, the first place they explore their new abilities is horary astrology. Horary provides the new astrologer a safe space to develop the interpretive skills that will be necessary when working with clients in natal consultations. It allows them to grow proficiency in clear and objective chart delineation.

A strong astrological practice requires us to concretely interpret the specific outcomes indicated by a chart. We must be able to come to definitive conclusions regarding a multitude of astrological combinations. In traditional astrology, this conclusion is known as a "judgement." The judgement we arrive at represents the most probable outcome based on a systematic approach to chart analysis. When students begin to grow their astrology skills in this way, they become detached and objective. They become more willing to make a definitive statement about whether a particular astral influence is describing a positive or a negative outcome.

This ability to define various astrological combinations as "good" or "bad" is a quickly dying component of our practice. It would seem as if the more modern and politically correct we become, the less willing we are to be honest about the nonexistent state of the emperor's new clothes. Through the modern over-emphasis on natal astrology, astrology itself has become over-personalized. This excessive self-indulgence has contributed to creating a generation of astrologers who cannot help but become personally offended when we speak about a bad aspect or an afflicted planet or a bad chart in general. Due to this lack of astrologers wanting to view a chart or combinations within a chart as bad, we find ourselves in an age of anti-negativity; one in which we hear statements such as "there is no such thing as a bad chart" – a statement which is emphatically untrue. Learning how to tell the difference between a bad chart and a good chart is the first concrete skill that needs to be developed by someone intending to become an excellent astrologer. Knowing how to answer specific questions based on the good or bad combinations in a chart is the second skill that the new astrologer must master.

When we begin our astrology training with less of an emphasis on person-based astrology and more of an emphasis on question-based astrology, it allows us to grow clearer, more objective powers of assessment. The purpose of cultivating these skills is so that we can be guided by the chart towards the specific truth it represents. Equipped with this truth, our objectivity then becomes the most helpful thing that we can offer our clients. In my opinion, there is no better sphere within which to acquire these skills than horary astrology.

Even though I believe horary astrology is a supreme teaching tool, I don't think it is sufficient as a stand-alone professional practice. Another issue that we currently find ourselves faced with is that of "certification culture" within our field. Students have the option of receiving specific certifications in specific branches of astrology. Subsequently, many of those students go on to elect themselves as the specialists within those areas. However, the classical astrologers have never been specialists. They have always been generalists – fully conversant in all branches of traditional astrology.

Today, horary astrology is at the forefront of astrological certification culture. It provides an easy, relatively affordable, and immediate entrance into the field of professional astrological practice. Students with little practical ability at all, armed with only their horary astrology certification can quickly and prematurely call themselves "professional astrologers specializing in horary astrology." However, in my humble opinion, horary only provides rudimentary skills that do not begin to encapsulate the full scope of what a student of astrology needs in order to begin a client-based practice.

As we read books on horary astrology from the late seventeenth and eighteenth centuries, we find a constant thread. The authors seem to all be in agreement that though horary astrology is useful, it isn't truly a substitute for natal astrology. In *Clavis Astrologiae Elimata* (1676), Henry Coley writes:

> ... if the Querent have but his own Radical Figure of Birth, he may draw the judgment of his Question from thence more safely, as upon a surer Foundation. For if the Nativity be known, a Horary Question is but of small validity, especially in general Questions such as these viz. shall I ever be rich, or attain to honor or preferment in the world? Shall I ever travel and see remote parts, etc. But if that cannot be procured, a Question is acceptable, it being as it were a Second Birth. The Question is the Birth or motion of the Mind.

In *A New and Complete Illustration of the Celestial Science of Astrology* (1794), English occultist and astrologer Ebenezer Sibly writes:

> Hence, the birth of the Question, like the nativity of a child, carries the story of the whole matter in hand upon its forehead. And hence also follows that skill in natural predictions by which the artist is enabled to demonstrate the particulars of the event required. However, the predictions that are made from the Questionary Way are by no means so perfect and correct as those deduced from nativities, and therefore I recommend all judgments of futurity to be made from Nativities when they can be procured, rather than from horary Questions.

There are also technical difficulties with horary astrology as a professional practice. One difficulty that I have encountered has to do with scheduling horary readings. A large portion of my clientele comes from the astrological community. I have had a number of astrologically-aware clients tell me that they'd never book a horary reading with me while Mercury is retrograde or when the Moon is void-of-course. We'll learn what both these concepts mean later on. I believe this level of conscious "tampering with the process" either partially or wholly destroys the fundamental element upon which all good divination is built: the suspension of our conscious ability to impose our will or ego onto the outcome. Despite this tampering, the actual moment when I produce the chart may not be exactly when the client planned for it to be. However, the fact that the client attempted to orchestrate an outcome in favor of the answer they were seeking has made me doubt whether or not that moment could truly be seen as valid from a divinational perspective.

Another scheduling related issue is less ethical than it is practical. Within my astrology practice, I have a set time that I meet clients: 11:30 AM and 1:30 PM daily. What this means, however, is that if I have a client today at 11:30 AM and a client tomorrow at 11:30 AM, both clients will have Ascendants for their horary charts that are within one or two degrees of each other. If 00° Aquarius happens to be rising today at 11:30 AM, it will take somewhere around three weeks for Pisces to begin to rise at 11:30 AM. Saturn is the "domicile ruler" of Aquarius. The planet that rules the sign on the cusp of the Ascendant signifies the querent. This means that every client who comes to me within that three-week period will have Saturn as their significator within the horary chart. This is highly out of alignment with the larger realities of human complexity that each client brings to a reading.

I have seen astrologers try to address these difficulties in different ways. Some erect the horary chart after they have read a question that was submitted via email. Others, upon receiving an emailed question, ask the client to call them to confirm the details of the question. They then cast the horary chart – not for the moment of reading the email, but for the moment of understanding the verbal question that they received via the phone call. World renowned astrologer Evangeline Adams, addressed a slightly different challenge that she saw within horary practice. In her book *Astrology: Your Place in the Sun* (1928), she makes the perfectly valid argument that two clients asking their question at the same time or in fairly rapid succession of each other, would end up with the same chart to answer their question. She writes:

> As stated in "The Bowl of Heaven," the Ancients, in their Horary Astrology, considered only the mundane position of the heavens at the time the individual sought an answer to his query. It can at once be seen that if two or more persons present their queries at exactly the same time, they would with this method get exactly the same diagnosis, irrespective of what their immediate need might be. Horary Astrology, as practiced by the author, considers also the position of the heavens in relation to the radical chart of the individual. With this method... each person would receive the information bearing on the particular problem involving his life at the moment...

All of these workarounds are satisfactory ways of dealing with this issue in horary astrology. However, due to my strong belief in the primacy of natal astrology, I lean more towards the approach outlined by Adams, combined with other timing considerations that I believe provide a more valid moment of divination.

Beyond using horary astrology as a teaching tool, there is also the reality of what I do in my professional practice. I believe that all astrology, if it is to be useful for the individual in a practical sense, must be referred back to that person's natal promise. Therefore, I practice and teach what I've come to call "natal-based horary astrology."

I consider horary astrology as it is usually taught to be a wonderful place for astrologers to sharpen their critical thinking and troubleshooting skills. However, I do not believe it should be used in isolation of a larger, more holistic natal-based approach. I hope to fully outline my method of natal-based horary astrology in a future publication.

## ELECTIONAL ASTROLOGY

Horary astrology teaches us how to judge the strengths of the planets and how to judge the overall condition of a chart. It teaches us what a fortunate chart looks like in comparison to an unfortunate one. These skills naturally lead to the practice of electional astrology.

Electional astrology is the practice of choosing the most auspicious moment to begin an action, project, or event based on the astrological factors active within that moment. An electional astrology chart is called an "election." Elections can be made for virtually everything. There can be elections for buying property, selling property, getting a haircut, planting a garden, signing a contract, submitting a thesis paper, starting a business, going on a trip, making an important phone call, getting a surgery, and even IVF implantation. Through applying the skills learnt in horary astrology, the astrologer can reverse engineer a chart to reflect a client's desired outcome.

I practice and teach a form of electional astrology that I call "natal-based electional astrology." My approach greatly differs from what most people practice as electional astrology today.

Within the modern approach to creating elections, many people believe that an election can be chosen that is generally good for the entire world. Personally, I don't find this to be that dissimilar from overly generalized Sun sign astrology columns that state that a particular day will be lucky for everyone born with their Sun in a particular sign. I do not believe in the use or the value of general elections, and neither did the astrologers of the Renaissance. Throughout the Renaissance literature, we find the repeated admonition against creating elections that are not rooted within the nativity of the person in question. In his book *Astrologia Restaurata* (1653), author William Ramesey has this to say on the matter:

> *In all authors that ever I yet met with, I find there can be no time elected (in this our astrological way of electing) advantageous to anyone whose nativity or time of birth is not exactly known; for according unto it must you frame your election, together with respect to the solar return of the year...*

He goes on to say that if the accurate birth time is not known, a horary chart should be used instead. However, he then reiterates all the reasons why the natal chart should be the root of all elections.

Henry Coley also speaks about the importance of natal-based elections. He writes:

> ... *From what hath been said, may be gathered that there are two kinds of Elections, the first from the Nativity, and the second (in a more general way, the Nativity not being known) from a Question... But the first [natal-based election] is only to be embraced, and the second [horary-based election] wholly to be rejected as erroneous and illegitimate... Thus 'tis clear to the eye of Reason, in my opinion, that except the Nativity be known, 'tis but a vain and foolish thing for any person to constitute an Election... And hence may be discovered, what necessity there is that the Nativities of Persons should be known, and therefore Parents should be more careful in recording them...*

I agree with these classical astrologers that all true elections must be aligned with the natal chart. There is no "one size fits all" approach. Without rooting the election in the realities of the nativity, the election itself may be nothing more than aspirational – the power of positive thinking at best.

## NATAL ASTROLOGY

I believe that after the foundations of classical astrology are learnt, followed by horary astrology, the student can venture into whichever other branch of astrology most interests them. However, most people enter astrology expecting to learn how to read their natal charts and the charts of others. Therefore, after FOCA and horary astrology, the next branch of astrology I teach is natal astrology.

Natal astrology is the practice of interpreting the nativity of a person. A more traditional name for natal astrology is "genethlialogy." The word "genethlialogy" comes from the Greek "genethliālogía," which denotes the casting of destinies through the interpretation of the birth chart. Similar to this is the classical word "geniture" – which is synonymous with "nativity" or "birth chart."

When we delineate or interpret a birth chart, we do so with the intention of explaining the destiny that person was born to fulfill. This person is referred to as the "native." The destiny that is interpreted from the natal chart is often referred to as the "natal promise."

The natal promise is an astrological description of the concrete reality we will be born into within this lifetime. It also describes the major formative circumstances we will experience. The natal promise describes our psychological orientation to the world, our physical constitution, finances, siblings, family, community, offspring, illnesses, marriage, death, travel, education, career, and friendships. It even outlines our less than desirable tendencies that we would rather keep hidden from the world. Combined, these topics – and the multitude of subtopics within them – constitute what is known as our "destiny."

Natal astrology is a far more complex branch of astrology than the two previously mentioned. It deals with the very life of a person, whereas horary and electional astrology focus on the multitude of micro-events that occur within that life. The astrologer takes on a huge responsibility when interpreting a birth chart. The birth chart isn't just the chart of some inconsequential question, or the chart for the launch of a business. It is the chart of the very precious life of an individual – a fact that should not be taken lightly. Natal astrology is not meant to be practiced by people who only have an entry level knowledge of astrology, and I daresay it is not an appropriate place to begin one's astrological studies.

## Sub-Categories of Natal Astrology

There are several sub-categories in natal astrology. These divisions are, in fact, complete fields of astrology within themselves. These include: financial, vocational, family, fertility, medical, and predictive astrology. There is also synastry, or the astrology of relationships and compatibility. With the exception of predictive astrology, which touches on all areas of life, each of these fields represent an expansion on the various topics that we find in the twelve houses of the natal chart. Financial astrology is a second house subject, fertility astrology is a fifth house subject, synastry is a seventh house subject, vocational astrology is a tenth house subject, and so on. We will learn the full significations of the twelve houses later on.

Though these topics can be localized to specific houses, there is a peculiar thing that occurs in natal astrology. When we put on the lens of one of these categories, the entire chart can be read as a commentary on that category. Psychological astrologers do this all the time when they read the entire chart as a commentary on the soul and psyche of the person. However, in financial astrology, the entire chart can be read purely in a financial sense. In synastry, the entire chart is read through the lens of love and compatibility. In medical astrology, the same chart that was read through a financial lens a moment earlier, can be utilized to give concrete commentary on the physical vitality, health, and constitution of the native. It is an extraordinary feature of astrology that the same chart with the same planets can be read in a completely different way through multiple, independent lenses. Each lens allows the chart to give a full and robust delineation of the various parts of a person's life.

I have often said that astrology is holographic. No matter how we divide the chart into various topics, the entire chart continues to act as a unified whole. The same planets that represent the immense difficulties that we had with our toxic fathers, can be the same planetary combination that describes our chronic digestive issues. I don't know of any astrologer who has an answer as to why this should be the case. However, this points us towards the truth that our lives, though complex in every way, are a singularity that express one specific story of human unfolding. All of our experiences are compounded and share a common thread. When we start to pull on one of these living threads, we find that it is deeply woven into the fabric of every other major formative event that we've experienced. Circumstances that seem vastly different in their impact often originate from a common source within us. Therefore, the vast experiences that have made us who we are can be expressed using the same astrological factors.

## MUNDANE ASTROLOGY

Mundane astrology is the astrology of world events. Cities, nations, large groups of people, weather, and environmental events are the subject of study within this branch of our discipline.

In *Raphael's Mundane Astrology or The Effects of the Planets and Signs Upon the Nations and Countries of the World*, popular astrologer Raphael (Robert T. Cross) wrote:

> *Mundane Astrology is that branch of the Science which treats of the influence of the Zodiac and Planets upon Nations, countries, cities, and divisions of the earth, and is the art of foretelling the chief events which will come to pass therein.*

Charles E. O. Carter writing in *An Introduction to Political Astrology*, tells us:

> *… under Mundane Astrology came not only the rise and fall of dynasties, and wars, but also earthquakes, droughts, epidemics, the founding and destinies of cities.*

A teacher of mine once asked me, "What do you do when you've learnt all the natal astrology there is to learn?" I didn't have an answer for her at the time. Her personal recourse was to study the astrology of world events. Today, I believe that mundane astrology would be a sensible next course of study for the astrological student if they are following the sequence outlined above. However, because of its non-personal nature, the student can choose to delve into mundane astrology at any point within their astrological studies.

Mundane astrology tends to be less popular than other branches because of its lack of a personal focus. However, I think that every astrologer should have some idea of the astrological factors that are impacting their immediate environment. Our personal destinies must inevitably be secondary to the collective destiny of our community, city, and nation. We cannot truly return to our "original harmony" on a personal level if we haven't first harmonized with our surroundings and understood our role within it. We must all ask ourselves the question: What is my presence meant to offer the collective social ecosystem that I am a part of?

Mundane astrology allows us to contextualize our individual stories against the backdrop of a larger societal framework. It also enables us to see and track cycles that repeat throughout history. While the study of all branches of astrology are vital to the development of the well-rounded astrologer, mundane astrology shows the very concrete ways astrology can manifest in the world at large. Seeing events unfolding through the practice of mundane astrology hopefully will inspire more students to trust in the concrete predictive value of astrology in their lives.

CHAPTER 2 QUESTIONS

1. What are the branches of astrology?
2. What does it mean that horary astrology is "divinational"?
3. Why do we consider all branches of astrology to be question-based?
4. What is one technical challenge we may face in practicing horary astrology? What is one way of dealing with that challenge?
5. Renaissance astrologers all agreed that general elections should be utilized because some days are luckier than others for everyone at the same time. True or False?
6. What is the natal promise?
7. What are three sub-categories of natal astrology?
8. Why is mundane astrology important?
9. Which branch of astrology are you most drawn to studying and why?

CHAPTER 3 OBJECTIVES

✳ Introduce several of the pre-Socratic philosophers, and discover how their teachings impact Western astrology.

✳ Learn how the elements fit within the ancient Greek and alchemical understanding of the evolution of the universe.

✳ Explore Eastern perspectives that are analogous to our ancient Western cosmogony myths.

✳ Discover how Hermeticism and alchemy preserve major classical ideas regarding the origins of the universe.

✳ Learn why the Sun and Moon played such an integral role in classical Western mysticism.

✳ Introduce the three alchemical principles of sulfur, mercury, and salt.

# CHAPTER 3

## HERMETIC PHILOSOPHY
## OF THE PRE-COSMOS

*Since the Creator made the whole cosmos, not with hands but by the Word, understand that he is present and always is, creating all things, being one alone, and by his will producing all beings. For such is his body: intangible, invisible, immeasurable, indivisible, like nothing else. It is not fire, nor water, nor air, nor breath, but through it, all things exist.* –CORPUS HERMETICUM, 4:1

MODERN ASTROLOGY TENDS TO BE taught without providing insight into its mystical and philosophical roots. In recognition of this absence of depth, there has been an eruption of New Age-based astrological systems in the twentieth century: from Alan Leo's esoteric astrology, to various transpersonal, karmic, and theosophical schools. Each has sought to "fill the gap" by supplying Western astrology with an underlying spiritual doctrine; one that is often heavily borrowed from the mystical teachings of the East. Yet, this supposedly missing link has always existed. Our Western ancestors have left us with a treasury of metaphysical philosophy regarding the structure of the universe and the role of astrology within it. Though time has restored many of these rich teachings to us, much of the astrological community remains unaware of the ancient mystical philosophy of this practice.

In order to understand the backdrop upon which astrology was built, we must study many schools of ancient philosophy. Classical Western astrology didn't fall out of the sky as one perfected system at the dawn of time. God didn't teach it to the angels who in turn taught it to us. There is no one hand of authorship behind what we call traditional Western astrology. However, within our practice, we can find certain philosophical, metaphysical, and cosmological threads; ideas that lead us back in time to wide-ranging schools of classical Western thought. The fact that these threads all intertwine within the tapestry of our astrology, proves that for the ancient fathers of philosophy, astrology existed as a natural extension of a complex, yet integrative vision of the world.

Astrology developed alongside our desire to understand more about the universe and our place within it. Classical philosophy and astrology never existed as two independent subjects. They were always deeply interwoven – as if the stars themselves inspired human beings to think and discover our inner genius. In teaching astrology, the metaphysical theories of the ancients should not be disregarded. They provide a sense of genuine heritage, culture, and of belonging to a tradition much larger than ourselves.

While a full treatment of classical Western philosophy and metaphysics is beyond the scope of this volume, I will share a synopsis of ideas from those teachings that relate to our present study. It is my hope that this glimpse into the ancient mind gives you a sense of being a part of a cosmic legacy that has been nurtured for thousands of years.

## Bereshit – In the Beginning

> *Some hold that the universe does not derive its elements from any source but is devoid of origin, that it ever was and ever shall be, without beginning as it is without end; it may be that ages ago chaos in travail separated the mingled elements of matter and that, having given birth to the shining universe, the darkness fled, banished to infernal gloom; perhaps nature after a thousand ages remains an aggregate of indivisible atoms, though doomed to dissolve and return to the same form, and the total sum is made up of practically nothing and will become nothing, and it is lifeless matter which has produced heaven and earth; possibly the universe was constructed out of fire and flickering flames, which have formed the eyes of heaven and dwell throughout the whole system and shape the lightning which flashes in the skies; the skies, perchance, were born of water, without which matter is parched and hardened and which quenches the very fire by which it is destroyed...* – MARCUS MANILIUS

### THE PRESOCRATICS

The Presocratics were a group of thinkers who flourished between the sixth and seventh centuries BCE. Presocratic philosophy is also known as "early Greek philosophy." "Presocratic" denotes that they were "before Socrates" – both chronologically and also in terms of the content of their study. This title "Presocratic" – coined in the eighteenth century by Johann Augustus Eberhard – has been argued to not be the most appropriate designation for them. It isn't entirely chronologically accurate; the last of the Presocratics were contemporaries of Socrates.

One of the key distinctions between the Presocratic and the later Socratic philosophers is that the Presocratics largely concerned themselves with the nature of the cosmos, whereas the Socratic philosophers were more concerned with ethics, morality, and politics. However, it should be noted that several Presocratic philosophers, including Pythagoras, also held within their philosophy teachings on morality, conduct, and methods by which to cultivate a higher quality of human life.

### THE MILESIANS

The beginning of philosophy can be traced back to the single question "What is the universe made of?" and those who sought to answer it. Within the recorded history of the Western world, the first people to answer this question were three ancient Greek thinkers: Thales, Anaximander, and Anaximenes. They are collectively known as "the Milesians," since they all hailed from the Ionian city of Miletus, in what is now modern-day Turkey. The combined teachings of the Milesians established the Ionian school of Presocratic philosophy. Ionia was an ancient region comprised of twelve Greek city-states, of which included Miletus.

The Milesians sought to discover the origins of the universe from natural causes. This is in distinct contrast to their predecessors, who explained nature primarily through supernatural causes and the actions of the gods. The Milesians began their inquiry into the origin of the cosmos by searching for the "theory of everything." Central to this search, was the discovery of the root substance out of which the entire universe emerged. This originating principle was known as the "archê" (AR-kai) to the ancient Greeks. The word "archê" denotes a beginning, origin, or the root of action.

THALES (circa 624-545 BCE)

Thales (THAY-leez) is hailed as the father of Western philosophy. He was the first person in recorded Western history to propose a theory concerning the archê. Not only did he offer his thoughts on the matter, he also justified his rationale based on an observation of nature. His efforts laid the foundation of what would later become codified as the scientific method. Others would follow his lead, offering their observations and conclusions. Notably, his student, Anaximander, and Anaximander's student, Anaximenes, both disagreed with his ideas. The first of many disagreements between classical Western philosophers was about the root of all existence.

Thales posited that the archê was water. In his influential work titled *Metaphysics*, Aristotle (384-322 BCE) writes:

> [Thales'] supposition may have arisen from the observation that the nourishment of all creatures is moist, and that warmth itself is generated from moisture and lives by it... and water for most things is the origin of their nature.

Reginald E. Allen in *Greek Philosophy: Thales to Aristotle* (1991) writes:

> He [Thales] seems to have supposed that the Earth floats on a vast body of water, a clot in a sea of liquid. The liquid itself he must have thought to be "unbounded" – not infinite, since the concept of the infinite had not yet been invented, but rather of indefinite extent. This conception of unbounded primordial water is not Greek; it is found in the myths of the great river-civilizations of Egypt and Babylonia, and in Genesis. The world itself was probably thought by Thales to have grown from this liquid, perhaps, Aristotle suggested, as an animal grows from the moist seed.

As Allen points out, the notion of primordial water existing before the creation of the world can also be found in the *Torah*. In the book of *Genesis* 1:1-4, we read:

> In the beginning of God's creating the heavens and the earth – when the earth was astonishingly empty, with darkness upon the surface of the deep, and the Divine Presence hovered upon the surface of the waters – God said, "Let there be light," and there was light.

Thales' sense of the preeminence of water within the universe is a core cosmological concept within Judaism and Christianity.

Another concept held by Thales was that the entire world was ensouled. Within his philosophy, everything – animate and inanimate – is filled with daimons or spirits that act as sources of divine life for the entities they inhabit. On this point, Aristotle writes in *De Anima*:

> *And some say that [soul] is intermingled in the universe, for which reason, perhaps, Thales also thought that all things are full of gods.*

For Thales, everything was alive and, therefore, capable of being in dynamic interaction and communication with everything else. Aetius (circa 100 CE) writes:

> *Thales said that the mind of the world is god, and that the sum of things is besouled, and full of daimons [spirits]; right through the elemental moisture there penetrates a divine power that moves it.*

This idea of universal ensoulment would later become one of the central pillars of Western astrology. In astrology, we hold a belief that there is one universal life force permeating the entire natural world; that the souls of every creature are connected as if by an invisible web. The incessant whirling motion of the planets sends waves of influence throughout the cosmos. These cosmic tides reverberate across the web of universal life. Thus, every ensouled being is impacted by these stellar forces that originate in the heavens above. In the *Astronomica*, Manilius writes:

> *This fabric which forms the body of the boundless universe, together with its members composed of nature's diverse elements, air and fire, earth and level sea, is ruled by the force of a divine spirit; by sacred dispensation the deity brings harmony and governs with hidden purpose, arranging mutual bonds between all parts, so that each may furnish and receive another's strength and that the whole may stand fast in kinship despite its variety of forms.*

This is in harmony with the philosophy of Thales. It is noteworthy that Thales was also an astrologer. The few tales that we have of his life from authors such as Plato, Aristotle, and Herodotus all mention his study of the heavenly bodies to gain fortune, avert disaster, and give timely counsel to the leaders of his day.

## ANAXIMENES (flourished circa 545 BCE)

Anaximenes does not chronologically follow Thales in the sequence of the Milesian Presocratics. He was the student of Anaximander, who was the student of Thales. However, Anaximenes does follow Thales in his assertion that the archê could be found in the elemental world. Anaximenes put forth that the archê was air. Aetius writes:

> *Anaximenes... of Miletus, declared that air is the principle of existing things; for from it all things come-to-be and into it they are again*

*dissolved. As our soul, he says, being air holds us together and controls*
*us, so does wind and air enclose the whole world.*

For Anaximenes, the rarefication and densification of air gave birth to the other elements of fire, water, and earth. As the root of the elements which composed the cosmos, air – for Anaximenes – was also the root of the cosmos itself.

In *Early Greek Philosophy* (1920), John Burnet states that Anaximenes was one of the philosophers on whom Theophrastus (circa 372-287 BCE) – successor of Aristotle – wrote a monograph. Theophrastus writes:

> *Anaximenes... also says that the underlying nature is one and infinite.*
> *He did not, however, say it was indeterminate, like Anaximander, but*
> *determinate, for he identifies it as air; and it differs in its substantial*
> *nature by rarity and density. Being made finer it becomes fire, being made*
> *thicker it becomes wind, then cloud, then (when thickened still more)*
> *water, then earth, then stones; and the rest comes into being from these.*

## ANAXIMANDER (610-546 BCE)

Anaximander said that the root source of existence could not possibly be something that was already existent in the material sense. He reasoned that if the root source of "all things" was in fact one of those "things," then that one thing would dominate and destroy everything else. On this, Aristotle writes:

> *... for the elements are opposed to each other (for example, air is cold,*
> *water moist, and fire hot), and if one of those were infinite, the rest*
> *would already have been destroyed.*

What then, in Anaximander's philosophy, would replace water, if neither water nor any other material substance could justifiably be the root of all existence? Anaximander posited that the archê was an endless presence that he called the "apeiron." The word "apeiron" can be translated as endless, infinite, and boundless. Allen writes:

> *Anaximander supposed the answer to lie in ridding the primordial*
> *principle of its association with any single sensible opposite and*
> *making it simply the Unbounded. This is a great leap of the creative*
> *imagination, an abstraction of very high order: Anaximander posited*
> *as explanatory of the world of sense perception a principle that had no*
> *characteristic found in the world of sense perception.*

The components of the unborn world originated in Anaximander's Unbounded as a collection of raw, pre-elemental qualities: hot, cold, wet, and dry. These warring pairs of opposites existed in the Unbounded as an undifferentiated field of infinite possibility. No one of these qualities had superiority over the other. None of them was truly manifest in a way that would threaten the existence of the other.

On their own, these qualities represented the pure spiritual natures of the elements. Bonatti writes:

> *Insofar as the elements are simple or pure in their own spheres, they have simple qualities ruling in them: fire, heat; air, moisture; water, coldness; earth, dryness. But insofar as they are connected and entangled, they have composite qualities with respect to each other, namely: fire, heat and dryness; air, heat and moisture; water, coldness and moisture; earth, coldness and dryness.*

As these qualities became enlisted in the creation of the physical universe, they densified, and in so doing, lost their original purity. Complementary qualities clung to one another and created the four elements of fire, water, air, and earth. The four elements are the building blocks of the universe from the perspective of the ancient Greeks. Though diverse in their operations, it is important for us to remember that in Anaximander's vision of the world, the four elements are derived from the One Thing that is the root of all existence.

We find a similar veneration of the elements occurring within our traditional astrological literature. Manilius writes:

> *… it may be that neither earth nor fire nor air nor water acknowledge a begetter, but themselves constitute a godhead of four elements, which have formed the sphere of the universe and ban all search for a source beyond them, having created all things from themselves, so that cold combines with hot, wet with dry, and airy with solid, and the discord is one of harmony, allowing apt unions and generative activity and enabling the elements to produce all things.*

What we find in the writings of Manilius is the idea that the entire universe is composed wholly of the four classical elements. He completes his reflections on this matter by outlining the Aristotelian theory of how the elements are arranged within the sublunary world. "Sublunar" refers to the world "beneath the Moon." Traditionally, this was used to describe the sphere within which the Earth existed in the Chaldean Order. The sublunar arrangement of the elements are: fire represented by the Sun, Moon, and stars above us; the air, which is a connective intermediary between the world below and the world above; water, which covers the body of the Earth; and lastly earth, representing the stability of our planet, which geocentrically stands at the midpoint of the cosmos. Manilius writes:

> *But however obscure its origin, all are agreed about the outward appearance of the universe, and the orderly arrangement of its structure is fixed. Winged fire soared aloft to ethereal reaches and, compassing the rooftops of the starry sky, fashioned the walls of the world with ramparts of flame. Air next sank down to become the tenuous breezes and spread out the atmosphere midway through the empty space of*

*the sky. The third place was allotted to the expanse of the waters and floating billows, as the level sea at its birth was poured abroad to form the whole ocean, to the end that water might breathe out and expel the subtle vapours and so feed air which draws the seeds of its being from water, whilst, set beneath the neighbouring stars, the breath of air might nourish the fire. Lastly at the bottom sank earth, moulded into a ball by its weight, and mud, mixed with shifting sand, collected as the light liquid gradually made its way to the top; more and more the moisture withdrew to form clear waters, the filtering of the liquid built up land, and the fluid plains came to rest in hollow valleys; so by degrees mountains emerged from the deep, and the round world sprang forth from the waves, but closed in on every side by the vast ocean.*

ALCHEMICAL WORLDVIEW OF THE UNBOUNDED

FIGURE 1: *Ouroboros*

Anaximander's theory of the Unbounded found many sympathizers in the various schools of Western alchemy. Later alchemical authors would come to describe this Unbounded through the image of the serpent Ouroboros, eating its own tail. This symbol of Ouroboros, represents the double power of life and death held within the Unbounded. For the alchemists, it represented the alchemical duality of "solve" and "coagula." *Coagula* signifies the force by which all things come into being, whereas *solve* is the force that reabsorbs all things into the "One Substance" out of which the universe arose. The serpent Ouroboros was thought to produce and destroy itself, thereby holding the secrets of immortality. Evola writes:

*"Nature takes pleasure in itself" and "Nature dominates itself." Here is the possibility of "nature" being desire, abandonment to itself, spontaneity, and identification with self-gratification. At the same time, it is the possibility of saying no to itself, of manifesting itself as that which acts against itself, that which dominates, and transcends itself, to the point of actually making the distinction between that which dominates ("masculine", active) and that which is dominated ("feminine", passive) ...*

This "distinction" creates the first division within the "prima materia," or original substance. This can be symbolized by the alchemical glyph of Salt, which we will learn about more fully later.

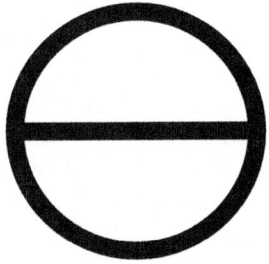

FIGURE 2: *Salt*

We see a similar idea of creating a partition within the "one substance" in the *Torah.* In *Genesis* 1:6-8 we read:

*God said, "Let there be a firmament in the midst of the waters, and let it separate between water and water." So God made the firmament, and separated between the waters which were beneath the firmament and the waters which were above the firmament. And it was so.*

This initial polarization creates the basis for every pair of opposites that exists within the universe. While the Unbounded remained the root of all things, it held within itself both a divine masculine and a divine feminine creative principle. These agents would ultimately create the universe. However, in order for this creative act to occur, nature first had to "dominate nature." The Unbounded would first have to bind its boundlessness in a sense; to carve out a hole in its own body where it could safely give birth to a material universe.

## TAO TE CHING ON THE ORIGINAL SUBSTANCE

The quest to discover the original substance of creation occupied the hearts and minds of ancient philosophers. Despite their technological limitations, many of them presented ideas that were elegant and well-reasoned for the period in which they lived. Their way of understanding nature lays out fascinating cognitive paths to explore. We might choose to follow the direction of primordial water described by Thales, or the very rational theory of the Unbounded laid out by Anaximander. The condensation and rarefication of air as outlined by Anaximenes could very well strike us as being explanatory of the material world from a philosophical perspective. Perhaps, like Heraclitus who came after, we might come to believe that the "One Thing" was composed wholly of flames, and that the world itself were "an everlasting fire." Regardless of whose philosophy we are most moved by, they all held that the universe, in all its complex wonder, developed from a single original matrix.

Lao Tzu (circa 600-501 BCE) was the first philosopher of Chinese Taoism. He is the alleged author of the *Tao Te Ching*. In that text, he describes the One Thing in the following manner:

> *The Tao that can be told is not the eternal Tao.*
> *The name that can be named is not the eternal name.*
> *The nameless is the beginning of heaven and earth.*
> *The named is the mother of ten thousand things.*
> *Ever desireless, one can see the mystery.*
> *Ever desiring, one can see only the manifestations.*
> *These two spring from the same source but differ in name;*
> *This appears as darkness.*
> *Darkness within darkness.*
> *The gate to all mystery.*

In the West, one of the names the ancient alchemists gave this pre-universal substance was "One the All." One the All was symbolically represented by the circle, which is ultimately a simplified representation of the serpent Ouroboros. The circle is a symbol of undifferentiated potential and the original Chaos out of which the universe was born.

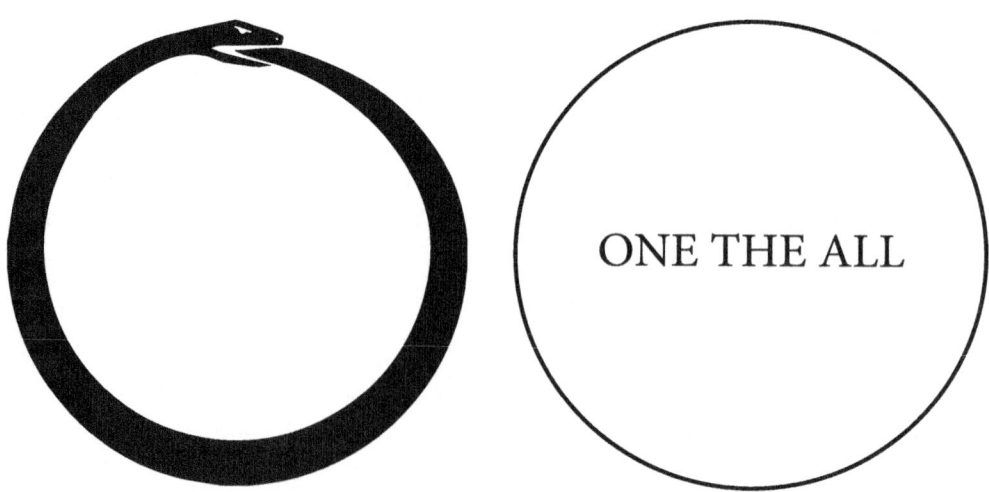

FIGURE 3: *Ouroboros & One the All*

One the All contains the masculine "desiring" or "dominating" principle within nature as well as the feminine "desireless" or "dominated" principle. These can further be divided into: light/dark, life/death, hot/cold, dry/wet, day/night, good/evil, limited/unlimited, up/down, masculine/feminine, growth/decay, and all other conceivable pairs of opposites.

Evola says that in the "One" and "All" splitting apart, they release one from the other. He writes:

> We can also say that in the One the All, the "One" and the "All" now crystallize as two distinct principles. The "One" takes on the meaning of a center that manifests in the heart of chaos (the "All") and affirms itself there as a principle of incorruptible fixity, stability, and transcendence. From the signature ○ – "the first matter" – we move on to ⊙, which is the ancient hieroglyph of the Sun. and that which in the originating matter was undetermined possibility, a passive potentiality for any quality, change, or chaotic transformation, is turned into a quite different principle, which in hermetism corresponds to the feminine symbol of the Moon ☽.

From this doctrine arises the two most foundational astrological symbols: the glyphs of the Sun and the Moon.

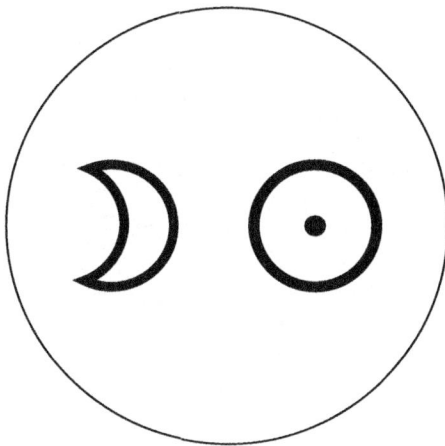

FIGURE 4: *Symbolic Representations of the Luminaries*

Sun and Moon represent the original duality within Hermetic thought. The Sun symbol signifies the desiring, masculine, dominant principle. It is the impulse to separate from the field of infinite possibility, and to manifest as an individual self. The glyph of the Sun depicts the rebellious seed that crystallizes within the heart of the Unbounded. It is the urge within all of us to call ourselves "I."

The Moon represents the original substance – the desireless, feminine, dominated principle. Within the teachings of alchemy, she epitomizes the raw, undifferentiated forces of nature; forces which are most closely aligned with how we would describe the Unbounded. She signifies the field of infinite potential that has not yet been acted upon by the dominant, individualizing, creative power of the Sun.

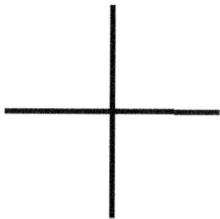

FIGURE 5: *Feminine & Masculine Symbolism of the Luminaries*

These solar and lunar principles were also expressed by the ancient alchemists through the symbols of the horizontal and the vertical lines. The horizontal line represents the Moon. It corresponds with the passive, feminine, receptive, and yielding principle within nature. It symbolizes relationships, understanding, and the womb in the most abstract sense. The vertical line represents the Sun. It corresponds with the active, masculine, resistant, and dominant principle within nature. It symbolizes achievement, conquest, and the phallus in the most abstract sense.

The Moon represents the "Not-I," whereas the Sun represents the "I." The ancient alchemists tell us that these two principles are fundamentally antagonistic towards each other. The struggle between these forces has a direct impact on our existence or nonexistence within the material world. In order for us to exist without the looming threat of our physical bodies and planet dissolving into a nonexistent state, the "I" (Sun) has to wage symbolic war against the "Not-I" (Moon) and win. The cross is a symbol of this battle.

FIGURE 6: *Equal-Armed Cross*

In the symbol of the cross, the solar "I" principle passes through the center of the body of the lunar "Not-I" principle in an attempt to dominate her. It is as if the masculine principle is demanding the feminine principle to give him access to her inexhaustible supply of unmanifest potential so that he can create something tangible.

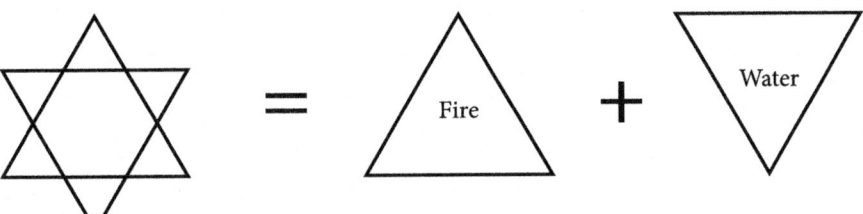

FIGURE 7: *Hexagram Deconstructed*

The hexagram maintains this symbolism, and provides even deeper symbolic meaning. In the hexagram, we come to understand that the material world of individual beings – represented by the upward pointing, masculine triangle – is fed and nourished by the infinite supply of the nonmaterial world – represented by the downward pointing, feminine triangle. Finites are supported by infinites. Conversely, the infinite is reflected in the multiplicity of finite, individual things. Evola writes:

> *If as we have suggested, the law of desire and of self-absorption is expressed by the descending direction of the symbol for water* $\nabla$ *, everything in the "one thing" that is on the contrary oriented toward the principle of the Sun can be expressed by the ascending opposite direction, that is, flame: whence the alchemical sign of Fire* $\triangle$ *.*

As we have come to expect from fairy tales, the hero – depicting the solar, individualizing principle – slays the dragon – signifying the lunar, universalizing principle. From a metaphysical perspective, the principle of stability, particulars, and order that the Sun represents conquers the principle of chaos, universals, and non-being that the Moon represents. From this solar victory, our material universe is born.

Though the Sun is successful in his conquest of the raw and chaotic lunar tides, the battle changes him as well. If we refer back to our glyph of the cross, we notice that the masculine vertical line and the feminine horizontal line that we began with, begin to transform into something else as soon as they connect with each other.

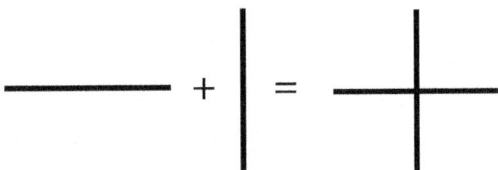

FIGURE 8: *Cross Deconstructed*

As the masculine principle passes through the feminine, he gets stuck, as if in a web. He is frozen, petrified, and trapped. In their crossing, these two principles become unified once more. However, it isn't the same unity they experienced when they existed as undifferentiated concepts within the Unbounded. Separated from the Unbounded, they are conceptually "denser" than they were previously.

This time, in their remerging, they give birth to a third concept distinctly different from themselves.

Though different, this third thing carries forward the dominating principle of the Sun in the densest sense. It creates the quality of physical stability that permeates the entire cosmos. The unindividualized (Moon) and the individualizer (Sun) give birth to the individual (Matter), as can be seen everywhere around us through the determinate existence of our physical universe. Here we see the triad of mother, father, and child. More specifically, the "son" is a reflection of the Sun. He carries out the purpose of his father through physical manifestation.

In describing the cross glyph, Evola writes:

> The first case defines the hermetic idea of the fixed (as opposed to volatile) taken in a negative sense. This is the state of petrification, arrest, suspension, and stagnation devoid of life. It is the "body" element in the widest sense where the Gold (or Solar principle), although present [within the body], is as restricted in its power as the opposite principle to which it has reacted. It is the negative side of individuation...

Positive individuation, in this context, refers to the existence of individual souls that are self-aware, but without a body. Negative individuation, therefore, is when a soul becomes encased in the dense chamber of a physical body and can no longer partake of the universal freedom that it previously knew. It is now bound to the material plane and trapped in a physical container that will go through all the phases of generation, preservation, corruption, and destruction, before it can return to a state of original freedom. The Sun only signifies the concept of individuation in a spiritual sense – where the individual soul breaks free from the neutralizing force of the cosmic field of all life. This is akin to the drop that separates itself from the ocean, or the flame that breaks free from the overwhelming grandeur of the Sun. Matter, on the other hand, signifies the realized concept of a separate entity in material form. The Sun serves as the inner star around which our individuality constellates. Matter represents this idea taken to the extreme through the formation of a physical body that serves as a container for the solar principle within all of us.

This is reminiscent of the myth of the Welsh goddess Cerridwen. In a shapeshifting race around the world, her enemy Gwion turned into a hare and she chased him as a greyhound. He transformed into a salmon, and she chased him as an otter. He transformed into a wren, and she chased him as a hawk. He transformed into a seed, and she – transforming herself into a hen – swallowed him whole. However, he did not die. He took root in her womb, and the goddess found herself pregnant with the reincarnated body of that same man. Though she was victorious in destroying her antagonist, she, too, had her individuality destroyed in the process. Evola writes:

> The "two" that become "three" are the two in their joining... ideographically, that can be expressed by the cross, the equivalent from this point of view to the seal of Solomon.

70

The cross has long been considered the symbol of the Earth and of the entire material universe. It represents the density of matter. It is the celestial sphere carried on the shoulders of Atlas. It is the stone to which Prometheus was chained. It is the cross upon which Jesus was said to have been crucified. In all of these myths, the heaviness of the material world is depicted as a burden on the immortal self within us. The Moon, Sun, and Earth are the primary triad of the ancient alchemists: the boundless, the binding, and the material, respectively. These principles exist everywhere within nature. In the alchemical tradition, they are also depicted through the substances of Mercury, Sulfur, and Salt.

## THE THREE ALCHEMICAL SUBSTANCES

FIGURE 9: *Mercury, Sulfur, & Salt*

For the alchemists, the earthy ideas of stagnation, arrest, and petrification were almost identical to the principle of Salt. Paul Foster Case in his treatment of the Salt principle in *Hermetic Alchemy: Science and Practice* writes:

> *Ordinary salt retards the chemical processes which cause decay. On account of this it is used to preserve meat. This is what is regarded as the main characteristic of alchemical Salt. It is due to the quality of inertia attributed to Tamas in Hindu philosophy. This quality is definitely associated with the idea of body.*

Alchemical Salt, therefore, was thought to preserve the individual solar identities of everything. This solar identity corresponds with the soul (Sol), whereas the earth or Salt principle corresponds with the body. It is through the agency of Salt that everything within the material universe inherits a gross, physical, material body to serve as its vehicle.

The alchemists extended the Sun and Moon metaphor into the physical substances of Sulfur and Mercury, respectively. Mercury represents all that is vibratory, fluid, sublime, and transcendental. It has an inherent plasticity. It can take on vastly different shapes and qualities when placed in different conditions. Therefore, like the lunar principle, it has no true form, and bears within itself the possibility of every form in creation. Sulfur is hot, active, fiery, dominant, and aggressive like the solar principle. Salt, on the other hand, is inert, dense, dull, stable, unchanging, and preservative; all qualities which naturally correspond with the Earth.

Philippus Aureolus Theophrastus Bombastus von Hohenheim (1493-1541) was a German-Swiss physician and alchemist who established the role chemistry played in medicine. He changed his name to Paracelsus, which means "above or beyond Celsus." He did this to indicate that his medical knowledge exceeded that of renowned first century Roman medical writer, Aulus Cornelius Celsus. Within the Western mystery tradition, Paracelsus is regarded as one of the greatest alchemists to have ever lived. *In The Hermetic and Alchemical Writings of Paracelsus* (1910), he writes:

> *Hermes truly said that all the seven metals [viz. the planets] were made and compounded of three substances... these three substances he named Spirit, Soul, and Body... Now, in order that these three distinct substances may be rightly understood, namely, spirit, soul, and body, it should be known that they signify nothing else than the three principles, Mercury, Sulfur, and Salt, from which all the seven metals [planets] are generated. For Mercury is the spirit, Sulfur the soul, and Salt is the body. The metal between the spirit and the body, concerning which Hermes speaks, is the soul, which indeed is Sulfur. It unites these two contraries, the body and the spirit, and changes them into one essence.*

This quote is of vital importance to our study. For the ancient alchemists, the seven planets were composed of the three substances of Mercury, Sulfur, and Salt. Developmentally, we can trace these back to the Moon, Sun, and Earth triad; from there, back to the duad of the Sun and the Moon – representative of the division between the One and the All, respectively; and from there, even further back to the "One Thing" or "One Substance" from which the universe arose. Hermes Trismegistus considered the seven planets to be the governors of fate and destiny – the rulers of the forces of time. From this quote of Paracelsus, we see how the planets can trace their roots back to the eternal. However, we all bear these planetary influences within ourselves. Every component of our soul, mind, and body corresponds with a planet or a combination of planets. In the same way as the planets can trace their bloodline back to the eternal, so can we.

MERCURY – GOD OF ALCHEMY

Mercury is the god of alchemy. He contains within his glyph all of the foregoing alchemical principles mentioned by Paracelcus.

FIGURE 10: *Mercury Deconstructed*

Though mythological Mercury is seen as being the servant of the gods, within the Western mystery tradition, Mercury is the most important of the ancient gods. It is Mercury who holds the key to fulfilling the "Great Work," the singular goal within the life of every alchemist. Mercury was also the god of astrology – a fact that was not lost on the ancients. In the opening pages of *Astronomica*, Manilius begins by honoring Mercury. He writes:

> *You, God of Cyllene [Mercury], are the first founder of this great and holy science; through you has man gained a deeper knowledge of the sky – the constellations, the names and courses of the signs, their importance and influence – that the aspect of the firmament might be enhanced, that awe might be roused not only by the appearance but by the power of things, and that mankind might learn wherein lay God's greatest power.*

### THE FOUR ELEMENTS

This universal unfolding does not stop with Mercury, Sulfur, and Salt. The cross gave birth to another level of symbolic ideas within the minds of the ancients. The two principles Moon and Sun unify to create the third principle, Earth. The Earth would go on to give birth to four separate things as indicated through its quadripartite glyph. These four things are the four elements of fire, air, water, and earth.

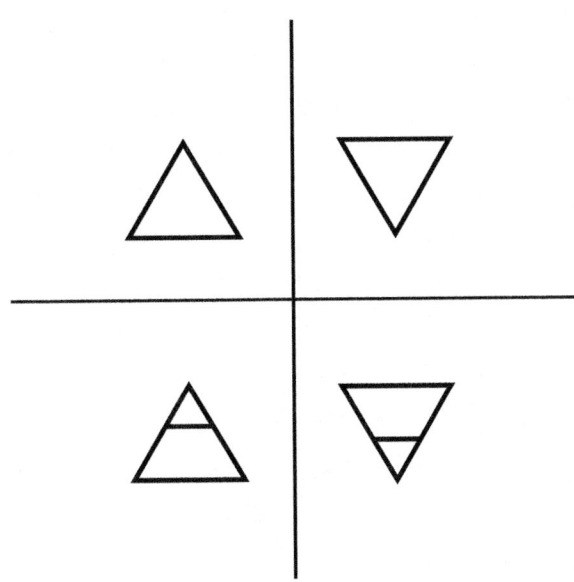

FIGURE 11: *Four Elements*

73

The glyph of Earth is meant to demonstrate that everything within our sublunary world is composed of the four elements.

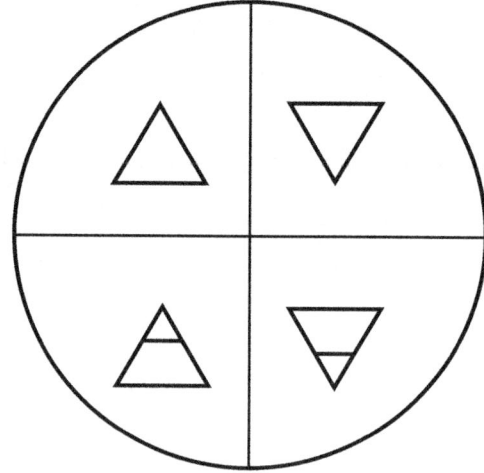

FIGURE 12: *Four Elements within the Earth Glyph*

It also symbolizes spirit (circle) being supplanted by matter (cross).

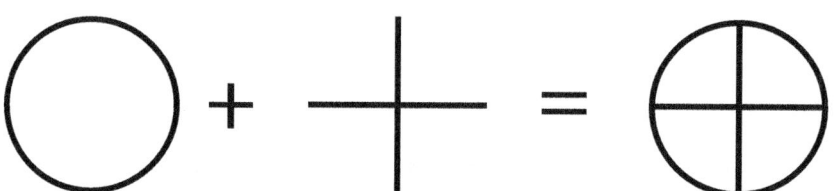

FIGURE 13: *Earth Glyph Deconstructed*

Ideographically, this carries the same meaning as the glyph of Saturn, in which we see the cross of matter superior to the crescent of spirit. We will learn more about the planet Saturn and his attributes later on.

FIGURE 14: *Saturn Glyph*

For the ancients, the four elements were the building blocks of the material universe. The three alchemical principles of Mercury, Sulfur, and Salt find their expression through these elements. Therefore, the One created the Two, the Two created the Three, the Three created the Four, and the Four ultimately reconstituted the unity of the One through the complex wholeness of the cosmos. Meditation upon the four elements provides us the key to understanding all forms of life within the material universe. This depth of insight into the operations of our material world ultimately leads us to the precipice of our understanding, beyond which there is nothing left to discover than godhead itself.

THE END IS IN THE BEGINNING

> *Ten Sefirot [divine emanations] – their end is tied in their beginning and their beginning is in their end, like a flame attached to an ember. For it is One Master that has no other, and before One what do you count?* – SEFER YETZIRAH

$$1 + 2 + 3 + 4 = 10$$

Pythagoras of Samos (circa 570-490 BCE) was an ancient Greek mathematician and philosopher. He claimed that everything in the universe, including music and astronomy, is mathematical in nature. According to Pythagoras, ten was the number of the universe in its completion. He depicted this concept in what is known as the "Tetractys of Pythagoras."

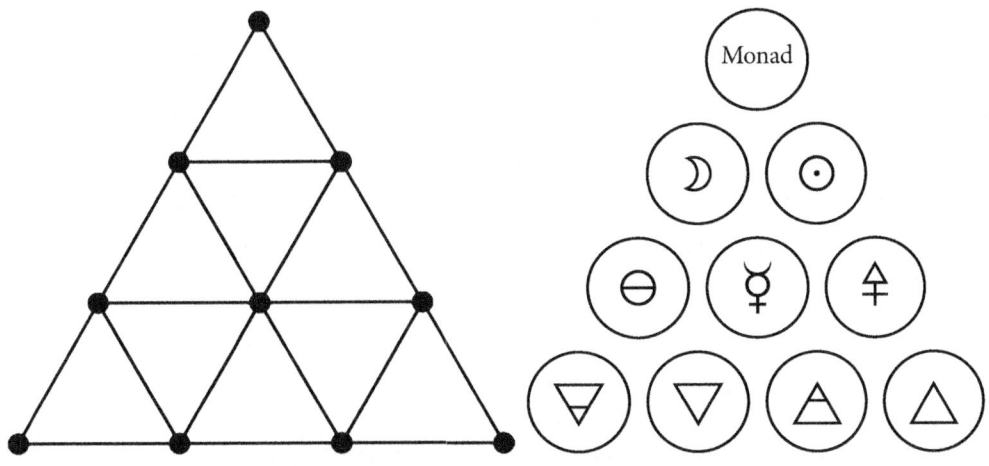

FIGURE 15: *Tetractys of Pythagoras*        FIGURE 16: *Alchemical Tetractys*

The first tier consists of the indivisible Monad: One the All. The Duad of Moon and Sun compose the second tier. The Triad of Mercury, Sulfur, and Salt constitute the third tier. The Tetrad of Fire, Air, Water, and Earth establishes the fourth and final tier.

Pythagoras wasn't the only ancient philosopher who held that the number ten represented the perfect completion of our material universe. The Kabbalah also asserts that the number ten is of central importance in the unfolding of God's power within the cosmos.

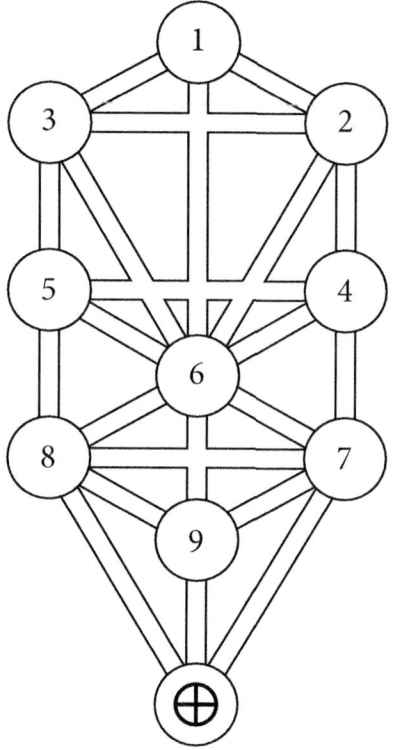

FIGURE 17: *Etz Cha'im (Tree of Life)*

In the Kabbalah, the Tree of Life consists of ten spheres or divine emanations. Each sphere represents the distillation of God's power from a field of infinite potential. This field is called "Ain Sof," meaning "without end." This Ain Sof is synonymous, in a sense, with the Unbounded of Anaximander. While the ancient philosophers surely influenced each other in their hypotheses about the origins of the universe, it is extraordinary to see how many of these Western schools of thought shared a common understanding.

Within the tradition of Western mysticism known as the Hermetic Qabalah, the ten divine emanations on the Tree of Life were thought to correspond with the Chaldean Order. The first sphere symbolized the Primum Mobile, the second, the fixed stars of the zodiac, and from the third onward are the spheres of the seven classical planets: Saturn, Jupiter, Mars, Sun, Venus, Mercury, and the Moon. The tenth sphere, hanging as a pendant to the other nine, symbolized our Earth.

Though the Tree of Life depicts the descent of God's divinity into the material world, it also symbolizes how – by ascending through the spheres – we can return to our rightful place in the dwelling place of the eternal. In the *Corpus Hermeticum*, Hermes describes this ascension of the soul. In Book I verse 25, he writes:

> *Thus, a man starts to rise up through the harmony of the cosmos. To the first plain [Moon] he surrenders the activity of growth and diminution; to the second [Mercury] the means of evil, trickery now being inactive; to the third [Venus] covetous deceit, now inactive, and to the fourth [Sun] the eminence pertaining to a ruler, being now without avarice; to the fifth [Mars] impious daring and reckless audacity, and to the sixth [Jupiter] evil impulses for wealth, all of these being now inactive, and to the seventh plane [Saturn] the falsehood which waits in ambush.*

After breaking free of the sphere of Saturn, Hermes states that we ascend into the eighth sphere. We join with the other beings present, to sing of the infinite splendor of the cosmos and its Creator. From there, we ascend even further until we are reabsorbed into the unbounded body of the eternal from which the universe first emerged.

When viewed through the lens of our modernity, this style of Hermetic and alchemical cosmology seems fantastical – remote from reality and out of harmony with science. As true as that may be, spirituality is not meant to teach us the laws of the material universe; it is meant to give us a means of living within it in a deeper, more reverential way. Exploring these teachings fills us with genuine compassion for all expressions of life. At its core, Hermetic philosophy is the philosophy of awe; it broadens the parameters that define who and what we consider to be worthy of our love.

As we study this metaphysical philosophy of the ancients, we are ultimately studying the infinite grandeur of the human mind – that sphere of the eternal that we all embody. We search for a sense of order and purpose within the outer universe with the ultimate intention of further understanding our inner cosmos. Learning how to explore the magnificence of the unbounded star fields within ourselves is the purpose of astrology.

CHAPTER 3 QUESTIONS

1. What did Thales believe was the root element out of which the universe emerged?
2. Which three elements did the various pre-Socratic philosophers believe could be the universal substance?
3. Which element did they exclude? Why do you think it was not considered as being the root substance for all universal life?
4. Write a list of at least ten pairs of opposites you can think of that correspond with the Sun and the Moon. You should end up with ten solar words and ten lunar words.

CHAPTER 4 OBJECTIVES

* Briefly explore the primary components of traditional Western astrology: planets, signs, elements, aspects, and houses.
* Learn about the divisions of the signs by triplicity, quadruplicity, gender, and sect.
* Learn the domiciles of each of the seven classical planets.
* Understand the design of the traditional square chart.

# CHAPTER 4

## A PRIMER IN
## ASTROLOGICAL SYMBOLISM

*Few are the seeds of God, but they are mighty, beautiful, and good.*
–CORPUS HERMETICUM 9:4

AS ASTROLOGERS, OUR FUNDAMENTAL premise is that astrology is a universal language through which we can describe and understand everything within our material universe. The symbolic components of astrology are miniscule when compared to the scope of our subject. From a traditional perspective, every chart can be described as a combination of the same core components: three quadruplicities (or modes), four triplicities (or elements), seven planets, five aspects, twelve signs, and twelve houses. If we were to whittle this down further to the most economic expression of our craft, we would be left with an astrology based purely on planet-to-planet contact. In that version of astrology, the factors to consider would be the planets, their locations within the zodiac, and the various aspect relationships they have to each other. If we included Uranus, Neptune, and Pluto to our celestial pantheon, we would end up with ten planets in total. Though these modern planets nuance how we astrologically speak about reality, a palette of ten colors seems not that different than a palette of seven in its inadequacy to express the infinite diversity that exists within our cosmos.

However, it *does* express that diversity, and it does so infinitely better than any other mystical system bequeathed to us by our ancestors. This seemingly limited set of ideas contains the entire treasure-house of meaning by which we describe everything that happens in our material world. The components of our astrology are like "the seeds of God": few in number, but "mighty, beautiful, and good." You will find in this chapter an outline of these components, all of which should be committed to memory by the aspiring astrologer.

### THE SEVEN CLASSICAL PLANETS

Astrology is the study of how celestial influences are reflected through our material world. These celestial influences manifest through the planets and their relationships with each other. The imprint of these relationships is registered from moment to moment. These planetary imprints are not measured "in" time, but rather "onto" time; as if time itself were a giant tapestry extending through the ages, with the planets as both the lords of its unfolding as well as its weavers. In traditional astrology, the seven classical planets are considered to be the primary rulers of the material universe. As we've previously learnt, the organization of the seven classical planets from Saturn to the Moon is known as the Chaldean Order. The Chaldean Order is: Saturn, Jupiter, Mars, Sun, Venus, Mercury, and the Moon.

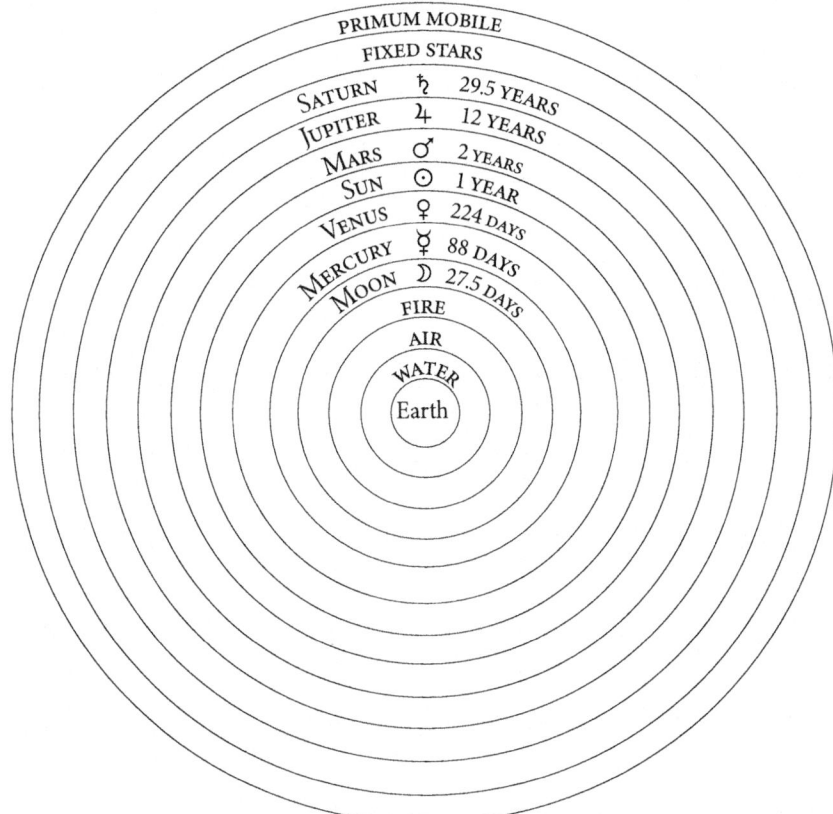

FIGURE 1: *The Celestial Spheres*

The seven classical planets were thought to consist of the following qualities:

TABLE 1: *Qualities of the Planets*

| | |
|---|---|
| ♄ | COLD & DRY |
| ♃ | HOT & WET |
| ♂ | HOT & DRY |
| ☉ | HOT & DRY |
| ♀ | HOT & WET |
| ☿ | WET & DRY |
| ☽ | HOT & WET |

This list of attributions comes from Claudius Ptolemy. You will notice the peculiar composition of Mercury. It is also interesting to note that none of these seven classical planets consist of cold and wet as their composition – the qualities associated with the water element in ancient Greek philosophy. This was an intentional omission of Ptolemy which we will learn more about later on.

### The Modern Planets

In the neo-classical astrology that I teach, I use the modern planets Uranus, Neptune, and Pluto. Since Uranus was discovered in 1781, Neptune in 1846, and Pluto in 1930, they do not receive any of the classical attributions of hot, cold, wet, and dry as the other planets do. They have no rulership, dignity, or debility as the other planets have. However, they have proven themselves to be extraordinarily relevant within our practice. The symbols for these ten celestial bodies can be found below.

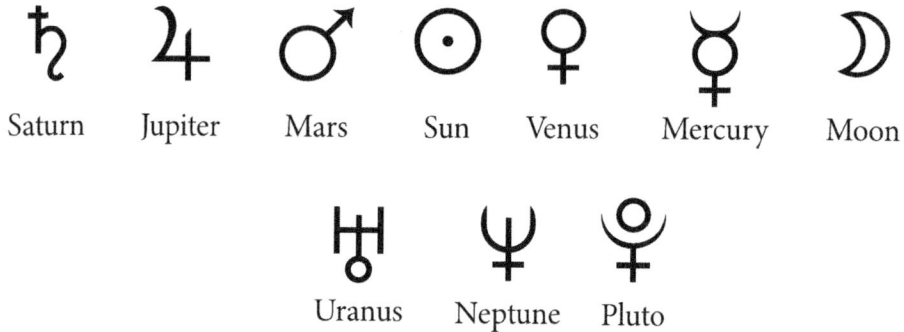

| Saturn | Jupiter | Mars | Sun | Venus | Mercury | Moon |

| Uranus | Neptune | Pluto |

FIGURE 2: *Planetary Glyphs*

### Nodes, Part of Fortune, and the Earth

Other celestial factors that can be found in traditional astrology charts are the Moon's North and South Nodes as well as what is called the "Part of Fortune." Though these are celestial factors, they are not planets. They are important calculated points that have no actual physical body.

The Moon's Nodes are the two points of intersection between the Moon's orbital path and the orbital path of the Sun, also known as the "ecliptic." Since these two orbits do not run parallel to each other, these paths cross in two locations. This crossing point is known as a node, which comes from the Latin "nōdus," meaning "knot."

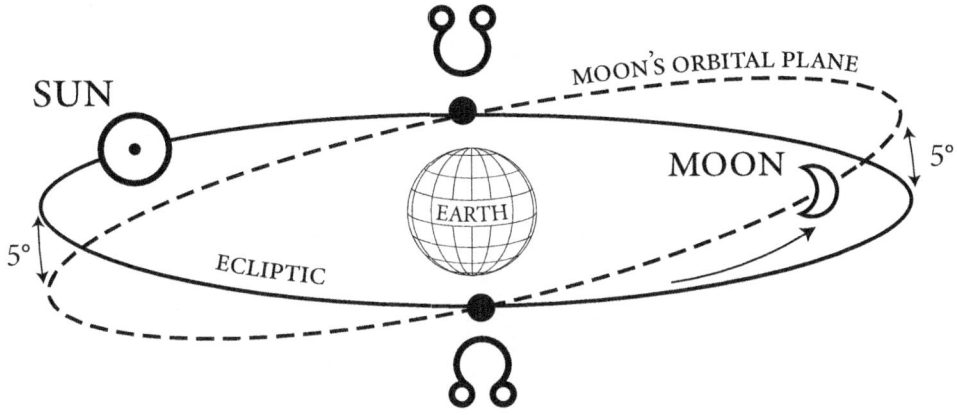

FIGURE 3: *Paths of the Luminaries and the Nodes*

The Part of Fortune (also known as Pars Fortuna, Fortuna, or Fortune) is an important mathematical projection used in astrology. It is derived from calculating the angular distance or arc between the Sun and the Moon and projecting that value from the Ascendant. The symbols for the nodes & the Part of Fortune are given below. The glyph for Earth is also included, since that glyph is often confused with the glyph of the Part of Fortune. Note that the Earth glyph contains an equal-armed cross, whereas the Part of Fortune glyph contains an x.

Part of Fortune     Earth     North Node    South Node

FIGURE 4: *Glyphs of the Nodes, Fortune, and the Earth*

## ASPECTS AND THE CONJUNCTION

An aspect is an angular relationship between two or more planets. As the planets move in their individual orbits, they form aspects with each other. Aspects let us know whether there is harmony or disharmony between the planets in question.

The four traditional aspects are: the sextile, which occurs when two or more planets are 60° apart; the square, which occurs when planets are 90° apart; the trine, which occurs when planets are 120° apart; and the opposition, which occurs when planets are 180° apart.

TABLE 2: *Traditional Aspects & the Conjunction*

| | | |
|---|---|---|
| SEXTILE | 60° | ✳ |
| SQUARE | 90° | □ |
| TRINE | 120° | △ |
| OPPOSITION | 180° | ☍ |
| CONJUNCTION | 00° | ☌ |

There is a fifth planetary relationship known as a "conjunction." A conjunction occurs when planets are conjoined to each other. Therefore, based on our system of measurement, planets in a conjunction are 00° apart. Though the conjunction is a relationship between two or more planets it is not technically an aspect. An aspect is an angular relationship between two or more planets. When planets are in a conjunction, they are 00° away from each other. Therefore, they have no angular relationship between each other, because there is no zodiacal distance between them. However, it was universally accepted amongst Medieval and Renaissance astrologers that though the conjunction was not truly an aspect, it should be considered amongst the other aspects. The conjunction functions in the same way that an aspect does. It brings together the influences of two or more planets, and shows a relationship between the concrete realities those planets represent.

The sextile and the trine are considered to be good aspects in traditional astrology. Conversely, the square and opposition are considered to be bad aspects in traditional astrology. The conjunction has always been somewhat in the middle. The conjunction is beneficial when positive planets are conjoined. However, it is considered to be a negative aspect when negative planets are conjoined. When good and bad planets are conjoined, the good planets are thought to "stave off the malice" of the bad planets. However, the bad planets still act in a challenging way, even if their impact is diminished.

## THE ZODIAC

Aspects are angular relationships between planets that are mathematically measured in space. In order for these angles to be measured, there has to be a backdrop to measure them against. There are several coordinate systems that allow us to measure where the planets are in relationship to each other. However, the most popular framework that we use to measure planetary positions in astrology is called the "zodiac." Within Western tropical astrology, the zodiac refers to the 360° belt in the sky where the Sun can be found travelling throughout the year.

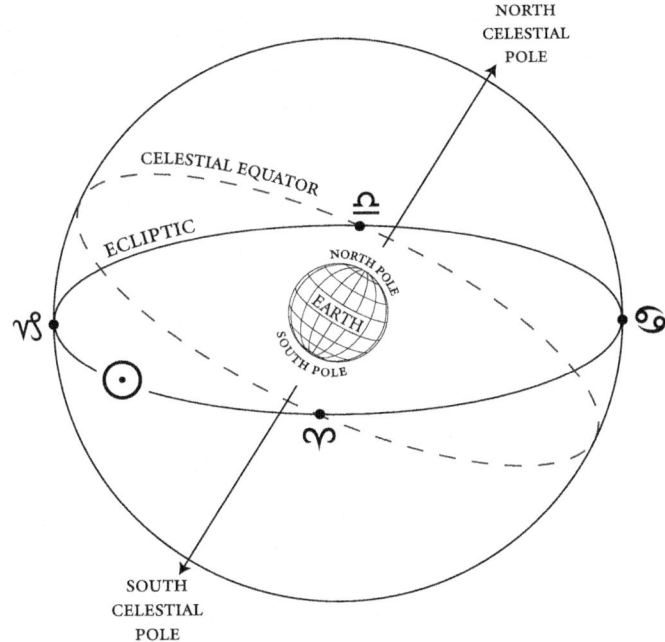

FIGURE 5: *Ecliptic*

The ecliptic is the path of the Sun. The ancients noticed that the planets travelled along a belt approximately 8° in width on either side of the ecliptic. The constellations within this belt became known as the "signs of the zodiac."

The Sun is the only planet that is constantly on the ecliptic. The other planets can be North of the ecliptic, South of the ecliptic, or on the ecliptic. When a planet is North or South of the ecliptic, it has ecliptic latitude.

While the other planets may not necessarily be "on" the ecliptic in the same way that the Sun never strays from it, we project their positions onto the ecliptic all the same. This helps us easily determine how far apart they are from each other, using the ecliptic as our convenient frame of reference and measurement. We measure this distance in terms of degrees of zodiacal longitude. A planet, star, asteroid, or some other celestial object can always be described as having an exact degree of zodiacal longitude.

Therefore, planets in a square relationship can be said to have a 90° arc opening between them. An "arc opening" is the distance between two points measured on a circular or rounded plane. Planets with a 90° arc opening can also be described as being separated by 90° of zodiacal longitude. They both mean the same thing.

Knowing how to easily identify the zodiacal longitude of a planet is a very important skill for the practicing astrologer. The range of degrees for each of the twelve signs of the zodiac is given below.

TABLE 3: *Zodiacal Longitude*

| | | | |
|---|---|---|---|
| ♈ | 00° - 29° | ♎ | 180° - 209° |
| ♉ | 30° - 59° | ♏ | 210 - 239° |
| ♊ | 60° - 89° | ♐ | 240° - 269° |
| ♋ | 90° - 119° | ♑ | 270° - 299° |
| ♌ | 120° - 149° | ♒ | 300° - 329° |
| ♍ | 150° - 179° | ♓ | 330° - 359° |

If a planet is located at 202° zodiacal longitude, it's location in the zodiac is 22° Libra. If another planet is located at 292° zodiacal longitude, it's location in the zodiac is 22° Capricorn.

$$292° - 202° = 90°$$

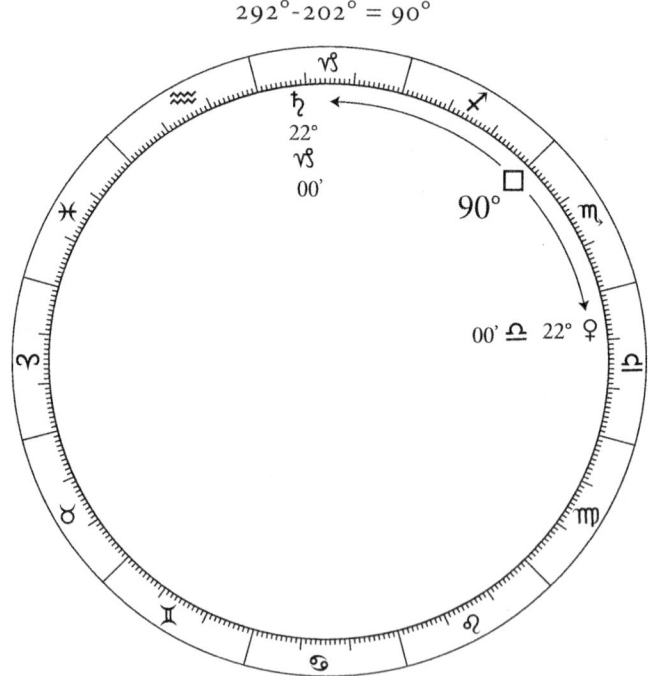

FIGURE 6: *90° Arc Opening Between Venus & Saturn*

These planets are 90° away from each other. There is a 90° arc opening between them. They are separated by 90° of zodiacal longitude, and therefore, are in a square relationship to one another. The list of zodiacal longitudes should be committed to memory by the serious astrology student.

## Zodiacal Placement vs. Zodiacal Longitude

When we refer to a planet at 22° Libra, we are referring to its zodiacal placement and not its zodiacal longitude. When we refer to a planet at 292° zodiacal longitude, we are referring to its zodiacal longitude and not its zodiacal placement. When we refer to a planet occupying any of the 30° of a specific sign of the zodiac, such as Mars at 12° Pisces or Moon at 27° Taurus, our frame of reference is specifically that sign, and nothing else. We are referring to the planet's placement in that sign. However, when we refer to a planet occupying any of the 360° of zodiacal longitude, our frame of reference is where that planet is in relation to the entire zodiac and everything else within it. Regardless of which of these two frames of reference we choose to use – zodiacal placement or zodiacal longitude – they both refer to the same location for the planet in question.

The zodiac is divided into twelve signs. Since the zodiac contains 360°, the twelve signs of the zodiac consist of 30° of zodiacal longitude each. The signs of the zodiac are: Aries, Taurus, Gemini, Cancer, Leo, Virgo, Libra, Scorpio, Sagittarius, Capricorn, Aquarius, and Pisces.

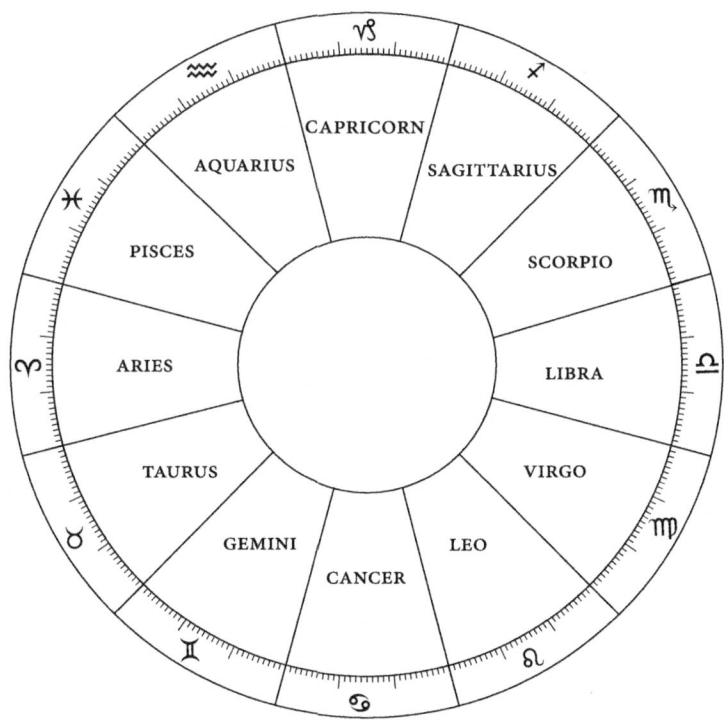

FIGURE 7: *Twelve Signs of the Zodiac*

## Divisions of the Signs of the Zodiac

There are many divisions of the signs of the zodiac.

THE TRIPLICITIES

The signs of the zodiac can be divided based on the element of each sign. This element-based division is known as "triplicity." Signs of the same triplicity all have a 120° trine or trigonal relationship to each other.

TABLE 4: *Triplicities of the Signs*

| FIRE | EARTH | AIR | WATER |
|---|---|---|---|
| ARIES | TAURUS | GEMINI | CANCER |
| LEO | VIRGO | LIBRA | SCORPIO |
| SAGITTARIUS | CAPRICORN | AQUARIUS | PISCES |

THE FOUR QUALITIES & THE ELEMENTS

In traditional astrology, the elements consist of the four qualities of nature found in ancient Greek philosophy: hot, cold, wet, and dry. Through merging, the four qualities create both the four elements and the four temperaments found in Medieval and Renaissance medicine: the hot and dry, fiery, choleric temperament; the cold and dry, earthy, melancholic temperament; the hot and wet, airy, sanguine temperament; and the cold and wet, watery, phlegmatic temperament.

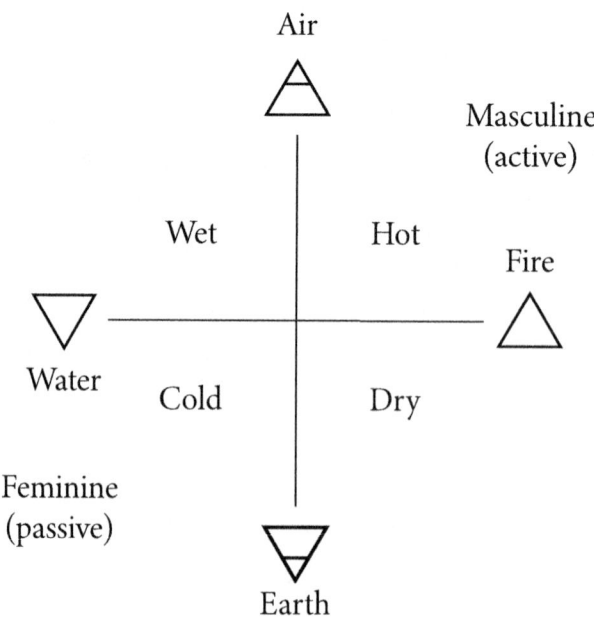

FIGURE 8: *The Qualities of the Elements*

The signs of the zodiac that belong to the same triplicity all consist of the same two qualities. Therefore, all the fire signs are hot and dry, all the earth signs are cold and dry, all the air signs are hot and wet, and all the water signs are cold and wet. We will explore this more deeply later.

## THE QUADRUPLICITIES

> *And so it was discovered that the signs should be only twelve, neither more nor less. There could not be more because each of these acts upon the four elements universally, and because each of these acts on the element assigned to it according to the three states of being, namely, beginning, middle, and end.* – GUIDO BONATTI

The signs can also be divided based on the period of a season that they correspond with. Since the signs of the zodiac are the backdrop of the Sun through his annual travel, each sign can represent a different part of one of the four seasons.

Each season has a beginning, a middle, and an end. These three parts of every season are directly related to the twelve signs of the zodiac in tropical astrology. This season-based division of the signs is known as "quadruplicity." The moveable or cardinal signs represent the beginning of the season, the immoveable or fixed signs represent the middle of the season, and the common or mutable signs represent the end of each season.

TABLE 5: *Quadruplicities of the Signs*

| MOVEABLE/CARDINAL | IMMOVEABLE/FIXED | COMMON/MUTABLE |
|---|---|---|
| ARIES | TAURUS | GEMINI |
| CANCER | LEO | VIRGO |
| LIBRA | SCORPIO | SAGITTARIUS |
| CAPRICORN | AQUARIUS | PISCES |

It should be noted that signs of the same quadruplicity have either a square or opposition relationship with each other.

A more detailed description of the various categories of the signs of the zodiac will be given in the chapter on the zodiac.

## DOMICILE RULERSHIP

The signs of the zodiac are the temples or the homes of the planets. Some planets have signs they "own" as their primary home or place of residence. The signs that are the permanent homes of the planets are called their "domiciles." The planets that are the "home-owners" of those signs are called "domicile rulers." The only planets that rule signs of the zodiac are the seven classical planets. Uranus, Neptune, and Pluto do not rule signs of the zodiac.

Below is a table of the classical planets and the zodiac signs they rule.

TABLE 6: *Domicile Rulership of the Planets*

| | | |
|---|:---:|---|
| CAPRICORN | ♄ | AQUARIUS |
| PISCES | ♃ | SAGITTARIUS |
| SCORPIO | ♂ | ARIES |
| | ☉ | LEO |
| TAURUS | ♀ | LIBRA |
| VIRGO | ☿ | GEMINI |
| CANCER | ☽ | |

## ON GENDER AND SECT

Fire and air are masculine elements. The fire and air signs are masculine signs. Earth and water are feminine elements. Earth and water signs are feminine signs.

All the masculine signs are called "diurnal signs." All the feminine signs are called "nocturnal signs." This division of the signs into diurnal and nocturnal categories is known as "sect" which will be discussed in detail later.

## ESSENTIAL DIGNITY & DEBILITY

When a planet is in its own domicile it is like a king in his castle. He has no one else to report to other than himself. However, domicile rulership is not the only level of rulership or comfort that planets have in the zodiac. Planets have signs that they enjoy being in as well as signs that they don't enjoy being in. Some planets enjoy being in certain parts of certain signs, while they have a difficult time being in other parts of that same sign. For example, Venus has a difficult time being in the entire sign of Aries. However, there are certain pockets of Aries that are a little bit easier for her to be in than others. This topic in classical astrology is known as "essential dignity and debility." Essential dignity and debility refers to how much intrinsic power a planet has in order to perform optimally. More will be said about this in the chapter on *Essential Dignities & Debilities in Practice*.

## THE TWELVE HOUSES

In order to bring these stellar influences down to Earth, the ancients devised a system of twelve houses. These houses represent different topics within the life of whoever or whatever the chart is being erected for.

The dividing line between one house and another is called a "cusp." Note that houses have cusps. Signs of the zodiac do not have cusps. Since there are twelve houses, there are also twelve cusps – one for each house. The twelve cusps, like the planets, are also projected onto the backdrop of the zodiac. Therefore, there is a sign of the zodiac on each house cusp.

Since every sign of the zodiac has one planet as the domicile ruler of that sign, that domicile ruler is considered to be the lord or representative of that house. No matter where that lord may be in the rest of the chart, he or she will always be responsible for the affairs of that house.

A house is considered strong or weak depending on planets in that house. However, the ruler of that house is the planet who will have the final say in terms of the outcome of what that house represents. That planet is the same planet that rules the sign on the cusp of that house.

The twelve houses and their associated topics are listed below.

TABLE 7: *Topics of the Terrestrial Houses*

| First | Self and health | Seventh | Marriage and partnership |
|-------|-----------------|---------|--------------------------|
| Second | Finances, moveable property | Eighth | Death, partner's money |
| Third | Siblings and community | Ninth | Foreign travel, religion |
| Fourth | Father and home | Tenth | Mother and career |
| Fifth | Children and pleasure | Eleventh | Friends and hopes |
| Sixth | Sickness and employees | Twelfth | Hidden enemies, self-undoing |

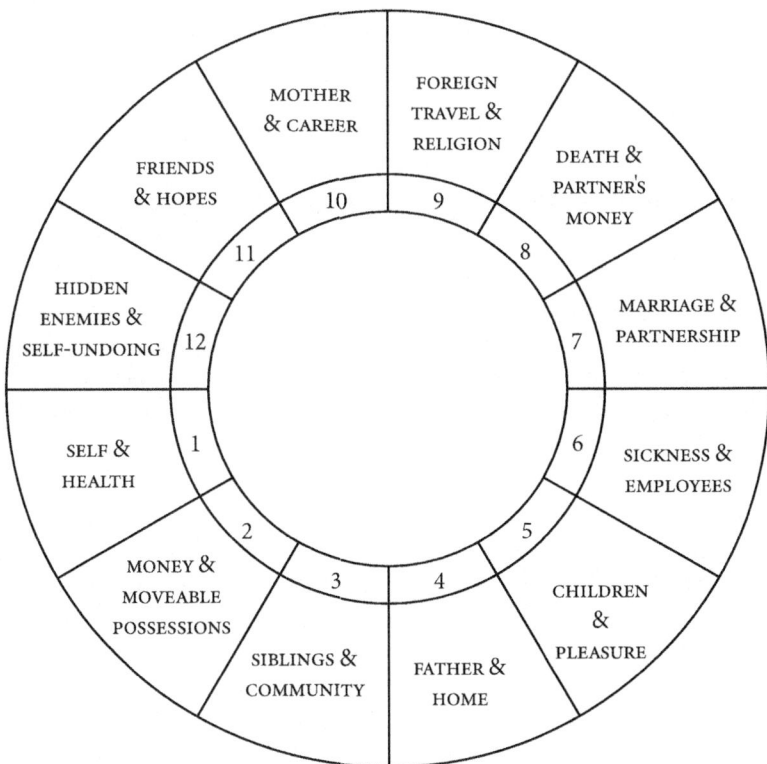

FIGURE 9: *Modern Chart Format (Round)*

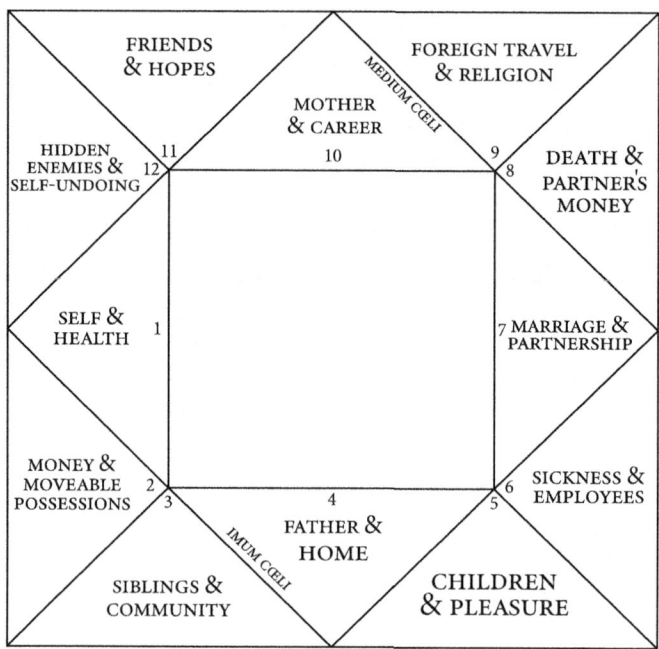

FIGURE 10: *Classical Chart Format (Square)*

## SQUARE VS. ROUND CHARTS

In the twenty-first century, it is customary for Western astrologers to present charts in a round format. However, in the Medieval and Renaissance periods, charts were almost always presented in a square format. Interestingly, in the Jyotish practiced in both North and South India, a square chart format is still used. However, the Indian square chart differs from the version that we commonly see in the Western astrology texts from the Renaissance.

As scholars of traditional astrology, it is important for us to understand how to read a square chart, even though our daily practice of astrology is conducted using round charts. One of the most important systems of divination in both the East and West is called "geomancy." Geomancy is a method by which a question can be answered through creating certain figures composed of rows of dots while holding a question within your heart and mind. These figures are then projected onto one of two formats: a shield-shaped chart or the traditional square-shaped astrological chart. The geomantic figures correspond to the elements, signs, and planets, making geomancy an astrological system of divination. Geomancy, like astrology, is one of the core practices within the Western mystery tradition. Those of us who aspire to expand our possibilities as practitioners of Western mysticism would do well to learn how to read square charts. It not only enables us to understand classical astrological chart examples, but it also gives us a means of exploring other fields of mysticism such as geomancy.

Whether we chose to use square charts or round charts, the meanings of the twelve houses remain the same.

### Regiomontanus – House System of the Seventeenth Century

I teach my students classical astrology that spans the Hellenistic, Medieval, and Renaissance periods. However, we constellate our efforts in the seventeenth century. The house system that was popularly used all across Europe during that time was the Regiomontanus house system. It was popularized by Johann Müller von Königsberg in the fifteenth century. Therefore, we use Regiomontanus houses exclusively for all branches of astrological practice.

With this, we have completed a survey of all the core elements of classical astrology. Everything to come in the following pages will be an elaboration on the topics presented here. The first topic which must come as a precursor to the others is astronomy. In the next chapter, we will explore the general astronomical principles that all astrologers should know. We will see how this subject directly impacts our practice of classical astrology in the twenty-first century.

CHAPTER 4 QUESTIONS

1. How many planets exist within traditional astrology?
2. How many modern planets are usually integrated into "neo-traditional" astrology? Which planets are they?
3. Define triplicity. List the four triplicities of the signs and the signs within each triplicity.
4. Define quadruplicity. List the three quadruplicities of the signs and the signs within each quadruplicity.
5. What is an aspect?
6. What might be one benefit of using a square chart versus a round chart?

# PART 2

*We are travelers on a cosmic journey, stardust, swirling and dancing in the eddies & whirlpools of infinity. Life is eternal. We have stopped for a moment to encounter each other, to meet, to love, to share. This is a precious moment. It is a little parenthesis in eternity.*

—THE ALCHEMIST

CHAPTER 5 OBJECTIVES

* Distinguish between geocentricism and heliocentrism.
* Understand the basic coordinate systems that directly impact our practice of astrology.
* Learn the difference between primary and zodiacal motion.
* Be able to differentiate between a great circle and a small circle.
* Learn about the three zodiacs commonly used today.
* Define "precession of the equinoxes" and outline how it impacts our practice.
* Discuss and define eclipses, retrogradation, and other forms of planetary motion that directly impact our astrology.

# CHAPTER 5

## ASTRONOMY OF ASTROLOGY

*There is nothing (besides first philosophy) in which the soul gains so much wealth as in astronomy or astrology. For through it, we know and understand impassable and unalterable creatures, and those not changing into another essence, as are the supercelestial bodies. And through those creatures we can reach an understanding of the Creator, and know about Him however much more the human mind can attain to and we can perceive him to be impassible and unalterable.* –GUIDO BONATTI

EVERY ASTROLOGER SHOULD HAVE a basic understanding of the astronomical principles that directly impact astrology. Though not the main purpose of this book, this chapter will outline in brief some of the key concepts the twenty-first century astrologer should know about astronomy.

### GEOCENTRIC VERSUS HELIOCENTRIC PERSPECTIVES

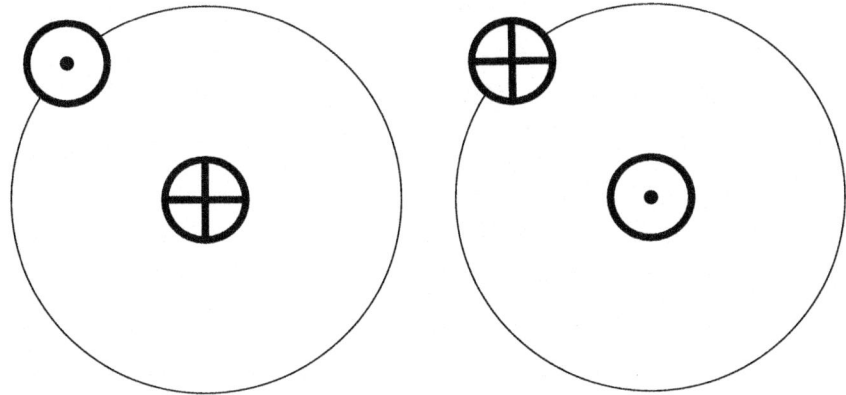

FIGURE 1: *Gecentric & Heliocentric Models*

The geocentric perspective begins by first assuming the viewer is on an unmoving Earth looking out at the heavens above. In contrast, the heliocentric perspective places the viewer on an unmoving Sun from which to look out at the universe. Most of the astrology practiced in the West is geocentric. Though we know we live in a solar system and not an Earth system, our Earth-based perspective allows us to make sense of our relationship to the heavens.

The crowning jewel of scientific achievement was discovering that our Earth endlessly orbits a relatively stationary Sun. It goes against everything our senses perceive to be true, and forces us to face the humbling fact that what we see pales in comparison to what is actually occuring. The heliocentric model was rediscovered and popularized by Nicolaus Copernicus (1473-1543). It was a part of his written works around the year 1514. However, before Copernicus, the heliocentric debate was one that reached far into the ancient world. Aristarchus of Samos in the third century BCE also proposed a heliocentric model. Hypatia in the fourth century CE discussed this controversial topic with her students of astronomy. She was subsequently killed by the burgeoning Christian movement for these ideas – ideas which they considered to be highly blasphemous.

Factual though it may be, our heliocentric understanding doesn't tangibly assist in our daily life. We set our alarms so we can wake an hour before "sunrise" to beat the early morning traffic, even though we know the Sun isn't actually rising and setting. Construction workers in the Caribbean start their days earlier to avoid the fierce heat of the high-noon Sun. It doesn't really matter to them that the Earth has changed location, and not the Sun. Many people build their diets so they eat closer towards the middle of the day and start to wind down their consumption of food as the evening approaches. They know that their bodies are more likely to utilize heavier food in the daytime as fuel as opposed to storing it as excess weight, something that is more prone to happen if we eat a hearty midday meal late at night. It would seem as if in the same way the Sun's power is modulated during the day, our digestive fires are modulated to rise, burn, slow down, and sleep as a part of maintaining our natural rhythms. Ayurveda, a traditional Indian approach to medicine, has long noted this relationship between our physiological rhythms and the daily ebb and flow of solar power. According to Ayurveda, in order for us to live in harmony with nature, we should model our energy based on these daily solar tides. We have built holidays and holy days, our concept of time, and the very practicalities of our daily life around the phenomena of the rising and setting Sun. Our objective understanding of the unmoving Sun seems out of step with the realities upon which our lives depend.

Scientists have sought to rail against astrology because of the geocentric principles that underlie our practice. However, what makes astrology such a vitally humane subject is that it is based in life. Astrology has never positioned itself to be more than a description of the events of our Earth-based lives as we experience them under an infinitely changing sky as we experience it. With human beings and our understanding of the world around us as the central subject matter of astrology, it would be absurd for us to practice an astrology based on us being located anywhere else in the solar system other than Earth. And if Earth is our location, then surely Earth must also be the point from which we extend our vision out into the cosmos in order to understand how we relate to the infinite sky above us. If the Earth is our home, then the Earth must also be the center of our self-knowing.

### THE CELESTIAL SPHERE

If we imagine that the stars in the sky are imprinted onto a giant black sphere with the Earth in the center, then we will have an image of what the ancients referred to as the "celestial sphere."

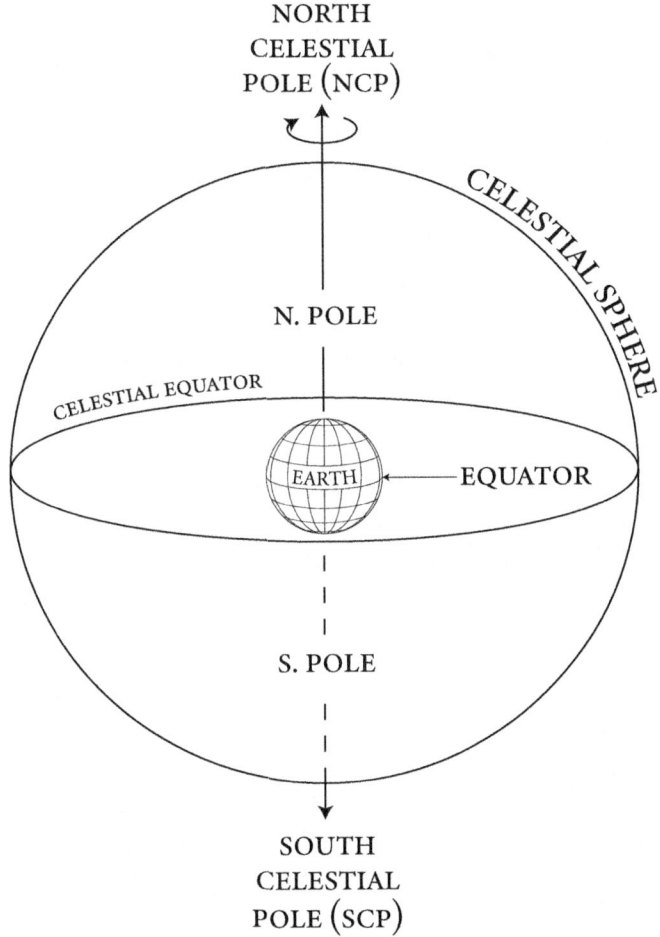

FIGURE 2: *Celestial Sphere*

The ancients considered the universe to consist of several concentric shells, seven of which belonged to the seven classical planets in the Chaldean Order. These planets are: Saturn, Jupiter, Mars, Sun, Venus, Mercury, and Moon. They believed that beyond the shell of Saturn was the shell of the firmament; the sphere of the fixed stars against which the planets etched their paths. Medieval mystics held that there was yet another two rings that lay beyond this firmament. In *Cosmographia* (1574) written by Peter Apianus, we read that the shell of the firmament:

*Is surrounded by the ninth sphere, called the crystalline or watery heaven, because no star is discovered in it. Lastly, the primum mobile, styled also the tenth sphere, encompasses all the beforementioned aethereal spheres, and is continuously turned upon the poles of the world, by one revolution in twenty-four hours, from the east through the meridian to the west, again coming round to the east. At the same time, it rolls all the inferior spheres round with it by its own force; and there is no star in it. Against this primum mobile, the motion of the other spheres, running from the west through the meridian to the east, contends. Whatever is beyond this, is fixed and immovable, and the professors of our orthodox faith affirm it to be the empyrean heaven which GOD inhabits with the elect.*

Apianus mentions two motions: the daily motion of the Primum Mobile from East to West, and the opposite motion of the planets from West to East that fights against the Primum Mobile. We will discuss this dual motion of the heavens below.

### PRIMARY OR DIURNAL MOTION

It was thought that the Primum Mobile, through its incessant whirling motion, caused the ceaseless turning of the sky around us. Though the most distant from Earth, the Prime Mover is the fastest moving element within the geocentric system. It is responsible for what is known as primary motion, which is the full revolution of the entire dome of heaven in twenty-four hours. By primary motion, everything within the cosmos rises in the East, reaches the highest point in their daily journey, and continues onward to set in the West. Under the Earth, and beyond our view, the dome continues to turn, our celestial travelers reach the lowest point in their daily journey, until they rise once more in the East. This corresponds with the rising, culmination, setting, and anticulmination of the Sun. However, in a geocentric model, everything in the sky goes through these four points due to the primary motion of the sky: Sun, Moon, planets, and stars. This primary motion is also known as "diurnal" or "daily motion."

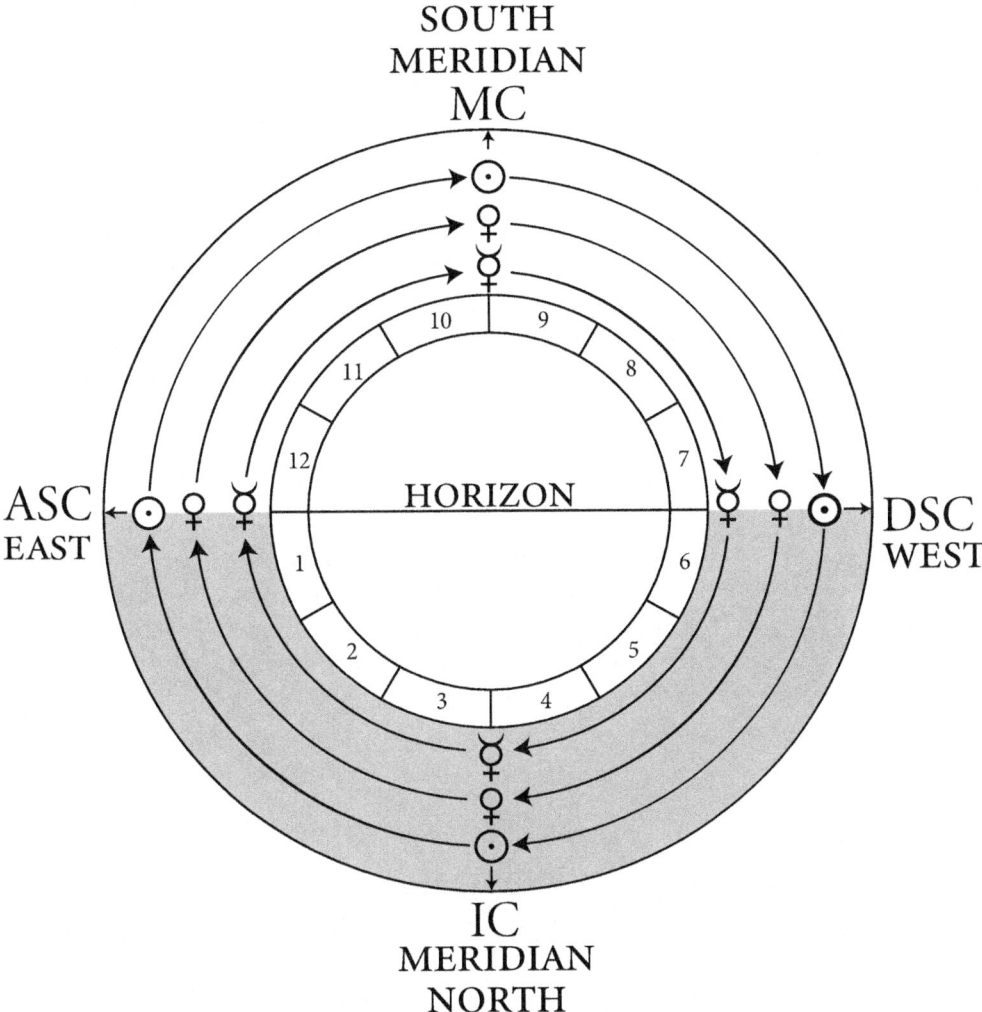

FIGURE 3: *Primary Motion*

## SECONDARY OR ZODIACAL MOTION

Though primary motion is responsible for our daily observance of the rising and setting sky, there is another, slower motion that occurs to the planets. This is the movement of the planets through the various signs of the zodiac. This is called "secondary motion." It is also known as "zodiacal motion." In secondary motion, the planets move from West to East, whereas in primary motion, the planets move from East to West, following the daily path of the Sun.

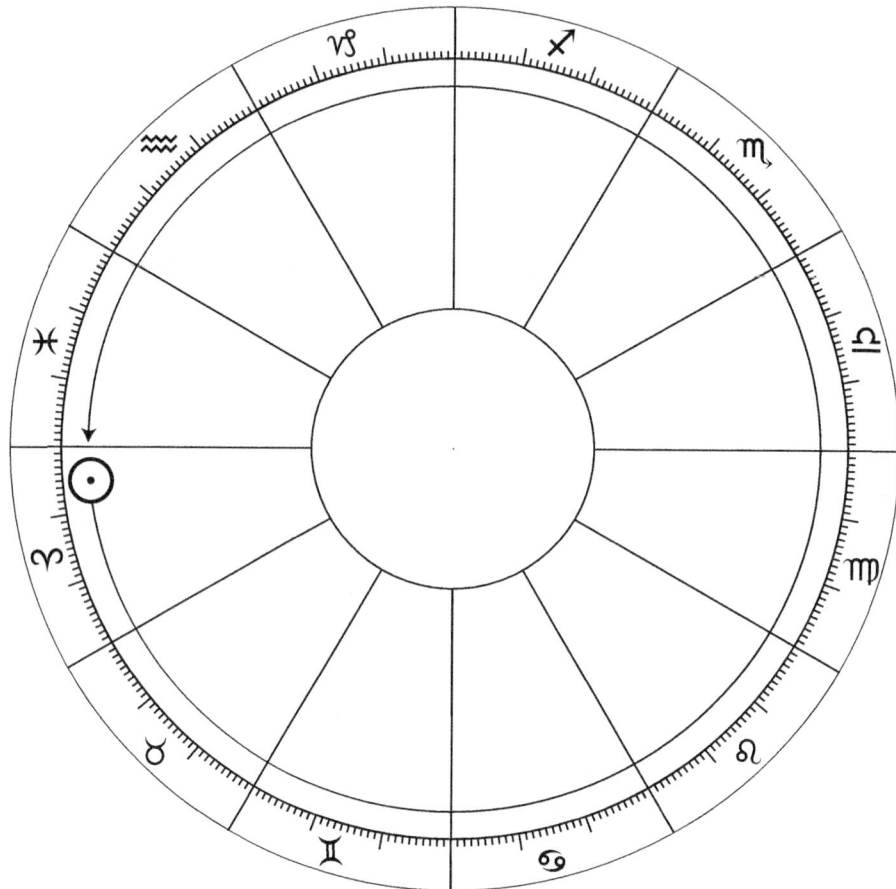

FIGURE 4: *Secondary Motion*

Everything within the sky undergoes these two forms of motion. Primary motion refers to the turning of the entire sky within the course of a day. Secondary motion refers to the movement of the individual planets through the signs of the zodiac, which in most cases is only noticeable over a longer period than twenty-four hours. The exception to this rule would be the Moon, who moves faster than her other celestial counterparts. However, even in the case of the Moon – moving at an average speed of 12° a day – her zodiacal motion throughout the course of the day or night may be imperceptible to the untrained eye.

Before getting deeper into this topic of the movement of the planets, it is necessary for us to speak about some of the circles that provide us with our astronomical coordinate systems. Astronomical coordinate systems give us different ways of mapping where a body is in the sky, in much the same way as a geographic coordinate system gives us a means of mapping where a location is on Earth.

## THE HORIZON CIRCLE

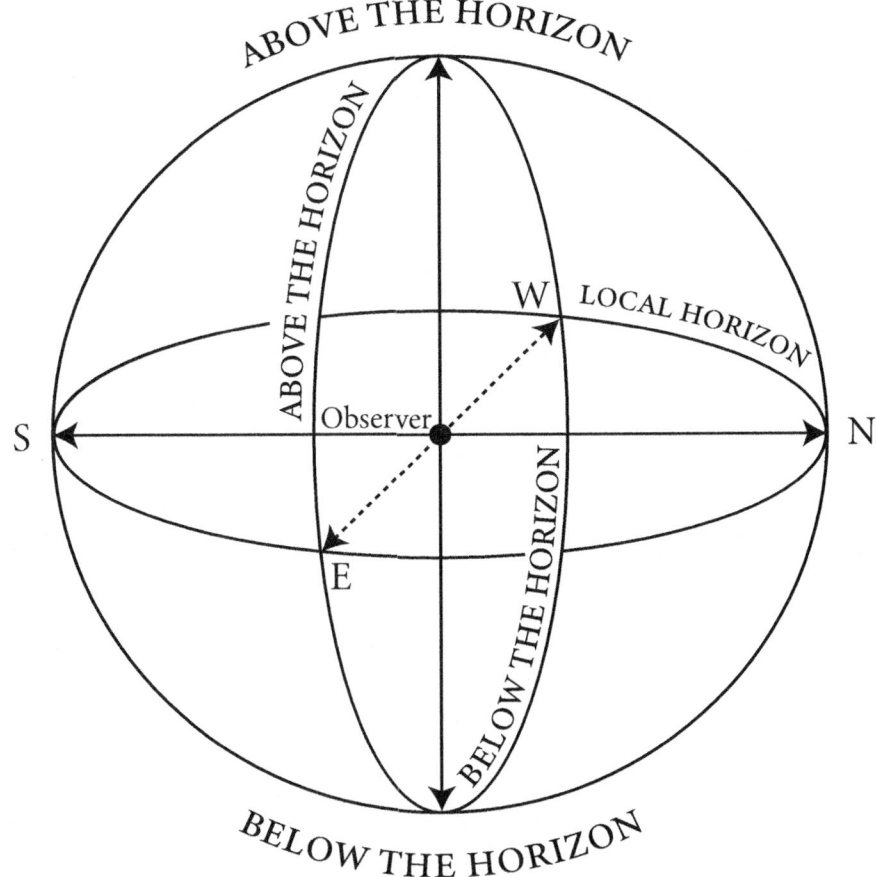

FIGURE 5: *Horizon Circle*

Each of us have a locational circle that is unique to us. This is our "horizon circle." If we were to stand in the middle of a large open field and look as far as the eye could see in all directions, we would be looking at our local horizon. The horizon circle is of extraordinary importance in astrology, particularly in the construction of the twelve houses of the horoscope.

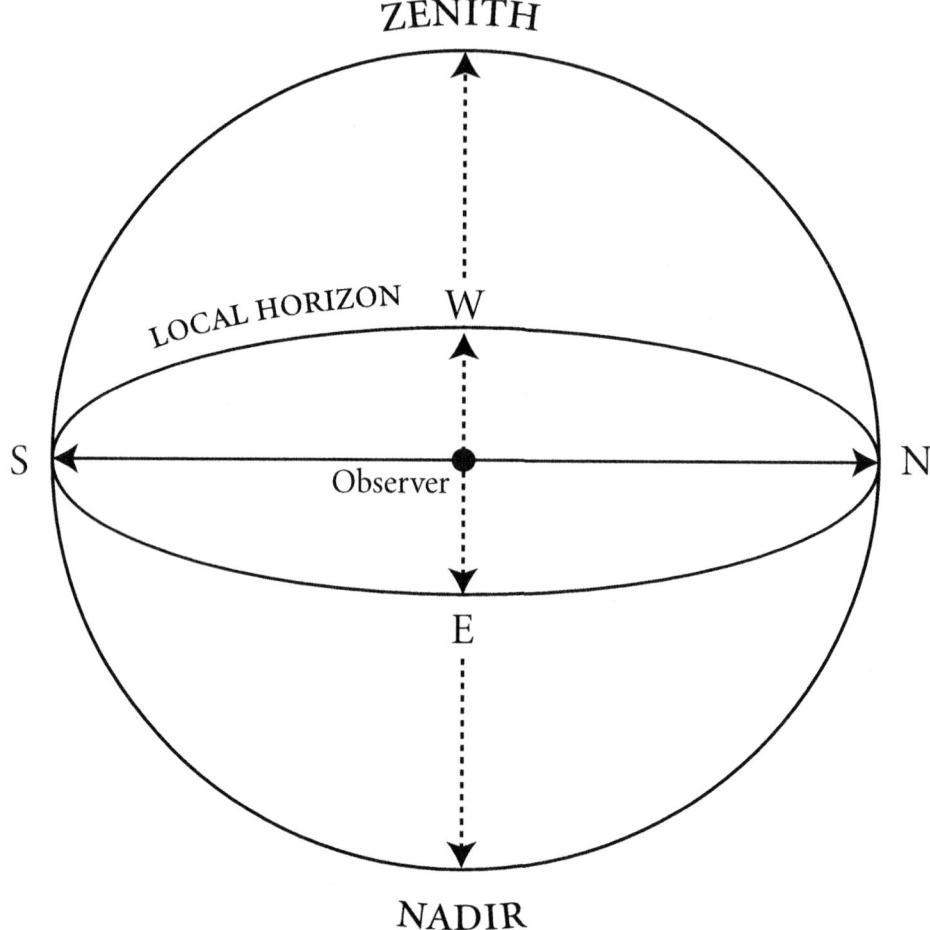

FIGURE 6: *Zenith & Nadir*

If we were to extend a line from the center of the Earth through the crown of our heads and project that line infinitely upward into space, the point that this line would create as it crosses the celestial sphere would be our "zenith." If we then projected that line downward through the center of the Earth, the exact opposite point to the zenith would be the "nadir." The zenith and the nadir are respectively the highest and the lowest points on the celestial sphere in relation to a particular location. Both the zenith and the nadir will always be 90° away from our observable, local horizon.

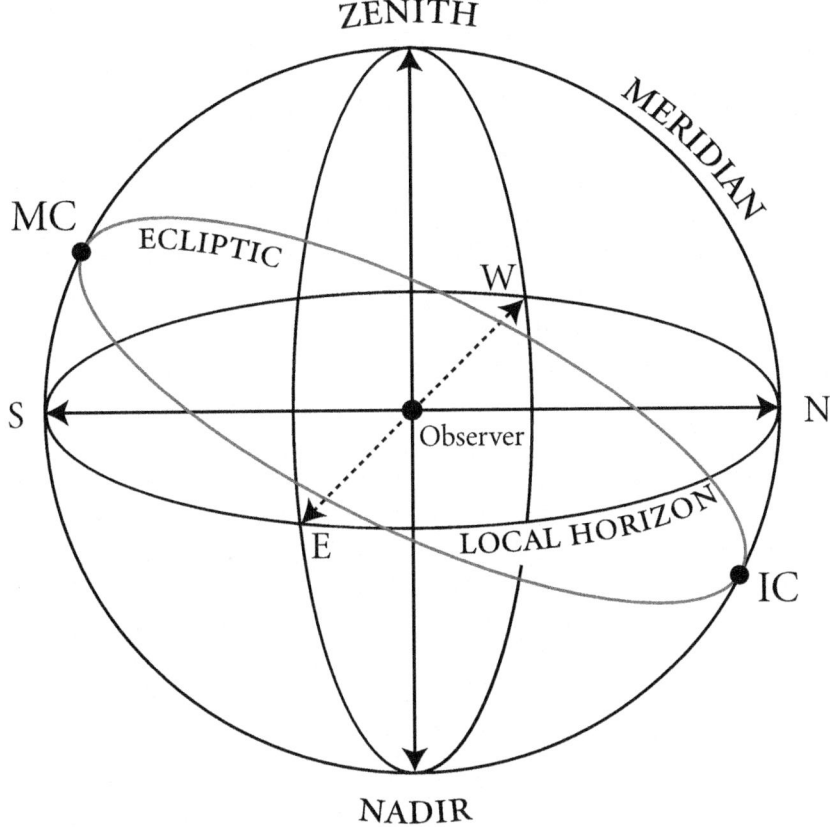

FIGURE 7: *MC in Relation to the Zenith*

A popular misconception in astrology is that the zenith is synonymous with the Midheaven (MC) and the nadir is synonymous with the IC. They are not. We will discuss this distinction more fully later within the chapter.

### PRIME VERTICAL

From the zenith, we can draw another circle. If we are facing due South in the Northern hemisphere, the East will be to our left and the West will be to our right. If we were to draw a line from our Eastern horizon through our zenith to the Western horizon through the nadir and back to our Eastern horizon, we will create what is known as the "prime vertical."

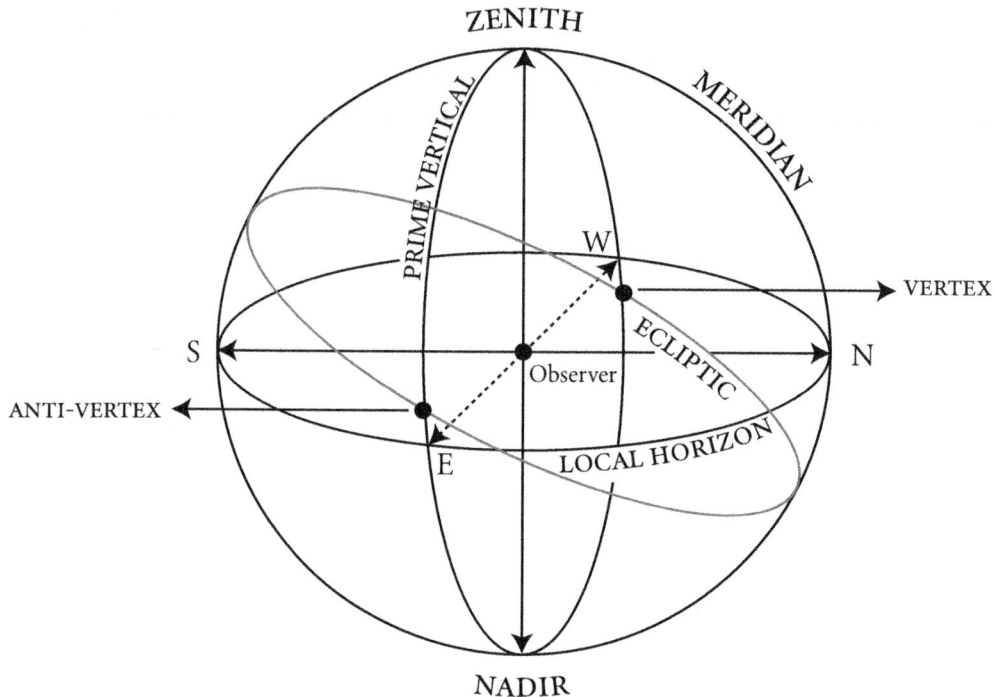

FIGURE 8: *Prime Vertical*

Where the prime vertical crosses the ecliptic in the West is known as the "Vertex" in astrology. Many astrologers use the Vertex and its opposite point known as the "Anti-Vertex" within their practice.

### ALTITUDE AND AZIMUTH

We can use the horizon circle as a means of locating the exact position of a stellar body at an exact moment in time. Every stellar body is in constant motion based on the diurnal motion of the celestial sphere. Therefore, when we locate the exact position of a stellar body based on its relationship to the horizon, this only accounts for where it is at that exact moment in time.

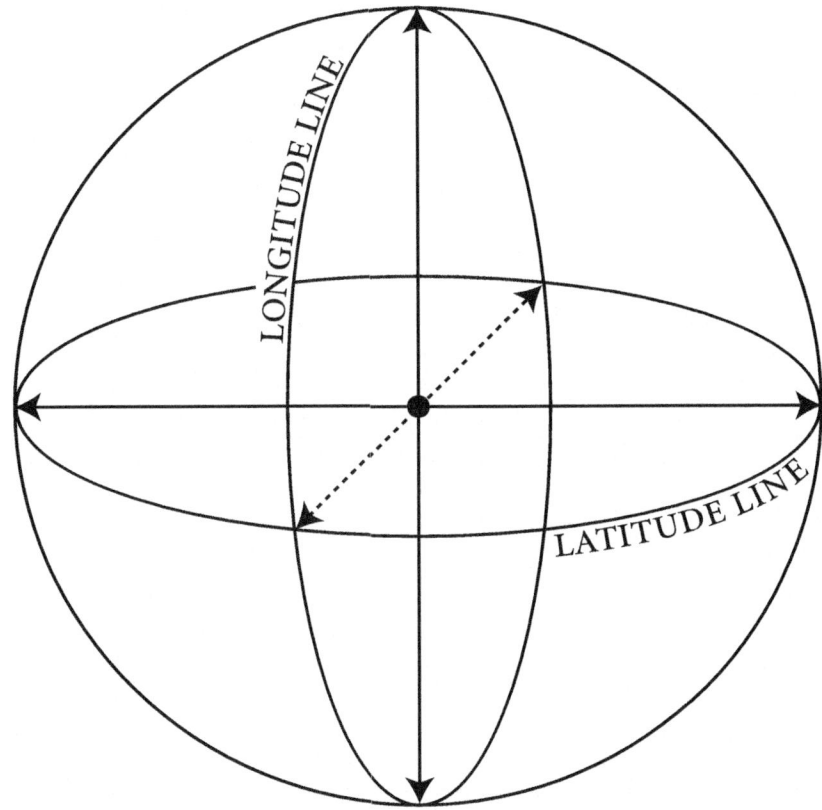

FIGURE 9: *Longitude & Latitude Lines*

In general, latitude lines are flat, horizontal lines. Longitude lines are vertical lines. "Lat" lies flat. "Long" stands strong. Latitude measures how wide or broad something is from side to side. Longitude measures how tall something is from top to bottom.

Planes of latitude that are parallel to our local horizon measure the angular distance between the stellar body in question and our local horizon. This measurement is called "altitude."

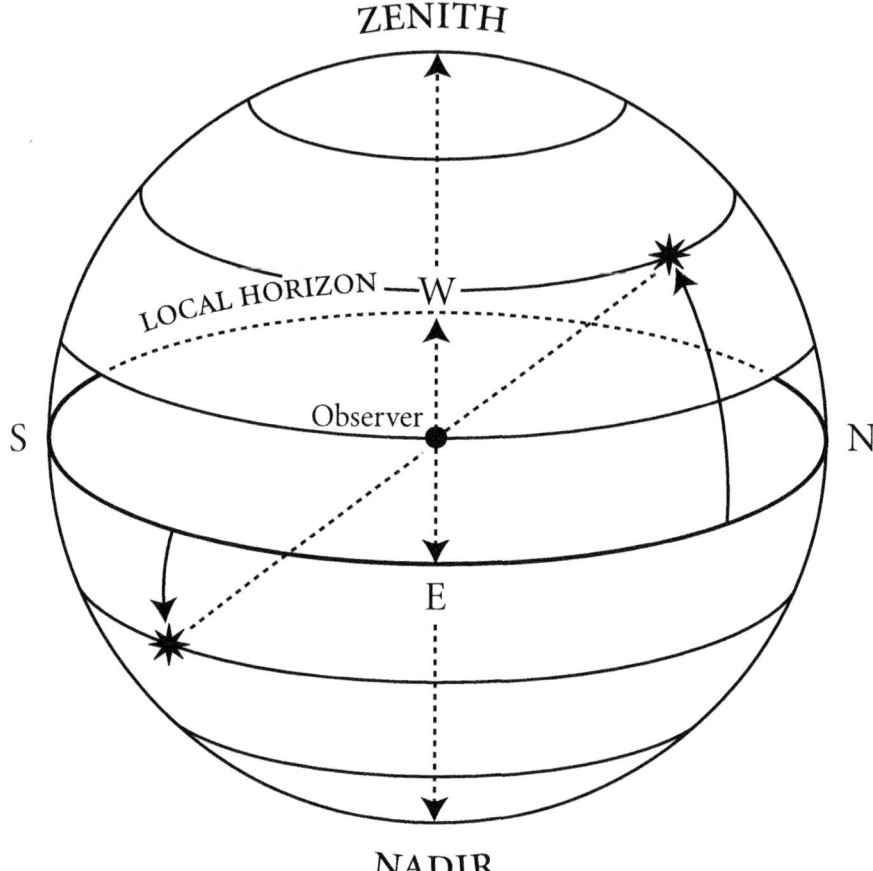

FIGURE 10: *Altitude Circles*

Altitude refers to how high or low a stellar object is in relation to our local horizon. The altitude of any visible object can be measured from 00° to 90°. If a celestial body is at 90°, this means that it is located directly overhead at our zenith. Conversely, if a stellar object had an altitude of -90°, that object would be directly below our feet, opposite to our zenith, and at our nadir.

This location by latitude isn't enough. In order to know the exact location of a planet in relation to our local horizon at a specific moment in time, we also need to know where it is longitudinally. In order to know its exact longitudinal location, we need a specific starting point on our local horizon to measure from. Exactly 00° North on the local horizon is usually the starting point for this longitudinal measurement. How far a planet is along the circumference of that 00° North starting point is known as its "azimuth."

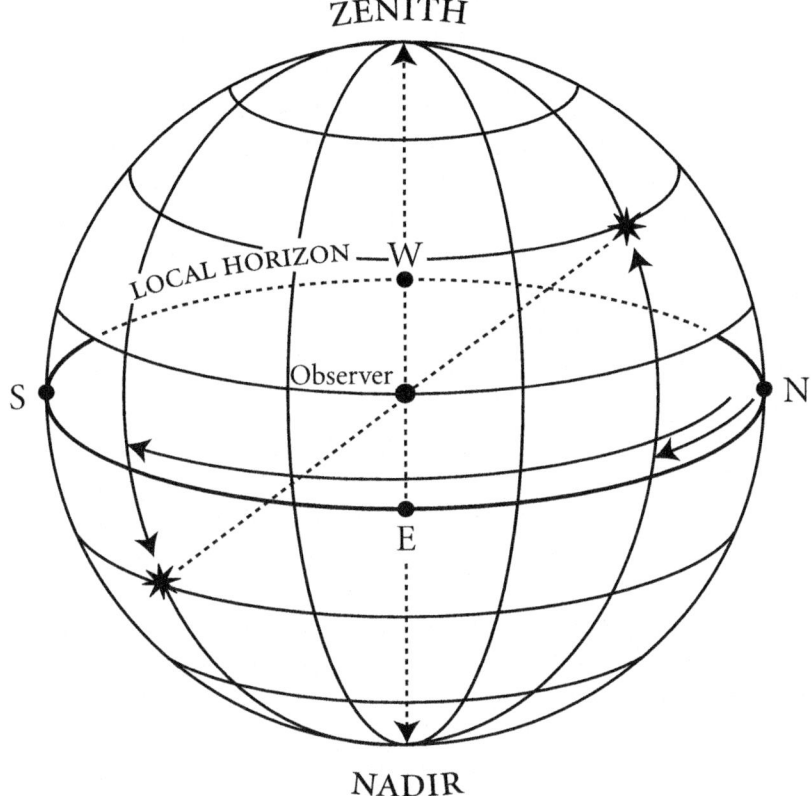

FIGURE 11: *Altitude & Azimuthal Circles*

The azimuth of an object is measured in degrees from 00° to 360°. 00° corresponds with North on the local horizon, 90° corresponds with East, 180° corresponds with South, and 270° corresponds with West.

Altitude and azimuth create what is known as the "horizon coordinate system." Notice that in the horizon coordinate system, the horizon was our specific frame of reference in order to determine where an object was in relation to it.

## THE EQUATOR

Zooming out from our exact location on Earth, we can also apply this concept of coordinate systems to our entire planet.

Just as our local horizon divides the sky above us from the sky below us, we can similarly divide our Earth into hemispheres. The Equator is the great circle that divides the Earth into a Northern and Southern hemisphere. It is also known as the "terrestrial equator" which differentiates it from the celestial equator which we will learn about later within this chapter.

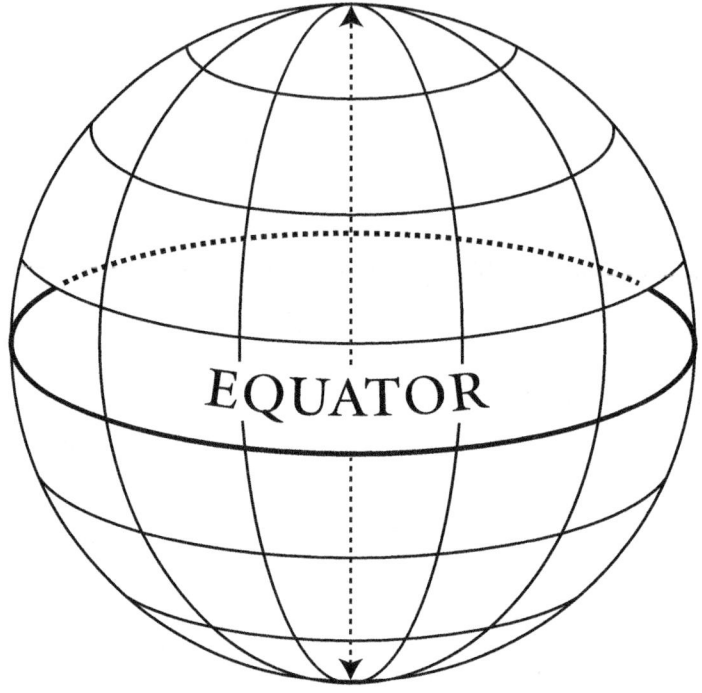

FIGURE 12: *Terrestrial Equator*

## On Great Circles

A "great circle" is any circle that passes through the center of a sphere. On the Earth there are lines of latitude and longitude that give us the exact coordinates of a specific location. All lines of longitude are known as "meridians."

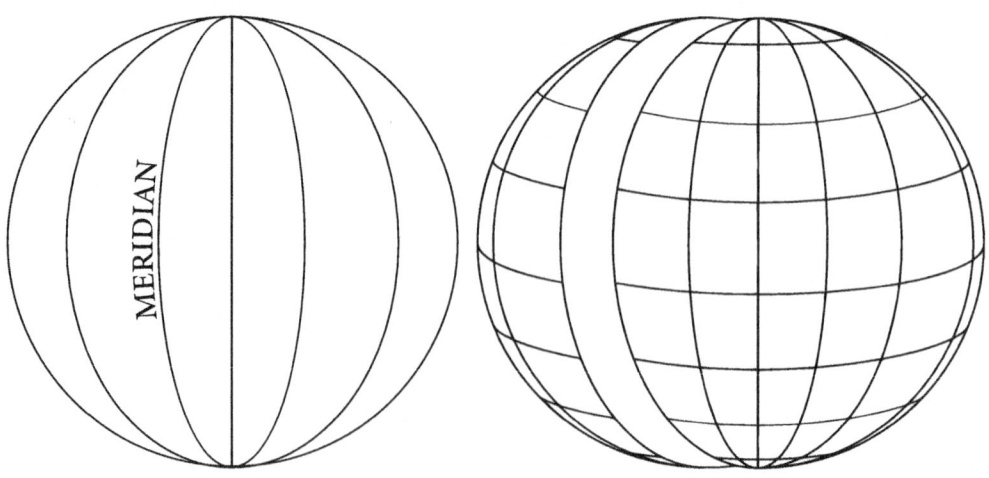

FIGURE 13: *Meridian Circles*

"Meridian" comes from "medius" (middle) and "dies" (day). The meridian of a place is determined by where the Sun will be located at midday, halfway between sunrise and sunset. All meridians run from North to South. This means that they all meet at the North and South Poles.

If we were to divide the Earth along any of these lines of longitude, we would end up with two clean halves. All meridians are great circles.

The Equator is a line of latitude. This means it lies horizontally on the surface of the Earth in contrast to the vertical North-South longitude lines. Remember: "long stands strong," suggesting that the longitude lines are upright or vertical. "Lat lies flat," suggesting that latitude lines are horizontal. While longitude lines run from North to South, latitude lines run from East to West. Like the meridians, the Equator is also a great circle because it passes through the center of the sphere of our planet.

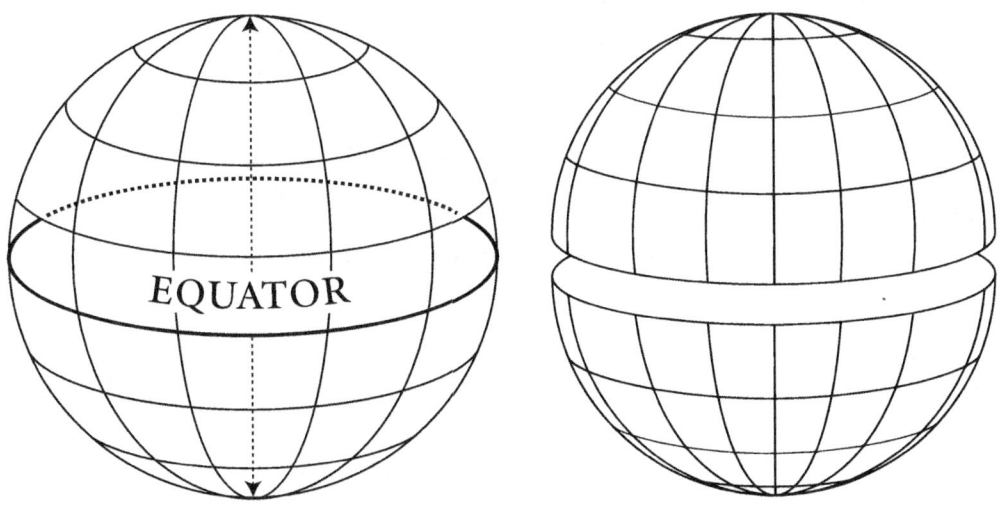

FIGURE 14: *Equator (Great Circle)*

Unlike the longitude lines which are all great circles, the Equator is the only latitude line that is a great circle. It is the only latitude lines that passes through the center of the Earth. All other latitude lines that run parallel to the Equator become smaller as we move closer to the North or South Poles. These smaller circles do not pass through the center of the sphere of our Earth. Therefore, they are called "small circles."

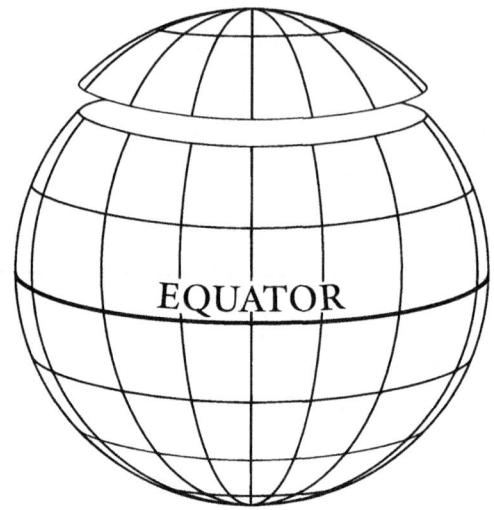

FIGURE 15: *Small Circle (parallel to the Equator)*

THE POLES

A "pole" is a line or plane that passes through the center of a sphere and is perpendicular to its own great circle. The North and South Poles are the poles of the Equator. They are exactly opposite each other and are both 90° away from the Equator. We can actually define the Equator as being the great circle that is exactly 90° away from the Earth's North and South Poles.

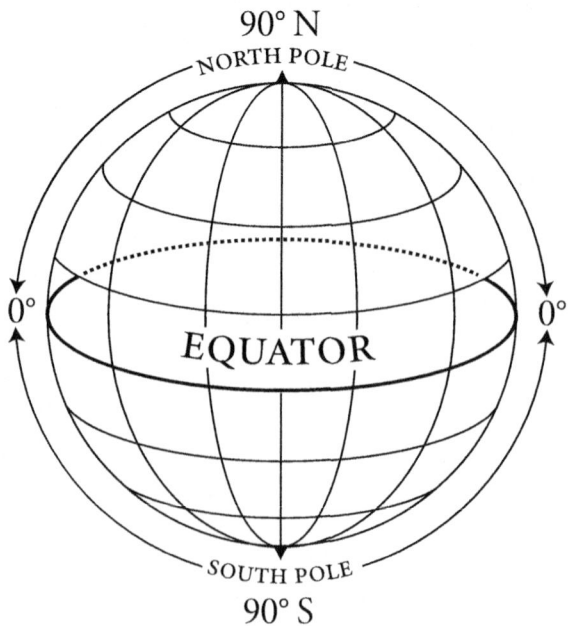

FIGURE16: *Poles 90° away from Equator*

## GEOGRAPHIC COORDINATE SYSTEM

The distance of a location on Earth can be expressed in geographical latitude and geographical longitude. How far North or South a particular location is from the Equator is known as its "latitude." Latitude begins with 00° at the Equator and ends with 90° North at the North Pole and 90° South at the South Pole.

Meridians are used to measure how far East or West a location is from a particular starting point on Earth. This starting point is known as the "prime meridian." The longitude at the prime meridian is 00°. In October 1884 the Greenwich Meridian was chosen to be the common 00° longitude for the entire world. This not only serves as an important reference point in the geographic coordinate system, but it also assists in establishing the time zones for various cities and countries on Earth.

The prime meridian divides the Earth into the Eastern and Western hemispheres. How far a location is East or West of the prime meridian determines its exact location in "longitude."

Our geographic coordinate system of latitude and longitude can be projected onto the celestial sphere to create a celestial coordinate system. When we project this system onto the sky around us, we have a means of mapping the exact location of a stellar body in relation to the center of the Earth. Note that this is different from our horizon coordinate system, which provides the location of a stellar body in relation to our local horizon.

## CELESTIAL EQUATOR

If we project the Earth's terrestrial equator infinitely out into space until it imprints on the celestial sphere, we create the "celestial equator." The celestial equator is Earth's terrestrial equator projected into space.

CELESTIAL POLES

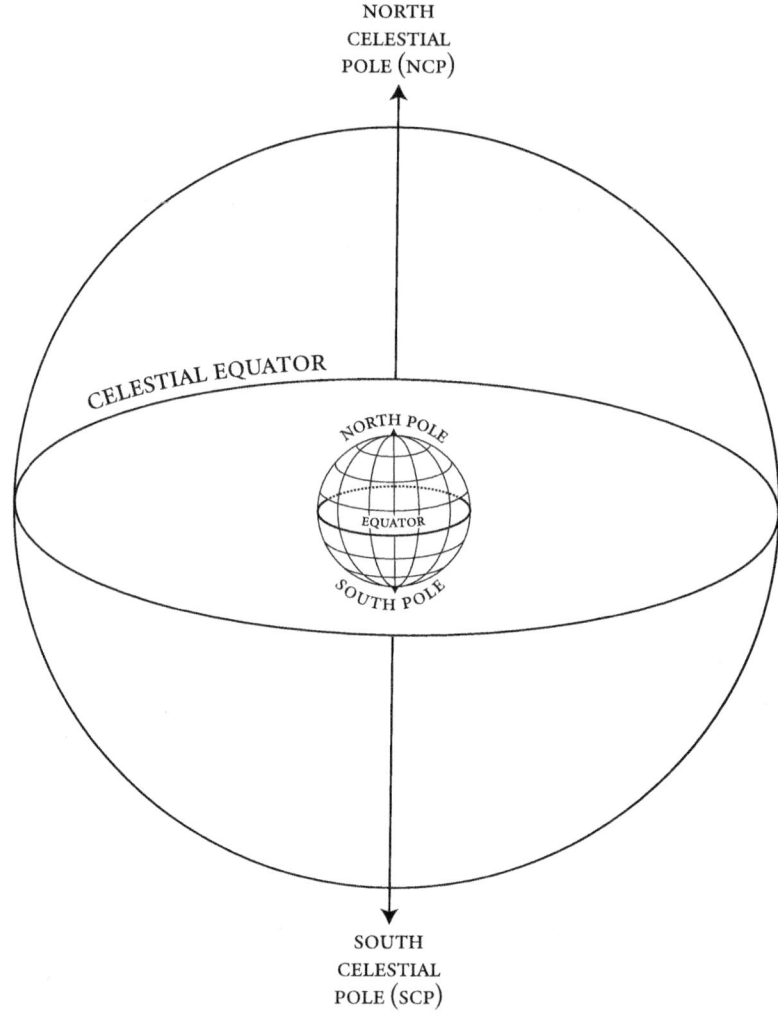

FIGURE 17: *Celestial Poles and the Celestial Equator*

If we extend the Earth's North and South Poles infinitely upward and downward until they intersect the celestial sphere, they create two points known as the "Northern Celestial Pole" and the "Southern Celestial Pole." The celestial equator is 90° away from the northern and southern celestial poles in every direction.

Every great circle has a pole that is exactly 90° away from its circumference. This pole establishes its axis of rotation. In the case of the Earth, the North and South Pole are the axis of rotation for our planet. The rotation of the Earth around its axis every twenty-four hours creates the phenomena of day and night.

THE OBLIQUITY OF THE EARTH

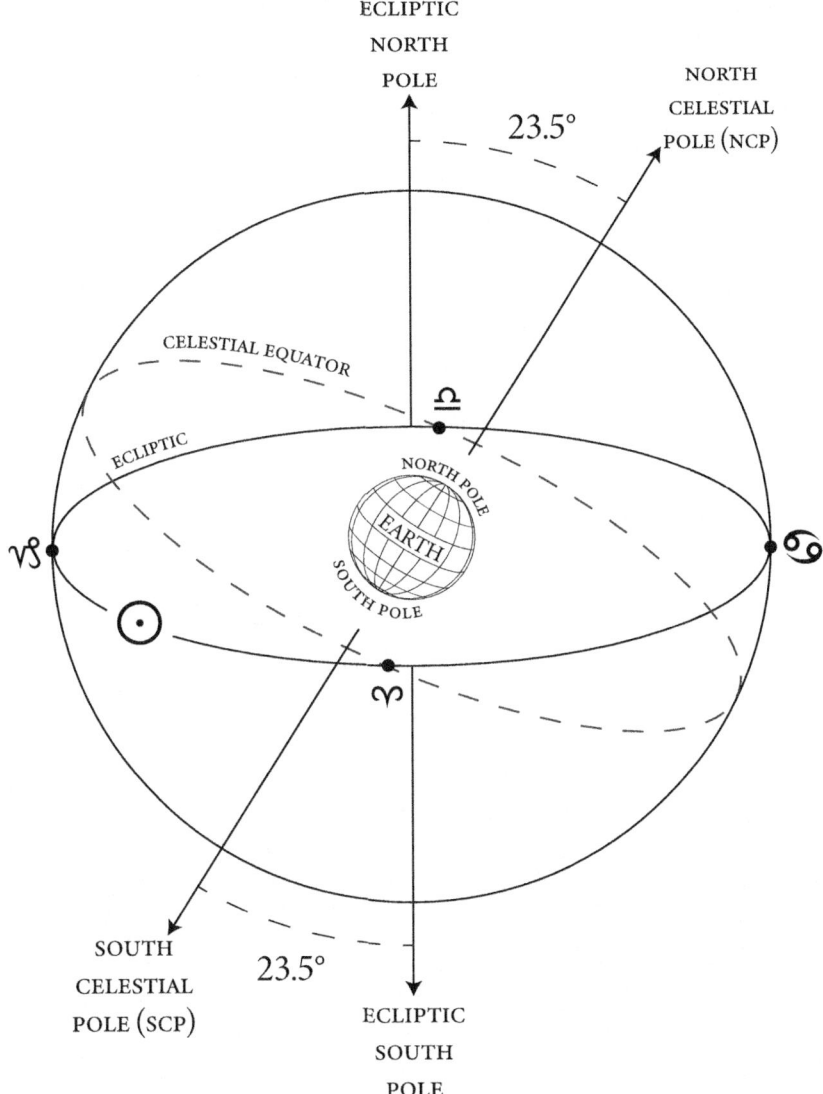

FIGURE 18: *Obliquity of the Earth*

Many of us have heard that the Earth is tilted on its axis. What this means is that the Earth is tilted on its orbital plane relative to the ecliptic. This angular difference between the pole of the Earth and the pole of the ecliptic is currently approximately 23.5°. Over the last million years, it has varied between 22.1° and 24.5° with respect to Earth's ecliptic plane. This tilt of the Earth on its axis is called the "obliquity" of the Earth.

As a result of the obliquity of the Earth, during different times of the year, one hemisphere of the Earth receives more direct sunlight, while the opposite hemisphere receives less direct sunlight.

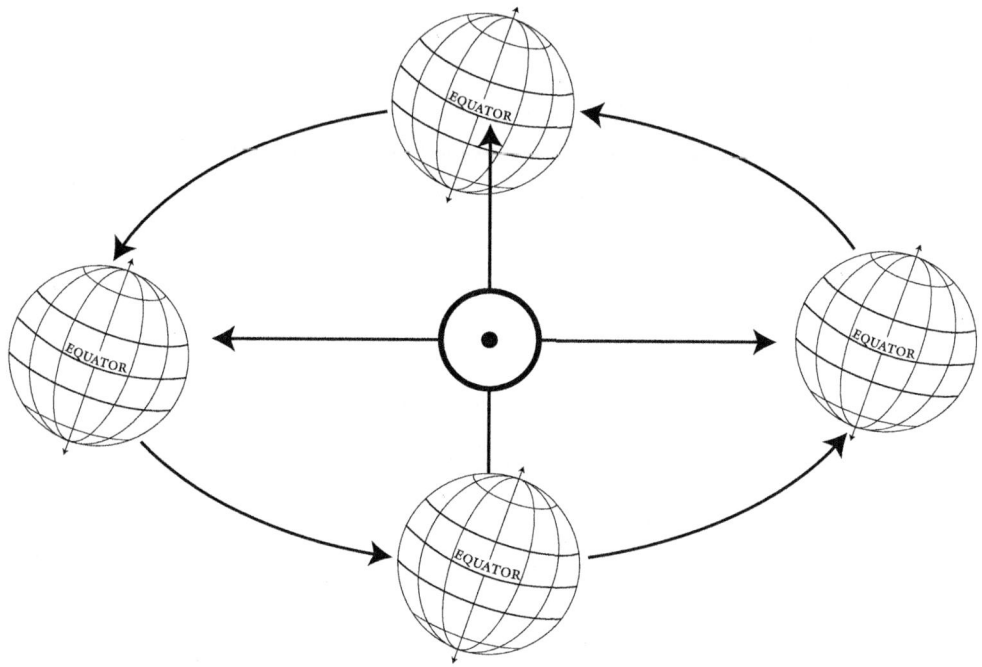

FIGURE 19: *Four Seasons*

This is why when it is Summer in North America, it is Winter in South America. The same is true for Spring and Autumn. Places located on or near the Equator have more temperate weather. Those countries tend toward being hot and humid, with a definite rainy season. However, the four seasons of Spring, Summer, Autumn, and Winter tend to be indistinguishable. The further North or South we travel away from the Equator and towards the poles the more distinct the four seasons become.

There is a theory that a planet the size of Mars collided into the Earth some four and a half billion years ago. This caused the Earth to be tilted on its axis. This *Giant Impact Hypothesis* is the prevailing theory regarding the obliquity of the Earth.

TROPICS

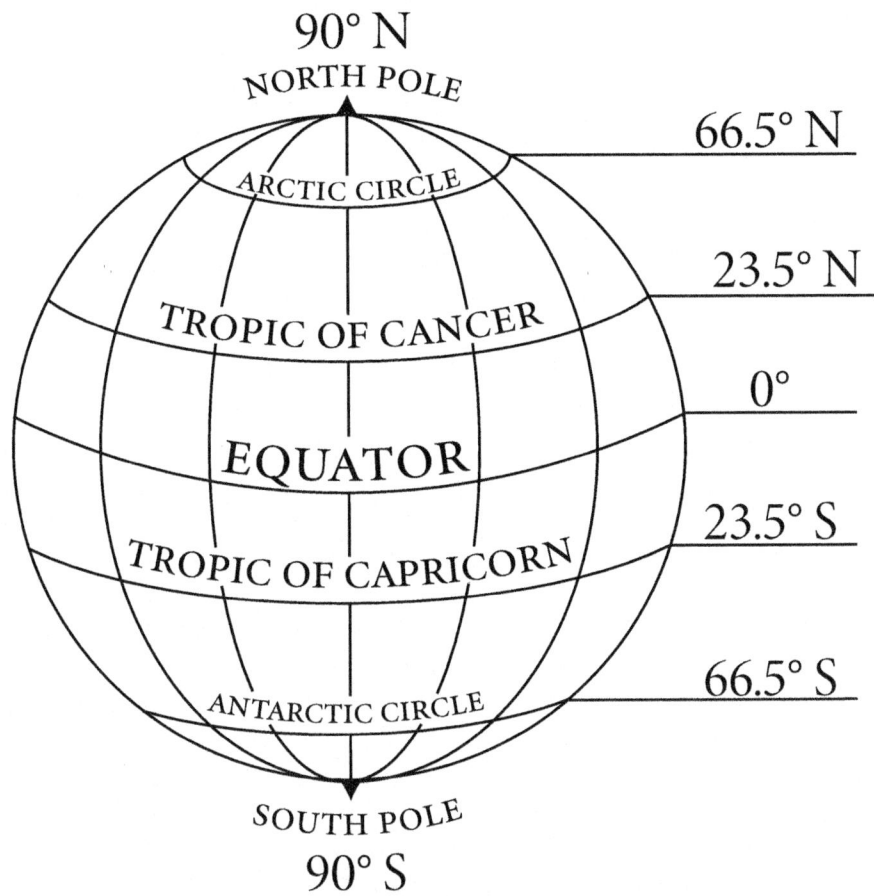

FIGURE 20: *Tropics of Cancer & Capricorn*

The "tropics" refer to the region of the Earth surrounding and adjacent to the Equator. The weather in the tropics tends towards being hot and moist. The "tropical region" is defined as the region between the Tropic of Cancer (23.5° Northern latitude) and the Tropic of Capricorn (23.5° Southern latitude). The Tropic of Cancer or the Northern Tropic refers to the most northerly circle of latitude at which the Sun can be directly overhead. This occurs at the Summer Solstice, when the Northern Hemisphere of the Earth is tilted towards the Sun to the maximum extent. The Tropic of Capricorn or the Southern Tropic refers to the most southernly circle of latitude at which the Sun can be directly overhead. This occurs at the Winter Solstice, when the Southern Hemisphere is tilted towards the Sun at the maximum extent.

ON THE ECLIPTIC & THE SEASONS

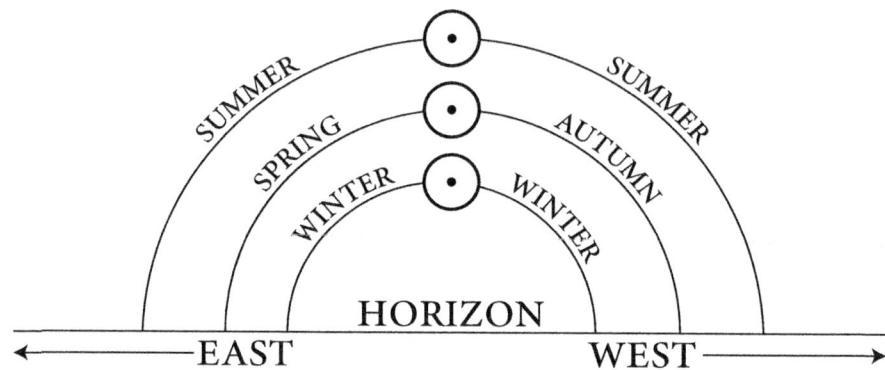

FIGURE 21: *Sun/Horizon Relationship during the Four Seasons*

From our geocentric perspective, the ecliptic is the annual path the Sun makes around the Earth. The exact point where the ecliptic crosses the celestial equator in the East is known as the "Vernal Equinox." The Sun begins his journey along the ecliptic at the Vernal Equinox at the beginning of Spring.

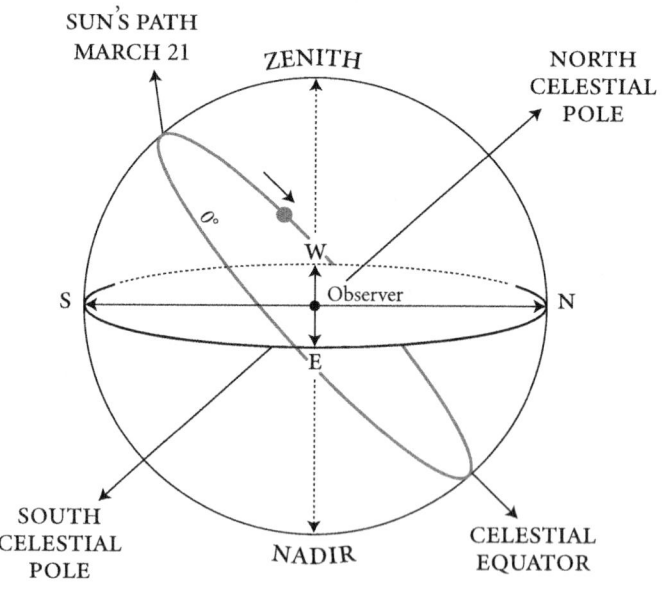

FIGURE 22: *Sun at the Vernal Equinox*

On the first day of Spring, both day and night are equal. This is where we derive the term "equinox." The word "equinox" is derived from the Latin "aequinoctium." "Aequus" means "equal" and "nox" means "night." During the days after Spring, the Sun can be seen to rise higher and higher in the sky. This means that the days become increasingly longer. The nights will become shorter.

In general, the Sun moves an average of 01° each day. However, due to the increasing periods of daylight during the Spring, the Sun spends a greater length of time above the horizon. In the Spring and Summer months, the Sun climbs higher in the sky and also appears to be moving slower. Therefore, he travels less than a degree a day during the Spring and Summer months.

This year, on 20 March 2022, the Sun was travelling at a rate of +00° 59' 36". The "+" means that the Sun was moving direct in the sky. In other words, he was not moving retrograde. "Retrogradation" refers to the apparent backward movement of the planets within the zodiac. For example, if a planet at 12° Aries moved backward in the zodiac to 11° Aries, this planet is said to be retrograde. We will speak more about the reasons for retrogradation closer to the end of this chapter. In the case of the Sun, he never moves in a retrograde direction from his normal course. The Moon is also never retrograde.

After 20 March 2022, due to the increased length of day, the daily travel of the Sun was:

TABLE 1: *Distance Traveled by Sun(April-June 2022)*

| +00° 58' 34" | 20 APRIL 2022 |
| +00° 57' 44" | 20 MAY 2022 |
| +00° 57' 15" | 20 JUNE 2022 |

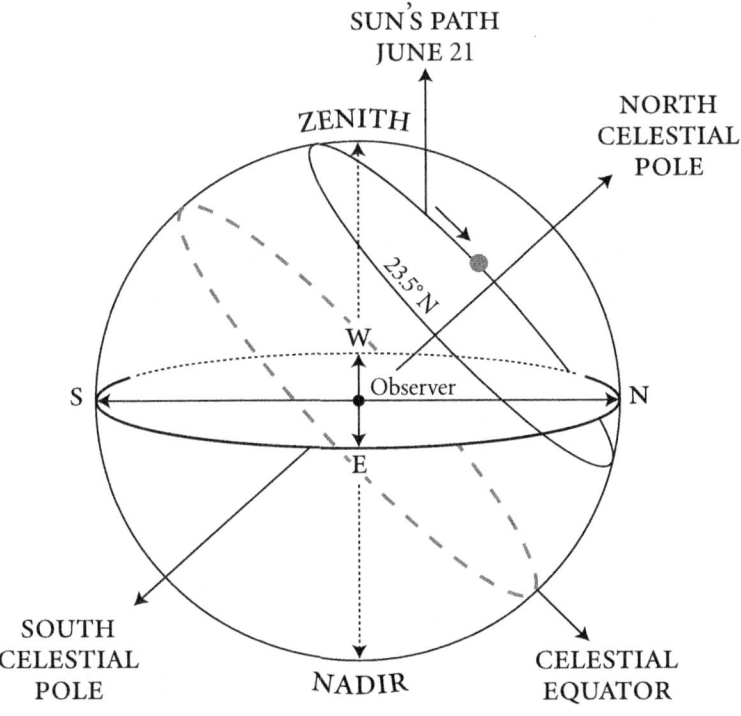

FIGURE 23: *Sun at the Summer Solstice*

This shows the daily decrease in the Sun's rate of speed during the Spring. From the equal length of day and night at the Vernal Equinox, we gradually see the Sun rising higher in the sky each day. He has further to travel in the same amount of time. The Sun during these months is appreciably moving at a slower rate creating longer days, and shorter nights.

The Sun continues to rise higher in the sky until at the Summer Solstice the Sun attains his highest elevation in the sky in relation to the horizon, marking the longest day of the year. The Sun seems to stand still, bracing himself for the descent to come. This is where we derive the word "solstice." "Solstice" comes from the Latin words "sol" which means "Sun" and "sistere" which means "to stand still."

In the Northern hemisphere the Summer Solstice of 2022 occurred on 21 June 2022. The Sun was moving at a rate of +00° 57' 15". For the first days of Summer, the Sun continued to decrease in the rate of his daily travel until arriving at 00° 57' 11" on 12 July 2022.

From there, the Sun increased his speed, travelling at a rate of:

TABLE 2: *Distance Traveled by Sun (July-September 2022)*

| | |
|---|---|
| +00° 57' 16" | 21 JULY 2022 |
| +00° 57' 47" | 21 AUGUST 2022 |
| +00° 58' 44" | 23 SEPTEMBER 2022 |

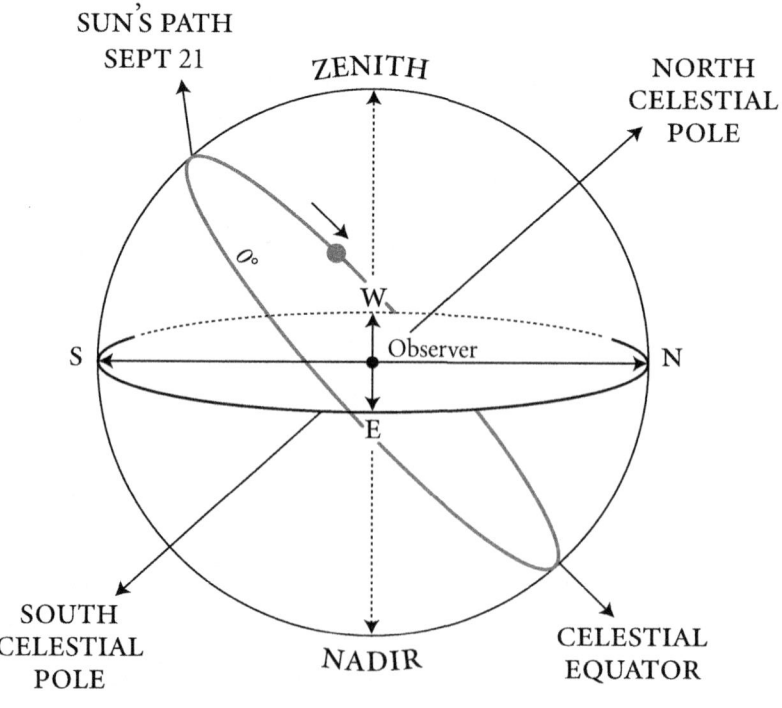

FIGURE 24: *Sun at the Autumnal Equinox*

By 23 September 2022, the Sun was within roughly a degree of the speed he was travelling at on the first day of Spring. This once again creates the effect of equal hours of day and night. From there on, the Sun's maximum daily elevation in relation to the horizon decreases, with the consequence of the days becoming shorter, and the nights becoming longer.

From the Autumnal Equinox, the elevation of the Sun in the sky continued to decrease. This means that the height of the midday Sun became gradually lower as we moved towards the Winter. His daily rate of travel continued to increase. He travelled at a rate of:

TABLE 3: *Distance Traveled by Sun (October 2022-March 2023)*

| | |
|---|---|
| +00° 59' 40" | 21 OCTOBER 2022 |
| +01° 00' | 21 NOVEMBER 2022 |
| +01° 01' | 22 DECEMBER 2022 |
| +01° 01' | 21 JANUARY 2023 |
| +01° 00' | 21 FEBRUARY 2023 |
| +00° 59' 38" | 20 MARCH 2023 |

Because of the decreased length of time the Sun stayed in the sky during the daylight hours, we perceived the Sun to move quicker in the Autumn and the Winter, than at other times in the year. Therefore, the Sun completed his daily arc in the sky in less time during the Autumn and Winter than during the Spring and the Summer.

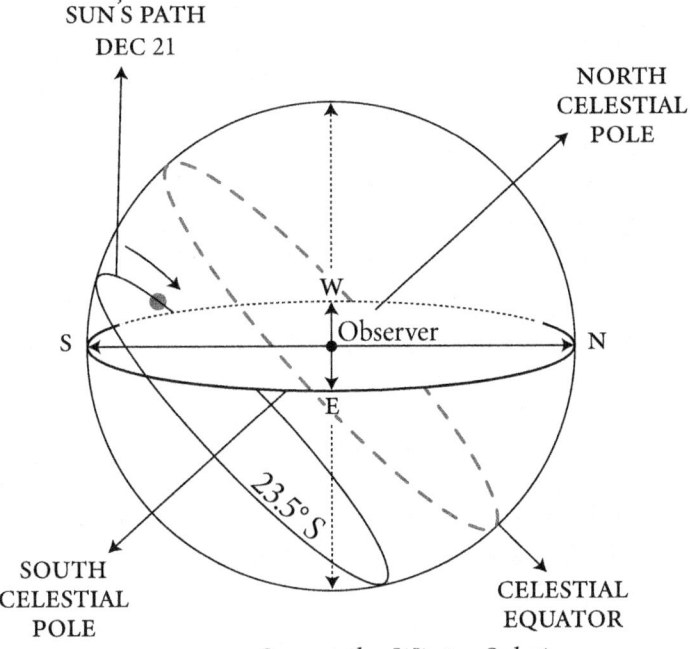

FIGURE 25: *Sun at the Winter Solstice*

This daily arc of the Sun between his rising and setting is called his "diurnal arc." A half of this arc is called his "semidiurnal arc." Whether we are considering the diurnal arc or the semidiurnal arc of the Sun during the Winter, it is shorter than his arc during the late Spring and Summer months. At the Winter Solstice, the diurnal arc of the Sun is as low to the horizon as possible, creating the shortest day and the longest night of the year. After the Winter Solstice, the length of the day gradually begins to increase until both day and night are equal once again at the time of the Vernal Equinox.

In the West, we primarily practice tropical astrology. This means that our astrology is based on this annual revolution of the Sun around the Earth, causing the changing seasons.

However, ours is not the final statement on what the zodiac is or how it works. The three major zodiac systems are: the constellational zodiac, the sidereal zodiac, and the tropical zodiac.

ON THE ZODIAC

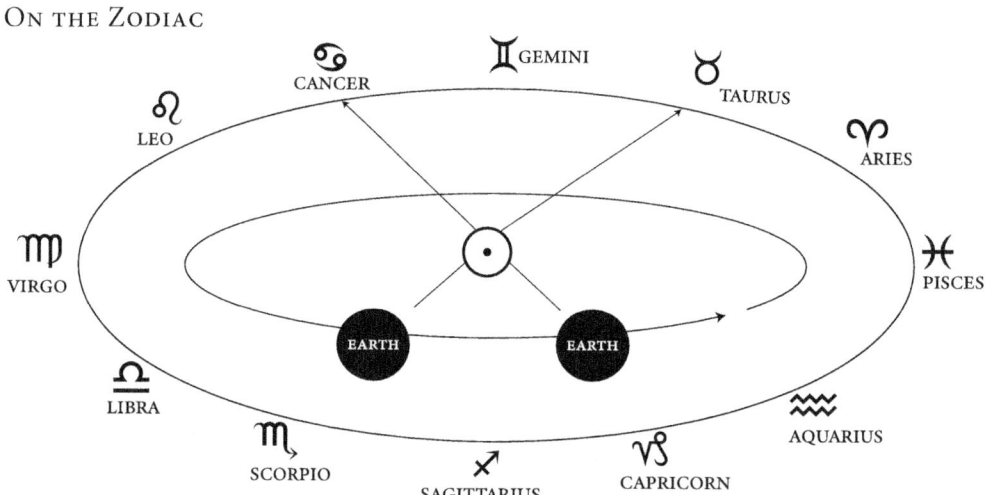

FIGURE 26: *Signs of the Zodiac*

The zodiac refers to the band of sky that is the backdrop of the Sun's ecliptic path. The ecliptic is in the middle of this band. The zodiacal belt extends 08° North and 08° South of the ecliptic. From a geocentric perspective, the zodiac can be thought of as the highway upon which the Sun, the Moon, and the planets travel in their orbits around the Earth. The zodiac is a useful reference for describing where the planets are in relation to each other and where they are as independent factors. However, there are a few discrepancies between what the zodiac is and what we consider the zodiac to be in Western tropical astrology.

## THE CONSTELLATIONAL ZODIAC

Technically speaking, the zodiac is the belt of the twelve constellations that are the "wallpaper" of the ecliptic. The "constellational zodiac" is the zodiac that uses the actual constellations as a framework of measurement for the planetary positions. This is not the case in either the sidereal or tropical zodiac.

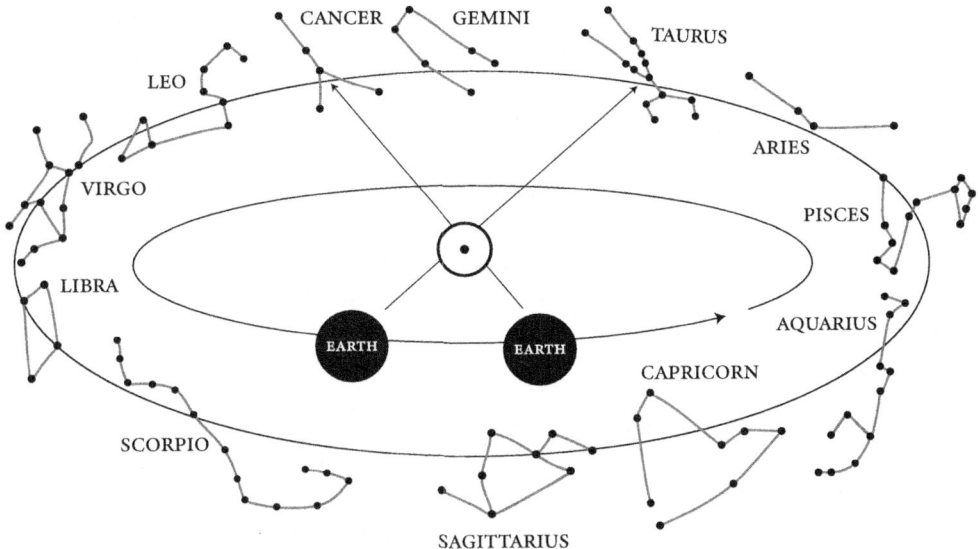

FIGURE 27: *Constellations of the Zodiac*

The first issue that we find in using the constellational zodiac is that the constellations vary in size. Some of the zodiacal constellations occupy far more than 30° of zodiacal longitude, whereas other constellations occupy far less. Though the constellational zodiac is more accurate when referring to the locations of the planets in space, it isn't the most practical measurement system. It would seem as if even the ancient Babylonians agreed with this. James Herschel Holden in *A History of Horoscopic Astrology* writes:

> *Babylonian constellations included the twelve zodiacal constellations...*
> *They were of uneven length with gaps between some of them. Later, in*
> *the 4ᵗʰ century, when the Babylonians began to invent mathematical*
> *theories for calculating solar, lunar, and planetary positions, they were*
> *obliged to invent the 360-degree circle and the "signs" of the zodiac.*
> *This was done for convenience in studying the past records of planetary*
> *positions and phenomena, not for astrological reasons. The "signs" had*
> *the same names as the corresponding constellations but were defined*
> *as having exactly 30 degrees each.*

From the very beginning of astrology in the West, there was a distinction that could be made between the constellation of the zodiac and the "sign" that bore the same name. Today, in order to distinguish between the constellation and the sign, we refer to the constellation by the figure it represents, and we refer to the signs by the names we are familiar with. We speak about the constellation of the Ram, and the sign of Aries; the constellation of the Bull, and the sign of Taurus, and so on throughout the constellation and sign pairs.

There is a growing community of people who use the constellational zodiac in the twenty-first century. However, it is more common to find people using either the sidereal zodiac and its variations or the tropical zodiac.

## THE SIDEREAL ZODIAC

The "sidereal zodiac" is largely used in Indian astrology, known as "Jyotish" (jee-OH-tish). It is also used in Western sidereal astrology. Like the ancient Babylonians, the siderealist bases their zodiac on the first degree of the constellation of the Ram and then divides the space of the zodiac into even 30° segments. This differs from the constellational zodiac. In the constellational zodiac, the constellations do not represent even 30° segments of space, whereas the signs of the sidereal zodiac do.

## TROPICAL ASTROLOGY AND THE AYANAMSHA

In the tropical zodiac, the starting point of the zodiac is the exact location of the Vernal Equinox. Remember: the Vernal Equinox is the exact crossing of the ecliptic and the Equator in the East. While the Vernal Equinox point is a fixed location on the Equator, it is not fixed in relation to the constellations. As a result of what is known as the "precession of the equinoxes," the Vernal Equinox point slowly moves backward against the backdrop of the fixed stars at a rate of approximately 01° every seventy-two years. This means that the stars that are the backdrop of the Sun on the first day of Spring in 2022 are very different stars than the ones that he rose in front of on the first day of Spring 2,000 years ago. Thus, 00° Aries in tropical astrology and 00° Aries in sidereal astrology refer to very different locations on the ecliptic. Robert DeLuce in his book *Constellational Astrology* (1963) writes:

> *The difference in longitude between the 0° Aries point of the constellations and the 0° Aries point of the signs (vernal equinox) is referred to by the Hindus as the ayanamsha, from the Sanskrit words, ayana, meaning "season of the year," and amsha, which means "a portion." The ayanamsha is used to calculate the constellational longitude of a celestial body or point when its position in sign longitude is known, such as is given in Western ephemerides.*

It may seem as if sidereal astrology is more accurate because it bases its zodiac on 00° of the constellation of the Ram. However, it is important to note that there is disagreement – particularly in the Indian sidereal community – as to the date of 00° ayanamsha. 00° ayanamsha would essentially refer to that period over 2,000 years ago when the Vernal Equinox aligned with 00° of the Ram constellation. If we aren't sure about the date of 00° ayanamsha, then we can't be sure about the exact deviation between the Vernal Equinox and 00° of the Ram.

In astrology, the exact time and date of things is of ultimate importance in erecting accurate charts. A popular ayanamsha amongst practitioners of Jyotish is called "Lahiri." Popular amongst Western siderealists is the Fagan-Allen ayanamsha. The ayanamsha that one uses is completely under the discretion of the astrologer and the tradition to which they belong. Regardless of these various paths within the sidereal tradition, sidereal astrology remains a formidable system in both the East and the West, and it demands our respect and consideration.

In tropical astrology, our zodiac is not bound to the constellations. Rather, it is bound to our Earth-Sun relationship. As tropical astrologers, we consider the Earth-Sun relationship to be far more personal in relation to our daily experience of the universe and our place within it. We see this season/time-based orientation of tropical astrology becoming even clearer when we consider some of the myths the ancients built around the four cardinal signs of Aries, Cancer, Libra, and Capricorn in the Northern hemisphere.

## CARDINAL INGRESSES OF THE SUN

When the Sun ingresses into Aries at the Vernal Equinox, Spring begins. The day and the night are equal. However, with each passing day, the days grow longer as the Sun increases in power. The Ram was thought to be a most appropriate symbol for this part of Spring, because at this time the ewes and the rams bring forth their young. Though they can give birth to multiple offspring, a pregnant ewe will usually give birth to one lamb. This is symbolic of the singularity of the newborn Sun in the springtime – individualized and in radiant expression. Metaphysically, the Ram of Spring represents the rushing force of the vital Sun breaking free from the shackles of Winter, fertilizing the Earth and giving birth to a new world.

The Sun continues to grow in his power until he attains his highest elevation in the sky at the Summer Solstice. This marks the longest day of the year. There, the Sun turns back on himself, like the backward moving Crab, and begins his descent towards the Equator. This crablike "turning back on himself" is what causes the length of day to decrease. The Sun continues his descent towards the Equator until he arrives at Libra, the Balanced Scales, where both day and night are equal once again. There, he goes hurtling into the underworld until he reaches his lowest point of decline (or declination) in relation to the Equator at his ingress into Capricorn. Just as the mountain goat has to climb the treacherous mountainsides in order to arrive at the summit of achievement, so too must the Sun climb up from the depths and make the perilous journey until he once again is reborn at the Vernal Equinox. Therefore, within Western tropical astrology, we find a mythological framework that mirrors our lived experience as observers of the natural world. We also find within this framework a doctrine of spiritual reincarnation. We come to know the immortality of the human soul through the unending death and rebirth of the eternal Sun.

### HIPPARCHUS & THE PRECESSION OF THE EQUINOXES

Hipparchus of Nicaea (circa 190-127 BCE) was a Greek astronomer, mathematician, and geographer. During the latter part of his illustrious career, he turned his gaze upward to measure the location of the stars based on the star catalogs of ancient Babylon. When assessing the fixed star Spica in comparison to the works of his predecessors, he discovered that the star seemed to have moved 02° in relation to the point that we define as the Autumnal Equinox. As a result of this, Hipparchus decided that the equinoxes were "precessing" backward against the backdrop of the zodiacal belt at a rate of around 01° every hundred years. He called this the "Precession of the Equinoxes."

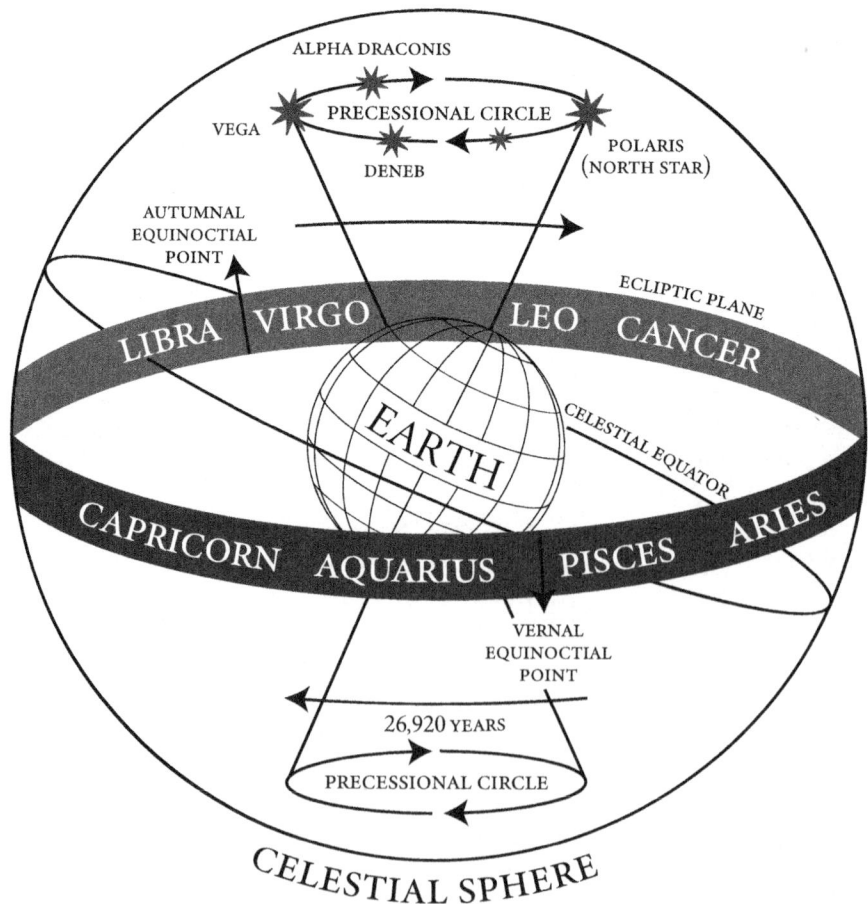

FIGURE 28: *Precession of the Equinoxes*

"Axial precession" can be defined as the slow and continuous change of a planet's rotational axis. Precession is caused by the gravitational pull of the Sun and the Moon on what is known as Earth's "equatorial bulge." Though we customarily think of the Earth as a sphere, it is actually an ellipsoid. This means that it bulges more at its Equator. Therefore, a person standing on the Equator is farther from the center of the Earth than a person standing on the North Pole. The bulge of the Earth at the Equator, along with the gravitational influence of the luminaries, causes the Earth to move backward against the backdrop of the fixed stars over the course of time. In particular, it causes the rotational axis (the North and South Poles) of the Earth to draw a cone shape in space over the course of 26,000 years. This means that Polaris, our current North Star, will not be the North Star 2,000 years from now.

The reality of precession has a direct impact on which zodiac we choose use in astrology. We have seen that the tropical zodiac, based on our Earth-Sun relationship, does not need to factor in the effect of precession on the Vernal Equinox point. The sidereal zodiac does need to factor in precession, since precession is the very foundation upon which that zodiac is built. This is a part of the appeal of sidereal astrology as a living, changing, organic system. It accurately reflects the changes that our place in the universe undergoes in relation to the universe around it. Both the tropical and the sidereal argument bear considerable merit. The topic of precession has been one of the arguments that the scientific community has used in attempts to discredit astrology, even though it is an astronomical fact that astrologers are deeply familiar with. Precession has also been a sore point within the astrological community between tropical and sidereal astrologers for generations.

## THE EQUATORIAL COORDINATE SYSTEM

There are two more coordinate systems for us to explore: the equatorial coordinate system and the ecliptic coordinate system.

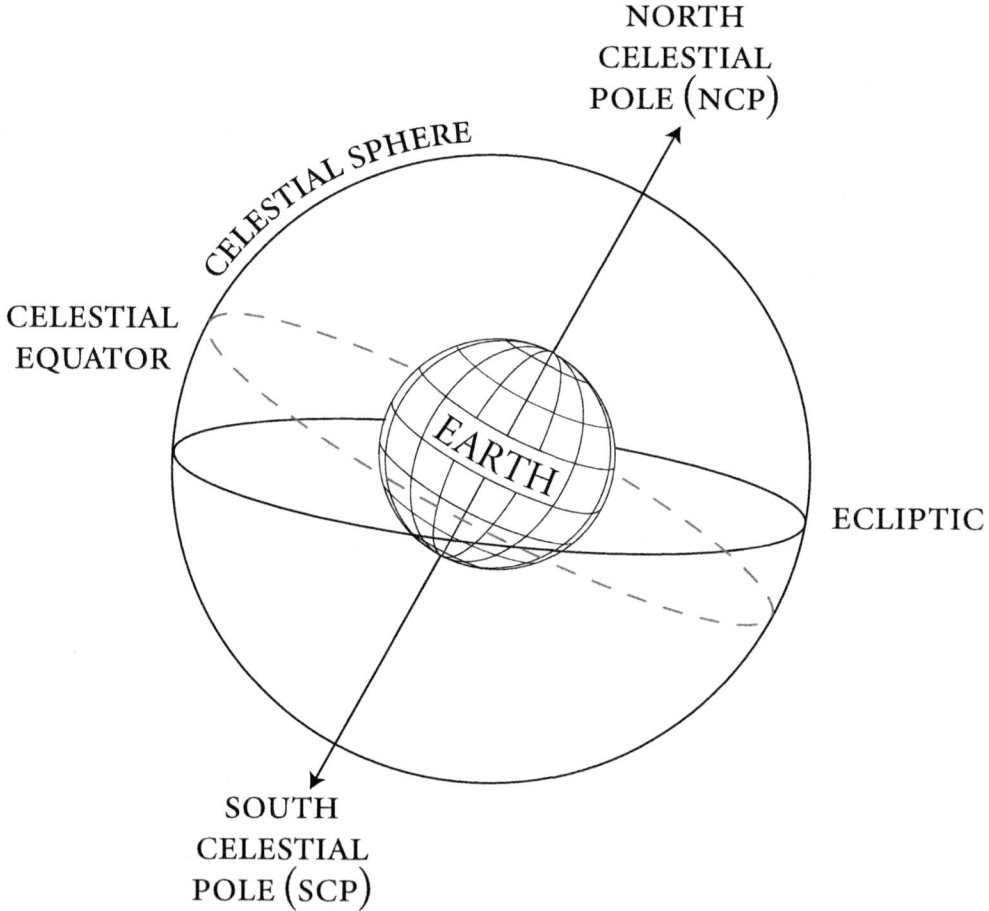

FIGURE 29: *Ecliptic & Equator*

As we've previously learnt, the celestial equator is the Earth's Equator projected into space. "Declination" is measurement North or South of the celestial equator.

"Right Ascension" (RA) is measurement eastward on the celestial equator, using the Vernal Equinox as its starting point.

Declination is measured in degrees, the farthest being 90° North or South of the celestial equator. Right Ascension is measured in hours, the maximum being twenty-four hours of right ascension on the celestial equator. Since the entire celestial sphere makes a full 360° rotation once every twenty-four hours, right ascension can also be expressed in degrees from 00° to 360°.

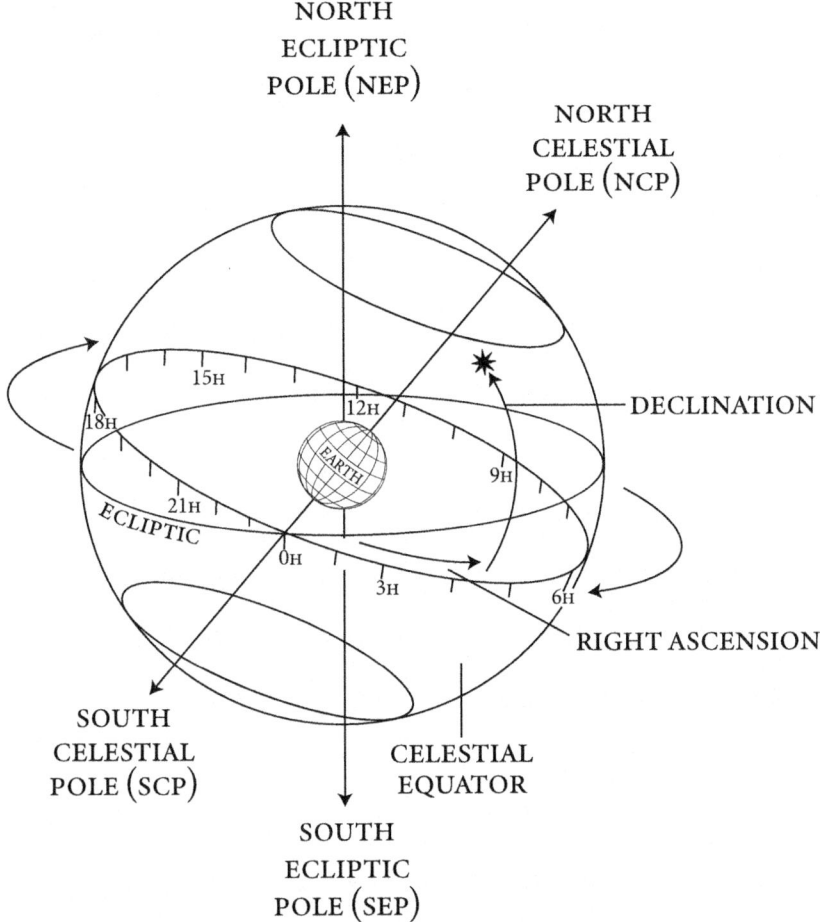

FIGURE 30: *Right Ascension & Declination*

Both of these systems of measurement are used in much the same way that we use the lines of latitude and longitude on Earth. The difference between geographic and stellar coordinate systems is that the former is used to identify locations on Earth, whereas the latter is used to identify the location of stellar bodies on the celestial sphere.

### ON ECLIPSES

Ecliptic sounds like "eclipse." This is because both solar and lunar eclipses can only happen when the Sun and the Moon are relatively near to where the orbital path of the Moon crosses the ecliptic. The Moon's orbital path has approximately a 05° inclination in relation to the ecliptic. This means that the orbital path of the Moon and the orbital path of the Sun do not run parallel to each other. This offset causes them to intersect in two places. The two points where the ecliptic and the Moon's orbital path cross are the North and South Nodes of the Moon.

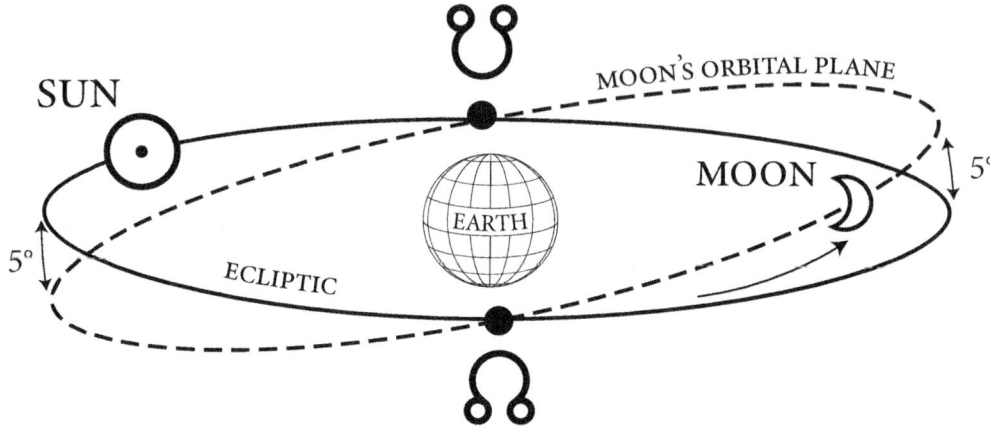

FIGURE 31: *Lunar Nodes*

All of the planets have a north and south node. A node is where two great circles cross. In the case of the other planets, their nodes represent where their paths cross the path of the ecliptic in the North and the South. For the Moon, the North Node is where she crosses from South to North of the ecliptic plane. The South Node is where she crosses from North to South of the ecliptic plane.

In order for an eclipse to occur, there are certain stellar conditions that have to be met. Firstly, an eclipse can only occur at a New or Full Moon. Solar eclipses happen at the New Moon. Lunar eclipses happen at the Full Moon. During a solar eclipse, the Moon gets in the way of the Sun and the Earth. She blocks the Sun's light and looks like a shadow crossing over the face of the Sun. If the entire Sun is obscured, we call this a "total solar eclipse." When only a portion of the Sun is obscured, we call this a "partial solar eclipse."

During a lunar eclipse, the Earth gets between the Sun and the Moon. The Earth blocks the light of the Sun and causes the Moon's light to fade away. If the entire surface of the Moon is obscured, we call this a "total lunar eclipse." If only a portion of the Moon's surface is obscured, we call this a "partial lunar eclipse."

Declination also plays a vital role in eclipses. In order for an eclipse to occur, the Sun and Moon need to be either conjunct (New Moon, solar eclipse) or opposite (Full Moon, lunar eclipse) each other and they also need to be conjunct or opposite each other in declination. A conjunction in declination is called a "parallel." An opposition in declination is called a "contra-parallel." We will fully discuss this type of planetary relationship in our chapter on *Aspects*. This added factor of declination is one of the reasons why not every New Moon is a solar eclipse and why not every Full Moon is a lunar eclipse.

The final condition necessary for an eclipse to occur is that the New or Full Moon in question has to occur near to either of the Moon's Nodes. During a New Moon, if the Sun and the Moon are also conjunct or near to a conjunction of either of the nodes, we have a solar eclipse. During a Full Moon, if the Sun and the Moon are conjunct both the nodes as they oppose each other, we have a lunar eclipse.

Robert Carl Jansky was one of the leading modern pioneers in astrology on the effect of eclipses within the birth chart. The following eclipse criteria are taken from his masterful work on the topic, *Interpreting the Eclipses* (1979).

A total solar eclipse occurs when the Sun and the Moon are within 09° 55' of either of the Moon's nodes. It must occur if they are within this range. It can, but does not always occur within a range of 09° 55' and 11° 15' of the Moon's nodal point.

A solar eclipse can occur within 18° 31' or less of the Moon's nodal point. It must occur if the range is 15° 21' or less. If the orb is 09° 55' or less, the eclipse will be a total eclipse. Between 09° 55' to 11° 15', it can be either partial or total. Between 11° 15' and 18° 31', it must be a partial solar eclipse.

A total lunar eclipse occurs when the Sun and Moon are 03° 45' from the Moon's nodes or closer. A total eclipse must occur if they are within this range. A total lunar eclipse may occur if they are a maximum of 06° 00' from the Moon's nodes.

In general, a lunar eclipse can occur when the distance from the Moon's nodes is less than 12° 15'. It will occur if the range is less than 09° 30'. From 12° 15' to 06° 00' it must be a partial eclipse. Below 03° 45' it must be a total eclipse. Between 03° 45' to 06° 00', the lunar eclipse can either be partial or total.

Eclipses are very important events, particularly in natal predictive astrology and mundane astrology.

## The Ascendant, the Midheaven, and the Twelve Houses

The Ascendant is where the ecliptic crosses our local horizon in the East. The Midheaven is where the ecliptic crosses our local meridian, above the horizon. The Descendant is opposite the Ascendant. The Imum Coeli (IC) is opposite the Midheaven. If we are in the Northern hemisphere, the ecliptic will cross our local meridian above the horizon in the South. If we are in the Southern hemisphere, the ecliptic will cross our local meridian above the horizon in the North. This Midheaven position represents the highest elevation the Sun will attain from the horizon on a particular day, at a particular moment in time.

If you are in the Northern hemisphere and you point your compass in the direction of the Sun at midday, you will see that the Sun is: 1) not directly overhead (unless your location is somewhere on the Equator), and 2) the compass will be pointing towards the South. If you live on the Southern hemisphere and point your compass toward the midday Sun, the direction will be towards the North.

As we've discussed previously, a common astrological misconception is that the zenith is synonymous with the Midheaven, and the nadir is synonymous with the IC. "Midheaven" is the astrological name for how the local meridian is expressed within a two-dimensional astrological chart. However, just as your local meridian and your zenith are not the same point in the sky, the Midheaven within our charts is not synonymous with our zenith. Neither the zenith nor nadir are represented within an astrological map of the heavens. The zenith and the MC will always be above the horizon, but they are not the same. The nadir and the IC will always be below the horizon, but they are not the same.

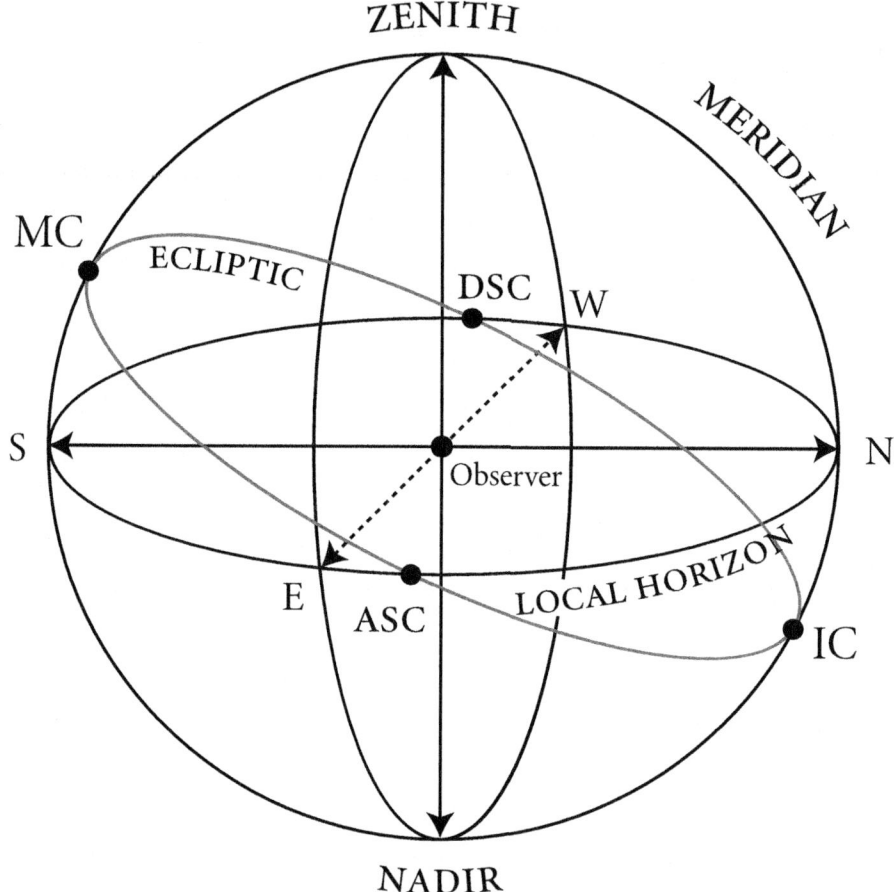

FIGURE 32: *Four Angles of Astrology*

The other twelve houses of a chart are derived from first knowing the exact location of the Ascendant and the Midheaven. Many astrologers throughout time have devised numerous ways of dividing the space between the Ascendant and the Midheaven in order to create the multiple house systems that exist in astrology today. As stated previously, we will only be using the Regiomontanus house system within this book. Regiomontanus is the house system that flourished during the seventeenth century – a period of time upon which much of the astrology within this book is based.

How the Planets move in relation to the Ecliptic

The final coordinate system we will explore is the "ecliptic coordinate system." This allows us to identify the exact location of an object in space based on its relationship to the ecliptic. In astrology, we tend to give everything within the sky a location in ecliptic or zodiacal longitude. "Ecliptic longitude" refers to how far East a planet may be from a specific starting point on the ecliptic. This starting point is 00° Aries, which is the same as saying 00° of ecliptic or zodiacal longitude.

Though we speak about all of the planets primarily based on their ecliptic longitude, there is another system of measurement that tends to be ignored by astrologers today. This other system is known as "ecliptic latitude." Similar to declination, which measures how far North or South a planet is in relation to the Equator, ecliptic latitude measures how far North or South a planet is in relation to the ecliptic.

All planets can have ecliptic latitude with the exception of the Sun. The other planets can be anywhere from 01° to 07° distant from the ecliptic. Pluto can be impressively further from the ecliptic than the other planets. What can be said for planets can also be said for the fixed stars, the majority of which have no relation to our ecliptic at all. The messy truth is that many of the stellar factors that we consider in traditional astrology can exist all across the infinite sky, not just on the organized stretch of sky that we call our zodiac.

How, then, do we have ephemerides and programs that tell us the locations of the planets as if they all were located on the zodiac? We project them there.

For example, in our diagram below, we see that the physical body of Jupiter has risen above the horizon before his projected ecliptic position does the same. This is because Jupiter can have Northern latitude in relation to the ecliptic. Conversely, if this Jupiter had southern latitude in relation to the ecliptic, his ecliptic position could rise before his physical body does.

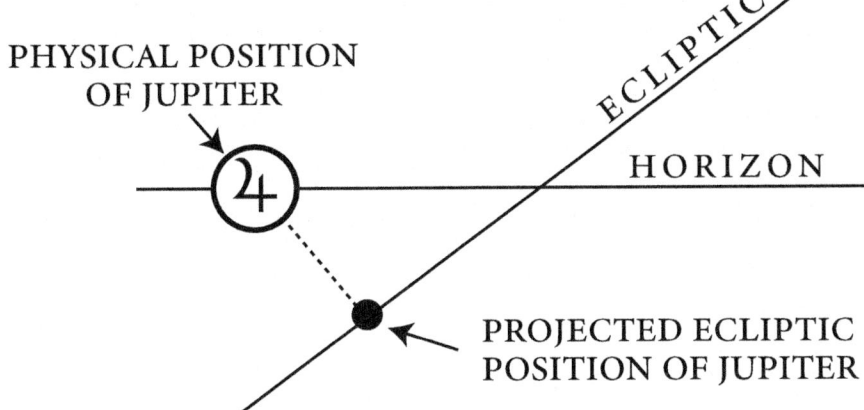

FIGURE 33: *Jupiter – Actual Location & Projected Location on the Ecliptic*

By the time that Jupiter's projected ecliptic degree rises in the East, he would have already been visible in the sky for quite some time.

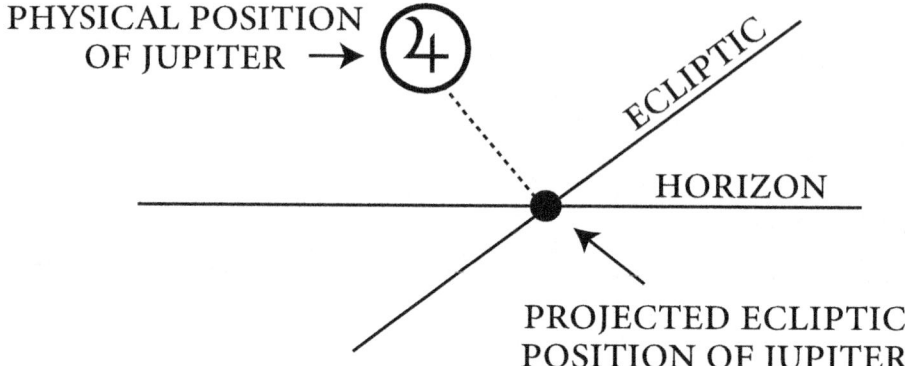

FIGURE 34: *Projected Ecliptic Position of Jupiter Rising*

In our next diagram, we see the actual location of the planet Jupiter. He is not located on either the ecliptic or the Equator. A great vertical circle has to be drawn from the ecliptic poles to determine his ecliptic location. Similarly, in order to find his equatorial location, a great vertical circle has to be drawn from the celestial poles. Most of the time when we are referring to the zodiacal location of the planets or their location in relation to the celestial equator, we are referring to their projected location, not their actual location.

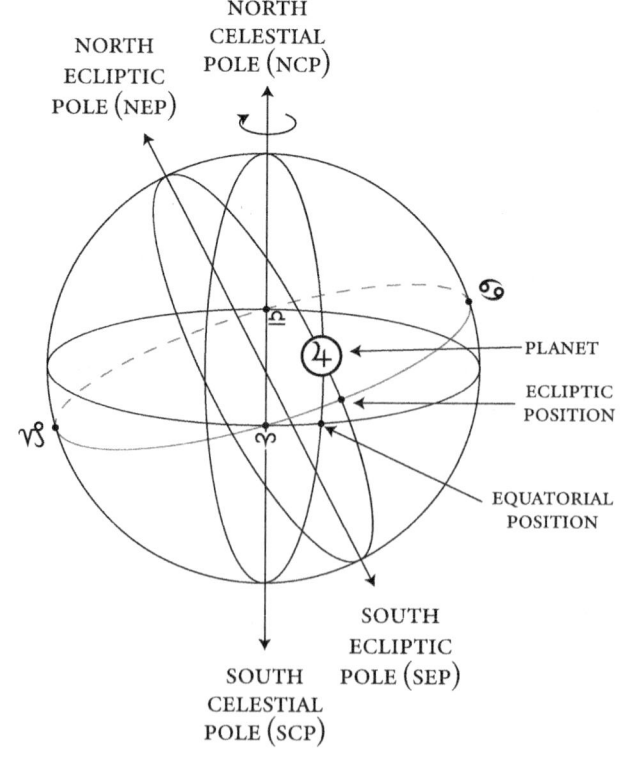

FIGURE 35: *Locating a Planet on the Equator & Ecliptic*

## POLES OF THE ECLIPTIC

The ecliptic is a great circle like the Equator. It also has a plane that is perpendicular to it. Just as the Equator has a North and South Pole, the ecliptic has a North and South ecliptic pole. The North ecliptic pole has a celestial latitude of +90°. The South ecliptic pole has a celestial latitude of -90°. The difference between the pole of the ecliptic and the pole of the Earth is 23.5°. When we say the Earth is tilted on its axis, what we are actually saying is that the pole of the Earth is tilted in relation to the pole of the ecliptic.

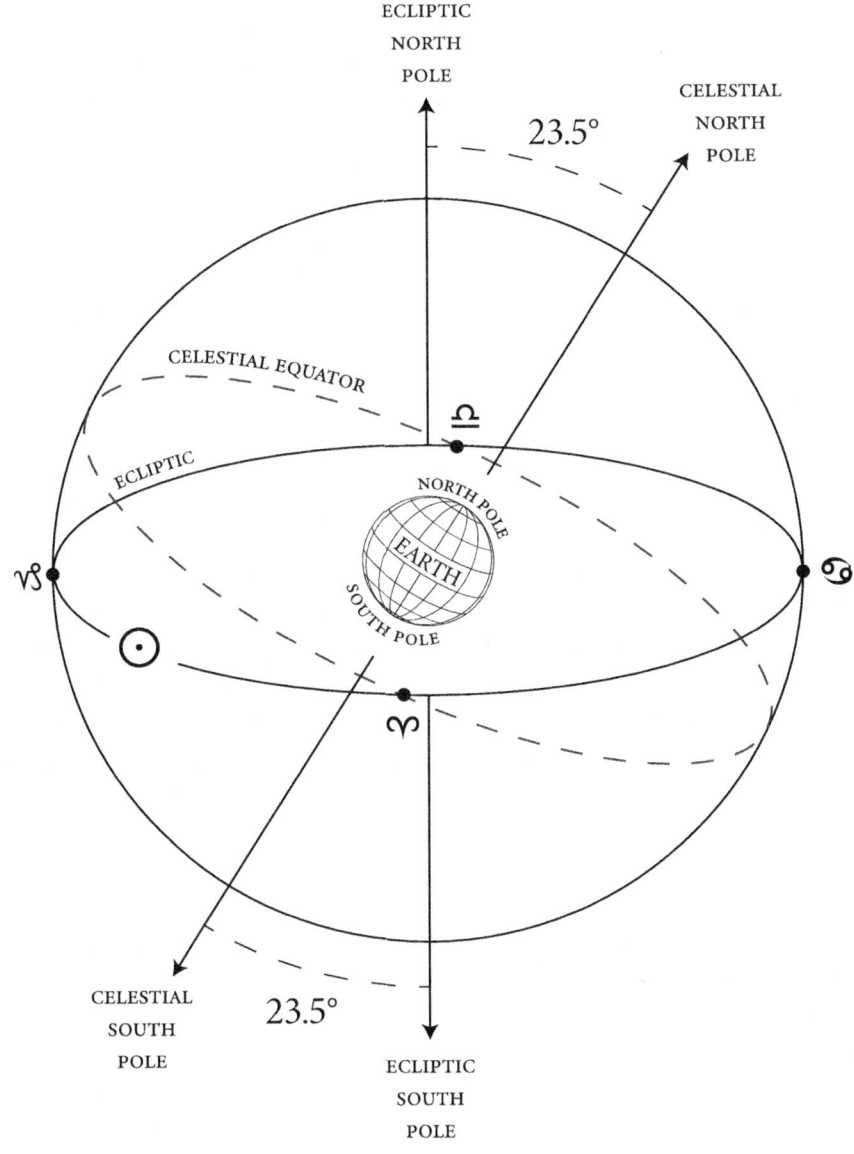

FIGURE 36: *Poles of the Ecliptic*

RETROGRADATION

Retrogradation is the apparent backward movement of a planet based on our location on Earth. Retrogradation is an optical illusion. The planets are not actually moving backwards in the sky. Due to the varying speeds of the planets in relation to the speed of Earth, our visual perception of how those planets move becomes distorted at different points in their orbit.

For example, the orbital period of Earth is approximately three hundred and sixty-five days. This is how long it takes Earth to orbit the Sun. It takes Mars approximately six hundred and eighty-six days to do the same. Similar to speeding pass a slower moving car, when the Earth passes Mars, Mars appears to move backward for a period of time in relation to the constellations behind it. Once the Earth pulls far enough ahead, the backward moving motion of Mars stops, and it appears to resume its forward or direct motion.

The same is true for the inner planets of Venus and Mercury. Venus and Mercury move faster than Earth and often overtake Earth in their orbital paths. The optical illusion that causes Mars to come to a standstill (or station), retrograde, and then move direct is the same thing that occurs with the inner planets of Venus and Mercury. With the exception of the Sun and Moon, the other planets exhibit direct motion, a stationing period, and retrograde motion. This first standstill is called their "retrograde station," and people often say that the planet has "stationed retrograde." They then turn retrograde. At the end of their retrograde period, they come to another standstill called their "direct station." People often say that the planet has "stationed direct." After their direct station, the planets continue in their forward motion until their next retrograde station.

CHAPTER 5 QUESTIONS

1. Why do we continue to use a geocentric model in traditional Western tropical astrology as opposed to a heliocentric model?
2. What is the difference between the zenith and the Midheaven?
3. What is the difference between primary and secondary motion?
4. What is the ecliptic?
5. What is the difference between the terrestrial Equator and the celestial equator?
6. What is the difference between altitude and declination?
7. What is the difference between azimuth and right ascension?
8. Give one pro and one con for choosing to use each of the three zodiacs: constellational, sidereal, and tropical.

## CHAPTER 6 OBJECTIVES

* Elaborate on Ptolemy's teachings regarding the nature of the seven classical planets.
* Discuss how the four qualities become the driving force behind how the planets express themselves in the material world.
* Demonstrate that some of Ptolemy's more controversial ideas regarding the natures of Venus, Mercury, and the Moon were also held within the teachings of other classical astrologers.
* Define the terms "benefic" and "malefic."
* Discuss the notion of gender in relation to the seven classical planets.

# CHAPTER 6

## PTOLEMY ON THE PLANETS

*I know that I am mortal and the creature of a day; but when I search out the massed wheeling circles of the stars, my feet no longer touch the earth, but, side by side with Zeus himself, I take my fill of ambrosia, the food of the gods.* –PTOLEMY

CLAUDIUS PTOLEMY (BORN C. 100 CE) IS ONE OF THE founding fathers of Western tropical astrology. His book the *Tetrabiblos* helps us understand the ancient orientation to nature, the cosmos, and the one life power shared between the seven classical planets and the Earth. In this chapter, we will explore Ptolemy's philosophy regarding the nature of the seven planets. We will also learn how his ideas fit into the classical Greek understanding of the structure of the universe.

Before we begin, it is important to know that Ptolemy's thoughts on the nature of Venus, Mercury, and the Moon are very out of sync with those of later ancient Greek and Medieval authors. Many astrologers have been satisfied to explain away this difference of opinion, stating that Ptolemy was just a collector of astrological data and not an actual astrologer; therefore, "Ptolemy didn't know what he was talking about." Since I, as a practicing astrologer, am in full agreement with Ptolemy's ideas concerning the natures of Venus, Mercury, and the Moon, I have supplied this chapter with quotes from other important astrologers of the ancient world whose understanding of these planets is in harmony with Ptolemy. One such author is Hephaistio of Thebes (born 380 CE). In the preface to the Project Hindsight translation of *Apotelesmatics* by Hephaistio, Robert Hand writes:

> But it is not only the completeness of this work and its explications of Ptolemy that makes it important. Hephaistio appears to have set himself the task of unifying what were by his time the two major schools of Greek astrology, that of Ptolemy and that of Dorotheus of Sidon.

Hephaistio's work does indeed represents an expansion in many regards of Ptolemy's original theories. However, in choosing to replicate Ptolemy's rationale regarding the natures of the inferior planets, Hephaistio shows us that, for him, Ptolemy's thoughts on these matters were philosophically and astrologically sound.

Rhetorius of Egypt (circa 6th or 7th century CE) is another noteworthy astrologer who will be referenced in this chapter. While he deviates from Ptolemy with respect to the nature of Venus and the Moon, he agrees with Ptolemy on perhaps one of Ptolemy's more controversial ideas. Rhetorius agrees that the nature of Mercury is "sometimes wet and sometimes dry" – a fascinating and daring leap within the well-structured cosmological models of the Hellenistic world. When compared to the painstaking strides the ancient Greeks made to rationally explain their universe, the idea of a wet and dry planet makes no sense whatsoever. However, with Rhetorius reiterating this teaching from Ptolemy, he – like Hephaistio before him – proves to us that this paradoxical understanding of the nature of Mercury could find a home within the heart of ancient cosmology.

### The Influence of the Planetary Orbs

The seven classical planets are Saturn, Jupiter, Mars, Sun, Venus, Mercury, and the Moon. According to Ptolemy, all of the planets derive their natures based on their relationship to and distance from the Sun, Moon, and Earth.

### Sun

⊙ *The Sun is found to produce heat and moderate dryness.* – PTOLEMY

According to Ptolemy, the Sun is the origin of the principles of heat and dryness within our universe. For the ancients, the combination of hot and dry corresponded with the choleric temperament. Hephaistio echoes these teachings, stating:

*The Sun, then, is taken as heating and drying at the same time.*

Ptolemy tells us that the very nature of the Sun is to create these two qualities. He even states that people from warmer climates tend to have a warmer, solar disposition. I always thought of this as a glimpse into ancient psychological astrology. As rudimentary as it is, it shows us that there was already thought being placed on what constituted the interiority of the human being at a psychological level. Modern astrology tends to say that classical astrology never paid attention to the personality of its subjects, only the physical realities of their lives. This is just not true.

### Moon

 *The Moon principally generates moisture... she has, however, a moderate share in the production of heat in consequence of the illumination she receives from the Sun.* – PTOLEMY

Ptolemy tells us it is obvious the Moon operates in the realm of moisture because of the clear effects she has on the Earth's waters. According to Ptolemy, the Moon further demonstrates her rulership over moisture through her involvement in the processes of birth, maturation, death, decay, and putrefaction. While he doesn't state how she is involved in these processes, one can imagine that for Ptolemy, there was an analogous relationship between the phases of the Moon and the phases of human life.

Putrefaction is the fifth and final stage of death following pallor mortis, algor mortis, rigor mortis, and livor mortis. It is when the body begins to decompose and breakdown into simpler forms. Through her influence over water, the Moon was thought to govern the level of relaxation necessary that would allow the previously formed animal body to loosen, become undone, give way to the tides of change, and be destroyed. The word "relaxation" is apt for the Moon because it represents anything that is diffuse and has no central organizing factor, much like the element of water which she governs. In Hermeticism, the Sun governs everything that is stable and fixed. He rules the process by which everything gains an individual self, separate from everything around it. The Moon, on the other hand, represents all things that are loose, relaxed, and still existing in a volatile state. Hermetically speaking, the Moon represents anything that has not yet taken on an individual identity.

The Moon also holds some measure of heat due to her relationship to the Sun. She draws the power she needs from the Sun that will fuel her light and radiance. Thus, within the *Tetrabiblos*, we find the Moon described as hot and wet. For the ancients, this combination of hot and wet corresponds with the sanguine temperament. Hephaistio agrees with Ptolemy in this regard. He writes:

> *The Moon, moistens and, as it were, ripens bodies, along with slightly heating.*

Within the Medieval period, astrologers dissented from Ptolemy, saying that the Moon couldn't possibly be hot and wet. As Ptolemy builds his theory of the natures of the planets, he only mentions three pairs of complementing qualities: hot and dry, hot and wet, and cold and dry. Ptolemy never refers to any of the seven planets as cold and wet, which is the last possible pairing of complementary qualities. Therefore, within Ptolemy's system, no planet is associated with the cold and wet, phlegmatic temperament. Many ancient astrologers could not accept this. In the Medieval period, it was widely accepted that the Moon (and Venus) were both cold and wet, and therefore phlegmatic. We will see why, within the well laid out rationale of Ptolemy, this cannot be the case.

## Saturn

 *Saturn produces cold and dryness, for he is most remote both from the Sun's heat and from the earth's vapours. But he is more effective in the production of cold than dryness. And he and the rest of the planets derive their energy from the positions which they hold with regard to the Sun and Moon... –* Ptolemy

After the Sun and Moon, Ptolemy goes on to describe the nature of Saturn. Since Saturn is as far removed from the Sun as possible, Ptolemy considered Saturn to be cold in a destructive and unyielding way. Saturn is also as far from the Moon and

Earth as possible. Thus, his second quality was dryness, having no ability to appropriate unto himself the moisture of either of those two bodies. Ptolemy viewed Saturn as a distant, desolate ice giant, who stood as sentinel and guardian on the very outskirts of the known universe. Hephaistio writes:

> *Kronos [Saturn] chills and slightly dries.*

As a cold and dry planet, Saturn has a melancholic temperament.

## MARS

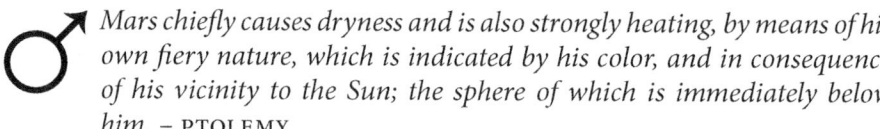 *Mars chiefly causes dryness and is also strongly heating, by means of his own fiery nature, which is indicated by his color, and in consequence of his vicinity to the Sun; the sphere of which is immediately below him. – PTOLEMY*

Mars, though not next in the Chaldean Order, comes next in Ptolemy's essay on the planets. Mars clearly proclaims his nature through his red and shining body. The ancients thought his red color to be symbolic of blood, slaughter, fire, and warfare. Therefore, they thought of Mars as intrinsically hot and volatile.

The amount of heat already in his nature also predisposed him to being dry. With his sphere directly above the Sun, that proximity only made him more destructively hot and unforgivably dry. Thus, the ancients considered Mars to be intemperately hot and dry, making him a choleric planet. Hephaistio writes:

> *Ares [Mars] chiefly dries and burns.*

One could imagine that if Mars is intemperately hot and dry, then the Sun must be even more extreme. However, the difference between Mars and the Sun is that Mars is a warrior while the Sun is the king. The fire held within the Sun must support and provide life for an entire cosmos. The Sun must hold this life-fire in a more dignified and controlled way than Mars ever can. Due to his role in the cosmos and him being the sustainer of all life, the Sun holds his fire temperately, with maturity, compassion, and wisdom. If he did not, we would all die by the force of his heat and power. Mars, on the other hand, has no such restraints. He lives by the sword and dies by the sword. His nature is to destroy by fire, and that is what he does.

## JUPITER

*Jupiter revolves in an intermediate sphere between the extreme cold of Saturn and the burning heat of Mars, and has consequently a temperate influence: he therefore at once promotes both warmth and moisture. But, owing to the spheres of Mars and the Sun, which lie beneath him, his warmth is predominant: and hence he produces fertilizing breezes. – PTOLEMY*

Standing above the double-burner of Mars and the Sun, Jupiter naturally absorbs the intense fire rising from beneath him. However, he is also directly below the desolate shell of frozen Saturn. Ptolemy tells us that Jupiter, through his heat, causes the ice of Saturn to melt. As the perspiration of Saturn falls downward, it lands within the sphere of Jupiter. Therefore, Jupiter – though primarily heating – also holds moisture within his constitution. This makes Jupiter hot and wet. Heat and moisture make Jupiter a sanguine planet. Hephaistio writes:

> Zeus [Jupiter] has a productive power that is temperate, heating, and moistening at the same time.

At this point, some keen student always points out that Saturn, because of his distance from the Moon and the Earth, can't possibly hold any moisture that Jupiter may be able to receive. While this is true in the purely rational sense, when we allow ourselves to move through a mythic framework, we must remember that we are dealing with a myth. Very often, myths are meant to convey an internal understanding of a process that occurs within nature, even if the steps involved in coming to that understanding don't make objective sense. This myth and myths in general are meant to point us in the direction of larger universal truths. Squabbles over the factuality of mythic frameworks are less important than knowing what the framework is and how it impacts the way we practice and think about astrology.

VENUS

 To Venus also the same temperate quality belongs (as Jupiter), although it exists conversely; since the heat she produces by her vicinity to the Sun is not so great as the moisture which she generates by the magnitude of her light, and by appropriating to herself the moist vapours of the earth, in the same manner that the Moon does. – PTOLEMY

After the three superior planets and the luminaries, we come to Venus. As the sphere of Mars is directly above the Sun, so too is the sphere of Venus directly below the Sun in a geocentric model. Due to her proximity to the Sun, Venus naturally absorbs his heat. Since she is close to the Moon and the Earth, she attracts the moist vapors contained within those two bodies. Hephaistio writes:

> And the star of Aphrodite [Venus] is temperately productive of the same things [as Zeus].

Therefore, like Jupiter and Ptolemy's Moon, Venus is hot and wet. These dual qualities make Venus a sanguine planet.

## Mercury

 *Mercury sometimes produces dryness, and at other times moisture, and each with equal vigor. His faculty of absorbing moisture and creating dryness proceeds from his situation with regard to the Sun, from which he is at no time far distant in longitude; and, on the other hand, he produces moisture because he borders upon the Moon's sphere, which is nearest to the earth; and, being thus excited by the velocity of his motion with the Sun, he consequently operates rapid changes tending to produce alternately either quality. – PTOLEMY*

Finally, we come to the most peculiar sphere of Mercury. Here Ptolemy tells us something altogether strange, even by Mercury's standards. He states that Mercury is wet because of the proximity he holds in relation to the Moon and Earth. However, Mercury is also dry because of his proximity to the Sun and the speed of his motion. When Mercury is wet, he is fully wet; when he is dry, he is fully dry. Therefore, in Ptolemy's universe, Mercury – unlike any other planet that exists – has the ability to be wet and dry. He is composed of two qualities that are completely destructive towards each other, yet somehow, he continues to exist. Since there is no temperament that combines the two qualities of wet and dry, the Mercury of Ptolemy's philosophy is without a temperament. Hephaistio follows Ptolemy's lead. He writes:

> *The star of Hermes [Mercury] is sometimes drying, other times moistening.*

Though Rhetorius adapts the more popular opinion that both Venus and the Moon are cold and wet, phlegmatic planets, he curiously agrees with Ptolemy on the nature of Mercury. He writes:

> *Mercury's nature is sometimes wet and sometimes dry...*

For something that many people have considered to be a mistake on Ptolemy's part, it is interesting to see it reflected in the written works of other reputable ancient astrologers. It begs us to consider that there is something within this doctrine of the wet and dry Mercury that is deeper than may initially be evident.

Later generations after Ptolemy could scarcely imagine a universe in which the Moon was not phlegmatic. Those same astrologers would never rest well knowing that history had left Mercury without a temperament. In choosing which two qualities they would bestow upon Mercury, they chose cold and dry, thus designating Mercury as a melancholic planet. This was an arbitrary decision based on Mercury having both his domicile and exaltation in Virgo – a cold and dry, melancholic sign of the earthy triplicity.

The ancients – in an attempt to bring order to our astrological universe – flattened the wild complexity that exists within our notion of who and what Mercury is. Nothing about the nature of Mercury is melancholic or earthy. In fact, in traditional astrology, melancholy is considered to be solely under the domain of Saturn. Just as there is nothing in common between Saturn and Mercury, there is also no overt similarity between the melancholic temperament and the swift-footed messenger of the gods. Inert melancholia and swift changeability exist in polar opposition to each other. I feel it to be deeply incorrect for us to view the inherent nature of Mercury through any melancholic characterization.

The true nature of astrological Mercury was a secret that Ptolemy knew and shared with us all. Upon this arcane teaching the entire Western mystery tradition would later be built. Ptolemy tells us that Mercury has the ability to be wet and dry, fully and separately, as two completely opposite states of being. What Ptolemy is really saying is that Mercury has the ability to balance contradiction within himself and not be destroyed by the force of those opposing powers.

In all the myths of Mercury, we find him able to do what no other god can. He can ascend to the highest heights of heaven and descend to the deepest portals of the underworld without being challenged or destroyed in the process. He can be himself as well as transform into the absolute opposite of himself. He has the power to shapeshift effortlessly between all multiplicities. No other god has that level of mastery over life that they can warp the very fabric of the universe to allow them to walk between worlds unscathed. This power of Mercury to be and become everything is the highest aspiration of the mystic and magician.

Within the wet and dry Mercury, we find what may be the earliest prototype of the right brain/left brain theory. This theory states that the right side of the brain governs the left side of the body, and with it our "wet" faculties of emotion, creativity, visualization, and artistry. The left side of the brain governs the right side of the body, and with it the "dry" and cerebral processes of analysis, rationalization, quantifying, and logic. Though these two parts of ourselves may be separate and strongly polarized, both of them working in unison give us the ability to live in a masterful way. Merging creativity and reason are necessities for living skillfully in the world.

The qualities of wet and dry are also close parallels to the alchemical Moon and Sun, respectively. The alchemical Moon represents the wet principle of dissolution, death, and a return to the original matrix of creation. The Sun represents the dry principle of a singular life, individualized and in radiant expression. Therefore, Mercury, more than any other planet, represents the idea that Nature both is dominated by herself (feminine, wet/lunar principle), and that Nature dominates herself (masculine, solar/dry principle) – a concept that we were introduced to back in chapter three. Holding these two principles within his constitution, Mercury becomes the master of both life and death. In *Proverbs* 18:21, we read:

> *Life and death are in the power of the tongue, and those who love it*
> *will eat its fruit.*

Curiously, within the human body, Mercury governs the brain, limbs, mouth, and tongue. These parts of our anatomy give us the creative power to change our world. This verse can be translated to mean that our words hold the power to create or destroy. Metaphysically, this can suggest that Mercury is the master and the reconciler of the opposing forces represented by the Sun and the Moon.

Life places us all in positions where we must take on the mercurial role of shape-shifting. Often, we find ourselves confronted with challenges that demand we break beyond the narrow framework of our individual temperaments, in exchange for a more expansive and adaptable approach. Acclaimed Austrian poet Rainer Maria Rilke (1875-1926) in his poem *As Once the Winged Energy of Delight*, wrote:

> *Take your practiced powers and stretch them out until they span the chasm between two contradictions... for the god wants to know himself in you.*

A melancholic, one-natured Mercury cannot show us the way to interacting with this multiplicity within ourselves. Only the wild, undefinable enigma that is the wet and dry Mercury can truly point us towards the path of the Mysteries and ultimately towards the doors of truth.

Mercury was singular amongst the gods in that he was also a hermaphrodite. This means that Mercury was both male and female. This continued use of contradictions to describe Mercury offers us a timeless piece of wisdom. In order for us to become masters of the world, we must first learn to transcend it. We must learn to alchemize ourselves in such a way that we can be both Self and Not-Self at the same time; I and Not-I, Thing and No-Thing, Being and Not-Being and every valence shell of possibility that exists between them. We must do this until we realize that all life exists on a continuum that is limited only by perception.

In a letter intended for the family of a recently deceased friend, Albert Einstein (1879-1955) wrote:

> *The distinction between the past, present and future is only a stubbornly persistent illusion.*

Mercury sees that illusion more clearly than any other planet. His mastery of that illusion has granted him mastery over magic, death, and life. To study the mysteries of the wet and dry Mercury is to study the very heart of mysticism itself.

The ibis-headed Thoth or Tehuti – god of science, art, and magic of ancient Egypt – is one of Mercury's incarnations. In describing the spiritual path laid out for us by Thoth/Mercury, Dr. M. Doreal (1898-1963) wrote:

> *He who by progress has grown from the darkness*
> *Lifted himself from the night into light,*
> *Free is he made of the Halls of Amenti,*
> *Free from the Flower of Light and of Life.*

*Guided he then, by wisdom and knowledge,*
*Passes from men to the Master of Life.*
*There he may dwell as one with the Masters,*
*Free from the bonds of the darkness of night.*

In no other planet do we find the promise of immortality or of mastery over all creation as we do in the wet and dry Mercury.

It should be clear to us that the philosophy erected by Ptolemy was a skillful and well-reasoned vision of the cosmos. It carries not only his observation-based understanding of the natural world; it also points us in the direction of deeper spiritual truths.

## BENEFICS AND MALEFICS

TABLE 1: *Benefic & Malefic Planets*

| BENEFIC | MALEFIC | VARIABLE |
|---------|---------|----------|
| ♃ | ♄ | ☉ |
| ♀ | ♂ | ☿ |
| ☽ | | ☽ |

Astrologically speaking, a benefic is a causer of good. A malefic is a causer of evil. According to Ptolemy, the natures of the planets can be characterized as either benefic or malefic based on the primary qualities they embody.

Earlier, we saw Ptolemy using the four qualities to build and describe the temperaments of the seven classical planets. Saturn is cold and dry, Jupiter is hot and wet, Mars is hot and dry, the Sun is hot and dry, Venus is hot and wet, Mercury is wet and dry, and the Moon is hot and wet.

Of these four qualities, Ptolemy tells us two are "nutritive and prolific." Only two of the qualities are supportive and life-sustaining. These qualities are hot and wet. He writes:

> *By them all of nature coalesces and is nourished.*

For this reason, things that are hot and wet are considered to be positive and good for humankind. Symbolically speaking, the Earth that nourishes us, our mother's womb, the food we eat, and even our physical bodies all have these two qualities of hot and wet in common. The hot and wet planets Jupiter and Venus are, therefore, our celestial allies. They have the ability to support, sustain, and nourish us. Jupiter is the greater benefic. Venus is the lesser benefic.

Here, we see a doctrine of analogies beginning to take shape. Ptolemy says the reason we like Jupiter and Venus is because Jupiter and Venus are both "like us." We find echoes of this within the Medieval writings of Jewish astrologer Abraham Ibn Ezra. In *The Book of Reasons* he writes:

*He [Jupiter] is a benefic planet, whose nature in life is to increase
fortune and generosity, for he is of the nature of man, which is warm
and moist. He signifies children because warmth and moisture are
essential for procreation, and wealth because he is a benefic planet.*

Ptolemy goes on to tell us that the Moon is also a benefic because she, too, like
Jupiter and Venus, is hot and wet. It is clear that Ptolemy did not make a mistake
earlier in his writing by identifying these as the qualities of the Moon. He never had the intention of describing her as a cold and wet, phlegmatic planet. In
building a cohesive doctrine of how the planets function, his description of the
qualities of the Moon was meant to ensure that she would be considered as one
of the benefics.

The Moon is benefic during her waxing period and malefic during her waning.
While the Moon is a benefic planet in general, her waxing is more analogous with
the proliferation of life. Her waning is more analogous with the corruption and
ultimate destruction of life. This may be the root of the rough and ready rule of
electional astrology that if we want things to prosper, we align those activities with
the waxing Moon. Conversely, if we want things to shrink, die, and be banished
from our lives, we should align those intentions with the waning Moon.

Ptolemy continues by stating that two qualities are noxious and destructive, and
that by them "all matter is decayed and dissipated." These qualities are cold and
dry. It is for this reason that the two planets that abound in these two qualities are
considered destroyers of life. These planets are Saturn and Mars. Saturn is destructive due to his excess of coldness. Mars is destructive due to his excess of dryness.
Saturn is the greater malefic. Mars is the lesser malefic.

If we were to consider where we want to live in the world, most people may
choose to live in a temperate climate that is warm and moist. The chances of this
would be exponentially increased if the only other options were a climate that is
intemperately cold and dry and another that is destructively hot and dry. In a similar manner, we find Ptolemy stating this case for the benefics and the malefics. We
like the benefics because they feel good and because we know they are less likely to
do us harm. We tend to dislike the malefics because they don't intrinsically mean
us well and – in those iconic words found inscribed on Harry Potter's *Marauder's
Map* – they are "solemnly sworn to be up to no good…" Most of the time.

The Sun and Mercury are neither benefic nor malefic according to Ptolemy.
Both of them, he tells us, are variable. They are benefic with benefic planets and
malefic with malefic planets. By the Medieval period, we find the Sun being
considered to be benefic in general. However, he is thought to be benefic by
aspect, and malefic by conjunction. Remember: an aspect is an angular relationship between two or more planets. In the case of a conjunction, which is
the zodiacal "union" of two or more planets, there is no aspect because there
is no angular relationship. Though conjunctions represent important planetary
connections, they cannot rightfully be called aspects. As far as relationships to

the Sun are concerned, it's nicer to receive the blessings of the benefic Sun from a distance than to sit in the throne room with him in his full power. A trine to the Sun is nice. A bodily conjunction with the Sun? Not so nice.

Medieval Mercury retains his nature of being good with good planets and bad with bad planets.

The titles "greater malefic and benefic" and "lesser malefic and benefic" apply to Saturn, Jupiter, Mars, and Venus, respectively. The Moon, though a benefic planet, does not have a designation of "greater" or "lesser."

## MASCULINE AND FEMININE

TABLE 2: *Masculine & Feminine Planets*

| MASCULINE | FEMININE | HERMAPHRODITE |
|:---:|:---:|:---:|
| ♄ | ♀ | ☿ |
| ♃ | ☽ | |
| ♂ | | |
| ☉ | | |

Ptolemy goes on to tell us that there are two sexes: male and female. He says that the feminine gender abounds in moisture. Venus and the Moon, because of their great moisture, are feminine. While he doesn't necessarily say that "the masculine planets abound in heat," he does consider Jupiter, Mars, and Sun to be masculine planets. Though cold and dry, Saturn is included amongst the masculine planets. At the time of Ptolemy writing the *Tetrabiblos*, it was universally accepted throughout ancient Greece and Rome that Saturn/Kronos was the father of the gods.

As always, magical, mystical, mysterious Mercury is neither masculine nor feminine because "he produces wetness and dryness and each in equal ratio." Mercury is considered masculine with masculine planets and feminine with feminine planets. We consider Mercury as "he" because that is how he is traditionally depicted. However, Ptolemy reasserts that Mercury is common to both genders.

CHAPTER 6 QUESTIONS

1. What are the four qualities that compose the natures of the planets?
2. From which planets do the other planets derive their nature?
3. What are the qualities of the moon within Ptolemy's philosophy?
4. What do all the benefic planets share in common?
5. Besides being dry, what quality does Saturn and Mars share in common? What about them makes them both malefic?
6. Explain Ptolemy's rationale behind the composition of Mercury.

## CHAPTER 7 OBJECTIVES

* Gain a basic understanding of the speed and motion of the planets.
* Provide an introductory outline of the principal correspondences that each planet has on Earth.
* Give commentary on how each of the planets manifests through the psychological constitution of a human being.
* Discuss the lunar nodes and their significations.
* Briefly discuss the Arabic Parts and how the Part of Fortune is used in traditional astrology.
* Introduce the three modern planets Uranus, Neptune, and Pluto and their terrestrial significations.

# Chapter 7

## Planetary Correspondences

*For the planets have their own faculties and divine wisdom. Animated by pure reason they tirelessly obey that highest divinity, the ruling God who has organized all things under the rule of law to protect the eternal pattern of creation.* –FIRMICUS MATERNUS

WITHIN ASTROLOGY, THE PLANETS ARE considered to be the chief governors of destiny. They are vehicles of cosmic influence who describe through their myriad combinations the multitude of events we experience on Earth. Through the universal law of correspondences, everything within our physical world can be represented by the specific nature of individual planets or through combinations of planets working in unison. The planets represent the building blocks of our reality.

The purpose of astrology is largely to understand the planets and how they interact with each other. The student who has an in-depth knowledge of the combinations of these stellar influences has a far greater advantage in the practice of astrology than the student who only has a psychological understanding of the signs of the zodiac.

In this section, I will provide a brief outline of correspondences for each of the seven classical planets. I will also provide similar descriptions for the lunar nodes and the Part of Fortune, since they also populate the sky of traditional astrology. Since I use Uranus, Neptune, and Pluto within my work, I will provide outlines for them as well.

I will use the term "celestial houses" interchangeably with "signs" in relation to the signs of the zodiac. Traditionally the domiciles of the planets were referred to as their "houses" or "celestial houses." This is distinctly different from the twelve terrestrial houses that represent the various topics shown within a chart. It is easy to believe that all references to "houses" is meant to suggest the twelve terrestrial houses with which most students of astrology are familiar. However, we must not. My use of the term "celestial houses" in relation to the domiciles of the planets is not meant to add to the confusion over what the word "house" means. My purpose is to familiarize students with the multiple ways in which our astrological ancestors expressed their understanding of these various concepts.

Beyond this traditional use of the term "celestial houses," I have tried to simplify the terminology in this section as much as possible. I typically do not find it useful or kind to maintain the use of ancient language in the twenty-first century. I've tried in every way possible to rid these planetary correspondences of the heavy classical language used in the ancient, Medieval, and Renaissance periods, and hopefully have created a more useful body of work as a result of those efforts.

I have added sections on the corresponding body parts, colors, and flavors associated with the planets. Students of astrology should have a more thorough understanding of how the ancients viewed the magical correspondences that underpinned their vision of the world. Hopefully, the inclusion of these correspondences will provide students with a deeper understanding of the planets themselves.

As far as Uranus and Neptune are concerned, I have taken the liberty to reference books from astrologers in the early nineteenth century, while giving my own observations. As far as Pluto is concerned, I have referenced twentieth century authors such as Reinhold Ebertin, Barbara Watters, and other modern astrologers operating within the 1930s-1970s. This is mainly out of an appreciation for the style of the writing within that era. I have not referred to the written works of any twenty-first century astrologer on the meanings of the modern planets. Rather, I have based my understanding on how these planets manifest on a psychological and concrete level in my own client work.

*

*We must now turn to the essential characteristics of the planets uncomplicated by any other influence, because the relation of the planets to the signs is such that when they enter them they undergo certain alterations; for the planets like the signs are spiritual forces which change the nature of bodies submitted to their influence, a retrograde planet for example, may change a temperament into a choleric one, or a joyful or anxious one, according as one of the four elements becomes preponderant and alters the activities of the spirit and the conditions. –* AL-BIRUNI

# THE TRADITIONAL PLANETS

Saturn, Jupiter, Mars, Sun, Venus, Mercury, and the Moon represented the celestial pantheon of the ancient world. In a world devoid of the ability to see beyond the rings of Saturn, these seven represented the governors of fate, and the motive-forces behind all manifestations of life within our world.

## SATURN

*They called Saturn the Father of the gods, and temperatour of times, saying that he was high and a great Lord, sage, prudent, wise, foreseeing, witty, ancient, and of a great profoundness in knowledge and understanding, knowing the thoughts of men, and boldening them in high enterprises and acts valiant, the keeper of things secret and hid, and a great Lord over life and death.*
– CHRISTOPHER CATTAN

| | |
|---|---|
| ORBITAL PERIOD: | 29.5 years |
| LENGTH IN EACH SIGN: | 2.5 years |
| MEAN DAILY MOTION: | 00° 02' 00" |
| TASTES: | Sour, bitter, sharp. Astringent. |
| DAYS: | Saturday day, Tuesday night. |
| COLORS: | Black. |
| METALS: | Lead, coal, or the dross of all metals. Detritus. |
| STONES: | Sapphire, lapis lazuli. |
| DIRECTION: | West (according to al-Biruni). |
| CELESTIAL HOUSES: | Aquarius is his day house and Capricorn is his night house. Aquarius is his celestial house of joy. |
| HUMOR: | Author of Melancholy. |

GENERAL PLANETARY NATURE:

Cold and dry, intemperate, melancholic, an enemy and destroyer of the nature and life of man, diurnal, masculine, evil, and the Greater Misfortune. Slow in effects, ponderous, weighty, terrible in all aspects, always fixed. Author of Solitariness. Barren. Leaden pale color to our eyes. In his *Essays on the Foundations of Astrology*, English astrologer CEO Carter tells us:

> *By limiting the outgoing activities of fire, [Saturn] causes checks, delays, and disappointments, and so becomes the planet of fate which sets definite bounds to our efforts.*

IN THE HUMAN BODY:

Saturn rules the bones, teeth, cartilage, and the entire skeletal framework. Saturn rules the skin, hair, fingernails, and all the protective coverings of the body. Saturn also is said to rule the spleen, right ear, bladder, and retentive faculties through the whole body. Saturn rules waste material in the body, which the ancients referred to as "black bile."

PROFESSIONS:

Saturn represents religious officials such as priests, popes, bishops, pastors, nuns, ascetics, hermits, or anyone who turns their back on worldly pleasures. Saturnians may be interested in professionally studying occult and hidden things, as is the case with historians, antiquarians, and archaeologists. Saturn represents people who are older – elders and ancestors. Saturnians may gravitate towards hard manual labor jobs, such as construction work. Saturn can also represent architects, masons, potters, and real estate agents – jobs that concern the use, cultivation, and sale of the earth. Saturn also represents farm workers and agriculturists.

Saturn can represent a stable or orthodox form of employment. He represents government employees, or people who work in a traditional, practical field. As the planet of burdens, he can represent people who work with large animals or "beasts of burden." Traditionally, Saturn was associated with dirty jobs. He rules tanners – people who convert animal skins to leather; janitors, garbage collectors, and other low-paying service work. As a god of death, he can represent people who work with death: morticians, grave-diggers, and taxidermists. Saturn has also been called "the god of humblings." As such, Saturn represents comedians and clowns – people who are socially mocked for a living.

MYCHAL'S COMMENTARY:

Saturn gives people deep introspection, judgment, and imagination. Saturnians have a rich inner world which may manifest as outer silence. Saturnian people are responsible. They feel the needs of the community are their personal duty to fulfill. They can come across as argumentative, or chronically pessimistic. Saturnian people can have a very sobering and potentially depressive outlook on life. They can be stubborn and unwilling to change. Bonatti writes:

> *If a Saturnian man undertook to esteem someone (which rarely happens), he will esteem him with true esteem. And if he undertook to hate someone (which often happens), he will hate him with an extreme hatred, and will hardly or never desist from that hatred.*

Saturnian people think with the future in mind and are always preparing for the worst. Since they constantly plan for a rainy day, they love wealth, stability, and the security that money can buy. They can be frugal, mean, unwilling to share, and always seeking a bargain. Abū Maʿšar writes:

> *... and when he shows provisions, he shows much, and when he takes away, he takes away much.*

Saturnians do well in positions of management. They enjoy being able to organize and control the affairs of people around them. Because Saturn represents the furthest reaches of our perception, he also represents the universal power that teaches us about the limits of our reality. However, this can turn into a crippling sense of limitation and over-materialism. I often make the distinction between the higher Saturn and the lower Saturn. The higher Saturn is who we think of when considering the sign Aquarius. The lower Saturn is who we think of when considering the sign Capricorn. The higher Saturn can lead us toward paths of ingenuity and social progress. The lower Saturn – only seeing that which is below him – comes into the world thinking he has to maintain the order of the material universe as it currently is. The lower Saturn tends to be who people think of first when describing Saturn. He represents the Law of Matter, which can manifest as a strict orthodoxy.

Saturn can represent someone who is a master at physical arts and creations. He also represents poverty and living in depressive states. Vettius Valens tells us that Saturn is a god who causes people to fall on their faces. Saturn reminds us of our mortality, thus keeping us humble.

Saturnians have a deep memory and they hold deep emotions. They feel as if nothing can be gained without hard work and effort. They are likely to be found working extremely hard at things that don't really require that much work at all. Saturnians may be largely missing out on the sweetness of life. However, the Saturnian person is willing to work for that sweetness, and enjoys the fruits of their labor later in their old age.

Ill-dignified Saturnians are people who are always suspicious of others and deeply mistrustful. They may be envious, jealous, and may think that good things do not happen for them. They may harbor a deep and constant fear. They may never truly be content, and may be chronic complainers. Ill-dignified Saturnian people may find themselves constantly in survival mode. They may always be seeking to fulfill their goals and objectives in life without much care as to the impact this way of living has on others around them.

# ♃

## JUPITER

*Jupiter is called a Father, named in the old time, the King of Heaven, invincible, bold, blessed, pleasant, amiable, merciful, and of goodwill, honest, honorable, sage, and surpassing all others in goodness.* – CHRISTOPHER CATTAN

| | |
|---|---|
| ORBITAL PERIOD: | 12 years |
| LENGTH IN EACH SIGN: | 1 year |
| MEAN DAILY MOTION: | 00° 05' 00" |
| TASTES: | Sweet and oily things. |
| DAYS: | Thursday day and Sunday night. |
| COLORS: | Blue, purple. |
| METALS: | Tin & pewter. |
| STONES: | Amethyst, emerald, topaz, marble. |
| DIRECTION: | North (East according to al-Biruni). |
| CELESTIAL HOUSES: | Sagittarius is his day house and Pisces is his night house. Sagittarius is his celestial house of joy. |
| HUMOR: | Author of Sanguine. |

GENERAL PLANETARY NATURE:

Hot and moist, sanguine, a friend and preserver of the life and nature of man, masculine, diurnal, and is called the Greater Fortune.

IN THE HUMAN BODY:

Liver, left ear, lungs, blood, semen, veins, diaphragm, sides, muscles.

PROFESSIONS:

Jupiter, like Saturn, also has rulership over religious officials, especially those who take on a benevolent parental role. Jupiter represents religious leaders who inspire kindness and mercy in their followers. Judges, lawyers, dignitaries, justices of the peace, people of wealth and influence, young scholars, doctors, students in general, teachers and professors are all represented by Jupiter.

Jupiter can also represent people who travel as a part of their profession: photo-journalists, documentary makers, and people who enjoy visiting far distant places. The Jupiterian is a citizen of the world, with big dreams and high ambitions. They enjoy professions that bring freedom, autonomy, and wealth. They can work in mass communication, public relations, and human resources. Less positively, they can be swindlers – people who gamble and make big risks with money. Jupiter can also represent people who do not want to work. Jupiter can represent people who simply want to enjoy the good things in life and who get by due to the good-will of others.

MYCHAL'S COMMENTARY:

Jupiterians are naturally charitable and loving people. They seek to create a world of justice and cooperation for everyone around them. They are kind, open-heart-ed, generous, and optimistic. They don't have the ability to stay depressed for very long. They are naturally idealistic. They tend to see the good in every situation and in every person. The Jupiterian person needs both crowds and community to feel fulfilled. They are interested in meeting people from foreign lands and cultures so that they can create wider social connections with others. They will not hesitate to step into the role of financial provider for those in need. They do not have a clear understanding of limitation, which can manifest as a problem. Their purpose in life is to alleviate the world of some of the pressures and restrictions of Saturn.

Because of their lack of inner limitations, they may overdo everything. They may love too deeply, travel too far, spend too much, eat too much, and live a life of gluttony. They may have a very high pleasure craving and sex drive. Harmony needs to be created between the expansive qualities of Jupiter and the restrictive qualities of Saturn in order to create a balanced individual.

They have a rich and boisterous laugh. It makes them wonderful people to have around and also makes them loved by others. They are people's people.

Jupiter ill-dignified can create wasteful people. They can burn through their in-heritance by spending excessively. They overcommit themselves, and therefore, can't stay true to their promises. They have too many buns in the oven and may not be able to support or sustain any of them. Sometimes ill-dignified Jupiterians can become overly zealous and dogmatic. They can also be hypocrites – espousing a beautiful philosophy that they don't uphold. They may have a hard time settling down or being loyal. They may be continuously unfaithful to their spouses. CEO Carter writes:

> *Under affliction, it runs to excess of energy, optimism, and self-indulgence. The faith becomes an unbounded belief in luck and a reckless disregard of consequences, so that – although seldom anyone's enemy but his own – the Jovian often ruins himself by pushing his luck so far, taking unreasonable hazards, gambling, and wasting time, money, and energy.*

## Mars

*Mars is called Mavors, which is as much to say, as mighty in war, bloody, of high courage, and not to be subdued, valiant in arms, strong, furious, invincible, whom none can resist that would do him harm, he putteth down the mighty, and taketh kings, emperors, and potentates out of their places, he is Lord of heat, and governor of Fire, a planet of blood, and encourageth and maketh hardy people in fight.* – CHRISTOPHER CATTAN

| | |
|---|---|
| ORBITAL PERIOD: | 1.88 years |
| LENGTH IN EACH SIGN: | 2.5 months |
| MEAN DAILY MOTION: | 00° 31' 00" |
| TASTES: | Bitter, tastes of gall, sharp tastes. Pungent. |
| DAYS: | Tuesday day and Friday night. |
| COLORS: | Red, yellow, fiery. |
| METALS: | Iron, steel, arsenic, brimstone, and red vermillion. |
| STONES: | Bloodstone, jasper. |
| DIRECTION: | South. |
| CELESTIAL HOUSES: | Aries is his day house and Scorpio is his night house. Scorpio is his celestial house of joy. |
| HUMOR: | Choleric. |

GENERAL PLANETARY NATURE:

Immoderately hot and dry. CEO Carter tells us:

> *[Mars is] fiery and in many respects resembles the Sun. It's actions, however, are more energizing and less stable.*

He is choleric, masculine, nocturnal, evil, and the Lesser Misfortune, enemy to man's nature, hurtful by conjunction, square, or opposition. Of a shining, bloody color, similar to fire burning in its strength. Mars is the Author of Strife, Quarrels, Controversies, and Contentions. He is the author of anger, hate, haste, and choler, and rules these dispositions within us. He is the Star of Malevolence.

### IN THE HUMAN BODY:

The gall and gallbladder, the genitals, the mesentery, the attractive faculty. He governs and fortifies the sense of smell. Through his rulership of Aries, he rules the face. Mars rules our capacity for apprehension. The ancients said that this is why choleric people tend to be so quick-witted.

### PROFESSIONS:

Mars rules martial, combative people and martial, dangerous jobs. He can represent police officers, soldiers, and criminals. He represents the fighter as well as his opponent; athletes and sports in general. Mars represents people who work in defense occupations: he is the lawyer who is not afraid of a fight, as well as the person working in cybersecurity. Martian people enjoy knives, machines, and firepower. They can easily work in engineering or mechanical fields. Skillful with a knife, the Martian can excel at surgery as well. They can be great carpenters, barbers, cooks, tailors, blacksmiths, bakers, or watchmakers.

### MYCHAL'S COMMENTARY:

Martians tend towards being hotheaded, impulsive people who cannot be controlled. They want to have absolute freedom to move as they please, to do what they want, and to be the only governing power in their lives. Martians are bold, courageous, and dynamic. They are restless. They always want to do something with their extraordinary energy and power. Martians are trailblazers. They willingly step into the line of fire in order to feel passion and excitement. They live for war and crisis, and rush into the heat of the flames when other people may think twice. They listen to no one, but speak loudly so that everyone can hear them.

Martian natives are intellectually sharp and full of words. Renaissance texts tell us that men who are Martian are prone to talk about their great manhood. They are boastful and enjoy telling the world about their great acts. They fear neither God nor man, and hate the thought of being a loser or subservient to anyone. They will not hold onto anyone or anything if their survival is on the line. They can quickly sever connections with others if they feel it will be best for them. They may find it hard to forgive and forget the past, which may make them always ready to strike back or get revenge. They are easily angered, and can often act first and think later only after they've done the wrong thing. Oftentimes Martians need to slow down and seek outside counsel. If left to their own devices, they will likely run into trouble because of their lack of planning, forethought, or consideration.

They can be fiercely loyal friends or fierce enemies. Either way, they do everything in life with ferocity and stamina. Martians can be cutting in both their words and their actions. The masterful Martian can be incisive and penetrating, and can be extremely focused in ways that other people cannot even imagine. When dignified, they can be pioneering and enterprising and can be the force necessary to start a positive new initiative. They have the fire of beginnings to their advantage, and in their highest expression, they can achieve whatever goal or surmount whatever challenge they are faced with. They have to learn to do this through self-mastery and discipline and not through violence and impulsiveness.

Ill-dignified Mars creates people who are always angry. They may consistently start things they cannot finish. Ill-dignified Martians look for a fight where no fight is necessary, and create conflict just to feel alive. They tend to be scattered in their energy and cannot bring themselves fully to support a singular goal. They can frustrate themselves and others through their intensity. They need to learn to calm down and relax, though they may hate being told that. They are the Type A personality – overachieving and over-reaching in every way. They may do underhand things to destroy a person if they think that person is ahead of them or progressing at a faster rate.

The ill-dignified Mars is underhanded in general, and is capable of doing things that are criminal and unjust in order to get ahead in life. They are independent in a way that makes them feel they have to do everything for themselves. This can lead to them living an isolated life. They do not know how to feel other emotions that aren't hot and fiery. This can make them violent, harsh, and abrupt with people around them. They can speak in a hurtful manner and consciously seek to weaponize their words for the purpose of hurting others. They have strong sexual cravings that they seek to fulfill constantly and may cause them to lead a destructive lifestyle. They have poor family connections and may have come from a violent family background. In their interactions with others, they fluctuate between feeling weak and oppressed to being the ones that oppress and dominate others.

## SUN

*The Sun is the most glorious and resulgent body of all the planets,
and of Philosophers is called Oculus Mundi, the Eye of the World, and Fons Lucus,
the Fountain of Light, from the (Hebrew) word Shemesh, because when he arises or
ascends any horizon, by the dispersing of his rays, he obscures
the lesser light of the Moon and stars, and causeth them to disappear,
and by reason of which the Greeks called him Helios, intimating thereby, his super-
sufficiency to be, appear, and rule alone. He is indeed Rex Planetarum,
the King of the Planets, for whereas the other six do move sometimes
by Retrogradation, and other times by Direction and at sometimes not at all,
and mostly are observed soon to be on this side, soon on the other side
of the Ecliptic Line, this Princely Body is never found to deviate, but keeps one certain
place, viz. the ecliptic, as his mansion house, and is always
to be found there. –* JOHN GADBURY

| | |
|---|---|
| ORBITAL PERIOD: | 365.25 days |
| LENGTH IN EACH SIGN: | 1 month (approximately) |
| MEAN DAILY MOTION: | 00° 59' 00" |
| TASTES: | A mix of sweet and sour. Things that are salted just right. Pungent. Sharp. |
| DAYS: | Sunday day and Wednesday night. |
| COLORS: | Yellow, saffron, scarlet. |
| METALS: | Gold. |
| STONES: | Ruby, carbuncle. |
| DIRECTION: | East. |
| CELESTIAL HOUSES: | Leo is his day and night house. Leo is his celestial house of joy. |
| HUMOR: | Choleric. |

# PLANETARY CORRESPONDENCES

## GENERAL PLANETARY NATURE:

Hot and dry, and yet he is more temperate than Mars. Masculine, diurnal, fortunate by aspect (sextile and trine in particular, but not square or opposition), unfortunate by corporal conjunction. The fountain of life. Celestial Lamp, Lux Mundi, Light of the World.

## IN THE HUMAN BODY:

He rules the heart, brain, the right eye in men, and the left eye in women; the arteries. The attractive faculty throughout the whole body.

## PROFESSIONS:

The Sun is a universal significator of men. Solar people usually seek out professions of dignity and honor. They desire careers that allow them to get recognition within the world. They can be bosses, CEOs, or a part of the administration of an organization. They can work in the financial industry as managers of wealth or can work amongst wealthy people. Solar people enjoy doing rarefied work that sets them apart from others. They can be actors or performers; anyone who enjoys being in the limelight. They are great at identifying the talents that other people have and can be good career consultants and coaches. They can work as jewelers, and can have a special liking for gold. Sometimes they can be tyrannical in their pursuit of power or authority. They can often represent people in positions of power who don't actually deserve to be there. Less positively, sometimes Solarians are people who feel bigger and better than any profession. They may find themselves constantly unemployed.

## MYCHAL'S COMMENTARY:

Solar people know their worth, and they are not afraid to let you know it as well. They are bold and content, because they feel they have everything they need to make it in life. They enjoy being the center of attention. Solarians can be warm, big-hearted, and affectionate. They have the ability to identify the best in others. They can have abundant vitality, and may live a long life. A Solarian is a generous and honorable person to everyone. As a result of their deep self-confidence, they can be very convincing. They are unwilling to allow themselves to look bad, even if they aren't doing well in life. There is an air of pride and dignity about them that they carry into all of their interactions.

Solar natives can be self-absorbed, self-obsessed, and in love with their own reflection. They aren't necessarily competitive; they already feel they've won and as if they are the best at everything they do. They may be dramatic, even a bit of a performer, and are flashy with the things they own. However, we all still love them and want to stand in their warm light.

When ill-dignified, these people have no substance. They talk a big talk, but can't actually back it up. They promise much, but perform little. They are always on the verge of a greatness that they never attain. They speak loudly because they feel small. They lack personal power and presence.

Ill-dignified Solarians can be tyrannical leaders, who are arrogant, egotistical, and don't care for the people they lead. They can overdramatize their own glories and sorrows, because they need the attention of others constantly. They do not know who they are, and therefore, try to graft themselves onto society or onto social causes in order to give them a sense of personal identity. They may enter partnerships in order to dominate those partnerships. This allows them to feel a sense of personal power and control.

Ill-dignified Solarians can easily be driven to excess. Because of their extravagant lifestyle, they can burn through their wealth, and easily become bankrupt. They may gamble in order to regain wealth that they have lost. This may keep them in a constant state of lack. They may also take risks with other people's resources, while selfishly trying to protect their own.

## Venus

*As soon as Kronos had lopped off the genitals [of Ouranos] with the sickle he tossed them from the land into the stormy sea. And as they were carried by the sea a long time, all around them white foam rose from the god's flesh, and in this foam a maiden was nurtured. There this majestic and fair goddess came out, and soft grass grew all around her soft feet. Both gods and men call her Aphrodite, foam-born goddess, and fair-wreathed Kythereia; Aphrodite because she grew out of aphros, foam, that is, and Kythereia because she touched land at Kythera. – HESIOD*

| | |
|---|---|
| ORBITAL PERIOD: | 224 days |
| LENGTH IN EACH SIGN: | 23 days to 2 months |
| MEAN DAILY MOTION: | 01° 12' 00" |
| TASTES: | Sweet oils and fatness; moist, odiferous foods. Rich. Greasy. |
| DAYS: | Friday day and Monday night. |
| COLORS: | Light blue, white, green. |
| METALS: | Copper, brass, mirror materials of all kinds. |
| STONES: | Turquoise, beryl, chrysolite, carnelian, lapis lazuli because it dispels melancholy, alabaster, marble. |
| DIRECTION: | North (according to al-Biruni). |
| CELESTIAL HOUSES: | Libra is her day house and Taurus is her night house. Taurus is her celestial house of joy. |
| HUMOR: | Sanguine. |

General Planetary Nature:

Hot and moist, temperate, sanguine, feminine, nocturnal, of good nature, and is called the Lesser Fortune. Venus is a star of a bright and shining color. She is called *Hesperus* or Evening Star from her being seen after the setting of the Sun, and *Lucifer*, the Morning Star, from her rising and being seen before the Sun rises. She is the Author of Voluptuousness and Pleasure.

In the Human Body:

Throat, breasts, buttocks, womb, kidneys, genitals.

Professions:

Venus can represent artists of every kind. These include dancers, painters, musicians, and poets. She enjoys all things that have to do with fashion, design, and a fine aesthetic sense. She enjoys designing aesthetically pleasing experiences for others. She can represent people who work in the creative industry, from interior to graphic design. She can work in the beauty industry as a hair stylist, make-up artist, nail technician, massage therapist, and dermatologist. She can specialize in working with women, and industries that serve to adorn them. She can be a fashion designer, model, or a person who gets paid to be beautiful.

Venusians tend to be conflict averse, and can be great counsellors, therapists, and healers. She can work in the fine arts and be a trader of jewelry and fine linens. She can also work with perfumes or be a spice merchant; she takes pleasure in all things that appeal to the senses. She enjoys sensual work that brings pleasure to both herself and others.

Mychal's Commentary:

The Venusian person is soft and gentle. Venusians are unwilling to be in environments that are cruel and harsh. They are lovers of the joys of this life. They are often well-dressed, and love to be in aesthetically pleasing spaces whether they create them or frequent them. They enjoy beauty and cleanliness. Venusians have a highly developed sensitivity; they long for balance and harmony within their lives. They are not inclined to hard work, and can sometimes be very lazy. They would rather everyone else do the heavy lifting around them, while they sit back and continue to enjoy the comforts of the world.

Venusians are peaceful and peacemakers. They are wonderful at calming a fight, and can be great mediators between warring parties. Venusians are wonderful friends. They easily fall into the role of being people pleasers. They work best with others, and need to be a part of the group in order to feel fulfilled. However, sometimes the group can be too much for them, especially if there is disharmony. This is why one-to-one relationships are important for them. They are likely to feel the inclination towards finding love at a very young age.

They can be drawn to the arts and other creative pursuits. They can equally be drawn to counselling. Venusians can naturally create an environment in which people feel heard and held. They are caring people – lovers of children, animals, and plants. They win others over, not through force, but through attraction. People are drawn to their lovely energy.

Venus ill-dignified can make people lazy. They can overdo their dressing. They come across as flashy and superficial. They may be driven only by the fulfilment of their pleasures, which can place them in many odd relationship situations. Ill-dignified Venusians may be in an unintentional love triangle. They want to be in a relationship so badly that they don't really think about who they are connecting with. The ill-dignified Venusian can lead a wasteful, reckless, riotous life.

## MERCURY

*Dry but changing according to the nature of that to which it is joined into something different, melancholic but burning.* – JOHANNES SCHÖNER

| | |
|---|---|
| ORBITAL PERIOD: | 88 days |
| LENGTH IN EACH SIGN: | 14 to 30 days in a sign (or up to 10 weeks if retrograde) |
| MEAN DAILY MOTION: | 01° 23' 00" |
| TASTES: | Sourish, and sharp flavors. Acidic. |
| DAYS: | Wednesday day and Saturday night. |
| COLORS: | "Sky colors;" a mix of colors and patterns in combination. |
| METALS: | Quicksilver. |
| STONES: | Agate, red marble, topaz, marcasite. |
| DIRECTION: | North (East according to al-Biruni). |
| CELESTIAL HOUSES: | Gemini is his day house and Virgo is his night house. Virgo is his celestial house of joy. |
| HUMOR: | As a wet and dry planet, Mercury governs no humor. |

GENERAL PLANETARY NATURE:

He is like a Hermaphrodite, participating of both sexes: he is masculine when joined by conjunction or aspect to a masculine planet, feminine when with a feminine, good and fortunate when joined with the fortunes, bad and mischievous when joined with the Malevolents.

IN THE HUMAN BODY:

Mercury rules the brain and tongue. Mercury also rules the legs, feet, arms, hands, fingers, and nerves.

Professions:

Mercury can represent mathematicians, public speakers, writers, philosophers, and people who tend to be very intelligent and good at everything. Mercury represents astrologers, diviners, and inventors – people who plug themselves into larger currents of intelligent design and inspiration for a living. Mercury is the god of mercantile endeavors. As such, he represents people who work in stocks and trading; merchants of every kind. As the messenger of the gods, Mercury also represents people who can work as personal assistants, secretaries, and servants. As the god of writing, Mercury represents religious scribes such as the sofrim STA"M in Judaism and calligraphers in general. Mercury represents people who represent others: advocates, ambassadors, attorneys. The Mercurian may also be prone to entrepreneurship. They are highly skillful multitaskers.

Mychal's Commentary:

Mercurians are constantly changing like the wind and cannot be held down or contained. They love to communicate and interact with diverse groups of people. If you try to hold them down physically, they will escape mentally, and you will know that they are gone because of the distant look on their faces. They are the supreme multitaskers. The word "multitask" was created to describe Mercurial people. They are witty and intelligent, and always know a little bit of something about everything. They tend to keep things very superficial in general, and you seldom know what is going on deep within their hearts. Mercurians are good with things that require counting and accounting. They can be very good in roles of support or as assistants. They are very intellectually gifted and can be self-trained in most of their endeavors. They learn things easily. They are very imaginative. Mercurians can help you get the word out, if you have something you want to say to society at large.

Ill-dignified Mercurians can be scatterbrained busybodies who don't have the ability to focus very long on anything at all. They can be aimless wanderers who jump around from one thing to the next without any real sense of focus. They can be exaggerators, often to the point of dishonesty. They can also confuse people with their disorganized words and use of language. Sometimes ill-dignified Mercury can represent people who have a speech impediment or people who are mute. The ill-dignified Mercurian can spend a lot of time and money investing in things that will never come to pass. They can be great gossipers. They can boast of great knowledge, when in fact they may have no actual skills to support their claims.

## MOON

*The Moon is below the planets and because she is the closest to the earth, she indicates of the body of man and the beginning of every deed and thought... She has rulership over the whole body because in her light she is like the light of man that grows until a prescribed time and then diminishes.*

— ABRAHAM IBN EZRA

| | |
|---|---|
| ORBITAL PERIOD: | 27.5 days (geocentrically) |
| LENGTH IN EACH SIGN: | 2.5 days |
| MEAN DAILY MOTION: | 13° 11' 00" |
| TASTES: | Fresh, flat waterish tastes. Salty (according to Valens). |
| DAYS: | Monday day and Thursday night. |
| COLORS: | White, pale, sea green. |
| METALS: | Silver. |
| STONES: | Diamond, crystal, pearl, marcasite, selenite, and soft stones. |
| DIRECTION: | North-West. |
| CELESTIAL HOUSES: | Cancer is her day and night house. Cancer is her celestial house of joy. |
| HUMOR: | Phlegm. |

GENERAL PLANETARY NATURE:

The Moon is considered to be cold and moist by many classical authors. However, as we've seen in the *Tetrabiblos* her nature is primarily moistening, though her relationship to the Sun also gives her a part in the generation of heat. She is a feminine, nocturnal planet. Since she is the closest planet to our sublunary world, she transfers the light and influence of all the other planets to us. She is fortunate with benefic planets, and infortunate with malefic planets.

IN THE HUMAN BODY:

The brain, the left eye in men and the right eye in women, menstruation. Intestines, stomach, vulva. The Moon with Mars rules the expulsive faculties of the body. She rules apprehension and what Jean-Baptiste Morin calls the "universal appetite."

PROFESSIONS:

The Moon, like Venus, represents all women in general. She represents women in power, from queens to bosses. Lunarians can be people who work with fluids, such as wine merchants and pharmacists. She represents people who have a maternal role in the world at large, and professions that help to make people feel at home. She can represent gardeners or home decorators. She gives people the desire to take care of all forms of life. She represents veterinarians. Lunarians can be chefs, restaurant owners, nurses, and midwives. As the goddess of the water, she can represent people who work on or near the water. As the fastest moving planet, she can represent people who enjoy travelling or moving about in their immediate or distant environments, such as sailors, pilgrims, and mailmen.

MYCHAL'S COMMENTARY:

Lunarians are caring, compassionate, and gentle. They are sensitive, emotional, mothering, and nurturing. They hold things together: families, businesses, and family businesses. Lunarians enjoy being the stability within their family. However, they are not always the most stable member of the tribe. Like the Moon in the sky, Lunarians fluctuate, and do so regularly. At times they are highly happy and optimistic; at other times they are sad and depressive. Lunarians are shy, and don't naturally open up to others quickly. When they do, however, they are wonderful, protective, and loving people to be around.

Lunarians may also hold a great deal of natural fear. This may make them that much keener to establish earthly stability for themselves. They have expectations that other people will be sensitive to their emotions because they are sensitive to other people's emotions, but this isn't always the case. Lunarians also have expectations that other people will naturally know how they are feeling. When others don't pick up on the unspoken cues of the Lunarian, they can feel very hurt, unloved, or misunderstood. When they feel mistreated – whether it really happened or not – they often turn away from the world.

When ill-dignified, Lunarians are constantly moving, searching, and generally lost in life. They can be wanderers – never truly satisfied with where they live, and constantly searching for a place to call home. Their turbulent emotions prevent them from finding rest. They can develop anxiety, fatigue, depression, and a general lack of motivation to do much of anything or become much of anything. The ill-dignified Lunarian can experience feelings of isolation and loneliness, even when they are surrounded by people. Their mood swings can negatively color their view of the world, which can create problems in the home.

# NORTH NODE OR HEAD OF THE DRAGON
## (CAPUT DRACONIS)

*The head of the Dragon is in all points like to Mercury, good with the good Planets, and evil with the evil: for being joined with the good planets, he doth increase their goodness, and with the evil their malice.* – CLAUDE DARIOT

| | |
|---|---|
| ORBITAL PERIOD: | 18 years and 225 days |
| LENGTH IN EACH SIGN: | 1.5 years |
| MEAN DAILY MOTION: | 03° 11' 00" |

Bonatti tells us that the North Node is masculine, and of the nature of Jupiter and Venus. Therefore, Caput Draconis has a benefic influence.

Unlike Dariot – who believes that the North Node increases the evil of evil planets – Bonatti states that when the North Node is joined with evil planets, he lessens their malevolence. This is important to know because this is a view held by many practitioners of traditional astrology. However, I have not found Bonatti's view to be true within practice.

Similar to Dariot, I have found that the North Node always has an amplifying quality. I have observed that the North Node increases the good of the good planets as well as amplifies the evil of bad planets, especially if those planets are already very debilitated. An example of this would be Saturn at 29° Leo 59' rx. conjunct the North Node. The evil of this debilitated Saturn would be amplified because of his connection to the North Node, not weakened.

## THE NORTHERN BENDING

The first square to the North Node is called the "Northern Bending." From the North Node, if we continue to move forward in the zodiac, the square that follows the North Node is the Northern Bending, as opposed to the square that is behind it.

For example, if the North Node is in Taurus, then the first square to the North Node moving forward in the zodiac will be in Leo. If the North Node is in Gemini, then the first square to the North Node will be in Virgo. If the North Node is at 16° Capricorn, the Northern Bending will be at 16° Aries. If the North Node is at 20° Pisces, the Northern Bending will be at 20° Gemini.

I usually use a very small range of exactitude when it comes to planets being conjunct the Northern Bending. I feel comfortable within a range of 03°-05°.

Therefore, if the North Node is at 13° Leo, the Northern Bending will be at 13° Scorpio. However, I'd willingly say that a planet that is within 05° of 13° Scorpio on either side is still at the Northern Bending.

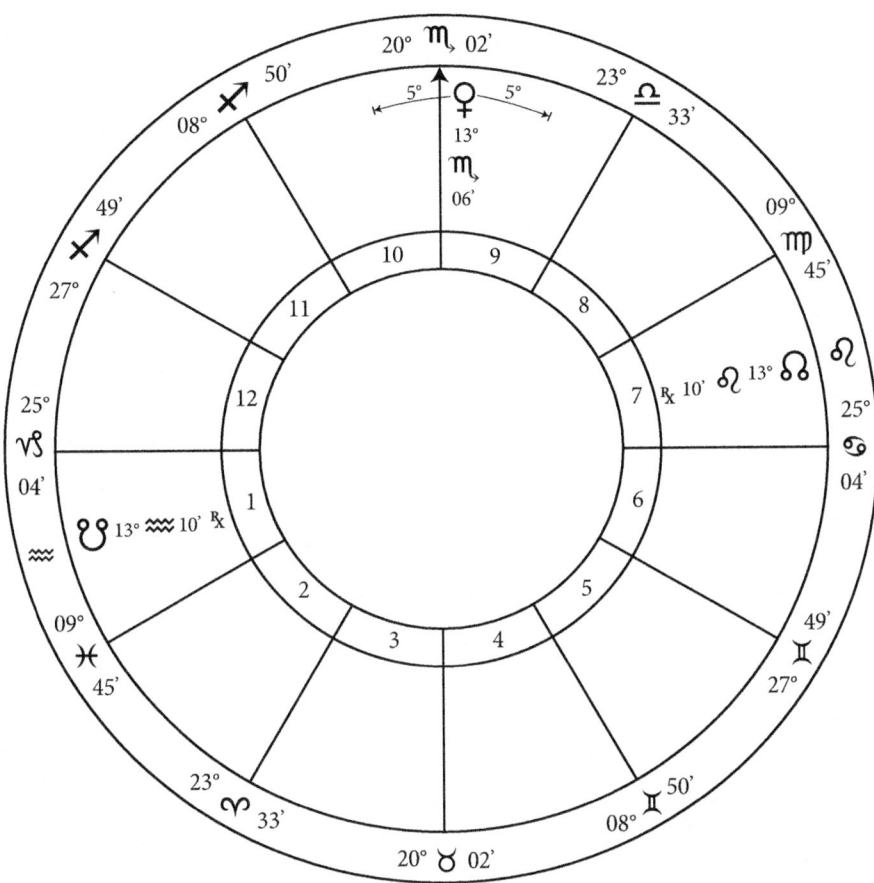

FIGURE 1: *Northern Bending (5° Orb)*

When a planet is conjunct the Northern Bending it represents a topic that we find ourselves at a crossroads about in life. It can represent an area of life that we are challenged to grow around. The house that the planet rules may be an area of concern where a person finds their most potent challenge to grow.

Beyond this concept of the Northern Bending representing a challenging area of life, when a traditional planet is either conjunct the nodes or at either the Northern or Southern Bending, it is something worth paying close attention to. This is especially the case if that planet is important to the topic that we may be investigating within the chart. In general, planets at the bendings tend to be in duress.

## SOUTH NODE OR TAIL OF THE DRAGON
### (CAUDA DRACONIS)

*The tail of the Dragon is contrary to the head, for he is evil with the good and good with the evil, so that he doth diminish the malice of the evil planets, and in like manner doth hinder the goodness of the good.* – CLAUDE DARIOT

| | |
|---|---|
| ORBITAL PERIOD: | 18 years and 225 days |
| LENGTH IN EACH SIGN: | 1.5 years |
| MEAN DAILY MOTION: | 03° 11' 00" |

It has largely been held traditionally that the South Node is malefic in general. Bonatti writes:

> *... its nature is composed of the nature of Saturn and Mars. And it signifies decrease, namely dejection and a fall and poverty, and the decrease of every good thing and every fortune. And the same philosophers said that the peculiar property of the Tail is to diminish...*

However, how the South Node operates when joined to a malefic planet has been a source of debate throughout the classical astrological world. In general, our consensus tends to be that if strongly dignified benefic planets are conjunct the South Node, those planets suffer. Bonatti and Dariot both believed that when a malefic is conjunct the South Node, its malice is decreased. William Lilly (1602-1681), in his seminal work *Christian Astrology* (1647), has this to say on the matter:

> *When joined with the evil planets, their malice or the evil intended thereby was doubled and trebled, or extremely augmented. And when he chanced to be in conjunction with any of the fortunes who were significators in the question, though the matter by the principal significator was fairly promised and likely to be perfected in small time, he [the South Node] created many rubs and disturbances, much wrangling and controversy before a perfect conclusion could be had. And unless the principal significators were angular, and well-fortified with essential dignities, many times unexpectedly the whole matter came to nothing.*

I agree with Lilly on this point. When evil planets are conjunct the South Node, I have found that their malevolence is increased.

## THE SOUTHERN BENDING

The first square to the South Node is called the "Southern Bending." From the South Node, if we continue to move forward in the zodiac, the square that follows the South Node is the Southern Bending, as opposed to the square that is behind it.

For example, if the South Node is in Aries, then the first square to the South Node moving forward in the zodiac will be in Cancer. If the South Node is in Virgo, then the first square to the South Node will be in Sagittarius. If the South Node is at 16° Libra, the Southern Bending will be at 16° Capricorn. If the South Node is at 20° Scorpio, then the Southern Bending will be at 20° Aquarius. I usually use a very small range of exactitude when it comes to planets being conjunct the Southern Bending. The same range of 03°-05° that I applied for the Northern Bending is also applicable here.

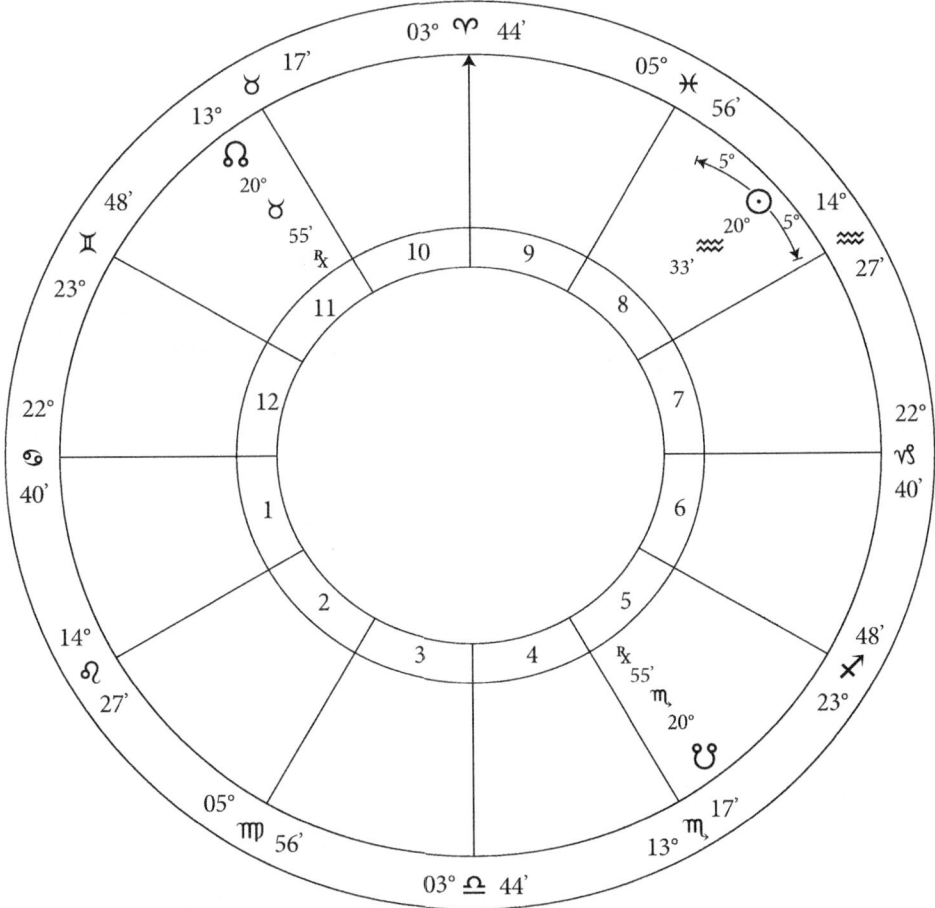

FIGURE 2: *Southern Bending (5° Orb)*

When a planet is conjunct the Southern Bending, it can represent a topic concerning which we are being asked to make a major sacrifice. It can manifest as an affliction to that planet as well as to the things represented by the houses that it rules. This is especially the case if the planet in question is already severely essentially or accidentally debilitated. For example, if the South Node were at 27° Capricorn 00' RX., the Southern Bending would be at 27° Aries. If Saturn were at 29° Aries 42' RX. ruling the first house, he would be within the allowable range of a conjunction to the Southern Bending. Since the first house rules the health and life of the person who owns the chart, this could manifest as having a very detrimental impact on the health and vitality of the person. This would especially be the case if health and vitality were the topics being investigated within the chart.

In general, both the North and South Node are always retrograde. In astrology, we can choose to either use the true node or the mean node. The true node demonstrates deviations from the constant retrograde motion of the nodes, whereas the mean node maintains a constant retrograde motion. Since the mean node is what was utilized in the seventeenth century – and since this is primarily a Renaissance astrology textbook – my preference is to use the mean node within my client work and teaching.

## FACTORS OF DEPLETION WITHIN THE UNIVERSE

I consider there to be four major factors of depletion in our astrological universe. They are: the twelfth house, Neptune, the South Node, and the Southern Bending. All of them work through draining planets of their power, which can feel like a slow leak on the planet in question. When a factor is conjunct the South Node, this is considered to be a negative thing. It can indicate something that is being taken away from a person, a challenging part of their life, or something that may need to be sacrificed.

## PART OF FORTUNE OR PARS FORTUNA

*The Part of Fortune shows the quality of life, the amount of inheritance,*
*and the course of good or bad fortune.*
– JULIUS FIRMICUS MATERNUS

The Part of Fortune is another significant chart factor in traditional astrology. It is one of several mathematical projections in a chart that are known as the "Arabic Parts." The name "Arabic Parts" is a misnomer, as they are not Arabic in origin. The doctrine of the parts hails back to ancient Greece. Resultantly, we typically refer to them simply as "parts" or "lots."

A part is a mathematically derived placement within a chart that has no physical body. It can be used as a representative of a subject within a chart. Different topics have different parts, such as the Part of the Mother, the Part of the Father, the Part of Siblings, the Part of Bravery, and the Part of Fortune.

Abū Maʿšar (787-886 CE) was the most highly regarded astrologer of the Middle Ages. In his book *The Great Introduction to Astrology*, he writes:

> *The Ancients among astrologers mentioned the lots [parts] universally and we see almost all our predecessors in this art mention their power... when they wanted to examine something specifically, such as wealth, brothers, children, or other things, they did not look at that place [terrestrial house], nor its lord, nor the condition of all the planets for them, but they used to look at the lot of that thing, at its position and the lord of its place, and they used to make a judgment on that for whatever they desired of that specific theme.*

A part acts as a unique representative of a topic within a chart. Planets can specifically signify several things, especially when those planets rule multiple houses.

For example, a person with Taurus on their second house cusp, may very well end up with Libra on their seventh house cusp. Resultantly, Venus would be the planet meant to signify their money as well as their marital partner. While this doesn't actually pose an interpretive problem in traditional astrology, the parts allow us to conduct a more focused delineation. If we wanted to specifically investigate money in this person's life, we could do so through the Part of Fortune or another part associated with the second house. If we wanted to discuss marriage, we could surely do so through the ruler of the seventh house. However, we could also do so through the Part of Marriage. The use of the parts ensures that the exact thing we are investigating in a chart corresponds with the exact part we are investigating. The ruler of the tenth house traditionally represents the mother as well as one's authority in the world. However, the Part of the Mother only represents the mother. The Part of Rulership and Authority only represents one's authority.

The Part of Fortune is used as a secondary indicator of wealth or fortune within a chart. In natal astrology, it can also be used to indicate an area within a person's life that they may find a great deal of pleasure or joy in. Along with the second house of money, planets in the second house, the ruler of the second house, and aspects to the ruler of the second house, the Part of Fortune can be another indication of how financially fortunate or unfortunate a person may be within this lifetime. It can also represent the transient state of a person's wealth in horary astrology.

There are two different formulas for calculating the Part of Fortune. These formulas depend on whether or not the chart in question is a diurnal chart or nocturnal chart.

The formula for calculating the Part of Fortune in a diurnal chart is:

Ascendant + Moon – the Sun = the Part of Fortune.

The formula for calculating the Part of Fortune in a nocturnal chart is:

Ascendant + Sun – the Moon = the Part of Fortune.

What this means is that we take the zodiacal longitude of the Ascendant and the luminaries and apply them to the formulas above. This will give us the appropriate Part of Fortune based on the sect of the chart. How to convert the zodiacal degree of a factor to zodiacal longitude can be found in the chapter entitled *A Primer on Astrological Symbolism*.

In the seventeenth century, we find many astrologers only using the diurnal Part of Fortune formula for both daytime and nighttime charts. However, in the Medieval tradition, it was more customary to use a formula that corresponded with the sect of the chart. I follow the Medieval tradition of using the diurnal Part of Fortune formula for diurnal charts and the nocturnal formula for nocturnal charts.

## THE MODERN PLANETS

Now that we've established a world within which the classical celestial factors of astrology exist, it is time for us to explore the new: Uranus, Neptune, and Pluto.

### URANUS

*Ouranos, Uranus, or heaven, is said to have been the father of Saturn, who, jealous lest another son should appear, mutilated him with his scythe... This planet swims lonely in the vast abyss that separates Saturn from Neptune... if we have called Neptune the soul of the sea, then Uranus is the essence of volcanic fire. There is no planet so strange, so revolutionary, so occult and mysterious, or so contradictory. For this is the shocking story of Uranus, the principle of heaven bereft of fatherhood by the jealousy of time.* – ALEISTER CROWLEY

| | |
|---|---|
| ORBITAL PERIOD: | 84 years |
| LENGTH IN EACH SIGN: | 7 years |
| MEAN DAILY MOTION: | 00° 00' 42" |
| TASTES: | None. |
| DAYS: | None. |
| COLORS: | Sky blue. |
| METALS: | Uranium and aluminum. |

IN THE HUMAN BODY:

Uranus has been associated with the nervous system in general. Moon/Uranus or Moon/Mars/Uranus hard aspect combinations can potentially point towards issues of womb health and fertility in general. Mercury/Uranus hard aspect combinations can potentially indicate insomnia or an attention deficit of some kind. However, Mercury/Uranus combinations can also indicate an exceptional ability to process complex information. This combination produces a brilliant mind. When present in the natal chart, it can indicate someone who can excel at astrology.

PROFESSIONS:

Uranus can represent engineers, airplane pilots, scientists, science teachers, inventors, freelancers, hackers, and people who make money through technology in general. It can represent people involved in e-trading. It represents people with a revolutionary mind, inspired leaders, geniuses, eccentric people in general, and astrologers.

MYCHAL'S COMMENTARY:

Uranus represents lightning, sudden events, accidents, strokes of genius, ingenuity, rebellion, the impulse towards freedom, and going against the grain. Uranians are people who are before their time. They see the world around them differently than everyone else and may become outcasts because of this perspective early in life. People don't understand their way of viewing things. They tend to think in a big way that is even larger than Jupiter can handle. Uranians see a completely new way in which the world can be run and are often trying to usher the world in that direction. They can be brilliant thinkers, savants, and capable of a level of problem solving that leave people awed. However, they can also be very erratic. Uranian people have been given life experiences that haven't left them with the most stable relationship to the world and the people in it.

Often people who have Uranus rising are people who came from an unstable household. They may have moved allot, been in a military family that made moving a requirement, or come from a home that left them jostled and probably even deeply disembodied. When people have Uranus conjunct their fourth house cusp, they may have come from families where the parents divorced. Uranus conjunct the seventh house cusp has long been considered to be a sign of divorce between the native and their spouse. It can also indicate the inability to hold together a stable or long-lasting relationship in general. Uranus conjunct the tenth house cusp can often represent instability within the work environment. However, more often than not, Uranus in the tenth can represent a career in the technological industry or the sciences. It can represent people who excel in their rapidly changing and constantly moving career. In all cases, the impact of Uranus is one that is sudden and unsettling.

People who are heavily Uranian can have insomnia, restless leg syndrome, or some other nervous or anxiety-based issue that prevents them from being in a state of deep rest. The Uranian mind is one that moves a thousand miles an hour. It can be hard for them to turn off the mental chatter. People with a strong Uranian influence can either be officially or self-diagnosed with some form of hyperactivity or attention deficit. As children, these people may have been medicated for just being themselves. The world wants them to slow down. While moving more slowly might indeed do them well, they would just as strongly benefit from being given the opportunity to discover intriguing passion projects within which to burn off their excess energy. Uranian people are creators and inventors. They can benefit the world through their ability to be master craftsmen at whatever they pursue in life.

Freedom is a must for the Uranian. Their love of freedom often makes them disregard the sort of stability that money can bring. Uranian people can sometimes be anti-money in their approach to the world and to life in general. Money doesn't matter to them as much as the freedom to do as they desire. They are hard to keep up with. Stability and commitment may frighten them deeply. However, home, family, and stable friendships are exactly what they need to ground the immense amount of lightning they draw down into the world.

## NEPTUNE

*Ah, Neptune is the soul! And does not this fit the sea? Is not the sea at once infinitely calm and infinitely air-hungered? Does not the sea take strange shapes, break up the light into a myriad [of] fantastically-colored flaws? Illusion, and art, chameleon and dragon, that is the sea! Is not the sea now tender and adorable, sun-kissed; now terrible in its torment, a whirl of insatiable desires? Did not Sappho fling herself into the sea, and did not Undine draw thence the bitter joy of her veins? Are not the seas' depths unstirred, unplumbed, and do they not harbor monsters more terrible than the fancy of antiquity ever invented?* – ALEISTER CROWLEY

| | |
|---|---|
| ORBITAL PERIOD: | 164 years |
| LENGTH IN EACH SIGN: | 14 years |
| MEAN DAILY MOTION: | 00° 00' 24" |
| TASTES: | None. |
| DAYS: | None. |
| COLORS: | Sea-green, iridescent pearl hues. |
| STONES: | Pearls, coral, and other wealth of the sea. |

### IN THE HUMAN BODY:

Neptune is said to have rulership over the endocrine system. Hard aspect combinations of Moon/Neptune or Moon/Mercury/Neptune can have to do with intense food allergies. Venus/Neptune or Venus/Jupiter/Neptune in hard aspect combinations could potentially point in the direction of hormonal imbalances.

### PROFESSIONS:

Neptune can represent inspirational teachers, religious followers and leaders; people working within the spiritual industry in general. It represents poets, artists, musicians, dancers, graphic designers, and people working in film and television. Venus/Neptune as a specific combination can represent photographers. Neptune can represent pharmacists, chemists, people who work on or near the water. It can represent any type of selfless, volunteer-based work, or even paid work that has a selfless component such as nursing and medicine in general. Neptunians can be people who work with psychedelics and plant medicines, such as herbalists.

MYCHAL'S COMMENTARY:

Neptune represents spirituality, psychic ability, dreams, confusion, illusion, delusion, devotion, romance, idealism, water, drowning, depression, and addiction. Neptunian people move through the world without skin. They feel everything with a hypersensitivity that makes it seem as if they've come into this life less prepared for the hardships of this world than others. Their extreme sensitivity makes them amazing in helping, healing, and counseling professions. That same hypersensitivity can also make those professions extraordinarily draining for them to participate in.

Neptunians can be lost at sea most of the times. As a result, they need something to devote themselves to, perhaps more than others, in order to truly feel at home within the world. Once devoted, their entire life becomes deeply engrained in that one thing with a deep religiosity that they can very well lose themselves in. They tend to be idealistic, seeing no flaws within what they have committed themselves to, whether it is a person, a thing, a religion, or an ideal. Resultantly, they can hold onto something far longer than they should, even after that thing has proven itself to be a source of disappointment. They often need the assistance of others around them to point out the fact that they've been misguided in the use of their energy.

Neptunian people, unlike Martian people, tend to only feel wet emotions: deep romance, deep depression, deep sorrow, and often deep apathy. Neptunian people can get caught in a spiral of belief where they think nothing is working out well for them and that nothing can ever work out well for them. Their hypersensitivity makes them believe that other people feel the same way about them, which only furthers the depth of their suffering. Often the hardest lesson for a Neptunian person to learn in life is how to separate fact from fantasy.

They may come into the world feeling physically weaker than others, and may find themselves in a body that does not perform at the same level as others. Neptune is one of four "cosmic toilet bowls" in my vision of astrology (the other three being the twelfth house, the South Node, and the Southern Bending). The Neptunian person can feel as if they are at a disadvantage in life or as if their vital power is being slowly drained away either because of being in a body that doesn't work or in a life that doesn't work.

They tend to want to pacify these tendencies through escaping from the stark realities of life. Very often Neptune is culpable in cases of severe addiction, ranging from alcoholism to the misuse of narcotics or even gambling. Neptunians can find themselves needing to do things that take the sharp edge off life, and substance abuse can often be a very direct means of accomplishing that.

However, Neptunians can also excel at art, poetry, and particularly in music because of the ways these interests enable them to find freedom from the harshness of the world.

The sensitivity of the Neptunian gives way to a very strong sense of artistry and an understanding of the sublime divinity of beauty. Neptunians make fine musicians, artists, dancers, and photographers because of their innate desire to preserve what is beautiful. The well-adjusted Neptunian can be an infinite source of inspiration for others around them.

## PLUTO

*He who has perceived it, cannot perceive any other; he who has contemplated it cannot contemplate any other; he cannot hear of any other, he cannot even move the body. Ceasing from all bodily movement and sensation he stays still. When it has illumined the whole mind, and the whole soul, it flames up again and draws the entire man out of the body and transforms him into his essential being. It is impossible, my son, for the soul who has beheld the beauty of the Supreme Good to become God while in the body. – CORPUS HERMETICUM, 10:6*

| | |
|---|---|
| ORBITAL PERIOD: | 248 years |
| LENGTH IN EACH SIGN: | 10 to 20 years |
| MEAN DAILY MOTION: | 00° 00' 15" |
| TASTES: | None. |
| DAYS: | None. |
| COLORS: | Black. |
| STONES: | Black tourmaline, clear quartz, lava stone, moldavite. |

IN THE HUMAN BODY:

In modern medical astrology, Pluto has been said to play a major role in the reproductive system. This may be the result of the erroneous Pluto/Scorpio/Eighth house connection. In general, Pluto seems to operate through intense pain, abnormal growths, and malfunctioning of whatever body system it afflicts. Moon/Pluto or Moon/Mercury/Pluto hard aspect combinations can indicate painful stomach and/or intestinal issues. Venus/Pluto or Venus/Mars/Pluto hard aspect combinations in a woman's chart can indicate painful reproductive health issues.

PROFESSIONS:

Pluto can represent forensic scientists, psychologists, trauma surgeons, morticians, sanitation workers, taxidermists, and doctors who specialize in either the reproductive system or the excretory system. Pluto can represent large amounts of generational wealth, and therefore, represents banking and the financial industry in general. Pluto represents hypnotherapists, private detectives, and investigators. In its less pleasant manifestations, it is the planet of organized crime, murderers, and gang violence.

MYCHAL'S COMMENTARY:

Pluto is the god of death and dying, who made his abode in the underworld. As such, Plutonians come into this world with a deep sense of isolation, power, and severity. Plutonians have to learn very early in life the lessons of power and powerlessness. Very often, because of early powerlessness, the Plutonian seeks to have power over others in later life. These people are forceful, commanding, and demanding. They know how to handle adversity well and can deal with any hand they've been dealt. They are exceptionally resilient and resourceful. This probably arises out of their keen awareness that nothing truly lasts forever. They can enjoy dark things: dark clothing, dark music, dark literature; things that would often make others very uncomfortable. They aren't afraid of the topic of death, and may very well have hobbies such as taxidermy, fungus farming, and other things that directly involve the dead.

Plutonians can live intensely. This also comes from their knowledge that all things will end, including their own lives. Drugs, sex, and rock n' roll exists on one end of the Plutonian spectrum. Sky-diving, sense deprivation tanks, and sitting in a tub full of ice and freezing water exists on another end of this spectrum. The violin and the cello are deeply Plutonian instruments. Red wine, black coffee, and red meat are deeply Plutonian foods.

They may live their lives as if they inhabit a fortress of solitude and self-protection. They can either have a voracious hunger in love or can deprive themselves of love entirely. In all things, they are able to go distances that other people cannot comprehend: in sex, in abstinence from sex, and in all areas of life.

I have often joked that if the world were to burn to the ground, the life-forms that would survive to rebuild it would be the rats, the roaches, and Plutonian people. Their ability to survive adversity is unparalleled. Their survival skills often ensure that they will find a position of wealth and power for themselves in the world to come. However, it can also leave them with an in-built feeling of survivor's guilt, and a deeply rooted stress response from previous traumas experienced in life.

CHAPTER 7 QUESTIONS

1.  List the planets in the Chaldean Order.
2.  List the days of the week associated with each planet.
3.  Which metals are associated with each of the seven classical planets?
4.  What are the four qualities that we find amongst the seven classical planets? These are the same qualities found in the elements.
6.  How are those qualities combined in each of the seven classical planets?
7.  List one positive and one negative psychological attribute belonging to each of the ten planets spoken about in this chapter.
8.  If the North Node were in Leo, which sign would the Southern Bending be in?
9.  If the South Node were in Pisces, which sign would the Northern Bending be in?

CHAPTER 8 OBJECTIVES

* Outline the role that planets play in traditional astrology.
* Describe the difference between universal and specific signifacators.
* Define the term "determination" within the seventeenth century astrology of Jean-Baptiste Morin.
* Show why the specific determinations of the planets is such a cornerstone of traditional astrology.
* Briefly outline the main points of Morin's teachings regarding the various states of the planets.

# CHAPTER 8

## PLANETS IN THEORY & PRACTICE

*I shall not here take notice of any Poetical Fictions, concerning the names of the Seven Planets, or their governments and rules; as of* SATURN *reining in the Golden Age, when the Earth brought forth without tillage; or of* JUPITER, *his being the son of Saturn, who, because his father would have devoured him, expelled him his kingdom, and gave the rule of Hell to* PLUTO, *to* NEPTUNE, *the Water, and took Heaven and Earth to himself, or how that* MARS *was produced of Juno without the concourse of Royal Jupiter, and so being the Son of Discontent, was called the God of War; of* VENUS, *her being the Goddess of Love and Beauty,* MERCURY, *the God of Eloquence, and Messenger in chief to all the rest of the Gods. I shall not, I say, take notice of any such, they being but the witty inventions of aspiring Pates, and carry a far greater show of rhetoric than Reason in them.*
–JOHN GADBURY

WITHIN TRADITIONAL ASTROLOGY, the planets are understood in one of two ways. Planets can either be "universal significators" or "specific significators." Astrologically speaking, a significator is a symbolic representative of anything within our physical world. Planets will always represent certain themes or ideas universally. Venus, for example, is the universal significator of love and marriage. When Venus, or any planet for that matter, is viewed purely through the universal theme it represents, that planet is known as a "universal significator."

A planet becomes a specific significator when – in a specific chart – it is given rulership over a specific house or houses within that chart. A planet rules a house when it rules the sign that is on the cusp of that house.

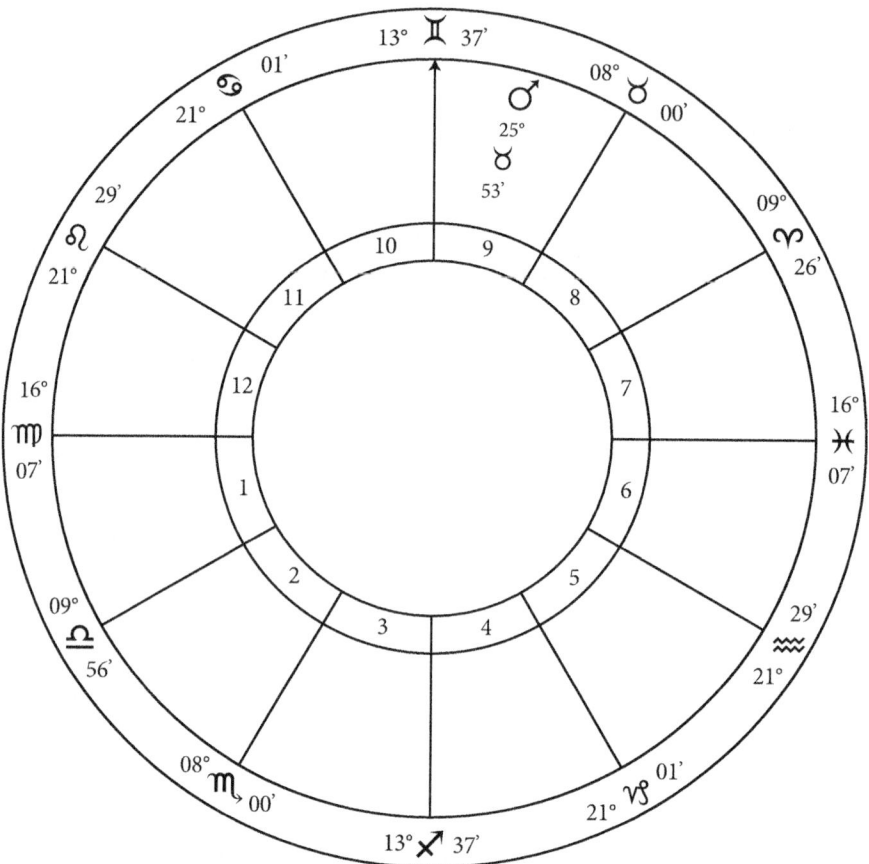

FIGURE 1: *Mars Ruling the Third House*

Mars rules Scorpio. Therefore, if Scorpio is on the cusp of the third house, Mars has circumstantially become the governor or the ruler over the affairs of the third house. This has nothing to do with the intrinsic nature of Mars or his universal meanings. When a planet rules a house, it is the accidental ruler of that house.

ACCIDENTAL RULERS

This term "accidental ruler" may lead you to believe that houses have "natural rulers." However, this is not the case. Though there may be accidental rulers, there are no natural or universal rulers for the twelve terrestrial houses of a chart. Some planets have universal meanings that naturally incline them towards certain houses. However, these planets are not universal rulers of the houses with which they share similar qualities.

A planet does not need to have a natural connection or similarity between its universal meanings and a house that it rules.

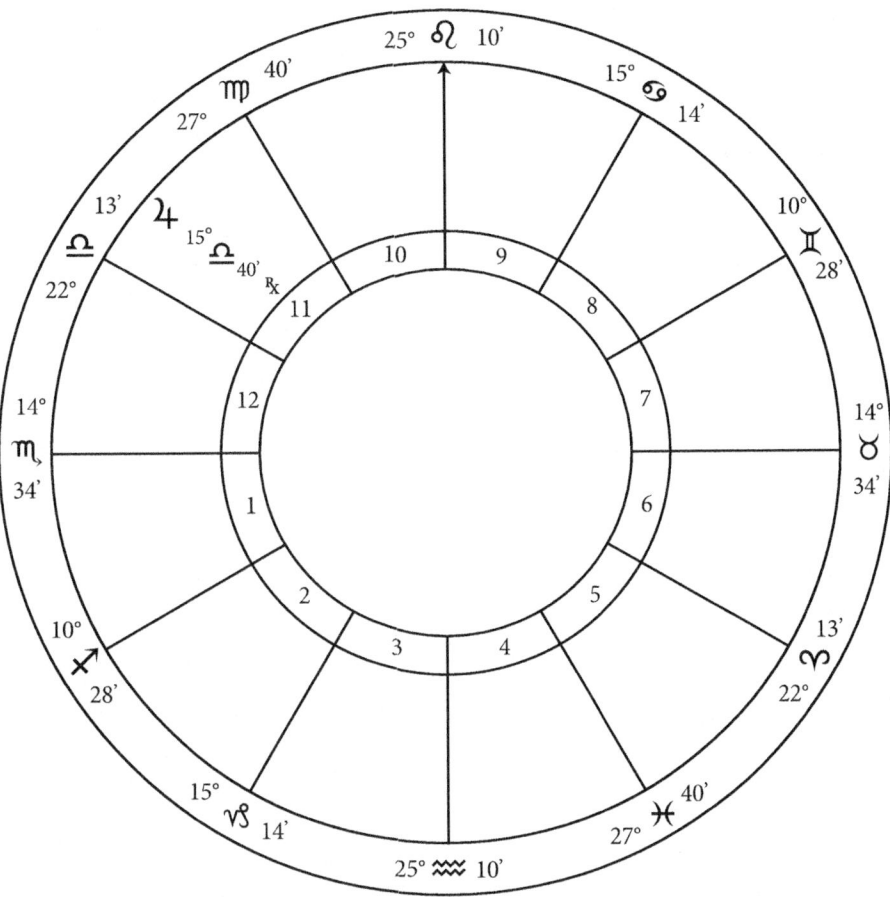

FIGURE 2: *Jupiter Ruling the Second House*

If in a given horoscope, Jupiter just so happens to rule the second house of money, this is purely based on the specific time and location when that chart was erected. Two hours later, it could very well be Saturn ruling that same second house, even though Saturn, the traditional god of death and limitation, doesn't have a natural relationship to the second house of wealth and abundance. It does not matter that Jupiter has a natural affinity with the second house or that Saturn in another example would not. What matters is that in this particular chart, Jupiter has been "chosen" to carry out the destiny of the second house regardless of whether that house corresponds to his universal significations or not. Within the chart in question, Jupiter's specific yet accidentally circumstantial role is to be the ruler of the second house. He has no choice in the matter.

This applies to all the houses. The ancients distinguished between the accidental things a planet ruled just by being the ruler of a sign on the cusp of a house versus the universal things that the planet rules that correspond with its nature. Though the

191

universal significator of the father might be the Sun, the specific significator of the father is whichever planet finds itself accidentally ruling the fourth house based on the exact moment that the chart was erected.

## UNIVERSAL SIGNIFICATORS

A universal significator is a planet that represents a theme in general. Every planet is like a magnet that attracts things that correspond to it from every level of existence. In this way, the planets become universal significators of ideas, emotions, types of people, careers, gems, fragrances, foods, animals, metals, qualities of weather, places, and a myriad of other correspondences. For example, Saturn is the universal significator for all things that are old and dying; Jupiter is the universal significator for wealth and higher learning; Mars is the universal significator for war and litigation; the Sun is the universal significator of fathers and kings; Venus is the universal significator of love and pleasure; Mercury is the universal significator for writing and communication; and the Moon is the universal significator of the family and motherhood in general.

The planets are each a tiny microcosm, bearing a universe within themselves full of concepts that all have some similarity or relationship within the physical world. The Sun, for example, is the universal significator of kings. Therefore, he represents all kings: human kings and people in kingly positions, gold as the king of metals, diamonds as the king of gems, lions as the king of beasts, and the sunflower which is his namesake. Each planet is a wellspring of concrete correspondences. When we study these correspondences, no matter how unrelated to our specific field of astrology they may be, it creates a deep psychic momentum within us that allows us to pull information together that is rich in interpretive value. This information will serve us when we need it the most: in an actual astrological reading.

## SPECIFIC SIGNIFICATORS

When using the planets as specific significators, the intrinsic nature of the planets becomes secondary in importance. One might even go as far as to say those intrinsic qualities become irrelevant. When viewed as specific significators, the planets become pawns that represent topics, and nothing more. Our main concern with specific significators is which houses those planets specifically rule within that specific horoscope. Within a traditional astrology reading, the main function of the planets as specific significators is to represent the affairs of those houses. When viewed as the proxies for the houses they rule, who those planets are intrinsically becomes far less important than how strong they are, where they are, and what they're doing in relationship to other planets within the chart. The relationship between one house ruler and another house ruler describes the concrete way those areas of our lives interact with each other in the material world. Understanding how planets operate as specific significators is the secret to accurately describing concrete events through traditional astrology.

Through their strength or weakness, significators show how strong or weak the things they signify may be. If, for example, we were using Saturn as the specific significator of a person, the internal state of Saturn tells us how strong that person is to support themselves in the larger ecosystem of the chart in which they exist. This would be true whether we use the planets as universal or specific significators.

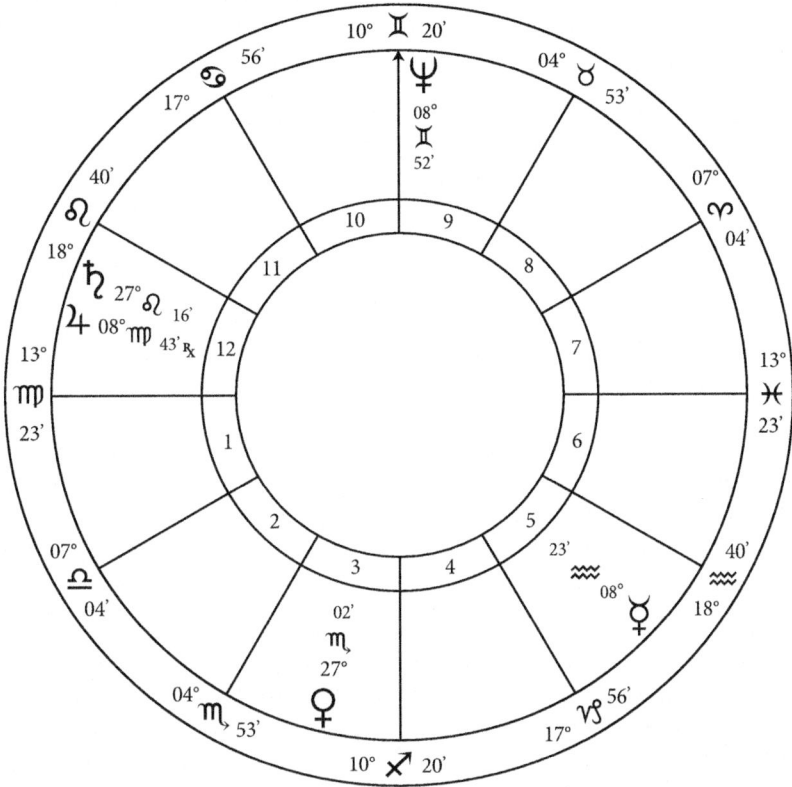

FIGURE 3: *Weak Seventh House Ruler & Debilitated Venus*

A severely debilitated Venus might greatly negatively impact a person's love life, but so would a severely debilitated ruler of the seventh house of love and marriage. More specifically, a severely debilitated Venus could greatly hinder the affairs of the house that she rules within the chart in question. This is because, as the specific significator or ruler of that house, she is the planet entrusted with delivering on the promise of how well the topics of that house will manifest for a person within this lifetime.

## STRENGTHS OF THE PLANETS

This internal state of strength or weakness is known as "essential dignity or debility." However, this isn't the only thing that impacts how well a planet will perform within a chart. There are also external, surrounding factors that occur to the planets such as house placement and aspects to other planets. These environmental factors tell us how much environmental support that planet is receiving in order to accomplish their goals within that chart. These external augmenting factors are known as the "accidental fortitudes or debilities" of the planet.

For example, the Queen is always the Queen. On a human level, she has attained the highest state of "dignity" possible through her very station in life. It stands to reason that she would still be the Queen whether she was in her palace or if she were standing in a field of animal feces. Clearly, she would rather be in an external environment that is in harmony with her internal state of dignity. She may be less than thrilled to be in a field of manure, and may struggle a great deal there. It doesn't change the quality of who she is on the inside, even if it makes it a bit more difficult for her to access the level of power her inner queenly state represents. Planets, like the Queen, can be essentially strong, but accidentally weak.

Conversely, planets can be essentially weak, yet accidentally strong. This reminds me of those turkeys who get pardoned on Thanksgiving by the us president. The birds are technically in no position to free or pardon themselves, and yet they are supported by their environment to at least live another year. Planets can be strong essentially and accidentally, which would be particularly amazing for those planets, the turkeys, and the Queen. They can also be essentially and accidentally weak, which would be awful for the planets and the things they signify. We will treat these topics of essential dignity and debility and accidental fortitude and debility more fully later on.

## Universal vs. Specific Significators – a Traditional Dilemma

While the universal significations of the planets may be valuable in a general sense, they do not represent the core of our interpretive ability when applied in practice. When we ignore the specific significations of the planets as house rulers and base our interpretations purely on what they represent universally, we run into a number of difficulties. Chief amongst these is the fact that planets universally represent multiple things. Therefore, which of the things are we referring to when we interpret that planet universally?

Jean-Baptiste Morin (1583-1656) was a French mathematician, doctor, and astrologer. He outlines this conundrum very bluntly in Book 21 of his *Astrologia Gallica.* He writes:

> ... *although each of the planets differs from the others in its nature and quality, each does have an analogy to the various classes of sublunary things which correspond to its essential nature. For example, the Sun stands for the health, the father, the rank or position, etc. But because this analogy is based on the essential nature of the Sun and the influence of the Sun is completely universal and indifferent, the Sun could not by analogy alone indicate the health any more than it could the father, the husband, the king, or the position... But because of this general indifference*

*one could not assume that the Sun specifically means one of these things any more than another. If it were taken to stand for everything – that is, the father, husband, position in life, etc. – everyone would agree that that would be absurd and contrary to experience.*

It is true that much of traditional astrology is based on the specific determinations of the planets as rulers of houses. However, it is also true that much of traditional astrology throughout time has focused on the interpretation of charts based on the universal significations of the planets within them. We see this in Ptolemy's *Tetrabiblos*, where he writes:

*In conformity with nature, the Sun and Saturn are allotted to the person of the father; and the Moon and Venus to that of the mother.*

Many astrologers, myself included, have interpreted this to mean that the Sun and the Moon represent the parents in diurnal charts. A diurnal chart is one where the Sun is above the horizon at the time the chart is erected. Saturn and Venus would, therefore, represent the father and mother, respectively, in nocturnal charts. A nocturnal chart is one where the Sun is below the horizon at the time the chart is erected. This understanding is echoed by Morin, who writes:

*Ptolemy, Cardanus, and others were also in error when they claimed that in every diurnal horoscope judgment concerning the father of the native is to be made from the celestial state of the Sun, and in a nocturnal horoscope from the condition of Saturn, but they do not see that this is absurd, because if the Sun were in Leo, and, for example, conjunct or trine Jupiter or Venus no child would be born anywhere on earth during the course of that day whose father would not be fortunate and long-lived, or on the other hand, unfortunate and short-lived if the Sun were badly placed. And of course, as this aspect would remain in effect for several days it is clearly foolish to suppose that during this period every child born would have the same kind of father. This is not only contrary to experience but would also render meaningless the significance of the houses.*

Although often in disagreement with Cardanus, Morin does agree with him on a point he made regarding universal significators. Of Ptolemy's using one planet to indicate multiple things, Morin writes:

*Cardanus seems to ridicule this very idea in ch. 6 of his Liber de Revolutione in the Commentary when he states that Ptolemy introduced a great deal of confusion when he assigned several meanings to one significator, and made the Moon, for example, the significator of the body, the morals, the health, the wife, mother, daughters, maid-servants, and sisters. Says Cardanus: "What then must be the condition of the Moon in the horoscope of one whose wife had died in childbirth but himself lived a long life, who had many healthy daughters but also maid-servants who ran away, who had a sound body but a mother who died young, and who himself showed a poor moral character?"*

This is a very valid argument. It highlights the necessity of considering each planet first through their specific determinations as the rulers of houses and the occupants of houses, before taking into account anything that they indicate generally.

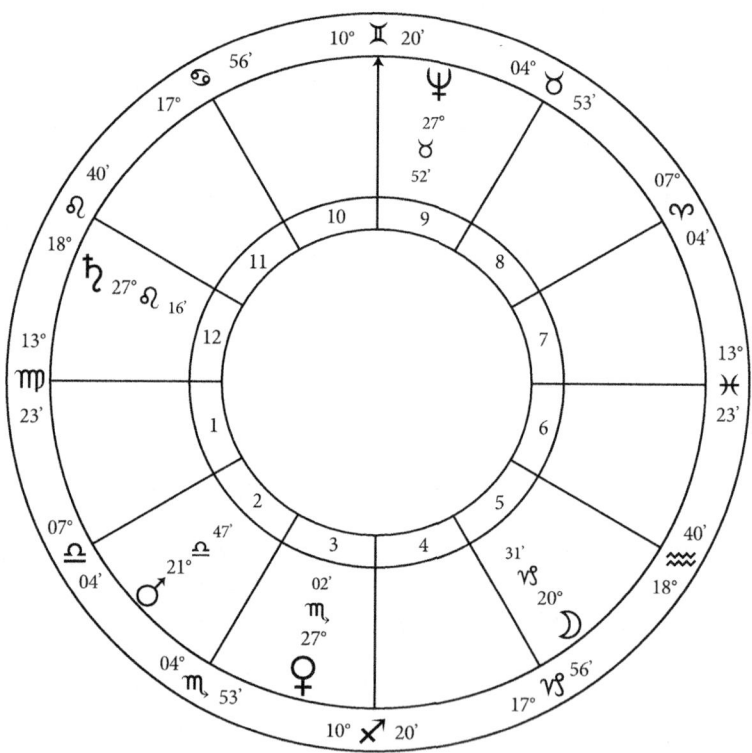

FIGURE 4: *Moon & Venus in Detriment with Hard Aspect to Malefics*

And yet, universal significators do work. More often than not an afflicted Moon in Capricorn, the sign of her "fall," who is also in hard aspect to malefic or bad planets does indicate highly challenging relationships within the family and specifically with the mother. An afflicted Venus in hard aspect with malefics frequently indicates a highly challenging love life. It would be reasonable to take on Morin's argument against universal significators. However, experience shows that the conditions of planets as universal significators is often reflected within the lives of people in the areas that those planets universally signify.

An afflicted Sun often does indicate weakness of the body and a lack of constitutional vitality. An afflicted Mercury often does represent difficulties in communication, and the possibility of a speech impediment.

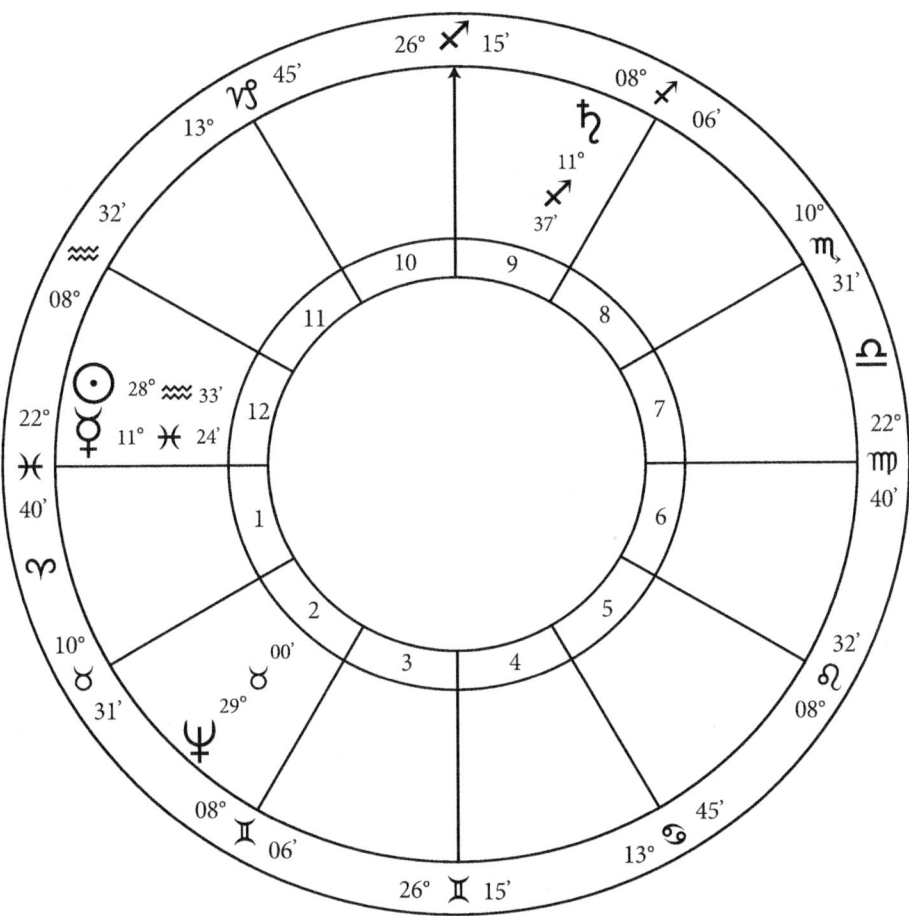

FIGURE 5: *Afflicted Sun & Mercury*

A full treatment of how to skillfully navigate the waters of universal and specific significators is beyond the scope of this present work. However, from a sequencing perspective, it is helpful to first interpret what the planets are doing as specific significators, and then interpret what they are doing as universal significators.

For example, to know the love destiny that a particular chart describes, delineate the relationship between the ruler of the first house and the ruler of the seventh house. What is happening to them individually and collectively? Then look at what is happening to the Venus in the chart. Venus is the universal significator of love. Often, the state of the Venus can further corroborate the conclusion you've already come to through studying the first and seventh house rulers. If it doesn't corroborate that conclusion, then it is wise to stick with the original treatment of the specific significators. That conclusion is often far more tailored to the realities of that chart and those people than anything the universal significator of love may say.

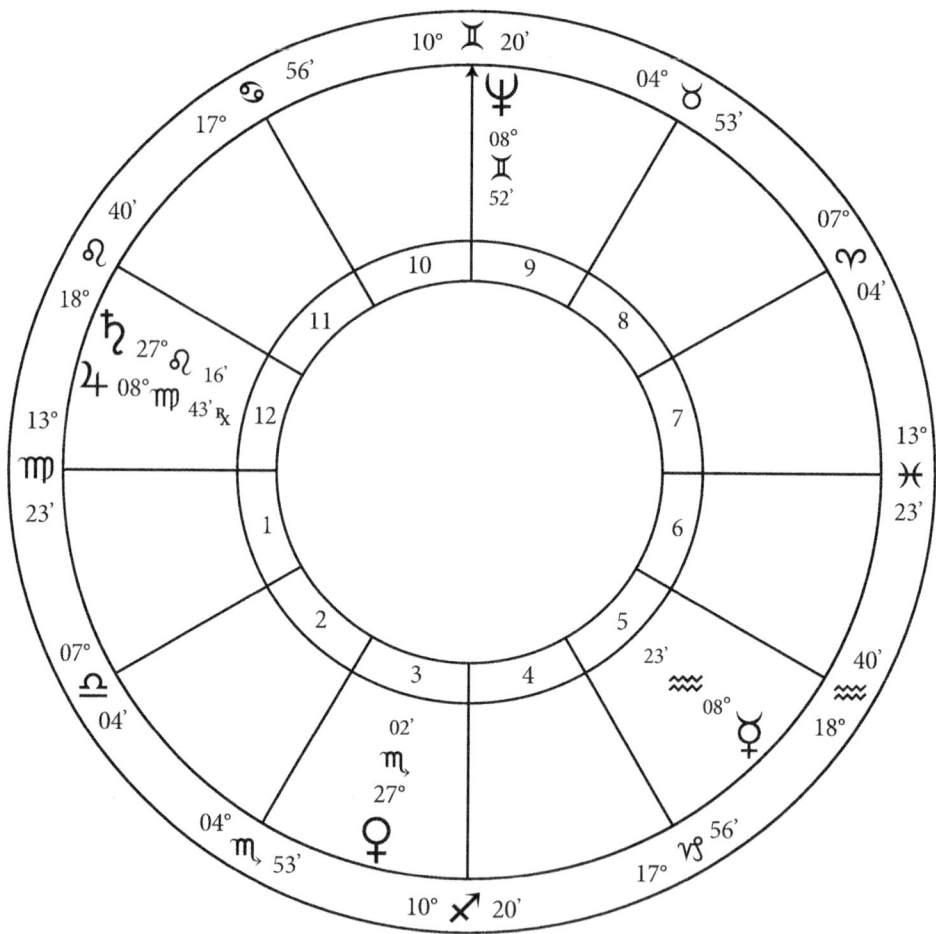

FIGURE 6: *Lord 1, Lord 7, & Venus*

It is helpful to remember that when we say a planet rules a house, we are referring to that planet ruling the sign that is on the cusp of that house.

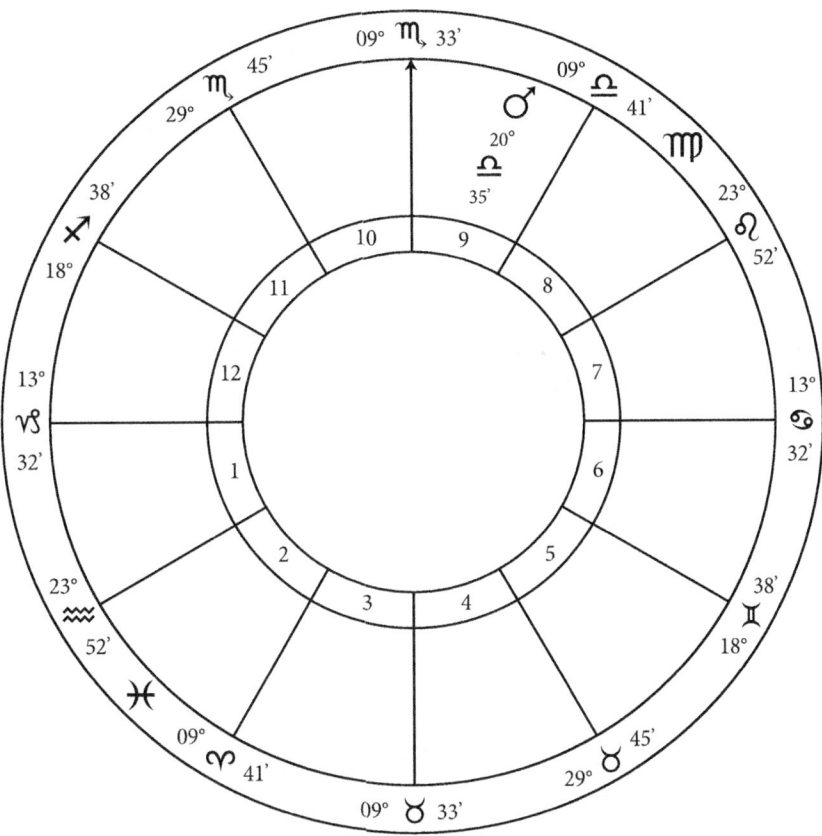

FIGURE 7: *Mars Ruling the Third & Tenth House*

If Aries is on the cusp of the third house of siblings and community, then Mars is the ruler and the representative of the third house. We know that Mars doesn't only rule Aries. He also rules Scorpio. Therefore, if Mars rules the house cusp that Aries is on, he will also rule the house cusp that Scorpio is on. Sometimes, when Aries is on the third house cusp of siblings and community, Scorpio may be on the tenth house cusp of mother and career. In that case, Mars will be the ruler of both the third house and the tenth house. This means that Mars will represent the affairs of the third house and the tenth house, no matter where Mars may be in the chart.

The topic of house rulership or the specific determination of the planets is one that we should pay close attention to as aspiring masters of traditional astrology. In concluding his thoughts on this matter, Morin writes:

> *For the Moon's celestial state does not indicate the moral nature any more than (she represents) the mother or the wife, etc., because in order to refer to any one of these rather than another*

*a specific determination is required – that is, the Moon's rulership in the horoscope or aspects with the rulers of the houses to which these matters pertain... And so, careful attention should be paid to the planets' location by house, or their house rulerships, and to whether they aspect favorably or unfavorably a planet having an analogy with the meanings of these houses, and what the celestial state and determinations of this other planet may in turn be. From all this a very accurate prognostication can be made, for herein lie the secrets of Astrology.*

As stated previously, I cannot fully agree with Morin on this, particularly as it relates to the Moon in natal astrology. Very often the condition of the Moon does give potent commentary on the condition of the family life of the native. However, so do the rulers of the fourth and the tenth houses. It is my hope to fully show how we apply this doctrine of natal significators in a future volume dedicated to natal astrology.

Traditional astrology is the only school of astrology that has brought this study of house rulership to a level of unparalleled excellence. The lineage that was handed down to us by Morin has done far more to refine this interpretation of the rulers of the houses than any of his contemporaries. Other schools of astrology such as Uranian astrology and Cosmobiology have developed our understanding of planet-to-planet relationships by leaps and bounds. However, understanding the relationships between one house ruler and another is just as extraordinary an art, if not more so. The only reliable template we have for how this should be done comes directly out of traditional astrology.

A MODERN DILEMMA

All of traditional Western astrology is deeply planet-based. Whether those planets are universal significators or specific significators, traditional astrology is a planet-heavy subject. However, many schools of modern astrology have gone in a somewhat different direction. Beyond the general disinterest in saying anything particularly concrete or "fatalistic" at all, today we find many astrologers practicing in a way that requires no actual skill or technical ability – and being certified to do so! In the place of master astrological technicians, we now exist in a field saturated by creative, intuitive astrologically-inspired wordsmiths. The colleague of a student of mine once told her that all she needed to be a good astrologer was a background in English literature, poetry, mythology, and a sprinkling of counselling skills. The overwhelming trend amongst people calling themselves astrologers today strongly confirms these suspicions.

These astrologers go about reading charts through counting all the elements that a person has represented in their chart, followed by all the modes, followed by the number of planets in masculine or feminine signs, followed by the hemisphere that is emphasized in the chart, followed by the quadrant that is emphasized. After tallying their scores, they go on to interpret what these numbers mean. Then, as if that wasn't time-consuming enough, in comes the assessment of the lunar phase of the chart, followed by the chart shape, followed by the interpretation of the intercepted signs, followed by whether the aspects in your chart make the shape of a kite, a mystic rectangle, or the finger of God. Then comes the interpretation of the house. However, it isn't quite like what Morin described earlier. Today, the completely arbitrary *size* of the house has interpretational value. So, if heaven forbid, a person had a spatially tiny first house and a humongous eighth house, one can only imagine the perils that person faces on a daily basis. If a house were "cursed" with the affliction of being empty, I've recently come to learn that this means the native has nothing going on in that area of their life... at all. How greatly must everyone on the planet have suffered before the discovery of Uranus in the year 1781! Even if we include Neptune, and Pluto, our astrological cosmos still only contains ten possible occupants to fill twelve houses. Out of fear of having empty houses, people have gone on to populate their birth charts with every transiting piece of floating gravel as a means of averting misfortune and personal calamity. After this two-hour long marathon of astrological prowess, you might be surprised to know that your reading has only just begun. Next comes the interpretation of the sign and house placement of the North and South Nodes – an hour-long discussion at best. If there is any time left, you hopefully may get a reading of the position of your natal Pluto. Pluto! Pluto who spends upward of twenty years in a sign of the zodiac has become the staple planet of a modern astrologer's toolkit. After an assessment of your Pluto placement (PLUTO!), potentially then you may get to hear what it means to have your "Sun, Moon, and Rising" in the signs of the zodiac they inhabit.

If you are an astrologer and your annoyed response to reading this is "That's not me. I start my readings with the Sun, Moon, and Rising first," then you've missed the point entirely. Being able to recite from memory what it means for a person to have five planets in fire, two in air, three in earth, and none in water isn't real astrology. Telling someone what it means for them to have the upper hemisphere of their chart more populated than the lower hemisphere requires no true technical astrological skill. And with approximately three hundred and eighty thousand babies being born every day, I can scarcely imagine that myself along with at least two million other babies my age were destined to deal with life in the same way because we were all born with a "bucket" chart pattern in the first week of May 1992.

I am not saying that these methods can't add value to a reading. I've seen masterful astrologers use these approaches very skillfully in ways that add tremendous insight to their larger chart delineation. What I'm saying is that as far as our professional practice is concerned, these non-technical additions aren't necessarily something we should lead with. As a rule, I never, ever interpret a natal chart by talking about a person's "Big Three" of Sun, Moon, and Rising, because up until quite recently in our astrological history, no one ever did. I hardly know how many planets I have in water signs in my own chart, and I definitely don't know how many anyone else has. Often when I've seen people try to "prove" astrology to others, they do so by using these dubious methods; methods which are severely subjective, often don't work, and don't have the structural fortitude to support their claim that "astrology is real" in a robust or tangible way.

On the other end of the spectrum, I've seen astrologers try to substitute actual astrological talent through the acquisition of counselling skills. However, counselling skills do not make up for a lack of actual technical astrological ability. In my life, I have only ever seen concrete astrology demonstrated through Jyotish, Uranian astrology, Western sidereal astrology, or traditional Western tropical astrology, and even those branches of astrology have their drawbacks. I've seen Jyotish astrologers get lost in esoteric terms and technicalities that don't actually translate into useable astrology. I've seen Uranian astrologers who can calculate the formulas for every planetary picture but who can't read a chart. And I've seen traditional astrologers become completely crippled by knowing too much and getting deeply engaged in every argument about whose technique is older, without being able to show why those techniques are useful to begin with.

I believe the astrology we practice is only as valuable as what we dedicate that astrology to. I have chosen to dedicate my practice to practical, helpful, concrete, accurate, event-based demonstrations of astrology. Ironically, the people who have demonstrated that type of astrology the best to me have not always been traditional astrologers. The first astrologer who was able to prove her practice to me in a way that was truly remarkable was a person who made it her civic duty to practice astrology in a concrete way. She isn't a traditional astrologer; in fact, she is an extremely modern astrologer. However, she carries the concrete pragmatism of traditional astrology within her practice. Without having that as a core intention, our astrology becomes weak – unable to stand the test of credibility. I believe that astrology is absolutely provable. Though astrology is a spiritual practice, good astrology is also a concrete skill. Concrete skills can and should be demonstrable.

## DIVING DEEPER WITH SPECIFIC SIGNIFICATORS

Back to the planets. As we mentioned before, planets can be:
1. Universal significators of human concepts such as love, war, lack, success, and speech; or
2. Ambassadors of the houses they rule.

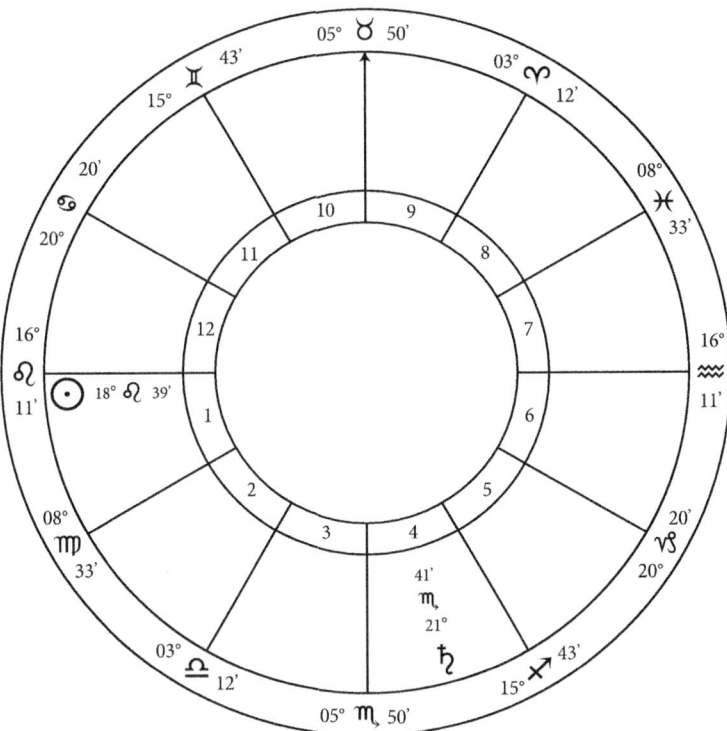

FIGURE 8: *Lord 1 Square Lord 6*

It is one thing to know that Sun square Saturn could represent difficulties with the father. However, suppose that Sun is the ruler of the first house of health and Saturn is the ruler of the sixth house of stress and sickness? This can indicate someone who is highly stressed or working in a high-stress environment. It can represent someone with a weakened physical vitality and severe pet allergies. If the person is self-employed, it can represent a bad relationship with the employees who works within their business. These possibilities are only increased or decreased based on the state of the planets in question, and based on their own webs of relationships with other planets within the chart.

Astrology is like a cosmic game of chess. The planets become the various players on the chessboard who have strategic alignments with each other. These alignments represent a statement of what they will do next, and how they will function within our lifetime. In natal astrology, each planet is entrusted with fulfilling different aspects of our natal promise based on which houses they govern within our charts. Some planets are all powerful in this regard, while others are weak. Some planets are naturally more inclined to deliver a positive result – based on who that planet is and what it rules – while others aren't. Knowing how to interpret all these considerations leads to a clear and accurate practice of astrology.

### JEAN-BAPTISTE MORIN'S PLANETARY INSIGHTS

Jean-Baptiste Morin wrote profusely on the topic of astrology in his encyclopedic work *Astrologia Gallica* (or French Astrology). In Book 21 of that work, he outlines his doctrine of natal astrology. Below is a brief summary of some of his key points that are pertinent to our understanding of how the planets function.

### MORIN'S THEORY OF DETERMINATION

For Morin, the relationship between the planets and the houses that they both ruled and occupied was of utmost importance in astrological delineation. In the twenty-first century, there are fully functional systems of astrology such as Uranian astrology and Cosmobiology where the houses are not important factors. However, in Morin's worldview – and in all traditional astrology in general – the houses are indispensable. The houses give the various planets within the chart their specific determination.

The word "determination" in this context means that a planet is "determined" towards a particular type of destiny or activity based on its house rulership and placement. In traditional astrology our ability to interpret a chart depends on our ability to assess planets based on their specific determinations.

### DETERMINATION BY LOCATION IS IMMEDIATE

In general, planets located in a house are more powerful than the ruler of that house if it is located elsewhere. In Section 2, Chapter 2 of Book 21, Morin tells us:

> ... *a planet's presence in a house has a greater effect than rulership over that house by a planet located elsewhere, because determination by location is immediate.*

This means that a planet's actual residency in a house will have more impact on that house than if that house's ruler was present in some other house of the chart. If I live in a house that I rent from someone who lives on the other side of the country, my ability to do great or awful things for that house will be immediately more impactful than that of my landlord. This is because I physically inhabit that house. My landlord may take days to get back and extinguish the fire that I start in his apartment, even if he is an Olympic gold medalist for being the fastest man in the world. Planets in a house will usually be more noticeable to us in our initial encounter with that house. However, the ruler of that house has the final say regarding what the ultimate destiny of that house will be.

This is particularly true in natal astrology. In horary astrology much more of our interpretation is based on the house ruler and not the house occupants. The planets that occupy houses in horary charts tend to be secondary to the actual rulers of those houses in our interpretation.

## STRONG PLANETS

Morin goes on to tell us that planets that are strong are strong for the entire world. Strength in this instance refers to planets that are strongly essentially dignified in their domicile, exaltation, or a combination of major and minor dignities. Other things that strengthen the planets environmentally are when planets are direct, not combust because of being too close to the Sun, receiving positive aspects from benefics and no harmful aspects from malefics. Planets that fulfill all of these requirements are universally strong. This is especially the case when those planets are essentially dignified. These planets may be considered benefic regardless of what their intrinsic nature is. This is even true for Saturn and Mars, who are technically malefic planets.

Dorotheus of Sidon (circa 75 CE) was a first century astrologer and writer. In his *Carmen Astrologicum*, he writes:

> *Every planetary fortune [benefic planet], if it was in its own house, or in its own triplicity or its elevation [exaltation], then when it indicates of the good will be powerful [and] increasing. And an infortune too [malefic planet], if it was in its own place, then its evil will become lighter and decrease.*

Strongly dignified malefic planets are planets that seek to support and build, even though their nature is to destroy. Jupiter and Venus when strongly dignified are a blessing for the entire world, because their intrinsic nature is already one that leans in the direction of blessedness.

When a chart is erected, the strength of the planets receives a specific determination based on the houses they rule in that chart. This determination will also impact the houses they are placed in. If those planets are strong, they will still operate in a powerful and positive way. However, they will do so in relation to their specific determination based on their house rulership and house location. They will also benefit the planets they aspect based on the houses those planets specifically reside in and rule.

The Sun in Leo trine Jupiter in Sagittarius and Mars in Aries, while also sextile Saturn in Libra is a powerful Sun universally. Surely, that is a powerful sky in general. When a snapshot of that sky is taken for the creation of an astrological chart, those powerful planets and that highly supported Sun become specifically determined to: 1) reside in houses, and 2) rule houses.

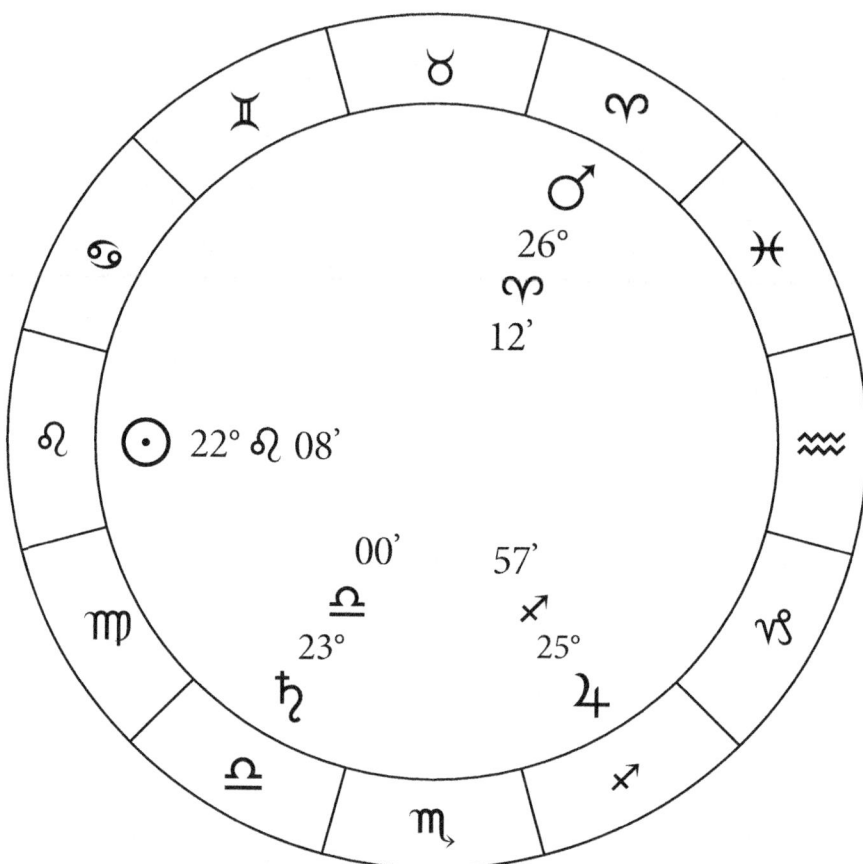

FIGURE 9: *A Powerful Sky*

They maintain their high level of strength and virtuosity. However, now they exercise those powers through the specific framework of the houses they rule and the houses they reside in. If in a chart, the Sun rules the Ascendant and he trines Jupiter in the fifth ruling the fifth, then the person has great fortune from his father and may in turn grow to become a great and prosperous father himself. If he has a trine to Mars, ruler of the ninth in the ninth, then he possibly also has a great passion for travel and for seeing the wider world. He may fancy himself to be an explorer or a connoisseur of foreign cultural experiences. With Mars also ruling the fourth house of his father, the trine can indicate that there was a great relationship between the two of them.

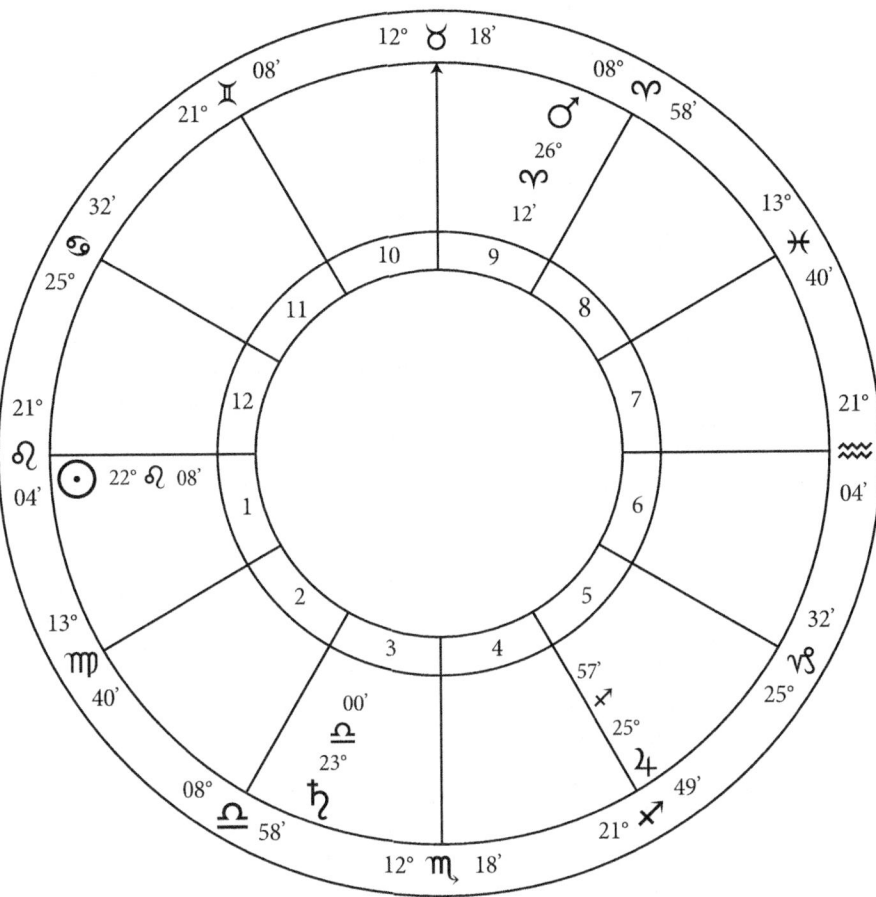

FIGURE 10: *Specific Determination of a Powerful Sky*

The ninth house is the sixth house from the house of his father. In astrology, we would call this his father's "derived sixth house." We will learn more about this topic in our chapter *On the Twelve Houses*. Since the ninth house is his father's derived sixth house, Mars in Aries as lord four (L4) placed in the ninth house can indicate that his father was overworked, but possibly very successful and passionate about what he was doing. This may have further inspired the native's own desire to work and become successful in the world. This is only one example. However, the seasoned astrologer has the ability to consider the thousands of possibilities that exist within any given chart and speak about them skillfully with clients.

WEAK PLANETS

Planets that are weak are weak for the entire world. Weak in this context refers to planets that are essentially or accidentally debilitated. Essentially debilitated planets may be in detriment, fall, or peregrine – terms which we will discuss further in our chapter *Essential Dignities & Debilities in Practice*. Some accidental debilities are when planets are retrograde, combust, conjunct the South Node, in hard aspect to the malefics and receiving no positive aspects from the benefics. These planets are considered to be malefic universally, even if they are Jupiter and Venus, who are technically benefic planets. In these conditions, they are weak, debilitated, and can't do much good for anyone. This is especially true for Saturn and Mars who are malefic planets by their very nature. However, unlike Jupiter and Venus who become weak when essentially debilitated, the intrinsically malefic planets are more harmful when in that state. The negative state of being essentially debilitated matches who those planets are intrinsically.

When brought down to the level of a chart, all severely weakened planets become functional malefics based on the houses they rule and the houses they are located in. These planets have very little ability to deliver on the promises of those houses. Planets can only function based on their intrinsic strength or their supplemental external strength. If neither of these strengths are available, then those planets will deny, impede, destroy, or negatively alter the things represented by the houses they rule.

## WORKING WITH DEBILITATED PLANETS

The weakened force of debilitated planets is truer in horary and electional astrology than it is in natal astrology. Each of these branches of astrology concerns itself with a different relationship to time. Horary and electional astrology are more immediate. Therefore, if a planet is debilitated in one of these branches of astrology and that planet is the chief significator for something that is being asked about or planned for, then that planet is likely to deliver unfavorable results.

Natal astrology is different. When debilitated planets are built into our birth charts, we often learn how to work skillfully with those planets over time. We have had our entire lives to figure them out. Things that were challenging before, once understood, become unique parts of our individuality.

CHAPTER 8 QUESTIONS

1. What are the two main headings under which the planets fall in traditional astrology?
2. What does it mean for a planet to be a universal significator?
3. From the chapter, name one thing that each of the seven classical planets are universal significators of.
4. What is Morin's chief argument against the notion of universal significators?
5. From the text, what are two systems of astrology that deal purely in planet-to-planet relationships as universal significators?
6. What is "determination by location"?

CHAPTER 9 OBJECTIVES

* Define the term "Thema Mundi."
* Understand the rationale behind the construction of the Thema Mundi.
* Learn the celestial joys of the planets.
* Learn the division between the solar and lunar halves of the zodiac.
* Understand the doctrine of the aspects through the relationships within the Thema Mundi.
* Know what is meant by "aspects of aversion" and how they can be applied to our astrology.

# CHAPTER 9

## THEMA MUNDI:
## BIRTH CHART OF THE UNIVERSE

*[So,] understand the houses of the planets: for truly Cancer is the house of the Moon, and Leo the house of the Sun, and Capricorn and Aquarius the two houses of Saturn, and Sagittarius and Pisces the two houses of Jupiter, and Aries and Scorpio the two houses of Mars, and Taurus and Libra the two houses of Venus, and Gemini and Virgo the two houses of Mercury.* –DOROTHEUS OF SIDON

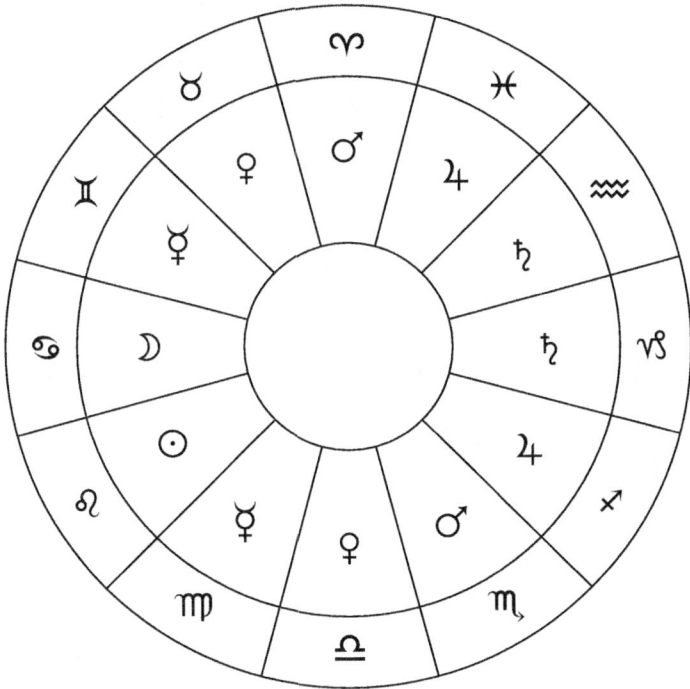

FIGURE 1: *Thema Mundi*

THE THEMA MUNDI IS A PICTORIAL KEY that was used in Hellenistic astrology as a teaching tool. It offers an explanation of essential dignity, sect, and aspects within traditional astrology. "Thema Mundi" can be translated as "Theme of the World." It is thought to represent the birth chart of Mother Earth. While purely symbolic, it represents a cohesive and logical demonstration of the relationship between core astrological concepts that serve as the backbone of all Western astrology.

The Thema Mundi begins with the idea that the signs of the zodiac already exist as divisions of the year and temples in the sky. Each sign is thought to have qualities such as a gender, sect, and element. Each sign already bears a relationship to the seasons and the wheel of the year. Within this zodiac the ancients sought to give a home to the seven planets based on the natural harmony that existed within the organization of the planets and the order of the signs. However, the myth begins with the signs unruled and uninhabited by the gods of heaven. They have not yet been enlivened by the bodies of the living creatures they are meant to host. Therefore, when we enter the mythological landscape of the Thema Mundi, we find ourselves in the middle of the divine unfolding of the universe. All the constituent parts of the Universe have already been set in their rightful place, save for this final act. The Prime Mover has to decide where the seven governors of heaven should call their homes within the twelve temples of the zodiac.

## THE MOON – MOTHER OF THE WORLD

As the birth chart of the World Mother, our first duty is to decide which planet will be her significator. The ancients agreed that this designation should go to the Moon. Within the ancient Western world, the Moon has often been considered a Mother Goddess. Of the seven celestial governors, she not only is physically closest to Earth, but she also represents the stellar deity who is most capable of this maternal role. She is the guardian and keeper of our planet.

Aristotelian metaphysics defines our world as the "sublunary sphere." This term "sublunar" refers to the fact that our planet is physically under the sphere of the Moon. It is through her sphere that the influence of all the other planets is delivered to us. The Moon is the closest celestial ambassador we have between our planet and the wider universe. She serves as a mother and a shield, making sure that whatever she gives us from the other planets can be digested and turned into creative energy within our world.

## A HOME FOR THE MOTHER GODDESS

After determining who our mother would be, the next order of business was to see which of the celestial temples most corresponded with her nature. Since the role of motherhood is benefic beyond any other post in life, the Moon Mother required a temple that also had an inherent benefic quality. This temple had to match the characteristics of the three benefic planets Jupiter, Venus, and the Moon, according to the doctrine outlined in Ptolemy's *Tetrabiblos*.

These three planets are considered benefic because they all bear the two qualities of hot and wet. The temple of the mother had to be wet enough to nurture the unborn seed, as well as warm enough for it to grow. It couldn't be wet in an utterly destructive way that would wash away the seed's chances of survival, and neither could it be hot in a way that would destroy it by fire. It had to be feminine since it would be the house of the Queen of Heaven. It would need to have a natural relationship to birth and fertility, and therefore would need to be one of the fruitful signs. The fruitful signs of the zodiac are the three water signs – Cancer, Scorpio, and Pisces. Therefore, the house of the Moon would also have to be a water sign. Like the Moon, it would have to be a nocturnal sign, even while maintaining a responsibility for the preservation of heat.

The only sign of the zodiac that fit all of these requirements was Cancer. Cancer and the Moon abound in wetness. However, the moisture of Cancer is tempered and young, since it is a cardinal sign. Its force does not wash away the seed of the unborn life. Cancer and the Moon both participate in the birthing or generation of heat. Though a water sign, Cancer bears a natural relationship to "young heat" and fire since it corresponds with the beginning of Summer. The young heat of the princely Sun continues to grow in the womb of Cancer. However, the Sun does not yet have the royal and destructive heat that he will acquire when he moves into (or "ingresses") Leo. The motherly heat that is held within Cancer is the heat that inspires all life to awaken, evolve, and grow.

Ptolemy tells us that the Moon bears this same responsibility in generating heat due to the light she naturally gains from the Sun. Just as Ptolemy's *Tetrabiblos* begins by describing the constitution of the luminaries, so too does the Thema Mundi myth begin by describing their domiciles. Within the Thema Mundi doctrine, Leo, the domicile of the Sun, follows Cancer, symbolizing the eternal relationship of the Moon and the Sun as the Queen and the King of Heaven.

Bonatti builds his explanation of the Thema Mundi starting with the Sun and not the Moon. He writes:

> *(Cancer) is more near to the domicile of the luminary from which the Moon receives the light (the Sun) than any other moveable or cold or moist sign that agrees with the nature of the Moon. And the Moon is even called the luminary of the Sun, because she receives light from him, and those two domiciles are brighter and more splendid, and agreeing more with the natures of the luminaries than any of the other domiciles in all the climes and in all the regions in the world.*

The heat of the Moon is a nurturing and life-supporting fire, more tempered than that of the Sun. This fire within the Moon is identical to the quality of heat that we find in Cancer. Both planet and sign correspond with conditions that are thought to be necessary for generating new life. Resultantly, Cancer is the sign that occupies the Ascendant within the world chart, with the Moon residing there as Queen and Mother.

Though there are other water signs, none of them bears an analogous relationship to the Moon in the same way that Cancer does. As a fixed water sign, the frozen nature of Scorpio would prevent the heat of the growing Sun from ever taking root in the world. Also, as the heart of Autumn, Scorpio represents the death of solar power as opposed to it's proliferation. Mars, the ruler of Scorpio, is more concerned in mid-Autumn with poisoning the air than with preserving life. Of the Sun's ingress into Scorpio, Bonatti writes:

> *Then the Sun enters the Scorpion and the cold is increased above the heat. Things become somewhat cold and somewhat warm. The air is made distemperate and there are rains. Grievous ills are generated, pestilences and death-bearing things as deadly as poisons and the like. For this reason, this sign was named for the poisonous scorpion.*

As a mutable water sign, the unbounded nature of Pisces would surely drown the princely Sun through its oceanic force. As the end of Winter, Pisces represents the slow reawakening of aquatic life underneath the frozen rivers and lakes. It does not have the life power necessary to serve as the container for the adolescent Sun.

We will recall that the Ascendant represents the soul and psyche of the person whose life the nativity describes. Within the birth chart of the world, no other sign more adequately describes the World Mother than the motherly, nurturing, fruitful Cancer rising, ruled by the Moon.

## The Sun – Father of the World

Since Cancer was chosen to be the home of the Mother of the World, it was then necessary to find a temple for her consort, the Sun. The Sun has been called *Rex Planetarum* or "King of the Planets." He is the only celestial body that equals and overpowers the Moon in her influence upon us in both apparent size and strength. The tradition of viewing the Moon and Sun as consorts eternally bound to one another is one that goes deep into antiquity. The temple of the Sun would have to be similarly bound to the temple of the Moon. The temple of the Sun would have to correspond to his nature in the same way that the Moon's temple corresponded to hers.

The Sun is hot and dry, choleric, diurnal, king of the planets, and source of fire. He is the strongest planet that exists in the cosmology of traditional astrology. He is the natural significator of fathers and kings, eternally demanding honor and glory unto himself. The temple of the king would require the same attributes. Leo, which follows Cancer in the zodiac, is the only sign that can honor the Sun in this way. It is hot and dry and, therefore choleric. It is represented by the kingly and majestic lion, which is analogous to the kingly nature of the Sun. Leo is considered to be the strongest sign of the zodiac. It represents the middle of the Summer when the heat of the day is sweltering and often hardly bearable. It represents a formidable time in the journey of the Sun when he is known beyond a shadow of a doubt to be the ruler of the world. This heat ripens the world and calls upon the fertility within the plant kingdom to rise and bear fruit. He ripens and over-ripens through the fullness of his light.

While there are other fire signs, none quite bears such an analogous relationship to the Sun in this way. Aries, the first sign of the fiery triplicity, has only just battled off the icy chains of Winter. Neither the days of Spring nor the sign of Aries have the full power necessary to be the constant temple of the Sun. It would be incompatible with nature. Sagittarius, the last sign in the fiery triplicity, is so far removed from the fierce heat of the Summer that it was chosen to be the sign to usher in the Winter. Furthermore, both the qualities of cardinality that we find in Aries and mutability that we find in Sagittarius do not reflect the constant and everlasting nature of the Sun. Only fixed Leo could represent the domicile of the undeviating and noble Sun. Therefore, in the Thema Mundi, the second celestial house was given to Leo, with the Sun as its ruler.

Within traditional astrology, the second house is called "Anaphora" or "Exit from the Gates of Hades." John Gadbury tells us that it was given this name because all things that find themselves there bear the promise of ultimately rising to the Ascendant and being born anew. Thus, the second house holds the promise of life, abundance, wealth, and blessedness. In the Thema Mundi, the Sun provides this vitality as an infinite source of supply for the Moon. The Moon is as supported by the light and the power of the Sun as we are supported by the wealth and abundance that is held within our own natal second houses. Though the ingress of the Sun into Cancer represents when the Sun has reached his maximum Northern distance from the Equator, the Sun doesn't enter the fullness of his majesty until he descends into the sign of Leo. Similarly, though our Ascendant represents the wellspring of power that is allotted to us in this lifetime, we do not have a means of fully flourishing within the world until we tap into the abundant supply of food and riches found in our second house. Both the Moon and the Sun are rightfully placed as the Lady of the first house and the Lord of the second house of the world, and the rulers of Cancer and Leo, respectively. These are both their domiciles as well as their celestial houses of joy.

## The Celestial Joys of the Planets

> *Of these therefore Aquarius is Kronos' [Saturn] preference, Zeus [Jupiter] is pleased in Sagittarius, Ares [Mars] in Scorpio, Cypris [Venus] brightens up in Taurus, Hermes [Mercury] gladdens in the Maiden [Virgo]; one house there is for each light.* – HEPHAISTIO OF THEBES

The term "joy" has two meanings in traditional astrology. A planet can have a celestial joy or a terrestrial joy. The terrestrial joys refer to whichever of the twelve terrestrial houses a planet prefers to be in. While different systems of terrestrial joys exist, the one most popularly referenced today is based on the sect of the planet and the location of the house in relation to the horizon.

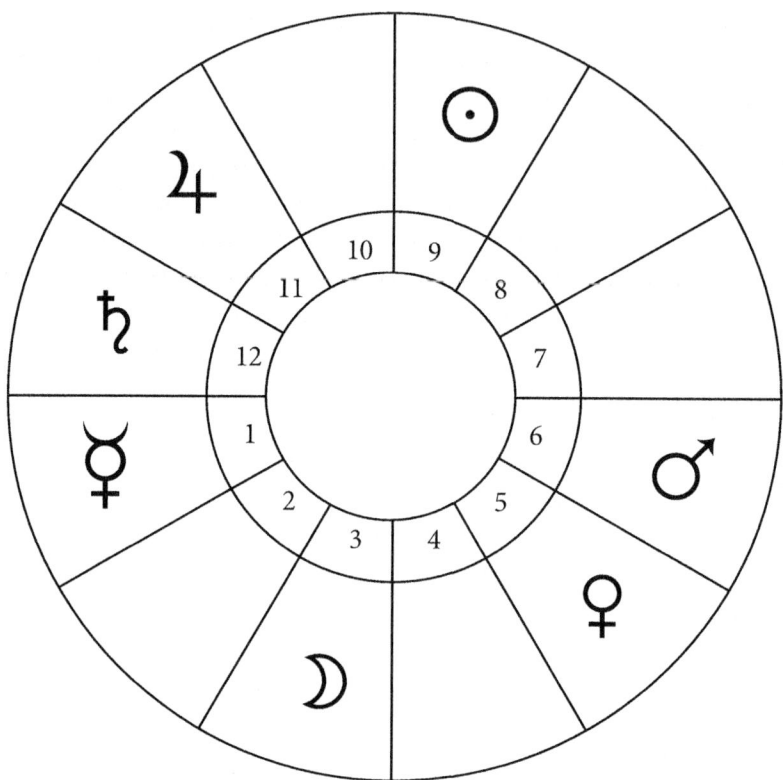

FIGURE 2: *Terrestrial Joys of the Planets*

The terrestrial joy of Mercury is the first house, the terrestrial joy of the Moon is the third house, the terrestrial joy of Venus is the fifth house, the terrestrial joy of Mars is the sixth house, the terrestrial joy of the Sun is the ninth house, the terrestrial joy of Jupiter is the eleventh house, and the terrestrial joy of Saturn is the twelfth house.

Note that the nocturnal planets all have their terrestrial houses of joy in the nocturnal hemisphere of the chart. The diurnal planets all have their terrestrial houses of joy in the diurnal hemisphere of the chart. Mercury, a planet that is neither diurnal nor nocturnal, has his terrestrial joy in the first house. Even though the first house is below the horizon, it is the bridge between the darkness and the dawn at the beginning of a new day, just as Mercury is the bridge between every pair of opposites.

The celestial joys refer to the specific domicile of a planet that the planet in question prefers to be in. Planets have their celestial houses of joy in whichever of their domiciles corresponds to their sect. The Moon and the Sun, due to the singularity of their natures as the Queen and King of Heaven, are afforded one sign each. Therefore, the celestial house of joy of the Moon is her only domicile of Cancer. The celestial house of joy of the Sun is his only domicile of Leo. However, the remaining five planets in the Chaldean Order are afforded two signs each. They each have a masculine and a feminine domicile. The masculine sign is the diurnal domicile of that planet while the feminine sign is the nocturnal domicile of that planet.

Diurnal planets have their diurnal domiciles as their celestial houses of joy. Nocturnal planets have their nocturnal domiciles as their celestial houses of joy.

Note that I have used the terms "diurnal and nocturnal" when specifically referring to the planets and their celestial houses of joy. This is because the celestial joys are based on sect, not gender. In traditional astrology, sect and gender are not synonymous. This is an important distinction, particularly in the case of Mars. When we discussed Ptolemy's astrological worldview, we learnt that Mars is a masculine planet, who also happens to be a nocturnal planet. Therefore, his nocturnal domicile of Scorpio is his celestial joy. Though he is a masculine planet, his celestial house of joy is not his masculine domicile. This is because the concept of celestial joy is completely based on sect and not gender. Also note that "celestial house of joy" and "celestial joy" are synonymous. Terrestrial houses refer to the twelve houses of an astrological chart. However, celestial houses always refer to the domiciles of the planets, which is why "celestial joy" is always a reference to their domiciles.

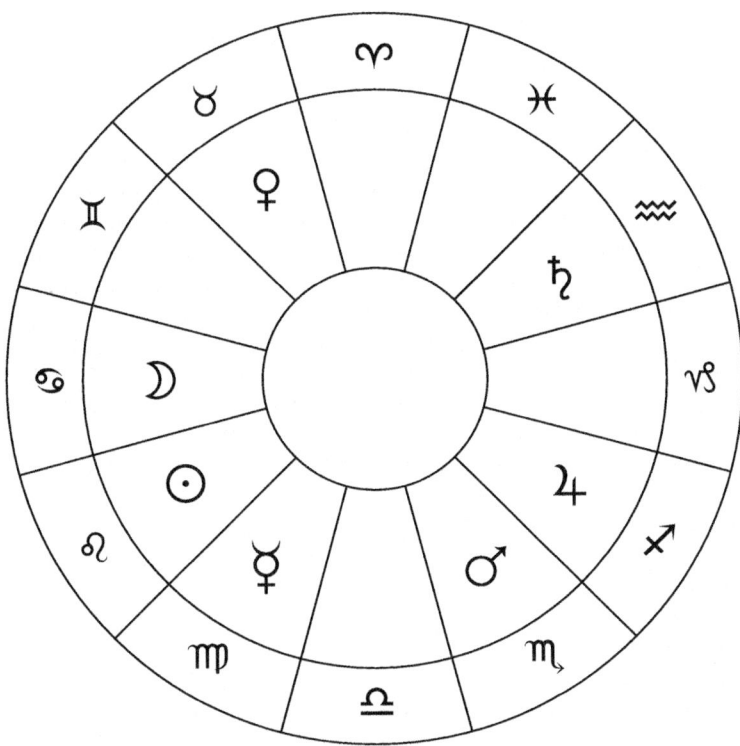

FIGURE 3: *Celestial Joys of the Planets*

TABLE 1: *Masculine (Diurnal) & Feminine (Nocturnal) Signs*

| MASCULINE/DIURNAL | FEMININE/NOCTURNAL |
|---|---|
| ARIES | TAURUS |
| GEMINI | CANCER |
| LEO | VIRGO |
| LIBRA | SCORPIO |
| SAGITTARIUS | CAPRICORN |
| AQUARIUS | PISCES |

Saturn, a diurnal planet, has two domiciles: diurnal Aquarius and nocturnal Capricorn. Aquarius, Saturn's diurnal domicile, is the celestial joy of Saturn, a diurnal planet.

Jupiter, a diurnal planet, has two domiciles: diurnal Sagittarius and nocturnal Pisces. Sagittarius, Jupiter's diurnal domicile, is the celestial joy of Jupiter, a diurnal planet.

Mars, a nocturnal planet, has two domiciles: diurnal Aries and nocturnal Scorpio. Scorpio, the nocturnal domicile of Mars, is the celestial joy of Mars, a nocturnal planet.

The Sun, a diurnal planet, has one domicile: diurnal Leo. Leo, the only domicile of the Sun is the celestial joy of the Sun, a diurnal planet.

Venus, a nocturnal planet, has two domiciles: diurnal Libra and nocturnal Taurus. Taurus, the nocturnal domicile of Venus, is the celestial joy of Venus, a nocturnal planet.

Mercury is a planet without a sect of his own. He has two domiciles: diurnal Gemini and nocturnal Virgo. Virgo happens to be both the domicile of Mercury as well as his exaltation – a condition that exists nowhere else in the entire zodiac for any other planet. Virgo is the celestial joy of Mercury. This does not mean that Mercury is an intrinsically earthy planet, and neither does it mean that Mercury is a nocturnal planet. In all ways, the path of Mercury is different from how we expect the planets to function. The same is true here.

The Moon, a nocturnal planet, has one domicile: nocturnal Cancer. Cancer, the only domicile of the Moon is the celestial joy of the Moon, a nocturnal planet.

We will revisit this topic of sect more fully later on.

TABLE 2: *Celestial Joys of the Planets Based on Sect*

| SECT | PLANET | JOY |
|------|--------|-----|
| DIURNAL | ♄ | ♒ |
| DIURNAL | ♃ | ♐ |
| NOCTURNAL | ♂ | ♏ |
| DIURNAL | ☉ | ♌ |
| NOCTURNAL | ♀ | ♉ |
| VARIABLE | ☿ | ♍ |
| NOCTURNAL | ☽ | ♋ |

## SATURN – THE WATCHER AT THE THRESHOLD OF THE UNIVERSE

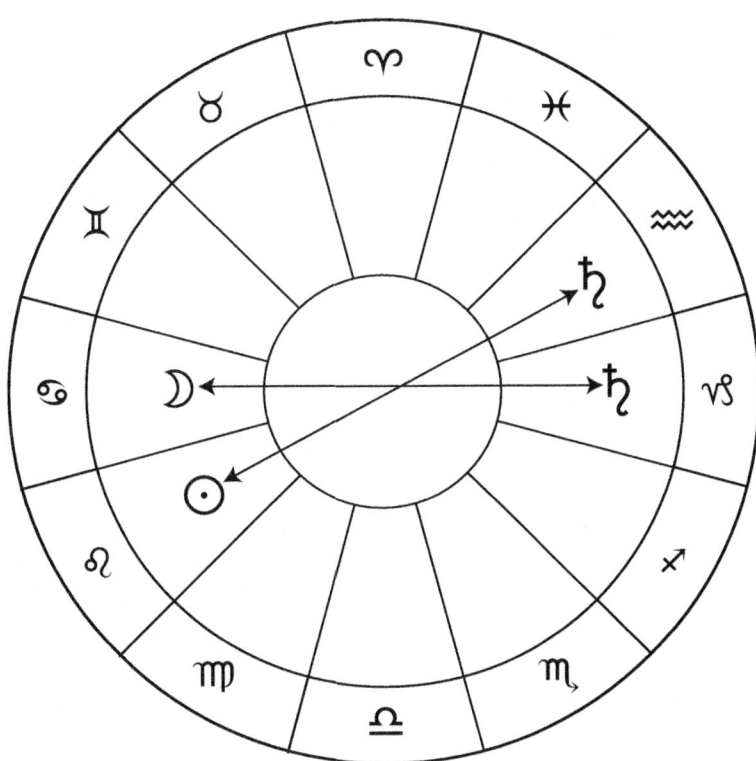

FIGURE 4: *Domiciles of Saturn Opposite the Domiciles of the Luminaries*

Once we have identified a home for the luminaries, the next thing that becomes possible is to allocate the natural homes for the planet farthest from the luminaries. We remember that in the Chaldean Order, Saturn is both farthest from the heat and light of the Sun, as well as farthest from the wetness and the moisture-filled vapors of the Moon and Earth. Saturn is farthest from the Sun and the Moon, simultaneously. Therefore, the domiciles of Saturn have an oppositional relationship to the domiciles of the luminaries. Capricorn is 180° distant from Cancer, while Aquarius is 180° distant from Leo. Ptolemy writes:

> Saturn, therefore, since he is cold and inimical to heat, moving also in a superior orbit most remote from the luminaries, occupies the signs opposite to Cancer and Leo: these are Aquarius and Capricorn; and they are assigned to him in consideration of their cold and wintry nature; and because the configuration by opposition does not cooperate towards the production of good.

Just as Saturn is considered to be hateful to the Moon and the Sun, the signs of Saturn are in an unfriendly relationship to the signs of the Moon and the Sun.

## Lunar and Solar Halves of the Zodiac

This opposition between the temples of the luminaries and the temples of Saturn creates a division in the zodiac. The six signs from Cancer to Aquarius exist in that half of the zodiac belonging to the Moon. The six signs from Leo to Capricorn exist in that half of the zodiac belonging to the Sun.

If we divide the zodiac along the Cancer/Capricorn axis, we end up with the Moon as the Queen of Heaven on one side of six signs, and the Sun as King of Heaven on another side of six signs. Ptolemy writes:

> It has hence resulted, that the semicircle from Leo to Capricorn has been ordained solar, and the semicircle from Aquarius to Cancer, lunar; in order that each planet may occupy one sign in each semicircle, and thus have one of its houses configured with the Sun and the other with the Moon, conformably to the motion of its own sphere, and the peculiar properties of its nature.

This provides one lens of rationale for the structure of the Thema Mundi and the concept of domicile rulership. While philosophically interesting, there are other divisions of the zodiac that are more important to maintain in our awareness. Beyond its value as a way of describing how and why the Thema Mundi is constructed in the way that it is, I have not found this solar and lunar division of the zodiac to be significant in actual chart interpretation.

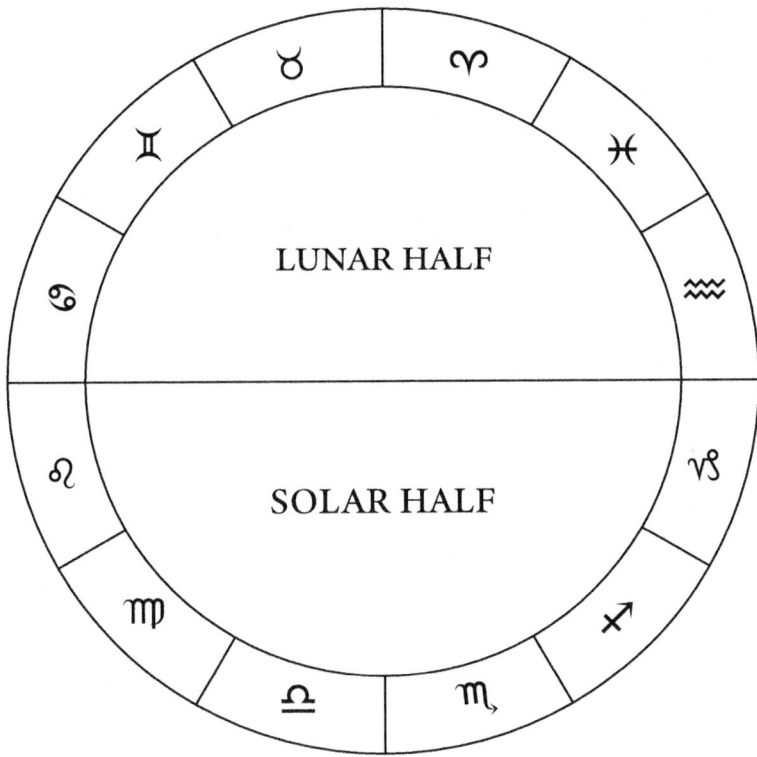

FIGURE 5: *Lunar & Solar Halves of the Zodiac*

With the exception of the opposition, all of the aspects that the temples of the luminaries receive from the other ten signs of the zodiac are taken from their own side. In other words, the aspects that the sign Leo receives from the other signs of the zodiac are those that come from its own side containing the signs of Leo, Virgo, Libra, Scorpio, Sagittarius, and Capricorn, while its opposition to Aquarius comes from across the line of the Cancer/Capricorn axis. Bonatti writes:

> *But you could say that Gemini aspects Leo and Virgo (aspects) Cancer. Still, this does not have a role in this case; because according to this consideration, no sign is said to aspect the domicile of any luminary from any aspect such that the domicile of the other luminary falls within those boundaries. Whence Gemini is not said to aspect Leo, because Cancer (the domicile of the Moon) falls within those boundaries…*

We know that Gemini does aspect Leo by sextile. However, for the purpose of teaching the doctrine of aspects using the Thema Mundi, it is useful for us to view the aspects to the domiciles of the luminaries as coming from the side that belongs to that luminary. This is important because the aspects carry the nature of the planets whose domiciles form those aspects to Cancer and Leo. As we will learn in the following pages, trines are "of the nature of Jupiter." This is because the domicile of Jupiter that trines Leo is Sagittarius, which is on the same side of the oppositional divide as Leo. Similarly the domicile of Jupiter that trines Cancer is Pisces, which is on the same side of the oppositional divide as Cancer. However, Sagittarius does not trine Cancer, and Pisces does not trine Leo. There is a name for the relationship that Sagittarius has to Cancer and that Leo has to Pisces. It is called a "quincunx," which we will discuss later within this chapter.

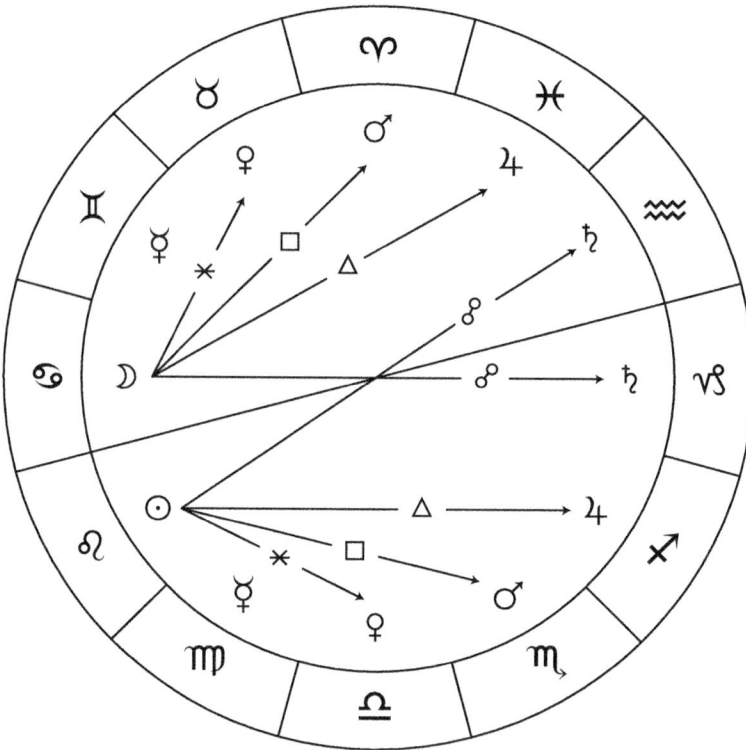

FIGURE 6: *Division of the Aspects within the Zodiac*

WHY TRADITIONAL ASTROLOGERS CONSIDER OPPOSITIONS TO BE BAD

Since the primary opposition in the zodiac comes from the relationship between the domiciles of the luminaries and the two domiciles of Saturn, the opposition was considered to be Saturnian in nature. Since Saturn is the greater malefic in traditional astrology, the aspect that comes from his domiciles to those of the luminaries is also considered to be malefic in nature. In the Renaissance, we find the opposition called an aspect of "Perfect Hatred." Ptolemy considered Saturn's nature to be noxious and unsupportive of life. Therefore, the aspect Saturn makes through the force of his two signs to the signs of the luminaries is also considered to be an aspect of absolute destruction.

As a child growing up with astrology, I considered it very weird that two signs ruled by the same planet would follow each other. I had even read some authors say that it was a "mistake" that the ancients made, because thousands of years ago, they didn't have any other planet to rule Aquarius. This lack of understanding of the ancient roots of astrology has left many modern astrologers in a self-righteous position. Many astrologers think they need to amend the errors of the ancients by modifying classical concepts such as domicile rulership. Understanding the Thema Mundi allows us to see the rationale that underpins the concepts of domicile rulership and aspects. There is no place within the framework of traditional astrology at all for the concept of "modern rulers." This does not mean that there isn't space in traditional astrology for modern planets. This means that the doctrine of sign rulership is unalterable from a traditional perspective. Just because we use the modern planets does not mean that those modern planets rule signs.

After the temples of Saturn were established in relation to the temples of the luminaries, the organization of the other planets in their domiciles follows the Chaldean Order.

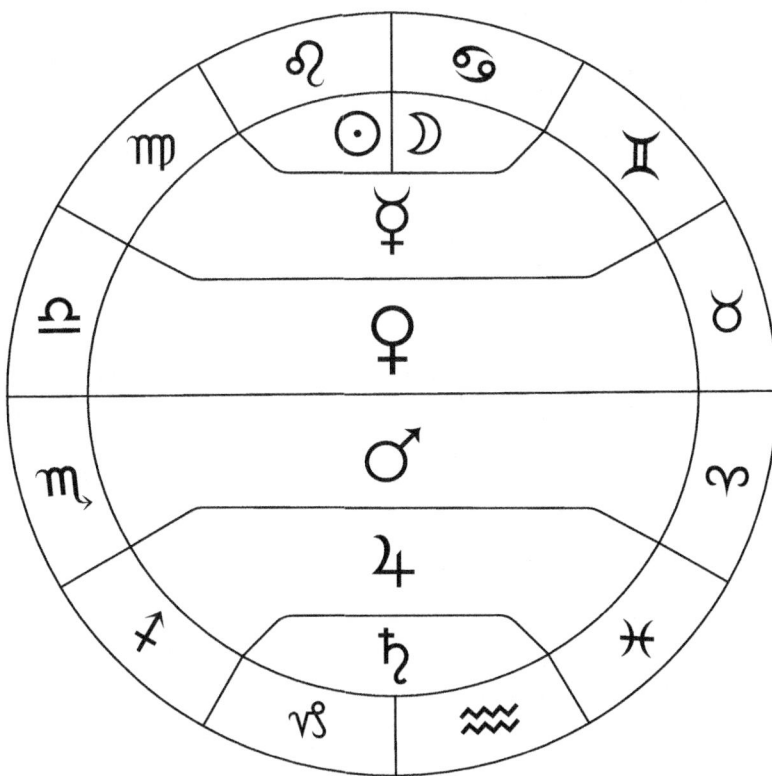

FIGURE 7: *Domiciles of the Seven Planets*

From the domiciles of Saturn, we find the domiciles of Jupiter on either side, followed by the domiciles of Mars on either side. Since the Sun has moved from his place in the Chaldean Order to join the Moon at the birthing of the world, his domicile does not follow that of Mars. We continue with the domiciles of Venus flanking the domiciles of Mars. Finally, we come to the domiciles of Mercury on either side of the domiciles of Venus. The two domiciles of Mercury also flank the domiciles of the luminaries on either side. Thus, our Chaldean Order within the Thema Mundi becomes: Saturn, Jupiter, Mars, Venus, Mercury, and the luminaries.

### ASPECTS WITHIN THE THEMA MUNDI

An aspect is the angular relationship between two or more celestial factors. However, if we use the first degree of all the signs of the zodiac as our reference point, then we can just as easily say that the signs of the zodiac form various angular relationships with each other. In this way, we can say that Aries aspects Cancer, Libra aspects Leo, and continue to make our way around the zodiac, until we find that each sign has a particular aspect relationship to each other sign. As far as aspects within the Thema Mundi are concerned, our primary objective is to identify the aspects that are made between the other signs of the zodiac and the domiciles of the luminaries.

Just as Saturn established an oppositional relationship to the luminaries through his domiciles, the other planets in the Chaldean Order also form aspect relationships to the luminaries through their domiciles. In our 360° circle of the twelve signs of the zodiac, we find twelve equal parts of 30° each. All of the aspects that we use in traditional astrology are thought of as being similar in nature to the planets whose domiciles make those aspects to the domiciles of the Sun and the Moon.

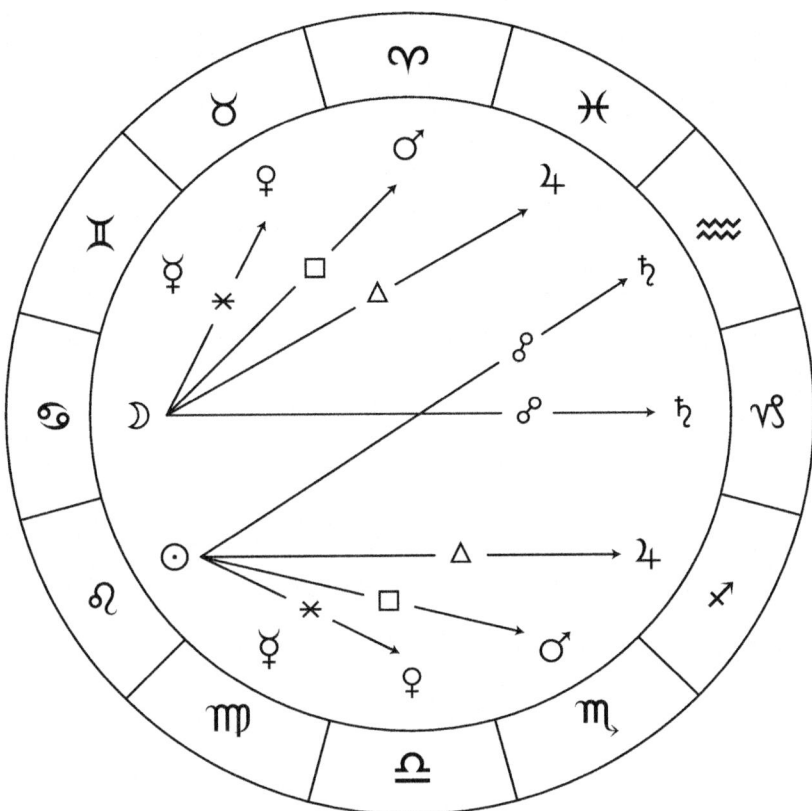

FIGURE 8: *Aspects within the Thema Mundi*

## SAGITTARIUS AND PISCES – DOMICILES OF JUPITER

Jupiter's domiciles are Sagittarius and Pisces. They are on either side of the domiciles of Saturn. Sagittarius casts its aspect to Leo, in the same way Pisces casts its aspect to Cancer. If Saturn's domiciles of Capricorn and Aquarius are 180° away from Cancer and Leo, respectively, then Jupiter's domiciles will form a 120° aspect to those signs. This 120° aspect is called a trine. Sagittarius is in a 120° trine relationship with Leo, and Pisces is in a 120° trine relationship with Cancer.

Jupiter is the greater benefic. Therefore, the aspects that Jupiter's domiciles make to the domiciles of the luminaries is considered to be a benefic aspect. Ptolemy tells us:

> But Jupiter has a favorable temperament, and is situated beneath the sphere of Saturn; he therefore occupies the next two signs, Sagittarius and Pisces. These signs are airy and fruitful in consequence of their trine distance from the houses of the luminaries, which distance harmonizes with the operation of good.

Of these signs, Ptolemy says they are "airy and fruitful." Through Jupiter being their ruler, they both take on some of the naturally life-supportive qualities that he holds. Jupiter is a hot and wet, sanguine planet. The element of air was also considered in Ptolemy's time to be hot and wet. Therefore, though neither Sagittarius or Pisces is an air sign, they both contain some of the fertilizing properties of that element.

In the Renaissance, we see the trine aspect being called an aspect of "Perfect Love and Friendship." Just as the opposition is considered to be the most debilitating and antagonistic aspect because of its inherent relationship to Saturn, the trine is considered to be the most supportive or harmonious aspect because of its analogous relationship to Jupiter.

## QUINCUNX – THE ASPECT THAT ISN'T AN ASPECT

So far, we have consistently ignored the relationship of Leo to Capricorn, and Cancer to Aquarius. We have similarly ignored the relationship of Cancer to Sagittarius, and Leo to Pisces. The distance between these signs is 150°. Traditionally we consider this to be a relationship of aversion. It is also commonly called a "quincunx."

The quincunx is a peculiar relationship that I use very heavily in my work. When two planets are in a quincunx, it means that they have gone as far out of their way as possible to not be in aspect with each other. They have made such a big statement about not being in a relationship, that they've created a new relationship called a "non-relationship." This is similar to two women by the names of Mary and Martha who are so repulsed by each other, that Mary wears a shirt that says "I don't talk to Martha" and Martha wears a shirt that says "I don't talk to Mary." Their determination to not be in connection with each other is so noteworthy that their lack of a connection has a name. The name of their non-relationship is "quincunx" or "aversion," and it technically isn't an aspect. However, though it isn't an aspect (it is literally *the* non-aspect), for the purpose of chart reading I include it amongst the other aspects when delineating planetary relationships. I believe the quincunx is well-worth our consideration in traditional astrology.

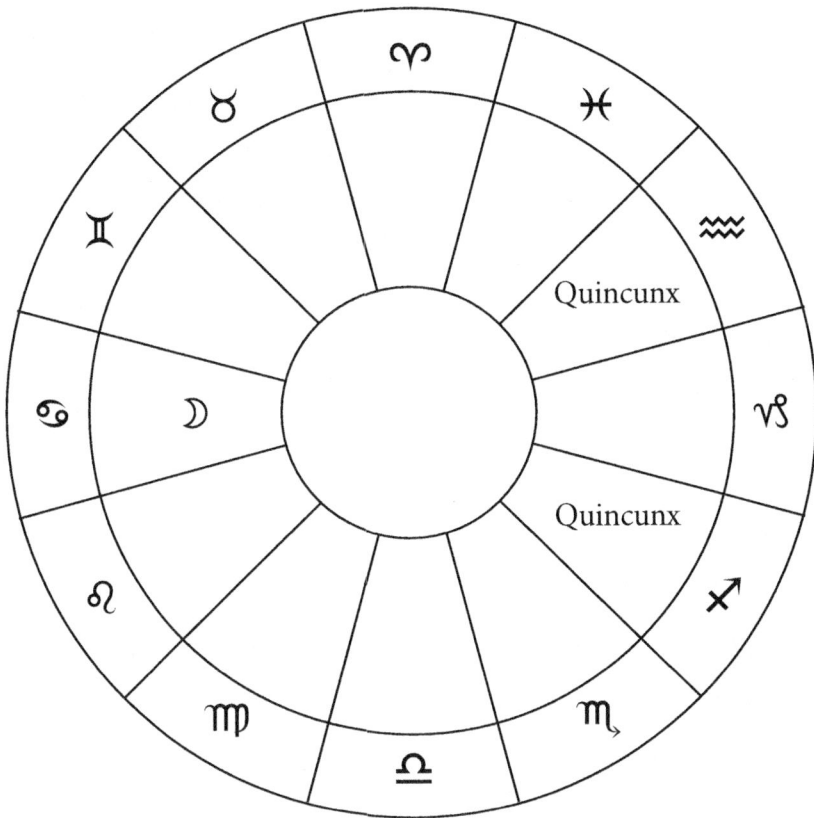

FIGURE 9: *Quincunxes*

A sign is always in a quincunx with the two signs that are on either side of its opposition sign. Therefore, Cancer is opposite Capricorn, and quincunxes Sagittarius and Aquarius. Leo is opposite Aquarius, and quincunxes Capricorn and Pisces. A table of all the quincunxes between the signs of the zodiac can be found below.

TABLE 3: *Quincunxes*

| | | | | | | | |
|---|---|---|---|---|---|---|---|
| ARIES | → | ♍ | ♏ | LIBRA | → | ♓ | ♉ |
| TAURUS | → | ♎ | ♐ | SCORPIO | → | ♈ | ♊ |
| GEMINI | → | ♏ | ♑ | SAGITTARIUS | → | ♉ | ♋ |
| CANCER | → | ♐ | ♒ | CAPRICORN | → | ♊ | ♌ |
| LEO | → | ♑ | ♓ | AQUARIUS | → | ♋ | ♍ |
| VIRGO | → | ♒ | ♈ | PISCES | → | ♌ | ♎ |

## QUINCUNXES ARE USEFUL

Many astrologers ignore quincunxes. However, I have found that if two classical planets are in a quincunx with each other, there is or will be disharmony between those two planets as well as the houses they rule. If the ruler of the first house is in a quincunx with the ruler of the tenth house of the mother, this can indicate a person who had a very difficult relationship with their mother. If the ruler of the first house is in a quincunx with the ruler of the second house of money, this may be a person who struggles constantly to make ends meet. If the ruler of the first house is in a quincunx with the ruler of the seventh house of marriage, this can be a person who finds it difficult to have a healthy, long-lasting relationship. At all times, it is important to do a full reading of the chart in order to see how strongly or weakly other factors confirm or deny our assessment. These are just general guidelines to get you thinking in a more concrete astrological way.

## ARIES AND SCORPIO – DOMICILES OF MARS

The next aspects to consider are the squares. The domiciles of Mars are Aries and Scorpio. They flank the domiciles of Jupiter on either side. In the same way as Jupiter's domiciles are 120° away from the domiciles of the luminaries, the domiciles of Mars are 90° away from the domiciles of the luminaries. Aries casts a 90° square aspect to the sign of Cancer. Scorpio casts a 90° square aspect to the sign of Leo. 90° is a half of 180°, the aspect of Perfect Hatred. Therefore, the Mars-like 90° square aspect is considered in the Medieval and Renaissance periods to be an aspect of "Imperfect Hatred," containing half the force of the Saturn-like opposition. Ptolemy writes:

> *Mars is dry in nature, and beneath the sphere of Jupiter: he takes the next two signs of a nature similar to his own, viz. Aries and Scorpio, whose relative distances from the houses of the luminaries are injurious and discordant.*

This follows what we know to be true about Mars and Saturn in general. Saturn is the greater malefic and Mars is the lesser malefic. It makes sense that the aspects that carry their natures also show this modulation of intensity. Though the square aspect isn't as forceful as the opposition, it still packs quite the punch because of its war-like Martian nature. Traditionally speaking, two planets in a square are planets in a tense and volatile relationship.

## LIBRA AND TAURUS – DOMICILES OF VENUS

By subtracting 30° from the 90° square, we arrive at the 60° sextile. The domiciles of Venus are Taurus and Libra. They flank the domiciles of Mars on either side. Just as the domiciles of Mars are 90° away from the domiciles of the luminaries, the domiciles of Venus are 60° away from the domiciles of the luminaries. Taurus casts a 60° sextile to the sign of Cancer. Libra casts a 60° sextile to the sign of Leo. 60° is a half of the 120° trine, which we've already referred to as the aspect of Perfect Love and Friendship. Ptolemy writes:

> *Venus, possessing a favorable temperament, and placed beneath the sphere of Mars, takes the next two signs, Taurus and Libra. These are of a fruitful nature, and preserve harmony by the sextile distance; and this planet is never more than two signs distant from the Sun.*

Therefore, the Venus-like 60° sextile is considered in the Medieval and Renaissance periods to be an aspect of "Imperfect Love and Friendship," containing half the force of the Jupiter-like trine.

This follows what we know to be true about Venus and Jupiter in general. Jupiter is the greater benefic and Venus is the lesser benefic. It makes sense that the aspects that carry their natures also show this modulation of intensity. Though the sextile isn't as forceful as the trine, it still creates a harmonious interaction and exchange between the planets in question because of its Venusian nature. Two planets forming a sextile are planets in a harmonious relationship.

Ptolemy mentioned that Venus is never more than "two signs distant from the Sun." From a geocentric perspective the two inferior planets, Venus and Mercury, are bound to the Sun and will always be near him. Venus can only be a maximum of 48° away from the Sun. Mercury can only be a maximum of 28° away from the Sun. When either of those planets attain that maximum distance, they station, and turn retrograde.

## Gemini and Virgo – Domiciles of Mercury

> *Mercury never has greater distance from the Sun than the space of one sign, and is beneath all the other planets: hence he is placed nearest to both luminaries, and the remaining two signs, Gemini and Virgo are allotted to him.* – CLAUDIUS PTOLEMY

Finally, we come to the domiciles of Mercury flanking the domiciles of Venus on either side. The domiciles of Mercury are Gemini and Virgo. By subtracting 30° from the 60° sextile, we attain the 30° semi-sextile. Strictly speaking, the semi-sextile is not an aspect that we use within traditional astrology. Though we do find astrologers such as Morin using them in the seventeenth century, semi-sextiles are not widely held as being aspects by the ancients. The semi-sextile is an aspect of aversion, or a non-aspect, in the same way as the 150° quincunx is an aspect of aversion. However, in practice, I have found the 150° quincunx to be far more potent and far more disharmonious than the 30° semi-sextile. As a rule, I never use the semi-sextile aspect. On the rare occasions when I have commented on it in a class setting, I have always done so as an afterthought, and not as a major consideration in my chart interpretation.

On Semi-Sextiles, Quincunxes, and Aversion

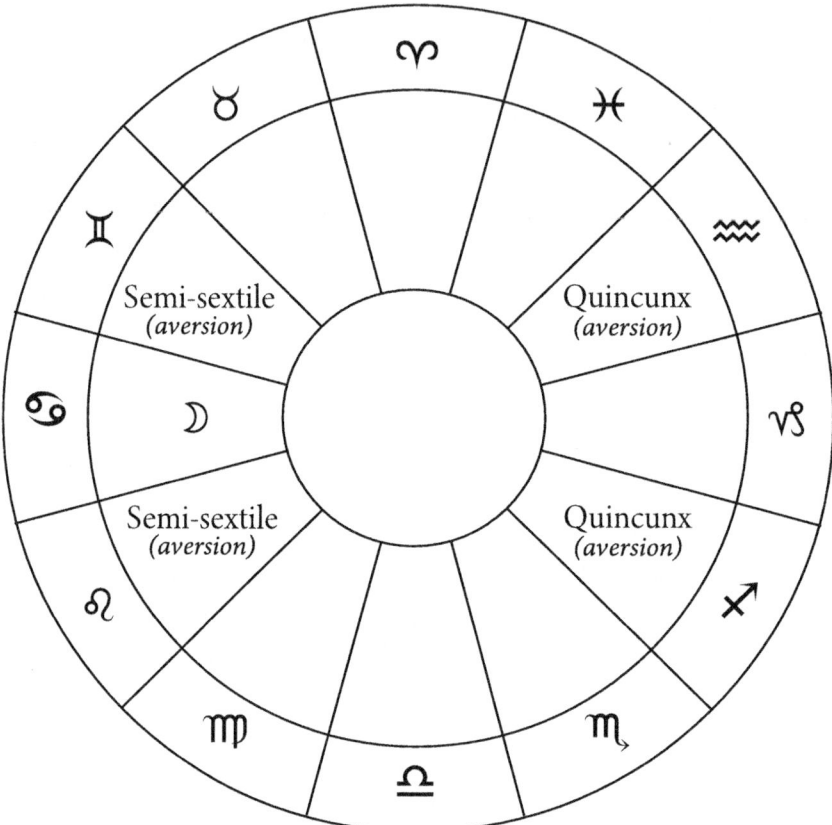

Figure 10: *Semi-Sextiles & Quincunxes*

Semi-sextiles and quincunxes are both aspects of aversion. However, only the 30° aversions are called "semi-sextiles," and only the 150° aversions are called "quincunxes." All aversions are not semi-sextiles. All aversions are also not quincunxes. A semi-sextile is not a quincunx, but it is an aversion. A quincunx is not a semi-sextile, but it is an aversion. Of the four aversions, the quincunxes seem to work out in a determinately malefic way; while the semi-sextiles, if they are to be considered at all, range from mild to ineffectual in their actual ability to create concrete events.

The reason why the 30° semi-sextile is considered to be an aspect of aversion is because the ancients held the belief that signs directly adjacent to each other could not "see" each other. Manilius writes:

> But no friendliness towards one another has been granted to adjacent signs: sympathy between them is blunted because the sight of each other is denied them. Their attentions are bestowed on distant signs which they can see.

Therefore, since Gemini is directly adjacent to Cancer, planets in Gemini and planets in Cancer can't see each other. Similarly, planets in Virgo and planets in Leo can't see each other because of their proximity. This was thought to be most unfortunate, particularly in the case of planets that we want to be in a relationship. Much of traditional astrology is based on the relationships between planets. If two planets do not have a relationship, they cannot communicate, and if they cannot communicate, it is likely that – unless they are strongly fortified in some other way – they won't be able to do much good in supporting or sustaining each other. Planets that are in aversion with each other are typically planets that cannot support one another. This is especially true for the quincunx. However, it does not seem to be as true for the semi-sextile.

It is important to remember that any one of the twelve signs of the zodiac will always have four signs that are in aversion to it. These signs will be the two signs that are adjacent to it on either side, and the two signs that are on either side of its opposition sign.

Aries is in aversion to Pisces and Taurus which are directly adjacent to it on either side. Aries is also in aversion to Virgo and Scorpio, the two signs which are on either side of Libra, the opposition sign of Aries. All of these signs are in aversion to Aries: Pisces and Taurus which are 30° away from Aries, and Virgo and Scorpio which are 150° away from Aries. However, only the signs that are 150° away from Aries – Virgo and Scorpio – are in a quincunx with Aries.

❋

This concludes our discussion of the Thema Mundi. As we can see, the Thema Mundi is built on ideas that are central to traditional astrology. These ideas are rooted in a series of harmonies that exist between numbers, qualities, and nature. It is wholly dependent on a metaphysical understanding of the structure of the universe as conceived by the ancients, and the rulers of heaven as they perceived them from Earth.

Our modern astrological studies show us that there are many more planetary relationships than the aspects made possible through the Thema Mundi. However, the Thema Mundi still serves as a logical entry point into understanding the aspects and the planets which influence their nature. The more we orient ourselves within this classical understanding of astrology, the more our practice will feel natural, stabilizing, and organized. These are the hallmarks of classical astrology, and these are qualities that we should all seek to embody within our astrological practice.

CHAPTER 9 QUESTIONS

1. What is the Thema Mundi?
2. Why are the Moon and Cancer so important in the construction of the Thema Mundi?
3. Why are the domiciles of the luminaries next to each other?
4. Why are the domiciles of Saturn opposite to the domiciles of the luminaries?
5. What is the chief consideration underlying the celestial joys of the planets?
6. Describe the intrinsic natures of the four traditional aspects based on the Thema Mundi.
7. What does the word "aversion" mean?
8. What is the similarity between semi-sextiles and quincunxes? What is the difference between semi-sextiles and quincunxes?

CHAPTER 10 OBJECTIVES

* Define the term "aspect."
* Understand the importance of aspects within traditional astrology interpretation.
* Differentiate between applying and separating aspects.
* Define the terms "orb" and "moiety."
* Differentiate between the Medieval and the Renaissance concept of the width of the orb of the planets.
* Learn the seven aspects of traditional astrology.
* Introduce the concept of harmonics as it relates to aspects.
* Understand how to view conjunctions.
* Introduce other important ways in which the planets can be in relation with each other.

# CHAPTER 10

## ASPECTS

*Worship the Immortal Gods with an understanding as to their order and function in the universe. for it is impossible to worship unless you understand to some extent the nature and function of that which you worship. The Gods do not occupy their position by accident, nor from carelessness on the part of the Great Architect, nor are they isolated units independent of each other, but rather are they linked together in such a way as to form one perfect whole, like the different parts of one animal.* – GOLDEN VERSES OF PYTHAGORAS

AN ASPECT IS THE ANGULAR RELATIONSHIP between two or more celestial factors in the zodiac. These include planets, house cusps, nodes, and other important considerations within a chart. We measure these angles in degrees, minutes, and seconds of arc. Within traditional astrology, the relationships – or lack thereof – between celestial factors bears great interpretational value. These relationships let us know how these factors will act together within the chart in question. From here on, I will use the word "planet" to refer to both planets as well as non-planetary celestial factors in describing how aspects function.

The distance between two planets is called their "arc opening." In traditional astrology, there are specific arc openings that are more powerful than others. These are the four traditional aspects. They are: the 60° sextile, the 90° square, the 120° trine, and the 180° opposition. Many people also consider the conjunction to be an aspect. However, this is not the case. A conjunction is when two or more planets are conjoined to each other degree-to-degree. These planets have no arc opening between them. Therefore, they are not forming an aspect. A conjunction represents an important planetary connection that should never be ignored, but it cannot rightly be called an angular relationship – which is the basic definition of what an aspect is.

### WHY ARE ASPECTS IMPORTANT?

Aspects are important because they signify the action potential between planets. While aspects don't make things happen, they do allow things to happen between two or more planets. In other words, they facilitate a particular quality of planetary relationship. Some aspects facilitate a positive, harmonious relationship. Other aspects facilitate a negative, warlike relationship. We call harmonious aspects "soft aspects." We call difficult aspects "hard aspects."

The aspectual relationship between planets holds vital interpretive information. Aspects show us how planets will cooperate and whether or not they will support each other in fulfilling their outcome. Will they be friendly or warlike? Will they harmoniously cooperate or will they try to divide and conquer each other? While the essential dignity of two planets tells us how strong they are to deliver on the promise they've been entrusted with in the chart, the aspects show us what the quality of their working relationship will be. Two weak planets could work very harmoniously together. Two strong planets could be the worst of enemies. Through harmonious aspects, a weak planet and a strong planet can figure out how to forge forward towards some common good for both of their interests. Through difficult aspects, a strong planet and a weak planet can actively seek to destroy each other. Aspects show a broad array of connections that reflect both our human relationships as well as the relationships that exist between the various areas of our lives, such as finances and family, or job and spouse.

## APPLYING ASPECTS

In general, an aspect can be applying, exact, or separating. An applying aspect is one in which the faster moving planet has not yet arrived to the exact degree of the slower moving planet that it is aspecting. However, it is within a range that allows the slower moving planet to "feel" its presence.

An example of this would be if we had Mercury at 15° Scorpio applying to the square of Mars at 20° Aquarius.

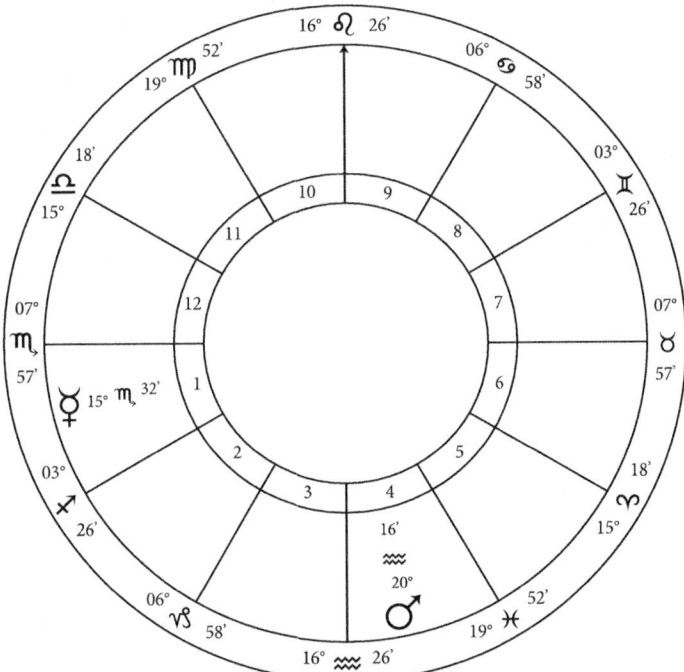

FIGURE 1: *Mercury Applying to a Square with Mars*

This is an applying square. Here, Mercury has not fully made his way to the perfect square of Mars, but still has "a little way to go." This "little way to go" is the orb between Mercury and Mars. The "orb" is the distance between two planets before they come to their perfect aspect.

When two planets are within range of aspecting each other, but are not at the same degree, they are in a "platick aspect." A platick aspect is an aspect that is occurring within the range of an allowable orb. Mercury at 15° Scorpio is in an applying square to Mars at 20° Aquarius. Another way we could say this is that Mercury is applying to a square with Mars within a five degree orb. This means that Mercury has five more degrees of arc between him and Mars before he comes to the exact square aspect with Mars. If Mercury were to take five "steps" forward in the zodiac, with each step representing a degree of zodiacal longitude, then Mercury will come to the exact square of Mars.

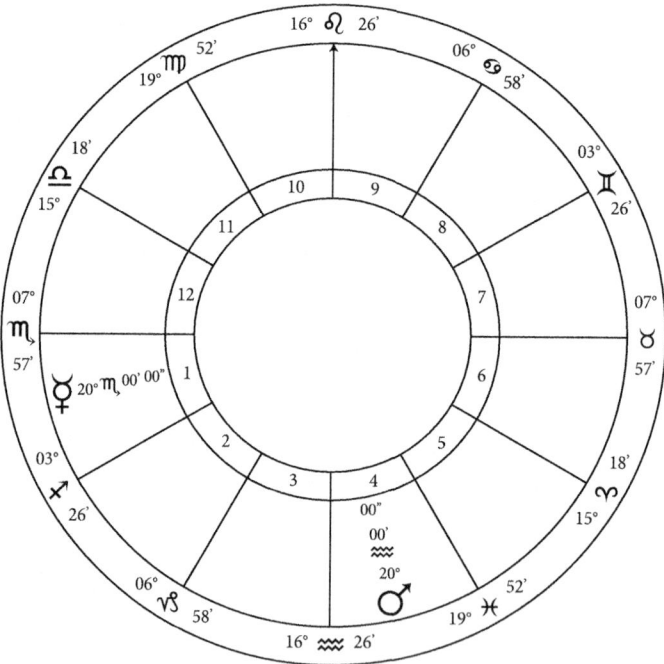

FIGURE 2: *Exact Square between Mercury & Mars*

EXACT ASPECTS

A perfect aspect occurs when two planets share the same degree, minute, and second of arc in their respective signs and form an aspect. This is also known as an "exact aspect." If Mercury at 15° 00' 00" Scorpio made his way to 20° 00' 00" Scorpio, he would then be in a perfect or exact square with Mars at 20° 00' 00" Aquarius. An exact or perfect aspect is one in which there is no orb between the planets. If a square is exactly 90°, then the planets in question are exactly 90° apart. Not 91°, not 89°, but 90°. Exact is exact.

236

In FIGURE 2 both Mercury and Mars are exactly 90° apart in the zodiac. This is the same as saying Mercury and Mars are 90° apart in zodiacal longitude. This is also the same as saying Mercury and Mars have a 90° arc opening, or that there is a 90° arc opening between Mercury and Mars. One can also say there are 90° of arc between Mercury and Mars. While these all mean the same thing, it is useful to know the various ways whereby aspect relationship can be spoken about.

## PARTILE ASPECTS

A partile aspect occurs when two or more planets share the same degree in their respective signs. However, they may differ in terms of minutes and seconds of arc.

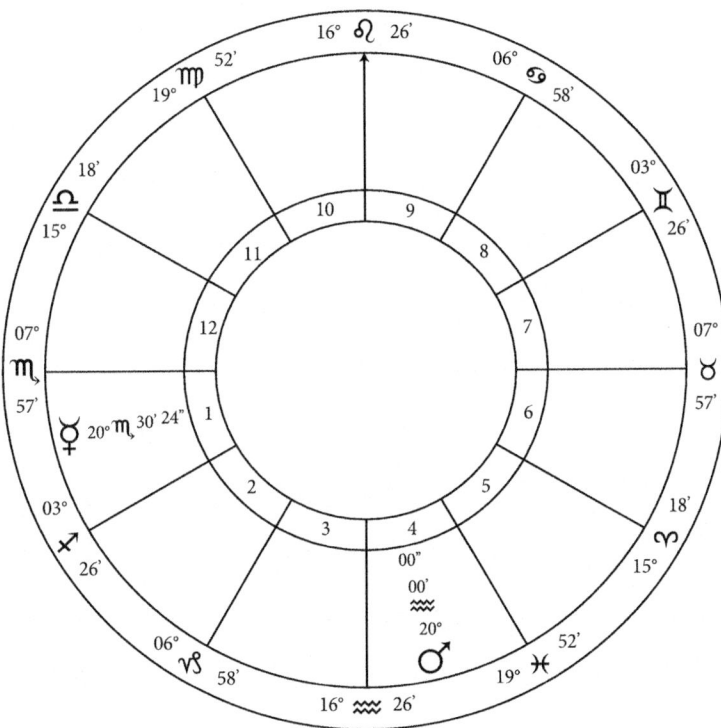

FIGURE 3: *Partile Square between Mercury & Mars*

Mercury at 20° 30' 24" Scorpio is in a partile square with Mars at 20° 00' 00" Aquarius. Though they are partile, they are not in a perfect or exact square any longer.

## SEPARATING ASPECTS

After Mercury has applied to a conjunction of Mars by square, he will eventually separate from that aspect. Mercury at 20° of Scorpio will eventually move to 21°, 22°, and 23°, ultimately leaving Mars far behind him. In our example, in the time it would take for Mercury to travel to 25° Scorpio, it is likely that Mars would have only travelled forward in the zodiac to about 21° Aquarius. Though the aspect is no longer applying or partile, it is still considered to be an aspect. This is because Mercury at 25° Scorpio is still within the allowable range or orb necessary for him to be in a square aspect with Mars at 21° Aquarius.

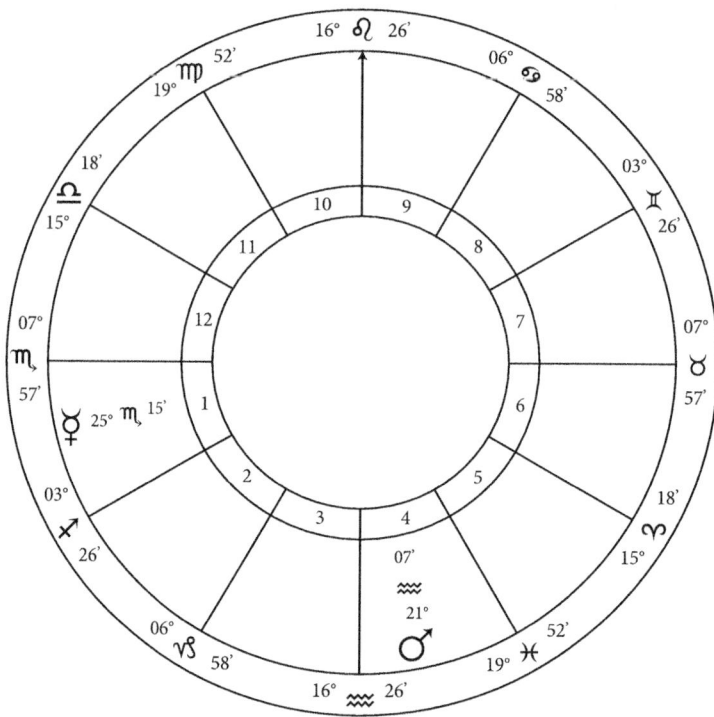

FIGURE 4: *Separating Square*

Remember, aspects that aren't partile, but are still within the allowable range to be considered an aspect are called "platick aspects." This is true for applying as well as separating aspects. In our example of Mercury at 25° Scorpio and Mars at 21° Aquarius, Mercury is in a platick square with Mars. However, it isn't just any square. Platick doesn't tell us whether the square is separating or applying – a piece of information that is very important in both horary and natal astrology. Because Mercury has separated from the exact square to Mars, we would say that Mercury is in a separating square "from" Mars. If we wanted to split hairs, we would say that Mercury is in "a platick separating square from Mars" to distinguish him from being in "a platick applying square to Mars" or "a partile square with Mars." However, it is not necessary to use "platick" when describing applying or separating aspects. There is no such thing as an "applying partile square" or a "separating partile square." If an aspect is applying or separating and not yet exact, it must be a platick aspect. Therefore, we can say "applying square" and "separating square" knowing that both of them, by definition, are also platick.

### WHAT ARE THE ALLOWABLE ORBS GIVEN TO THE PLANETS?

There are two definitions for what an orb is. Firstly, an orb can be defined as the entire radiant field of influence that is emitted from a planet. A half of this radiant field is called the "moiety" of the planet.

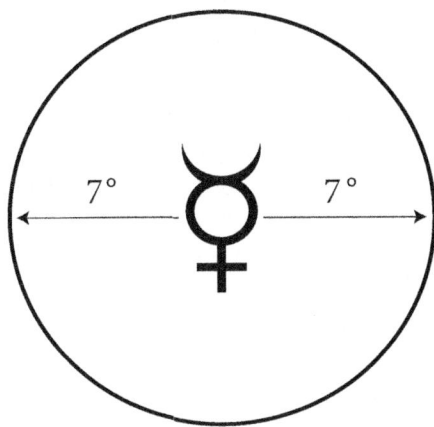

FIGURE 5: *Orb of Mercury*

Secondly, an orb can also be defined as the combined half-radiations of two planets. When two planets are within the range of their combined half-radiations, they are aware of each other's presence, and they can begin to communicate with each other. If two planets are not within the range of their half-radiations, they cannot interact with each other.

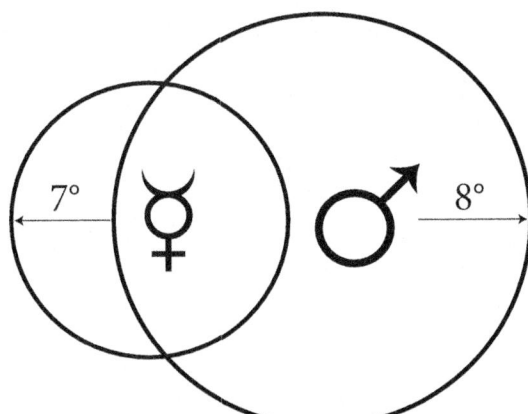

FIGURE 6: *Mercury & Mars within Orb of Each Other*

Planets have orbs. Aspects do not have orbs. Modern astrology incorrectly says that aspects have orbs. However, this is based on a misunderstanding of what an orb actually is. An orb is the radiation of a living body. Therefore, only things that have a living body can have an orb. "An aspect hath no orb, because an aspect hath no body" – said no one ever. Four hundred years ago, it was just assumed that no one would ever think that empty space could radiate an influence that was qualitatively different from another patch of empty space without actual planets involved.

An aspect is a distance between planets. The key players here are the planets, not the distance. The distance between two planets is created as a result of the living bodies of those planets themselves. Therefore, the distance is secondary to the planets who create it. An aspect can have no orb because empty space has no influence if it does not span the distance between a beginning point and a terminus.

In traditional astrology we do not say "a trine has a 10° orb" or "a square has an 8° orb." This would be absurd. There is no trine just floating around in empty space waiting for two planets to enter it. There are, however, the bodies of the planets that emit their radiations through space. Each planet extends its 60° hexagonal ray, its 90° tetragonal ray, its 120° trigonal ray, and its 180° diametrical ray. This is like a web of cosmic influence extending from the body of that planet outward into space.

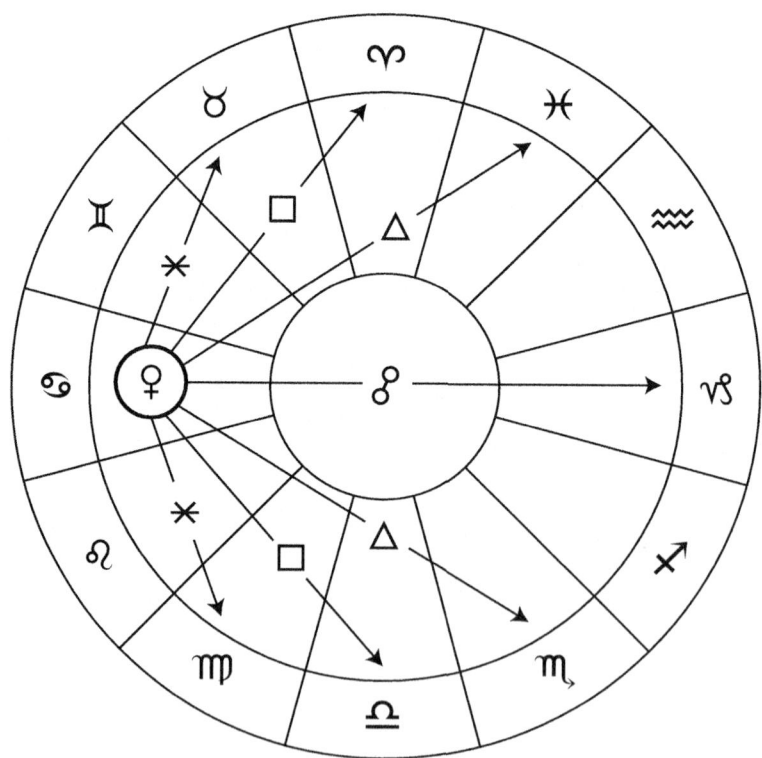

FIGURE 7: *Venus Extending Her Aspects through Space*

When other planets enter the necessary range for those rays to become active, those planets lock into a particular relationship. For example, if Venus moves into the appropriate range of Saturn's square ray, then Venus and Saturn will lock into a square aspect relationship. If Mercury moves into the appropriate range of Jupiter's trigonal ray, then Mercury and Jupiter will lock into a trine relationship. At all times, the planets carry and project their aspects. The aspects do not project the planets.

## THINGS THAT HATH NO ORBS

In the Renaissance, we see reference to the aspects as "radiations" and "rays." As mentioned before, these aspect radiations are from the bodies of the planets themselves and do not exist independent of them. This is why stellar factors such as the angles, the Part of Fortune, and the nodes – all of which do not actually have a physical body – "casteth no rays." While they have the ability to receive aspects and are very strongly impacted by them, they can't actually make an aspect to anything. The Ascendant of your radical chart will never aspect your Sun. The Sun will aspect your Ascendant. The North or South Node will never be conjunct Pluto; Pluto will be conjunct either the North or South Node. The Part of Fortune will never square Saturn. Saturn will square the Part of Fortune. In every case, the planet becomes the initiator of the aspect whereas the angles, the Part of Fortune, or the nodes are considered to be the termini of the aspect.

What if there is an aspect between the angles, the nodes, and the Part of Fortune? Whether this is standard practice or not, I've grown accustomed to viewing the angles as the immoveable framework within which the rest of the chart is built. Therefore, I would never say that the angles were aspecting anything else. I would say "Fortuna conjunct, sextile, square, trine, or opposite the Ascendant." And instead of saying Fortuna opposite the Ascendant, I'd say "Fortuna in the seventh house" or "Fortuna conjunct the seventh house cusp/Descendant." I'd also say "Fortuna conjunct or square the nodes," as opposed to "nodes square Fortuna."

The only aspects I take to the nodes are the conjunction and the square of any planet. I do not use sextiles or trines to the nodes. Neither would I use the quincunx. I wouldn't say "Venus is conjunct the North Node and opposite the South Node, therefore..." Neither would I ever say "Venus opposite the North or South Node." Since the nodes are always in an exact opposition to each other, it is a given that if something is conjunct the North Node it will be opposite the South Node. Therefore, the opposition to a node is inconsequential and is never worth mentioning. The conjunction to the nodes, however, is very important to note.

## THE ORBS OF THE PLANETS

The orb of a planet is the full diameter of that planet's radiation field. This is measured from the center of its body to the circumference of its radiant sphere. This means that if we were to place a planet in the middle of a circle which outlines its "field of influence," the orb of that planet extends from the center of its body to the circumference of its "aura" from side to side.

Abraham Ibn Ezra (circa 1089-1164) was an eminent twelfth century astrologer and Jewish biblical commentator. In *The Beginning of Wisdom*, Ibn Ezra gives us the following range of influence for the seven classical planets:

TABLE 1: *Orb of the Planets (Ibn Ezra)*

| PLANET | IBN EZRA |
|--------|----------|
| ♄ | 09° |
| ♃ | 09° |
| ♂ | 08° |
| ☉ | 15° |
| ♀ | 07° |
| ☿ | 07° |
| ☽ | 12° |

For Ibn Ezra, these degrees indicate how far forward and backward in space the planets project their influence. Therefore, though we use the term "orb" to indicate the full circumference or radiant field of a planet's influence, Ibn Ezra used similar language to refer to a half of that radiant field. This became the seed of much confusion in later centuries. Ibn Ezra's ranges of influence for the planets were only the echoed thoughts of the astrologers who came before him on this matter. Abū Maʿšar in his *Abbreviation to the Introduction*, writes:

> *...and so the Sun has 15° of his power in front of himself and the same amount behind himself. The Moon, 12° in front and the same amount behind. Saturn and Jupiter, 09° in front and the same amount behind. But Mars, 08° in front and the same amount behind. Finally, Venus and Mercury: 07° in front and the same amount behind.*

This, in my opinion, is wretchedly large as far as the orbs of planetary influence are concerned. This means that if the Sun is at 15° Leo, both a planet at 00° Leo and another at 29° Leo would still be in orb of a conjunction with the Sun.

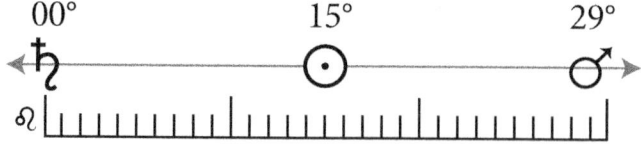

FIGURE 8: *Medieval Orb of the Sun*

We find the remnants of this train of thought coming all the way down to the sixteenth century, where French astrologer Claude Dariot (1533-1594) rehashes these ancient numbers. In *A Briefe and Most Easie Introduction to the Astrologicall Judgement of the Starres* (published in 1598), he outlines the orbs of each planet. And just to ensure that we are not mistaken as to what the implications of these orbs are, he writes:

> *For Saturn casteth his beams circularly, 09° forward, and so much backward, wherefore the half diameter of his radial circle containeth*

*09°, and the whole diameter 18°. The radial circle of Jupiter is of the same quantity and bigness. But the circle of Mars containeth in his diameter only 16°, which is 08° for his half. The Sun casteth his beams in compass 15° upon every part, which maketh the whole diameter of his circle [to] contain 30°, and the one half 15°. Venus and Mercury cast their circular beams 07° every way in length, so their whole diameter is 14°. Finally, the Moon sendeth forth her beams on every side 12° for the half of the diameter, and the whole containeth 24°.*

He ends on a more sober note, saying that the half of the half-diameter of the planetary orbs can be taken as the range of their influence. Therefore, Saturn, though projecting 09° in every direction, would be allowed a half of his diameter as his range of influence if he were in aspect with another planet. The same would be true for the other planet. Instead of his 09°, Saturn would now be given a modest 04° 30' by which to be in aspect with another planet. He referred to this as the "moiety of the half diameter of the circle radiant of Saturn." We'll discuss more about this word "moiety" in the next section.

By the seventeenth century, what Dariot considered to be the half diameter of the complete orb of the planets evolved into the actual complete orb of the planets. Saturn no longer was considered to have a complete orb of 18° with a half diameter of 09°. For many of the notable seventeenth century astrologers, the complete orb of Saturn was 09°. Therefore, Saturn's moiety was thought to be a very reasonable 04° 30'.

In Henry Coley's *Clavis Astrologiae Elimata* (1676), he lists the following as the orbs of the planets:

TABLE 2: *Orb of the Planets (Coley)*

| PLANET | COLEY |
|--------|-------|
| ♄ | 09° |
| ♃ | 09° |
| ♂ | 07° |
| ☉ | 15° |
| ♀ | 07° |
| ☿ | 07° |
| ☽ | 12° |

This is far more reasonable, and more within keeping with how I practice astrology. The more refined orbs of the Renaissance allow for tighter and more potent connections between planets. If you would like to stay true to a traditional astrology orb limit for the planets, I'd suggest you use the orbs outlined by Coley above.

The orbs seem to be based on the bodies of the planets. The larger the planet, the bigger the orb. The Moon, which we know is clearly not bigger than Saturn or Jupiter, is given a larger orb because she is that much closer to Earth. She is also the only stellar body that can rival the disk of the Sun in size from our Earth-based perspective.

Clearly, Uranus, Neptune, and Pluto weren't given orbs by astrologers in the seventeenth century. However, since we do use them so consistently within our astrological practice, it is only fair to afford them some influence in traditional terms. I suggest that we give them an orb of 5°-7°, since their power is far more impactful at a closer range.

## A Modern Dilemma Between Traditionalists

There are those who would argue that my understanding of this doctrine concerning the orbs of the planets is incorrect; that the orbs of the Renaissance are exactly the same as the orbs of the Medieval period, and that the only difference is the language used to describe them. I highly and emphatically disagree.

In William Ramesey's *Astrologia Restaurata* (1653), he gives the following example when describing the separation of two planets.

> *Separation is, where two Planets have been either in Partile Conjunction or aspect, and are going from it; as if Saturn be in 8 degrees of Aries, and Jupiter in 9; here Jupiter is separated one degree from the Partile Conjunction, yet he shall not be said to be totally separated till he be the full half orb of Jupiter, and his own half orb distant from him; for every Planet both in Conjunction and Aspect is admitted his half orb and the half orb of the other Planet joined unto him; as the half orb of Saturn you have heard is 4 degrees 30 minutes, and so likewise Jupiter, the which being added together make 9 whole degrees; and therefore till Jupiter be thus many degrees elongated or separated from Saturn, he shall not be said to be fully separated, neither shall their signification be ineffectual for that time; understand the same of an aspect still admitting or allowing the half orbs of both Planets.*

Ramesey's point is more than sufficiently clear. The half orb of Saturn is 4° 30'. Though in his outline of the significations of each planet, he uses the same Medieval orbs to radiate "before and after any aspect," his above example of the separation of two planets paints a very different picture of what he practiced. Ramesey's example is distinctly different from Dariot's understanding. Dariot states:

> *For Saturn casteth his beams circularly, 09° forward, and so much backward, wherefore the half diameter of his radial circle containeth 09°, and the whole diameter 18°.*

It is very evident that in the interval of time between these two authors, another understanding of the orbs of the planets emerged.

This isn't to say that every seventeenth century astrologer was of the opinion of William Ramesey on this matter. Richard Saunders was a medical astrologer who practiced during that period. He wrote a text entitled *The Astrological Judg-*

*ment and Practice of Physick* (1677). In it, he outlines several sublevels of aspect combinations that have largely fallen into disuse. However, he echoes the sentiments of Dariot and the Medieval astrologers before him. In describing platick aspects, he writes:

> *The Platick Aspect is, when two Planets or more do differ from a perfect Aspect, more than the Semidiameter of either of them, yet so that this distance doth not exceed the sum of both their Semidiameters; as if Saturn were in the 7th degree of Aries, and Mars in the 20th of the same Sign, here should be a Conjunction Platick between Saturn and Mars, because the distance they differ from a true Aspect is 13 Degrees, which is more than the Diameter of either of them, and yet less than the sum of both their Semidiameters: and this Aspect is of the least effect of all the rest, because they do not behold each other from their Centre, but by Contaction of Beams.*

He then goes on to outline the semi-radiant circles of the planets – in other words, their moieties.

TABLE 3: *Semi-Radiant Circles of the Planets (Saunders)*

| PLANET | SAUNDERS |
|--------|----------|
| ♄ | 09° |
| ♃ | 09° |
| ♂ | 08° |
| ☉ | 15° |
| ♀ | 07° |
| ☿ | 06° |
| ☽ | 12° |

John Gadbury on the other hand – one of the most notable seventeenth century astrologers – follows in the spirit of Ramesey by using the "modern" understanding of the orbs of the planets. The "orb" within the astrology of Ramesey and Gadbury is distinctly different from the "semi-radiant circle" or "moiety" of Saunders listed above. Gadbury writes:

> *Here you see that Saturn's Orbs are 10°, the mediety [moiety] of which are five; and Mars his Orbs are 7° 30' the half of which are 3°45'; whence it results, that the Platique Aspect of Saturn and Mars remains until they are 8° 45' distant from their true aspect.*

TABLE 4: *Orb of the Planets (Ramesey & Gadbury)*

| PLANET | RAMESEY | GADBURY |
|--------|---------|---------|
| ♄ | 09° | 10° |
| ♃ | 09° | 12° |
| ♂ | 07° | 07° 30' |
| ☉ | 15° | 17° |
| ♀ | 07° | 08° |
| ☿ | 07° | 07° |
| ☽ | 12° | 12° 30' |

He further clarifies what is meant by the "orb" and "moiety" of the planets in his definition of "separation." He writes:

> Now Separation, as it hath a beginning, so it hath a time of continuance and ending. It continues all the time the Planets are within Orbs; and ends when they are past them. To know which artificially, do thus: Get the moiety of each Planet's Orb, and add them together; and the sum tells you how long it is before they be fully separated: as in the example of the Sun and Moon: the Orbs of the Sun by the foregoing Table, are 17°, half of which, is 8° 30'. The Moon's Orbs are 12° 30', half of which is 6° 15' which added to 8° 30' (the half of the Sun's Orbs) the sum is 14° 45' and so many degrees and minutes must the Moon recede from the Sun, before she can be said to be fully separated from him. Now the Sun and Moon being in 10° 10' of Aquarius, if you add 14° 45' thereunto, it tells you, that until the Moon have passed the 24° 55' of Aquarius, she cannot be said to be beyond the Orbs of the Sun.

I cannot imagine more straightforward examples than those outlined above. In the astrology of both Ramesey and Gadbury – two highly influential and prominent astrologers of the seventeenth century – we see clear evidence that their conception of the orbs of the planets differs tremendously from the orbs commonly agreed upon by Medieval astrologers.

In a universe other than the one that we inhabit, if indeed we were to still use the Medieval orbs of the planets – which, hopefully, we do not – this would take us back to the ridiculous circumstances that would allow any planet within 15° of the Sun to be in a conjunction with the Sun, as depicted in FIGURE 8. This would also mean that if Saturn were at 05° Gemini and Mars were at 20° of Gemini, they would still be within the allowable orb of a conjunction because their combined Medieval moieties allow them to continue to have an effectual relation if they are within 17° of one another. I do not know a single colleague of mine who would consider Mars and Saturn to be in a conjunction if there were a 17° orb between them. I know I wouldn't – regardless of what the ancients did.

MOIETY OF THE PLANETS

> *A platique aspect is when two planets behold each other within the moiety of their orbs.* – HENRY COLEY

Moiety means "each of two parts into which a thing is or can be divided." The moiety refers to one half of the orb of the planets.

TABLE 5: *Orbs & Moieties of the Planets*

| PLANET | ORB | MOIETY |
|--------|-----|--------|
| ♄ | 09° | 4.5° |
| ♃ | 09° | 4.5° |
| ♂ | 07° | 3.5° |
| ☉ | 15° | 7.5° |
| ♀ | 07° | 3.5° |
| ☿ | 07° | 3.5° |
| ☽ | 12° | 06° |

With this as our basis, now we can speak about the allowable orb between the planets.

The allowable orb between planets is the sum total of their moieties. The allowable orb or distance between Venus and Saturn would be:

4.5° (SATURN'S MOIETY) + 3.5° (VENUS'S MOIETY) = 8°

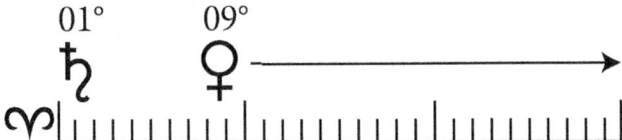

FIGURE 9: *Venus Applying to a Bodily Conjunction with Saturn*

Venus and Saturn can be a maximum of 8° of arc from making a perfect aspect and still be within the allowable orb of that aspect. If Venus is at 1° Aries and Saturn is at 9° Aries, the two of them are within their 8° allowable orb. In our example, Venus is in an applying conjunction to Saturn.

FIGURE 10: *Venus Separating from a Bodily Conjunction with Saturn*

If Venus is at 9° Aries and Saturn is at 1° Aries, they are in a separating conjunction within an 8° orb.

This rule would also apply if the two planets were in a sextile, square, trine, or opposition. When a faster moving planet is either applying to or separating from an aspect with a slower moving planet within their allowable orb, those two planets are considered to be in aspect with each other. It is more common to find a chart containing platick aspects than to find a chart primarily consisting of partile aspects. This is why it is important for us to know what the allowable orb is for any combination of planets.

I have simplified the orbs and moieties for my students. I have done this by using a scale of hot, hotter, and hottest. If planets are 05°-07° degrees apart they are in the hot range. They are still within a valid aspect combination and are still close by most traditional standards. However, they are on the verge of being too far apart for our consideration. If planets are 03°-05° degrees apart they are in the hotter range, and are close enough to be powerfully felt. If planets are 00°-03° apart, they are in the hottest range and are in a tight aspect with each other.

TABLE 6: *Acceptable Orbs for Modern Practice*

| HOT | 05°-07° | STRONG |
|---|---|---|
| HOTTER | 03°-05° | STRONGER |
| HOTTEST | 00°-03° | STRONGEST |

As a traditional astrologer who also practices Uranian astrology, I am accustomed to using very tight orbs within my astrological practice. Though the above-mentioned orbs may be considered to be too restrictive for other traditional astrologers, this is the system I teach to my students.

If we take the planet with the largest moiety (the Sun) and add it to the smallest moiety (Venus or Mercury for example) we would get:

7.5° (SUN'S MOIETY) + 3.5° (MERCURY'S MOIETY) = AN 11° ORB

If we take the sum of the smallest moieties, we would get:

3.5° (VENUS) + 3.5° (MERCURY) = 07° ORB

The orb that I use is only as large as the smallest moiety based on seventeenth century standards. I believe that tight is right. The tighter the orb, the stronger the aspect. If you are just learning astrology, I strongly suggest you use this measurement of "hot, hotter, and hottest" as a guide for judging the strength of aspects.

## WHICH PLANETS CAN ASPECT WHICH OTHER PLANETS?

Faster moving planets aspect slower moving planets. The Chaldean Order is organized from the slowest moving planet (Saturn) to the fastest moving planet (Moon). If we include the three modern planets, the planets from slowest to fastest moving would be: Pluto, Neptune, Uranus, Saturn, Jupiter, Mars, Sun, Venus, Mercury, and the Moon. The diagram below shows us which planets can aspect other planets based on their orbital speed.

FIGURE 11: *Planets that Aspect Each Other*

## WHEN SLOWER MOVING PLANETS ASPECT FASTER MOVING PLANETS

John Gadbury states that there are three ways in which planets can apply to each other. He writes:

> *First, when two Planets (being both direct in motion, but the one a more light and swift Planet than the other) do apply... Secondly, when both Planets are Retrograde... Thirdly when one Planet is Direct in Motion, and the other Retrograde... Note also, that the superior Planets are never said to apply unto any (unless they are Retrograde), but the lesser or inferior (as it is among men) make application unto them.*

The superior planets are the planets that are above the sphere of the Sun in the Chaldean Order. These planets are Saturn, Jupiter, and Mars. The inferior planets are the planets that are below the sphere of the Sun in the Chaldean Order. These planets are Venus, Mercury, and the Moon. In general, any planet that is inferior to another planet will aspect that other planet.

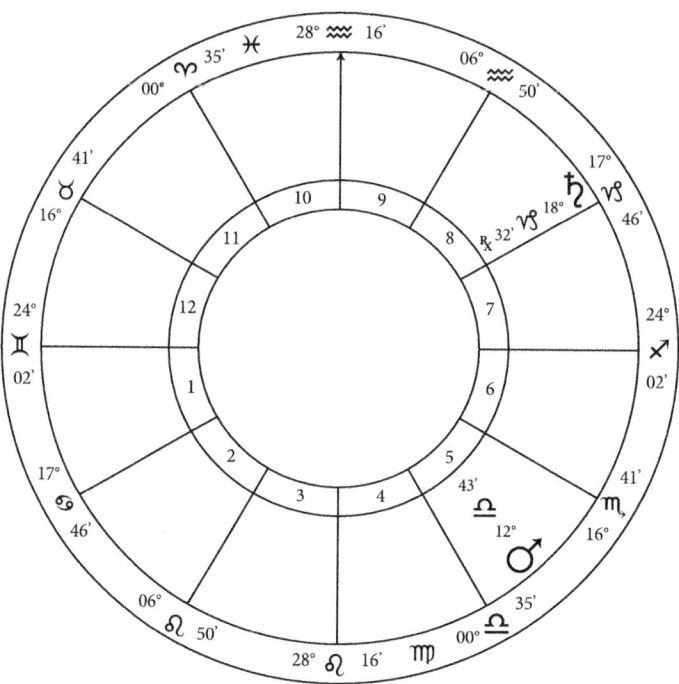

FIGURE 12: *Saturn Applying to Mars by Retrograde Motion*

When a slower moving planet is retrograde, it can aspect a faster moving planet. For example, Saturn 18° Capricorn, RX., can – through his retrograde motion – apply to the square of Mars at 12° Libra. Since Mars in this example is direct, he is applying to Saturn. Since Saturn is retrograde, he is applying to Mars. They are mutually applying to each other. While we could very well say "Mars is applying to the square of Saturn," we could also say "Saturn is applying to the square of Mars through his retrograde motion" or "both Mars and Saturn retrograde are mutually applying to the square of each other." All of these variations would be correct. In the case of Saturn applying to Mars, we would need to indicate that Saturn is applying to Mars through his retrograde motion. Otherwise, it would be inadequate to say that Saturn is applying to Mars, since we know that generally speaking, slower moving planets do not apply to faster moving planets. Faster moving planets apply to slower moving planets.

## HOW MANY ASPECTS ARE THERE?

Traditionally speaking there are only four aspects.

TABLE 7: *Arc Openings of Traditional Aspects*

| SEXTILE | 60° | ✳ |
|---|---|---|
| SQUARE | 90° | ▢ |
| TRINE | 120° | △ |
| OPPOSITION | 180° | ☍ |

Though there are only four aspects, three of them can be projected either forward or backward in the zodiac. This means that each planet projects from its body a forward sextile and a backward sextile, a forward square and a backward square, a forward trine and a backward trine. Aspects projected forward in the zodiac are known as "sinister aspects." Aspects projected backward in the zodiac are called "dexter aspects." By "forward in the zodiac" I mean aspects that follow the natural direction of the zodiac signs. Aspects projected backward in the zodiac go against the natural direction of the zodiac signs. Therefore, there are really seven aspects in traditional astrology.

1. Dexter sextile
2. Sinister sextile
3. Dexter square
4. Sinister square
5. Dexter trine
6. Sinister trine
7. Opposition

If the Sun in Aries aspected Saturn in Gemini, the Sun would have to cast his rays forward in the zodiac in order to make that aspect occur. This is a sinister aspect. A sinister aspect occurs when a faster moving planet aspects a slower moving planet that is ahead of it in the zodiac. In our example, the Sun is the faster moving planet and Saturn is the slower moving planet.

When saying the signs of the zodiac, we say "Aries, Taurus, Gemini." I often tell my students to think about sinister aspects as if Planet A were sneaking up on Planet B from behind. In this case the Sun is behind Saturn in the zodiac. Therefore, the Sun is creeping up on Saturn and about to catch him completely unaware; a very "sinister" thing to do.

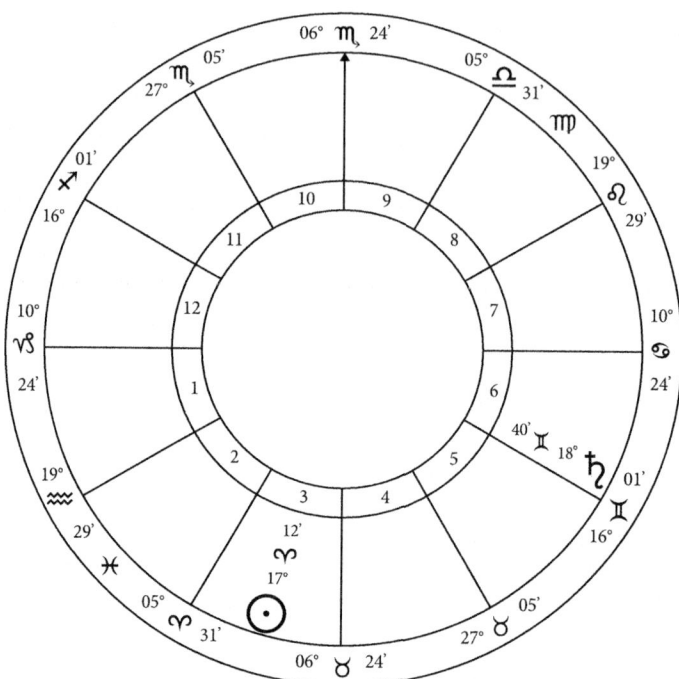

FIGURE 13: *Sinister Sextile*

If the Sun were in Aries and Saturn were in Aquarius, the Sun would have to muster all his power to cast his rays backward in the zodiac to aspect Saturn. This is a dexter aspect. A dexter aspect occurs when a faster moving planet aspects a slower moving planet that is behind it in the zodiac. In our example above, the Sun is the faster moving planet and Saturn is the slower moving planet.

When saying the signs of the zodiac, we don't say "Aries, Pisces, Aquarius." It takes more cognitive effort to recite the signs of the zodiac in reverse order. It also takes greater planetary effort for a planet to cast its rays backward in the zodiac. It is easier for planets to aspect other planets that are in the front of them. It's a bit more effortful for planets to aspect planets behind them. This is why when a planet aspects another planet behind itself in the zodiac, like our Sun in Aries aspecting Saturn in Aquarius, it is thought of as being a stronger and more forceful aspect relationship. William Lilly writes:

> *Observe the dexter aspect is more forcible than the sinister... dexter aspects are contrary to the succession of signs, sinister in order as they follow one another.*

Rolling a boulder downhill is less of an accomplishment than rolling a boulder uphill. Therefore, rolling the boulder uphill and actually accomplishing that task is more noteworthy. It requires more effort and is a stronger demonstration of power. Similarly, dexter aspects are said to be stronger in nature because of the increased effort associated with their creation.

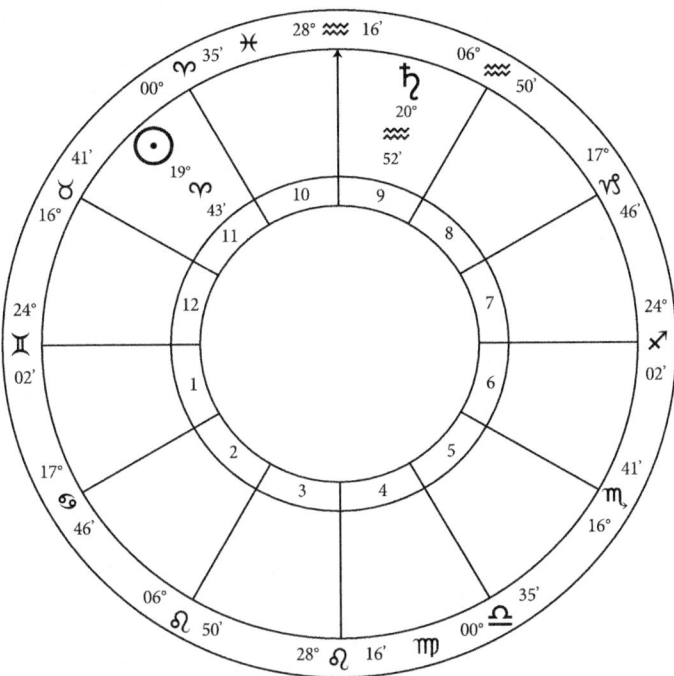

FIGURE 14: *Dexter Sextile*

All the aspects have a dexter and sinister counterpart except for the opposition. No matter which way a planet casts its 180° radiation in the zodiac, forward or back, it will still end up landing in the same degree of the same sign. From 18° Aries, the dexter opposition would be 18° Libra. From 18° Aries, the sinister opposition would be 18° Libra. No matter if we are going forward or backward in the zodiac, the opposition of Aries will always be Libra, the opposition of Taurus will always be Scorpio, the opposition of Gemini will always be Sagittarius, the opposition of Cancer will always be Capricorn, the opposition of Leo will always be Aquarius, and the opposition of Virgo will always be Pisces. We don't speak about "dexter or sinister oppositions," and no one ever has. We just say "opposition."

REVISITING THE THEMA MUNDI

Every aspect is of the nature of the planet that creates that aspect to the luminaries in the Thema Mundi.

TABLE 8: *Planetary Nature of the Aspects*

| GLYPH | ASPECT | QUALITY | ARC OPENING | NATURE |
|-------|--------|---------|-------------|--------|
| ☍ | OPPOSITION | MALEFIC | 180° | ♄ |
| △ | TRINE | BENEFIC | 120° | ♃ |
| □ | SQUARE | MALEFIC | 90° | ♂ |
| ✳ | SEXTILE | BENEFIC | 60° | ♀ |
| ⚻ | QUINCUNX | MALEFIC | 150° | - |

ASPECT HARMONICS

Today, many astrologers employ many more aspects than those utilized by the ancients. These aspects are all based on the division of the 360° of the zodiac by a number from which we can derive equal subdivisions. These equal subdivisions are called "harmonics." Harmonics refer to the number by which we divide the zodiac and the family of aspects that we derive based on that division.

TABLE 9: *Harmonics*

| HARMONIC | DEGREE | ASPECTS |
|----------|--------|---------|
| FIRST | 360° | conjunctions |
| SECOND | 180° | oppositions |
| THIRD | 120° | trines |
| FOURTH | 90° | squares |
| FIFTH | 72° | quintiles, bi-quintiles |
| SIXTH | 60° | sextiles, trines |
| SEVENTH | 51.42° | septiles, bi-septiles, tri-septiles |
| EIGHTH | 45° | semisquares, sesquiquadrates |
| NINTH | 40° | noviles, bi-noviles, quadra-noviles |
| TENTH | 36° | deciles, bi-deciles, tri-deciles |

The conjunction is a part of every harmonic. This is because a conjunction has no arc opening. A true corporal conjunction has an angular distance of 00°. In the same way as the number zero can be said to belong to every family of numbers, the conjunction also belongs to every family of aspects.

## ON CONJUNCTIONS

*There is no doubt that the strength of a conjunction is greater than that
of an aspect.* – ABRAHAM IBN EZRA

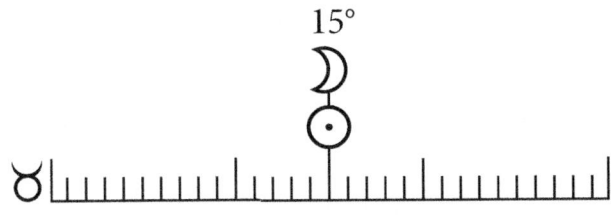

FIGURE 15: *Corporal (Bodily) Conjunction*

As we have learnt, a conjunction is not an aspect. An aspect is the angular relationship between two or more celestial factors. In a true conjunction, there is
no angular relationship between planets, because in a conjunction the planets in
question are essentially "on top" of one another in zodiacal longitude. The word
"conjunction" means a "coming together." When speaking about conjunctions, we
are usually referring to planets coming together to form a "bodily" or "corporal/
corporeal" conjunction. This means that the two planets are occupying the same
degree of the same sign with their physical bodies. They have physically conjoined
and there is no arc opening between them.

### EVERY ASPECT IS A CONJUNCTION

Even though the conjunction is not an aspect, every aspect is a conjunction. A
conjunction is the coming together of two or more planets to form a relationship.
This relationship links those two planets in their universal significations as well as
in the things those planets specifically signify within the chart. When two planets
come together to form an aspect, they are forming a "conjunction by aspect." This
is different than when they form "a bodily conjunction." Thus, two planets can
form a conjunction by sextile, a conjunction by square, a conjunction by trine, and
a conjunction by opposition. All of these represent conjunctions by aspect as opposed to a conjunction by body.

The distinction between conjunctions and aspects is a well-established component of traditional astrology. However, since at least the Middle Ages, astrologers
have conceded that though conjunctions can't rightfully be called aspects, in writing about aspects, the conjunction should be listed amongst them.

### OTHER TYPES OF ASPECT RELATIONSHIPS

Beyond the seven traditional aspects and the conjunction, there are other planetary relationship that are significant in my style of chart delineation. These are
antiscia/contra-antiscia and parallels/contra-parallels.

ANTISCIA

Antiscia (an-tish-uh) refer to reflection points on either side of the Cancer/Capricorn axis. The singular of antiscia is "antiscion" (an-tish-uhn). If we were to draw a line vertically from 00° Cancer to 00° Capricorn, it would divide the zodiac into two halves containing six signs each.

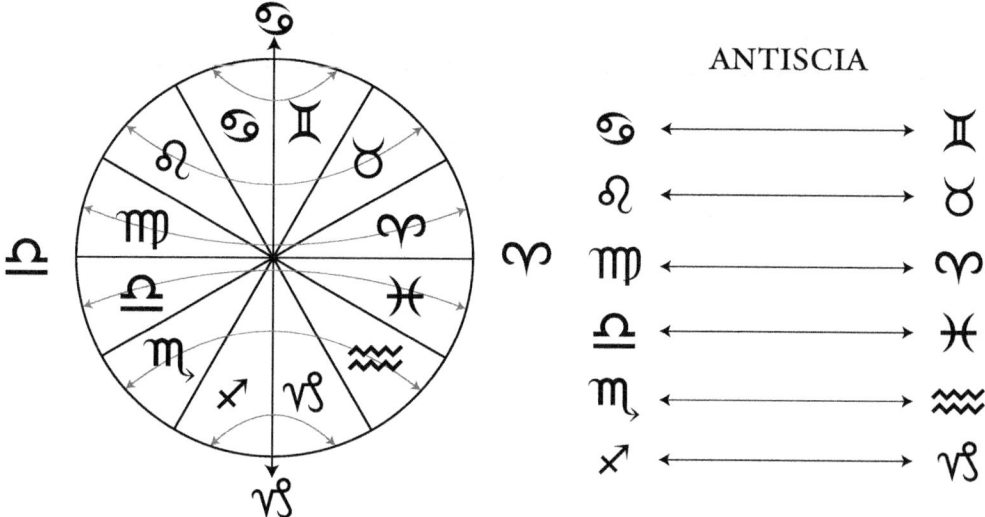

FIGURE 16: *Antiscia*

Therefore, if a planet is in Libra and another is in Pisces, those two planets inhabit signs that have an antiscia-based relationship.

However, to be in signs that are each other's antiscion isn't sufficient. There must also be exactitude by degree. All signs of the zodiac have 30°. The antiscion degree of a planet will be the degree that – when added to the degree of the planet in question – will equal 30°. It's quite a simple technique.

TABLE 9: *Corresponding Degrees by Antiscia/Contra-Antiscia*

| 29° → 01° | 24° → 06° | 19° → 11° |
|---|---|---|
| 28° → 02° | 23° → 07° | 18° → 12° |
| 27° → 03° | 22° → 08° | 17° → 13° |
| 26° → 04° | 21° → 09° | 16° → 14° |
| 25° → 05° | 20° → 10° | 15° → 15° |

For example, we already know that the antiscion sign of Gemini is Cancer. If we have Mars at 04° Gemini, what will his antiscion be? Sometimes students will say that 04° Gemini has its antiscion at 04° Cancer. This is incorrect. 04° + 04°

does not equal 30°. We have to find what number completes the number thirty if we add it to the degree of the planet in question. In this case, the planet is Mars at 04° Gemini. What number completes the number four on the pathway of thirty? Twenty-six. Therefore, the antiscion of Mars at 04° Gemini is 26° Cancer.

Let's say we have the Sun at 19° Sagittarius. We know that the antiscion sign of Sagittarius is Capricorn. Therefore, the only thing we need to figure out is what degree reflects the number nineteen on the pathway to thirty. The answer is definitely not 19° because 19° + 19° = 38°. What number can we add to nineteen that would give us the number thirty? Eleven. Eleven is the only number we can add to nineteen to give us the number thirty. Therefore, the antiscion of the Sun at 19° Sagittarius is 11° Capricorn.

In traditional astrology, we believe that antiscia operate like conjunctions. We would interpret the conjunction of two planets in the same way we would interpret them occupying each other's antiscion.

Antiscia represent very sensitive and important relationships between planets. In determining whether a planet is occupying the antiscion of another, I suggest using only a 01° orb.

## CONTRA-ANTISCIA

Contra-antiscia are another important type of planetary relationships. They work in the same way as antiscia, with one exception. Instead of using the Cancer/Capricorn axis as our reflection plane, we use the Aries/Libra axis.

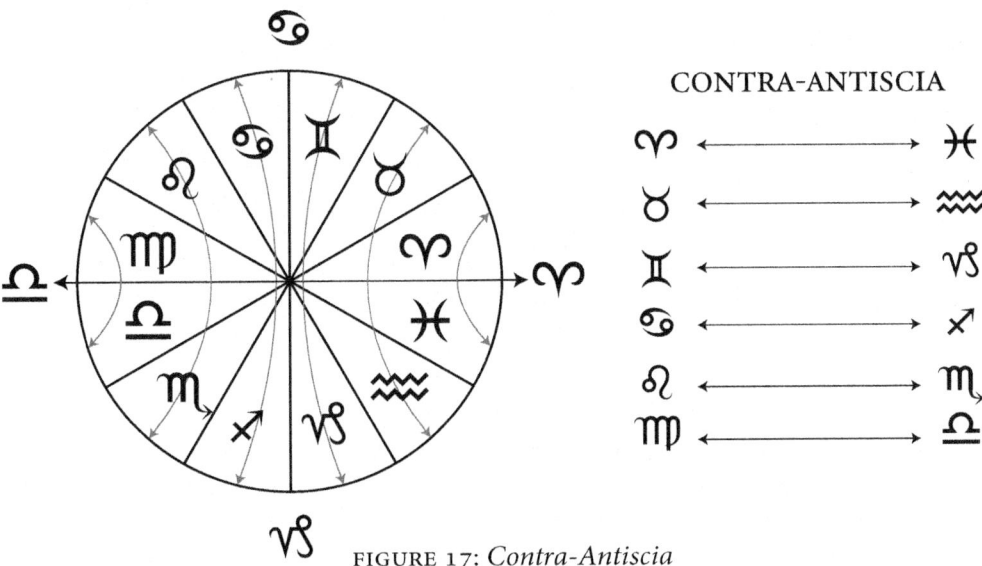

FIGURE 17: *Contra-Antiscia*

The reflective degrees are the same as those used for antiscia. 29° reflects 01°, 28° reflects 02°, and so on.

For example, suppose we are looking for the contra-antiscion of Venus at 13° Scorpio. The contra-antiscion of Scorpio is Leo. The number that gives us thirty when added to 13° is seventeen. Therefore, the contra-antiscion of Venus at 13° Scorpio is 17° Leo.

If you've already memorized the antiscia signs, you don't need to memorize the contra-antiscia. The contra-antiscion of any sign will be the opposite of its antiscia sign. The antiscion of Cancer is Gemini. Therefore, the contra-antiscion of Cancer will be Sagittarius. Sagittarius is the opposite sign of Gemini; therefore, it must be the contra-antiscion sign of Cancer.

In traditional astrology, we believe that contra-antiscia operate like oppositions. Therefore, whatever we would say about the opposition aspect can be applied to two or more planets in a contra-antiscion relationship.

## ON DECLINATION

Declination refers to measurement North or South of the celestial equator. We will recall that the celestial equator is the great circle that divides the celestial sphere into a Northern celestial hemisphere and a Southern celestial hemisphere. Just as the latitude lines on the Earth allow us to measure terrestrial locations that are North or South of the terrestrial Equator, declination provides us a means of measuring stellar bodies that are North or South of the celestial equator.

## OUT OF BOUNDS PLANETS

From our Earth-based perspective, the Sun can only attain a maximum distance of approximately 23.5° North or South of the celestial equator. Therefore, the path of the Sun defines a set boundary in relation to the celestial equator that is relatively unchanging. Planets that are further North or South of this set boundary of 23.5° are "out of bounds." They are beyond the boundary of the Sun's highest and lowest declination.

## DECLINATION – ASTROLOGY'S HIDDEN TREASURE

The value of declination in twenty-first century astrology has been underestimated. As recently as the early twentieth century, observing declination relationships between planets was still a staple of Western astrology. However, this practice slowly fell into disuse.

In astrology, the aspects formed by planets sharing the same declination are called "parallels." When two planets are on the same side of the celestial equator and also share the same degree of declination, they are in a parallel relationship. When two planets are on opposite sides of the celestial equator and share the same degree of declination, they are in a contra-parallel relationship.

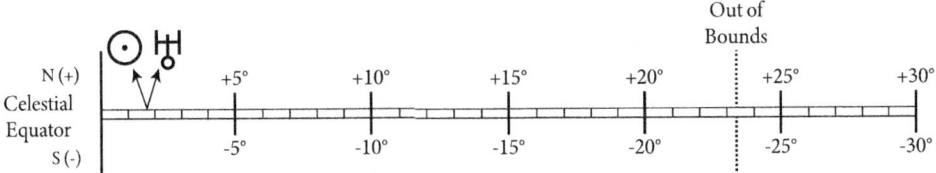

FIGURE 18: *Parallel of Declination*

If the Sun and Uranus are on the Northern side of the celestial equator, they both have Northern declination. If the Sun and Uranus are both at 01° North 47', then they are parallel one another.

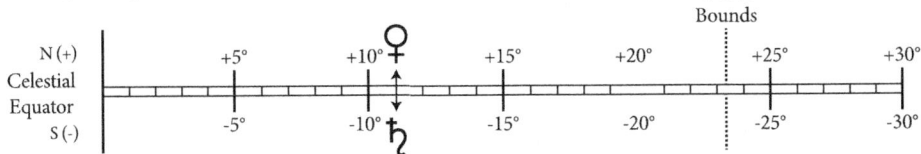

FIGURE 19: *Contra-Parallel of Declination*

If Venus is on the Northern side of the celestial equator, she has Northern declination. If Saturn is on the Southern side of the celestial equator, he has Southern declination. If Venus is at 11° North 00' declination and Saturn is at 11° South 00' declination, then Venus and Saturn are contra-parallel one another.

Parallels and contra-parallels are as strong as any of the regular traditional aspects. They are, in fact, as strong as the strongest traditional aspects, which are: the conjunction, the square, and the opposition. In general, most astrologers consider parallels to be equivalent to conjunctions, whereas contra-parallels are equivalent to oppositions. We wouldn't ignore conjunctions and oppositions in astrology. Neither should we ignore parallels and contra-parallels of declination.

Like antiscia and contra-antiscia, I only use a 01° orb for parallels and contra-parallels. Like most aspect relationships in astrology, the tighter the orb, the more evident the impact. We have found that when planets share a tight orb in declination, those planets work together, either positively or negatively, based on the nature of those planets and what they universally signify.

Reinhold Ebertin (1901-1988) was a German astrologer, who founded the school of Cosmobiology. His most important astrological book is undoubtedly *Combinations of Stellar Influences*, also known as COSI (1972). In my opinion, COSI provides the clearest path for understanding the meaning of various planetary combinations. It is the only text I use when teaching students how to interpret the universal significations of planets that are in an antiscia, contra-antiscia, parallel, or contra-parallel relationship within the context of natal astrology. Therefore, a parallel of the Sun and Uranus would be interpreted in COSI as:

> (+) *Originality, consciousness and concentration upon an objective or aim, a far-seeing mind, love of freedom, tendency to strive for reforms, mobility.*

A Venus/Saturn contra-parallel could be interpreted as:

> (-) *Emotional inhibitions, the state of being unsatisfied, hardhearted, an unhealthy expression of the sex urge, self-torment, jealousy.*

When interpreting planets purely through their universal significations, what those planets represent as specific significators within a chart tends to not be important. Similarly, when interpreting planets purely through their specific significations as house rulers, what those planets represent as universal significators is of no relevance.

This completes our chapter on the aspects. Aspects represent one of the most important parts of traditional astrology and should be thoroughly understood by students who desire to be masters within this field. In the beginning, they represent very black and white qualities of planetary interaction. However, as we progress, our understanding of the aspects becomes more nuanced. The more refined our practice becomes, the less we see the astrological world in terms of good aspects or bad aspects. While the doctrine of "good aspect" vs. "bad aspect" is an important one for beginner students to learn, it isn't where this topic ends.

## CHAPTER 10 QUESTIONS

1. What is an aspect?
2. Why are aspects so important in traditional astrology?
3. What is the difference between an applying and a separating aspect?
4. Define "orb."
5. Define "moiety."
6. What is the key difference between the orbs used in the Medieval period vs. what were used in the Renaissance.
7. What are the seven aspects of traditional astrology.
8. Why is the conjunction not an aspect, even though every aspect is a conjunction?

CHAPTER 11 OBJECTIVES

* Identify the importance of the Moon within traditional astrology.
* Define the term "tidal locking."
* Understand the difference between the sidereal and solar month.
* Learn the various arc openings between the luminaries for each of the eight lunar phases.
* Explore the use of the eighth harmonic aspects within traditional medical astrology.
* Learn about the critical role the Moon played in traditional medical astrology timing techniques.

# Chapter 11

## Lunar Cycles

*There is one glory of the sun, and another glory of the moon, and another glory of the stars: for one star differeth from another star in glory. So also is the resurrection of the dead. It is sown in corruption; it is raised in incorruption.* – 1 CORINTHIANS 15:41-42

ASTROLOGY IN THE WEST HAS BECOME a distinctly solar subject. Even alleged teachers and practitioners of traditional astrology find themselves engaged in in-depth discussions about the Sun signs of people; as if the Sun sign could actually begin to provide an explanation as to why two people – born in the same astrological month – may choose the same profession in life. The over-emphasis on Sun sign astrology has led us into a veritable form of Sun-worship, and a glorification of all that the Sun God represents – the ego, the self, and the frail victory won by the individual "I" over the larger sphere of Nature from which it originated.

Though the Sun expresses changeability based on the annual ebb and flow of his power, his face is ever the same: ever brilliant, ever beaming, eternally in the morning of his life. Even the revolution of the Sun expresses the ideas of consistency and permanence. Guido Bonatti writes:

> *Moreover, his motion is practically uniform, and is not varied nor altered, but always keeps the same similar advancement annually. And his motion is most noble above the motions of the other planets, nor does he go retrograde like the others go retrograde.*

On an esoteric level, the apparent everlastingness of the Sun leads us inward towards deeper truths about the immortality of our indwelling spirit. However, it doesn't reflect the relentless variability of our earthly bodies, the nontangible emotional tides that so greatly affect us, or the daily oscillations of this physical world in which we "live, breathe, and have our being." In order for us to contemplate the wild forces that govern growth and decay within our material universe, we must turn our attention away from the fixed certainty of the Sun, and towards the fluctuating face of the Moon.

Of the seven planets in the Chaldean Order, our astrological forebears thought the Moon was most analogous to us. This was due both to her proximity to the Earth, as well as to the alterations she demonstrates through her constantly changing shape. This incessant metamorphosis was thought to mirror the transiting of our earthly existence through the four life stages of generation, preservation, corruption, and destruction. Ibn Ezra writes:

*She has rulership over the whole body because in her light she is like*
*the light of man that grows until a prescribed time and then diminishes.*

Ibn Ezra associated the Moon with our humanity because she represents the cyclical principles of what Aristotle defined as "coming-to-be and passing-away." The relationship between the Moon and human mortality was held even by astrologers more ancient than Ibn Ezra. Manilius writes:

*...[She] reflects human mortality in the dying edges of her face.*

In the Qabalistic Tarot, the esoteric title for The Moon card is *The Ruler of Flux and Reflux: Child of the Sons of the Mighty*. This title represents the deep lunar truth that despite the apparent firmness of things, impermanence is the organizing principle that serves as the nucleus of our material world.

One of the most dramatic astronomical displays of the principle of impermanence is the eightfold lunar cycle. Monthly, the Moon passes through periods of waxing and waning, assuming eight very distinct relationships with the Sun. When the Moon is waxing, the illumination of her visible surface increases. When waning, her illumination decreases. Though rich in mythological meaning, the eightfold lunar cycle is wholly dependent upon specific hard aspect relationships between the Sun and Moon.

Though the Moon is considered to be a luminary in traditional astrology, she does not produce her own light. The Moon, like all the planets in our solar system, reflects the light of the Sun, just as a mirror reflects what it is facing. The various shapes we associate with the Moon are due to how much of her Earth-facing surface is illuminated by solar light at any point in time.

## Tidal Locking

I refer to the Moon's "Earth-facing surface" because we have only ever seen one half of the Moon in the sky – and it has always been the same half. This is because the Earth and Moon are in synchronous rotation. Synchronous rotation can be compared to two dancers spiraling around each other, while always facing one another. Synchronous rotation is more commonly known as "tidal locking." Tidal locking occurs when an orbiting body takes as long to rotate around its axis as it does to revolve around its host star or gravitational partner. The Moon takes twenty-seven days to rotate once on her axis, and twenty-seven days to orbit the Earth once.

Though we only see one side of the Moon, that does not mean she has a side that is permanently dark. The Sun illuminates the Moon in her entirety as she circumambulates our Earth, even if only one of her surfaces is constantly visible to us. Remember – the Earth revolves around the Sun and the Moon revolves around the Earth. Though we only see one face of the Moon, every surface of her body receives the illumination of the Sun over the course of approximately one month, as both the Earth and the Moon make their orbits through space.

## SIDEREAL MONTH VS. SOLAR MONTH

The Moon's orbit can be measured based on either her relationship to the Earth and the fixed stars, or based on her solar phases. The Moon takes approximately 27.3217 days to orbit the Earth once and return to her starting position in relation to the fixed stars behind her. This is called the Moon's "sidereal month." However, this is not the same length of time it takes for her phases to repeat – from Full Moon to Full Moon, or New Moon to New Moon, for example. The phases of the Moon are based on the relationship between the Moon and the Sun, and what we can see of that relationship from our place on Earth. The length of time it takes for the Moon to orbit the Earth is of no importance as far as her solar phases are concerned. Due to the Earth orbiting the Sun simultaneous to the Moon orbiting the Earth, the Moon has to make more than a complete orbit around the revolving Earth in order to repeat the phase she had in relation to the Sun a month previously. The time interval necessary for the lunar phases to repeat is approximately 29.5306 days.

## MOON PHASES

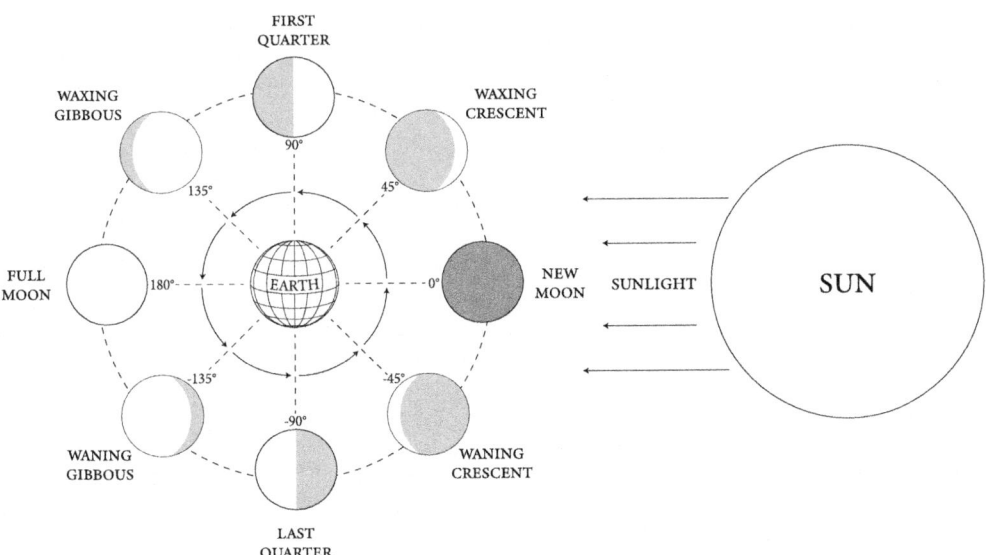

FIGURE 1: *Eight Lunar Phases*

When we speak about the lunar phases, we are referring to a particular arc opening that the Moon has in relation to the Sun. Each lunar phase lasts for approximately 3.5 days. While we call each of these arc openings a "lunar phase," we reserve the word "lunation" to specifically refer to the corporal conjunction of the luminaries at the New Moon. Though some people have taken to calling the Full Moon a lunation as well, specifically speaking, in traditional astrology, this word only applies to the New Moon.

## New Moon (00° – 45° arc opening from the Sun)

*Aspect: corporal conjunction*

The New Moon occurs when the Sun, Moon, and Earth are relatively aligned with each other. Since the Sun is illuminating the far side of the Moon that is invisible to us, the surface of the Moon that we can see appears to be dark.

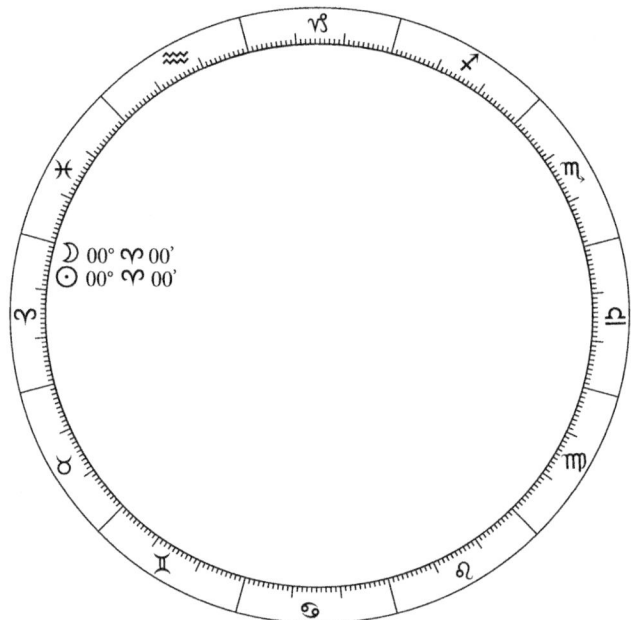

FIGURE 2: *New Moon (Conjunction)*

In an astrological chart, this is depicted as the Sun and Moon being in a corporal or "bodily" conjunction. This means that they are standing with each other in the same degree and minute of zodiacal longitude.

## Waxing Crescent (45° – 90° arc opening from the Sun)

*Aspect: opening semi-square*

As the Moon separates from the Sun, a thin crescent begins to appear on her Earth-facing surface. This is the Waxing Crescent of the Moon.

The Waxing Crescent occurs when the Moon is 45° separated from the body of the Sun in zodiacal longitude.

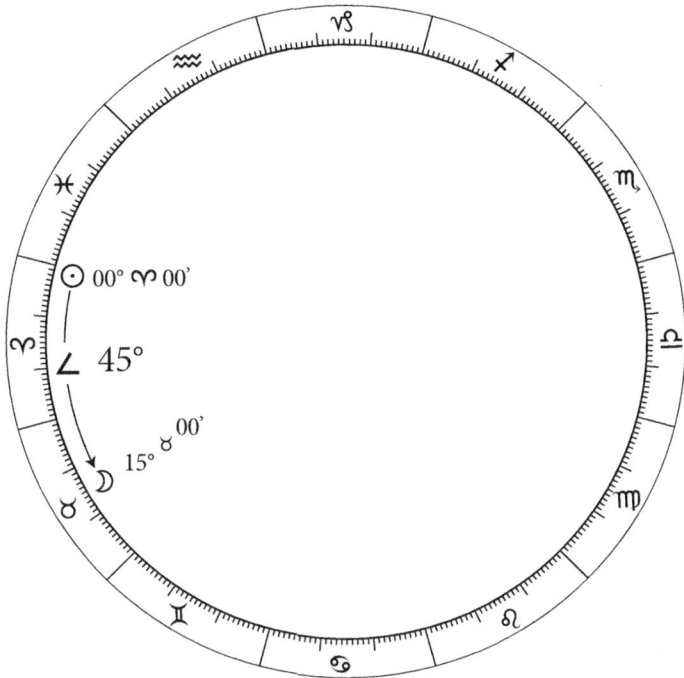

FIGURE 3: *Waxing Crescent (Opening Semi-Square)*

This aspect is called a "semi-square." The semi-square is not one of the aspects we find being used in in the general application of classical astrology. However, since the phases of the Moon are measured in 45° increments, this aspect is highly important when discussing the lunar cycles. As we learned in the previous chapter, 45° is the basis of the eighth harmonic aspect series. This is because 45° divides the 360° zodiac into eighths. The eighth harmonic aspects are: the semi-square, square, sesquiquadrate, and opposition. We treat the conjunction as if it were an aspect, even though it is not. Since its value is 00° it is considered to belong to every family of aspect harmonics, including the eighth harmonic aspects.

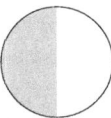

## FIRST QUARTER (90° – 135° ARC OPENING FROM THE SUN)

*Aspect: opening square*

As the Moon pulls farther away from the body of the Sun, her waxing crescent grows until a quarter of her surface is illuminated by the Sun's light. This is known as her First Quarter.

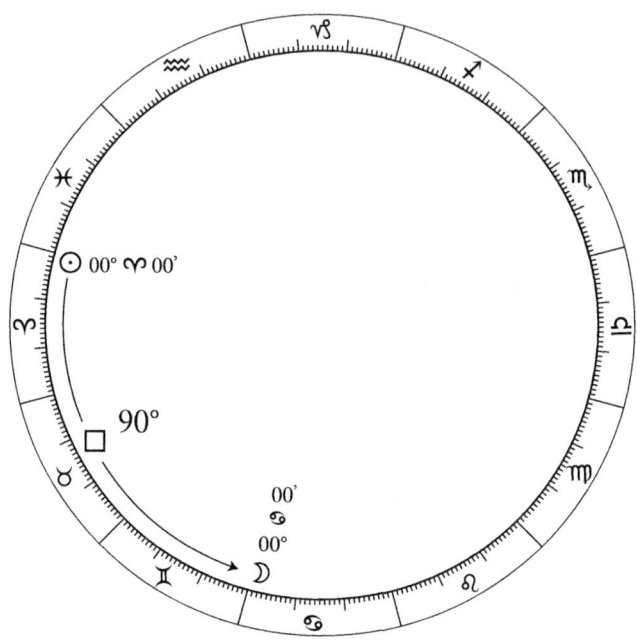

FIGURE 4: *First Quarter (Opening Square)*

In astrological terms, the Moon is forming her opening square with the Sun. We could also say that she is forming a dexter square with the Sun. This means that the Moon is forming a square with the Sun while the Sun is physically "behind" her in the zodiac. For example, if the Moon at 00° Cancer were in her First Quarter phase, the Sun would be at approximately 00° Aries.

WAXING GIBBOUS (135° – 180° ARC OPENING FROM THE SUN)

*Aspect: opening sesquiquadrate*

As the Moon continues to march forward in the zodiac from her First Quarter phase, the portion of her illuminated surface increases in size. When the Moon has separated from the Sun at a distance of 135°, she has entered her Waxing Gibbous phase. *Oxford Learner's Dictionary* defines "gibbous" as:

> *(of the moon) with the bright part bigger than a semicircle and smaller than a circle.*

In astrological terms, when the Moon has entered her opening sesquiquadrate with the Sun, she is in her Waxing Gibbous phase. If the Sun were at 00° Aries, the Moon would perfect her opening sesquiquadrate – her Waxing Gibbous – at 15° Leo.

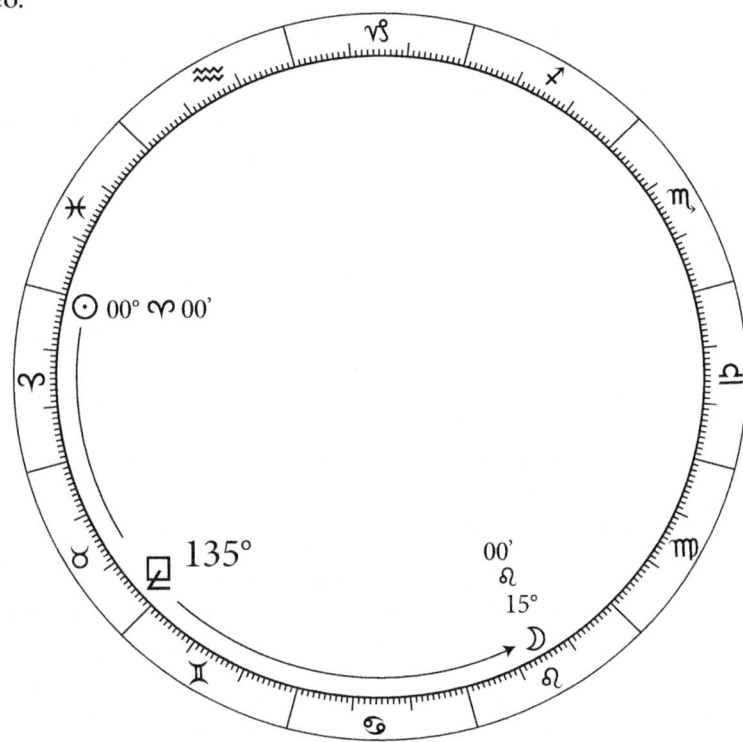

FIGURE 5: *Waxing Gibbous (Opening Sesquiquadrate)*

While we know that Aries and Leo have a trine aspect relationship in general, when we apply different harmonics to the zodiac – such as the eighth harmonic – we find more dynamic relationships between the various degrees of the signs that would be elusive to us if we only used the traditional aspects.

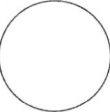

## FULL MOON (180° – 225° ARC OPENING FROM THE SUN)

*Aspect: opposition*

The Moon continues to pull forward in her orbit until she comes into a 180° relationship with the Sun. Now, the Earth stands between the Moon and the Sun. When this occurs, her Earth-facing side is also facing the Sun, resulting in the full illumination of her disk from our geocentric perspective. This is called a "Full Moon."

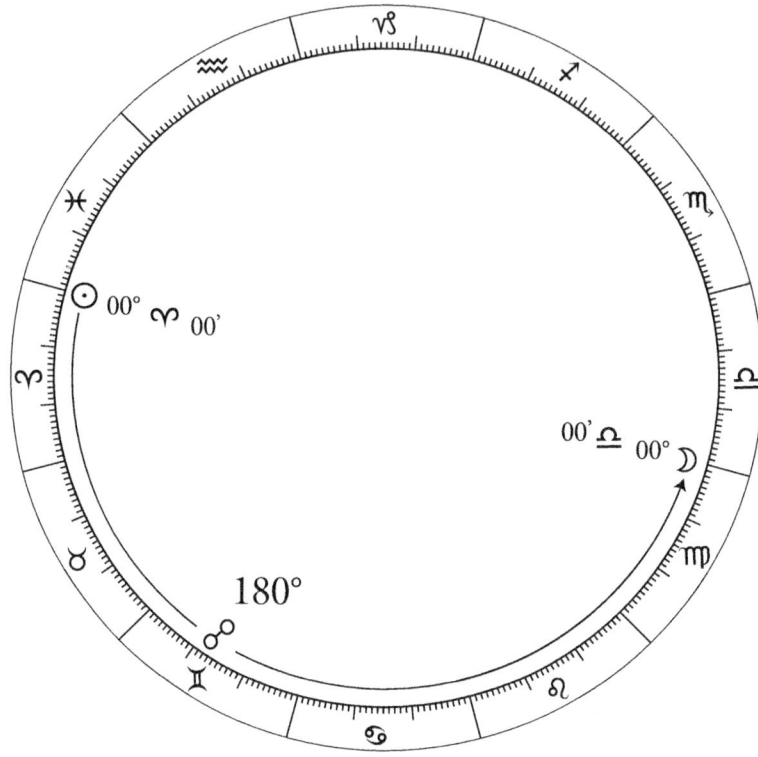

FIGURE 6: *Full Moon (Opposition)*

If the Sun were at 00° Aries, the Moon would perfect her opposition to the Sun at 00° Libra.

## WANING GIBBOUS (225° – 270° ARC OPENING FROM THE SUN)

*Aspect: closing sesquiquadrate*

The Moon continues in her orbit until her sphere is once again "bigger than a semicircle, but less than a circle." This is the second gibbous phase she experiences within her solar cycle. This is known as her "Waning Gibbous." During this phase, her surface is visibly decreasing in light. She is in her closing sesquiquadrate with the Sun.

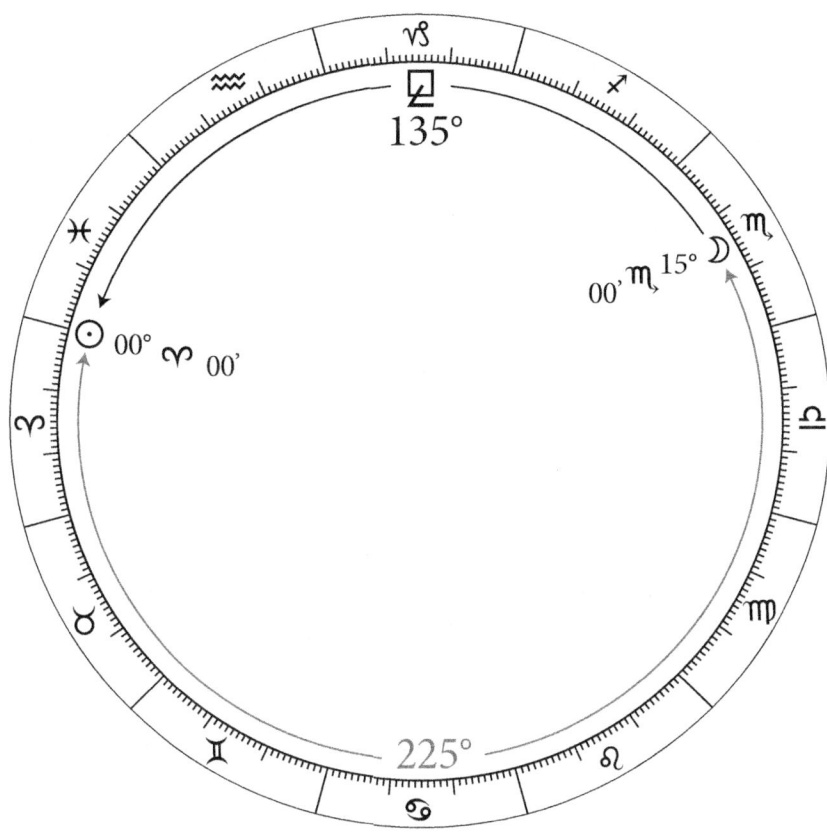

FIGURE 7: *Waning Gibbous (Closing Sesquiquadrate)*

Having reached her furthest elongation from him at her opposition, every aspect she now makes will only close the distance between their two bodies. The roles have reversed. She is now behind the Sun in zodiacal longitude. Thus, in her Waning Gibbous she is in her sinister sesquiquadrate, since she is sinisterly "creeping up on him from behind."

## LAST QUARTER (225° – 315° ARC OPENING FROM THE SUN)

*Aspect: closing square*

From her Waning Gibbous, she continues onward – old, dreary, world-worn, and knowing that her end is nigh. She comes to her Last Quarter where once again only one half of her face is illuminated; the other, consumed by the encroaching darkness. Astrologically, she is in her closing or sinister square with the Sun.

271

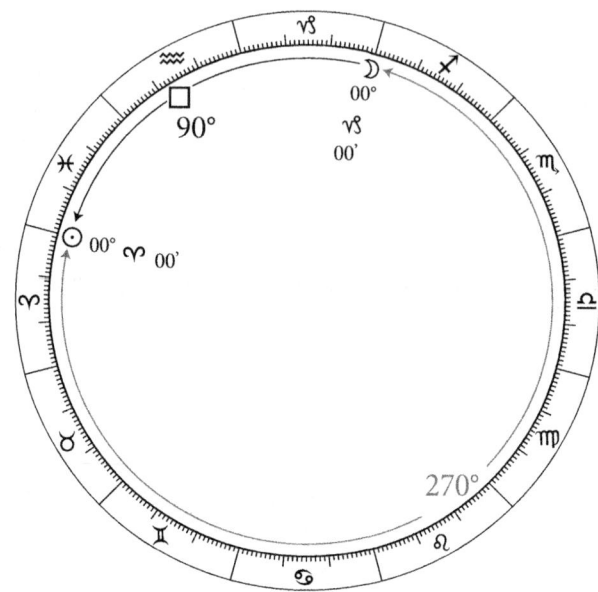

FIGURE 8: *Last Quarter (Closing Square)*

## WANING CRESCENT (225° – 315° ARC OPENING FROM THE SUN)

*Aspect: closing semi-square*

Onward she continues until she reaches the next climactic moment within her journey.

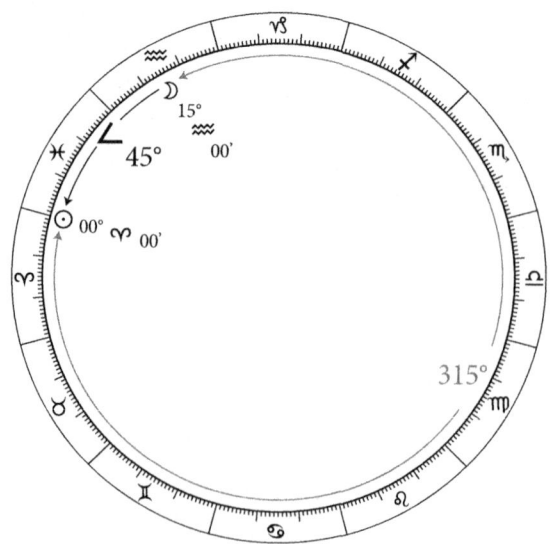

FIGURE 9: *Waning Crescent (Closing Semi-Square)*

She is now a mere 45° of arc distant from the body of the Sun. The darkness has all but fully overtaken her. She is weak and devitalized – ready for death by glorious fire. Astrologically, we refer to this as her "balsamic" phase. Angularly, she is forming a sinister or closing semi-square with the Sun.

## New Moon (315° – 360° arc opening from the Sun)

*Aspect: corporal conjunction*

Here, at her last gasp, she has taken her ultimate step forward; like a wandering lover who finally enters the flaming embrace of her beloved. At the New Moon, she returns to the body of her King – to burn, to die, and to spend a brief period in the ecstatic endlessness of non-being – only to be reborn 3.5 days later to repeat her cycle once again. During this period, the Moon is in a corporal conjunction with the Sun. At the exact moment of the lunation, the luminaries have no arc opening between them.

## Periodicity Exists within Everything

What we find in both the cycles of the Sun and the Moon is the root of the occult axiom that periodicity exists in everything. In this way, everlastingness is preserved – through the endless cycles of coming-to-be and passing away. Within the cycles of the luminaries, we find stellar evidence of the immortality of nature; evidence that would go on to inspire religion and philosophy into the belief that though the body may perish, the indestructible soul lives on to be reborn in a body anew. It is undoubtedly this observation of the natural world that led St. Paul to write this moving passage regarding his observations of death:

> *Behold, I show you a mystery; We shall not all sleep, but we shall all be changed, In a moment, in the twinkling of an eye, at the last trump: for the trumpet shall sound, and the dead shall be raised incorruptible, and we shall be changed. For this corruptible must put on incorruption, and this mortal must put on immortality. So when this corruptible shall have put on incorruption, and this mortal shall have put on immortality, then shall be brought to pass the saying that is written, Death is swallowed up in victory. O death, where is thy victory? O grave, where is thy sting?*

## Eighth Harmonic – Aspects of Material Manifestation

As far as aspects are concerned, the eight phases of the Moon reflect two very important ideas. On the one hand, they show us the way in which the major hard aspects (conjunction, squares, and oppositions) correspond with tangible, dramatic, concrete events. Though it is common to see lunar cycle diagrams that depict the eight phases of the Moon, it is not uncommon to see diagrams that only depict her four primary quarters: New Moon, First Quarter, Full Moon, and Last Quarter. These four quarters are known as the "primary phases" of the Moon. As we have learnt, these four quarters correspond with the major hard aspects.

On the other hand, the eight phases of the Moon also show the importance of the hard aspect intervals that occur between her primary phases. These intervals are represented by the 45° semi-square at the waxing and waning crescent, and the 135° sesquiquadrate at the waxing and waning gibbous. These four intervals between primary phases are known as the "intermediate phases" of the Moon. Just as we would not ignore the Moon in her crescent or gibbous phases, many astrologers have come to the agreement that the semi-square and sesquiquadrate are also potent aspects as far as the manifestation of concrete events is concerned.

This idea is a core principle within the German schools of Uranian astrology and Cosmobiology. In *Applied Cosmobiology* (1972), Ebertin writes:

> *Although in the past great significance has always been attributed to the sextile and trine, I cannot reconcile this with my own experience. As I have said elsewhere on many occasions my repeated experience has been that sextiles and trines seem to relate to more passive conditions whilst those angles divisible by 45° appear to point to the actual manifestation of events.*

### Eighth Harmonic Aspects in Traditional Medical Astrology

This idea that the 45° hard aspect angles represent the manifestation of concrete events wasn't just discovered in the twentieth century. Though not used within traditional natal chart delineation, the 45° group of aspects have been a cornerstone of traditional medical astrology for centuries. We find the greatest use of these 45° lunar aspects within traditional medical horary astrology.

A "decumbiture" is the chart that is cast for the moment of a person falling ill. If that exact moment is not known, then the moment the person is first counselled by their doctor also qualifies as a valid decumbiture. Traditionally, these charts were used to predict the critical points within a person's period of illness. They could also be used to determine how long an illness would last. While the motion of the Sun could be a valid predictive index in more chronic conditions, the Moon's transits were often taken to indicate the development of these "critical days" in cases that were more acute. For the ancients a "crisis" was any noteworthy event that occurred to a person health-wise during their course of being unwell. It did not matter if the crisis was good or bad. For traditional astrologers, it was more important that a concrete event could be predicted for the sick person in question. Seventeenth century astrologer Richard Saunders writes:

> *Crisis is no other thing, than a Duel or Contention betwixt Nature and the Infirmity; if Nature at the time of the Crisis overcome the Malignity of the Disease, it's a good Crisis; if Sickness prevail, it's a pernicious and ill Crisis. Or, Crisis is no more than this, viz. a sudden alteration of man's body when he is sick, tending either to health, or further sickness; for when this Crisis [occurs], there's a sharp fight, as it were, betwixt Nature and the Disease, whether of them shall overcome.*

Curiously, the hard aspects of the Moon often indicated these crises for the classical medical astrologer. In *Sefer Ha-Me'orot*, acclaimed Medieval Jewish astrologer Abraham Ibn Ezra writes:

> But the root of the crisis takes place when the Moon is in quartile to its place at the onset of the disease, and [on] the fourteenth day when [the Moon is] in opposition [to its place at the onset of the disease], and on the twentieth day or on the following day [when the Moon is] in the second quartile, and [on] the twenty-seventh or twenty-eighth day when the Moon returns to its position [at the onset of the disease].

Here we see Ibn Ezra confirming something that both traditional and modern astrologers tend to agree on: hard aspects make things happen. And, even for those amongst astrologers who do not believe that the planetary combinations are causal *per se*, it still cannot be denied that there is often a mirrored relationship between the momentary hard aspect configurations of the planets, and the concrete events that simultaneously unfold within our lives. This theory was applied by Ibn Ezra, his precursors, and his contemporaries specifically within their medical astrology practice. However, within the twenty-first century, we have come to discover that the material impact of the hard aspects stretches far beyond medical astrology.

Most fascinatingly, Ibn Ezra goes on to discuss the intermediate 45° hard aspect combinations that occur in the intervals between the primary phases of the Moon. He continues:

> The fourth day resembles a crisis day because it is a demi-aspect [opening semi-square], like the keys of the Moon, and the same applies to the eleventh [opening sesquiquadrate], seventeenth [closing sesquiquadrate], and twenty-fourth [days] [closing semi-square].

Saunders takes this idea further. He says that the midpoint between the beginning and the end of any 45° segment of the Moon's sojourn through the zodiac, can also denote days that indicate a change within the condition of the sick person. Thus, for Saunders, the 22° 30' increments of the Moon were also worth considering. He writes:

> Now for right distinction and calculation of Time, observe in what degree of the Zodiac the Moon was at the decumbiture, and to that degree add 22° 30', which is half the time between the Crisis and the Indicial time, and this shows (when the Moon comes to that degree) the first Indicative... time [of change within the course of sickness]; then to this former time add 22° 30' more, and that makes the Indicial time; to which, when the Moon comes, it is accounted a Judicial day; which is when the Moon is gone 45° or half a Quadrate from the first Crisis; then to this last Indicial time add 22° 30' more, which makes 67° 30' from the first Crisis; and this is the second Indicative day... as falling between the Crisis and Judicial day; to which again add 22° 30'

*more, and you have the first perfect Crisis from the decumbiture, viz. 90°; and adding 22° 30' more, makes the next Judicative day, when the Moon comes to it, and so on through the whole Zodiac, and over it again, if the Disease Terminate not in that time...*

If we divide our 360° zodiac by 22° 30', we end up with sixteen equal divisions. Today, we refer to this as the "sixteenth harmonic." Both the eighth and sixteenth harmonic are used extensively within the German school of Uranian astrology. For both the Renaissance medical astrologer and the Uranian astrologer, all hard aspects that can be derived from dividing the circle of the zodiac into eighths represent aspects that correspond with the manifestation of material events. Today, many astrologers believe this insight originated out of a study of the harmonies that exist within numbers. However, from our study of the Moon and her primary and intermediate phases, it is more likely that this understanding arose out of an observation of the lunar phases.

These eighth and sixteenth harmonic aspects hold very special relevance within my natal astrology practice. The way in which I apply these harmonics go well beyond the purpose of this introductory textbook. Nevertheless, it is worth our present consideration to understand other forms of aspect relationships that are as equally rooted in an observation of nature as any trine or opposition may be. It is also important for us to remember that these insights were derived through contemplating the eightfold phases of the Moon. Our study of the Moon and her relationship to the Earth and Sun inevitably points us deeper towards the heart of mastering concrete, event-based astrology.

## CHAPTER 11 QUESTIONS

1. Why do we call the Moon a luminary?
2. What is meant by the term "tidal locking"?
3. Why is the sidereal and the solar month different lengths of time?
4. What is the arc opening between the luminaries during the eight lunar phases?
5. What is meant by the Moon's "opening" and "closing" aspects?
6. What is a decumbiture chart?
7. What is the arc opening for the other hard aspect that is smaller than the 45° semi-square? This arc opening was mentioned by Richard Saunders in his discussion of the critical days.

CHAPTER 12 OBJECTIVES

* Define essential dignity and essential debility.
* Learn about the point system for the various levels of essential dignity and debility.
* Learn how to skillfully interpret a planet that is minorly dignified, yet majorly debilitated.
* Interpret the various levels of essential dignity and debility.
* Define the term "almuten."
* Differentiate between dignity-based almutens and topic- based almutens.

TABLE 1: *Essential Dignities & Debilities*

| Sign | Houses of the Planets | Exaltation | Triplicity of Planets | The Terms of the Planets | | | | | The Faces of the Planets | | | Detri ment | Fall |
|---|---|---|---|---|---|---|---|---|---|---|---|---|---|
| | | | D N P | | | | | | | | | | |
| | +5 | +4 | +3 | +2 | | | | | +1 | | | -5 | -4 |
| ♈ | ♂ D | ☉ 19 | ☉ ♃ ♄ | ♃ 6 | ♀ 14 | ☿ 21 | ♂ 26 | ♄ 30 | ♂ 10 | ☉ 20 | ♀ 30 | ♀ | ♄ |
| ♉ | ♀ N | ☽ 3 | ♀ ☽ ♂ | ♀ 8 | ☿ 15 | ♃ 22 | ♄ 26 | ♂ 30 | ☿ 10 | ☽ 20 | ♄ 30 | ♂ | |
| ♊ | ☿ D | ☊ 3 | ♄ ☿ ♃ | ☿ 7 | ♃ 13 | ♀ 21 | ♄ 25 | ♂ 30 | ♃ 10 | ♂ 20 | ☉ 30 | ♃ | |
| ♋ | ☽ D/N | ♃ 15 | ♀ ♂ ☽ | ♂ 6 | ♃ 13 | ☿ 20 | ♀ 27 | ♄ 30 | ♀ 10 | ☿ 20 | ☽ 30 | ♄ | ♂ |
| ♌ | ☉ D/N | | ☉ ♃ ♄ | ♄ 6 | ☿ 13 | ♀ 19 | ♃ 25 | ♂ 30 | ♄ 10 | ♃ 20 | ♂ 30 | ♄ | |
| ♍ | ☿ N | ☿ 15 | ♀ ☽ ♂ | ☿ 7 | ♀ 13 | ♃ 18 | ♄ 24 | ♂ 30 | ☉ 10 | ♀ 20 | ☿ 30 | ♃ | ♀ |
| ♎ | ♀ D | ♄ 21 | ♄ ☿ ♃ | ♄ 6 | ♀ 11 | ♃ 19 | ☿ 24 | ♂ 30 | ☽ 10 | ♄ 20 | ♃ 30 | ♂ | ☉ |
| ♏ | ♂ N | | ♀ ♂ ☽ | ♂ 6 | ♃ 14 | ♀ 21 | ☿ 27 | ♄ 30 | ♂ 10 | ☉ 20 | ♀ 30 | ♀ | ☽ |
| ♐ | ♃ D | ☋ 3 | ☉ ♃ ♄ | ♃ 8 | ♀ 14 | ☿ 19 | ♄ 25 | ♂ 30 | ☿ 10 | ☽ 20 | ♄ 30 | ☿ | |
| ♑ | ♄ N | ♂ 28 | ♀ ☽ ♂ | ♀ 6 | ☿ 12 | ♃ 19 | ♂ 25 | ♄ 30 | ♃ 10 | ♂ 20 | ☉ 30 | ☽ | ♃ |
| ♒ | ♄ D | | ♄ ☿ ♃ | ♄ 6 | ☿ 12 | ♀ 20 | ♃ 25 | ♂ 30 | ♀ 10 | ☿ 20 | ☽ 30 | ☉ | |
| ♓ | ♃ N | ♀ 27 | ♀ ♂ ☽ | ♀ 8 | ♃ 14 | ☿ 20 | ♂ 26 | ♄ 30 | ♄ 10 | ♃ 20 | ♂ 30 | ☿ | ☿ |

# CHAPTER 12

## ESSENTIAL DIGNITIES &
## DEBILITIES IN PRACTICE

*The ancient Astronomers have found out and tried by experience,
that the Planets do show and utter their force & strength, much
more in some certain places of the Zodiac than in other-some,
and therefore are said to be more strong & better fortuned in
those places than in others, the which thing happeneth because
the nature of those places and of the Starres which are in those
places, do accord & agree better with the nature of the Planets,
insomuch that there is a certain Sympathy or agreement between
the nature of the one and the other. And for this place also they
are called the Essential dignities of the Planets. – CLAUD DARIOT*

ESSENTIAL DIGNITY REFERS TO ZODIACAL conditions that support a planet in being more of itself. Essential debility refers to zodiacal conditions that prevent a planet from being more of itself. When a planet is essentially dignified, it can strongly support itself and fulfill its agenda. When a planet is essentially debilitated, it is gravely limited in its ability to bolster itself from within. It has a more difficult time functioning in general, and cannot truly do what is specifically being asked of it when brought into a chart.

Within traditional astrology, the seven classical planets all have a specific job to fulfill in relation to the houses they rule and the houses they occupy within a chart. Every planet has a mission to carry that agenda out to its fullest, most successful completion. However, not every planet can guarantee a successful outcome in this regard. Essential dignity and debility refer to how internally strong or weak planets may be to successfully complete the tasks with which they have been entrusted.

Within a chart, there are many ways in which a planet can be supported. Planets can be supported based on the houses they occupy, aspects to other planets, their spatial relationship to the Sun, and many other environmental factors. All of these auxiliary supports are known as "accidental fortitudes," and will be discussed more fully later on. None of these environmental supports are as significant as the planet's internal condition.

Essential dignity affects the very heart of how the planet operates. It gives the planet more ability to be itself. Planets who have the ability to express themselves in a pure way are usually more naturally predisposed to delivering successful outcomes. Essential dignity gives a planet power and mastery. This is why when beginning an assessment of a planet from a traditional perspective, it is a great idea to assess the state of that planet's essential dignity or debility first, before taking into consideration other things that are happening to it.

Essential debility has the opposite effect on a planet than essential dignity does. When a planet is essentially debilitated, that planet is weakened in its very core. It has no self-awareness, and cannot contribute in any powerful way within the chart in question. Even if that planet is drawn into action, the sort of action the deeply essentially debilitated planet can offer is hardly worth relying on. That planet is dependent on the good graces of other accidental fortitudes within the chart to assist it in delivering on its promise.

A powerfully essentially dignified planet can be likened to a king within his castle: strong, authoritative, and fully able to be the highest version of himself possible. A very weakly essentially dignified planet – such as a planet in its own "face" – only has the minimum amount of strength by which to express its essential nature. A planet only having dignity by face is not far from being essentially debilitated and is only holding on by threads of power. It can be described as a "man on his last gasp;" desperate and unfortunate, though still dignified.

QUANTIFYING ESSENTIAL DIGNITY AND DEBILITY

The different levels of essential dignity are: domicile rulership, exaltation rulership, triplicity rulership, term/bound rulership, and face/decan rulership. They all represent different qualities of planetary power, from strongest to weakest. If a planet is in any one of these states of essential dignity, then we have a piece of information that has great interpretational value. There is also interpretational value if a planet is in a state of essential debility by being in its detriment, fall, or in a degree of the zodiac where it is peregrine. We will elaborate on the meanings of all these levels of essential dignity and debility further within this chapter.

Our astrological ancestors developed a point system for the different levels of essential dignity. This allowed the strength of a planet to be calculated and easily expressed numerically. It also made it possible to identify which planets were essentially the strongest and which were essentially the weakest.

TABLE 2: *Levels of Essential Dignity*

| | |
|---|---|
| DOMICILE | +5 points |
| EXALTATION | +4 points |
| TRIPLICITY | +3 points |
| TERM/BOUND | +2 points |
| FACE, DECAN/DECANATE | +1 point |

While planets at all levels of essential dignity are considered to be essentially dignified, I make it a point to distinguish between planets being strongly essentially dignified by having domicile or exaltation rulership and planets being weakly essentially dignified by only having term or face rulership. Triplicity rulership is the middle of the entire scheme and, therefore represents a planet middling in strength.

There is also a point system for planets that are essentially debilitated.

TABLE 3: *Levels of Essential Debility*

| DETRIMENT | -5 points |
|---|---|
| FALL | -4 points |
| PEREGRINE | -5 points |

For me, it has always been a sufficient enough debility if a planet is either in its detriment or its fall or peregrine. Some astrologers have found it necessary to say that x planet is both in detriment and peregrine when in x sign, or x planet is both in fall and peregrine when in x sign.

Though this isn't what I do, I understand the rationale behind it. A planet may be in detriment, but still in its triplicity, term, or face. This means that though it is in detriment, it is not also peregrine versus if it were in detriment and also not occupying any of its minor dignities. The planet in detriment and not occupying its minor dignities is definitely in detriment and peregrine.

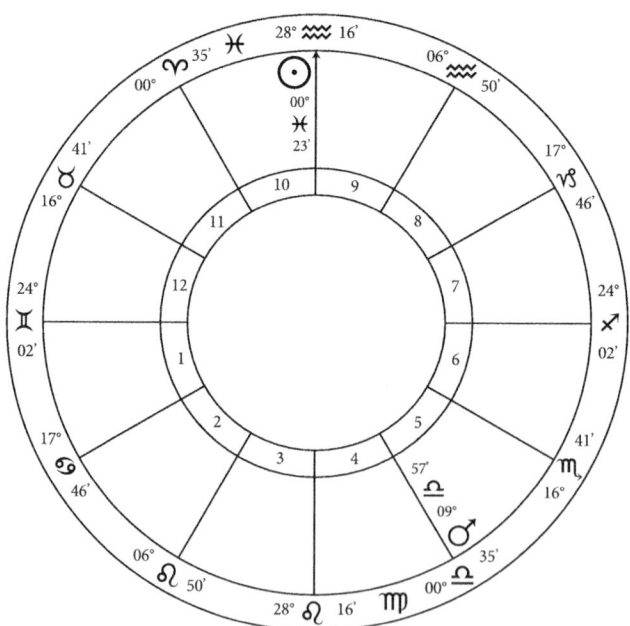

FIGURE 1: *Peregrine Planets*

For example, Mars at 09° Libra 57' in a diurnal chart is in detriment and also peregrine. He is in the domicile of Venus, the exaltation of Saturn, the triplicity of Saturn, the term of Venus, and the face of the Moon. He has no essential dignity at all in that degree and the general condition of Mars in Libra is that he is in his detriment throughout that entire sign.

Though this is a valid example, in my opinion, to say that a planet is in detriment or in fall is sufficient. This is because if a planet is in its detriment, but also in its triplicity or term or face, its minor dignity doesn't materially alter the fact that the planet is in its detriment.

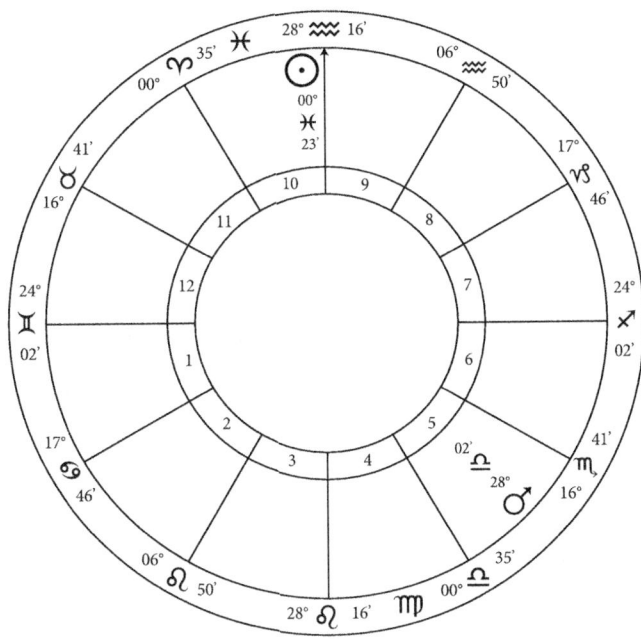

FIGURE 2: *Mars in his Term/Bound*

If Mars were at 28° Libra 02', he would be in his term in Libra which spans from 24° Libra 00' to 29° Libra 59'. Though he has dignity by term, he is still in his detriment. Of those two conditions, his detriment is a bigger statement than his minor dignity by term rulership. The same is true for a planet in its fall. I don't find it necessary to note when a planet is in detriment and peregrine, or in fall and peregrine, and I never actually do so in my practice. I reserve the condition of peregrination for when a planet does not have domicile, detriment, exaltation, or fall, triplicity, term, or face in a particular degree of a sign in which it finds itself.

DEBILITATED WHILE DIGNIFIED

With the point system, a planet in its detriment or fall can accrue enough points that would mitigate its essential debility. When this happens, I have seen many traditional astrology novices and veterans get very excited; as if they have found a cosmic loophole which causes their Venus in detriment in Scorpio to be better than it actually is. Incidentally, it is often the people who have their Venus in detriment in Scorpio who look for this loophole. However, in my opinion, they've missed the point about the point system.

The point system doesn't actually reflect the internal life and experience of the planets. The point system is a crude estimation of the amount of power or weakness a planet may have and feel within itself. It is as artificial as trying to put a percentage on the amount of happiness or sorrow a human being may experience at any moment in time. When we get lost in the numbers, we often miss the point that these planets are living entities, not just the representation of an accumulative score. As such, the actual quality of a planet's experience in a sign is far more vital than the score it receives for being there. The overarching reality of an essentially debilitated planet is the level of limitation that planet experiences for being in that state of debility. Minor dignities don't actually change the fact that for a planet to be in its detriment or fall goes against the very cellular matrix of that planet.

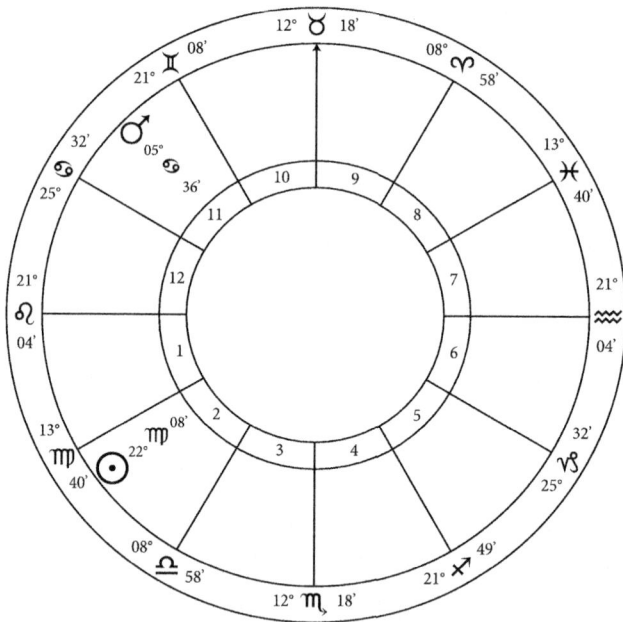

FIGURE 3: *Mars - Simultaneously Essentially Dignified & Debilitated*

If Mars were at 05° Cancer 36' in a nocturnal chart, the overarching reality of Mars is that he would be in the sign of his fall. He would be essentially debilitated. It does not matter that at 05° Cancer, he also is in his term in Cancer, giving him +2 points of essential dignity. It also doesn't matter that in a nocturnal chart he would have attained another +3 points of essential dignity for being the nocturnal triplicity ruler of water signs. The accumulative points that he gains for being at 05° Cancer 36' in a nocturnal chart is +5 points of essential dignity. However, these +5 points have to be added to the -4 points that he already has lost by being in that sign. In the end, Mars only would receive +1 point of essential dignity for being at 05° Cancer 36' in a nocturnal chart. This is the same amount of dignity he would have if he were in his face/decan. Many people would consider this to be an essentially dignified Mars. I disagree.

The numbers game above is something I would never do. In Ibn Ezra's *The Beginning of Wisdom*, we read:

> *When a planet is in its fall, it indicates worry, distress, and hardship.*

This isn't a conditional statement. The overall state of a planet in its fall is one that is negative and highly debilitating. Traditional astrology is, above all, pragmatic. It is better for a planet to not be in its detriment or fall, and have +1 point of essential dignity for being in its face/decan. This is preferable to that planet reverse engineering that +1 point of essential dignity through minor dignities while in a sign where it is in its detriment or fall.

Essential debility is like a mortal wound to the heart of everything the planet represents. Within my practice, I have particularly found this to be true in the case of Saturn in Cancer, Leo, or Aries; Jupiter in Capricorn; Mars in Libra, Taurus, or Cancer; Venus in Scorpio or Virgo; most definitely Mercury in Pisces; and the Moon in Capricorn or Scorpio.

## USING THE POINT SYSTEM

Regardless of the artificial design of the point system, it represents a form of astrological shorthand that every student should know.

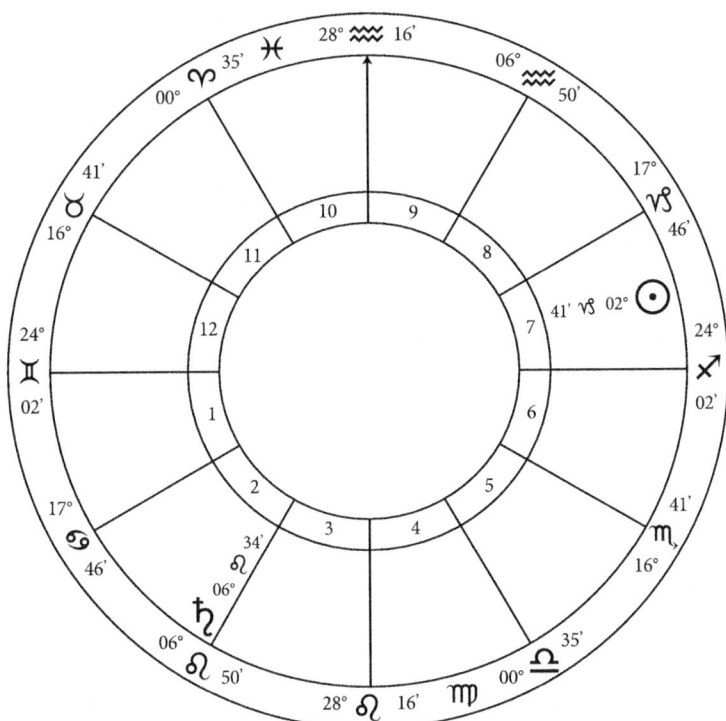

FIGURE 4: *Saturn - Simultaneously Essentially Dignified & Debilitated*

If Saturn were at 06° Leo 34' in a diurnal or nocturnal chart, he would have:

TABLE 4: *Essential Dignity & Debility Example I*

| | |
|---|---|
| IN HIS DETRIMENT | -5 points |
| PARTICIPATING TRIPLICITY RULER | +3 points |
| IN HIS TERM | +2 points |
| IN HIS FACE | +1 point |

Though essentially debilitated, Saturn has gained +6 points of essential dignity by being at 06° Leo 34'. If we add these +6 points to the -5 points he has lost by being in his detriment, Saturn would receive +1 point of essential dignity for being in Leo in the abovementioned scenario. Though the larger take away for me is that Saturn is still in the sign of his detriment, he is less debilitated in our example than if he were elsewhere within Leo where he didn't have term and face rulership.

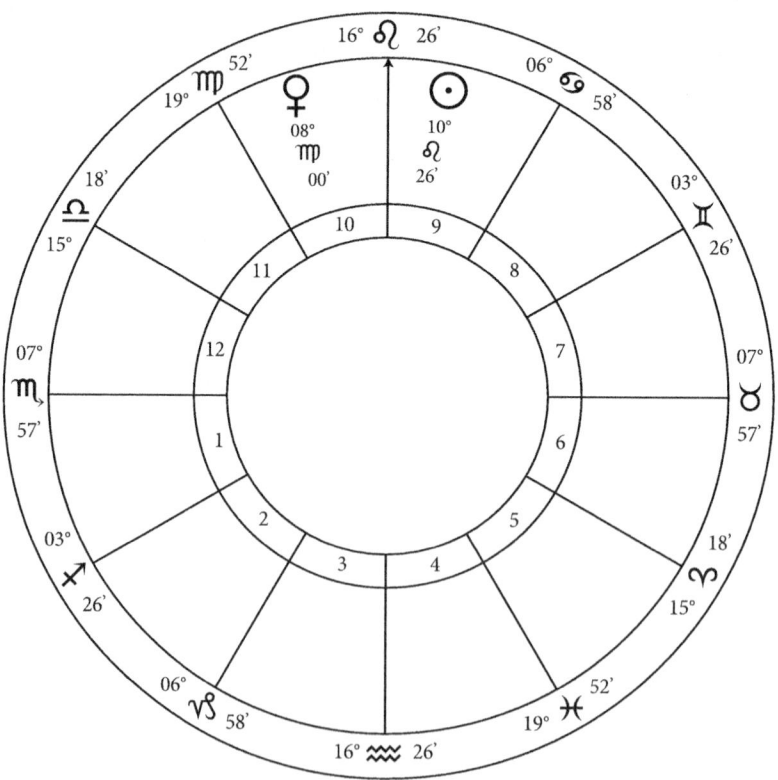

FIGURE 5: *Venus - Simultaneously Essentially Dignified & Debilitated*

If Venus were at 08° Virgo oo' in a diurnal chart, she would have:

TABLE 5: *Essential Dignity & Debility Example II*

| IN HER FALL | -4 points |
|---|---|
| DIURNAL TRIPLICITY RULER | +3 points |
| IN HER TERM | +2 points |

Though essentially debilitated, Venus has gained +5 points of essential dignity by being at 08° Virgo oo'. If we add these +5 points to the -4 points she has lost by being in her detriment, Venus would receive +1 point of essential dignity for being in Virgo in the abovementioned scenario. Though the larger take away for me is that Venus is still in the sign of her fall, she is less debilitated in this example than if she were elsewhere within Virgo where she didn't have term rulership or if it were a nocturnal chart.

## A COMPLICATION AMONGST THE LESSER DIGNITIES

What we have seen in our last two examples is that a planet can have essential dignity even in signs in which they are essentially debilitated. One of the places where this is most obvious is in the doctrine of the triplicity rulers. Several of the planets have triplicity rulership in signs of the zodiac in which they are essentially debilitated.

Fire signs are ruled by the Sun in the day and Jupiter at night, with Saturn as their participating triplicity ruler. Though Saturn is the participating triplicity ruler of all fire signs, he is in detriment in Leo and in fall in Aries.

Earth signs are ruled by Venus in the day and the Moon at night, with Mars as their participating triplicity ruler. Though Venus is the triplicity ruler of earth signs in the day, she is in fall in Virgo. Though the Moon is the triplicity ruler of earth signs at night, she is in fall in Capricorn. Though Mars is the participating triplicity ruler of all earth signs, he is in detriment in Taurus.

Air signs are ruled by Saturn in the day and Mercury at night, with Jupiter as their participating triplicity ruler. Though Jupiter is the participating triplicity ruler of all air signs, he is in detriment in Gemini.

Water signs are ruled by Venus in the day and Mars at night, with the Moon as their participating triplicity ruler. Though Venus is the triplicity ruler of water signs in the day, she is in detriment in Scorpio. Though Mars is the triplicity ruler of water signs at night, he is in fall in Cancer. Though the Moon is the participating triplicity ruler of all water signs, she is in fall in Scorpio.

What, then, do we make of this? How can something have essential dignity in the same sign in which it is majorly debilitated? It would seem silly that the Moon would be thought to have participating triplicity rulership over all the water signs including Scorpio, if the Moon is so majorly debilitated in Scorpio. Shouldn't she have less triplicity rulership in Scorpio than she does in Cancer or Pisces, since Scorpio is such a terrible place for her to be?

The answer is no. As astrologers, we are meant to be technicians who can stand in the gap of potentially contradictory realities without being overwhelmed or confused. We are meant to know that the Moon has participating triplicity rulership over all the water signs, and also has her fall in Scorpio because that gives us the ability to begin thinking in a more nuanced, nonlinear way. Astrology's contradictions are life's contradictions, and we see them around us all the time. Some people hate doing certain things that they are really good at. Other people may be respected in an environment in which they are simultaneously hated. Some people are given a cool glass of water to drink while they are walking through the molten lava fields of Hell. In the case of the Moon having triplicity rulership over Scorpio in which she also has her fall, she is the person being given cool water while walking through Hell.

What is important in our analogy above is the overarching reality in which the Moon finds herself. The overarching reality for the Moon in Scorpio is that she is in the sign of her fall, regardless of what other levels of dignity she may have there. This is as true for the Moon as it is for all the other planets. This is one of the most important things you will learn in this entire book.

## A Minor Good does not Alter an Overwhelming Evil

A minor good does not alter an overwhelming evil. If a planet is in a sign in which it has either detriment or fall, its minor dignities in that sign are of no importance. The fact that it has some form of minor dignity as well in that sign does not alter the overwhelmingly debilitated state that it finds itself in. This is because a minor good does not alter an overwhelming evil.

This is a point that many students of astrology struggle with, especially students who have become overly dependent on the point system in terms of understanding essential dignities and debilities. They will quickly point out the fact that the Moon in Scorpio loses -4 points for being in her fall, but gains +3 points for being the participating triplicity ruler, which means she actually only loses -1 point for being in her fall in Scorpio. This is good math and good logic. However, it isn't good astrology. It is disconnected from astrological reality and represents a form of cerebral astrology that ultimately is unhelpful in the trenches of actual client work.

The point system is beneficial for aiding us in a rudimentary understanding of planetary strength. However, it represents entry-level astrology that, as far as I can tell, was a convenient means of enabling a group of astrologers to be on the same page when discussing the planets. However, the point system does not represent an aid to interpretation; and neither do the points provide us an interpretational key within themselves. Saying that a planet has +1 point of essential dignity means nothing at all. Saying that a planet is in its own face offers a wealth of allegory and symbolic insight.

The only true aid to interpreting essential dignities and debilities is having a deep understanding of the internal nature of the planets. We must also know how that nature is modified based on all of the signs and segments of signs that the planets may find themselves in. This is several steps beyond being able to do quick math. In order to practice traditional astrology, we have to understand how the various components of our astrological ecosystem interact with each other as living creatures, and not just numbers that we can add or subtract.

This brings us back to the point: a minor good does not alter an overwhelming evil. The Moon in Scorpio may be less afflicted because she also has triplicity rulership there. However, this makes no difference at all in actual applied astrology. The Moon in Scorpio is still afflicted beyond measure in ways that would make her triplicity rulership over that sign seem absolutely negligible and of no value whatsoever. This is as true for the Moon in Scorpio as it is for Saturn in either Aries or Leo though they are of his same triplicity, Jupiter in Gemini, Mars in Cancer, and Venus in Virgo. In all of these cases where each of these planets has dignity by triplicity rulership, their minor strength does not alter their overwhelming weakness when in those signs of the zodiac.

The same rule applies for the lesser levels of essential dignity: term and face. Venus rules the second term and the last face of Aries. However, regardless of her being in either her term or face while in that sign, she is in her detriment within the entire sign. The overwhelming reality of her debility when in Aries is not materially altered by her having some minor essential dignity there.

It would seem obvious that once you have identified a planet in one of its major debilities, a great deal of your work is done. The same is true if we find those planets in their major dignities. Therefore, when it comes to calculating the essential dignity or debility of a planet, I tell students to begin by running through the major dignities and debilities first. Is the planet in its domicile, exaltation, detriment, or fall? This makes our assessment more efficient. For beginner students, first checking the major dignities and debilities is extraordinarily helpful. Many students tend to get lost in the more nuanced sections of the essential dignities table which includes triplicity, term, and face.

After going through the four major dignities and debilities, every student should still look at the lesser dignities in order to ascertain whether or not the planets have any additional strengths by being in their triplicity, term, or face. It is important to get in the habit of looking at all the levels of essential dignity even if they aren't domicile and exaltation rulership. It trains our eye and forces us to be meticulous and systematic in our understanding of each planet and how they are individually operating within a chart. One of the homework assignments I give students at this point is to calculate the points of essential dignity or debility of the seven classical planets within a chart. I'd encourage you to do this do this with your chart and the charts of people you know until the calculation of essential dignities and debilities becomes second nature to you.

## Levels of Essential Dignity

### Domicile Rulership

> *Every planet, whether benefic or malefic, if it is in its domicile or domicile of exaltation, will always indicate good.* – Abraham Ibn Ezra

When a planet is in its own domicile, it receives +5 points of essential dignity. It is like a king in his castle. A planet in its own domicile does not depend on another planet to be its ruler. It has full ability to express its essential nature. It is an ambassador only for its own interests. It will deliver whatever it promises with strength and vigor, especially if it is strongly supported by other factors within the chart. William Ramesey writes:

> *If you find a planet in his own house, and he significator, he shows a good state of the person or thing he signifieth in any scheme [chart] whatsoever.*

When a planet is in its domicile it is like someone in their own home. They are comfortable, and have the ability to deliver their promised results, usually in a benefic or positive way.

### Exaltation Rulership

> *A planet in its exaltation is like a person at his greatest rank.* – Abraham Ibn Ezra

When a planet is in its own exaltation, it receives +4 points of essential dignity. It is like a royal personage; a person larger than life who is a welcomed visitor within the home of another. However, this person is still a guest. He is dependent on the goodwill of his host. He is not a free agent in the same way he would be if he were in his domicile. He delivers not only on the promise that he represents, but he also has to deliver on the promise of his host. His host is the domicile ruler of the sign he is in. William Ramesey writes:

> *If a planet be in his exaltation, he shows a man of a high and majestical carriage and disposition, very high-minded, lofty and proud, taking more upon him than befitteth.*

In the seventeenth century, a planet in exaltation was thought of as a man "haughty and proud, assuming more of himself than is his actual due." When a planet is in its exaltation it is like a man who is lifted up on a pedestal. He thinks he is greater than he is. He is proud and sometimes arrogant. He has an inflated sense of himself.

This is distinctly different from the Medieval characterization of a planet in its exaltation. Guido Bonatti writes:

*And while in its own exaltation, it is like a man who is in his own kingdom and in his own glory... [or] other lay dignities which can forsake him before his own matters do.*

Exaltation is a highly positive state in Bonatti's writings. However, there is still a sense of impermanence connected with it, making it more unstable than the strength a planet has when it is in its own domicile.

## Triplicity Rulership

*A planet in its triplicity is like a person with his relatives. – Abraham Ibn Ezra*

When a planet is in its triplicity, it receives +3 points of essential dignity. William Ramesey writes:

*If a planet be in his triplicity, it shows a man meanly endued with the goods of this life, not meanly, nor very well descended; yet his present condition to be good.*

"Meanly endued with the goods of this life" means that the planet only has exactly what it needs to get by. It cannot live lavishly or abundantly, but it also is not in the pits of impoverishment. It is in the middle; living above the poverty line, but never actually able to increase its wealth or status within the world at large. He isn't doing terribly bad, but he also isn't doing wonderfully good.

Bonatti writes:

*And while it is in its own triplicity, it is like a man who is among his allies and his people... who obey him and follow him, who are not related to him out of kinship.*

This Medieval idea of the triplicity ruler having "followers" is a very apt description. When a planet is the triplicity ruler of an element, it has governance over all three signs of that triplicity, as well as all the planets that are in those signs.

## Term or Bound Rulership

*A planet in its bound is like a person in his residence [seat]. – Abraham Ibn Ezra*

When a planet has rulership by term/bound, it receives +2 points of essential dignity. William Ramesey writes:

*If a planet be in his terms, it shows a man rather participating of the temper and shape of the planet, than of the wealth, power or dignity signified by the nature of that planet.*

All throughout the Renaissance, we are told that a planet in its term isn't a planet that is strong *per se*. Rather, it is colored more by its natural characteristics and personality. An example of this could be Saturn in his term at 27° of Aries. This Saturn is allowed to be more Saturn-like (a more "Saturny" Saturn), but he isn't actually given power there.

If a planet is in the term of another planet, then the first planet becomes colored by the attitude, mode, or essence of the planet whose term it is in. Venus at 27° of Aries will be a more Saturn-like Venus (a "Saturny" Venus) because she is in Saturn's term. She may act in more melancholic and stoic ways, than if she were at 24° Aries where she would be in the term of Mars, where she might be more fiery, volatile, and aggressive.

We see a similar analogy to this in Medieval texts. Bonatti writes:

> And while it is in its own bound, it is like a man who is among his own kinsmen and blood-relatives and those related by birth, and by kindred, and kin by marriage, and those who relate to him by kinship.

Dignity by term/bound brings a sense of familiarity, even if it doesn't bring strength.

## Face/Decan/Decanate Rulership

> A planet in its face is like a person with [fine] ornaments and clothing.
> – ABRAHAM IBN EZRA

When a planet is in its own face, it receives +1 point of essential dignity. William Ramesey writes:

> A planet no otherwise fortified, than but being in face, and significator of any one, shows him signified to be, as it were, at the last shift, or as we say, at the last gasp, not knowing how to bestow himself, nor what course to take...

A planet that is only dignified by face rulership is not in a position to truly do any great amount of good. When a planet has face rulership, it is in a state that is better than being dead, but it is not that far from death. It is in a state of extraordinary desperation and despair, and is fearful of how it will support itself. A planet that only has face rulership is one that is minimally essentially dignified. When utilizing our point system to write a report regarding the strengths of the planets, I think it should be noted that the planet only dignified by face is "minimally essentially dignified" as opposed to "essentially dignified."

At first glance, the conception of a planet having face rulership in the Renaissance seems drastically different from how this is conceived in the Medieval period. Bonatti writes:

> And when in its own face, it is like a man who is among unknown people as sometimes happens to foreigners, and the like, though he lives among them because of an art and profession or service, or because of some other craftsman's or lay art.

For Bonatti, a planet in face is useful for what it can do, but not because of who it is intrinsically. For Ibn Ezra, a planet in face is like a very well-dressed person. Once again, this has more to do with the appearance and the outer garments of that planet, and not because of the planet's intrinsic value.

## On Essential Debilities

When a planet is essentially debilitated, it is in a state where it has no support to be who and what it is. It is weakened in its very essence, and cannot sustain itself, nor the things it signifies in a robust or powerful way. Whatever power it has is disrupted, confused, negatively altered, or destroyed. The way it performs will be notably more difficult or weaker than other more strongly dignified planets. It must rely heavily on whatever support it can find in its environment to assist it in delivering on its promise within the chart.

## Levels of Essential Debility

### Detriment

> *A planet in his house of detriment is like a person fighting with himself.*
> – Abraham Ibn Ezra

When a planet is in its detriment, it receives -5 points of essential debility. It is in a state of active destruction. It is in a sign of the zodiac that is in exact opposition to where it wants to be the most: its own domicile. It is in a sign where it is being corrupted; where what it naturally desires for itself is not available. It is in the exact opposite conditions than those that bring it the deepest amount of pleasure and joy. It is in a genuine state of misery and misfortune. The war that the planet is waging with itself is based on that planet asking itself the questions: What am I doing here? How did I end up here? Why would I do this to myself? These questions are true for the planet as well for the person the planet may represent in a reading.

### Fall

> *When a planet is in its fall, it indicates worry, distress, and hardship.*
> – Abraham Ibn Ezra

When a planet is in its fall, it receives -4 points of essential debility. It is in an exaggerated state of despair that is comparable to the exaggeration of being in its exaltation. It feels like it is falling down the side of a mountain, with no harness, no supports, and a clearly visible doom at the end of its descent. As far as the planet is concerned, it represents a most painful way to die. However, when a planet is in its detriment, it is far worse that when a planet is in its fall. Detriment represents what is most truthful about the suffering that a planet may be facing.

Fall represents an exaggerated state of suffering that, while terrible, isn't as bad as it seems. However, make no mistake: to be in fall is one of the worst things that can happen to a planet.

## PEREGRINE

> *A planet in a place where it has no dominion is like a person who is not in his own country.* – ABRAHAM IBN EZRA

When a planet is peregrine, it receives -5 points of essential debility. That planet has no essential dignity whatsoever. These planets are like people who are lost in the world: confused, wandering, and not knowing where to place themselves. These planets have neither a sense of direction nor a center of gravity, and are like disembodied souls roaming the Earth. They feel foreign and alien, as if they have fallen asleep and find themselves in the middle of some strange dream where they cannot adequately catch their bearings as to what is going on around them. Peregrine planet are anxious and uncertain.

## ALMUTENS

An almuten is the strongest planet that can be used to signify a thing within a chart. This strength can be measured in two ways. A planet can either be strong in terms of essential dignity or it can be strong based on it meeting a list of criteria.

It is important for us to make the distinction between an almuten of a degree versus an almuten of a topic. The term "almuten" can refer to a planet that has the most points of dignity within a particular degree of the zodiac. The use of this type of almuten was very popular within the seventeenth century. William Lilly writes:

> [The] Almuten of any house is that planet who hath most dignities in the sign ascending or descending upon the cusp of any house... [The] Almuten of a figure is that planet who in essential and accidental dignities is most powerful in the whole scheme of heaven.

If the almuten of a house is different from the domicile ruler of the sign on the cusp of that house, the almuten can technically be considered as a functional ruler of that house. When the points of essential dignity are fully tallied, it sometimes turns out that another planet has more points of essential dignity over a particular degree of the zodiac than the actual planet that rules that sign. When the degree in question falls on the cusp of a house we may be considering, the almuten of that degree may be considered all-powerful in carrying out the destiny of that house. This is further amplified if the domicile ruler of that house is essentially debilitated in the chart in which the almuten ruler is strong.

This frequently happens in the case of the signs Aries and Libra, where their exaltation rulers are often more powerful than their domicile rulers depending on which degree of those signs we are considering.

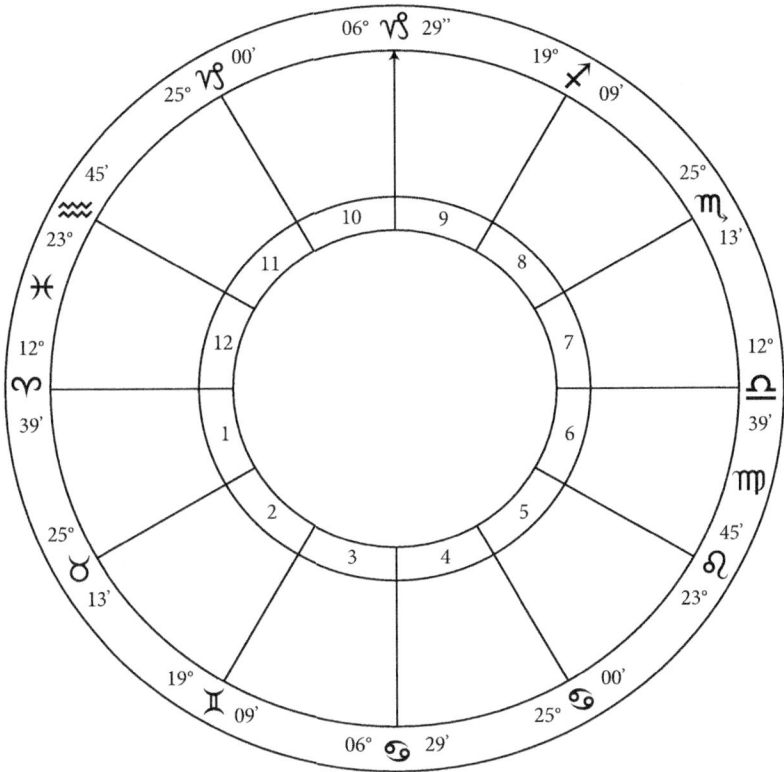

FIGURE 6: *Sun as the Almuten Ruler of 12° ARI 39' in a Diurnal Chart*

If in a diurnal chart, 12° Aries 39' were rising on the cusp of the Ascendant, the Sun would be the almuten of that degree. This is because the Sun is more dignified in that degree than the domicile ruler of Aries – Mars – is in the entire sign. Below is a table of the points of essential dignity various planets have at that degree.

TABLE 6: *Almuten Example Chart I*

| DOMICILE OF MARS | ♂ | +5 points |
|---|---|---|
| EXALTATION OF THE SUN | ☉ | +4 points |
| DIURNAL TRIPLICITY RULER | ☉ | +3 points |
| PARTICIPATING TRIPLICITY RULER | ♄ | +3 points |
| TERM OF VENUS | ♀ | +2 points |
| FACE OF THE SUN | ☉ | +1 point |

Below is a table of the total score each planet receives at that degree.

TABLE 7: *Calculating Almuten Ruler 1*

| | |
|---|---|
| ☉ | +8 points |
| ♂ | +5 points |
| ♄ | +3 points |
| ♀ | +2 points |

Mars will always be the domicile ruler over every degree of Aries in the daytime and the nighttime. However, in a diurnal chart the Sun will have more essential dignity at 12° Aries 39' than Mars will. The Sun would be the almuten of the Ascendant. He would be capable of representing the native or the querent just as much as Mars would under normal conditions.

The same is true in the case of Libra.

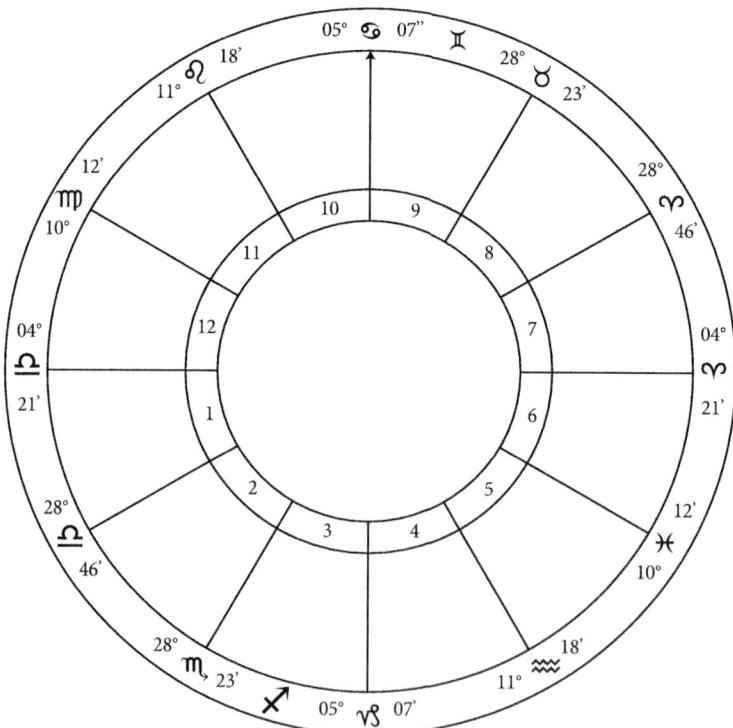

FIGURE 7: *Saturn as the Almuten Ruler of 04° LIB 21' in a Diurnal Chart*

If in a diurnal chart, 04° Libra 21' were on the Ascendant, Saturn would be the almuten of that degree. This is because Saturn is more dignified in that degree than the domicile ruler of Libra – Venus – is in the entire sign. Below is a table of the points of essential dignity various planets have at that degree.

TABLE 8: *Almuten Example Chart II*

| DOMICILE OF VENUS | ♀ | +5 points |
|---|---|---|
| EXALTATION OF SATURN | ♄ | +4 points |
| DIURNAL TRIPLICITY RULER | ♄ | +3 points |
| PARTICIPATING TRIPLICITY RULER | ♃ | +3 points |
| TERM OF SATURN | ♄ | +2 points |
| FACE OF THE MOON | ☽ | +1 point |

Below is a table of the total score each planet receives at that degree.

TABLE 9: *Calculating Almuten Ruler II*

| ♄ | +9 points |
|---|---|
| ♀ | +5 points |
| ☽ | +1 point |

Venus will always be the domicile ruler over every degree of Libra in the day-time and nighttime. However, in a diurnal chart Saturn will have more essential dignity at 04° Libra 21' than Venus will. Saturn would be the almuten of the Ascendant. He would be capable of representing the native or querent just as much as Venus would under normal conditions.

Though this is useful to be aware of, as always, I derive the core of my astrological interpretation from the domicile rulers of the signs on the cusps of the twelve terrestrial houses. Anything that I may gain from using the almutens only serves as a further corroboration of what is already being indicated within the basic chart delineation without overlaying additional techniques.

TOPIC-BASED ALMUTENS

The term almuten can also refer to a planet that most strongly represents a topic within a chart. For almutens of topics we find various formulae for deciding which planet will be most victorious in representing a specific topic.

Omar of Tiberias (died circa 815 CE) was a Persian astrologer from the Middle Ages. He wrote heavily about almutens within his work, *On Nativities*. He tells us that in order to find the almuten over sexual union, we must first examine:

> *The seventh [house] and its lord and see what planets may be in the seventh, also the Moon and Venus, and the Part of the Sexual Union and its lord; and according to the command of God you will examine the almuten of these places...*

I believe the almutens can be valuable corroborating factors for things that are otherwise already indicated in a chart. However, I will always build the core of my interpretation on the domicile rulers of the signs on the cusps of the twelve terrestrial houses.

## CHAPTER 12 QUESTIONS

1. What is essential dignity? What is essential debility?
2. Why is essential dignity and debility such an important planetary consideration in traditional astrology?
3. List the various levels of essential dignity, a brief definition of each, and their associated points in the point system.
4. List the various levels of essential debility, a brief definition of each, and their associated points in the point system.
5. Do you consider Saturn at 27° ARI 05' to be essentially dignified or debilitated? Give your rationale.
6. Define the word "almuten."
7. Which planet would be the almuten of 11° ARI 13' in a diurnal chart? Provide your rationale.
8. In traditional astrology, when we say "a small good does not mitigate a major evil," what do we mean? How does this relate to the topic of essential dignity and debility?

CHAPTER 13 OBJECTIVES

* Define the terms "reception" and "mutual reception."
* Identify the elements necessary for both of these planetary connections to occur.
* Discuss the difference between reception by major dignity and reception by minor dignity.
* Demonstrate the various forms of mixed reception.
* Explore the difference between planets being in reception and planets being in each other's generosity.
* Explore some of the linguistic issues we find in the various classical definitions of reception.

# CHAPTER 13

## ON RECEPTION &
## MUTUAL RECEPTION

*If a received planet were a fortune, its strength is augmented, but if a bad one, it will be diminished from its evil.* - ABRAHAM IBN EZRA

RECEPTION OCCURS WHEN A PLANET aspects its dispositor. In general, a "dispositor" is the planet that is the domicile ruler of the sign that another planet is in. However, a dispositor can also be the exaltation ruler of the sign in which a planet is located, or the ruler of two or more of the minor dignities of triplicity, term, or face that a planet may be in.

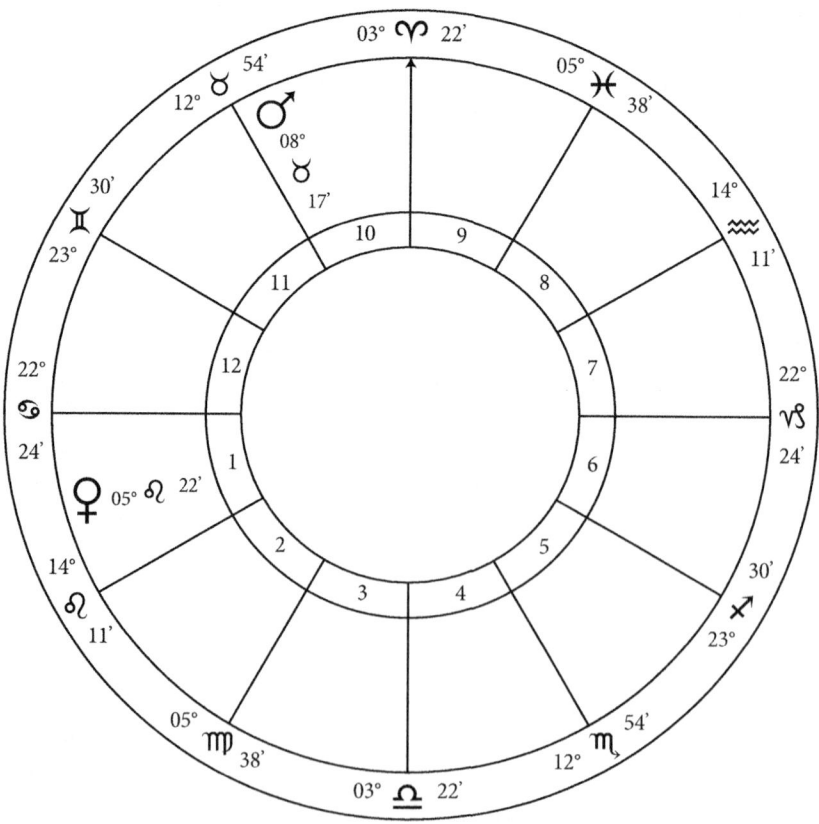

FIGURE 1: *Mars Received by Venus*

In reception, the planet can either be applying to the aspect of its dispositor, or its dispositor can be applying to the aspect of it. In the standard form of reception, where we have a faster moving planet applying to an aspect with its slower moving dispositor, the applying planet is called the "pusher." It is essentially pushing the intrinsic nature of its dispositor back to its dispositor from a sign in which its dispositor has essential dignity.

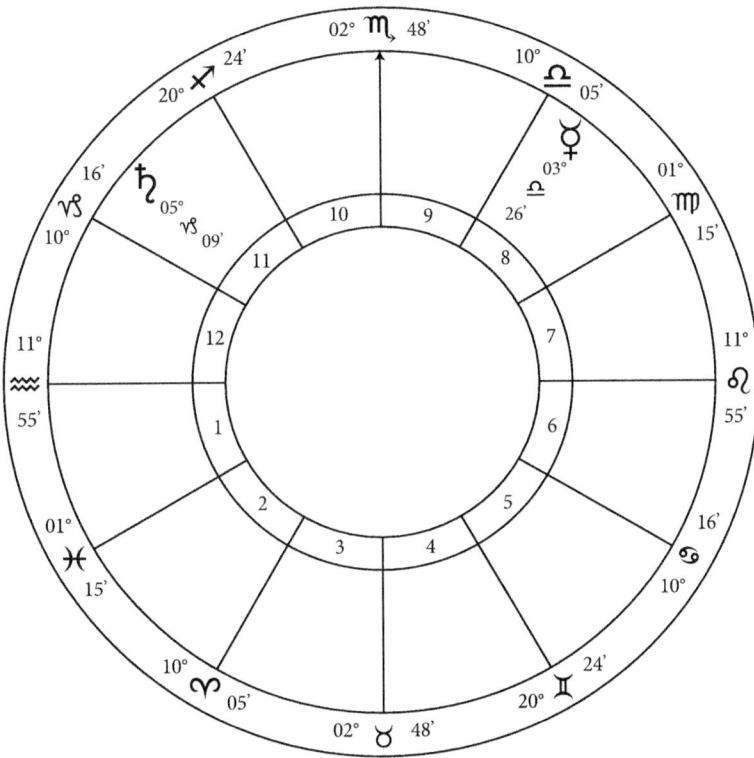

FIGURE 2: *Mercury Received by Saturn*

If Mercury in Libra were applying to Saturn in Capricorn, Mercury would be pushing back to Saturn something that Saturn is very familiar with receiving: the feeling of exaltation that he has while in Libra. Therefore, Saturn feels Mercury bringing him this gift of power. Resultantly, Saturn feels kindly towards Mercury. Saturn now wants to support Mercury in doing whatever it is he is trying to accomplish. The feeling or offering that Mercury has pushed towards Saturn inclines Saturn to help Mercury fulfill his destiny. This is what reception is – a receiving planet helping the planet it receives to fulfill its purpose within a chart.

The other version of reception is when a planet is being applied to by its dispositor. If Venus in Cancer were being applied to by the Moon in Virgo, the Moon would still be receiving Venus. This is true even though Venus is slower than the Moon. The Moon will still be predisposed to assisting Venus in fulfilling whatever her goal is while she is in Cancer. The Moon has now taken on the concerns of Venus and has made them her concerns.

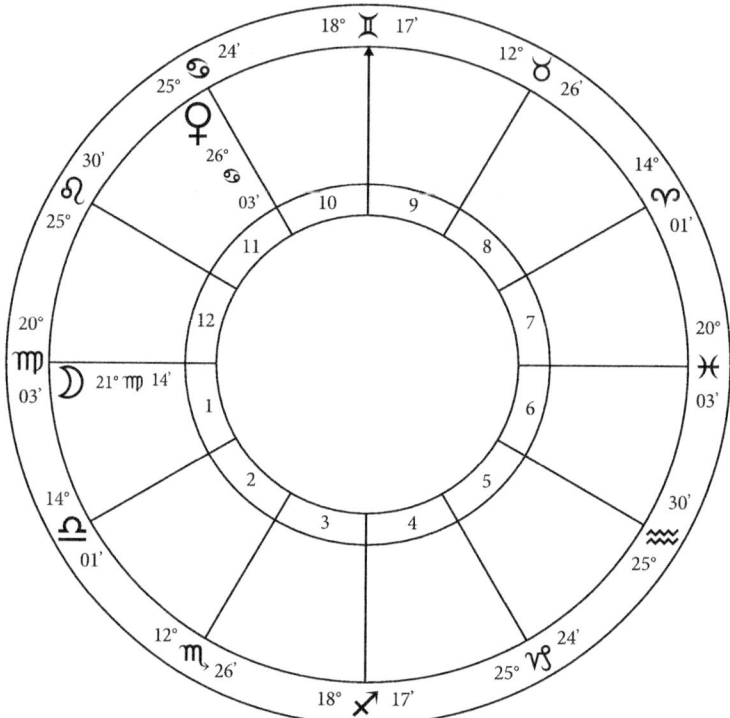

FIGURE 3: *Venus Received by the Moon*

In the first example, it was as if Mercury was reaching out to his dispositor for help. In this second example, it is as if the Moon is stretching out a hand to be of support to someone who she welcomes into her home.

Reception is highly supportive to the planet that is being received. It greatly assists that planet in fulfilling its promise. It is a blessing for planets that might find themselves in an otherwise challenging set of circumstances. It represents a source of aid and goodwill that helps the planet in charging forward towards a positive outcome.

In general, reception can be divided into two categories: perfect reception or minor reception. "Perfect reception" refers to when a planet is in one of the major dignities of another planet and is in aspect with that other planet. Medieval astrologer Sahl Ibn Bishr (circa 786-845 CE) tells us:

> *The reception of the planets is when a planet is joined to (another) planet by its own domicile or its own exaltation; then it receives it in a good spirit and in a perfect reception.*

"Minor reception" refers to when a planet is occupying at least two minor dignities of another planet and in aspect with that other planet. This is less powerful than perfect reception. However, it may still be beneficial for the planet being received.

Sahl writes:

> There is also another reception that is below this... viz. when a planet
> is joined to the ruler of its own triplicity and terms, or to the ruler of
> the terms and the face, i.e., when it is joined to a planet that has in
> its own place two or more of those minor dignities; and then it will be
> a true reception. But if it has only one (minor dignity), there will not
> be a reception there; and he says this [is] because something different
> was transferred from them, and by a skilled Astrologer it is said to be
> of no importance.

Sahl is saying that in order for minor reception to be valid, the planet being received has to be in either the triplicity and term or the term and face of the receiving planet. One minor dignity in isolation is not enough to qualify as reception. It is worth noting that Sahl does not mention triplicity and face being a potential combination.

Ibn Ezra is of another opinion. In *The Beginning of Wisdom*, he writes:

> ... if it is in its triplicity house, or bound, or face, it will not receive it
> by complete reception unless the two rulerships coincide, the triplicity
> with the bound or face.

Ibn Ezra is telling us that triplicity can be coupled with either bound or face in order to fulfill the requirements of minor reception. I tend to lean more in this direction. However, Ibn Ezra's requirements for minor reception also don't fully embrace all the combinations of minor dignities. For him, minor reception could include triplicity and term or triplicity and face. Within *The Beginning of Wisdom* we do not see him make mention of reception by term and face being an option.

What we see in both Sahl and Ibn Ezra is that reception by triplicity rulership is not enough. If we expressed this purely through the language of the point system, we may be led to believe that reception by only +3 points of essential dignity is not enough. This would suggest that reception by term and face combined would also be insufficient, since the accumulative value of their essential dignity score is +3 points.

Abū Maʿšar clarifies this point fully for us in his *Great Introduction*. He writes:

> However, if the conjunction were only with the Lord of the bound or
> the Lord of the triplicity, or with the Lord of the face, the reception will
> be weak, unless the bound and triplicity are being joined, or the bound
> and the face, or the triplicity and the face: because then it will be a
> perfected reception.

Thus, we see that reception can take place through a planet occupying either one of the major dignities of domicile and exaltation or two of the minor dignities of triplicity, term, or face of the planet that it is in aspect with. This allows us more possibility to find and use reception within our chart investigations.

## MUTUAL RECEPTION

> *The testimony of the significators, if in mutual reception, will indicate a thing coming to pass which had not been expected.* – ABRAHAM IBN EZRA

Mutual reception refers to when two planets are in each other's dignities and are in aspect with each other. In perfect reception, minor reception, and mutual reception we find that the planets must be in aspect with each other. The aspect relationship between the received and the receiving planet is a necessary component of our classical understanding of reception.

In the case of mutual reception, any combination of essential dignities is permissible. Mutual reception exists if two planets are in each other's domiciles such as the Sun in Aries trine Mars in Leo. Mutual reception exists if two planets are in each other's exaltations such as Venus in Cancer trine Jupiter in Pisces.

Mixed mutual reception is when planets are in each other's dignities, but the dignities are different. Amongst the major dignities, this would be if one planet was in the domicile of another planet while the other planet was in the first planet's exaltation.

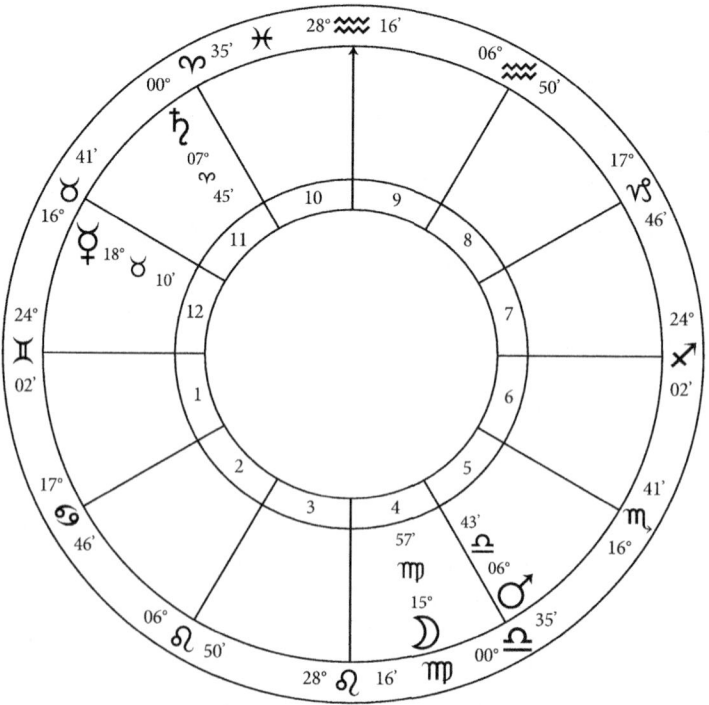

FIGURE 4: *Mixed Mutual Reception*

An example of this would be Moon in Virgo trine Mercury in Taurus. Another example could be Mars in Libra opposite Saturn in Aries. No doubt Mars in Libra and Saturn in Aries have very large problems to deal with since they are in their detriment and fall, respectively. However, this still qualifies as a mixed mutual reception, weak though it may be.

I think this brings up another important point. Reception or mutual reception is only as supportive for the planets in question based on how supported they are within themselves. A planet can only be supported within itself if it is essentially dignified. Mars in Libra square Saturn in Aries represents a mixed mutual reception between two very essentially debilitated planets. I believe that the essential natures of the planets will always be more important than the things that happen to those planets externally. Reception and mutual reception aid planets in achieving a successful outcome to their goals. However, if the planets are essentially weak to begin with, then reception and mutual reception can't truly be expected to do for those planets what they technically have no ability to do for themselves.

Another form of mixed mutual reception includes the use of the minor dignities. There can be several interesting combinations that we derive from this.

TABLE 1: *Mixed Mutual Reception Examples*

| PLANET A | PLANET B |
| --- | --- |
| IN THE DOMICILE OF B | IN THE TERM AND FACE OF A |
| IN THE EXALTATION OF B | IN THE TRIPLICITY AND TERM OF A |
| IN THE TERM AND FACE OF B | IN THE TRIPLICITY AND TERM OF A |
| IN THE TRIPLICITY AND FACE OF B | IN THE EXALTATION OF A |

All of these permutations represent different types of mixed mutual reception. In every instance, we either find two planets occupying each other's major dignities, one planet occupying the major dignity of the other while the other planet occupies two of the minor dignities of the first planet, or both planets occupying two of each other's minor dignities.

## OTHER MEANING OF RECEPTION

The other definition of reception is that any planet in any sign of the zodiac is already received by the planet that rules that sign, whether they are in aspect with each other or not. This definition of reception is synonymous with dispositorship, where a planet that rules a sign is the lord of the planets within that sign. While this definition of reception is also one that we find within classical literature, it isn't what most people would refer to when they use the word "reception." To minimize confusion, I never use it in this way.

## HOW NECESSARY IS THE ASPECT IN RECEPTION?

Classically, the aspectual relationship between a planet in a sign and the ruler of that sign was vital to the definition of reception. Mutual reception also traditionally required an aspect for it to be effectual. This tends to be the normative definition of reception within the Medieval literature on the topic. Nevertheless, there are still areas that make us doubtful regarding the full scope of what the ancients viewed as being valid criteria for reception.

I believe the aspect between planets is necessary for reception to occur. This is because there is already a name for when two planets are in each other's dignities and not connected by an aspect. When this happens, they are said to be in each other's "generosity." Abraham Ibn Ezra writes:

> *Generosity is when two planets are in each other's domicile, or exaltation, or some other rulership; even though they do not join nor aspect one another, there is (still) reception between them.*

By him saying "there is still reception between them," we find yet another technical issue. His use of the word reception skews our classical understanding that in order for reception to be valid, there must be an aspectual relationship between the received and the receiver. He wasn't the only one who did this. The word reception was commonly used amongst classical astrologers to describe many styles of planetary interaction. Al-Qabisi writes:

> *And there is another kind of reception: when some one of the planets occupies the trigon of the other, or the hexagon together with it, (but without an application, though reception with an application is stronger).*

What Al-Qabisi is saying is that if two planets are in each other's triplicity, then they are already in reception.

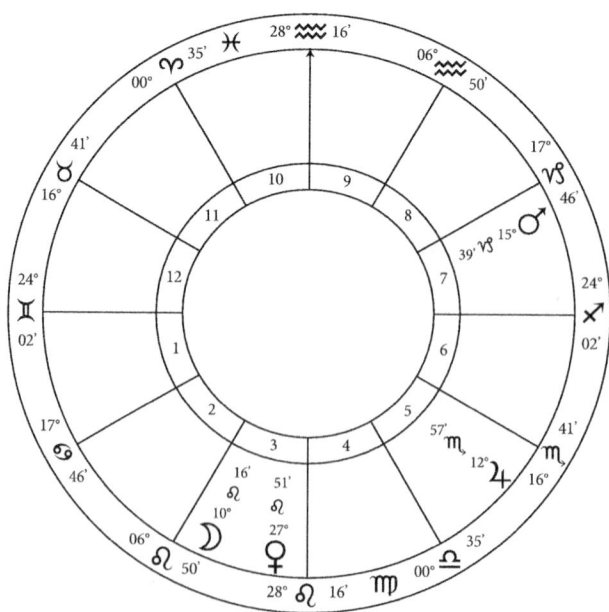

FIGURE 5: *Reception by Triplicity (Al-Qabisi)*

An example of this would be if the Moon, ruler of Cancer, were in Leo, a fiery sign, and Jupiter, ruler of Sagittarius, were in Scorpio, a watery sign. Just because they are in each other's triplicity, there would be some form of reception between them. Similarly, if Venus were in Leo of the fixed quadruplicity, and Mars were in Capricorn of the cardinal quadruplicity, Al-Qabisi is saying that there would be a type of reception between them. This is because Venus rules cardinal Libra that is of the same "hexagon" that Capricorn is in. Mars rules fixed Scorpio that is of the same "hexagon" that Leo is in.

As we read the classical literature on reception, we find that while several things end up being called "reception" throughout time, the indisputable definition of reception is when a planet is in aspect with its dispositor. Anything outside of this represents a weaker mode of planetary connection that many ancient astrologers considered to be a sort of reception. However, these connections still do not replace the power that the standard aspect-based reception holds.

I am more sympathetic to the idea of aspect-based reception. Aspects show interaction between planets. When we think of a planet being received by another planet, we think of those planets interacting with each other. In general, if there is no aspect between planets, there is no interaction between those planets. It seems logical that if two planets are not in an aspect relationship, then they also can't hope to receive or be received in our classical sense of those terms. Aspects allow planets to be aware of each other. I've dreamt about asking many people for help in life. However, the only times I actually received assistance from those people is when I reached out and asked them directly for their assistance. The only other times I've receive assistance from others is if assisting me was already on their agenda. In both scenarios, I needed to become a conscious thought within that person's mind. The same is true for planets. The only way the receiving planet can be aware of another planet's existence is if they can see each other. In astrology, the only way planets can see each other is through their aspectual relationship.

Within our classical literature, we see Medieval astrologers using whole sign aspects as valid forms of reception.

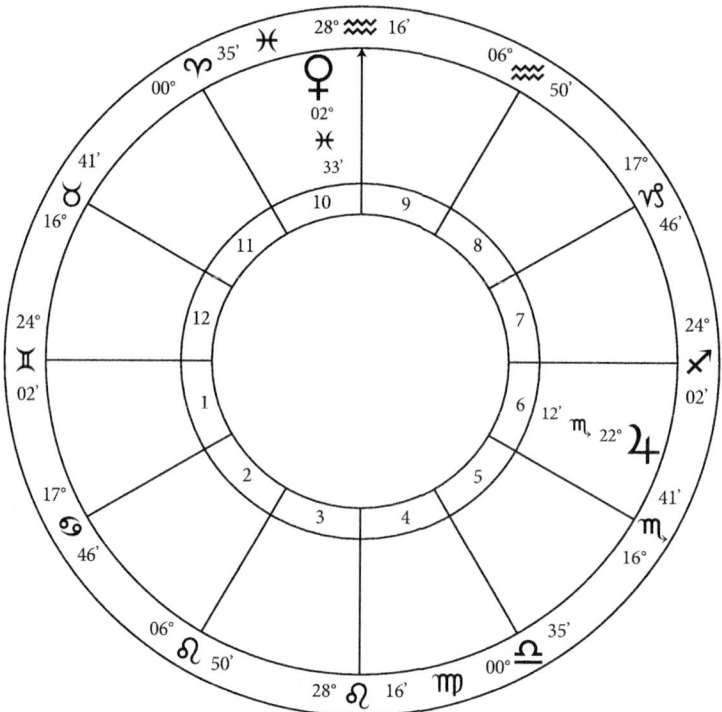

FIGURE 6: *Venus Received by Jupiter (Whole Sign)*

This means that Venus in Pisces and Jupiter in Scorpio would be in reception even if Venus were at 02° Pisces and Jupiter were at 22° Scorpio. As in all things, I prefer tighter orbs. I personally don't use whole sign aspects within my work with reception. I would give a maximum of a 10° applying orb for either the pusher to apply to its dispositor or for the dispositor to apply to its guest planet. Though this is wider than the orb I would normally use, these planets are already sensitive to each other's needs by being the received and the receiver.

I also prefer to only use applying aspects in my work with reception. It feels more in conformity with astrology and with nature that the applying aspect between a dispositor and the planet that it rules will be more powerful than a separating aspect between those two planets. However, in a world where many people utilize reception within a whole sign context, it is well worth deciding for yourself what seems most sensible to you and what yields the most accurate results within your practice of concrete astrology.

There is also a notion that reception is a blessing regardless of what the nature of the planets are who are in reception or mutual reception with each other. I fundamentally disagree with this. As far as traditional astrology is concerned, the intrinsic strength of the planet largely predetermines what that planet will be capable of within the chart.

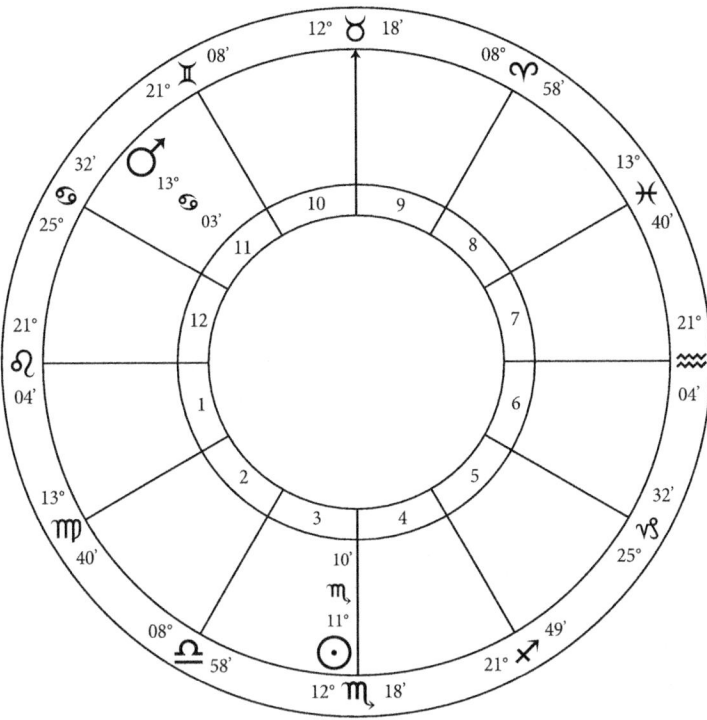

FIGURE 7: *Sun Received by Essentially Debiliated Mars*

For example, the Sun at 11° Scorpio 10' has Mars as his domicile ruler. However, if that Sun is trine Mars at 13° Cancer 03', I question how much that Mars can be of any assistance to the Sun. When planets are occupied with their own debility such as Mars in the sign of his fall, those debilitated planets have far bigger worries to attend to other than supporting other planets who may be asking them for help. In the case of our weakly essentially dignified Sun having face rulership at 11° Scorpio 10' and our essentially debilitated Mars in fall at 13° Cancer 03', the Sun has to find a way to take care of himself. Mars can render little to no assistance.

As far as reception is concerned, I am not inclined to use it excessively within my practice. I teach it to my students out of fidelity to traditional astrology. However, it doesn't feature very highly in my client work. I believe that having a deep understanding of how different planets feel when they occupy different degrees of the zodiac is a far better astrological aspiration than knowing how to judge how they operate together when in reception.

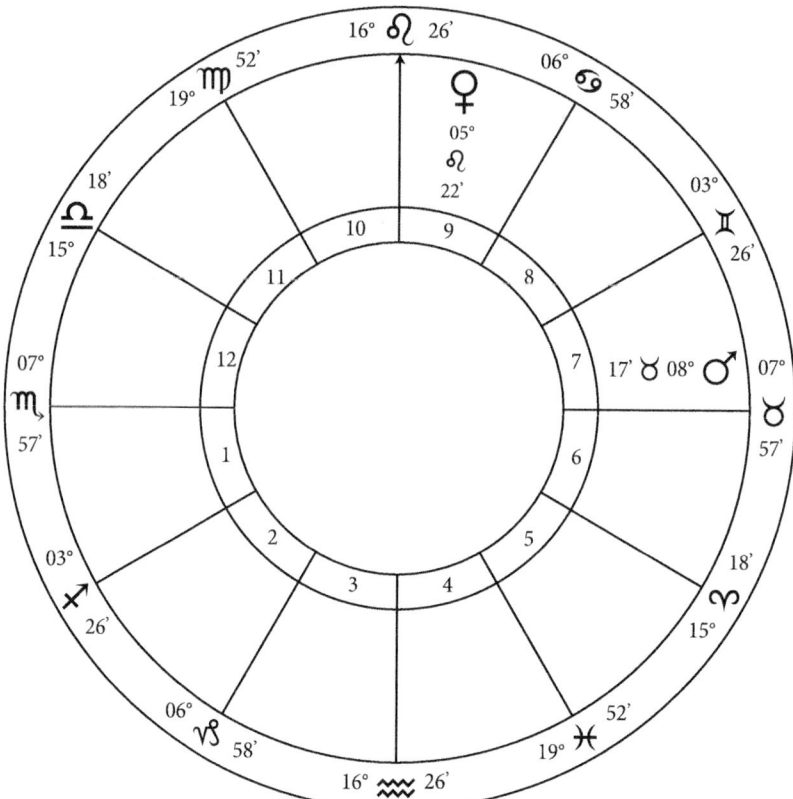

FIGURE 8: *Mars Received by Venus*

For example, Mars at 08° Taurus 17' is received by Venus at 05° Leo 22'. However, reception or no reception Mars in Taurus is powerfully essentially debilitated. The very nature of Taurus is not in conformity with the nature of Mars. When viewed from this perspective, this becomes less of a technical issue of how many points a planet gains or loses for being in a particular sign. It has more to do with how that sign makes that planet feel by being there in general. Taurus, a fixed earth sign, in no way shares a natural analogy with Mars, a fiery, fast, and volatile planet. How Mars feels in Taurus is more important than the number of points he gains for being received by Venus.

CHAPTER 13 QUESTIONS

1. What is reception?
2. What are the key elements necessary for reception to occur between planets?
3. What is mutual reception?
4. Give an example of two planets in mutual reception by major dignity.
5. Give an example of one planet being received by another planet through minor dignities. Remember that in order for minor reception to occur, the planet in question has to occupy two or more of the minor dignities of the receiving planet.
6. What does it mean for a planet to be in the generosity of another planet? How does this differ from planets being in reception?
7. If Mars at 12° CAN 37' received Saturn at 15° ARI 56' RX., how helpful do you think this would be for Saturn? Explain your rationale.
8. If strongly essentially dignified planets mutually receive each other, how do you think this will impact the things that both planets signify or promise within a given chart?

## CHAPTER 14 OBJECTIVES

* Understand the role exaltation plays within the five levels of essential dignity.
* Define the term "dispositor" and its appropriate use within traditional astrology.
* Discuss the difference between cardinal and ordinal numbers when outlining the degrees of exaltation and fall of the of the seven classical planets.
* Provide an explanation for why the planets have their exaltations and falls in the various signs of the zodiac.

# CHAPTER 14

## EXALTATIONS
## OF THE PLANETS

*When a planet is in its domicile, it has power in the whole sign,*
*and so it is in the sign of its exaltation; yet, at the [specific]*
*degree of exaltation, it has more power than in the rest of the*
*sign.* – ABRAHAM IBN EZRA

T HE THEMA MUNDI HAS SERVED US WELL in our understanding of the domiciles
and detriments of the seven classical planets. However, it hasn't given us very
much in terms of understanding the other levels of essential dignity and debility.
In this chapter, we'll unpack the second level of essential dignity: the exaltations
of the planets. We will also explore the opposition sign of each planet's exaltation.
This opposition sign is known as the "fall" of the planet.

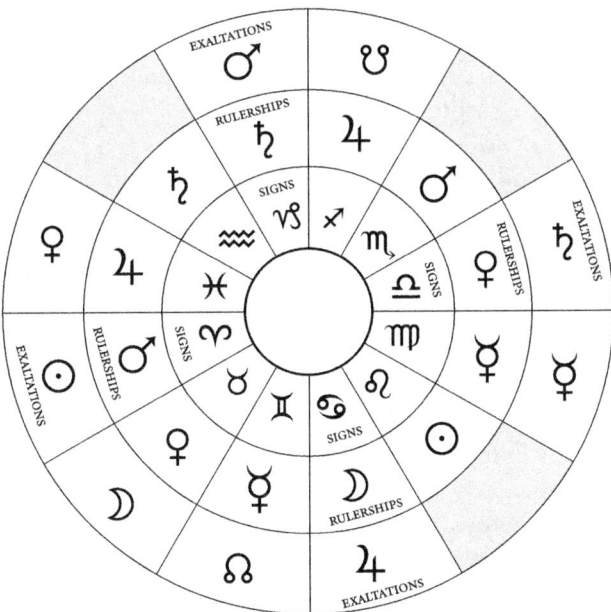

FIGURE 1: *Major Dignities of the Planets*

The exaltations of the planets refer to signs of the zodiac other than their
domiciles where they are strongly supported. When planets are in their sign of

exaltation, they can express themselves in a way that is harmonious with their nature. However, there is a major difference between exaltation and domicile. Whereas domicile refers to the sign that a planet specifically is the lord or owner of, exaltation refers to a sign where a planet is powerful, even though that sign belongs to another planet. When we speak about Saturn being in exaltation in Libra, we are saying that Saturn performs at a high level when he is there, even though Libra is the domicile of Venus. Though Saturn is treated like royalty when he is in Libra, he doesn't get to make the final decision in terms of what he does or how he does it. Venus is his ruler. Even if a planet is naturally very strong in a sign that it finds itself in, if that sign is not its domicile, then that planet is under the jurisdiction of the planet that is the domicile ruler of that sign.

Exalted planets have a great amount of power. They are well-positioned to fulfill their agenda successfully within a chart. In *The Beginning of Wisdom*, Abraham Ibn Ezra tells us:

> *A planet in its exaltation is like a person at his greatest rank.*

Guido Bonatti writes:

> *And while in its own exaltation, it is like a man who is in his own kingdom and in his own glory, like a kingdom, civil authority, a dukedom, and as are other lay dignities which can forsake him before his own matters do.*

Both Ibn Ezra's notion of "greatest rank" and Bonatti's "civil authority" show that exaltation refers to an honored title that is bestowed upon a planet. Though powerful, there is a sense of exteriority in exaltation; as if it is something the planet receives from the outside world. It is similar to being held in high social regard, as if the planet is being recognized for some great or valiant work. However, Bonatti adds that it also represents "… lay dignities which can forsake him before his own matters do." There isn't the same sense of permanence in exaltation that we find in domicile rulership. There isn't the same sort of genuine and unshakeable power. It isn't as natural or as effortless as being in domicile. It also doesn't provide the most grounded self-perception that a planet can have.

This should not lead us to believe that exaltation is a weak dignity. On the contrary, when a planet is in its exaltation, it has an extraordinary amount of power to fulfil whatever its promise is within a chart. This is further amplified if its dispositor is very strong in whatever sign it finds itself in. The strength is increased even further if the exalted planet is in a strong positive aspect with its ruler who is also strongly essentially dignified. This is one example of reception between planets, which we've previously discussed. Even if the ruler of the sign isn't strongly dignified, planets in their exaltation are more inclined to perform powerfully than if they were not in either of their two major dignities of domicile or exaltation.

On our five point measuring system for essential dignity, planets in their exaltation receive +4 points of dignity.

DISPOSITORSHIP

When Planet A is in the domicile of Planet B, Planet A is said to be ruled by Planet B. Traditionally, we would say that Planet B disposes Planet A. "Disposed" in this sense doesn't mean "to throw away or discard." It means "to determine the outcome of" or "to be responsible for." In the case of Saturn in Libra, though Saturn is in his exaltation in Libra, Venus disposes Saturn. Venus is the dispositor of Saturn. The word "dispositor" refers to a planet who presides over and is responsible for the affairs of another planet that is in the domicile of the first planet. Saturn in Libra is in the domicile of Venus. Therefore, Venus is the ruler or dispositor of Saturn when Saturn is in Libra.

The dispositor "disposes." The dispositor does not "disposit." *Disposit* is not a word. There are not planets that are "disposited" by other planets. A dispositor disposes. Every planet is disposed by its dispositor. Every planet is the dispositor of other planets who may be occupying their domiciles.

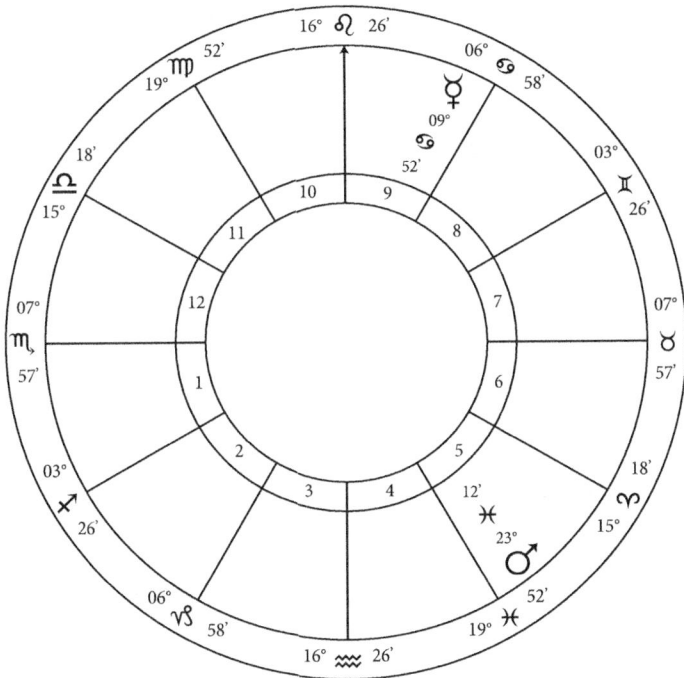

FIGURE 2: *Mars disposed by Jupiter, Mercury disposed by the Moon*

If Mars is in Pisces, his dispositor is Jupiter, he is disposed of by Jupiter, and Jupiter is his ruler. If Mercury is in Cancer, his dispositor is the Moon, he is disposed by the Moon, and the Moon is his ruler. The Moon will be the dispositor of Mercury for as long as Mercury is in Cancer. When Mercury leaves Cancer, the Moon will no longer be his dispositor. Every planet is the dispositor of the planets that are occupying their domiciles.

The exaltations of the planets are listed below as well as their dispositors when in those signs.

TABLE 1: *Exaltation Degree & Dispositors*

| PLANET | EXALTATION | | DISPOSITOR |
|--------|------------|---|-----------|
| ♄ | 21ST DEGREE OF | ♎ | ♀ |
| ♃ | 15TH DEGREE OF | ♋ | ☽ |
| ♂ | 28TH DEGREE OF | ♑ | ♄ |
| ☉ | 19TH DEGREE OF | ♈ | ♂ |
| ♀ | 27TH DEGREE OF | ♓ | ♃ |
| ☿ | 15TH DEGREE OF | ♍ | ☿ |
| ☽ | 3RD DEGREE OF | ♉ | ♀ |

Though each planet has its specific degree of exaltation, those planets are exalted within the entire sign. Though the Sun's exaltation degree is the 19th degree of Aries, he is in exaltation during his entire time in Aries.

Be mindful that I did not say "the Sun is exalted at 19° Aries;" but rather, that the Sun is exalted in the 19th degree of Aries. This is a very important distinction since the 19th degree refers to the ordinal placement of that degree within the sign of Aries. The number nineteen does not correspond with the number of the degree of the Sun's exaltation in Aries. In order to understand this, we first need to understand the difference between cardinal and ordinal numbers.

CARDINAL VS. ORDINAL NUMBERS

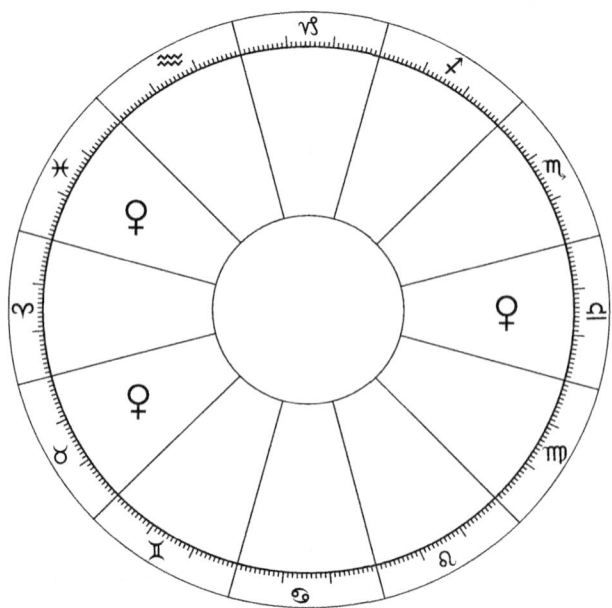

FIGURE 3: *Venus in her Domiciles & Exaltation*

The topic of exaltation is the first time we've had to become degree-specific in terms of essential dignity. When a planet is in its domicile, it is in its domicile at every degree of that sign. Venus is in her domicile from 00°00' to 29° 59' when she is in either Taurus or Libra. Even though she is exalted during her entire time in Pisces, when she is occupying the 27th degree of Pisces she is standing in the specific degree of Pisces where she is most exalted. In practice, I have not seen a planet in its exaltation degree doing any better than if that planet simply occupied its exaltation sign. Either of the major dignities of domicile or exaltation is usually sufficient without additional supports. However, this understanding of the degrees becomes particularly important especially when exploring the other minor essential dignities of term and face.

A cardinal number is a number used for counting (1, 2, 3, etc.). An ordinal number is a number used for denoting the position of a thing within a series (1st, 2nd, 3rd, etc.). We know that every sign of the zodiac has 30°. This means that we can count from the first degree of a sign to the thirtieth degree of a sign using the ordinal numbers of first, second, third, fourth, etc.

However, the first degree of a sign is not numbered "one." The first degree of every sign of the zodiac is numbered "zero." Even though there are 30° in every sign of the zodiac, when counting the degrees using cardinal numbers, we will never count a degree numbered "thirty." We will count from 00° of that sign to 29° of that sign, because 00° is the first degree of every sign of the zodiac. Therefore, degree number twenty-nine will be the thirtieth degree of every sign of the zodiac. If a planet is at the fourteenth degree of a sign, it is actually somewhere between 13° 00' and 13° 59' of that sign.

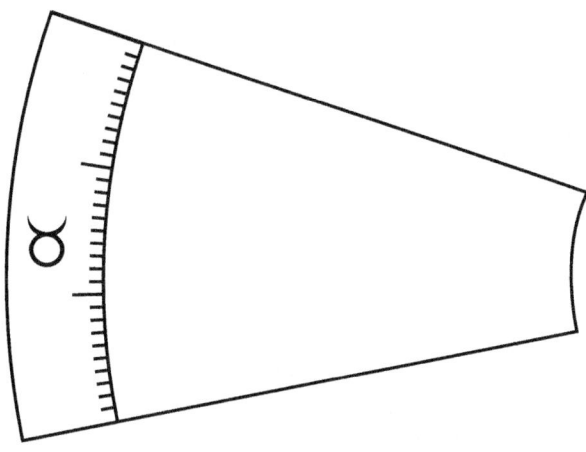

FIGURE 4: *30 ° of a Sign*

Though the exaltation degrees are listed in TABLE 1 using the ordinal system, this needs to be translated into cardinal numbers in order to understand where these degrees are in relation to the signs.

TABLE 2: *Exaltations*

| PLANET | ORDINAL DEGREE | EXALTATION | ZODIACAL RANGE |
|---|---|---|---|
| ♄ | 21ST DEGREE OF | ♎ | 20° 00' - 20° 59' |
| ♃ | 15TH DEGREE OF | ♋ | 14° 00' - 14° 59' |
| ♂ | 28TH DEGREE OF | ♑ | 27° 00' - 27° 59' |
| ☉ | 19TH DEGREE OF | ♈ | 18° 00' - 18° 59' |
| ♀ | 27TH DEGREE OF | ♓ | 26° 00' - 26° 59' |
| ☿ | 15TH DEGREE OF | ♍ | 14° 00' - 14° 59' |
| ☽ | 3RD DEGREE OF | ♉ | 02° 00' - 02° 59' |

The falls of the planets are the exact opposite sign and degree of their exaltations.

TABLE 3: *Falls*

| PLANET | ORDINAL DEGREE | FALL | ZODIACAL RANGE |
|---|---|---|---|
| ♄ | 21ST DEGREE OF | ♈ | 20° 00' - 20° 59' |
| ♃ | 15TH DEGREE OF | ♑ | 14° 00' - 14° 59' |
| ♂ | 28TH DEGREE OF | ♋ | 27° 00' - 27° 59' |
| ☉ | 19TH DEGREE OF | ♎ | 18° 00' - 18° 59' |
| ♀ | 27TH DEGREE OF | ♍ | 26° 00' - 26° 59' |
| ☿ | 15TH DEGREE OF | ♓ | 14° 00' - 14° 59' |
| ☽ | 3RD DEGREE OF | ♏ | 02° 00' - 02° 59' |

With the exception of Mercury in Virgo, in both the exaltations and the falls the planets are ruled over or disposed of by other planets.

Planets in their exaltation are strongly equipped to deliver on the promise they have been entrusted with within a chart. Planets in their fall are ill-equipped to deliver on the promise they have been entrusted with within a chart. Planets in their fall have to rely on environmental factors to support them and bolster their strength. Otherwise, they can't and won't deliver a positive outcome. A large part of our work in traditional astrology is to identify how strong or capable a planet is to deliver on what it has been specifically designated to do. The better our ability to measure planetary strength and come to a concrete decision about how it will materially manifest, the more skillful we become in traditional astrology.

Next, we will learn what the rationale is behind the exaltations and the falls of the planets as conceived of by the ancients.

SATURN

Saturn has his exaltation in Libra. Libra is where the Sun relinquishes his crown and begins his descent into the underworld. Cold and dry, cruel Saturn has his exaltation where the hot and dry, life-supporting Sun hurtles to his grave. In *A New and Complete Illustration of the Celestial Science of Astrology* (1826), astrologer Ebenezer Sibly writes:

> *Saturn, the most remote planet, is the author of cold, as the Sun is of heat, and is therefore exalted in that sign wherein heat is diminished and cold increased, viz. Libra…*

The fire signs cannot bring out the highest form of Saturn. The hot and outgoing fire is in direct contradiction to his cold and indrawn nature. The water signs only further increase his depressive melancholy. He is in detriment in Cancer. Scorpio – a fixed water sign ruled by malefic Mars – would only amplify the evil within him. The fixed nature of Scorpio would render his malice even more severe and destructive. Pisces is the absolute antithesis of everything Saturn represents. In the Qabalistic Tarot, the Eight of Cups corresponds with Saturn in Pisces. Its esoteric name is *The Lord of Abandoned Success*. Saturn requires stability that Pisces cannot provide. What Saturn builds, Pisces dissolves. The roots he seeks to establish never take hold in the infinite depth found in the oceans of Pisces. The earth signs correspond with his nature. He rules Capricorn. However, the mutability of Virgo does not conform to the concrete securities upon which his life depends. The harsh fixity of Taurus is far too unyielding. If his exaltation were in Taurus, the force of his gravity and weight would crush the universe he was charged with preserving. The air signs are his final recourse. However, he already rules Aquarius. The erratic instability and dispersive tendency of Gemini prevents him from maintaining the gravitational field of a central organizing purpose, which he so desperately needs and which we all need from him.

Libra, represented by the Balanced Scales, curbs Saturn's cruelty and transforms it into justice. Venus ruled, it softens his cruel resolve, and gives him the ability to enjoy the ease that is a natural byproduct of the stability he has been designated to create in the universe. It turns him away from harsh conservatism and unbending orthodoxy. In Libra, Saturn invests his energy in the maintenance of beauty through upholding the harmony of the natural world. Saturn in Libra is Saturn in the seat of the Fair and Honorable Judge.

Saturn falls in Aries. Aries is the exaltation of the newborn Sun after the cold Saturnian Winter that precedes the Spring. Saturn falls where the Sun rejoices. Sibly writes:

*...and his fall takes place in that sign where cold is diminished and heat increased, viz. Aries; which are quite contrary in nature to the Sun.*

Saturn in Aries is crushing and cruel. He squashes the life-giving potency that we associate with that sign. He diminishes the natural positive self-regard of Aries and can turn it into a boastful tyranny. He challenges the limits of responsible living in ways that are not always helpful or safe.

# ♃

## JUPITER

Jupiter is exalted in Cancer. He awakens the abundant fertility that Cancer holds within its womb. The ancients said that Jupiter was associated with the fertilizing Northern winds. This corresponds with Cancer, the sign of the highest Northern declination with regard to the Equator. Ptolemy writes:

> *Jupiter, since he is efficacious in exciting fruitful breezes from the north, and since he becomes most northerly, and augments his peculiar influence when in Cancer, accordingly obtains his exaltation in that sign...*

Sibly writes:

> *... for Jupiter delights in the northern part of the heavens, where he stirs up northern winds, which increase fertility and vegetation...*

The fire signs only increase his spirit of enterprise and authority. They cannot bring out his fertilizing power. Fire signs have long been considered barren – unable to sustain the new, moisture-craving life held in a seed. The earth signs also inhibit his ability to be fertile and prolific. Taurus, though ruled by benefic Venus, is a fixed earth sign. It is ultimately limiting to the growth of the wild fruit waiting to be borne in the cornucopia of Jupiter. He has his detriment in barren Virgo, and his fall in arid Capricorn. He is in detriment in Gemini, Libra begins the season of death, and Aquarius symbolizes the fruitless heart of Winter. Thus, the air signs could not be his "home away from home" as the exaltation signs are meant to be for the planets. Scorpio is even more associated with death than Libra. The promise of death that is foreshadowed in Libra, is fulfilled in Scorpio; which is in no way analogous to the fertility and vegetation that Jupiter has to offer. Pisces is his domicile. Thus, the only other temple that Jupiter could claim as his exaltation was Cancer.

Jupiter, as the all-seeding father of fertility and wealth, creates a feast of plenty when he is in nurturing, maternal Cancer. Jupiter in Cancer is the Father of the Endless Harvest, causing all the world to bring forth its vegetation in abundant supply.

Jupiter falls in Capricorn. Capricorn, the cold and dry domicile of cold and dry Saturn, is the herald of Winter. It is the sign that ushers in the end of life – cold and unyielding death by ice. It is hardly a sign in which Jupiter feels capable of delivering wealth, harvest, or abundant supply for anyone, including himself. Jupiter in Capricorn is a once rich ruler who has now fallen into poverty. He is a king without his crown who feels the deep level of indignation that comes from having fallen so far from his high station in life. What was once a wealth of joy and optimism has now transformed into a deep distrust that the structures of the world will be supportive or kind.

## Mars

Mars is in exaltation in Capricorn. Capricorn can temper the violent heat of Mars and turn it into something constructive. Usually, we would consider the nature of Mars and the nature of earth to be antithetical to each other. As such, Mars naturally has a deep hatred of being in the earthiest of earth signs, Taurus. What makes Taurus the "earthiest of earth signs" is that Taurus represents fixed earth. "Fixed earth" is earth as we expect it to be: unmoving, immoveable, and completely resistant to change. Action-oriented Mars does far better in the mutable earth of Virgo, and does extraordinarily well in the moveable or cardinal earth of Capricorn because those versions of earth create a mobile container for the power of Mars. The vehicle of Mars has to support the desire of Mars to do and to act. By its very nature, this is not something that Taurus can sustain or support.

The fire signs cannot tame the fire of Mars. They would only worsen his wrathful disposition. The water signs can tame his fire. However, they also can extinguish it. Only the wrathful Scorpion can channel the flames of Mars in a way that creates energy, as opposed to rendering him impotent. Mars feeds off of the erratic mental energy of the air signs. In Gemini, he develops a deep restlessness, anxiety, and an unfocused disposition. However, this lack of vigor comes through spreading himself too thin, and thus losing the motive force necessary for effective action in the world. He is in detriment in Libra. Aquarius, representing the frozen heart of Winter, would be equally debilitating to him. He would be held in a state of inactivity, much like the fate he encounters in Taurus.

Capricorn on the other hand is the perfect vehicle for the power of Mars. It is moveable earth ruled by Saturn. It can become a vehicle of war for Mars; a battle-ready tank that allows Mars to perform his duties in the world in a more organized and decisive way. Through the rulership of Saturn over Capricorn, Mars in Capricorn can become a master strategist. Mars in Capricorn is a Lord of Successful Works and Outcomes. He has more than sufficient energy and stamina to get the job done.

The ancients also considered Capricorn to be supportive of Mars because Capricorn has the furthest Southern declination in relation to the Equator. The South corresponds with the element of fire which is analogous to the hot, dry, and fiery nature of Mars. Sibly writes:

> *Mars is naturally hot and dry; and because his influence and effects are more powerful in Capricorn, a southern sign, where the Sun is generally hottest about noon, he is for this reason exalted therein…*

Mars is in fall in Cancer. His hot, dry, and violent nature is contrary to the maternal, nurturing container that Cancer represents. Mars in Cancer destroys the seed that lies dormant within Cancer's womb. He also poisons the feast at the family table. When Mars is in Cancer, he can easily facilitate hot and acidic emotions that destabilize familial harmony. Watery Cancer can also water-log his efforts towards the great and purposeful achievement of a singular and organized aim. Mars in Cancer is the Lord of the Subdued Flame, who feels bitter about the ways in which his family redirects his efforts towards their own needs and desires.

SUN

The Sun is in his exaltation in Aries. Aries corresponds with the surging fires of Springtime and heralds the returning power and light of the newborn Sun. The Sun's power is in the East. He is the awakener of the dead world after Winter and the Bringer Forth of Life. Sibly writes:

> *The Sun, which is the fountain of life, takes his exaltation in nineteen degrees of Aries, because he is then in the highest northern point of the ecliptic, making all things to spring and flourish, and producing fine warm weather, and length of days.*

The cold and dry earth signs could not provide him the freedom and expansion he needs to establish his power in the world. The weight of Taurus would force his power down into the core of the Earth, where it would be effective at sustaining life. However, it would also be invisible – a characteristic we do not associate with the Sun. Virgo heralds his quickly approaching demise in Libra. Capricorn is where he is at his weakest point in his annual cycle. The cold and wet water signs are collectively the polar opposite of everything he represents as the hot and dry creator of fire within the universe. Even Cancer, the watery womb that carries him as he steadily grows in strength and power, cannot truly testify of his greatness. He cannot find his exaltation amongst the air signs. Double-bodied Gemini does not contain the singularity of intention or purpose to serve as his exaltation temple. He is in fall in Libra and in detriment in Aquarius. Within the fire signs, he is in domicile in Leo. The fire within Sagittarius is the motive force that allows sickness to proliferate at the end of Autumn. It is the energy that continues to propel the Sun lower towards the horizon as the Winter approaches, until the shortest day and the longest night occurs at the Winter Solstice. Therefore, even Sagittarius was unfit for the king of heaven.

The Sun in Aries is the Sun at the dawn of the world. It is the Sun that represents new life; the solar hero driving away the dark beasts of the nighttime. The Sun in Aries perceives himself to be invincible. He is a source of constant energy – always keeping himself and the world around him healthy with the fire of his unwavering vitality. The Sun in Aries particularly corresponds with the life-force energy that is present all throughout the universe. The Sun in Aries is not the sweltering heat of midsummer. It is the vitalizing internal fire that rushes through all of us, granting both health and life. The Sun in Aries charges us all to move towards a loftier goal of what our lives can be. The Sun in Aries is the Lord of Leadership and Independence, individualized and in radiant expression.

The Sun is in fall in Libra. The Sun reaches his highest Northern declination when in Cancer, and the fullest expression of his power when in Leo. When he enters Virgo the heat and power of his radiance becomes trapped in the heart of every grain, fruit, and seed for the purpose of being harvested and utilized in another way. However, when he descends into Libra, he enters the Nighttime of the World. Sibly writes:

> And he is said to have his fall in Libra, because it is the opposite sign in the heavens to Aries, in which the Sun declines to the utmost southern point, and occasions shortness of days, and cold winterly blasts, destructive to the fruits of the earth.

The Sun loses his solar clarity and singularity of purpose when in Libra. His light becomes overshadowed by the thoughts, opinions, and needs of the world around him. This loss of his individuality diminishes his confidence and ability to act. The Sun in Libra sacrifices his crown for the sake of others. He enters the underworld so that the wheel of the year can continue to turn.

## VENUS

Venus has her exaltation in Pisces. Feminine, nocturnal, benefic Venus revels in feminine, nocturnal Pisces ruled by benefic Jupiter. All of these qualities are in conformity with her nature. Of Jupiter's two domiciles, Sagittarius and Pisces, Pisces is best suited to her nature. Fiery, quick-moving Sagittarius would rush and overstimulate her usual graceful movement through the world. It would force her to go far beyond what is pleasurable for her, and would disturb her native comfort.

In general, fire does not support the moisture that we associate with her. Aries is her detriment. She seems to enjoy Leo – a curiosity, since the ancient Babylonians held that Leo was her sign of exaltation. Venus in Leo enjoys a certain opulence and lavishness, that allows her to show the world her great beauty. However, Venus is also a goddess of fecundity. Leo, a barren sign, cannot support her function as a goddess of fertility and motherhood. With the exception of Taurus, the earth signs cannot support her essential nature. She is in fall in Virgo, and can grant no blessing of fertility in Capricorn. In Capricorn, she only has the bare minimum to take care of herself. She cannot support or nurture others as well.

Venus enjoys being in watery environments in general. She also does well in feminine, nocturnal Cancer. This may be because according to Ptolemy, the Moon is a benefic planet, similar to Venus and Jupiter. Venus hates being in Scorpio because Scorpio's association with deadly poison, cruelty, and the malefic planet Mars prevent Venus from feeling truly at home there. However, in Pisces she enjoys and supports the promise of new life that Pisces holds in its waters. There she feels lavish and fertile. Sibly writes:

> Venus is naturally moist, especially in Pisces, in which sign the spring is moistened and forwarded in the increase and strength of nature; and therefore she has the sign Pisces for her exaltation...

Venus in Pisces is akin to Aphrodite being born on the sea foam. She is a Goddess of Beauty. She considers herself to be the pearl of great price.

Venus is in fall in Virgo. Cold, dry, and infertile Virgo cannot support the parts of Venus that are soft, warm, wet, and desirous of the sensual pleasures of this world. Sibly writes:

> ...and, as Venus is the mother of generation and procreation, she has her fall in Virgo, in the autumn, when all things wither and fade.

Virgo dries all of her essential moisture, leaving Venus with only a knowledge of the hard and cold details of how to build a functional, working life. However, this strips her of the ability to cultivate a life of genuine, full-bodied pleasure. Virgo, the domicile of shapeshifting Mercury, can be far too cerebral for Venus to truly relax into the shape of a comfortable life.

## MERCURY

Mercury has both his domicile and exaltation in Virgo. This is peculiar because no other planet has the possibility of being in their exaltation while in their own domicile. This is one of several fascinating things about Mercury that gives us a clue that there is more to Mercury than meets the eye. He isn't just the lowly messenger of the gods. He is, in fact, the key to the entire Western mystery tradition.

Mercury in Virgo is the most powerful astrological placement a planet can hope to attain. Mercury is in exaltation in Virgo because he needs an earthen container to ground his often erratic and unstable energy. Taurus is too fixed to be the exaltation of the swift-footed messenger of the gods. Capricorn is ruled by domineering Saturn, the Lord of Boundaries – a concept that Mercury would rather not be trapped by. The fire signs do not make him more productive. They only increase his instability. The water signs drown his light freedom. The air signs trap him in constant and circuitous intellection. The only sign left for him to truly attain his highest glory is Virgo.

Mercury in Virgo is a skilled and intellectually masterful steward of humankind. He personifies the alchemical maxim "nature must be perfected by art." When in Virgo, he is the artisan chiseling away at that which nature is better off without. Mercury in Virgo is the Rectifier of the World.

Mercury is in fall in Pisces. Though Mercury tends toward a natural deficit of both concentrative ability and sustained attention, he is not intrinsically dissolute. His identity is not decentralized in such a way that he does not know who he is or what his primary motivations in life are. Pisces, the cold and wet, phlegmatic, mutable temple of Jupiter does not have the natural desire to become specific or to be concretized. It does not have the desire to ever attain a singular motivation in life. Its only desire is to dissolve for the purpose of absorbing back into its soul and psyche more of the world around it. The wet and phlegmatic way Pisces desires to become everything is antithetical to the cerebral and often removed approach that Mercury takes to the world he resides in. "Becoming everything" is different from "understanding everything," and understanding is more within the domain of Mercury. The absorption and lack of identity found in Pisces is destructive to the masterful specificity that is usually found in the mind and speech of Mercury.

☽

## Moon

The Moon has her exaltation in Taurus. The Moon is the fastest moving of our celestial governors. Therefore, she needs stability to balance her speed. She craves for a secure world more than any other planet. She represents the womb, the home, and the lineage of our family. She governs both culture and heritage. She weaves the threads that connect us to a larger ancestral tapestry. She connects us to our past.

As the stellar link to our ancestry and the accumulated wisdom that has contributed to us becoming who we are, she thrives best in conditions that feel safe, secure, and relatively unchanging. Taurus provides that for her more than any other sign.

The fire signs enflame her and make her even more unsettled. However, there is an exception with Leo. Leo, as the temple of the Sun, is more amenable to her needs than Aries or Sagittarius. Traditionally, we find that the Sun and the Moon have a slight bit of power in each other's domiciles. This is because of their close relationship as the progenitors of the universe. However, this "strength" is small and unquantifiable.

Sagittarius is also a fire sign in which the Moon is considered to have some level of comfort. This is because Sagittarius is ruled by Jupiter, and Jupiter is in exaltation in the Moon's domicile of Cancer. This causes Jupiter to also welcome the Moon into his domiciles of Sagittarius and Pisces. However, like the Moon in Leo, this "strength" or "comfort" that the Moon has in Sagittarius can't actually be quantified.

The Air signs also do not bode well for the Moon. She is peregrine in Gemini and Aquarius. She is only weakly dignified in Libra. However, the sign Libra poses other challenging conditions for the Moon. A large portion of Libra constitutes the malefic Via Combusta or "Burning Road," which is destructive to both luminaries. We will learn about the Via Combusta later on.

The water signs clearly do well for her. Her domicile is Cancer and she is welcome in Pisces because of Jupiter's rulership there. However, Pisces is unstable and does not give her the solid roots she needs in order to build a home for herself or others. Scorpio is the fall of the Moon. She cannot be honored there. Earth is the only element the Moon can find the stability she seeks. Mutable Virgo doesn't provide her a true sense of stable grounding, and Capricorn is her detriment. The only place she can find an environment stable enough to temper her own erratic nature is fixed, unchangeable, benefic-ruled Taurus.

The Moon in Taurus is a Patroness of Domestic Stability. She brings security through fertile, moist soil that offers food, health, and wealth to all. Taurus provides the Moon the walled enclosure that she needs to fully be at ease in the world.

The Moon has her fall in Scorpio. Both Libra and Scorpio are the two signs that represent the death of the luminaries. Libra is the fall or the death of the Sun, whereas Scorpio is the fall or death of the Moon. The Via Combusta – which spans 15° Libra to 15° Scorpio – is a portion of the heavens associated with death, sorrow, and annihilation. One of the reasons why this region of the zodiac is so noxious and harmful is because it is in opposition to Aries and Taurus, two signs that represent a gateway of life. Aries represents the renewal of the world in Springtime after the savage destruction that was endured through Winter. Taurus represents the firm establishment of that renewed Earth. Conversely, Libra represents the beginning of the death process in Autumn. For the ancients, Scorpio represented a slow poison that spreads throughout the entire natural world in mid-Autumn, causing everything in nature to become weakened and ultimately die. War-like Mars operates violence against the body of the Moon when she is found in Scorpio. The Moon in Scorpio is like a woman lost in the wilderness; a mother lamenting the demise of her children in the valley of the shadow of death. In this savage environment, she responds in kind – becoming feral and giving way to primal and animalistic means of self-protection. She is no longer the Goddess of Hearth and Home. The Moon in Scorpio is a Goddess of Fear-Filled Survival.

Within the exaltations, we find environments that allow the planets to amplify dimensions of themselves that complement their natures. In Libra, Saturn gains poise, and the ability to benevolently establish the law. In Cancer, Jupiter gains the ability to grant an inexhaustible supply of nourishment to all who need it. In Capricorn, Mars acquires the strategic powers necessary to build something of concrete significance within this world. In Aries, the Sun brings with him the promise that the wheel of the time continues to turn, and that even death bears no lasting signature. In Pisces, Venus grants us the ability to nurture our connections and relationships with others, teaching us to enjoy the quality of our experiences and not just the quantity of our acquisitions. In Virgo, Mercury grants us the wisdom of knowing that no one of us is an island. We are all our brother's and sister's keepers. Exalted Mercury teaches us that it is the duty of every one of us to rectify the world. The alchemical burden to transform the earth element into the highest expression of itself is all of ours to bear. In Taurus, the Moon grants us the security to grow and become wise from the inherited wisdom of our ancestors, so that we can pass those teachings on to future generations. When we understand how the planets find satisfaction and happiness within the universe, it opens insight into how we can collectively do the same.

CHAPTER 14 QUESTIONS

1. How many points does a planet receive if it is in its exaltation?
2. Define the term "dispositor."
3. When we say that the Sun is exalted in the nineteenth degree of Aries, what does that actually mean based on cardinal numbers?
4. As succinctly as possible, outline why the planets have their exaltations and falls in the various signs of the zodiac.

## CHAPTER 15 OBJECTIVES

* Define the term "triplicity" and identify what is meant by "triplicity rulership."
* Differentiate between the triplicity rulers of an element versus the domicile rulers who rule the individual signs within that element.
* Learn how the triplicity rulers are divided based on the sect of a chart.
* Identify the role of the participating triplicity ruler in both diurnal and nocturnal charts.
* Understanding the difference between the in-sect triplicity ruler and the out-of-sect triplicity ruler.
* Learn how to use triplicity rulers as a means of dividing the various topics of the houses.

# CHAPTER 15

## TRIPLICITY RULERSHIP

*And understand the lords of the triplicities of the signs. The triplic-*
*ity of Aries: its lords by day are the Sun, then Jupiter, then Saturn;*
*and by night Jupiter, then the Sun, then Saturn. The triplicity of*
*Taurus: its lords by day are Venus, then the Moon, then Mars; and*
*by night the Moon, then Venus, then Mars (and in Virgo Mercury*
*also has a share). The triplicity of Gemini: its lords by day are Sat-*
*urn, then Mercury, then Jupiter; and by night Mercury, then Sat-*
*urn, then Jupiter. The triplicity of Cancer: its lords by day are Ve-*
*nus, then Mars, then the Moon; and by night Mars, then Venus, then*
*the Moon. And I inform you that every thing which is decided and*
*indicated comes to be from the lords of the triplicities. And for ev-*
*ery thing of tribulation and hardship which afflicts the people of the*
*world and the generality of men, the lords of the triplicities decide it.*
—DOROTHEUS OF SIDON

TRIPLICITY RULERSHIP REFERS TO THE third level of essential dignity. This dignity assigns three planets to be the rulers over an entire triplicity of the zodiac.
These planets are the "triplicity rulers" or "triplicity lords" for that element. If we
thought of each element as a state composed of three cities (the three signs of that
triplicity), the triplicity rulers would be the governors of each state. Thus, the fire
state would have its three governors, as would the states of earth, air, and water.

Triplicity rulers are not necessarily the planets that have domicile rulership
over the signs of that element. For example, the triplicity rulers of fire are the
Sun, Jupiter, and Saturn. While the Sun and Jupiter are the domicile rulers of
two signs of the fiery triplicity, Saturn is not. Similarly, Mars is a triplicity ruler
of earth, though we know Mars doesn't have domicile rulership in any of the
earth signs. We will discuss the rationale behind this system later. The main
point is that while domicile rulers govern the three signs of a triplicity in a more
local and individual sense, they don't necessarily rule over the entire triplicity as
a collective. Rulership over a city is a very different level of rulership than rulership over a state. There may be three mayors of three adjacent cities who are
responsible for governing the affairs of their respective cities. This is similar to
our concept of domicile rulers – the local lords of the individual signs. However,
on a larger scale, those three cities collectively may constitute a state. When the
state is viewed as one entity, it gains three additional rulers. These rulers govern

the collective state, even though on a smaller scale each city within that state has its own mayor.

Just because a planet is the mayor of the city (domicile ruler) doesn't mean that it will not be elected to also be one of the three governors of the collective state (triplicity ruler). Some planets, like the Sun, are domicile rulers of a sign and also rulers of the entire triplicity in which we find that sign. Within our classical seven planet model, this is bound to happen. In the four triplicities of fire, earth, air, and water, we find several of the local domicile rulers taking on a dual role of being triplicity rulers over the triplicities in which their domiciles exist as well. All the planets take on multiple levels of responsibility throughout the various levels of essential dignity.

## Divisions within Triplicity Rulers

Each element receives three planets as its triplicity rulers. Every triplicity has a first triplicity ruler, second triplicity ruler, and a third triplicity ruler. The third triplicity ruler is always known as the "participating triplicity ruler" and it will always be the same planet based on that triplicity. For example, Saturn is the third triplicity ruler for fire signs. Similarly, Mars is the third triplicity ruler for earth signs. Jupiter is the third triplicity ruler for air signs. The Moon is the third triplicity ruler for water signs. This is because Saturn is the participating triplicity ruler of fire, Mars is the participating triplicity ruler of earth, Jupiter is the participating triplicity ruler of air, and the Moon is the participating triplicity ruler of water. Remember: the third triplicity ruler for any element will always be the participating triplicity ruler for that element.

### TABLE 1: *Order of Triplicity Rulers*

| ORDER | DIURNAL CHART | NOCTURNAL CHART | STATE |
|---|---|---|---|
| FIRST | DIURNAL RULER | NOCTURNAL RULER | IN SECT |
| SECOND | NOCTURNAL RULER | DIURNAL RULER | OUT OF SECT |
| THIRD | PARTICIPATING RULER | PARTICIPATING RULER | PARTICIPATING |

The first and second triplicity rulers will change depending on whether a chart is diurnal or nocturnal. A diurnal chart is one where the Sun is above the horizon. A nocturnal chart is one where the Sun is below the horizon. As we know, the Sun rises in the East. During his daytime journey, he will pass through houses twelve, eleven, ten, nine, eight, and seven. When the Sun is in any of those houses, the chart is diurnal. The Sun sets in the West by entering house number six, and then journeys through the night below the horizon through houses five, four, three, two, and one. When the Sun is in any of those six houses, the chart is a nocturnal chart.

The order of triplicity rulers is always first ruler, second ruler, and third or participating ruler. If a chart is diurnal, the order of the triplicity rulers will be: diurnal ruler as first ruler, nocturnal ruler as second ruler, followed by the participating triplicity ruler which will always be the third ruler no matter what.

If a chart is nocturnal, the order of the triplicity lords will be: nocturnal ruler as the first triplicity lord, diurnal ruler as the second triplicity lord, followed by the participating ruler which will always be the third triplicity ruler no matter what.

The doctrine of triplicity rulers is the only part of our essential dignity considerations that is impacted by the sect of the chart. This is another reason why it is important to clearly understand the implications of sect within traditional astrology. We will explore the philosophy of sect more fully in its own chapter.

We have seen the terms diurnal and nocturnal used in relation to the sect of the masculine and feminine signs of the zodiac. All the masculine signs are diurnal. That means all the signs of the fiery and airy triplicities are diurnal by nature. All the feminine signs are nocturnal. This means all the earthy and watery signs are nocturnal by nature.

The rulers of the various triplicities according to the sect of the chart are given below. It is also appropriate for us to review and consolidate several of the other concepts we have learnt thus far.

## FIERY TRIPLICITY

*Aries and Leo of flowing mane and Drawer of the Bow [Sagittarius] are of Helios [Sun] by day and Zeus [Jupiter] by night in alteration, dreaded Kronos [Saturn] got the third allotment.* – HEPHAISTIO OF THEBES

The hot and dry, choleric, masculine, diurnal, fiery triplicity consists of Aries, Leo, and Sagittarius.

Mars is the domicile ruler of Aries, the Sun is the domicile ruler of Leo, and Jupiter is the domicile ruler of Sagittarius.

The Sun is the exaltation ruler of Aries, Leo has no exaltation ruler, and Sagittarius has no exaltation ruler.

TABLE 2: *Triplicity Rulers of Fire*

| ORDER | DIURNAL CHART | NOCTURNAL CHART | STATE |
|---|---|---|---|
| FIRST | ☉ | ♃ | IN SECT |
| SECOND | ♃ | ☉ | OUT OF SECT |
| THIRD | ♄ | ♄ | PARTICIPATING |

In diurnal charts, the Sun is the first triplicity ruler of fire signs, Jupiter is the second triplicity ruler of fire signs, and Saturn is the third/participating triplicity ruler of fire signs.

In nocturnal charts, Jupiter is the first triplicity ruler of fire signs, the Sun is the second triplicity ruler of fire signs, and Saturn is the third/participating triplicity ruler of fire signs.

Note that in both cases of diurnal and nocturnal charts, the participating triplicity ruler stays the same.

EARTHY TRIPLICITY

> *Of Taurus, Virgo, and Capricorn are sovereign by day the Foam-born one [Venus], by night the heavenly Selene [Moon], and third to follow these the god who rules the wars [Mars], and in the present one [Virgo] it got as well the child of Maia [Mercury].* – HEPHAISTIO OF THEBES

The cold and dry, melancholy, feminine, nocturnal, earthy triplicity consists of Taurus, Virgo, and Capricorn.

Venus is the domicile ruler of Taurus, Mercury is the domicile ruler of Virgo, and Saturn is the domicile ruler of Capricorn.

The Moon is the exaltation ruler of Taurus, Mercury is both the domicile and exaltation ruler of Virgo, and Mars is the exaltation ruler of Capricorn.

TABLE 3: *Triplicity Rulers of Earth*

| ORDER | DIURNAL CHART | NOCTURNAL CHART | STATE |
|---|---|---|---|
| FIRST | ♀ | ☽ | IN SECT |
| SECOND | ☽ | ♀ | OUT OF SECT |
| THIRD | ♂ | ♂ | PARTICIPATING |

In diurnal charts, Venus is the first triplicity ruler of earth signs, the Moon is the second triplicity ruler of earth signs, and Mars is the third/participating triplicity ruler of earth signs.

In nocturnal charts, the Moon is the first triplicity ruler of earth signs, Venus is the second triplicity ruler of earth signs, and Mars is the third/participating triplicity ruler of earth signs.

Note that in both cases of diurnal and nocturnal charts, the participating triplicity ruler stays the same.

Also note that in the foregoing quote by Hephaistio, Mercury is given a sub-level of triplicity rulership in Virgo, though he is not given the same in the other earth signs. We also saw this in the quote at the beginning of the chapter by Dorotheus. Mercury, god of magic and the mysteries, consistently breaks the boundaries of what is expected of the planets. Once again, the connection between Mercury and Virgo is supremely fascinating in the overall landscape of classical astrology. Nevertheless, though ancient astrologers made room to mention this curious detail, in practice, we only see them using Venus, Moon, and Mars as the triplicity rulers of earth signs – including Virgo – and so should we.

AIRY TRIPLICITY

> *In Gemini, Libra, and Aquarius ice-cold Phainon [Saturn] took his portion daily, Argus-Slayer nightly [Mercury], the Son of Kronos [Jupiter] took the last of these.* – HEPHAISTIO OF THEBES

The hot and wet, sanguine, masculine, diurnal, airy triplicity consists of Gemini, Libra, and Aquarius.

Mercury is the domicile ruler of Gemini, Venus is the domicile ruler of Libra, and Saturn is the domicile ruler of Aquarius.

There is no exaltation ruler of Gemini, Saturn is the exaltation ruler of Libra, and there is no exaltation ruler of Aquarius.

TABLE 4: *Triplicity Rulers of Air*

| ORDER | DIURNAL CHART | NOCTURNAL CHART | STATE |
|---|---|---|---|
| FIRST | ♄ | ☿ | IN SECT |
| SECOND | ☿ | ♄ | OUT OF SECT |
| THIRD | ♃ | ♃ | PARTICIPATING |

In diurnal charts, Saturn is the first triplicity ruler of air signs, Mercury is the second triplicity ruler of air signs, and Jupiter is the third/participating triplicity ruler of air signs.

In nocturnal charts, Mercury is the first triplicity ruler of air signs, Saturn is the second triplicity ruler of air signs, and Jupiter is the third/participating triplicity ruler of air signs.

Note that in both cases of diurnal and nocturnal charts, the participating triplicity ruler stays the same.

WATERY TRIPLICITY

> *Cancer, Scorpio, and even Pisces last of all did Cypris [Venus] get as lot by day, and Pyroeis [Mars] by night, and after these quick glancing ones queen Selene [Moon] does have them.* – HEPHAISTIO OF THEBES

The cold and wet, phlegmatic, feminine, nocturnal, watery triplicity consists of Cancer, Scorpio, and Pisces.

The Moon is the domicile ruler of Cancer, Mars is the domicile ruler of Scorpio, and Jupiter is the domicile ruler of Pisces.

Jupiter is the exaltation ruler of Cancer, there is no exaltation ruler of Scorpio, and Venus is the exaltation ruler of Pisces.

TABLE 5: *Triplicity Rulers of Water*

| ORDER | DIURNAL CHART | NOCTURNAL CHART | STATE |
|---|---|---|---|
| FIRST | ♀ | ♂ | IN SECT |
| SECOND | ♂ | ♀ | OUT OF SECT |
| THIRD | ☽ | ☽ | PARTICIPATING |

In diurnal charts, Venus is the first triplicity ruler of water signs, Mars is the second triplicity ruler of water signs, and the Moon is the third/participating triplicity ruler of water signs.

In nocturnal charts, Mars is the first triplicity ruler of water signs, Venus is the second triplicity ruler of water signs, and the Moon is the third/participating triplicity ruler of water signs.

Note that in both cases of diurnal and nocturnal charts, the participating triplicity ruler stays the same.

## OUT-OF-SECT TRIPLICITY RULERS

If planets are in the signs they have triplicity rulership over, those planets will receive essential dignity for being in those signs. However, this will only be true for the first triplicity ruler and the third/participating triplicity ruler. The first triplicity ruler will always be the ruler who corresponds with the sect of the chart. If the chart is diurnal, the first triplicity ruler of any sign will be the diurnal triplicity ruler of that element. If the chart is nocturnal, the first triplicity ruler of any sign will be the nocturnal triplicity ruler of that element.

For example, the triplicity rulers of earth are Venus, Moon, and Mars. In diurnal charts, Venus would be the first triplicity ruler of earth signs. This is because she is the diurnal triplicity ruler of all earth signs. In a nocturnal chart, the Moon would be the first triplicity ruler. This is because she is the nocturnal triplicity ruler of all earth signs. In a diurnal chart, if Venus were in an earth sign, she would receive three points of essential dignity for being the diurnal triplicity ruler of earth signs. If Mars were in an earth sign, he would receive three points for being the participating triplicity ruler of earth signs. In this example, the Moon would receive no points of essential dignity by triplicity rulership. She is the triplicity ruler of earth signs only in nocturnal charts, and the chart in our example is diurnal.

Conversely, in nocturnal charts, the Moon would be the first triplicity ruler of earth signs. This is because she is the nocturnal triplicity ruler of all earth signs. In a diurnal chart, Venus would be the first triplicity ruler. This is because she is the diurnal triplicity ruler of all earth signs. In a nocturnal chart, if the Moon were in an earth sign, she would receive three points of essential dignity for being the nocturnal triplicity ruler. If Mars were in an earth sign, he would receive three points for being the participating triplicity ruler. In this example, if Venus were in an earth sign, she would receive no points of essential dignity by triplicity rulership. She is the triplicity ruler of earth signs only in diurnal charts, and the chart in our example is nocturnal.

The first triplicity ruler over an element is always going to be the triplicity ruler who corresponds with the sect of the chart. This ruler can also be called the "in-sect triplicity ruler." Naturally, this would make the second triplicity ruler become the "out-of-sect" triplicity ruler. In all cases, the third triplicity ruler is known as the "third" or "participating" triplicity ruler.

There is no essential dignity given to a planet that is the out-of-sect triplicity ruler of an element. The point of triplicity rulership is to determine which planet corresponds with the sect of the chart so that we can identify which planet should receive points of essential dignity by triplicity. Within triplicity rulership, it is also important to distinguish the sequence of the triplicity rulers of an element based on the sect of the chart. We will learn more about how this becomes useful later.

No matter who the in-sect triplicity ruler may be, the participating triplicity ruler co-operates with that planet as a co-ruler of the sect. Therefore, the only planets that get essential dignity by being triplicity rulers of an element are the in-sect triplicity ruler and the participating triplicity ruler. There is no dignity given to the out-of-sect triplicity ruler for being in its appropriate triplicity. Being in the appropriate triplicity doesn't matter at all if the planet is not in the appropriate sect based on the sect of the chart.

Here's an example. In a diurnal chart, the Sun is the in-sect triplicity ruler of fire signs, Jupiter is the out-of-sect triplicity ruler, and Saturn is the participating triplicity ruler. The Sun and Saturn, if they are in fire signs, receive essential dignity for being in their triplicity in a diurnal chart. In a diurnal chart, Jupiter does not receive the essential dignity of triplicity rulership by being in a fire sign. This is because out-of-sect triplicity rulership is not an essential dignity.

MAKING SENSE OF TRIPLICITY RULERSHIP

In general, diurnal planets are the triplicity rulers of diurnal signs. Nocturnal planets are the triplicity rulers of nocturnal signs.

The Sun was chosen to be the diurnal ruler of the fire signs because that designation is most in conformity with his diurnal nature. In a diurnal chart, he is first amongst the triplicity rulers of fire because the daytime receives its heat and light from him – he does not receive his heat or light from the day. He is the domicile ruler of Leo and the exaltation ruler of Aries. Jupiter, both a diurnal planet and the domicile ruler of Sagittarius, came next as the nocturnal ruler of the fire element. Jupiter, a warm and moist planet, holds moisture within himself that corresponds with the moistness of the nighttime. Saturn was elected to be the participating triplicity ruler of fire signs. The heat of the fire element staves off some of his destructive coldness; a coldness that is worsened in nocturnal signs and nocturnal charts.

Venus was elected to be the diurnal triplicity ruler of earth signs. As a hot and moist planet, the heat within her constitution corresponds more with the daytime than it does with the nighttime. She also is the domicile ruler of Taurus, which is the first sign within this triplicity. Though the Moon is also a hot and moist planet, she is more analogous with the nighttime than any other planet in the Chaldean Order. Similarly, the moisture within her constitution is greater than her heat. Her native moisture is identical to that of the nighttime. She is also the exaltation ruler of Taurus. Thus, she was chosen to be the nocturnal triplicity ruler of the earth element. Though a hot and fiery planet, the ancients elected Mars to be the participating triplicity ruler of the earth signs. The nocturnal signs in general stave off some of his inimical fire. He is also the exaltation ruler of Capricorn.

As we have seen earlier, the ancients also designated Mercury to be a triplicity ruler of sorts within the earth element. However, his triplicity rulership within this element extends only as far as his earthy domicile of Virgo. Be that as it may, the level of power by triplicity he receives while in that sign is not quantifiable. Therefore, Mercury does not receive +3 points of essential dignity for being in Virgo.

Saturn was elected to be the diurnal triplicity ruler of air signs. Though a cold and dry planet, he is also a diurnal planet. He is the domicile ruler of Aquarius, and the exaltation ruler of Libra. Therefore, he leads this triplicity in the daytime. Mercury was elected as the nocturnal triplicity ruler of air signs. Though neither a diurnal nor a nocturnal planet, his greatest zodiacal power is in his nocturnal domicile of Virgo. Therefore, it might have been thought that the nighttime was more analogous with his nature. Mercury also is far less forceful than Saturn, in the same way that the ancients thought the nighttime was far less powerful than the day. Mercury is a god of twilight – he is only seen just before sunrise and right after sunset. Therefore, it would seem as if his nature was more conformable to that of the nighttime. Jupiter is the participating triplicity ruler of air signs. Though he has no major dignity in any of the air signs, both Jupiter and the air element are hot and wet – sanguine, benevolent, and supportive of human life. Thus, Jupiter was elected to be the participating triplicity ruler of air signs.

Venus is the diurnal triplicity ruler of water signs. The heat within her constitution and her native proximity to the Sun makes her the best candidate amongst the nocturnal planets for the role of being the diurnal triplicity ruler of the water element. She also has her exaltation in Pisces. Mars was elected as the nocturnal triplicity ruler of water signs. The ancients perceived him to be less malevolent in the nighttime than in the daytime. They also considered him to be tamer in his domicile of Scorpio than in his domicile of Aries. The Moon was elected to be the participating triplicity ruler of the water signs. Whether in the daytime or the nighttime, the water element is analogous to her nature. As the Sun is to fire, she is to water. The water was born of her; she was not born of it. Thus, she has governance over that element in both the daytime and the nighttime.

## PTOLEMY'S SYSTEM OF TRIPLICITY RULERS

The two great schools of Hellenistic astrology are the schools of Claudius Ptolemy and the school of Dorotheus of Sidon. Therefore, it makes sense that the major systems of triplicity rulers in traditional astrology are the Ptolemaic and the Dorothean systems.

One of the distinguishing factors of Ptolemy's astrology is the use of the planets as the universal significators of topics and themes within the life of a person. Dorotheus, on the other hand, championed using the planets through their specific significations based on the houses they ruled. Thus, the astrology of Dorotheus is more house-oriented, while the astrology of Ptolemy is more planet-oriented.

The first major difference between their triplicity systems is that the Ptolemaic system has only two triplicity rulers – a diurnal and a nocturnal ruler, whereas the Dorothean system has three – a diurnal, nocturnal, and participating triplicity ruler. For Ptolemy, the triplicity rulers only represented another level of essential dignity. The triplicity scheme of Dorotheus, on the other hand, served the same purpose as the Ptolemaic system, but it also was used as a means of fine-tuning the significations of the houses. To this end, it was overwhelmingly popular amongst Medieval astrologers who seem to have primarily used the Dorothean system within their practice. They refined a system whereby each terrestrial house received three triplicity rulers based on the sign that was on the cusp of that house. Each of these rulers signified a subtopic that was directly pertinent to the overarching significations of that house.

For example, though the first house represents the life and health of the native in general, when we use the Dorothean triplicity rulers, we can divide the life of a person into three segments: beginning, middle, and end. If a person had Virgo on their first house cusp in a diurnal chart, the triplicity rulers of the earth element would govern the three stages of the native's life. Venus would govern the first stage of life since she is the diurnal triplicity ruler and our example chart is a diurnal chart. The Moon would govern the second stage of life since she is the out-of-sect triplicity ruler in this diurnal chart. Mars would be the third triplicity ruler and govern the third part of the life of the native, since he is the participating triplicity ruler of the earth element. We will learn more about this very useful technique closer towards the end of the chapter. Conversely, Ptolemy's two-triplicity ruler system cannot be used in this way because it was not designed for this purpose.

TABLE 6: *Dorothean & Ptolemaic Systems of Triplicity Rulers*

| ELEMENTS | DOROTHEAN SYSTEM | | | PTOLEMAIC SYSTEM | |
| | DAY | NIGHT | PART. | DAY | NIGHT |
| --- | --- | --- | --- | --- | --- |
| FIRE | ☉ | ♃ | ♄ | ☉ | ♃ |
| EARTH | ♀ | ☽ | ♂ | ♀ | ☽ |
| AIR | ♄ | ☿ | ♃ | ♄ | ☿ |
| WATER | ♀ | ♂ | ☽ | ♂ | ♂ |

Ptolemy only uses a diurnal and a nocturnal ruler within his system of triplicity rulers. They follow the same organization as the diurnal and nocturnal triplicity rulers of the Dorothean system, with one exception. Whereas the Dorothean system designates Venus as the diurnal triplicity ruler of water and Mars as the nocturnal triplicity ruler of water, in Ptolemy's system, Mars is the triplicity ruler of the water signs both diurnally and nocturnally. After dividing the other six planets amongst the fire, earth, and air elements, only Mars remains. Ptolemy writes:

> *The fourth triplicity, formed by Cancer, Scorpio, and Pisces, is left to the remaining planet, Mars, who has right in it by means of his house, Scorpio.*

However, Ptolemy does not stop there. He writes:

> *But as the signs which compose this triplicity are feminine, the Moon by night and Venus by day, through their feminine condition, govern it together with Mars.*

For the water element, we see Ptolemy doing something that he has not done for the other elements. Though he tells us that Mars governs the watery triplicity both diurnally and nocturnally, he also designates Venus and the Moon as joint rulers who govern this triplicity in partnership with him. Thus, all the other triplicities have two triplicity rulers in Ptolemy's system, while the element of water has three.

Clearly, this doesn't work as elegantly as the system of triplicity rulership outlined by Dorotheus. However, some may argue that Ptolemy's rationale – at least in the case of fire, earth, and air – is more rooted in nature. We have daytime and we have nighttime. Thus, it only makes sense for us to have a diurnal and a nocturnal ruler within an element. For the most part, all things astrological are divided into the diurnal and the nocturnal sect. There is no "participating" sect. Similarly, we do not call any portion of our twenty-four-hour day "participating." Nevertheless, Ptolemy's system of triplicity rulers can take us only as far as awarding a planet extra points of essential dignity if it is in its appropriate triplicity. The system invented by Dorotheus is far more useful and versatile.

By the Renaissance, there was a distinct desire within the heart of the Western astrologer to revitalize the astrology of Ptolemy. Thus, we see it being ubiquitously agreed upon – particularly amongst the English astrological community – that Ptolemy's system of triplicity rulers was the one worth using. I disagree. Though I root much of my astrological philosophy within the metaphysics of Ptolemy, I only use the Dorothean triplicity rulership system within my professional practice and teaching.

## Practical Application

Triplicity rulership has several applications within traditional astrology. Triplicity rulership is an additional layer of planetary strength. It assists us in determining the level of essential dignity that a planet should be awarded. Since much of our assessment of the strength of the planets comes from calculating the essential dignity of the planets, dignity by triplicity rulership becomes an invaluable addition. Planets receive +3 points of essential dignity for being in their correct triplicity based on the sect of the chart.

Secondly, Abraham Ibn Ezra tells us that the triplicity rulers of the sect ruler of the chart gives us qualitative information about the three divisions of the life of the native. This helps us know which third of life will be fortunate or unfortunate. The sect ruler of the chart is the luminary who corresponds with the sect of the chart. If the chart is diurnal, the sect ruler is the Sun. If the chart is nocturnal, the sect ruler is the Moon.

Let's use a diurnal chart as an example. If in this chart the Sun is in Virgo, he is in the earthy triplicity. As far as triplicity rulership is concerned, he is ruled by Venus because she is the diurnal triplicity ruler of all earth signs. He will also be ruled by Mars because he is the participating triplicity ruler in all earth signs, diurnally or nocturnally. The Moon, who is the out-of-sect triplicity ruler of the Sun, cannot be said to govern the Sun in the same way that Venus and Mars act as governors of the triplicity, because the Moon is the out-of-sect triplicity ruler. Therefore, she is of no consequence in the actual affairs of the Sun. The governors that the Sun has to pay taxes to are Mercury for being the domicile ruler of Virgo, Venus for being the diurnal triplicity ruler of earth signs, and Mars for being the participating triplicity ruler of earth signs in the day and night.

However, when specifically using Ibn Ezra's system, all three of the triplicity rulers play a role: in-sect, out-of-sect, and participating triplicity rulers.

### INTEGRATING THE OUT-OF-SECT TRIPLICITY RULER

The out-of-sect triplicity ruler becomes a necessary planet to consider when using the system outlined by Ibn Ezra. The out-of-sect triplicity ruler will govern the second third of the life of the native. Thus, the first triplicity ruler of the Sun in a diurnal chart will govern the first third of the life of the native. The second triplicity ruler of the Sun in a diurnal chart will govern the second third of the life of the native. The third or participating triplicity ruler of the Sun in a diurnal chart will govern the final third of the life of the native. According to Ibn Ezra, these planets will govern the quality of the fortune, vitality, and happiness a person can hope to experience in these parts of their lives. This is dependent on the condition of those planets and other factors that may either be supporting or debilitating them essentially or accidentally.

What can be said about the Sun in a diurnal chart can also be said for the Moon in a nocturnal chart. If a person is born at night, that person is born with the Sun below the horizon of their chart. The Moon will be the sect ruler of the chart, regardless of whichever side of the horizon line she is on. She will govern the entire life of the native in a general sense, and the happiness, vitality, and prosperity he or she may hope to attain in this lifetime. The triplicity rulers of the Moon will begin with the in-sect triplicity ruler, followed by the out-of-sect triplicity, and finally the participating triplicity ruler. From a rulership perspective, the Moon in a nocturnal chart will specifically be governed by the domicile ruler, nocturnal triplicity ruler, and the participating triplicity ruler of whatever sign she is in. However, when looking at the three parts of the life of the native, all three triplicity rulers are used. The joy, abundance, vitality, and happiness of the native as represented by the Moon will be signified by the three triplicity rulers of the sign the Moon is in.

This is something I seldom, if ever, use in my daily client practice. However, it's an important artifact of traditional astrology, and may still have relevance in fields such as traditional medical astrology.

TOPICS OF THE HOUSES

Triplicity rulers can also be used to divide the various topics of the twelve terrestrial houses. This is a classical technique that I frequently use in my practice.

The twelve terrestrial houses represent the various topics of life. However, some houses contain multiple topics. For example, the seventh house is the house of marriage, open enemies, and business partners. A very logical question would be: which of those three topics is being discussed when we assess the seventh house? The sixth house represents sickness, small animals, and employees. Unless we are planning to have small animals for employees who make us sick, chances are we will need to separate the different topics that the sixth house represents in a way that allows us to interact with each topic individually.

The ancients devised a way for this to be done through the use of the triplicity rulers. First, we note the sect of the chart. Is it a diurnal chart or a nocturnal chart? If the chart is diurnal, the triplicity rulers of the twelve houses will be ordered from the diurnal ruler first, to the nocturnal ruler second, and finally the participating ruler as the third triplicity ruler. If the chart is nocturnal, the order of the triplicity rulers for each of the twelve houses will be: nocturnal triplicity ruler first, diurnal triplicity ruler second, and the participating triplicity ruler will be the third and final triplicity ruler. These three rulers will individually represent three different topics for each house. Each of the twelve houses will have a sign of the zodiac on their cusps. If an earth sign is on the first house cusp in a diurnal chart, the diurnal organization of the three triplicity rulers will be used: Venus, Moon, and Mars. If the fifth and ninth houses also have earth signs on their cusps in this diurnal chart, they, too, will have the same order of triplicity rulers: Venus, Moon, and Mars.

The triplicity rulers of the first three houses are pretty straightforward. For the first house, the triplicity rulers represent happiness and vitality at the beginning of life, middle of life, and end of life. For the second house, they represent wealth at the beginning of life, middle of life, and end of life. For the third house they represent the oldest sibling, middle sibling, and youngest sibling. Clearly, this isn't a perfect system. For a person with ten siblings, a system like this would be inadequate. However, it represents the beginning of working with the houses in a more incisive way.

Below is a list of the thirty-six topics of the twelve houses and how they are divided within each house. While this list was primarily compiled from *The Beginning of Wisdom* by Abraham Ibn Ezra, I have also referenced Guido Bonatti's *Liber Astronomiae* and Claude Dariot's *A Briefe and most easie Introduction to the Astrologicall Judgement of the Starres* for a more thorough treatment of this topic.

TABLE 7: *First House Triplicity Rulers*

## First House ✳ Self & Health

| FIRST TRIPLICITY RULER | *Life, our characteristics; our desires, the overarching theme of the beginning of our lives. It represents our likes, dislikes, and cravings.* |
|---|---|
| SECOND TRIPLICITY RULER | *Our bodies and our strengths in the middle of our life.* |
| THIRD TRIPLICITY RULER | *The same as the above for the end of our life.* |

TABLE 8: *Second House Triplicity Rulers*

## Second House ✳ Finances & Moveable Property

| FIRST TRIPLICITY RULER | *Money at the beginning of our life.* |
|---|---|
| SECOND TRIPLICITY RULER | *Money in the middle years of our life.* |
| THIRD TRIPLICITY RULER | *Money at the end of life.* |

TABLE 9: *Third House Triplicity Rulers*

## Third House ✳ Siblings & Community

| FIRST TRIPLICITY RULER | *Older Siblings.* |
|---|---|
| SECOND TRIPLICITY RULER | *Middle Siblings.* |
| THIRD TRIPLICITY RULER | *Younger Siblings.* |

TABLE 10: *Fourth House Triplicity Rulers*

## Fourth House ✳ Father & Home

| FIRST TRIPLICITY RULER | *Father.* |
|---|---|
| SECOND TRIPLICITY RULER | *Land, Property & Real Estate.* |
| THIRD TRIPLICITY RULER | *The End of all Matters, Prisons & Death.* |

## TABLE 11: *Fifth House Triplicity Rulers*

### *Fifth House* ✳ *Children & Pleasure*

| First Triplicity Ruler | *Children & the Property of Ancestors.* *First child.* – ABRAHAM IBN EZRA |
|---|---|
| Second Triplicity Ruler | *Pleasure ("Love" According to Dariot).* *Second child.* – ABRAHAM IBN EZRA |
| Third Triplicity Ruler | *Ambassadors, People who represent our interests in the world.* *Third child.* – ABRAHAM IBN EZRA |

## TABLE 12: *Sixth House Triplicity Rulers*

### *Sixth House* ✳ *Sickness & Employees*

| First Triplicity Ruler | *Sickness & our ability to recover.* |
|---|---|
| Second Triplicity Ruler | *Servants (Employees) & Small Animals/Cattle.* |
| Third Triplicity Ruler | *Whether our servants, small animals, or employees are profitable or not.* |

## TABLE 13: *Seventh House Triplicity Rulers*

### *Seventh House* ✳ *Marriage & Partnership*

| First Triplicity Ruler | *Our spouse.* |
|---|---|
| Second Triplicity Ruler | *Wars and contentions, people who we are publicly at battle with (open enemies).* |
| Third Triplicity Ruler | *Business partners; al-Qabisi says it represents us entering into covenants (or contractual agreements).* |

TABLE 15: *Eighth House Triplicity Rulers*

## Eighth House ✳ Death & Partner's Money

| | |
|---|---|
| FIRST TRIPLICITY RULER | *Death.* |
| SECOND TRIPLICITY RULER | *Anything ancient.*<br>*Fear, so if the planet is unfortunate, the native*<br>*will be fearful.* – ABRAHAM IBN EZRA |
| THIRD TRIPLICITY RULER | *Inheritance.*<br>*Worries, mental stress/distress.* |

TABLE 16: *Ninth House Triplicity Rulers*

## Ninth House ✳ Foreign Travel & Religion

| | |
|---|---|
| FIRST TRIPLICITY RULER | *Travel; Pilgrimage & what we will encounter on*<br>*Long Journeys.* |
| SECOND TRIPLICITY RULER | *Faith & Religion. Our Eminence & Proficiency in*<br>*Religious Matters.* |
| THIRD TRIPLICITY RULER | *Dreams, Wisdom, & Education. The Knowledge*<br>*of the Stars & their Truth; our Ability in Divina-*<br>*tion & Astrology.* |

TABLE 17: *Tenth House Triplicity Rulers*

## Tenth House ✳ Mother & Career

| | |
|---|---|
| FIRST TRIPLICITY RULER | *Mother (I exclusively use the first triplicity ruler*<br>*of the tenth house to represent the mother).*<br><br>*Power, work, & exaltation; attainment of the*<br>*highest success.* |
| SECOND TRIPLICITY RULER | *Our rank within our chosen profession.*<br>*The power and boldness within our voice.* |
| THIRD TRIPLICITY RULER | *The profession.* |

TABLE 18: *Eleventh House Triplicity Rulers*

## Eleventh House ✳ *Friends & Hopes*

| | |
|---|---|
| FIRST TRIPLICITY RULER | *Hopeful thoughts; our ability to be confident within our aims & objectives.* |
| SECOND TRIPLICITY RULER | *Friends.* |
| THIRD TRIPLICITY RULER | *Whether we have loyal or untrustworthy friends.* |

TABLE 19: *Twelfth House Triplicity Rulers*

## Twelfth House ✳ *Hidden Enemies & Self-Undoing*

| | |
|---|---|
| FIRST TRIPLICITY RULER | *Grief ("Secret enemies" according to Dariot).* |
| SECOND TRIPLICITY RULER | *Prison ("Work, labor, & sorrow" according to Dariot).* |
| THIRD TRIPLICITY RULER | *Enemies ("Beasts for riding, cattle, flock animals" according to Dariot).* |

CHAPTER 15 QUESTIONS

1.  How many points does a planet receive for being the triplicity ruler of a particular triplicity?
2.  What is the difference between the triplicity rulers of a sign versus the domicile ruler of that same sign?
3.  In a diurnal chart, what would the organization of triplicity rulers be?
4.  In a diurnal chart, what would the organization of triplicity rulers be?
5.  In a nocturnal chart, what would the organization of triplicity rulers be?
6.  How many points of essential dignity does the out-of-sect triplicity ruler receive?
7.  What is meant by "participating triplicity ruler"?
8.  In a nocturnal chart, how many points of essential dignity do each of the three triplicity rulers receive?
9.  What was a major application of the triplicity rulers in Medieval astrology?

CHAPTER 16 OBJECTIVES

* Define and explain the two minor dignities.
* Discuss the differences in opinion regarding Ptolemy's terms and the Egyptian terms.
* Understand the rationale behind the thirty-six decans.
* Understand why the zodiac begins and ends with the decans of Mars.

# CHAPTER 16

## MINOR DIGNITIES

*Although the sign itself is the home of a planet, yet the degrees of this sign are divided among all the planets.* – FIRMICUS MATERNUS

NOW THAT WE'VE EXPLORED THE major dignities, it's time for us to look at the lesser-known minor dignities. These are dignity by term/bound and face/decan.

### TERM/BOUND

The terms refer to five uneven divisions of each of the twelve signs of the zodiac. They are also known as "bounds" since they represent definite boundaries within the individual signs of the zodiac that each have a distinct planetary ruler. Each of these divisions is ruled over by one of the seven classical planets with the exception of the Sun and the Moon. This means that in each sign, there is a term of Saturn, Jupiter, Mars, Venus, and Mercury. Nowhere in the zodiac do we find terms/bounds for the luminaries.

Term rulership is considered a minor dignity. They don't carry the same level of strength as domicile, exaltation, and triplicity rulership. However, they are worth our consideration since they can bolster the strength of an otherwise weakened planet. If a planet is in its own term (or face/decan for that matter) and that is the only dignity it has where it is, it cannot truly be said to be in essential debility. Term and face count as valid essential dignities. A planet that only has dignity by term receives +2 points of essential dignity. A planet in its own face receives +1 point of essential dignity. However, if a planet is both in its own term and face, it receives +3 points of essential dignity, which gives it the same level of strength as if it were in its own triplicity. Therefore, two minor dignities can give a planet the same sort of functional capacity as triplicity rulership, which is considered to be a relatively strong dignity.

### WHOSE TERMS SHOULD WE USE?

While the dignities of domicile, exaltation, and triplicity rulership have been more or less agreed upon through the ages, dignity by term has historically been a very controversial topic. The primary systems of terms in use today are the terms of the Egyptians and the terms of Ptolemy. This brings up the issue of having to decide which set of terms to use within our practice. Additionally, there is no clear logic behind the divisions of the signs by term. Unlike domicile, exaltation, and triplicity, we cannot trace a clear or easily understandable system behind the development of the terms.

I prefer to use the terms that were used in the seventeenth century. Most people consider these to be the Ptolemaic terms. However, I have found discrepancies between the Renaissance terms and the terms found in Ptolemy's *Tetrabiblos*. I believe we should use the techniques that are appropriate for the period of astrology in which we find ourselves practicing. Therefore, I use the terms that were in use during the seventeenth century because that is where a great deal of my astrology is rooted.

Many respected astrologers have argued against the use of the seventeenth century terms, saying that historically speaking, they are not accurate. The wider consensus in the traditional astrology community is that we should use the terms of the Egyptians. The Egyptian terms represents the only system of terms employed within ancient horoscopic astrology. Nevertheless, I am not overly compelled to use the Egyptian terms because 1) I only consistently use the terms in my practice of horary astrology, which I use more as a method of teaching than as a stand-alone practice by itself; and 2) in natal astrology, which makes up a large portion of my practice, I do not refer to or utilize the terms at all. In practicing concrete, event-based astrology, the terms have not added anything vital to the accuracy of the readings I give. Therefore, I don't use them in my natal work.

Two of the consistent features we will notice about the terms are that the first term ruler for each sign is a triplicity ruler of that sign and the last term ruler for each sign is always a malefic. This is true with the exception of Virgo, where Mercury, the domicile and exaltation ruler of Virgo, rules the first term of that sign, even though he is not a triplicity ruler of earth signs. Though Mercury is not one of the three main planets we consider to be the triplicity rulers of earth, we do find a special exception being made for him as it relates to his domicile and exaltation of Virgo. Dorotheus of Sidon, in listing the triplicity rulers for the four elements writes:

> *The triplicity of Taurus: its lords by day are Venus, then the Moon, then Mars; and by night the Moon, then Venus, then Mars (and in Virgo Mercury also has a share).*

We see this idea of Mercury having some form of triplicity rulership in Virgo coming up in the writings of other ancient authors as well. From this perspective, Mercury being the first term ruler in Virgo continues to follow the model of having one of the triplicity rulers of a sign be the first term ruler of that sign.

The last term of each sign is always ruled by either Saturn or Mars. This very likely contributed to the notion that ending degrees of the signs, especially the twenty-ninth degree, are unfortunate within traditional astrology. Other points of interest are that: Mercury is the first term ruler for both of his signs, Jupiter is the first term ruler for both of his signs. Interestingly, the signs of Jupiter and Mercury are all the mutable or common signs of the zodiac. Venus is the first term ruler of Taurus, her own domicile and her celestial joy, whereas Saturn is the first term ruler of Libra, his exaltation, followed by Venus, the domicile ruler of that sign. Aquarius is the celestial joy of Saturn and he is the first term ruler of that sign. Scorpio is the celestial joy and nocturnal domicile of Mars and he is the first term ruler of that sign. His term in Aries is placed closer to the end of that sign, perhaps as a means of taming his fire.

TABLE 1: *Terms (Bounds)*

| The Terms of the Planets | | | | |
|---|---|---|---|---|
| +2 | | | | |
| ♈ ♃ 6 | ♀ 14 | ☿ 21 | ♂ 26 | ♄ 30 |
| ♉ ♀ 8 | ☿ 15 | ♃ 22 | ♄ 26 | ♂ 30 |
| ♊ ☿ 7 | ♃ 13 | ♀ 21 | ♄ 25 | ♂ 30 |
| ♋ ♂ 6 | ♃ 13 | ☿ 20 | ♀ 27 | ♄ 30 |
| ♌ ♄ 6 | ☿ 13 | ♀ 19 | ♃ 25 | ♂ 30 |
| ♍ ☿ 7 | ♀ 13 | ♃ 18 | ♄ 24 | ♂ 30 |
| ♎ ♄ 6 | ♀ 11 | ♃ 19 | ☿ 24 | ♂ 30 |
| ♏ ♂ 6 | ♃ 14 | ♀ 21 | ☿ 27 | ♄ 30 |
| ♐ ♃ 8 | ♀ 14 | ☿ 19 | ♄ 25 | ♂ 30 |
| ♑ ♀ 6 | ☿ 12 | ♃ 19 | ♂ 25 | ♄ 30 |
| ♒ ♄ 6 | ☿ 12 | ♀ 20 | ♃ 25 | ♂ 30 |
| ♓ ♀ 8 | ♃ 14 | ☿ 20 | ♂ 26 | ♄ 30 |

FACES/DECANS

The final level of essential dignity is that of the faces or decans. The faces refer to 10° divisions of the twelve signs of the zodiac. Each sign can be divided into three faces of 10° each. This gives us a total of thirty-six faces in the entire zodiac.

The faces follow the Chaldean Order repeatedly throughout the entire zodiac. Starting with Mars ruling the first face of Aries, we continue with the second face of Aries being ruled by the Sun, and the third face of Aries ruled by Venus. Then we continue onto the first face of Taurus ruled by Mercury, the second face of Taurus ruled by the Moon, and the third face of Taurus ruled by Saturn. We continue in this familiar pattern of Saturn, Jupiter, Mars, Sun, Venus, Mercury, and Moon until we finally arrive at the last face of Pisces, ruled by Mars.

TABLE 2: *Faces (Decans)*

| **The Faces of the Planets** | | | |
|---|---|---|---|
| **+1** | | | |
| ♈ | ♂ 10 | ☉ 20 | ♀ 30 |
| ♉ | ☿ 10 | ☽ 20 | ♄ 30 |
| ♊ | ♃ 10 | ♂ 20 | ☉ 30 |
| ♋ | ♀ 10 | ☿ 20 | ☽ 30 |
| ♌ | ♄ 10 | ♃ 20 | ♂ 30 |
| ♍ | ☉ 10 | ♀ 20 | ☿ 30 |
| ♎ | ☽ 10 | ♄ 20 | ♃ 30 |
| ♏ | ♂ 10 | ☉ 20 | ♀ 30 |
| ♐ | ☿ 10 | ☽ 20 | ♄ 30 |
| ♑ | ♃ 10 | ♂ 20 | ☉ 30 |
| ♒ | ♀ 10 | ☿ 20 | ☽ 30 |
| ♓ | ♄ 10 | ♃ 20 | ♂ 30 |

## DECANS BEGIN AND END WITH MARS

If the thirty-six faces are meant to follow the Chaldean Order, then why would they begin with Mars and end with Mars? One reason for this is that fire is needed in order to overcome the depths of Winter. We could not end the Winter in the decan of Saturn no more than we could begin the Spring in the decan of Saturn. Saturn is the antithesis of the thawing of the frozen world that we find at Winter's end. He does not correspond with the return to the abundant outpouring of life that we find at the beginning of Spring. The rebirth of the world can only occur through fire. Though the external manifestation of this fire may seem minimal to us as observers, one can only imagine how extraordinary that cosmic fire must be that the cold clutches of Saturn's Winter would be forced to release the world from its grasp. This doubling of Martian fire is necessary because it delivers us from the harsh cold of death and reignites the engine of the world.

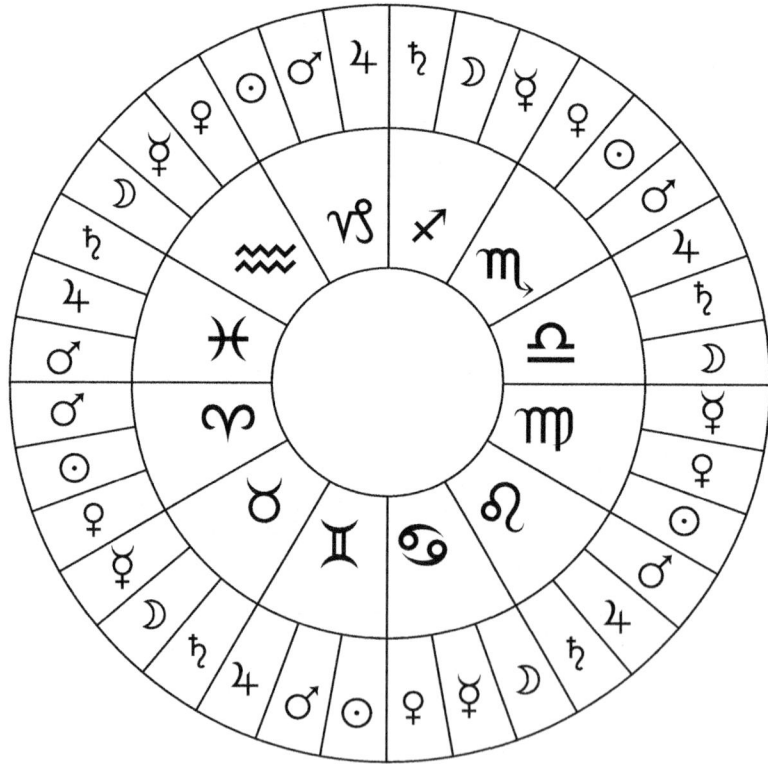

FIGURE 1: *36 Faces (Decans)*

## CARDINAL VS. ORDINAL NUMBERS AMONGST THE MINOR DIGNITIES

We were first introduced to the concept of cardinal and ordinal numbers in the chapter on the exaltations. There, we learnt that cardinal numbers are numbers that we use to count by (1, 2, 3, 4, etc.), whereas ordinal numbers are numbers that we use to ascertain the location of a factor within a sequence of other factors (first, second, third, etc.). The minor dignities are highly degree sensitive. This means that we need to know which degrees correspond specifically with which minor dignities.

It is important to remember that the essential dignities table lists the essential dignities using ordinal numbers. Therefore, when we see 30° on the essential dignity table, it is actually a reference to the thirtieth degree of a sign, which ranges from 29° 00' of that sign to 29° 59'.

The faces are the most straightforward. A face or decan divides a sign of the zodiac into a 10° segment. On the essential dignities table, we find the following face of Aries:

TABLE 3: *Faces (Decans) of* ♈

| 10° | 20° | 30° |
|---|---|---|
| ♂ | ☉ | ♀ |

The cardinal ranges of these degrees can be found in the table below.

TABLE 4: *Faces (Decans) of* ♈ *(Cardinal Range)*

| 00° 00' to 09° 59' | 10° 00' to 19° 59' | 20° 00' to 29° 59' |
|---|---|---|
| ♂ | ☉ | ♀ |

Though the actual essential dignities table shows these values as 10°, 20°, and 30°, what it actually means to convey is that the face of Mars in Aries extends from the first degree (00° 00') up to the end of the tenth degree (09° 59'). The face of the Sun extends from the eleventh degree of Aries (10° 00') up to the end of the twentieth degree (19°59'). The face of Venus extends from the twenty-first degree of Aries (20° 00') up to the end of the thirtieth degree of that sign (29° 59'). All of the thirty-six faces should be understood in this way.

For example, suppose we had Jupiter at 19° SCO 47'. Whose face would Jupiter be in? In Scorpio, Mars rules the first face, the Sun rules the second face, and Venus rules the third face. This means the extent of the range of each decan is:

TABLE 5: *Faces (Decans) of* ♏ *(Cardinal Range)*

| 00° 00' to 09° 59' | 10° 00' to 19° 59' | 20° 00' to 29° 59' |
|---|---|---|
| ♂ | ☉ | ♀ |

Jupiter at 19° SCO 47' would be in the face of the Sun.

A trickier example would be if we took the boundary between one face and another. For example, suppose we had Mercury at 10° TAU 00'. If we look at our essential dignities table, we may be confused as to whether or not this Mercury were in the face of Mercury or the face of the Moon. That is because, our essential dignities table lists the following as the faces of Taurus:

TABLE 6: *Faces (Decans) of* ♉

| 10° | 20° | 30° |
|---|---|---|
| ☿ | ☽ | ♄ |

The cardinal ranges of these degrees can be found in the table below.

TABLE 7: *Faces (Decans) of* ♉ *(Cardinal Range)*

| 00° 00 to 09° 59' | 10° 00' to 19° 59' | 20° 00' to 29° 59' |
|---|---|---|
| ☿ | ☽ | ♄ |

Therefore, even though Mercury is on the exact boundary between his own face and the face of the Moon, if he is at 10° TAU 00', he most definitely is in the face of the Moon.

The terms/bounds of the signs only seem more complicated. They are as simple to ascertain as the faces or the degrees of exaltation. Below is a table of the terms of Aries.

TABLE 8: *Terms (Bounds) of* ♈

| 06° | 14° | 21° | 26° | 30° |
|---|---|---|---|---|
| ♃ | ♀ | ☿ | ♂ | ♄ |

The cardinal degree ranges for these terms are given in the following table.

TABLE 9: *Terms (Bounds) of* ♈ *(Cardinal Range)*

| 00° 00' to 05° 59' | 06° 00' to 13° 59' | 14° 00' to 20° 59' | 21° 00' to 25° 59' | 26° 00' to 29° 59' |
|---|---|---|---|---|
| ♃ | ♀ | ☿ | ♂ | ♄ |

Though all of the terms are unevenly divided within the twelve signs of the zodiac, all the terms follow this same logic. Remember: all of the degrees on the essential dignities table are listed using ordinal numbers. In order to know what degree the table is refering to, we need to convert that number to its ordinal equivalent.

Therefore, if we see 26° on the essential dignities table, it's actually referring to the twenty-sixth degree (25° 00' to 25° 59'). If we see 30° on the essential dignities table, it's act actually referring to the thirtieth degree (29° 00' to 29° 59'). If we see something that spans the distance between 13° and 19°, this actually is referring to the distance between the thirteenth degree and the end of the nine-teenth degree (12°00' 18° 59').

With this, we have come to the end of everything you need to know in order to assess the various states of essential dignity and debility for the seven classical planets. What follows is an in-depth analysis of the twelve signs of the zodiac, and ways in which we can start thinking about them in a more traditional way.

## CHAPTER 16 QUESTIONS

1. What are the two minor dignities?
2. How many points of essential dignity does a planet receive for being in its terms/bounds?
3. How many points of essential dignity does a planet receive for being in its face/decan?
4. What is the rationale behind the organization of the thirty-six decans?

CHAPTER 17 OBJECTIVES

* Explain the solar mythology behind the names of the twelve signs of zodiac based on the seasons in the Northern hemisphere of the Earth.
* Discuss how the elements correspond with the four life processes of generation, preservation, corruption, and destruction.
* Explain the quadruplicities through both an astrological and alchemical framework.
* Propose explanations for the lesser-known divisions of the signs of the zodiac.

# CHAPTER 17

## THE ZODIAC:
## TEMPLE OF THE LIVING CREATURES

*How great is the space occupied by the vault of the heavens &*
*how great the territory within which the twelve signs of the*
*zodiac move, we learn from reason, reason that no barriers*
*or huge masses or dark recesses withstand; all things yield to*
*reason, & it can penetrate the sky itself.* – MARCUS MANILIUS

THE WORD "ZODIAC" COMES FROM THE Greek "zoidion," which refers to living
creatures or animals. With the suffix "-ion" referring to a place or location, zo-
dion can be translated to mean "locations of the living creatures." Many astrologers
view these "living creatures" to be the various animal characters that are found
amongst the twelve signs of the zodiac. On an esoteric level, I consider the "living
creatures" to be a reference to the planets that occupy the signs of the zodiac as
their celestial mansions. Therefore, the zodiac becomes a temple for the governors
of destiny – the designated homes of the ancient gods.

### MYTHIC CYCLES OF THE SUN

The tropical zodiac describes the modulations of solar power throughout the
course of the year. Each sign of the zodiac represents another alteration of the solar
force based on the season with which that sign corresponds. The seasonal mythology that arises out of the relationship between the Sun and the signs of the zodiac
corresponds more readily with the seasons of the Northern hemisphere than the
Southern hemisphere. This is because Western tropical astrology was born in the
Northern hemisphere of the Earth, and mirrors our understanding of the wheel of
the year based on how the seasons are perceived above the Equator.

ARIES starts the cycle. The Sun bursts from the cold slumber of Winter to reini-
tiate life in the Springtime. The Sun is fierce like the Ram, demanding that the cold
sting of death yield to the increasing light of life. The ancients tell us that rams
bring forth their young during the Spring, often one babe at a time; mirroring the
singularity of the reborn solar child at the Vernal Equinox.

TAURUS continues the cycle. Just as the power of a bull is greater than that of a
ram, the Sun increases in power when he travels through Taurus. The heat of the
Sun establishes itself more firmly within the world during this time. When the
Sun is in Taurus, there is a definite change in the air towards the establishment

of the solar power, with the same resilience as the fixed and immoveable Bull. When the Sun is in Taurus, the cattle also begin to produce their young.

When the Sun ingresses into Gemini, the sheep give forth their young, often as twins. The solar force doubles, becoming greater than what it was in Aries. The air becomes split – one part still holding onto the remnant Spring, the other part ushering in the coming Summer. The ancients tell us that the air in Gemini is double-bodied, changing and volatile, vacillating between the season that has left and the season that is coming.

When the Sun enters Cancer, he has reached his highest Northern declination. He now begins to turn backward towards the celestial equator, like the movement of the Crab as it crawls. The day has lengthened as long as it can, heralding the birth of Summer. The Summer Sun, still in a process of development and increase, has not yet come into the fullness of his power. He grows within the watery womb of Cancer gaining in strength with each passing day.

When the Sun ingresses into Leo, he is as powerful as he will ever be. He sits firmly on his throne in the heavens, proud and regal like the Lion, king of all the beasts. He is in the fullness of his power, fierce and terrible, yet majestic in his strength. At this time, he is unmistakably *Rex Planetarum*, king of the planets. However, though radiant and mighty, his days are numbered. The only thing that he can do after attaining his highest glory is to begin his decline. By the time the Sun ingresses into Leo, he has already begun his course to the underworld.

When the Sun ingresses into Virgo, the fullness of his might is absorbed into the grains of the Earth. The harvest is full of the life and the light of the waning Sun. The power that was once fully contained in his orb, now lives in the ripened bounty of the crop. His solar rays are stored in the grain, the wheat, and the barley that is harvested by the devout Virgin. This food will go on and feed the world in the Winter months ahead.

At the Libra ingress, the elderly Sun reaches the threshold of the underworld. The Summer days are over; daylight no longer reigns supreme. Both day and night are equal at the time of the Autumnal Equinox. As the days of Autumn progress, the night rises in power. The Sun king dies, reawakening the coldness of Winter.

When the Sun ingresses into Scorpio, the Autumn establishes its might. The spirit of this season pierces deep into the heart of the vegetable kingdom, like the cruel sting of the Scorpion, spreading poison and death. The leaves die and fall from the trees that once held them. Death pulls at the heart of all that once lived. The coldness sticks to the air longer as the period of daylight grows shorter and frailer. Winter is coming.

When the Sun ingresses into Sagittarius, the cold shoots erratically through the air like the far-flung arrows of the Archer. Warm days are punctuated by days of cruel frigidity, where the ice-winds cut through all that lives. Many fall ill under the frozen arrows of the approaching Winter. Hunters take this time to cut down their prey, so that the flesh of the fallen may feed their families during the coming months.

When the Sun ingresses into Capricorn, Winter walks across the land. We in the North are burdened under the cloven hoof of the coldest season and the longest night. We all must gain tenacity and the will to survive, like the mountain Goat navigating her way up the craggy cliffs of stone and ice. The Sun, too, begins his long and treacherous journey back up to the celestial equator from this point of his lowest declination. The journey uphill is a treacherous one. He, like the Goat, will face many hardships along the way.

When the Sun ingresses into Aquarius, Winter establishes itself as a force of death upon the land. All is frozen and all is wet, as if the world has been plunged into the ice-cold urns of the Water-Bearer. Water and ice have their rule. The only place where life can be found is in the ocean, that has remained volatile and alive through its formidable strength.

When the Sun ingresses into Pisces, he has risen that much further towards the celestial equator. Nature can sense his return, even if the force of his presence cannot be fully felt. He evidences his power through the volatile changes of the air. During this time, some days the world is covered by blankets of snow, and on other days torrential rains pour down from above. The ponds begin to loosen their frozen grip. The fish begin to multiply. Though the animals of Earth continue to sleep, the rivers and lakes are teeming with life. As the days increase, the solar power strengthens, until the Sun is born anew at the Vernal Equinox.

## Triplicities

> *Those signs whose nature as regards two qualities is identical, are situated in the zodiac at the angles of right-angled triangles; they are consequently known as triplicities and are recognized as entities, although three in number, the effects of each being identical or similar.*
> – Al-Biruni

### TABLE 1: *Triplicities of the Signs*

| FIRE | EARTH | AIR | WATER |
|:---:|:---:|:---:|:---:|
| ♈ | ♉ | ♊ | ♋ |
| ♌ | ♍ | ♎ | ♏ |
| ♐ | ♑ | ♒ | ♓ |

Triplicities refer to divisions of the zodiac based on the four elements. The four elements in astrology are the same as in other parts of the Western mystery tradition: fire, earth, air, and water. We have learnt that triplicities are connected with the elements from our previous chapter on the triplicity rulers. Another way to easily recall this connection between the word "triplicity" and the elemental divisions of the signs, is by remembering that signs of the same triplicity have trine relationships with each other.

There is another model of the elements in the West which includes a fifth element known as the "quintessence" or "spirit." This fifth element is the root substance out of which the four elements emerge.

The reason we do not include spirit amongst the triplicities is because the signs of the zodiac are modulators of planetary influences upon the material world. Though spirit is the root of all the elements, it exists in a pre-elemental world of its own and cannot be compared to any material substance. The building blocks of physical reality must have a means of tangibly expressing themselves in physical reality. Fire, earth, air, and water are capable of material expression. Spirit cannot be qualified, captured, or crystalized in the way the other four elements can. Therefore, it cannot have a triplicity within the zodiac.

## The Four Principles of the Life Power

The four elements also represent the four life processes that occur within the material world: generation, preservation, corruption, & destruction. These four processes are eternally in orbit around the axis of Necessity. Life leads to death and death leads to life through the constant turning of the wheel of time.

Within these four life processes, generation corresponds with FIRE. All life forms contain a central spark, a battery of soul and vitality that is analogous to this element. This life spark serves as the quantum of energy that every living being is endowed with at the beginning of life to fuel the entire process of their unfolding. This life spark grows in strength and power, as the entity grows and evolves. It is nourished by the heat of activity and desire; the will within the entity to be and become a unique expression of divinity clothed in flesh. With the continued development of the life spark, the being becomes more established in its own radiant identity.

Fire best corresponds with this principle. Fire separates and isolates one spark of life from the other, which allows each life spark to crown itself with the title of "I, the Individual." It is the urge of the fire principle within each of us that demands that we come into life and separate ourselves from the watery cave of our mother's womb.

Preservation corresponds with EARTH. To preserve is to make something fixed – to guard it against the destructive forces inherent in time. That which was birthed through the specializing power of fire, now has to be captured or fixed in the frame of the physical body. The body must protect the life power, be a vehicle for it, and remain a fit container for it to find expression in the world. The life process of preservation is one that protects and nourishes the fiery unit of Self within each of us, giving it the stability it needs to grow and gain wisdom through embodiment.

Earth best corresponds with this principle. Earth serves as the container within which every seed finds the stability to mature into what it is destined to become.

The entirety of our physicality – our flesh, sinews, organs, bones, nerves, and veins – has been created with the single purpose of giving the life power a vehicle through which to express itself. The containment of our earthen bodies gives us all the illusion for a while that permanency is the order of life; that youth will last forever, and that we will never die. This illusion is a necessity in our formative years. In its absence would rise a crippling paranoia that would steal the joy out of being born in the first place. Thus, the calming, stabilizing imprint of earth on the psyche of every individual becomes a balm for the incarnated being, allowing us to build a life based on exploration, discovery, and personal evolution.

Corruption corresponds with AIR. When a thing is corrupted, it is altered into a form that has less structural integrity than its original state. The state of air is to be in constant flux. The air principle not only dries the vital youth out of the earthen body with time; it also makes the body that much more susceptible to alteration. We speak of the "winds of change" when referring to the impact that time has upon the material universe. Air causes the dense stability of the body to become brittle over the course of years. It weakens the physical framework of the body in ways that facilitate its ultimate destruction.

Interestingly, in the traditional Indian system of medicine called "Ayurveda," the latter period of life is characterized by "vata," a principle associated with the air element. It represents the weakening of the body; when a body that was once solid now acquires "wind within the bones." This hollowing of the bones is a process of corruption, leaving the body more frail and more breakable.

Air best corresponds with the principle of corruption. If a container has more air within it than matter fortifying it, the container is weak and can easily shatter. Air corresponds with that which is fickle and constantly yielding. Its presence and activities remind us that change is the only immutable law within the universe. Even in our process of breathing, we come to know the meaning of corruptibility. In the continuous exchange of one inhalation for one exhalation, we realize that nothing can be held onto forever. As we all lie in our final hour in wait of death, the exhalation always wins.

The body, devoid of breath, loosens at its seams and gives way to the process of death. Destruction corresponds with WATER. Water is the universal solvent. It represents the dismantling of any individualizing influence that fire creates. Everything that has a physical form or an individual identity becomes completely reabsorbed into the morphic field of pre-cosmic possibility through the principle of water. It represents the voracious hunger of death; the loving call of the Dark Goddess of the Nighttime, beckoning each of us back into her womb.

The hidden truth within water is that every act of love or union is an act of destruction. Many mystical traditions have described the act of sexual union as one of losing oneself completely in ecstatic bliss. In French, sexual climax is referred to as a "tiny death." The process of becoming enlightened is also akin to dying. In enlightenment, we give up our tiny spark of personal consciousness in order to become part of a much larger field of undifferentiated universal intelligence. This is similar to returning a drop of water to the ocean, a flame to the body of the Sun, or the breath back to the wide and open sky. All of these acts represent the dissolving of the particular into the universal. This dissolution is both an act of destruction as well as the discovery of a much larger concept of life than physical embodiment can ever give us.

Within this model, water, death, enlightenment, and ecstasy are all synonymous ideas. Our earthen bodies, pass through the processes of generation, preservation, corruption, and destruction like everything else within our material universe. The soul that was once individualized in a corporeal form, responds to the call of death and returns to the limitless ocean of Chaos that exists as the backdrop of our reality. Though the body dies, the ocean continues. Hermeticism teach us that the goddess Necessity ultimately urges those souls back into material embodiment. Through the process of reincarnation, those souls burn brightly again within the dark cosmic fields of infinite possibility; they descend through the order of the heavens, back into the physical world for yet another journey on this Earth. In this way, we all live, grow, and become wise through the passage of lifetimes and the slow march of eternity.

FIRE

*The first triplicity is formed of Aries, Leo, and Sagittarius, all of which are fiery in their nature, withering and heavy, while the special domain of each is: for Aries, fires in ordinary use; for Leo those present in minerals and plants; and for Sagittarius that which is distributed from the heart of animals throughout the body.* – AL-BIRUNI

TABLE 2: *Fire*

| PRINCIPLE: | Generation |
|---|---|
| GLYPH: | △ |
| QUALITIES: | Hot & Dry |
| HUMOUR: | Red (YELLOW) bile |
| TEMPERAMENT: | Choleric |
| SEASON: | Summer |
| SIGNS: | ♈ ♌ ♐ |

The signs Aries, Leo, and Sagittarius all have fire as their chief operating system. When fire is the chief operating system, the mode of action tends to be active, volatile, fierce, expressive, confident, courageous, dignified, and optimistic. The fiery person's willpower causes them to dare to scale extraordinary heights. Their visionary ability gives them the perspective of the distances they will have to travel and the effort they will need to exert in order to make their dreams possible.

Fire signs fittingly lead the zodiac. They tend to gravitate more towards positions of leadership and authority. They enter life with the soul memory of being at the Beginning; of being the active spark that brought a universe into existence. They are creative and exciting. They can rouse even the dreariest of companions to launch forward into action. They challenge all of us to awaken and to seize the day, out of an acknowledgement that the day is often all there is. They can see farther than others around them. As a result, they inspire us to follow their lead because their vision of the future tends to be very clear.

They are sources of warmth and encouragement. Their presence in any space can lighten the room and make it feel more alive and engaging. They attract others to themselves like moths to a flame. They can use this natural spark to make a successful path for themselves in the world.

They are born knowing how powerful they are, which is often a blessing and a curse. The ferocious fiery native can lean towards hot and dry emotions such as irritation and anger far quicker than cold and wet emotions, such as sorrow and depression. They can be quick to a temper, and may appear to be angry when they are excited, or may actually rise to a sudden anger if they feel blocked or inhibited in any way. The fiery person is best when they remain in control of their temper and curb their natural inclination to act impulsively.

As a result of impulsive action, the fiery person can act without thinking. They can often find themselves biting off more than they can chew. Mars-ruled, the Aries native may burn their way through life. They may focus on winning at all costs, even if the cost is their relationships with others. They may commit to a project to avoid seeming weak or incapable, even if that project doesn't really excite them. The Solarian Leo may say "yes" to everything – pushing their limits to the extreme. What the ancients called the "super-sufficiency of the Sun's light" may actually be a bit overwhelming for people around them. They can push themselves and others beyond the point of exhaustion and need to be reminded that we are all just human, and we must all take rest. The jovial Sagittarian may dream beyond the scope of their current possibilities. All-providing like the Sun, the Jupiter-ruled native may also be inclined to saying "yes" to everything, and may frequently experience the fatigue of being burned out by their many interests and commitments.

The lesson of humility and self-reflection is one that the fiery native should learn. Though they carry the soul memory of being first to be born at the dawn of the universe and, therefore, first to rise to the call of action, they should also know that they live in a world that is built on the connections they form with others. They should lean into those connections more often as points of support and security. They should listen closely when others tell them that they are moving too hastily in the world.

The fiery person often views the world through the lens of conquest and exploration. When operating at their maximum, they quickly find their way in life, and follow their path without pause or deviation. The fiery person can get enflamed with passion. They know who they are and how they want to be perceived by others. They step into this life with their purpose branded on their foreheads. The rest of the world often watches in awe as they fulfill their destiny at all costs.

EARTH

*The second triplicity composed of Taurus, Virgo, and Capricorn is earthy, generous with its wealth; and the interpretation of its effects is that Taurus is responsible for pastureland which is not sown; Virgo for plants which have neither berries nor seeds and small trees; Capricorn for sown crops and large and tall trees.*
– AL-BIRUNI

TABLE 3: *Earth*

| PRINCIPLE: | Preservation |
|---|---|
| GLYPH: | ▽ |
| QUALITIES: | Cold & Dry |
| HUMOUR: | Black Bile |
| TEMPERAMENT: | Melancholic |
| SEASON: | Autumn |
| SIGNS: | ♉ ♍ ♑ |

The signs Taurus, Virgo, and Capricorn all have earth as their chief operating system. When earth is the chief operating system, the mode of action tends to be grounded, practical, pragmatic, calculated, slow, stabilizing, harmonizing, structured, and driven by security. Earthy people desire to live in a world that will not shift or change suddenly. They strive to create an environment that they can trust for their peace of mind and that of others around them. The bottom line is often their first consideration in most life experiences. They are keen to know the value of things.

Materially driven, earth people exist on a spectrum. At one end of the spectrum, they may cut no costs when it comes to creating a life that feels certain and secure, leading them to lavish abundance and material comfort. On the other hand, out of a fear that the material world around them is always moments from failing them completely, the earthy person may be frugal and miserly, fearing to part with their money and readily letting others cover the expenses. Earthy people are devoted to the pursuit of financial success as a means of creating a more stable life for themselves.

Earthy people don't like to be jostled. They build a life around them that feels increasingly more stable and secure with each passing year. This can be a response to having been raised in a jostling and unstable environment. The earthy person who has been raised to suffer hunger – either emotionally or physically – may vow to themselves to never be hungry again. Food often becomes their panacea. This is particularly true for the Venus-ruled Taurean. Since Venus leans more readily in the direction of comfort, feasting, sweet delights, and extravagant sensual pleasure, the fixed earth Taurean may find their greatest comfort through food. Food serves as a satisfying reminder that the world is indeed a stable place. Unfortunately, this can create health problems later.

Earth people tend to be slow moving, and seem to carry more gravity and weight both energetically and physically. In some instances, their slow-moving nature can be a sign of meticulousness. In other cases, it can be an indication of laziness. In all instances, the earthy person needs to be inspired, goaded, or lifted into a greater level of activity to help them burn off what can settle as stagnancy and inflexibility within their constitution. Even the highly Virgoan person – as activity bound as they may be – needs to be guided into doing other things that break away from the monotony of their set schedules and unalterable routines. The Mercury-ruled Virgoan can lose themselves in tiny details with ant-like devotion. This can cause them to miss out on more expansive life experiences.

The earthy person can be caring and compassionate, placing themselves readily in the role of taking care of others in a way that is both nurturing and supportive. They tend not to shy away from being the pillars upon which the society around them is built, and can be depended on in roles of support. As a result of living in such an earth-conscious way, the earthy person can fall towards heavier emotions such as melancholy, depression, anxiety, fear, and lack of enthusiasm. Saturn-ruled, the Capricorn native may see themselves as being the dutiful guardian of the firmness of the Earth. They may take on this role of being responsible, mature, and dependable at an early age. They should be mindful not to let this tendency steal the joy that they deserve out of life.

The earthy person with a purpose is a force to be reckoned with. When put to the test, they often have far more stamina and a greater level of endurance than any other triplicity. If they are convinced that the final outcome of their actions is increased security for themselves and those that depend on them, there is nothing that will stand in the way of them attaining their objective. Dutiful to their last breath, a purposeful earthy person will create a good life for themselves and their loved ones.

AIR

*Gemini. Libra, and Aquarius form the third triplicity which is airy in nature, sending winds abroad, and in detail Gemini is characterized by that quiet air which produces and sustains life, Libra by that which causes trees to grow, fertilizes them and produces fruit, and Aquarius by destructive storms.* – AL-BIRUNI

TABLE 4: *Air*

| | |
|---|---|
| PRINCIPLE: | Corruption |
| GLYPH: | △ |
| QUALITIES: | Hot & Wet |
| HUMOUR: | Blood |
| TEMPERAMENT: | Sanguine |
| SEASON: | Spring |
| SIGNS: | ♊ ♎ ♒ |

The signs Gemini, Libra, and Aquarius all have air as their chief operating system. When air is the chief operating system, the mode of action tends to be connective, expressive, communicative, cerebral, logical, objective, sociable, and friendly. The airy person seeks to spread information and disseminate ideas with others. They want to build bridges through words and thoughts. They often find themselves in roles of communication and public relations. Their way of being in the world is to engage with it intellectually – through stimulating discussions, debates, and exchanges. They are creatures of society and are likely to be the organizers of social dialogue around things that are affecting humanity.

Sometimes the airy person can communicate just for the sake of expressing themselves. They may not do so from a place of great depth or meaning. They are excited about exchanging ideas, whether or not it actually has an objective. They are often the spokespeople for others. This enables them to represent other people's point of view through their own interpretation. Airy people can be very good lawyers or counselors.

Airy people are keen on analysis and dissection. They can intellectually reduce an experience to its nuts and bolts to the point of no longer being able to enjoy it. The airy person can convince themselves that they are seeing things in the correct way, which may cause them to dismiss the opinions of others. This is often the case with Saturn-ruled Aquarius.

Venus-ruled Libra on the other hand cares so much about maintaining the peace, that they can be at constant war internally about their thoughts and the thoughts of everyone else. They can get lost in cycles of indecision and may lack the ability to stand firmly on anything, out of a concern that it may cancels someone else's opinion or point of view.

Mercury-ruled Gemini tends to have no loyalty to the point of view they came up with yesterday, and feel no anxiety surrounding dropping an opinion for something more interesting or exciting. They can be great wordsmiths, communicators, and representatives of a cause. They are eager to learn and excited to share, especially when it comes to sharing their own ideas. They tend towards being autodidactic – capable of teaching themselves anything. While they have all the requisite skills in life to "go it alone" they would rather not, preferring always to be in community or partnership with the world around them.

For people so partnership driven, they can come across as disinterested when others are sharing deeply emotional information with them. Even Venus-ruled Libra can miss the mark at understanding how to respond emotionally in a situation. They "get it" but may not really "get it, get it," which may be frustrating to others who would prefer that the airy native communicate from a place of greater emotional intelligence. Notoriously, the Libra can sit down and listen to someone pour their hearts out, but may not comfortably share with the same level of abandon. The Gemini native often finds themselves avoiding the subject of deeply emotional revelations altogether, preferring far more interesting and emotionally superficial conversations that have nothing to do with their own mysterious emotional inner life. The Saturn-ruled Aquarius will quickly explain to you that "emotion" should actually be written as "e-motion" because it represents "energy in motion," while completely circumambulating the fact that someone is having a meltdown about the recent divorce they've undergone.

The air native can be wonderfully impartial intermediaries for others, and are often thrust into the role of being a mediator, moderator, or some other go-between. They can excel in counseling, law, human resources, and ambassadorship on behalf of a company or brand. They can relay a message and make it theirs, whether they fully believe in it or not. The ability to engage and convince may be far more stimulating for them, than actually tackling the wider issues of faith and belief.

Water

*All the water and all its fruits come forth from the element of water; but they are not the element itself... From [water] emanates nothing but water.* – Paracelsus

TABLE 5: *Water*

| | |
|---|---|
| Principle: | Destruction |
| Glyph: | ▽ |
| Qualities: | Cold & Wet |
| Humour: | Phlegm |
| Temperament: | Phlegmatic |
| Season: | Winter |
| Signs: | ♋ ♏ ♓ |

The signs Cancer, Scorpio, and Pisces all have water as their chief operating system. When water is the chief operating system, the mode of action tends to be internalized, introverted, changeable, passionate, creative, intuitive, and intense. The water native comes into the world with a heightened level of sensitivity and perceptiveness. They feel their way through the world with greater awareness than others. While their highly evolved perceptive abilities may be a blessing, it can also be a burden. Many water natives feel they are missing a fundamental layer of protection that everyone else around them has naturally. This causes them to automatically seek to find shelter far sooner than others, because they tend to realize the coarseness of the world around them far sooner than others. The nature of water is to find the lowest, most stable ground at all times as an act of security and self-preservation. This also helps it establish a place where it can gather without being harshly thrown about by life. The watery person seeks this peace more than anything else.

Watery people are deeply aware of the intangibles of life. They are sensitive to feelings and the unexpressed motivations that may guide the actions of others. They often move through the world with a sort of psychic sensitivity that can accurately assess a person's true intentions. However, as people who may rely heavily on their emotions to give them an accurate assessment of what is going on around them, their psychic sensitivity is often as inaccurate as it is accurate. This may cause them to assume that a threat exists where one does not. The trust of a watery person may be earned slowly and broken quickly, and depending on which water sign we are referring to, may never actually be won again.

Watery natives are passionate and deeply devoted. Moon-ruled, the Cancerian is dedicated to family, home, the land, and their children. The Cancerian desires to serve through providing a warm meal and a safe living environment so that the people under their care can thrive. The Martian Scorpio is a fierce protector of everyone who has earned their love. Regardless of their gender, they will ferociously protect their young with a primal maternal instinct. They will pour both heart and soul into preserving the beauty and the sacredness of what they have built. Jupiter-ruled, Pisces is devoted to the wellbeing of all sentient beings. The Piscean can lose themselves in an ocean of humanitarian causes or interests. The care for the people, the animals, the environment, and the world. They viscerally experience the larger tides of change that occur within the collective soul of the planet. They are deeply aware of the sanctity of every form of life.

The water signs find it difficult to express themselves in words that can explain the depth of their emotional experiences. The Piscean may struggle with this most of all since Pisces is both the detriment and fall of Mercury, the god entrusted with the gifts of speech and communication. The watery person can communicate in other ways. They can express themselves artistically and can demonstrate an otherworldly sense of creativity and inspiration. They may have an uncanny understanding of the complex inner workings of the human soul and psyche. Art created by a water person can bring others into an experience of deeply healing catharsis.

The watery person needs to find something real to anchor themselves in. For the water native, the deepest feeling is the only thing that is real. What they commit themselves to has to have heart, soul, and meaning. They gravitate towards practices of spirituality and service to humanity. They can also be drawn to intense service jobs that other people either despise or fear, but that are necessary for the continuation of the human species. Love, loyalty, and something to devote themselves to can settle the soul of the watery person. These three things are often all it takes for them to truly flourish within the world.

QUADRUPLICITIES

*The first sign of each season is called tropical as it is the turning
point, the second fixed, because when the Sun is in it the season is
established, and the third bicorporeal [double-bodied].*
– AL-BIRUNI

TABLE 6: *Quadruplicities of the Signs*

| SIGN | QUADRUPLICITY | DIVISION OF THE SEASON | ALCHEMICAL PRINCIPLE |
|---|---|---|---|
| ♈ ♋ ♎ ♑ | MOVEABLE (CARDINAL) | BEGINNING | 🜍 |
| ♉ ♌ ♏ ♒ | IMMOVEABLE (FIXED) | MIDDLE | 🜔 |
| ♊ ♍ ♐ ♓ | COMMON (DOUBLE-BODIED) | END | ☿ |

Quadruplicities refer to divisions of the zodiac based on the beginning, middle,
and end of the four seasons. The quadruplicity of a sign is also referred to as its
"mode." Signs that correspond with the beginning of a season are called "moveable
signs." Today, these signs are more commonly referred to as "cardinal signs." Signs
that correspond with the middle of a season are called "fixed signs." These were traditionally called "immoveable signs." Signs that correspond with the end of a season are called "common" or "double-bodied signs" because they represent the end
of one season and the beginning of another. Today, these signs are more commonly
referred to as "mutable signs." One way to easily recall this connection between
the word "quadruplicity" and the modal divisions of the signs, is by remembering
that signs of the same quadruplicity have square ("quadrangular") or oppositional
relationships with each other.

On an esoteric level, I believe these three divisions of the seasons correspond
with the three alchemical substances: sulfur, salt, and mercury. Sulfur represents
the fiery impetus within nature that drives everything towards growth and evolution. Salt represents the fixed quality within nature that holds everything in its
specific shape. It preserves the integrity of the individual entity by preventing it
from dissolving and infringing upon the individuality of other sentient beings. It
represents the principle of stability that exists within our material universe. The
salt principle provides us with a body: a physical vehicle for the life power – represented by sulfur – to express itself within each lifetime.

Alchemical mercury refers to a substance, and not the planet. However, both
the alchemical principle and the planet share many similarities. Alchemical
mercury is a shapeshifter. It exists as both particle and wave. It can be solid,
liquid, or gaseous. It is the principle of both life and death as two sides of the

same reality. It is an indefinable quality that transcends the salt principle of "being" and the sulfuric principle of "becoming." The signs that correspond with alchemical mercury are rightly called "mutable" or "double-bodied." They exist in the yawning void between that which was and that which will be.

## MOVEABLE (CARDINAL)

*Each one of these is related by quartile to the others of its kind, and thus Aries, Cancer, Libra, and Capricorn form the tropical tetragon, the indications of which are gentleness, purity, and sociability with a tendency to science and details. – AL-BIRUNI*

TABLE 7: *Moveable (Cardinal)*

| SIGN | SEASON | PRINCIPLE |
|:---:|:---:|:---:|
| ♈ | BEGINNING OF SPRING | |
| ♋ | BEGINNING OF SUMMER | |
| ♎ | BEGINNING OF AUTUMN | ☿ |
| ♑ | BEGINNING OF WINTER | |

Aries, Cancer, Libra, and Capricorn are called "cardinal signs." Traditionally, they were known as "moveable signs." Abraham Ibn Ezra tells us that this name was chosen for them because when the Sun is transiting through any of these four signs, "at that time the air does move and change shape from what it was." These signs mark the beginning of a new season within the wheel of the year.

Aries begins the season of Spring, Cancer begins the season of Summer, Libra begins the season of Autumn, and Capricorn begins the season of Winter. Each of these signs represents a catalyzing impulse within their respective elements.

In classical Western alchemy, this principle of cardinality is reflected by the alchemical substance of sulfur. Sulfur represents the fiery, volatile, impulsive, action-oriented, life spark within nature. It represents the ability of nature to metabolize food and turn it into fuel for all sentient beings. Sulfur is the unstoppable kinetic energy in a waterfall. It is the momentum behind the avalanche, and the motive force within a hurricane. It is a power of desire. It represents the impulse of every being to pursue their destiny through expressing their individual will. It is what inspires all of us to awaken with the rising Sun, and to seize the day through our activities and involvement with the world around us. In Samkhya philosophy this is called "rajas." It is the heating fire of inspiration that causes everything to aspire to become something greater. It is the internal vital force that gives everything the will to live.

This can also be understood on a human level. Aries manifests this initiating principle through the desire to be independent. Aries, as a fire sign, embodies the burning principle of sulfur and cardinality more than the other signs of this quadruplicity. Mars-ruled, Aries is self-motivated, self-starting, and unafraid to charge into action, even if it doesn't have the longevity to see things through to completion.

Cancer manifests this initiating principle through the impulse to create a safe container for itself through home and family. There is a burning desire within the Cancerian to create comfortable spaces that have all the amenities necessary to live happily within the world. This same sulfuric fire can drive them to hoarding things – filling their home with far more belongings than necessary. They acquire things and acquire people, which ensures that they will always have a large domestic life.

Libra manifests this initiating principle through the impulse to create beauty in the world through words, relationships, and aesthetically pleasing physical spaces. The fires of sulfur create a hunger within the Libran to be in dialogue with the world around them. They want to build community and intimacy with others, as a means of deepening their knowledge of their environment and of themselves within it.

Capricorn natives manifest this initiating principle by creating stability for themselves through career, responsibility, and financial security. Capricorns manifest the sulfuric fires by driving themselves to attain their material goals and ambitions. They desire the power that comes through tilling the soil. Their hard work within the world convinces them that they have earned the right to exist.

All of the signs manifest this impulse to create, based on the motivations of their ruler and the element through which they operate.

## FIXED

*Then Taurus, Scorpius, Aquarius, and Leo form the fixed tetragon, the indications of which are mildness, thoughtfulness, and justice, in many cases of litigiousness and pugnacity, and sometimes of endurance in adversity and patience in trouble and injustice.*
– AL-BIRUNI

TABLE 8: *Fixed*

| SIGN | SEASON | PRINCIPLE |
|:---:|:---:|:---:|
| ♉ | MIDDLE OF SPRING | |
| ♌ | MIDDLE OF SUMMER | ⊖ |
| ♏ | MIDDLE OF AUTUMN | |
| ♒ | MIDDLE OF WINTER | |

Taurus, Leo, Scorpio, and Aquarius are the fixed signs. Abraham Ibn Ezra tells us that when the Sun is transiting through any of these signs, "the air is fixed and firmly established in what it is." They represent the full unfolding of the season that they are in. Taurus is the most established period of Spring, when the air is firmly fixed in the definite shape of the Springtime. Leo is the most established period of Summer, when the season is ablaze with the light of the triumphant Sun. Scorpio is the most established period of Autumn, when the air is pregnant with the Scorpion's poison that sucks the vitality out of the Earth, causing the leaves to decay. Aquarius is the most established period of Winter, when the air is fixed and the world freezes over.

In classical Western alchemy, this quality in nature corresponds with salt. Salt is the alchemical principle that solidifies and stabilizes everything in the material world in their individual forms. It is the principle that captures the descending soul and keeps it tied to the physical body. It preserves this connection so that all living beings can experience an incarnate life.

In Samkhya philosophy, it is called "tamas." Tamas represents a dull, inert, sleep state. It is the principle that prevents organisms from suddenly transforming into something else. Tamas, at its best, creates a container for the fertile expansion of an individual life. Tamas, at its worst, is a stifling, inflexible stubbornness, that causes an organism to be lost in the unbending gravity of its base desires. All fixed signs express this quality through their psychological approach to the world.

Taurus, a fixed earth sign ruled by Venus, expresses this through the slow building of a materially comfortable life. As fixed earth, Taurus runs the risk of being the heaviest of the signs physically and mentally, and may need far more goading in order to mobilize itself into action. Even Taureans that have a physically smaller built body can still move in a way that is deliberate and slow, to the point of it appearing as no movement at all.

Leo, as a fixed fire sign ruled by the Sun, tends to have more power and energy at its disposal than other signs. It can establish its vital presence within the world without the support of others. The proud Leo can stubbornly commit to an action long after that action has proven itself to be ineffective. The Leo may also be blinded by the effulgence of their own fire, which may cause them not to see how that fire impacts others around them.

Scorpio, as a fixed water sign ruled by Mars, manifests this principle through becoming unbending in what they believe to be emotionally true. This creates walls of defense and security for them as they move through life. It makes them keenly aware of when those walls of self-protection are being violated. They can become fierce adversaries, even when given evidence that there is no war to fight.

Aquarius, as a fixed air sign ruled by Saturn, manifests this principle through fixing a thought or a vision in their mind and projecting it onto their environment. They can become overly invested in this vision. Saturn-ruled, Aquarius believes that their vision of how the world can work, is the right way that the world *should* work. They hold onto these beliefs even if their point of view is out of step with the current world around them. They can stubbornly hold true to this vision and convince others to do the same.

All the fixed signs manifest this fixed quality based on their native element and the influence of their ruler.

## Common or Double-Bodied (Mutable)

> *Gemini, Virgo, Sagittarius, and Pisces, the bicorporeal [double-bodied] tetragon, indicates amiability, levity, playfulness, thoughtlessness, discord in business, capriciousness and duplicity.* – Al-Biruni

TABLE 9: *Common or Double-Bodied (Mutable)*

| SIGN | SEASON | PRINCIPLE |
|:---:|:---:|:---:|
| ♊ | END OF SPRING | |
| ♍ | END OF SUMMER | ☿ |
| ♐ | END OF AUTUMN | |
| ♓ | END OF WINTER | |

Gemini, Virgo, Sagittarius, and Pisces are known as common, double-bodied, or mutable signs. According to Ibn Ezra, these signs indicate when "the air is leaving that which it represented before while turning to that which will be." Common signs are the threshold of the seasons. They correspond with that period of time that stands between the season that is passing away and the season that is coming-to-be. During these volatile periods, nature gives us unexpected bursts of the fading season intermingled with glimpses of the season that is on the horizon. At the end of Winter during the period of Pisces, we experience both the sudden blizzard as well as the Springtime rain. At the end of Spring during the period of Gemini, we experience the cool chill of the reborn year as well as unexpected days of perfect Summer warmth. At the end of Summer during the period of Virgo, we experience days of sweltering heat, intermingled with the crisp winds of Autumn. At the end of Autumn during the period of Sagittarius, we experience the crisp winds of the dying year pierced by the frozen arrows of the newborn Winter.

In classical Western alchemy, this principle corresponds with mercury. For the alchemists, mercury was a volatile pre-cosmic substance out of which the entire universe arose. It was highly regarded as the metal of the magicians for its flexible, mutable nature. It has the ability to hold contradiction within itself – to be both a solid and a liquid, without being destroyed by the impossibility of those opposite states. It represents the spiritual part of every being. It is the dual nature of humanity: seemingly physical because of existing in a material body, but simultaneously composed of nothing other than pure spirit.

Mercury was traditionally used in the creation of mirrors because of its ability to reflect its environment. Ptolemy writes:

*Mercury sometimes produces dryness, and at other times moisture, and each with equal vigor.*

No other planet can hold two completely opposite principles within its constitution. Of the old gods, Mercury alone was hermaphroditic – both male and female – and therefore, something altogether transcendent of both. In Samkhya philosophy, alchemical mercury refers to the quality of "sattva" – the luminous, fluidic, expansive state that transcends both action (sulfur/rajas) and rest (salt/tamas). It is a state of pure reflective awareness. It is something altogether above and beyond the dualities of this material world.

All of the common signs express this quality through their psychological approach to life.

Gemini, a double-bodied air sign ruled by Mercury, seems to capture this principle more than all the others through its restless, highly mind-based orientation. The Gemini, more than other mutable signs, seems to be both here and there, as if living in two worlds simultaneously.

The Virgo, a common earth sign ruled by Mercury, is the most masterful at living in this dual way. The Virgo can hold the reins of the wild opposition they embody, and beat the chaos around them into the shape of an organized new world.

The Sagittarius, a mutable fire sign ruled by Jupiter, experiences a yearning to go as far as their flaming arrow can fly, as if seeking to reintegrate a long-lost part of themselves back into their soul.

The Pisces, a double-bodied water sign ruled by Jupiter, is an ocean within themselves. They seek to reabsorb an entire universe back into their being, and can often lose themselves through the ecstasy of becoming no-thing, of dissolving from the world, and participating in a universal life that has no central organizing principle.

All the common signs manifest this dual quality based on their native element and the influence of their ruler.

### TABLE 10: *Masculine & Feminine Signs*

| MASCULINE | ♈ ♊ ♌ ♎ ♐ ♒ | EXTROVERTED, ACTIVE, EXPANSIVE |
|---|---|---|
| FEMININE | ♉ ♋ ♍ ♏ ♑ ♓ | INTROVERTED, PASSIVE, CONTRACTIVE |

## MASCULINE

The masculine signs are the fire and air signs. These are Aries, Gemini, Leo, Libra, Sagittarius, and Aquarius. Masculine signs operate in an extroverted, active, and expansive way.

Feminine

The feminine signs are the earth and water signs. These are Taurus, Cancer, Virgo, Scorpio, Capricorn, and Pisces. Feminine signs operate in an introverted, passive, and contractive way.

Sect of the Signs

> *There is a general agreement that all the male signs are diurnal and the female nocturnal. The diurnal planets are powerful in the day signs and the nocturnal in the night ones.* – Al-Biruni

Masculine signs are diurnal. Feminine signs are nocturnal. Manilius writes:

> *There are those who fancy that the masculine signs are diurnal and that the feminine class rejoices in the safe cover of darkness.*

TABLE 11: *Diurnal & Nocturnal Signs*

| SECT | SIGNS |
|---|---|
| DIURNAL | ♈ ♊ ♌ ♎ ♐ ♒ |
| NOCTURNAL | ♉ ♋ ♍ ♏ ♑ ♓ |

Other Divisions of the Zodiac

While the division of the signs by triplicity, quadruplicity, and gender is common knowledge amongst astrologers today, there are other ways in which the signs can be divided. I've chosen to include a few of them here that tend to come up frequently within classical astrological works.

Fruitful Signs

> *The Crab's kind is especially fertile, and fertile too are the sharp-stinging Scorpion and the Fishes that fill the ocean with their spawn.* – Marcus Manilius

TABLE 12: *Fruitful Signs*

| FRUITFUL | |
|---|---|
| | 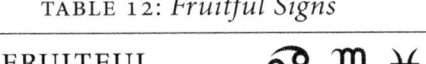 |

The water signs – Cancer, Scorpio, and Pisces – are fruitful or fertile signs. Classically, they were thought to represent the possibility for an abundant number of offspring. This was especially the case when these signs were on the Ascendant or the fifth house cusp; or if the ruler of the Ascendant, ruler of the fifth, or the Moon was placed in one of these three signs.

While this may hold some truth, the astrological assessment of fertility is a complex field, and no single indication or sign placement can say whether a person will be fertile or not. Through a more modern lens, the fertility represented by the fruitful signs could indicate creativity, idea generation, and extraordinary imaginative powers, which each water sign possesses in abundant supply.

SEMI-FRUITFUL SIGNS

> *Between the two groups (of fruitful and barren signs) fall Capricorn*
> *of compound form and the Centaur who glitters with his Cretan bow;*
> *also intermediate is the Ram who counts of like estate the equinoctial*
> *Scales, the Twins, and the Bull.* – MARCUS MANILIUS

TABLE 13: *Semi-Fruitful Signs*

| SEMI-FRUITFUL ♈ ♉ ♎ ♐ ♑ ♒ |
| --- |

The most commonly agreed upon semi-fruitful signs in traditional Western astrology are: Aries, Taurus, Libra, Sagittarius, Capricorn, and Aquarius.

Aries has reduced "fruitfulness" because it is a fire sign. The fire signs in general are not conducive to fertility because of their hot and dry nature. They do not readily facilitate the watery process of birthing life. Aries is also ruled by Mars – a malefic, fiery, destructive planet. Nevertheless, Aries represents the beginning of Spring, when all the world is born anew. The hard, oppressive, cold of Winter must be broken by an equally aggressive force: the fiery vitality of nature that desires to sweep across the land once more. Though full of passion, drive, and motivation, the life that is renewed in Aries is still fragile and weak. Aries is not very well-equipped to support life in general. However, it takes some part in the renewal of life based on where it falls on the wheel of the year.

Taurus is ruled by benefic Venus, and is thus considered to be somewhat fruitful. However, it is a fixed, earthy, cold and dry, melancholic sign, all of which is very similar to the nature of Saturn. For life to truly be born and nurtured, the earth must yield. The double effect of being fixed and earthy stifles some of the nutritive and birth-supporting fertility that Taurus can offer.

Libra is ruled by benefic, sanguine, hot and wet Venus. It is also a hot and wet, sanguine sign, which corresponds with the substance of blood within the human body. As an air sign, it also corresponds with the breath. Blood and breath were thought to be the vital substances necessary to animate a human being. Perhaps this is why it is considered as a somewhat fertile sign. However, Libra represents the beginning of Autumn – the time of the year when all life moves towards death and the world prepares itself to descend into the underworld. It is also the exaltation of Saturn, the god of the harvest who devoured his own children. The ancients considered Saturn to be a generally destructive planet. Though Libra has some fruitfulness because of being the domicile of Venus, the larger reality of this sign is that it is deeply associated with death and the dying process.

Sagittarius is ruled by benefic Jupiter. However, Sagittarius is a fire sign, which – like Aries – is not conducive to the nurturing waters of birth. It is limited in its ability to generate life. Sagittarius also represents the end of Autumn and the beginning of Winter. The harsh arrows of Sagittarius seal the fate of the world and usher it into the most barren time of the year, where only the fit survive.

Capricorn is ruled by malefic Saturn, the destroyer of his own offspring. It also represents the beginning of Winter. Neither of these factors is supportive of life. However, Saturn was also a god of agriculture, which gives him some association with fertility.

Aquarius, like Capricorn, is also ruled by malefic Saturn. While Aquarius represents the worst and the most barren period of Winter, it is also a sanguine sign, like Libra. The sanguine, hot and wet temperament, corresponds to blood, the bodily humor most analogous to life. While Saturn was a destroyer of his offspring, he was a father of the gods who populate the heavens. This is possibly why the ancients thought to give Aquarius this peculiar designation of being a semi-fruitful sign.

Collectively, the semi-fruitful signs have the ability to use both right and left brain thinking in order to navigate their way through life. However, they may still lean more toward paths of logic, stability, and reason. Though Aries natives are keen on fighting, even they can be skillful at tactically planning a path towards success.

BARREN

*Barren is the Virgin, as also her neighbor the Lion; and the Waterman fails to receive seed or, if he does so, he spills it.* – MARCUS MANILIUS

TABLE 14: *Barren Signs*

| BARREN | ♊ ♌ ♍ |
|---|---|

Gemini, Leo, and Virgo are all considered to be barren signs in many traditional Western sources.

Leo is a barren sign because the fire signs in general are not predisposed to supporting fruitfulness. The ancients thought the Sun would "burn the seed" of the unborn offspring, which would dispose the overly fiery person to having little or no children.

Virgo is the sign of the virgin. It goes without saying that cold and dry, Mercury-ruled Virgo should be considered a barren sign. She does not represent fecundity. Rather, she represents the harvesting of what was grown by a force other than herself.

Gemini is a very volatile sign. Between Gemini and Virgo, Gemini is most analogous to the unstable nature of Mercury. Within the wheel of the year, Gemini is an erratic sign, flipping constantly between the cool days of Spring and the hot days of Summer. It does not possess the stability necessary to be a fruitful sign.

In the quote by Manilius above, we see the "Waterman" also being listed as a barren sign. Though the inclusion of Aquarius amongst the barren signs fell into disuse by the seventeenth century, it would make sense that Aquarius would be considered barren. Aquarius is a fixed sign. Fixity goes against the versatile adaptation necessary for pregnancy and birth. It is also ruled by the greater malefic Saturn, who the ancients viewed as a destroyer of life. Aquarius corresponds with the middle of Winter, a most barren portion of the year in many parts of the world.

Though not "fruitful," Gemini, Leo, and Virgo can be very good at getting to the point of things. Their ability to see the big picture, plan, and delegate, makes them skillful in areas in which the fruitful signs may not excel.

MUTE SIGNS

> *... having no voice are Cancer and its triplicities. When Mercury is in a sign which has no voice and it does not aspect by good aspect, i.e. it is made unfortunate, the native's tongue or his sense of hearing is harmed, and he sometimes becomes deaf or dumb...*
> – ABŪ MAʿŠAR

TABLE 15: *Mute Signs*

| MUTE | ♋ ♏ ♓ |
| --- | --- |

The water signs Cancer, Scorpio, and Pisces are the mute signs. The animals they are represented by do not have a voice that is audible to human ears. A person who has very important chart factors such as the Ascendant, ruler of the Ascendant, or a majority of planets in water signs may be someone who finds it difficult to articulate their feelings in words. They may assume that other people will be able to pick up on their nonverbalized signals, which may leave them feeling let down when others can't or don't.

SIGNS WITH HALF A VOICE

> *And of the signs, certain ones are said to be having half a voice, as are whose which are shaped in the image of animals bleating, lowing, and roaring: as are Aries, Taurus, Leo, and Capricorn, and the last half of Sagittarius.* – GUIDO BONATTI

TABLE 16: *Signs with Half a Voice*

| HALF A VOICE | ♈ ♉ ♌ (LAST HALF OF ♐) ♑ ♐ |
|---|---|

The bestial signs Aries, Taurus, Leo, the last half of Sagittarius, and Capricorn are all signs with half a voice. As bestial signs, they tend to operate more based on impulse than a clearly defined logic. Even stoic Capricorn is driven more by the instinct of survival, than by anything deeply cerebral. For the ancients, having a voice was thought of as a sign of intelligence and rationality. Though these signs have the ability to articulate their intentions, they are much more action-oriented. They prefer demonstration over explanation.

HUMANE, RATIONAL, & SIGNS OF BEAUTIFUL VOICE

> *Al-Qabisi said, that of the signs four whole ones are called rational, namely Gemini, Virgo, Libra, Aquarius – and the first half of Sagittarius – whose images are shaped in the images of humans. And they are said to have beautiful voices...* – GUIDO BONATTI

TABLE 17: *Humane Signs*

| HUMANE, RATIONAL & A BEAUTIFUL VOICE | ♊ ♎ ♍ (FIRST HALF OF ♐) ♒ |
|---|---|

All of the air signs are considered to be humane signs. This is largely because these signs either represent the shape of a human or something that is manmade, as is the case with the scales of Libra. Virgo is a humane sign since she is in human form. The first half of Sagittarius is humane because up until the fifteenth degree of that sign (00° 00' to 14° 59') we find a human shape, while the last half of that sign is in the shape of a horse. All of these signs are thought to have a high level of intellectual aptitude and the gift of refined communication skills.

BESTIAL

> *Aries, Taurus, Leo, and the latter half of Sagittarius are the signs of the quadrupeds, and the first half of Capricorn sometimes indicates the same.* – ABŪ MAʿŠAR

TABLE 18: *Bestial Signs*

| BESTIAL | ♈ ♉ ♌ (LAST HALF OF ♐) ♑ |
|---|---|

The bestial signs represent animals that all have four feet. These were also called "quadrupedal signs," which means "four-footed." These signs are Aries, Taurus, Leo, Capricorn, and the last half of Sagittarius. Being bestial suggests that these signs act in a more instinctive and primal way. They are driven by a very strong predisposition towards survival, and seek to fulfill that impulse as a fundamental part of how they operate in the world.

LONG AND SHORT ASCENSION

Within a twenty-four-hour day, we would imagine that all signs have an even two-hour rising period on the Eastern horizon. This is not the case. Some signs rise in less than two-hours while other signs rise in more than two-hours.

Signs that rise in longer than two-hours are called "signs of long ascension." In the Northern hemisphere, these signs are: Cancer, Leo, Virgo, Libra, Scorpio, and Sagittarius. These signs are also called "direct/straight" or "commanding signs."

Signs that rise in less than two hours are called "signs of short ascension." In the Northern hemisphere, these signs are: Capricorn, Aquarius, Pisces, Aries, Taurus, and Gemini. These signs are also called "indirect/crooked" or "obeying signs." Al-Qabisi writes:

> And those ascending crookedly obey those ascending directly: that is, two signs which were of one longitude from the beginning of Cancer obey each other: as Gemini [obeys] Cancer, Taurus Leo, Aries Virgo, and Pisces Libra, Aquarius Scorpio, and Capricorn Sagittarius.

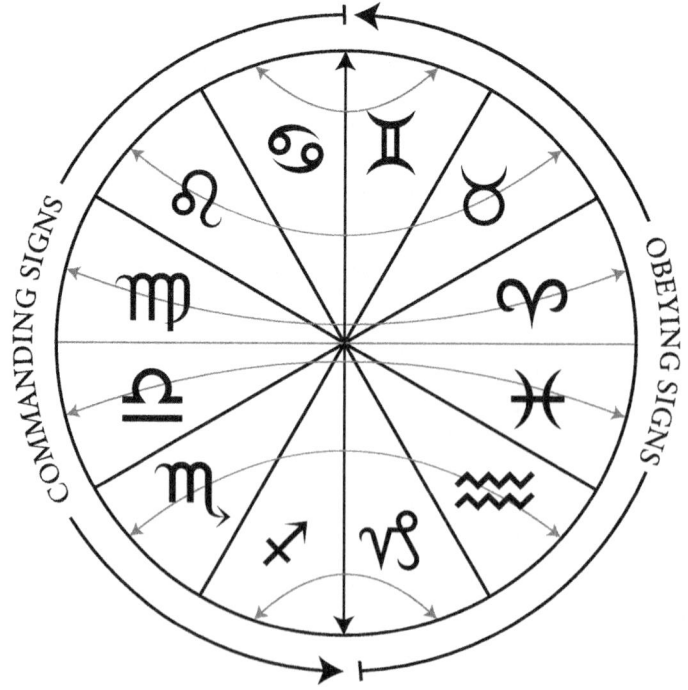

FIGURE 1: *Commanding & Obeying Signs I*

This model is based on signs that reflect each other on either side of the Cancer/Capricorn axis. We have learnt already that this is also known as "antiscia."

There is another ancient model of the commanding and obeying signs. Paulus Alexandrinus writes:

> The commanding [zoidia] have this order: Taurus commands Pisces and Pisces obeys it, Gemini [commands] Aquarius, Cancer Capricorn, Leo Sagittarius, Virgo Scorpio, [Libra obeys Aries].

In this system, all of the signs that are North of the celestial equator (Aries through Virgo) command the signs that are South of the celestial equator (Libra to Pisces). Bonatti writes:

> The northern ones are six, namely those which are from the beginning of Aries up to the end of Virgo (Aries, Taurus, Gemini, Cancer, Leo, Virgo). And they are called "northern" because they are of the northern direction from the equator of the day. The remaining six are those which are from the beginning of Libra up to the end of Pisces. And they are called "southern" because they are of the southern direction from the equator of the day.

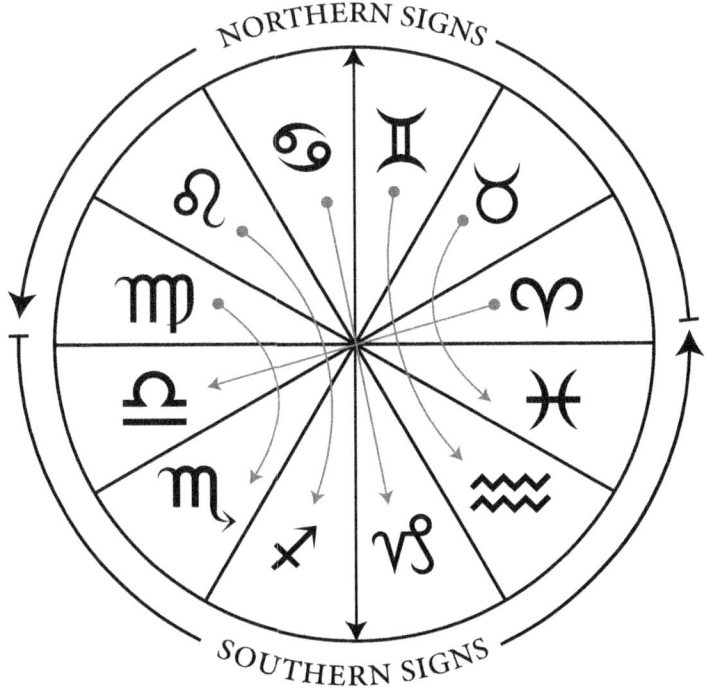

FIGURE 2: *Commanding & Obeying Signs II*

I prefer to teach the model in FIGURE 1 to my students, since it reinforces antiscia within their memory.

This designation of commanding and obeying becomes useful in questions regarding power or the likelihood of one party having an upper hand over another. This can occur in a battle, a legal case, or anything where we need to determine which of two parties has the advantage. If one planet is in a commanding sign and the other is in an obeying sign, and that is the only thing that will differentiate which of the two parties is stronger, the planet in the commanding sign will represent the stronger party. While this is a part of our astrological tradition, I have never had to use this in my practice.

CHAPTER 17 QUESTIONS

1. Within the mythology of tropical astrology, why are the four cardinal signs associated with the symbols of the Ram, the Crab, the Scales, and the Goat?
2. What are the four life processes and how do the four elements correspond with them?
3. What are the three alchemical substances? How do they correspond with the three quadruplicities?
4. Why are the water signs considered fruitful signs in traditional astrology?

CHAPTER 18 OBJECTIVES

* Discuss the impact Sun sign astrology has had on our field.
* Provide descriptions for the twelve signs of the zodiac that fully deconstructs each sign based on its triplicity, quadruplicity, and planetary affiliations.

# CHAPTER 18

## SOUL & PSYCHE OF THE ZODIAC

*Resplendent in his golden fleece the Ram leads the way and looks back with wonder at the backward rising of the Bull, who with lowered face and brow summons the twins; these the Crab follows, the Lion the Crab, and the Virgin the Lion. Then the Balance, having matched daylight with the length of night, draws on the Scorpion ablaze with his glittering constellation, at whose tail the man with body of a horse aims with taut bow a winged shaft, ever in act to shoot. Next comes Capricorn, curled up within his cramped asterism, and after him from urn upturned the Waterman pours forth the wonted stream for the Fishes which swim eagerly into it; and these as they bring up the rear of the signs are joined by the Ram. – MARCUS MANILIUS*

TODAY, MANY PEOPLE BELIEVE ASTROLOGY is only a way of describing our personality. The emphasis on character assessment within astrology over the last hundred years also brought with it a decline in the use of astrology to describe and predict concrete events. The esoteric, karmic, psychological, humanistic, transpersonal, archetypal, and evolutionary approaches to astrology that have arisen during that period, have used astrology as a backdrop to discuss larger, non-astrological themes. These themes often include a heavy emphasis on mythology, storytelling, philosophy, and psychology. Though, like astrology, these ideas are far-reaching and broad enough to include the experiences of everyone, these concepts are not representative of traditional astrological practice. This overemphasis on the non-tangible structure of the human psyche, has often come at the cost of disregarding the concrete realities of our world that shaped that psyche to begin with.

Though I am not inspired to practice astrology in a purely psychological way, I do understand the allure. Astrology has infinite potential as a language to describe reality. Our psychological constitution is central to how we perceive the world. It is very easy to understand how astrologers, in seeking to justify their right to exist and practice, would build their practice on describing the psychological constitution of human beings. However, the accurate assessment of personality has always been the low hanging fruit of astrology, and at best, represents an entry-level natal astrology skill. As astrologers, we know that astrology is an unparalleled tool in giving insight into the very specific body of complexes that make us uniquely who we are. The full scope of astrology, however, is greater than that.

## THE MULTI-PRISMATIC HOROSCOPE

The same chart that can be read as a psychological assessment of a person can also be read as a means of describing a person's career trajectory. Through another lens, it is an indication of a person's love potential in this lifetime. It is a useful index of not just their previous love experiences, but of how they deal with the topic of love in general. Through yet another lens, it can be used as a barometer of constitutional strength or weakness, and can indicate areas within the body that may be prone to illness. From a more general perspective, it can definitely be used as an album that contains the outline of all the major event structures we are bound to experience within a lifetime. The birth chart in its fullness is like a multifaceted prism that carries our totality within itself.

## THE TYRANNICAL REIGN OF THE UNDYING SUN

While no single factor carries the entire signification of the birth chart on its own, the version of astrology that is most prevalent in the world today would have us believe otherwise. Much of the astrology that the general public concerns itself with centralizes one astrological factor: the sign placement of the natal Sun. This is problematic for many reasons.

Every individual factor of a chart is impacted by the entire ecosystem of the chart as a whole. There is no one astrological factor that can sum up the entirety of an individual's self-knowledge, not even the all-powerful Sun. The Sun sign has become the astrological default for the general public because it requires virtually no skill whatsoever to determine what it is. While this is an understandable point of ignorance for the uneducated public, it is disappointing that many people who practice and teach astrology continue to do so from the perspective of the Sun sign. This furthers the public belief that there is nothing more to being an astrologer than knowing a laundry lists of adjectives to describe the twelve signs of the zodiac. In an age of such rapid advancement in our field through the revival of ancient techniques and modern discoveries, the continued glorification of Sun sign astrology is no longer a satisfactory baseline of astrological practice.

The dumbing down of astrology is a modern convention. Our astrological ancestors were master technicians. They had an organic understanding of the sky, that our minds – poisoned by the neon lights of modernity – will never be able to fathom. They practiced an astrology that was far more intricate than what we refer to as "Sun sign astrology," and so should every astrologer worthy of the title.

A professional astrologer should be equipped with greater tools than the Sun sign alone to describe the complexities of the psychological constitution of a person. That astrologer knows that there are multiple things that impact the soul and psyche of the individual, not just the placement of the natal Sun. Even seasoned professional astrologers who lead their readings by assessing the Sun position first, do not root their entire understanding solely based on that one factor.

Our predicament as astrologers becomes even more dubious when we consider that Sun sign astrology has become the template for how many aspiring astrologers interact with the other planets in a chart. The vast majority of practicing novice astrologers in the twenty-first century focus on interpreting the sign position of the various planets in a chart as their first line of defense when set to the task of giving someone a reading. Even more disconcerting is that these "astrologers" offer readings in which their disclaimer is that they'll only be able to cover the "Big Three" of Sun, Moon, and Rising sign within the hour-long session, as if any of those three factors requires that much time. The more ambitious amongst them will interpret the sign placement of your natal Mercury, Venus, Jupiter, and Saturn, as if the zodiacal position of your natal Jupiter by itself is more deeply personalized for you than the other several million babies who were born that same year while Jupiter was in that sign. The Type A personality astrological enthusiast will even interpret the sign placement of your natal Uranus, Neptune, and Pluto, just so as to leave no stones unturned.

However, this "sign language" of astrology is far from sufficient. The "astrologers" who end up on a televised program to prove astrology are often "astrologers" whose singular competency is that they have ingested a cookbook of astrological keywords, enabling them to describe the signs of the zodiac in which a person's planets at birth are found. Unfortunately, these well-meaning "astrologers" do more harm than good through their public demonstrations. Insofar as the accurate delineation of the life events of a person is concerned, a sole reliance on the meanings of the twelve signs of the zodiac will always be woefully inadequate.

And yet, there is something curious afoot within Sun sign astrology. Though the tools that we employ to fully assess the character of a person are vast, there still seems to be something about the Sun sign that has a way of describing at least the baseline or some core feature of who a person is. This is even more so the case when there is a confluence of planets within that sign. This is especially true when those are faster moving planets such as the Sun, Moon, Venus, Mercury, and Mars. When three or more traditional planets gather in a sign of the zodiac this is called a "stellium."

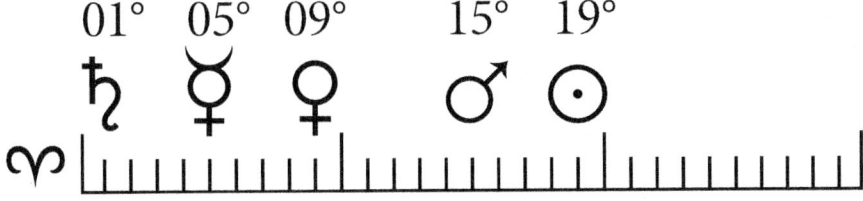

FIGURE 1: *Stellium*

Though the signs have some distinct qualities, they are not all-powerful. A sign is only a filter that expresses the will of its ruler, its element, and its mode. Devoid of those things, there is nothing intrinsically causal in the sign itself. There is no Scorpio without Mars, water, or the fixed principle that exists within nature. Therefore, when interpreting the signs of the zodiac, I always interpret them as if they were a direct reflection of their ruler, in a particular element, operating through a particular mode. Instead of thinking of Scorpio as one compact idea, I ask myself: what would Mars act like if he were in water that was of a fixed nature? Furthermore, what does fixed water feel like? What are the implications of Mars on ice? What would be his modus operandi if he were in a freezing cold environment? The deconstruction of "Scorpio" bears far more interpretive value than studying Scorpio as if it were an independent monolith. When we think about a sign as a composite of several stellar factors as opposed to an immutable idea within itself, it allows us to do more detailed work in terms of what we have to say about that sign.

I carry this philosophy into my interpretation of planets in signs as well. Instead of viewing Venus in Scorpio as having a meaning *per se*, it is more useful to think about how Venus and Mars operate in combination with each other, and how they would express their interaction through a fixed, water filter. I view planets in signs as being somewhat analogous to those planets being in conjunction with the rulers of those signs. For me, Venus in Gemini, can be interpreted somewhat as a Mercury/Venus conjunction. Moon in Aquarius can be interpreted similarly to a Moon/Saturn conjunction. This deconstructive method of interpretation forces us to think in terms of combinations of stellar influences as opposed to the textbook definition of what a planet in a particular sign may mean.

Here are some guidelines for how to include the signs into your practice. My goal is to point us all back to the planets as being the movers within our astrology. While this isn't a book about natal astrology, it is only fitting that an introductory astrology textbook should contain psychological descriptions of the twelve signs of the zodiac. At this point in our astrological history, it has come to be expected. Because what sort of astrology textbook would this be if you didn't learn what to expect if you were dating an Aries?

## Psychological Constitution of the Signs of the Zodiac

The following descriptions are best used when describing the rising sign in a natal chart. This is the sign that is on the cusp of the Ascendant. However, these descriptions can also be used as a generic outline of the sign position of the natal Sun if that is something you feel inclined to do.

The triplicity, quadruplicity, gender, domicile ruler, exaltation ruler, planets essentially debilitated in the sign, the body parts associated with the sign, and all the other subcategories of the sign serve as sources of information in understanding how that sign works in describing the native. I will demonstrate how some of these ideas can be used interpretively in the following delineations.

Aries

*They called this twelfth-part Aries the head of the cosmos, house of Ares [Mars]...* – Hephaistio of Thebes

Aries is a moveable, hot and dry, choleric, fiery, diurnal sign ruled by Mars. The chief operating system of Aries is fire. Fire predisposes the native to being ambitious, extroverted, passionate, excitable, and optimistic. It makes the native visionary and action-oriented. It fills them with confidence and the desire to seize life by the horns. It can also make this person someone who is rash and impulsive, not given to thinking before acting, and prone to feelings of burnout.

As a moveable sign, this further adds speed and impulse to the psyche of the Aries native. They desire to burn through life, conquering and overcoming all that stand in their way. Moveable fire people know no limits. However, moveability doesn't give them the greatest amount of endurance. Their fire may be sudden and erratic, projecting from them in quick bursts of intense force, but may easily be redirected to other aims if they find their efforts unable to alter the challenges before them.

Moveable fire makes the Aries native more equipped for the sprint than for the marathon. Mars-ruled, the fiery Aries can be fierce and violent in their ways, living with an excess of force and power. They can be hot-blooded and ready for arguments and debates, and untiring in their pursuit of victory and freedom. Mars, as the warrior of the gods, gives the Aries native a fearlessness in the face of adversity, which may also cause them to put themselves in dangerous situations that might have been avoided.

Aries is the exaltation of the Sun. Resultantly, the Aries-native can challenge themselves to be the absolute best in all things. In the competition of life, they can't fathom themselves as second to anyone. The solar exaltation in Aries predisposes these people to be able to rise to the occasion of leadership. As a result of the dignity received by both the Sun and Mars in this sign, it inclines them to create a life where they find dominion in all of their endeavors.

Aries is the detriment of Venus. These people may lack social graces and courtesies. They may appear rash and crude in their ways. Their ability to get turned on by people and things may have more to do with passion and desire, than a genuine sense of deep and lasting love. They can be an extraordinary source of energy and vitality socially. However, their inability to self-regulate may cause them to go overboard in terms of the things they say – which may lack tact and diplomacy. They are heavily invested in their own agenda, sometimes to the point of disregarding the larger society they inhabit. They are not prone to please or appease, and they may find it difficult to realize that an apology can often be used to build a bridge, and is not just a sign of weakness. They'd rather be alone than to feel themselves bested by someone who has "won" an apology from them, and therefore, find themselves alone more often than not. Positively, this lack of a strong allegiance to Venus means they will not wait on others to initiate action. They can self-start and self-motivate to attain their own successes in life.

Aries is the fall of Saturn. The Aries-native does not do well with barricades, walls, or places of confinement. They resist all things Saturnian such as restriction, regulation, or authority. They would rather no one ever have the pleasure of claiming to have ruled over them. This may even manifest as a dislike of them ruling over themselves, which may lead to a lack of self-discipline. They are hot, dry, and choleric, whereas Saturn is cold, dry, and melancholic. The Aries native burns up depression and throws it off of themselves like a plague. They would rather be anxious and angry than sad and depressed. If backed into a corner by the authorities – which can often happen – the Aries native will always find a way to escape and make their way back to freedom.

Within the physical body, Aries corresponds with the head and the face. As people who smash their way through life, they are often found with scars on their faces. They can have excess heat in their faces and heads, which can lead to migraines, acne, or facial blemishes.

TAURUS

> *Next is the twelfth-part Taurus, which ascends as far as the neck of the cosmos, the house of Aphrodite [Venus]....* – HEPHAISTIO OF THEBES

Taurus is a fixed, cold and dry, melancholic, earthy, nocturnal sign ruled by Venus. The chief operating system of Taurus is earth. Earth predisposes the native to being grounded, pragmatic, slow-moving, and gentle; responsible, dependable, unyielding, and stubborn. Being earth-ruled gives the Taurus native the understanding that things need to be supported and cared for. Earth-ruled, the Taurus native is distinctly aware of the value of the material world. They don't take for granted the sort of pleasure that having a financially stable life can bring. The Taurus native wants things: things of value, things of beauty, things that represent the fertility of the world. The acquisition of material creature comforts is more within the domain of Taurus than any other sign.

As fixed earth, the Taurus native can be slow, plodding, and at times downright unmovable. They can stubbornly commit themselves to one type of comfort that works for them. They can remain unchanging in their convictions. Fixed earth people appear both unwilling and incapable of changing from their set habit patterns. This blocks them from experiencing the joy of other things life has to offer. This can make them loyal and dependable, even though their dependability may come into question from time to time based on how slowly they move. The great deal of effort necessary for them to self-motivate can be annoying to people who are depending on them to be quick.

As a fixed earth sign ruled by Venus, the Taurus native knows how to both find and create comfort. The Taurus native can be entrusted with bringing things into the home that make it feel warm and nourishing, including good food, soft pillows, a comfortable sofa, and a warm bed. For the Taurus native, comfort is synonymous with security. They are unlikely to cut costs if it puts them in a position to be uncomfortable.

This Venusian creature is gentle, soft, and a wonderful companion. They have the ability to calm and stabilize the environment around them, bringing everyone into a vibration of peace and gentle affection. They can make others feel comfortable, cared for, and nurtured.

The fixed earth nature of Taurus gives them more gravity in the energy they project into the world. It can also make them more heavy-set physically. Even Taurus natives who are more slender still seem to have a thick and sweet aura around them. They exude an energy that is deliberate and sensual, like bubbles rising within honey or the slow flow of molasses. The Taurean will take their time to savor the moment and enjoy the deliciousness of life. Food can become the chief comfort of the Taurus native. It reminds them of the pleasures of the material world.

Being Venus ruled and fixed, Taurus can run the gamut of being sensually slow moving, to being downright lazy. It takes an extraordinary amount of willpower for them to goad themselves into action, and they will stubbornly resist change if they feel they are being goaded by someone else. Their path is the path of least resistance. They can quickly fall back into states of docile inactivity if given the opportunity, especially insofar as physical exercise and routines are concerned. However, when motivated the Taurus native can stick to the fulfillment of a task with far greater stamina than most of its other zodiacal companions.

Taurus is the exaltation of the Moon. The Taurean can nurture, love, support, and take care of all those within their immediate environment with lunar affection. Taurus provides a stabilizing environment for the volatility of the Moon. This is shown through the benevolence and the will to support others that is often found in the Taurus native. They nurture projects that are in the early stages of development; projects that will grow into a material empire that supports the multitudes. Their way of showing care is physical – through touch, through smell, through food, and through providing material security. Their greatest fear is that they may not be able to create material comfort for themselves and the ones they love. On a symbolic level, this is the same as the fear of hunger, or not being able to feed themselves.

Taurus is the detriment of Mars. The will-to-act is often lost within the soul of the Taurus native. They can be frustratingly slow, to both themselves and others. They may not be willing to upend the peace they've found for the sake of growth, evolution, and adventure. They may not know how to skillfully process anger. They may lash out at the world, often as a response to their own lack of mobility. Sometimes their efforts may feel blunted, as a result of them getting in their own way. They have a great fear of being lost in the world, something that Mars fearlessly embraces. For the Taurean, security may be more important than achievement.

Taurus corresponds with the neck and throat within the human body. As such, the Taurus native can have a beautiful and handsome voice: one that is deep, soothing, and healing.

GEMINI

> *The twelfth-part Gemini, which is taken for the shoulders [of the cosmos], is the house of Hermes [Mercury]....* – HEPHAISTIO OF THEBES

Gemini is a mutable, hot and moist, sanguine, airy, diurnal sign ruled by Mercury. The chief operating system of Gemini is air. Air predisposes the native to being intellectual, inquisitive, broad-minded, conversant in many areas, able to communicate ably with others, and friendly. Being air-ruled gives the Gemini native the instinctive desire to share their thoughts and ideas with people, whether they've been requested or not. It allows the native to easily separate themselves from being emotionally engaged in a subject, so that they can gain a more objective view. This causes the air-ruled Gemini to see things as they are. They have a deep appreciation for the diversity that exists within this world. The drawback of the air element is that it can be fickle: here today and gone today. It gives the native a roving spirit that may not easily find rest or satisfaction. This can lead to restlessness, over-intellectualization, and an ability to rationally justify why they, yet again, have dropped the ball.

Being mutable causes the airy Gemini to be fast moving, fast talking, and as flexible as the wind. They find it difficult to stay: in one train of thought, in one place, in one interest, in one conversation, and in most things that involve serious, far-reaching commitment. Mutable air can be a joyous combination and can enliven the minds of everyone it touches with a sparkling, crisp, and exciting gust of words and thoughts. However, the tendency of mutable air is to alter its course quickly, which doesn't provide the airy native a great deal of concentrative power.

The mutable Gemini may have an attention deficit if it doesn't find itself chasing things that move quicker than it does. Things that are slow and sequential may feel extraordinarily burdensome to the Gemini native, especially if they don't provide mental stimulation or surprising plot-twists. The Gemini mind may be more predisposed to Jenga than it is to chess. All the same, the mutable Gemini native may be an extraordinary problem solver. They are very apt to find short-term consultancy work, or a role that involves the rapid turnover of products in a way that provides constant bursts of stimulating activity.

Mercury-ruled, the Gemini native has a natural dexterity, agility, and a sharp, well-developed mind that may move far faster than others around them. They can be joyful, and seem eternally youthful in their wit, humor, and excellent conversation skills. Mercury corresponds with the tongue, the arms, hands, and fingers. The Gemini native can tell an epic tale while simultaneously using their nimble hands to juggle the lion, the witch, and the wardrobe.

Of all the signs of the zodiac, Gemini seems to be the only one who can truly claim to be a master of multitasking. However, there's a catch. The Gemini native already acts as if they are operating under the influence of too much coffee, and would be better off avoiding it. They have excess mental energy, which can lead to difficulty in resting their overactive mind, either in sleep or in downtime. They may suffer from fatigue and burnout long before they actually show it, and often need to be forced to take breaks. The Gemini native can be prone to nervousness. They expel this nervous energy through speaking in a way that is often disembodied. This means that they can launch into an unending stream of talking without noticing that they haven't stopped to catch a breath, or to let the other person get a word in edgewise. Being Mercury-ruled, the Gemini may find ways to take shortcuts or detours. They may skip steps for the sake of getting to the final goal quicker. If they can learn how to plan and organize, they may be able to harness their often scattered and unbridled energy towards extraordinary ends.

Though Gemini is the detriment of Jupiter, the way this works out seems to be less problematic than other planet and sign combinations. Jupiter in Gemini even further broadens the naturally scattered brain of the Gemini, causing them to be scattered on even higher and more rarified planes. The Gemini can often lack a centralizing reason or purpose behind their efforts, two things that are at the core of how Jupiter operates. They often lack the Jupiterian farsightedness to see what the end result of their efforts will be. It is for this reason why many Gemini natives can fall into the trap of dropping a project before its completion or moving on to some more exciting aim. Their efforts often lack purpose. However, this can be countered by other stabilizing factors within their charts. They can easily find themselves doing things for the sake of doing things. This may be exciting, but may not lead to great fulfilment in the end. If the Gemini native can figure out their purpose and their reason for being on this planet, they will be able to organize their efforts in such a way that they become more impactful in the long run.

Gemini corresponds with the lungs, arms, hands, and fingers. The Gemini cares about reaching out and grasping the world around them, twirling it in their fingers, and releasing it again. The Gemini can learn how to be ambidextrous, possibly quicker than others. They have fine motor skills when it comes to the use of their hands. They can excel in knitting, calligraphy, and other things that require refined hand-eye coordination.

CANCER

> *The twelfth-part Cancer, which is taken for the breast and ribs [of the cosmos], is the house of the Moon...* – HEPHAISTIO OF THEBES

Cancer is a moveable, cold and wet, phlegmatic, watery, nocturnal sign ruled by the Moon. The chief operating system of Cancer is water. Water predisposes the native to being soft, sensitive, caring, compassionate, deep-feeling, easily disturbed, and emotionally very complicated. For the water native, a decision has to first make sense in their gut before an intellectual argument can be agreed with. "It feels like the right thing to do" can be a motto for them. They will always act in a way that aligns with their values, regardless of how subjective those actions and values may be. Being so reliant on non-tangibles as the foundation of their lives, the water native needs to be given similar non-tangibles in order to gain their trust: loyalty, devotion, honesty, and an unbreakable love. Anything less can throw the watery person into a fierce state of self-protection; a sort of clamming up and withdrawal that they are inclined to do in any event. The watery native may not be able to articulate their feelings because they are in touch with ineffable realities. Nonetheless, if we stay around them long enough, the true motivation behind their intentions becomes evident.

As a moveable water sign, the Cancer native desires to initiate the things that make them feel nurtured and protected. These include building a home and nurturing a stable, well-fed family unit. All the watery signs are easily jostled. This is unavoidable. The watery Cancer tries to curb this by creating a safe container for themselves in a home that has all the amenities that are both necessary and unnecessary for comfort. This can make their home an overly comfortable, and at times excessively opulent environment. Whether male or female, the Cancerian is often the matriarch of the family, the mother hen of the roost. They often find themselves in places of being the one with their finger on the pulse of the family whether they like it or not.

Moon-ruled, the Cancer native is creative, emotionally sensitive to the needs of others, and can tend toward rapidly changing moods. The Cancerian can be fiercely protective of things having to do with home and heritage. They can be very patriotic as a result. They often find themselves in the role of protecting the underdog in the form of people, animals, and in particular, other people's children. The Cancerian either wants children or wants things or people within their lives who they can treat like children – animals, plants, pet projects, or coworkers. They can always be depended upon for a sense of lunar motherhood and care.

Cancer signifies containers: from an empty pot to the container of the mind. Resultantly, the Cancerian holds the memories of everything that happens to everyone. They particularly carry the memories of everything that has ever happened to them. They have no qualms with using the past wrongs of others against them to prove a point or come out on top in an argument. For all their sensitivity, the Cancerian can seldom identify their handiwork in what goes wrong in a relationship dynamic, and may need others to hold them accountable for their actions.

Trust is of utmost importance to all water signs. It allows them to feel safe in an unpredictable world. Each water sign responds to broken trust in a unique way. Moon-ruled Cancer often holds the burden of the sins of the family on their shoulders, and yet must still feed and attend to the needs of the family no matter what. The Cancerian mode of dealing with broken trust is to hold onto the memory of what was done forever, and serve as a living library of the transgressions of everyone else. The Cancerian is not beyond using guilt as a means of getting their way in life.

Like all water signs, the Cancer is considered to be a mute sign. The Cancer native may not be the greatest communicator in the world. Since they do so much to make an environment feel like a home, they often assume that other people will meet them with the same sensitivity and understanding. They may not say what they need when they need it because they think others should just know. Most people aren't mind readers. This is a harsh reality that can often leave the Cancerian feeling let down, disappointed, and in need of retreat from everyone else around them for the sake of self-care and self-nurturing.

Saturn is in detriment in Cancer. The Cancerian often doesn't realize how they spill into the personal space of others. They can become deeply interwoven in the affairs of those around them. They particularly do not have this self-awareness when it comes to people they share a home with. If left unchecked, this unhealthy tendency can make others feel smothered, suffocated, and incapable. Since everyone knows the natural sensitivity of the Cancer, no one may actually want to point out this toxic characteristic. When it finally is pointed out by others, they can feel like they've been mortally wounded. This can send detrimental ripples out into the larger environment and home that they share with their loved ones.

Jupiter is exalted in Cancer. The love a Cancer can provide is abundant and unbridled. There is a genuine sense of how much they care for others, and how much of a protector they want to be for those in need. No plate is ever empty and no glass is every dry in the Cancerian home. They will make sure that everyone has the base necessities of life met, as well as all the comforts one can ask for. Everyone needs something to believe in. What the Cancerian believes in is the family, the collective, the home, and the tribe.

Mars is in fall in Cancer. The Cancerian is very deeply invested in the stability of the home and family life. For the Cancerian, the family identity has to remain untarnished. This may cause them to skirt around the genuine pain that people may experience as a result of being a part of that particular family unit. Cancerians may not consider themselves to be outwardly angry people. However, when they are in a negative mood, they can respond to others with anger's watery counterparts: bitterness and spite. The Cancerian should learn how to view anger and arguments as necessary parts of holistic self-expression. When the Cancerian submerges their anger under the weight of the overall happiness of the family, it may lead to greater feelings of bitter negativity in the end.

Cancer corresponds with the containers of the body: the breasts, the stomach, the womb, and the lower portion of the lungs. The Cancerian knows how to hold the vital material necessary for the continuance of life. This makes them an extraordinary source of support and nurturing for everyone around them.

LEO

*The twelfth-part Leo, which is considered as the heart [of the cosmos and the places around it, is the house of the Sun... –* HEPHAISTIO OF THEBES

Leo is a fixed, hot and dry, choleric, fiery, diurnal sign ruled by the Sun. The chief operating system of Leo is fire. Fire predisposes the native to being warm, affectionate, outgoing, and brave; passionate, action-oriented, rash, and extroverted. The fiery Leo is apt to live from the front – through complete engagement with others and the world around them. This makes them feel like they're exploring all that life has to offer. It makes them driven to experience the fullness of life in a way that leaves no stone unturned. It opens them up to a life of great adventure. It causes them to demand more of themselves, which makes them extraordinary in leadership positions. This can lead to an even more extraordinary burnout, which is often the result of them over-exerting themselves. The fiery Leo native lives loudly in the world. Their lives are filled with vibrancy and color.

As a fixed fire sign, Leo can be steadfast and dependable; full of force and vigor. They are often trusted to bring visionary works to life. Their fixed fire is the fire that nurtures and nourishes. Other people come to them for comfort, warmth, and support. It's as if the fire of the Leo makes other people feel better about themselves. Because they represent fixed fire, their way of life may be onward and upward, causing them to push themselves and also others to live from the absolute highest level of self-expression and goal realization.

Sun-ruled, the Leo is expressive, grand in their actions, vitalizing in their impact on others, and can often be the proverbial center of attention. The Sun needs no other star to affirm his light, and the Leo native may need no one else around them to convince them of how powerful, extraordinary, and capable they are. The Leonian may move through the world feeling as if they are the best at everything they set themselves to. They have an inextinguishable understanding of their self-worth. Like the Sun, the Leo can sometimes give off far too much energy which may be overwhelming to others.

One of the challenges of the Leo is that they don't need to accomplish anything in life for them to believe they are the best. Nothing about their psychological constitution demands that they earn this title before claiming it. They may just believe they are the best at life in general, which is unwarranted and can rub people the wrong way. The effective Leo creates something of tangible value in the world upon which they can stake their claims of mastery and achievement.

Just like the Sun, the promise of the Leonian capacity may not actually be as everlasting as it seems in the moment. As powerful as the Sun is, it, too, has other obligations elsewhere which causes its power to diminish with the turning of the year. The Leo may promise a great deal to others from a place of genuine sincerity, but may not be the best at delivering on those promises. They may be far better at doing a task if you can get them to do it in that moment, rather than waiting for them to fulfill their promise at a later date.

Nothing can really stop the Leo from being pleased with the shape of their lives. The magnificence they experience on a daily basis is something they often feel compelled to tell others about. The rest of the world tends to be okay with it. Since the Leonian is often such an extraordinary performer, we get caught up in the drama of the telenovela that is their lives. However, even that can feel overdone; as if it were an exaggerated tale rather than a true depiction of life. Leos can make extraordinary actors. However, it can also make actors who look like they are acting, which is never quite as satisfying as seeing an actor who is truly a natural at their craft.

The Leo native is a complex character because few Leos are actually "Leo" in the textbook sense. I've often said that it takes a lot to be a textbook Leo, while it takes very little to completely shatter the Leonian complex. The person who has Leo rising, but also has the Sun in Cancer in the twelfth house, Sun in Pisces in the eighth house, or the Sun anywhere at all in hard aspect to Saturn or Neptune, will not be able to live up to the Leonian expectations of grandeur, dramatics, and unending exuberance. They might actually be quite shy, reserved, and introverted. Therefore, when delineating a horoscope in which there is Leo rising, it is very important to make sure that the Leo native doesn't also have one of these conditions at play. If you ignore this, your assessment may end up being very wrong. The shy, silent, withdrawn, depressive, overly serious, stern, and melancholic person you may meet, may not fit any of the descriptions that we typically assign to the flaming Lion.

Leo is the detriment of Saturn. The Leonian luminosity can infringe upon the light of others around them. This may inadvertently cause others to feel automatically "second place" by association, which may not be the healthiest thing in the world in terms of establishing deep and meaningful relationships. Also, the Leonian often doesn't have a sense of their physical limits or healthy boundaries in terms of how much effort they exert in a given task, or how long to exert it. This causes them to make too high demands of their energy and their bodies. They can push themselves until the very last straw, which may lead them to being bedridden with fatigue and burnout. Their recuperative powers are extraordinary, and they often bounce back quickly. However, them knowing this about themselves can cause them to continue to work, even when they have already been knocked off their feet. The Leonian person is one who feels they will die with their work-boots on. Like the Sun, they trust that the show cannot go on without their active involvement. It can.

Leo corresponds with the heart and spine. The Leo native stands as a pillar of support and assurance within the world, just as the spine is a pillar of support in the human body. As the heart is the battery around which we organize ourselves in this lifetime, the Leo native may consider themselves to be the radiant star around which an entire universe constellates.

VIRGO

*The twelfth-part Virgo, which is itself taken for the belly [of the cosmos], will be the house and exaltation of Hermes [Mercury]... –* HEPHAISTIO OF THEBES

Virgo is a mutable, cold and dry, melancholic, earthy, nocturnal sign ruled by Mercury. The chief operating system of Virgo is earth. Earth predisposes the native to being practical, stable, and collected in their approach to life. The earthy Virgo is someone who thinks first about the bottom line. They seek to orient their lives and their environment toward stability and peace. They cherish the feeling of the unmovable earth beneath their feet, and often go to great lengths to feel more fortified on it. They can similarly be great supports for others around them – for society, the workplace, their colleagues, and family. They can be trustworthy and dependable. The earth gives the Virgo native the ability to stick to a course of action, especially if that action leads to an even greater sense of peace and stability within their environment. They have the patience to watch things grow and develop, which is a part of the reason why earth people can exceed at both building and gardening.

As mutable earth, the Virgoan has a very peculiar lot in life. Naturally, the earth doesn't like to be forcefully moved or drastically disturbed. However, the very nature of mutability is that it is never in a state of true rest or peace. Therefore, the Virgoan has a heightened sense of anxiety and stress as they navigate the world around them. They do not feel genuinely secure in the world. They can find themselves regularly in a state of feeling as if the world is going to give way at any moment, falling into disaster and calamity. It is for this reason why the Virgoan approaches life with the seemingly self-appointed role of being the "rectifier of the world." The anal retentiveness that is often attributed to Virgo comes from this. They do not know how to delegate or let others take the reins. They do not believe others will pay as close attention to the details of a project as they can. This may also make them unforgivingly cruel in terms of their criticism of the work of others. They can often find the thinnest pencil line on the pure white wall, or the fallen eyelash that somehow made its way into the soup. This level of hypercritical living can cause them to be extraordinary when it comes to jobs that require troubleshooting or micro-level detective work. However, it can create difficulties in their intimate relationships when they don't know how to switch out of that role.

With their natural distrust that life will remain free from chaos, they tend to invest their efforts in controlling the one thing in life that is fully within their power: their physical bodies. This is why many people who are heavily Virgoan can be hypervigilant about their diets and food consumption. It has less to do with being healthy, and more to do with being able to control the effects of material deterioration that all physical things must endure through time. This is how they "rectify the earth" that they have been entrusted with.

Mercury-ruled, the Virgoan is agile and extraordinarily capable at getting many things done. Of all the signs of the zodiac, the Virgoan is perhaps the only one who can lay claim to being able to multitask in a way that is genuinely effective or efficient. Their ability to do things in what is often an impeccable way is why they are given roles of heightened responsibility within their various public circles. While they may naturally thrive in these roles, the extent of their responsibilities may also be psychologically taxing. No matter how financially secure the Virgoan is in life, they may always feel overworked and underpaid. Extraordinarily intelligent, the Mercury-ruled Virgoan learns best through physical experience. They can be thrown into a role that they learn how to perform on-the-spot.

Not only is Virgo the domicile of Mercury, but Mercury is also exalted there. The restlessness of Mercury is channeled through the life of the Virgoan towards the fulfillment of tangible goals and objectives. However, whether we are referring to Gemini or Virgo, Mercury has a bad habit of finding ways to enter a maze of micro-activities with ant-like devotion, no matter how straightforward the task at hand may be. Therefore, the Virgoan may continue to work on something until it bleeds under the pressure of their excessive fine-tuning. This is especially true if it is something that they are preparing to present to the world as a representation of themselves. They do not know when it is time to submit the final manuscript. The self-portrait of the Virgoan is never complete; neither is the Virgoan's autobiography, composition, or masterpiece. The final product may have to be pried from their cold hands at death, only for the world to discover that it was a masterpiece all along.

Jupiter is in detriment in Virgo. The Virgoan may lack a wider sense of perspective that allows them to actually think and work with the end in mind. So committed are they to perfecting every detail of the task at hand, they may miss out on the proverbial forest due to their hypercritical analysis of each and every tree. A broader outlook is often required for the Virgoan to realize that everything is okay; and that there is more world to see than the world that they currently have under the lens of their microscope.

Venus is in fall in Virgo. Through their regimental life, the Virgoan can miss out on some of the sweet and tender joys of living. On their deathbed, they may regret never having eaten that key lime pie or going out more frequently when they were invited to by others. They have a peculiar relationship to love and the expression of romance in general. So deeply invested are they in the art of taking care of things and taking care of others, they may miss out on the opportunity to interact with love in the organic, wet, messy, and overwhelming way that it frequently manifests. Their love language may be one of creating an environment for their loved ones where all their needs are met. However, the Virgo should learn to rest in the warm bosom of romantic love more often. They should bask in the genuine and raw feeling of love as it is; instead of doing something to prove love through taking care of another. A heartfelt "I love you" can go a long way out of the mouth of the Virgo native.

Virgo corresponds with the small and large intestines. Because of the connection between the brain and the gut, their heightened levels of stress can often have a direct impact on their digestion. Similar to the intestines digesting and processing food, the Virgoan has perfected the art of processing life's experiences. They know how to weigh the pros and cons of every situation. They can extract from a garbled mess of information a clear, methodical outline. They know how to extract from life what is absolutely essential for them to function.

Libra

> *The twelfth-part Libra, which is taken for the hips [of the cosmos], is the house of Aphrodite [Venus]...* – Hephaistio of Thebes

Libra is a moveable, hot and moist, sanguine, airy, diurnal sign ruled by Venus. The chief operating system of Libra is air. Air predisposes the native to being cerebral, communicative, and a lover of human connection in general. It causes them to feel a deep kinship with others, which is further supported through their highly developed conversation skills. The air native has a natural knack for observing social graces. They can get even the most noncommunicative guest at the party to enter a rousing discussion. The airy Libra has a broad way of seeing things. They can create an environment where everyone's truth is valid. However, they need to find ways to relieve themselves of the cognitive pressure of engaging with so many external perspectives all at once and all the time.

A moveable air sign, Libra readily creates the opportunities for dialogue and social exchange. They enjoy having the opportunity to be in conversation and being the person responsible for making connections occur. The Libran can desire intimate friendship or romantic partnership very early in life. This allows them to constantly use another person as a reference point for their own self-understanding. However, just because they are responsible for starting a conversation doesn't necessarily mean they have the wherewithal to continue it. They often trail away out of a desire to engage with other circles where other discussions are taking place.

Being an air sign, they may bore easily. The Libran who started the conversation with the best of intentions may find themselves anxious to move on if they are required to engage too deeply with the conversation that they started.

Venus-ruled, the Libran has a natural sense for the beautiful and the aesthetically pleasing. They shy away from things that are brusque and unpleasant. They can't fathom being in environments that don't make everyone feel welcomed. They live their lives in a beautiful way; from their home to their words, to the way they carry themselves in the world. Venus is social, loving, kind, and receptive. The Libran knows how to be a perfect host and create an environment where people feel comfortable. As Venusians, they are open to hearing about the cares and concerns of others. The Libran can magnetically attract people from all walks of life who feel deeply compelled to share their life stories with them. The Libran can nod, agree, and goad people on in revealing their deepest, darkest secrets. However, when the roles are reversed, the Libran often resorts to holding their cards close to their chest. This isn't because they don't want to engage with others. Rather, they'd prefer not to be completely exposed to other people – warts and all. The concept of political correctness is a Libran invention. They can navigate even the most challenging interactions with dignity and poise. As Venusians, they are not likely to tolerate discomfort for very long. They are skillful at making others feel in control and as if they are winning. However, in the end it is the Libran who often comes out on top; having crafted a set of circumstances completely to their liking.

They do best as an intercessor between two parties, and often shine in roles of counseling, talk therapy, deep listening, journalism, public relations, poetry, or anything that has to do with skillfully and beautifully representing others and themselves in the world at large.

Mars is in detriment in Libra. The Libran often can allow themselves to take on the shape of their interactions and relationships, reflecting to others what they think others want to see. This can severely impact their ability to be firmly determinate about anything. One of the key characteristics of the Libran is that they are comfortable standing in the middle of the road on most topics – never quite being able to make a decision that they feel wholeheartedly convinced by. The Libran can benefit from sharpening the edges of their opinions and beliefs. This will aid them in being decisive in a quicker, more efficient way. This can also increase an overall sense of trust in the power of their presence and beliefs in the world.

Saturn is in exaltation in Libra. Though the Libran native is often indecisive about the affairs of their own life, when placed in roles of authority, they can make a judgment call about the affairs of others with clarity and objectivity. They tend to always have a sense of what constitutes the course of right action in all things. They do well in human resources or management roles. They have the ability to see all sides of every argument, while still holding the book of the law as the underlying basis for the decisions they will ultimately make. This causes them to be fair judges most of the times.

The Sun is in fall in Libra. So ready is the Libran to take on everyone else's tasks and goals, that they may find it difficult to prioritize themselves. They need to strengthen their sense of pride in their individuality. They need more opportunities in life that validate their self-worth. They create value and beauty in the world around them. However, they may shy away from opportunities to put themselves first and to claim proud ownership of their hard work. The Libran needs to learn how to stand separate from their partnerships and associations so that they can truly shine in the world on their own.

Libra corresponds with the kidneys, pelvis, and the lumbar region of the spine. The kidneys help remove waste and assist us in maintaining the chemical balance of the body. The Libran correspondingly assists people in maintaining a sense of peace, balance, and easeful exchange with the larger environment in which they live.

SCORPIO

> *The twelfth-part Scorpio, which is taken for the genitals [of the cosmos],*
> *is the house of Ares [Mars]...* – HEPHAISTIO OF THEBES

Scorpio is a fixed, cold and wet, phlegmatic, watery, nocturnal sign ruled by Mars. The chief operating system of Scorpio is water. Water predisposes the native to being deep, devoted, sensitive, self-protective, intuitive, creative, moody, and introverted. As a water native, Scorpios seek to cultivate a life that is driven by deep, internal motivations. They want to feel a profound connection to everything they're doing. They'd prefer not to live superficially. Like all water natives, their moods fluctuate aggressively. However, as a fixed water sign, they seldom show these fluctuations on the surface.

As fixed water, the Scorpio native can seem constantly calm, put together, and well-composed externally. They take no joy in having other people see them struggle, sweat, or panic. They know the world is already in a constant state of chaos. They excel at concealing how affected they are by it. As a fixed water person, the Scorpio native lives by the motto "the deepest feeling is the reality." They seek depth, meaning, and purpose. In the absence of those things, they may experience a numbness to life and to their environment. Fixed water is also synonymous with ice, which can further increase their need for stimulation. This can cause them to pursue extreme experiences of exhilaration and adventure just to feel alive. In both sense fulfillment and sense deprivation, they enjoy themselves fully. For the Scorpio native, there is sweet nostalgia in the cool darkness of the nighttime and they revel in the ability to experience that pleasure alone. Driven by not living superficially, the Scorpionic native may frequently place themselves in the path of danger.

Mars-ruled, the Scorpio native has fierce convictions regarding what they believe. They are intensely passionate about things. However, in true nocturnal fashion, they may try to hide this excitement from others. With Mars as their cosmic undercurrent, it radiates from them nevertheless. They are ferociously loyal to their friends and family. They have no problem jumping into the line of fire for those they love, without fear of personal injury. The Scorpionic native doesn't think twice about the risk to self when it comes to rescuing, saving, or helping someone they care about. They place themselves in situations where the proverbial angels fear to tread. They may be involved with areas of life that others don't have the stomach for. These include surgery, trauma counseling, law enforcement, taxidermy, butchery, proctology, and other things that people may consider too difficult or too gross to do. Whatever they do, they do it with great vigor and pride.

The Scorpionic person has the ability to be "on" all of the time if they choose to be. Due to the full way in which they move through life, they have no problem severing ties with just as much ferocity. At the slightest sign of distrust or deception, they can unconsciously initiate a self-defense mechanism that begins to separate them from that relationship in real time.

As a fixed water sign ruled by Mars, the feelings of a Scorpio can be what they build their reality on. They can feel something so deeply that it becomes real for them, even before the truth has been fully established. The problem with this is that what they feel may be based on a wrong assumption. They may express very wet Martian emotions when they are disappointed or disillusioned by life. These emotions range from stone-cold reclusiveness to boiling anger and resentment. The Scorpio can find themselves in a state where they need to experience the full gravity of these negative emotions as a part of their ability to process them. However, very often they may not actually be processing them at all. They may just be sitting in them. This can be very painful for others, who may be trying to help the soggy Martian get out of their miserable rut. These attempts almost always prove fruitless. The Scorpion will get out of their own rut slowly, and even then, their level of re-engagement with the world may be cool and apathetic. The frozen Mars native can shut down completely and bury themselves in a hole of silent isolation like no other sign of the zodiac can. They have an unparalleled aptitude for going the distance and never being defeated by anyone. This means that if put to the test of who can be cold and silent for the longest time, the Scorpion will always win. This cutting-off self-defense is often done in excess, and should be moderated.

Trust is of utmost importance to all water signs. It allows them to feel safe in an unpredictable world. Each water sign responds to broken trust in a unique way. The Scorpionic mode of dealing with broken trust is to completely break the bond of that relationship forever in ways that are brutal and cold.

Scorpio is the detriment of Venus. What the Scorpio lacks in social grace and courtesy, they make up for in loyalty and passionate devotion to a cause. The Scorpio can often lean towards being alone on principle – a highly un-Venusian quality. They can enter states of prolonged isolation from lovers, family, and friends. This doesn't readily provide the Scorpio native with tools for finding warmth or outlets for bottled up emotions. It may block the Scorpionic person from settling into love or even thinking they need to be in a relationship to begin with. The Scorpionic person can benefit from greater social interaction – with friends, family, and the community at large. The warmth generated through loving interaction with others can remedy many of the afflictions that the Scorpio native may experience in life.

Scorpio corresponds with the vagina, penis, anus, and nose. The nose has always seemed to be an odd inclusion. However, pheromones are a secretion that can often trigger a sexual attraction. We detect these subconsciously through our nose. Similarly, the Scorpionic native can often "sniff out" the undercurrents that exist in their interactions with other people. They have an extraordinarily sharp perceptive faculty, which can predispose them to detective work, archaeology, and investigation in all its forms.

Sagittarius

> *The twelfth-part Sagittarius, as far as which the thighs [of the cosmos] ascend, is the house of Zeus [Jupiter]…* – Hephaistio of Thebes

Sagittarius is a mutable, hot and dry, choleric, fiery, diurnal sign ruled by Jupiter. The chief operating system of Sagittarius is fire. Fire predisposes the native to being courageous, optimistic, ambitious, energetic, passionate, driven, goal-oriented, and independent. The fiery native radiates from within and often find it difficult to be let down or depressed by things going on around them. Their ability to bounce back into action after some sad occurrence tends to be quicker than others. They can be inspirational to be around. However, they need to withdraw from action more often than not. They have the tendency of doing things in excess and overtaxing their physical constitutions in the process.

As a mutable fire sign, Sagittarius holds a very peculiar type of fire. They aren't as rash and volatile as the cardinally driven Aries, or as powerful and overwhelming as the fixed Leo. The fire of Sagittarius is scattered and light. It moves quickly and burns nothing: like a sudden blast of flame in the open air that feels like a welcome burst of warmth against the skin. The fire of the Sagittarius is a fire of exhilaration and freedom. It is the sudden fire that keeps a hot air balloon adrift. The mutable fire of Sagittarius represents the energy potential within the air element that allows a ship to take sail across a vast ocean. It is the force that enables the other elements to produce renewable energy in the form of the wind turbine or the hydroelectric power generated by a dam. It is the fire that pushes everything out into the wider world to fulfill some wider vision or quest. Grand in both their aim and their agenda, the Sagittarius native can often set impossible targets for themselves that they may not have the sort of internal concentrative ability to complete. The Sagittarian can be scattered and wild – favoring freedom over outcome, the dream over the deadline, and may resultantly struggle to manifest much in terms of physical security in this world. They need others around them to assist them in staying the course. It isn't that they don't have the ability to do so by themselves. It's just that they have so much ability to do so many things, it may be difficult to get them to commit continuously to doing one thing for very long without environmental support.

Jupiter-ruled, the Sagittarius is lighthearted, optimistic, broadminded, and benevolent. The Sagittarian cares about their friends and everyone they meet on their journey. They believe in having a good time and creating a good time for others. The Sagittarian can create an environment that stimulates others into action. They are very great motivators, coaches, and trainers. They can help other people see and attain the impossible. They move in big sweeping steps through the world, and can often have a very large gait. The Sagittarian can take up a great deal of space in a way that is witty, charming, and fun.

They have a desire to break free from the monotony of everyday life constantly. This may be in the form of excessive traveling or partying. Boredom is a crime against humanity that they seldom, if ever, allow themselves to experience. The Sagittarian can be an outdoorsman: a photojournalist, hiker, professional athlete, or someone who moves around the world constantly. When the Sagittarian isn't holding themselves accountable, they can defer their responsibilities to tomorrow far too often. They frequently find that when tomorrow comes, they are overwhelmed by the amount of work they have to complete. This may cause the Sagittarius native to work well "under pressure." However, the pressure is usually the result of their own misappropriation of energy towards things that represent joy and freedom, but that don't actually bring about the successful meeting of deadlines.

Sagittarius is the detriment of Mercury. Sagittarius tends to approach life in a broad and general way, preferring to see the full picture as opposed to the details. They can benefit from cultivating some of the mercurial faculties of analysis and attention to detail, which will be a blessing within the multiple odd jobs they pursue in life. The native Jupiterian can be very capable, but not necessarily meticulous. If the Sagittarian can bring in more of the attributes of Mercury in the forms of dexterity, skillfulness in action, and the ability to micromanage when necessary, they will create tangible things in the world that have a far greater impact and a more organized final result.

Sagittarius corresponds with the buttocks and thighs. This region of the body contains both the longest and the largest muscles in the human anatomy. Just as the hips and thighs give us locomotive power, the Sagittarian often has the ability to know ahead of time which direction they will head in next. They live their lives in a state of constant motion, with the desire to continuously scale more stimulating heights.

## Capricorn

*The twelfth-part Capricorn, which is taken for the knees [of the cosmos],
is the house of Kronos [Saturn]...* – Hephaistio of Thebes

Capricorn is a cardinal, cold and dry, melancholic, earthy, nocturnal sign ruled by Saturn. The chief operating system of Capricorn is earth. Earth predisposes the native to being methodical, slow, thoughtful, deliberate, practical, devoted, steadfast, and reliable. The earth native has a tendency to only trust things that are real. They only step forward when the way before them is tried, true, and proven to work. All earth natives may harbor a secret fear of their tangible assets slipping away. This is why the earth native works to establish a firm, inviolable life around them, with all the trappings of material comfort to reinforce their belief in the stability of their world. In this way, they lay a strong foundation for future success.

Cardinal Capricorn has a similar disposition to mutable Virgo. Both these signs operate through a lens of action that is contrary to their elemental nature. Capricorn is a moveable earth sign. The earth, as a rule, doesn't like to move. The Capricornian is hesitant to fully trust in the longevity of any of their partnerships. They may dutifully work into the late hours of the night to create a home or nest, because they know no one else will do it for them. So often have they experienced the earth moving from beneath their feet, they may come across as cynical and skeptical. They may have a shrewd sense of humor, and can often joke about the impermanence of the world.

There are certain signs of the zodiac that embody the full nature of their domicile ruler. Capricorn is one of them. In speaking about the nature of Capricorn, it often sounds as if we are directly speaking about Saturn. Between Saturn's two domiciles – Capricorn and Aquarius – Capricorn is more analogous to him. Saturn-ruled, the Capricorn native can be stern, silent, withdrawn, and focused; deeply dedicated and committed to the end result. Work is something they find pleasurable. A child with an angular Saturn may be wise beyond their years, and this is also true for the Capricornian native. They see the world through the eyes of maturity. They may have grown up very quickly. Perhaps they lost the fundamental glee of childhood far sooner than other children around them.

Saturn is the furthest visible planet from Earth. Thus, we have come to know Saturn as the gatekeeper, the guardian, and the sentinel who protects our tiny universe from the vast and wild unknown that lies beyond his rings. The Capricornian native can often find themselves in this position as well – that of protector, manager, and governor. They often find themselves thrust into roles of responsibility, whether or not it entails actual leadership. They can be depended upon to stick to the letter of the law. They realize that the responsibility to follow the rules lands more heavily on their shoulders than it does on the shoulders of others. The Saturn-ruled Capricorn may often comment on the fact that in life, they see others able to get away with far more recklessness than they can. As soon as the Capricorn puts a toe out of line, the consequences of their actions may seem instant. Therefore, the Capricorn may be found living on the straight and narrow path and demanding that others around them do the same.

Mars is in exaltation in Capricorn. The Capricorn native frequently has an extraordinary work ethic. They can drive themselves through the world like a vehicle of war, conquering and surpassing all who stand in their way. They have an extraordinary executive ability and will always know what is absolutely essential if put in a position to make cuts – both of a budget as well as of employment. They always know who in their battalion is working the hardest and who should be fired. They are sharp-shooters when it comes to strategy. They know how to plan a mission, especially in terms of the tactical action necessary to begin. In a world where many people struggle with taking the first step, the Capricorn will always have a well-thought-out starting plan.

Capricorn's capacity to hold Martian power can be a challenge when it comes to the formation of relationships. Sometimes the professional colleagues within the life of the Capricorn may feel expendable; as if their Capricorn counterpart or boss only views them through the duties they fulfill, as opposed to the values and characteristics that make them unique. This can cause the Capricorn native to seem insensitive to the human component of forming relationships with others.

The Moon is in detriment in Capricorn. The Capricorn may feel they were not given the coddling that other children received when they were growing up. They may have been the responsible one in their family, causing others to treat them like an adult far sooner than their siblings. Their love language may be through the provision of material security, as opposed to showing genuine affection. They may also be austere in their approach to domestic matters. They can benefit from viewing life and themselves through a softer lens.

Jupiter is in fall in Capricorn. The Capricorn may not readily avail themselves to a life of lavish abundance. They may be extremely frugal. Ruled by cold and distant Saturn, the Capricorn is accustomed to surviving on the bare minimum. They may even hold the narrative of having been left out in the cold to scale the desolate mountains of life on their own. Traditionally, the ancients considered Saturn to be a god of accumulation and hoarding. The Capricorn native isn't destined to a life of poverty. However, many of them live under this perception. They may be frugal with their finances even if it is not justified. They can easily fall prey to viewing life from a purely materialistic point of view. This will always prove to be limiting, especially to their deeper spritual yearnings, which they may be aware of, yet ignore. The Capricorn native can get all too accustomed to having to carry the cross of life alone. This can lead to feelings of depression and isolation. Even though the Jupiterian impulse towards freedom may be foreign to them, the Capricorn native can benefit from the perspective and optimism that Jupiter brings. Jupiter can broaden the horizons of the Capricorn's way of viewing the world. It can shake them from the doldrum of strict traditionalism and limiting beliefs that prevent them from accessing greater joy within their lives. Jupiter brings the message that there is more to life than the responsibilities and obligations that we may find ourselves born into. This is a message the Capricorn native should meditate on, especially when they feel burdened, overwhelmed, and exhausted by the gravity of life.

Capricorn corresponds with the knees in the human body. The knees have often been described as a precarious joint. They don't represent the finest biomechanics in the world, due to the amount of weight they carry. However, they still manage to do the job. The Capricorn may similarly feel as if they have started life off at a bit of a disadvantage, yet they learn to survive – and have an increasingly more heartfelt appreciation of life with the passing years. They tend to have good longevity, which gives them the decades necessary to appreciate life in a deeper way.

AQUARIUS

> *The twelfth-part Aquarius, which is taken for the legs [of the cosmos],
> is the house of Kronos [Saturn]...* – HEPHAISTIO OF THEBES

Aquarius is a fixed, hot and moist, sanguine, airy, diurnal sign ruled by Saturn. The chief operating system of Aquarius is air. Air predisposes the native to being communicative, social, intellectual, outgoing, quick-moving, objective, and broad-minded. They have sharp intellectual abilities which makes them great at strategic troubleshooting. They thrive on sharing their thoughts and ideas with the world around them. Air, a hot and wet, sanguine element, is highly sociable. The air native knows how to make others feel welcome and at ease.

As a fixed air sign, Aquarian natives tend to be very certain about their intellectual prowess and abilities. They can often be convinced that they see things in a way that is higher and even better than those around them. They can convince themselves of the rightness of their thoughts, and that those thoughts are right for others as well. They are quick to share these thoughts and suggestions as a means of progressing humanity.

As a fixed air sign, the Aquarian can crystallize a thought and build their entire lives on that version of reality. This can be exciting for others who are also looking for something to believe in. In this way, the Aquarian can become a thought leader –someone who is able to transfer a clear image of the reality that exists within their minds to the minds of others. However, this can also become dogmatic. The Aquarian needs to remember that the thoughts and opinions of others are valid as well. The fixed quality of Aquarius can cause them to freeze themselves in a way of seeing the world that may be out of step with the actual way the world works. This is a part of the reason why the Aquarian is viewed as a visionary and a pioneer. They are not lacking in bright ideas. Instead, they may lack the social graces necessary for them to share those thoughts without it seeming as if they are trying to create a new world order.

Saturn-ruled, the Aquarian is a fine organizer. They know how to organize both human and material resources. They want to do their part in being responsible for creating the world around them. The combination of air and Saturn causes the Aquarian to be driven by ideas of social justice and reform. The Aquarian can fight for the underdog and the disenfranchised and can be a member of boards, committees, coalitions, and unions. They come into the world with a vision of what a new world can look like. They often confuse their personal idea of a good time with what they believe is commonly good for everyone. They don't feel truly at peace, unless they have done their duty to further the interests of something much larger than themselves. They do well within the framework of the hive mind, both being a part of it and leading it. They do have an agenda: to create something that hasn't been built or seen before.

Their Saturnian disposition gives them a very early mastery of their mental faculties. They can be smarter than others around them and possess an effortless genius due to the combination of air and Saturn. The Aquarian who takes advantage of this can be a true force to be reckoned with in the world and may excel in the fields of mass communication, business, marketing, and public relations.

The Aquarian who does not manifest these qualities positively can run into problems. These people are burdened with a splendid mind, but often lack ambition to pursue a path of personal achievement. This other type of Aquarian may become the stereotypical unaccomplished genius: the person who knows the solution to every problem, but can't seem to find a way to fix their own. They are known for being able to talk a good talk. However, they have very little manifestation ability. They know they are brilliant and feel as if they are always one step away from changing the world. Resultantly, they may drag their feet in life, expecting to amaze others with their mental prowess, but may not put in the necessary effort to accomplish anything worthwhile. They may expect everyone to applaud their ingenuity, and may run the risk of pushing people and opportunities away because of it.

The Aquarian may seem cold and distant. They may be socially engaged, but remain an enigma to others. They may be a bit of an outsider and a self-proclaimed outcast, even when they are loved by everyone around them. As a Saturn-ruled air sign, they often fall into the role of being the organizer of all events. The party starts when they arrive. They are depended upon to facilitate the evening, even if it is at someone else's home. They know how to entertain, how to mingle, and how to give others the space to be who they are. Even amidst all of this social interaction, the Aquarian may still feel isolated and alone. All of these are true Saturnian dilemmas. It is useful to know which type of Aquarian one is dealing with – the socially engaged or the socially awkward – and adjust one's approach accordingly.

The Sun is in detriment in Aquarius. The commitment to the common good may make it difficult for the Aquarian to identify the individual needs of both themselves and others. What the Sun has that Aquarius tends to lack is the ability to clearly identify what serves their best interest, independent of how it ties into some larger social mission or calling. It would be useful for the Aquarian to commit themselves to figuring out what truly turns them on. They should discover what makes them shine their brightest in the world, separate from how their shining ties back into the commonwealth of the collective. The Aquarian finds it easier to identify what they are and what they do far faster than they can identify who they are. Sitting with the question "who am I?" can serve as a healthy point of meditation for Aquarians, who often identify themselves heavily with the role they fulfill within society.

Aquarius represents the shins and the calves. The shins play a vital role in giving us mobility. They bridge the gap between our service-oriented knees, and the feet which are the servants of the body. Therefore, the shins are a part of the continuum of selfless service to the world. The Aquarian is fundamentally helpful, and a part of the trinity of signs – Capricorn, Aquarius, and Pisces – that are the servants of humanity.

PISCES

> *The twelfth-part Pisces, which is taken for the feet and base [of the cosmos], is the house of Zeus [Jupiter]...* – HEPHAISTIO OF THEBES

Pisces is a mutable, cold and wet, phlegmatic, watery, nocturnal sign ruled by Jupiter. The chief operating system of Pisces is water. Water predisposes the native to being sensitive, thoughtful, caring, kind, devoted, loyal, imaginative, and moody. The watery Piscean can move through life feeling very sensitive to the world around them. They can be easily jostled and, therefore, deeply desirous of peace. As a water sign, they may be unable to express themselves through straightforward, direct language. They may turn to more creative means of self-expression such as music, art, and poetic forms of speech and writing. Their heightened sensitivity can cause them to pick up on the thoughts and emotions of others around them. This may be a lot for them to handle on a consistent basis. Seclusion works well for them. Being in nature helps them let go of the psychic overload they experience through excessive human contact. They may especially enjoy large bodies of water.

As mutable water, the Piscean tends to be uncomfortable in general. Their lot in life can often seem like far more to bear than others. Though they do not necessarily face more hardships than others, constitutionally, they tend to be more easily affected by the chaos of life. As mutable earth, Virgo doesn't like to be jostled. However, the Virgoan figures out very early on how to keep the world from shaking around them. Pisces, on the other hand, isn't naturally born with those skills. When the world shakes, they shake. Mutable water is always jostled, always thrown about, always shaken by the winds of change. Their very sensitive constitution can register all of these changes in the environment as visceral changes within their bodies. This can cause them to have a weaker physical constitution than even the other water signs. Their health may often be a concern for them.

As mutable water, they can have a very malleable body. This can be great for yoga, gymnastics, dance, and other performing arts that involve flexibility. On the other hand, the Piscean can have a very delicate homeostasis. The Piscean native can sometimes be the proverbial Typhoid Mary in their family – who has either just been sick, is currently sick, or is on the verge of becoming sick, whether this is actually happening or whether it is purely in their mind.

All of the water signs can have a propensity towards the healing arts. Pisceans can make extraordinary health and healing professionals. However, if they haven't learnt how to master their psychic sensitivity to the world around them, this fields may not be the best for them in the long term.

Mutable water means that they are deeply in touch with the nonphysical currents that shape our world. They are extraordinarily creative and visionary and can create art that seems to be divinely inspired. They can take this level of high-minded inspiration into all of their endeavors and turn raw material, concepts, or ideas into something truly remarkable. They know what the world wants and have their finger on the pulse of society. They can be deeply tuned into the large nontangible cultural yearnings that exist around them. Resultantly, they can excel in the field of advertising and marketing.

Jupiter-ruled, the Piscean has a boundlessness about them that makes them live life with both heart and arms wide open. They can care about everything and everyone because they feel the hurt of everything and everyone. The Piscean has a natural inclination to open animal shelters, orphanages, charities, and things that serve the greater good of the world. Being mutable, watery, and Jupiterian, the Piscean wants to melt: into life, into other people, into the ocean, into the universe. The Pisces native may desire to be reabsorbed into the cosmos to the point of disappearing completely. To deal with this impulse, the Piscean can turn to silent meditation, monastic living, religion, spirituality, and charitable work. They may do this with the intention of feeling as if they are expanding their physical and nonphysical parameters to the point of containing the world within themselves. Sensory deprivation tanks are on the Piscean spectrum of interests. Conversely, a full-on ecstatic rave is also a Piscean experience. The Piscean may seek out opportunities for their individuality to be lost in the larger ocean of the collective.

Jupiter expands the Piscean to higher levels of selflessness. This can cause them to engage in or be dependent upon things that directly bring about an even greater loss of self. Positively, this can be art, music, and spirituality. Negatively, this can be hard drugs, alcohol, cigarettes, or other addictive substances. They may use these things to numb their sensitivity and to help them navigate the world in a better way. It would serve them well to find higher spiritual ways of navigating the difficulties of their lives. As Expander-in-Chief, Jupiter can also cause the Piscean to imagine their lot in life as being substantially worse than everyone else around them; a peculiar brand of suffering that they may use to justify their addictive tendencies. They need positive reinforcement with a sprinkle of tough love to help them create a sense of structure within their lives.

Trust is of utmost importance to all water signs. It allows them to feel safe in an unpredictable world. Each water sign responds to broken trust in a unique way. The Piscean way of dealing with broken trust is to internalize it and turn it into a source of self-deprecation. They may feel as if something is wrong with them or that they are consistently taken advantage of by others. This can lead towards self-destructive tendencies.

Venus is in exaltation in Pisces. The Piscean has a deep connection to the beautiful. Their inner vision gives them access to streams of creativity, insight, and artistry that are highly refined. They also welcome everyone to them without judgement of who they are or what their past may be. They come closer to experiencing genuine unconditional love for others, potentially more than any other sign of the zodiac. While this is a rare and powerful ability, the Piscean needs to be mindful to not let people take advantage of their open-hearted kindness.

Mercury is in detriment and fall in Pisces. Mercury is the planet of communication and speech. Of all the signs of the zodiac, the Piscean may find it most difficult to articulate themselves clearly. They may speak too much, and in an incoherent way. Equally, they may be very silent and not speak at all for fear of being misunderstood. For the Piscean, it may always feel as if water is in their throat or in their phone lines, preventing them from being heard or understood by others. Speech therapy or coaching could be very helpful for them gain access to the power of their voice.

Pisces rules the feet. The feet are the servants of the body, and the Piscean can often feel like the servant of the world. It is important for them to realize that this is not actually the case. They need not martyr themselves – sacrificing their own joy and comfort for the sake of others. The Piscean should do things to remind themselves that they are a necessary part of humanity, and that their presence in this world matters.

CHAPTER 18 QUESTIONS

1. What is one positive and one negative impact Sun sign astrology has had on our field?
2. What are the three most basic components of each sign that provide important information regarding the interpretation of that sign?
3. Why do you think psychological approaches to astrology have become so popular within the twenty-first century?
4. Leo is said to correspond with the heart and the spine in traditional astrology. Based on what you know about those parts on the body as well as what you know about the astrological components that make up Leo, why do you think this correspondence exists? Please focus less on the idea of "Leo" the sign, and more on the various astrological components that constitute Leo (triplicity, quadruplicity, domicile ruler, etc.).

## CHAPTER 19 OBJECTIVES

* Explain the concept of sect within traditional astrology.
* Outline the divisions of the planets and the signs based on sect.
* Explore the rationale behind the sect of the malefics.
* Understand what sect does for a planet.
* Provide a rubric for identifying the sect of a planet.
* Explain what it means for a planet to be in hayz and in a contra-riety of hayz.
* Outline a method for finding the sect of Mercury.
* Explore the practical application of sect within our practice.

# CHAPTER 19

## ON SECT

*Whereas the whole is administered from the Sun and Moon, and no beings in the Cosmos are born without the mastership of these stars, it is necessary to teach both the solar and lunar sect, and what has been allotted (to each), and that through these (the Sun and the Moon), all unite.*
–PAULUS ALEXANDRINUS

TRADITIONAL ASTROLOGY IS BASED ON a keen observation of the natural world. One of the earliest observations of ancient astrologers was that everything in nature seemed to be dual. Everything seemed to be inherently masculine and feminine. Within that duality, however, some things seemed to lean more in the direction of the masculine – the definite, the concrete, and the dominant. Other things seemed to lean more in the direction of the feminine – the undefined, the fluid, and the passive. The ancient astrologer looked towards the heavens for a celestial template upon which to project this understanding of the bipartite nature of the material world. They found this within the most obvious division that we can perceive in nature: the division of day and night, and with it, the duality of the Sun and Moon who rule these two sectors of time.

What previously was thought of as masculine and feminine could now be understood through the lens of the luminaries. Since the Sun ruled the day, things that were considered solar or masculine in nature were also thought to correspond with the day. All things corresponding to the day, including the Sun, were called "diurnal." Diurnal means "of the day." Since the Moon rules the night, things that were considered lunar and feminine in nature were also thought to correspond with the night. All things corresponding to the night, including the Moon, were called "nocturnal." Nocturnal means "of the night." On these divisions of time, Ptolemy writes:

*The day and the night are the visible divisions of time. The day, in its heat and its aptitude for action, is masculine. The night, in its moisture and its appropriation to rest, feminine.*

Diurnal and nocturnal became the most basic divisions of most things astrological. This division later became known as "sect."

Sect refers to the division of the various components of traditional astrology into the categories of diurnal and nocturnal. Planets and signs can be either diurnal or nocturnal. Houses seven through twelve of a chart are in the diurnal hemisphere of the chart. They are above the horizon. Houses one through six are in the nocturnal hemisphere of the chart. They are below the horizon.

Astrology is largely based on analogous relationships between things. Things that have a natural analogy with one another will naturally be supportive of each other. A nocturnal planet in a nocturnal sign is going to feel more comfortable and supported in its operations than a nocturnal planet in a diurnal sign.

Sect supports the essential nature of a planet. However, it is not one of the levels of essential dignity. When a planet is fully supported by sect, it is strengthened in showing more of itself. This strength is akin to a planet receiving a spotlight. If a deeply essentially debilitated planet is supported by sect, it receives a spotlight that illuminates its debility. If a strongly essentially dignified planet is supported by sect, it receives a spotlight that illuminates its power. Sect provides emphasis, encouragement, and a spotlight for planets to reveal who they are – whether good or bad – within a chart.

## Divisions of the Planets by Sect

As mentioned previously, the planets can be divided by sect. The sect divisions of the planets are:

TABLE 1: *Sect of the Planets*

| Diurnal | Nocturnal | Variable |
|---------|-----------|----------|
| ♄ | ♂ | ☿ |
| ♃ | ♀ | |
| ☉ | ☽ | |

A planet supported by sect will be able to show more of who it is in an uninhibited way, regardless of its state of essential dignity or debility. If a planet is strongly supported by sect and strongly essentially dignified, then it will carry out its functions within a chart in a powerful way. If a planet is strongly supported by sect and strongly essentially debilitated, it will have great power to behave negatively within the life of the person. The essential dignity or debility of a planet predisposes it towards creating positive or negative outcomes in relation to what it specifically rules within a chart. If a planet is essentially dignified and ruling the first house, it could bode well for the health and constitution of the native. If a planet is severely essentially debilitated, and ruling the fourth house, there may be major issues within the native's life in relation to their father. If a planet is strongly essentially dignified, it is more predisposed to doing good. If a planet is strongly essentially debilitated, it is more predisposed to performing poorly within the life of the native. Sect supports bad planets in being bad. It also supports good planets in being good.

## ON SATURN AND MARS

Saturn and Mars were assigned to sects that would curb some of their natural tendency towards evil and destruction. Mars, though a masculine, fiery planet, was put in the nocturnal sect. Saturn, though a cold and dry, frozen planet, bordering on the icy darkness of space, was put in the diurnal sect. The coolness of the nighttime was meant to temper the raging fires of Mars, whereas the heat and radiance of the daytime was meant to soften the deadliness of Saturn's frigid resolve. Of Saturn and Mars, Ptolemy writes:

> Neither of them, however, is allotted to that division of time with which its nature accords (as heat accords with heat), but each is disposed of on a contrary principle. And for this reason, that, although the benefit is increased when a favorable temperament receives an addition of its own nature, yet, the evil arising from a pernicious influence is much mitigated when dissimilar qualities are mingled with that influence.

What Ptolemy is saying is that adding evil to evil only creates more evil. Ptolemy held that cold and dry Saturn has some of his evil minimized when he is forced to be in the sunlight. Saturn in diurnal conditions is less harmful than if he were in nocturnal conditions. Intemperately hot and dry Mars has some of his evil minimized when he is forced to be in the cool dampness of the nighttime. Mars in nocturnal conditions is less harmful than if he were in diurnal conditions. Ptolemy concludes:

> Thus each of these planets, being moderated by its combination, is placed in a condition calculated to produce a favorable temperament.

The theory of sect is conceptually sound, but very often doesn't hold up in applied practice. For example, Saturn is the domicile ruler of Aquarius and the exaltation ruler of Libra, both of which are masculine, diurnal signs. However, the remaining diurnal signs are Aries, in which he has his fall; Gemini; Leo, in which he has his detriment; and Sagittarius. In my observations, Saturn does not function well in mutable signs. Their mutability is not in harmony with his rigid, conservative nature. Thus, beyond Libra and Aquarius, no other diurnal sign really seems to be able to support Saturn in a way that enables him to function powerfully within a chart. A planet's ability to function maximally within a chart is based on its level of essential dignity. From the perspective of essential dignity, I am not convinced that Saturn in Leo, Aries, Sagittarius, or Gemini is more predisposed to operate with less malice than Saturn in nocturnal signs.

### WHEN A PLANET IS FULLY SUPPORTED BY SECT

When a planet is fully supported by sect, it is in a sign and chart of the same sect as it. It also must be on the side of the horizon that is most appropriate for it based on its sect.

Remember: all masculine signs (Fire and Air) are diurnal signs. All feminine signs (Earth and Water) are nocturnal signs.

It is also important for us to remember that the division of masculine and feminine doesn't always correspond with the diurnal and nocturnal sects. Mars, for example, is a masculine planet, but he is also of the nocturnal sect.

To discover the sect of the chart, we first need to know where the Sun is in the chart. If the Sun is above the horizon, the chart is diurnal. This means the chart was erected in the daytime. The Sun is above the horizon when he is above the horizontal Ascendant/Descendant axis. If the Sun is below the horizon, the chart is nocturnal. This means the chart was erected at night. The Sun is below the horizon when it is below the horizontal Ascendant/Descendant axis.

### Terrestrial preferences of the planets

If a chart is diurnal, that means the Sun is above the horizon. The diurnal planets will prefer to be above the horizon, with the Sun. This is the side of the chart that is most appropriate for them based on their sect.

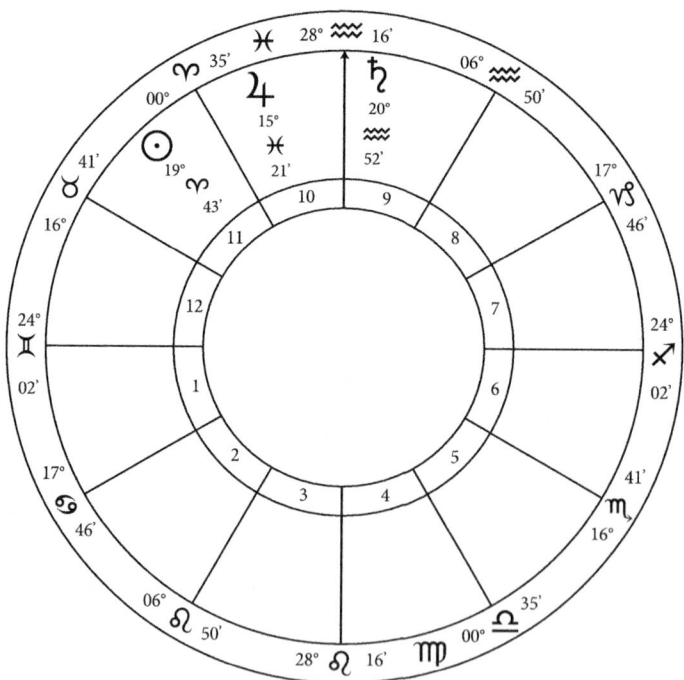

FIGURE 1: *Diurnal Planets Above the Horizon*

If a chart is nocturnal, that means the Sun is below the horizon. Please note: a chart being nocturnal has absolutely *nothing* to do with the position of the Moon. A chart being diurnal or nocturnal is solely based on whether the Sun is above or below the horizon. In a nocturnal chart, the diurnal planets will prefer to be below the horizon with the Sun. This is the hemisphere of the chart that is most appropriate for them based on their sect.

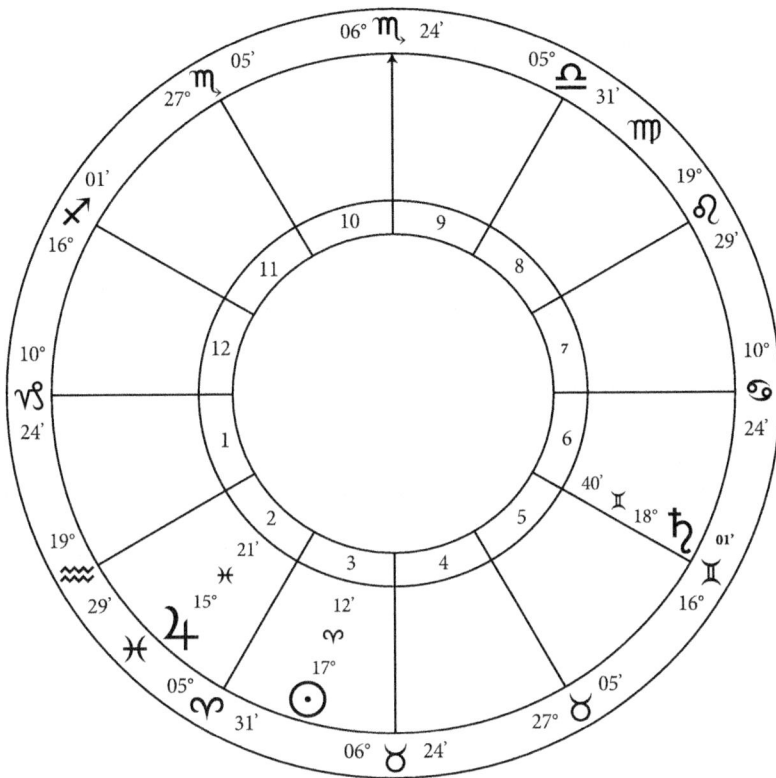

FIGURE 2: *Diurnal Planets Below the Horizon*

Diurnal planets will always prefer to be on the same side of the horizon as the Sun. It doesn't matter if it is a diurnal chart or a nocturnal chart. This is always going to be the case.

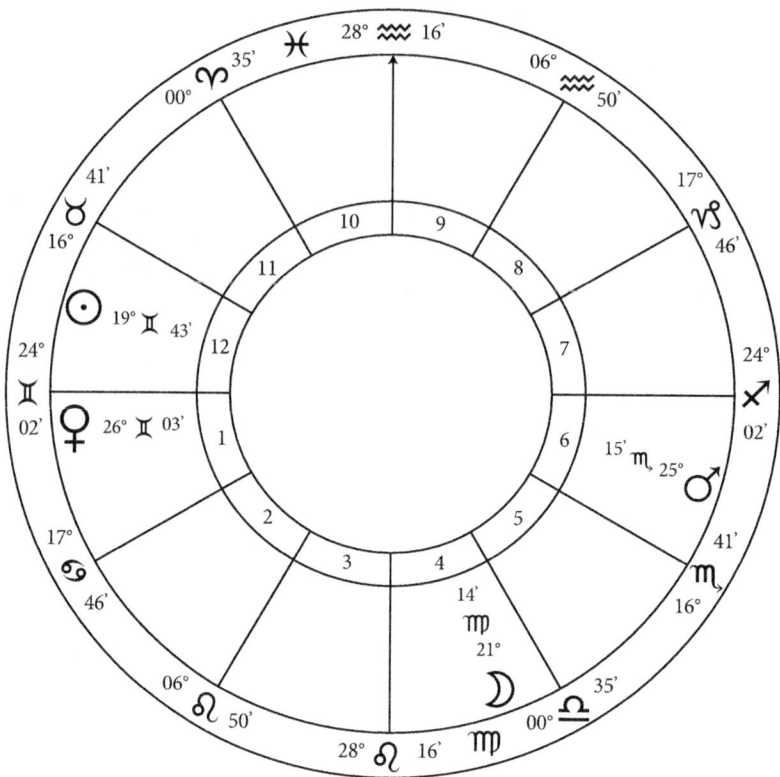

FIGURE 3: *Nocturnal Planets Below the Horizon, Sun Above the Horizon*

In a diurnal chart when the Sun is above the horizon, the nocturnal planets will prefer to be on the opposite hemisphere of the chart and away from the Sun. In a nocturnal chart, when the Sun is below the horizon, the nocturnal planets will prefer to be above the horizon and away from the Sun.

Nocturnal planets never want to be on the same side of the horizon as the Sun. It doesn't matter if it is a diurnal chart or a nocturnal chart. This means that in any chart, Mars, Venus, and the Moon prefer to be in the hemisphere of the chart where the Sun is not. As far as sect is concerned, Mars, Venus, and the Moon are not suited to be in the same hemisphere as the Sun.

## BUT ISN'T THE UPPER HEMISPHERE ALWAYS THE DIURNAL HEMISPHERE?

As we've learned, the upper hemisphere of a chart is always referred to as the "diurnal hemisphere." The lower hemisphere of a chart is always referred to as the "nocturnal hemisphere." Daytime is defined as when the Sun is in the upper hemisphere of the sky (and chart) and visible to us. Nighttime is defined as when the Sun is in the lower hemisphere of the sky (and chart) and invisible to us. Perhaps we could have avoided this confusion surrounding the words "diurnal" and "nocturnal" if we referred to the hemispheres as the "visible upper hemisphere" and the "invisible lower hemisphere." However, we don't.

Though the titles "diurnal hemisphere" and "nocturnal hemisphere" will always refer to the upper and lower hemispheres of a chart, respectively, this use of language means nothing at all as far as the topic of sect is concerned. Astrology requires us to be able to compartmentalize various encyclopedias of information within our minds. We cannot allow one complete symbolic framework to bleed unnecessarily into another. As far as the topic of terrestrial houses in astrology is concerned, the upper hemisphere of a chart is the diurnal hemisphere, and the lower hemisphere is the nocturnal hemisphere. As far as the topic of sect is concerned, the hemisphere where we find the Sun is where the diurnal planets want to be, whether that is above or below the horizon. The hemisphere where we do not find the Sun is the hemisphere where the nocturnal planets want to be, whether that is above or below the horizon. Everyone just wants to be comfortable. In the doctrine of astrological sect, that comfort is based on the location of the Sun and whether or not the planets naturally enjoy being with him or far away from him. Jupiter and Saturn prefer to be on the same side of the horizon as the Sun. Mars, Venus, and the Moon prefer to be on the opposite side of the horizon from the Sun. We will talk about Mercury later within this chapter.

I am emphasizing this point because this is consistently a major area of misunderstanding for both beginner students of astrology, as well as seasoned practitioners who have come to traditional astrology from other modern schools.

Hayz

In order for us to determine how supported a planet is by sect, we must:
1. Determine the sect of the planet.
2. Determine the sect of the sign it is in.
3. Determine the sect of the chart.
4. Determine where the planet is located in relation to the horizon.

If a planet fulfills all of these requirements by being in a sign of its sect, a chart of its sect, and on the appropriate side of the horizon that corresponds with its sect, that planet is in "hayz" (sounds like "highs" and rhymes with "eyes"). This means that the planet has full power to express itself, for good or evil within the life of the person. It is in the correct sort of spotlight that allows it demonstrate who it is to the world.

Hayz amplifies all of the essential and accidental conditions of a planet. Essential dignity or debility impacts the inner constitution of the planet. Accidental fortitude or debility impacts how strong or weak the planet is environmentally. After the essential and accidental factors have been considered, sect lets us know whether or not a planet has an additional spotlight that emphasizes its essential and accidental circumstances in a more pronounced way.

CONTRARIETY OF HAYZ

When a planet is in conditions that are opposite to what would cause it to be in hayz, it has no support "by light." When a planet is in a sign of the opposite sect, chart of the opposite sect, and on a side of the horizon opposite from where it should be based on sect, that planet is said to be in a "contrariety of hayz." This means that the planet is denied an additional spotlight by which to express itself loudly within the chart. The planet does not have an internal sense of luminosity.

As always, the full conditions of the entire chart must be taken into consideration, as well as the other essential and accidental circumstances the planet may find itself in. However, the sect condition of the planet gives us the most fundamental understanding of the intrinsic strength of that planet. It tells us how much that planet is supported by vital light, and if it has access to the light it needs in order to shine within a chart.

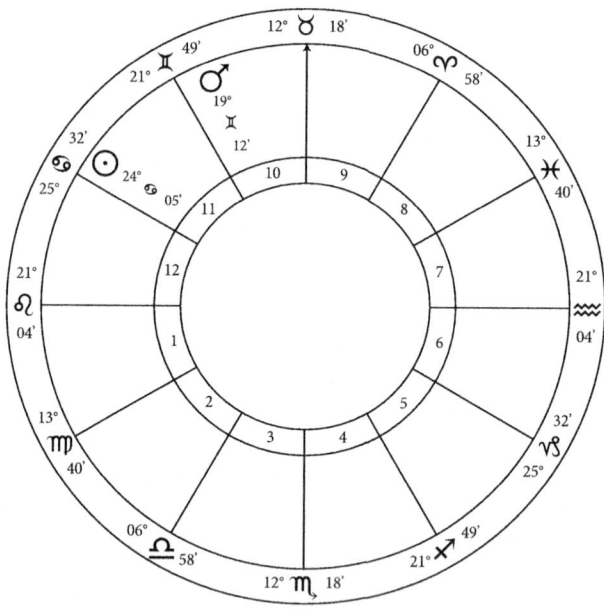

FIGURE 4: *Mars Above the Horizon in a Diurnal Chart*

For example, Mars is a nocturnal planet. At 8:00 AM EDT in The Bahamas, the Sun is above the horizon. Because the Sun is above the horizon, the chart is a diurnal chart.

Mars in our example chart is in Gemini. Gemini is a diurnal sign. Mars is a nocturnal planet. Therefore, Mars in Gemini loses one point of "light" or power by sect.

The next consideration is what type of chart Mars is in. In our example, Mars is in a diurnal chart. The Sun is above the horizon. Mars is a nocturnal planet and would rather be in a nocturnal chart. Therefore, Mars loses one point of power by light in terms of sect.

So far, our Mars is a nocturnal planet, in a diurnal sign, in a diurnal chart, above the horizon.

"Above the horizon" in a diurnal chart means that Mars is on the same side of the horizon as the Sun. Mars has no power in terms of sect. Mars is in a contrariety of hayz.

Let's take another example: the Libra Ingress chart of the USA for the Fall of 2022.

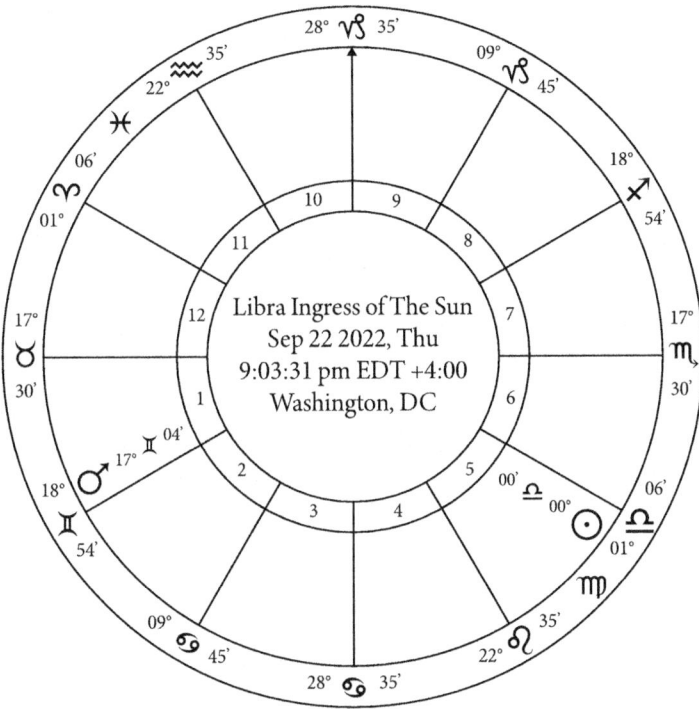

FIGURE 5: *Mars Below the Horizon in a Nocturnal Chart*

Nocturnal Mars in this chart is in diurnal Gemini. Thus, we know that Mars has lost one point of power by light.

In this chart, the Sun is below the horizon. This is a nocturnal chart. Mars is a nocturnal planet in a nocturnal chart. This is a good thing for Mars. Therefore, Mars has one point of power by sect.

Mars is below the horizon in this nocturnal chart. In other words, Mars is on the same side of the horizon as the Sun. Remember: diurnal planets want to be on the same side of the horizon as the Sun, irrespective of whether the Sun is above or below the horizon. Nocturnal planets, on the other hand, want to be on the opposite side of the horizon from the Sun, irrespective of whether the Sun is above or below the horizon.

Mars being on the same side of the horizon as the Sun is a problem. Mars has lost yet another point of power by light.

TABLE 2: *Power by Light (Mars Example)*

| Condition | Sect Power |
|-----------|------------|
| In a Diurnal Sign | -1 point |
| In a Nocturnal Chart | +1 point |
| Below the Horizon | -1 point |

Mars isn't in a contrariety of hayz, but he is close. As far as light is concerned, Mars is doing pretty poorly in terms of his "light nourishment." He will need other forms of support in order to bolster his level of expression within the chart.

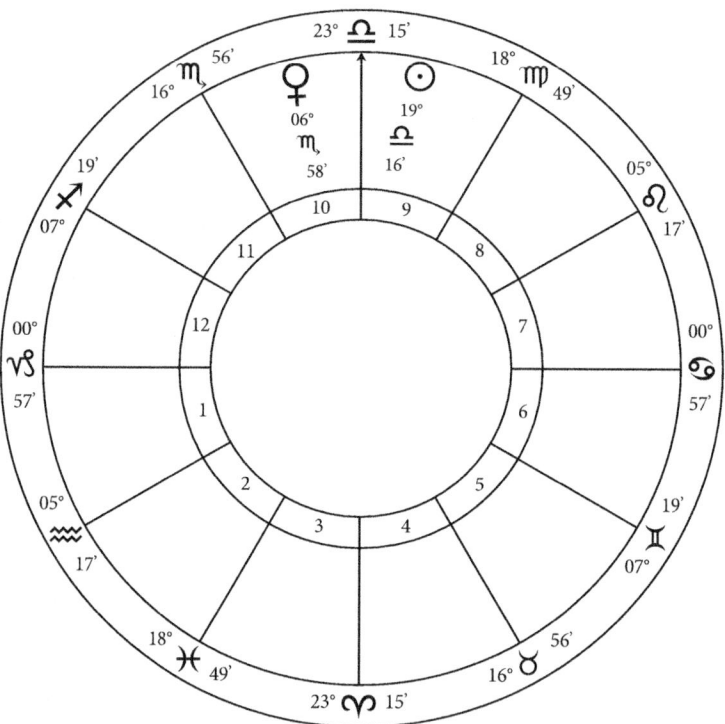

FIGURE 6: *Venus Above the Horizon in a Diurnal Chart*

Let's take the example of Venus in Scorpio at midday in Nassau, Bahamas. As we know, Venus in Scorpio is in the sign of her detriment. However, Venus is a nocturnal planet and Scorpio is a nocturnal sign. Therefore, Venus in Scorpio gets one point of power by light.

This is a midday chart. Since the Sun is above the horizon, it is also a diurnal chart. Venus is a nocturnal planet. Being in a diurnal chart is not good for Venus. Thus, she loses a point of power by light.

From a geocentric perspective, Venus can never be more than 48° of arc away from the Sun. Since this is a midday chart in Nassau, if the Sun is high above the horizon,

Venus will also be relatively high above the horizon. In terms of sect, this is not good for Venus. Therefore, Venus loses one point of power by light or sect.

TABLE 3: *Power by Light (Venus Example I)*

| CONDITION | SECT POWER |
| --- | --- |
| In a Nocturnal Sign | +1 POINT |
| In a Diurnal Chart | -1 POINT |
| Above the Horizon | -1 POINT |

Like Mars in our previous example, Venus isn't in a contrariety of hayz. However, she is in poor condition. She is in the sign of her detriment, which is a major essential debility. As I consistently remind my students, a major essential debility is not changed by a minor strength. This is because the major essential debility goes against the very nature and lifeblood of the planet. Adding her weakness by sect, we see that Venus does not have much strength to truly deliver on the promise she has been entrusted with in this chart. We expect for there to be complications, challenges, and a blockage of vital expression with whatever she ultimately delivers.

Let's continue to use our Venus in Scorpio in one more example.

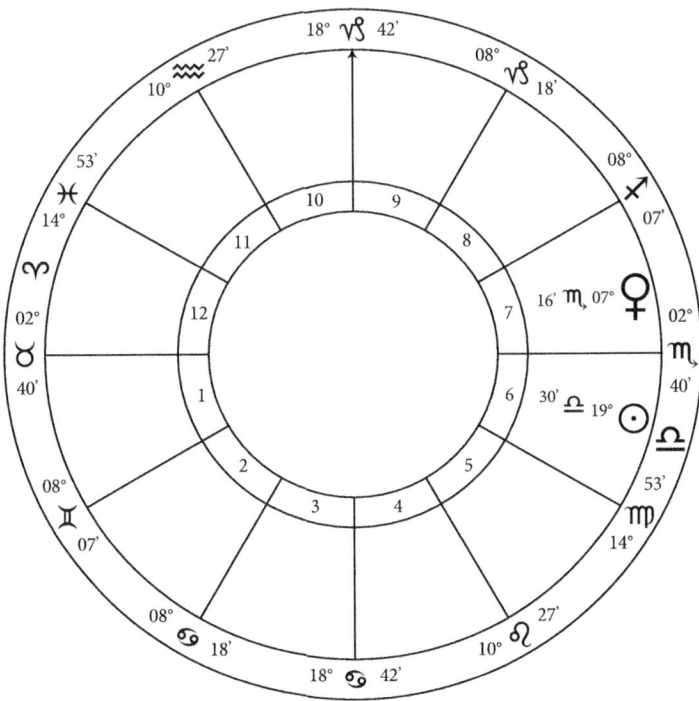

FIGURE 7: *Venus Above the Horizon in a Nocturnal Chart*

Here we have a chart for 7:00 PM EDT in Nassau, Bahamas. The Sun has already set. Venus, however, still remains in the sky. Not only is she in the sky, but she is there and angular since she is in the seventh house. When a planet is in an angular house, it has full visibility to be seen in the world. By her terrestrial placement in the seventh house, she is already positioned to be powerfully expressive within this chart.

TABLE 4: *Power by Light (Venus Example II)*

| CONDITION | SECT POWER |
|---|---|
| In a Nocturnal Sign | +1 POINT |
| In a Nocturnal Chart | +1 POINT |
| Above the Horizon | +1 POINT |

This Venus in Scorpio is completely in hayz. She is a nocturnal planet, in a nocturnal sign, in a nocturnal chart, and on the opposite side of the horizon from the Sun. From the perspective of sect, she is in a comfortable state. She is being nourished by the appropriate sort of light necessary for her to express herself in a powerful way in this chart.

Though she is in hayz and angular, we do not believe she will behave well. We do believe that she will behave in a prominent way for everyone to see. Being in hayz gives her a spotlight to show who she is more fully than if she were not in hayz. Her angularity also gives her 100% visibility – both in the sky and in this chart. However, her detriment tells us that what she is putting on public display isn't something very positive. In fact, it may not be the sort of thing that the owner of this chart would want the public to see. Just because an essentially debilitated planet is supported through both light (sect) and visibility (angularity) doesn't mean that what it represents will be altered from bad to good.

Essential dignity refers to the quality with which a planet will function. House placement refers to where a planet will function and how visible it will be. Sect power refers to the prominence with which a planet will carry out its functions.

The other things occurring to this Venus, both essentially and accidentally, must be taken into consideration in order to fully judge her strength within this chart. However, the initial judgement of her power by light lays a foundation upon which we can further build our understanding about how she will function.

## WHAT ABOUT MERCURY?

Due to his mysterious nature, even the topic of identifying the sect of Mercury has been a great debate throughout the ages. According to Ptolemy, Mercury is diurnal when he rises before the Sun and nocturnal when he rises after the Sun. This is the simplest way to judge the sect of Mercury in a chart. Mercury, like Venus, is bound in how distant he can be from the Sun. Whereas Venus can attain a maximum distance of 48° of zodiacal longitude from the Sun, Mercury can only attain a maximum distance of 28°. This contributes to Mercury rarely being seen. He is so close to the Sun that he is often made invisible by the Sun's solar light. Thus, if the Sun is high above the horizon, then Mercury will be above the horizon as well. If the Sun is low beneath the horizon, then Mercury will be beneath the horizon as well. Like Venus, the only times Mercury can be on the opposite side of the horizon from the Sun is in the morning – shortly before or after the Sun rises, or in the evening – shortly before or after the Sun sets.

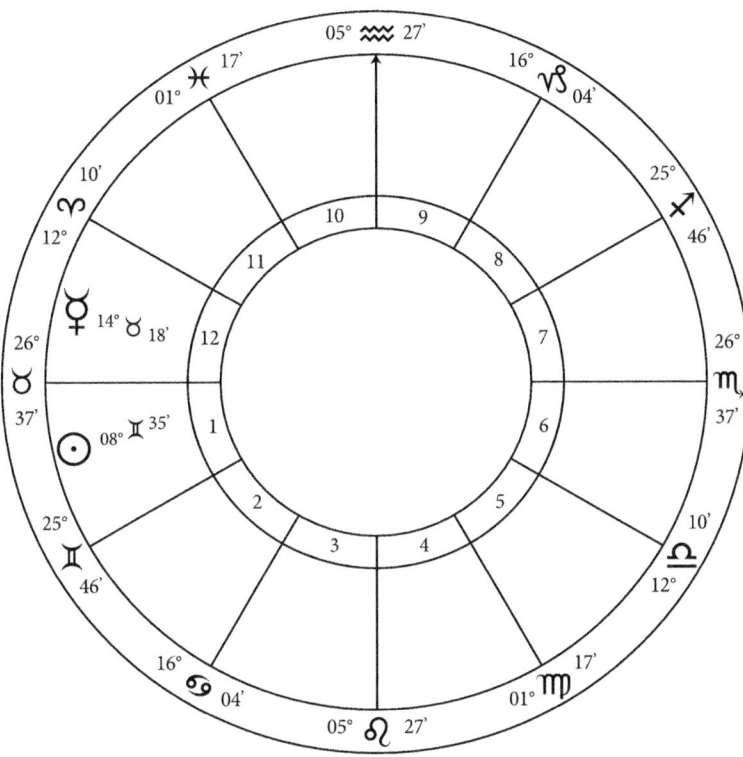

FIGURE 8: *Mercury Above the Horizon in a Nocturnal Chart*

If at 6:00 AM, Mercury has already risen and the Sun has not, then Mercury is a diurnal planet even though it is still a nocturnal chart. When Mercury, Venus, or any planet rises before the Sun, they are considered to be "matutine." Matutine means "rising in or just before the dawn." When the planets rise after the Sun has already risen, they are considered to be "vespertine." Vespertine means "related to, occurring, or active in the evening."

TABLE 5: *Power by Light (Mercury Example)*

| CONDITION | SECT POWER |
|---|---|
| In a Nocturnal Sign | -1 POINT |
| In a Nocturnal Chart | -1 POINT |
| Above the Horizon | -1 POINT |

Mercury is in a contrariety of hayz. He is not supported by the light he needs to carry out his functions within the chart. He may be essentially and accidentally strengthened in other ways. However, in terms of sect, he is weak.

## APPLICATION OF SECT IN CONCRETE ASTROLOGY

Sect doesn't factor that highly in my overall approach to chart reading. Very often the overarching story within a chart is said more loudly and by more obvious things. Those obvious things are largely the essential dignity or debility, accidental fortitude or debility, and the aspect relationships between the planets. A thorough and detailed treatment of these three subjects within a chart analysis is more than sufficient to read a chart with great depth and insight. What information we may find from analyzing the sect of the planets usually corroborates the larger story that we have already established through interpreting the dignity, debility, fortitude, and aspects between the planets.

Less tends to be more in terms of chart interpretation. However, it takes far more proficiency to be able to read a chart with less things to analyze. Having a streamlined and clean approach to chart analysis demands the astrologer to have a greater mastery of their tools. Sect can be a great inclusion to our practice. However, I haven't found it to be an essential part of my interpretation of how the planets are operating within a chart.

## OTHER PLACES WHERE SECT IS IMPORTANT

Sect is the primary consideration behind assigning the planets to their celestial houses (or signs) of joy. We learnt about this earlier in our chapter on the Thema Mundi. Sect is also important in the assignment of the terrestrial houses of joy to the planets, which we will learn about more fully in the following chapter.

The place where sect becomes an important consideration within my practice is in the calculation of the Arabic Parts. The Arabic Parts are sensitive points within a chart that are calculated based on the distance (or arc opening) between two planets or points, projected from a third planet or point. In Renaissance astrology, the most popular Arabic Part was the Part of Fortune (or Pars Fortuna). Traditionally speaking, Pars Fortuna can only be calculated correctly if we take into consideration the sect of the chart. Though this consideration was lost during the Renaissance period, it was a central idea in Medieval astrology, and is well worth considering today.

In a diurnal chart, the formula for calculating the Part of Fortune is:

Ascendant + Moon - Sun = Pars Fortuna

This means that we take the exact degree of the Ascendant in zodiacal longitude and add that to the degree of the Moon in zodiacal longitude. Then we subtract the position of the Sun in zodiacal longitude from the sum of the Ascendant and the Moon. This will give us the degree – in zodiacal longitude – of our Pars Fortuna in a diurnal chart.

For example, in FIGURE 9 we have a diurnal chart. Our Ascendant is 13° PIS14', the Sun is 11° AQU 26' and the Moon is 05° SAG 18'. In order to find the Part of Fortune, we have to first turn those zodiacal degrees into zodiacal longitude. In order to do this, we will refer to our zodiacal longitude conversion table on page 86. 13° PIS 14' converted to zodiacal longitude would be 343° 14'. 11° AQU 26' converted to zodiacal longitude would be 311° 26'. 05° SAG 18' converted to zodiacal longitude would be 245° 18'.

Applying this to our formula above, our diurnal Part of Fortune will be:

$$343° \, 14' \, (\text{ASC}) + 245° \, 18' \, (\text{MO}) - 311° \, 26'(\text{SO}) = 277° \, 06' \, 00'' = 07° \, \text{CAP} \, 06'$$

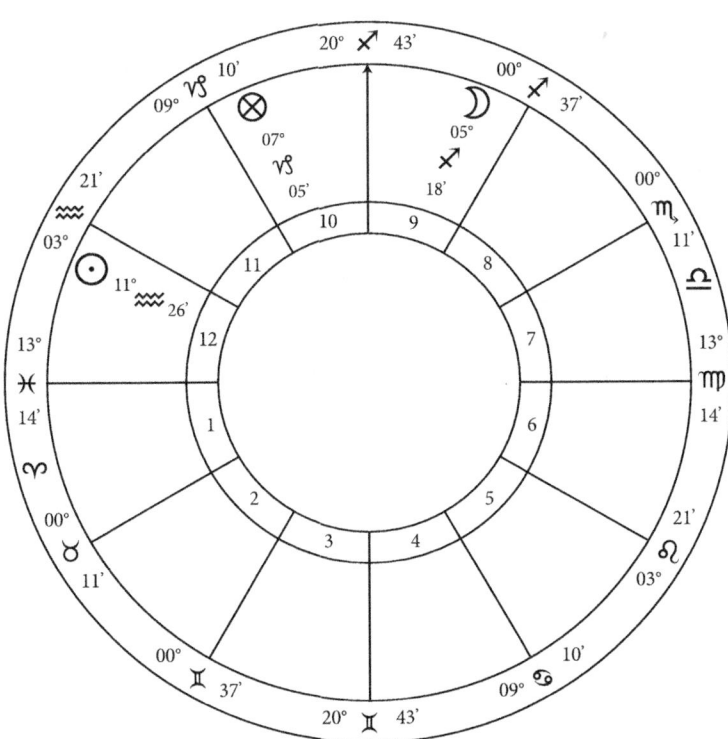

FIGURE 9: *Part of Fortune (Diurnal Formula)*

In a nocturnal chart, the formula for calculating the Part of Fortune is:

ASCENDANT + SUN - MOON = PARS FORTUNA

This means that we take the exact degree of the Ascendant in zodiacal longitude and add that to the degree of the Sun in zodiacal longitude. Then we subtract the position of the Moon in zodiacal longitude from the sum of the Ascendant and the Sun. This will give us the degree – in zodiacal longitude – of our Pars Fortuna in a nocturnal chart.

For example, in FIGURE 10 we have a nocturnal chart. Our Ascendant is 17° PIS 15', the Sun is 07° LEO 43' and the Moon is 25° SAG 27'. In order to find the Part of Fortune, we have to first convert those zodiacal degrees to zodiacal longitude. In order to do this, we will refer to our zodiacal longitude conversion table on page 86. 17° PIS 15' converted to zodiacal longitude would be 347° 15'. 07° LEO 43' converted to zodiacal longitude would be 127° 43'. 25° SAG 27' converted to zodiacal longitude would be 265° 27'.

Applying this to our formula above, our nocturnal Part of Fortune will be:

$$347° \ 15' \ (\text{ASC}) + 127° \ 43' \ (\text{SO}) - 265° \ 27' \ (\text{MO}) = 209° \ 31' = 29° \ \text{LIB} \ 31'$$

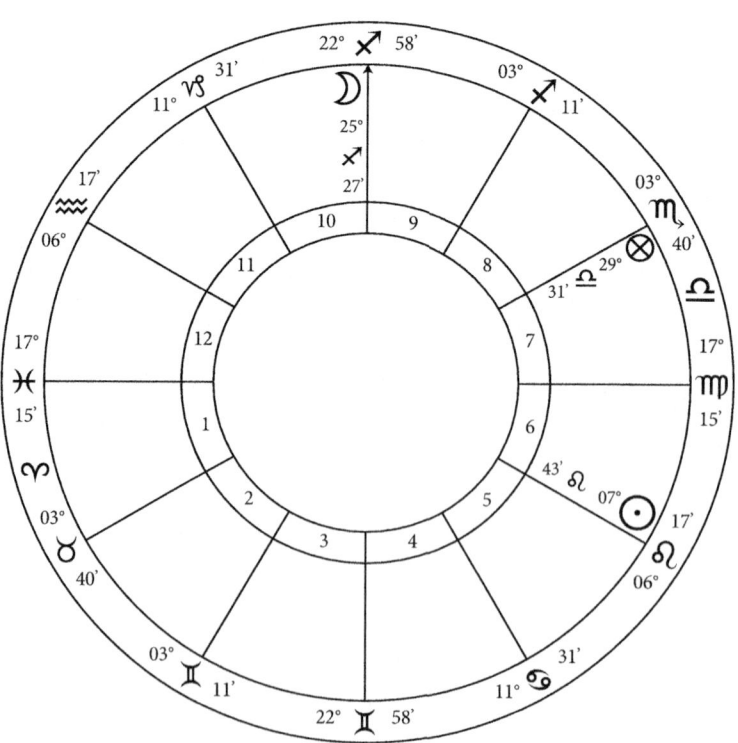

FIGURE 10: *Part of Fortune (Nocturnal Formula)*

The Part of Fortune is a proxy of the second house. It represents wealth, fortune, and our ability to find happiness and joy in life. It is a vital part of traditional astrology and should be calculated for every chart.

CHAPTER 19 QUESTIONS

1.  Define "sect" within traditional astrology?
2.  Which planets are diurnal? Which planets are nocturnal?
3.  What makes Mercury a diurnal or a nocturnal planet?
4.  Why is cold and dry Saturn considered to be a diurnal planet?
5.  Why is hot and dry Mars considered to be a nocturnal planet?
6.  Define "hayz."
7.  Define "contrariety of hayz."
8.  Where is one area in traditional astrology where the doctrine of sect is still important?

# PART 3

*... we must be aware that God the Creator, copying nature, has made man in the image of the universe, a mixture of four elements – fire, water, air, and earth – so that a well-proportioned combination might produce the living being as a divine imitation. With his divine skill he so composed man that the whole force and essence of the elements is collected in that small body. This spirit, though fragile, is nevertheless a likeness of the spirit of the universe. Thus man, like a tiny universe, is sustained by the everlasting fiery movement of the five planets and the Sun and Moon.*

FIRMICUS MATERNUS

CHAPTER 20 OBJECTIVES

* Define the term "terrestrial house."
* Briefly discuss various house systems that exist.
* Define "interception" and discuss how it impacts the rulership scheme within a chart.
* Explore the concept of co-rulership and where it might be useful within practice.
* Define "derived house."
* Explore various conditions that make a house strong or weak in traditional astrology.
* Outline the classical scheme of the four quadrants of the houses.
* Explain the rationale behind the angular, succedent, and cadent houses.
* Elaborate on the concept of the "three most evil houses of heaven" in traditional astrology.
* Outline the five-degree rule in traditional astrology.

# CHAPTER 20

## ON THE TWELVE HOUSES

*There is nothing appertaining to the life of man in this world, which in one way or other hath not relation to one of the twelve Houses of Heaven... so now we are come to relate the nature of the twelve houses, the exact knowledge whereof is so requisite, that he who shall learn the nature of the Planets and Signs, without exact judgment of the houses is like an improvident man, that furnisheth himself with variety of household stuff, having no place wherein to bestow them. –* WILLIAM LILLY

A THOROUGH UNDERSTANDING OF THE terrestrial houses is one of the most important acquisitions for an aspiring traditional astrologer to attain. The twelve houses, sometimes called "mundane houses," represent major areas of life that we can investigate through astrology. Abraham Ibn Ezra writes:

*These twelve houses are fundamental in the nativity of a person, in inquiries [horary], in elections, and also in judgment for the world in general.*

In horary astrology, the appropriate houses are chosen based on the question being asked. In electional astrology, we seek to fortify the houses that indicate the project we would like to be successful. In natal astrology, the houses represent the sphere of concrete experiences that a person has within their lifetime. In mundane astrology, the houses refer to the areas of collective life that affect the world at large. In all branches of traditional astrology, the houses are the way we organize our understanding of how the life of a person, place, or thing unfolds through time.

In natal astrology, the houses – and other factors dependent on the houses, such as the Part of Fortune – are the only things in our chart that we can claim as ours. We share the zodiacal planetary positions and aspects with everyone who was born on the same day as we were. Only the houses specifically modulate those stellar influences to reflect the unique individuality that each life contains.

Planets can be universal significators or specific significators. Planets signify concepts universally based on the level of natural analogy or correspondence they have with those concepts. This is demonstrated when we think of the Sun as the universal significator for fathers, and the Moon as the universal significator for mothers. Those planets will always represent those concepts based on their intrinsic natures. However, planets become specific significators when their domiciles bond to the various boundary lines between the houses. These boundary lines are called "cusps." A cusp is the starting point of an astrological house. There are twelve houses, which means there are twelve house cusps. Houses have cusps. However, signs do not have cusps.

When the domicile of a planet becomes linked to the cusp of a house (or perhaps it is better to say when the cusp of a house becomes linked to the domicile of a planet), the ruler of that domicile takes that house under its rulership. The planet that rules the sign on the cusp of a house is the ruler or lord of that house. If Scorpio is on the third house cusp, then Mars is the ruler or lord of the third house. Mars would be "Lord Three" (L3). If Pisces is on the cusp of the sixth house, then Jupiter is the ruler or the lord of the sixth house. Jupiter would be "Lord Six" (L6). However, Jupiter would also be the ruler or lord of whichever house(s) we find his diurnal domicile of Sagittarius on the cusp of. This is true for all planets. A planet will be the lord or ruler of whichever cusps its domiciles are on.

## MULTIPLE HOUSE SYSTEMS

Though we speak about the "houses" as if this were a homogenous term, there are many systems of houses that people use in astrology. Some of the house systems are: Porphyry, Alcabitius, Campanus, Regiomontanus, Placidus, Koch, Equal, and many others. There is even a system in which each house is considered to be one whole sign of the zodiac. The diversity that exists amongst the house systems is vast and sometimes very confusing. The easiest way to circumvent this is to utilize the house system that is appropriate for the tradition of astrology that we are practicing. Astrologers who practice seventeenth century astrology are more prone to use Regiomontanus houses than astrologers who practice thirteenth century astrology, who may prefer to use Alcabitius houses. Within this book, all the example charts have been casted using Regiomontanus houses. For your ease of practice, I'd suggest that you also use Regiomontanus houses while working through these charts.

While the mathematics of the houses go well beyond the scope of this current text, it is important to know that there was a time when we calculated charts by hand using logarithms, geographical coordinates, and an ephemeris. An ephemeris (pl. "ephemerides") is a book that tracks the movement of stellar objects on a daily basis. Today the computer does virtually all of this work for us with the click of a button. Nevertheless, knowing how to calculate a chart by hand is a great skill to have. It sharpens our mind and teaches us to live with astrology in a more tactile way.

As far as astrology software is concerned, computers get most things right. However, with lesser-known Arabic Parts that are sensitive to whether a chart is diurnal or nocturnal, the formula that a software uses as a default may be incorrect. Many programs, for example, are preset to only calculate the Part of Fortune based on the diurnal formula. In my opinion, the Part of Fortune should be calculated based on the sect of the chart. This is also true for any other sect-sensitive Arabic Part. If you use a software, ensure that it is applying the correct formula for the Arabic Part in question.

## On Interceptions

While all signs of the zodiac have 30° each, houses do not. Unless you are using some equal house division such as Equal houses or Whole Sign houses, you will end up with unequally spaced houses within your chart. The further from the Equator the latitude of a location is, the more disproportionate the houses of a chart will be. In charts such as these, it is normal to see one signs of the zodiac appearing on two or even three house cusps. Since there are twelve signs of the zodiac and twelve house cusps, if one sign appears multiple times on several house cusps, then it will cause other signs not to show up on any house cusps at all. This is known as "interception."

Interception is when a sign does not appear on the cusp of a house because the full 30° of that sign is contained within a house. This means that the sign that comes before it will be on the cusp of that house, and the sign that comes after it will be on the cusp of the next house. However, the intercepted sign itself will not show up on either of those two house cusps. Naturally, if a sign is intercepted on one side of a chart, its opposition sign will be intercepted on the opposite side of the chart. In any given chart, there may be one or two pairs of signs that are intercepted. In charts casted in locations that have very extreme latitudes, we may find even three pairs of signs intercepted.

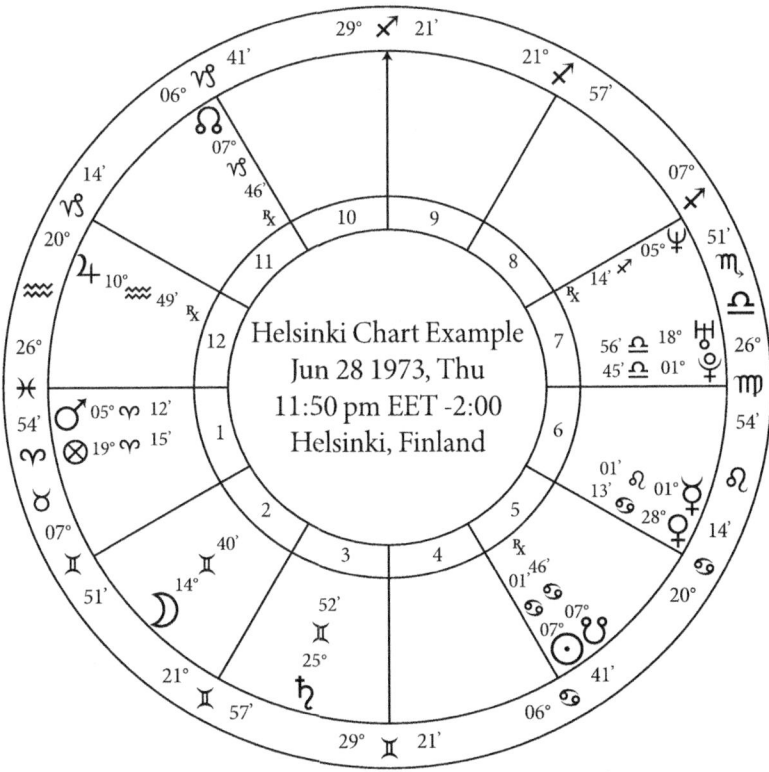

FIGURE 1: *Helsinki Chart (Non-Proportional Houses)*

439

For example, on 28 June 1973 at 11:50 PM EET, in Helsinki, Finland, we find that Aries, Taurus, and Leo are intercepted within the chart. This means that they do not appear on the cusps of any houses. This also means that their opposite signs of Libra, Scorpio, and Aquarius also don't appear on the cusps of any of the houses. The reason for this type of distortion is the extreme Northern latitude of Helsinki which lies at 60° N 10' 15" in relation to the Equator of the Earth.

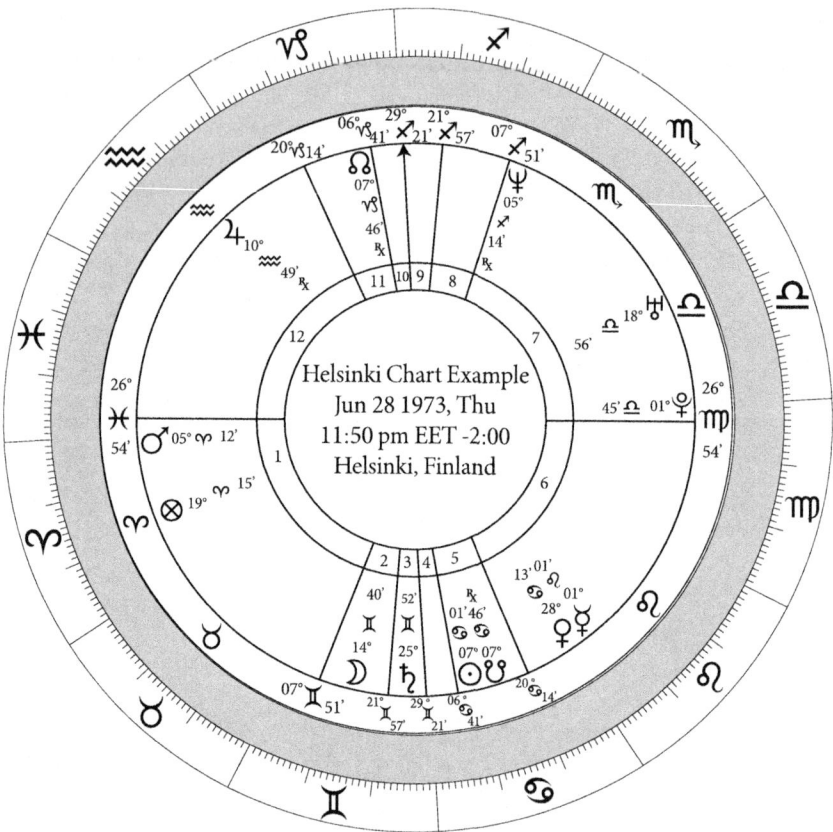

FIGURE 2: *Helsinki Chart (Proportional Houses)*

Interception is a mathematical anomaly that occurs as a result of the computational limitations of whichever house system we may be using. Signs that may be intercepted when using Regiomontanus houses, may not be intercepted at all if we chose to use Placidus houses instead. This is one of the reasons why I believe it is incorrect for us to impose interpretational value on intercepted signs. Modern astrology, sign-based as it is, tends to read very deeply into the meaning of which signs are intercepted within a person's chart. Within that form of astrology, the intercepted sign is often considered to represent an aspect of the person's psyche that is blocked, and that desires to be integrated into the fullness of their being. I personally am baffled by this idea and do not see how an intercepted sign can yield this type of information. I believe there are far more skillful ways of astrologically interpreting what proficiencies and deficits a person may carry within their psyche without interpreting their intercepted signs.

## ON THE CO-RULERSHIP OF HOUSES

Within traditional astrology, there is a tendency to call the domicile ruler of the intercepted sign the "co-ruler" of the house within which it is intercepted. We see this happening throughout the work of Jean-Baptiste Morin.

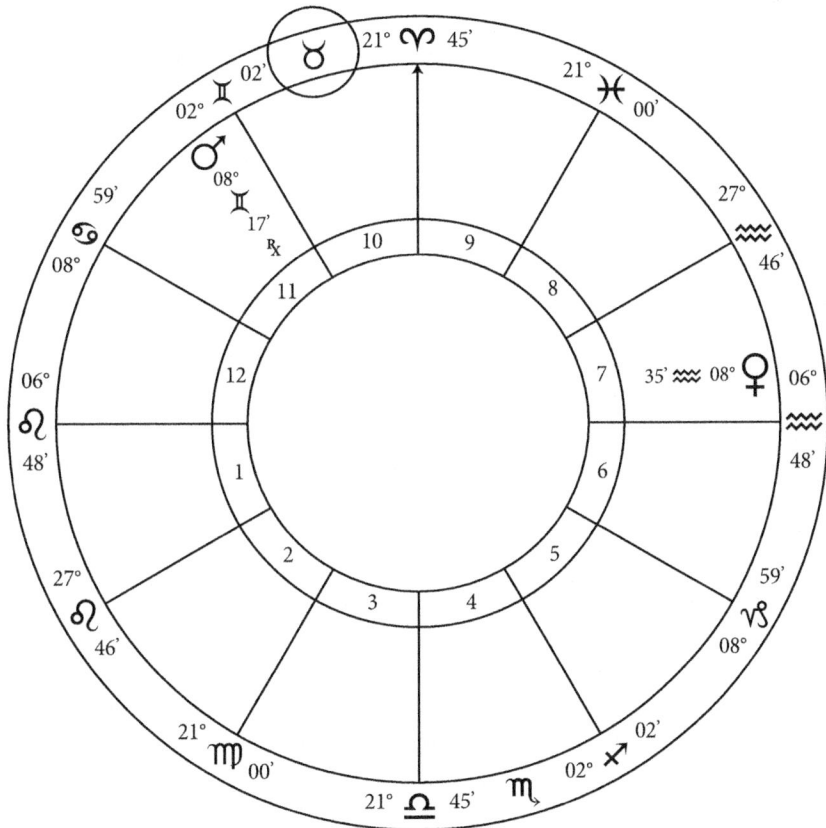

FIGURE 3: *Taurus Intercepted in the Tenth House*

If Aries is on the tenth house cusp with Gemini on the eleventh house cusp and Taurus intercepted in the tenth, then Venus would be the co-ruler of the tenth house. Mars would be the primary ruler. Though I love much of the corpus of Morin, I seldom if ever use this concept of co-rulership. The only time I may use co-rulership is if I find the co-ruler corroborating what I have already said about that house from the primary lord. This primary lord will always be the domicile ruler of the sign on the cusp of the house in question. The primary lord of a house will always be the primary planet entrusted with the outcome of the affairs of that house.

## THE PEOPLE WITHIN OUR HOUSES

In traditional astrology, the houses don't just reflect our psychology. They also identify the people who indelibly impact our lives. Our natal charts are heavily peopled. Our siblings, their spouses, our parents, children, employees, our spouse, their siblings, our grandparents, teachers, bosses, friends, enemies – anyone who impacts our lives profoundly can be found within our individual horoscopes.

Many Western astrologers feel this level of definitive practice only exists in Indian astrology. Jyotish has always predisposed itself to concrete astrological delineation. This is something that has been severely lost within the modern Western astrological community. We've gotten so caught up in talking to people about their "Sun, Moon, and Rising," that we've pushed the burden of concrete, event-based astrology onto the shoulders of our Indian colleagues. However, the more we look into the history of Western astrology, the more we find the concrete abilities of the Jyotish astrologer also existing in our Western tradition. After generations of disuse, our abilities may not be as highly refined as practitioners in the East. However, our Western legacy of concrete, event-based astrology is there in full-blood, waiting for us to reclaim it.

In modern traditional astrology, the skillset of the astrologer has to be twofold. The astrologer has to clearly outline and define, in planetary terms, the image of the person for whom he or she is consulting. After establishing the stellar image of the native, the astrologer then needs to define the material events that have occurred in that person's life that have contributed to them becoming who they are. The events that profoundly impact us don't just make us who we are; they also determine how we will respond to future events that may arise. There is an infinitely powerful feedback loop between the formation of self and the "cosmic event environment" in which we exist. The challenge as an astrologer becomes knowing how to astrologically identify and interpret the concrete events that have left behind psychological imprints which serve as the basis of our character.

Every major action or event that we participate in must leave their imprints within our soul. These imprints become themes within our lives that create the cosmic structure pattern of the events we continue to experience. The things we experience become a part of our subconscious treasure house of images; which all too often is simultaneously a subconscious house of nightmares. The internal psychic content of our accumulative life experiences – and the subconscious expectations we have of life as a result of those experiences – project from us out into the world with magnetic force. This projection of our interiority onto the world around us is like a radiation field that we carry with us everywhere. It attracts to us the events that reflect both who we are as well as who we've come to think we are based on our life experiences. Everything we have encountered, all of our joys and all of our sorrows, provide us continued opportunities to reinforce and reveal our conditioned persona to the world around us. Curiously, the word "persona" comes from the Latin word meaning "mask." It stands to reason that who we present to the world and to ourselves is but a mere mask, incapable of reflecting the fullness of our being.

In the formation of self, we tend to attract events that justify our lived experience; whether that experience is one of joy, suffering, victory, or defeat. The houses provide a systematic way to thoroughly investigate the events that have played a pivotal role in the formation of our lives. Within traditional astrology, the houses are important because they show us how the parts of our stories organically grow out of every other part. In this way, astrology can serve as an invaluable tool for continued self-study.

## Houses within Houses

When a chart is used only to refer to the primary subject it represents, it is called the "radical chart." For example, my birth chart is my radical chart. The primary subject matter of my chart is me and the unfolding of my life. This chart can also be referred to as the "radix," a Latin word which means "root," from which the word "radical" is derived. When a radical chart is used to refer to some secondary topic that differs from the primary subject of the chart, it is called a "derived chart." Though I am the primary subject matter of my birth chart, I can also use it to inquire into the lives of my mother, father, sister, and lover.

When we use the derived chart, we are taking the primary chart and using it to give us insight into some other person represented by a house in our chart. The radical house that represents that other person is used as the Ascendant of that person. In this way, we end up with a series of "derived houses." The second house from that person's Ascendant becomes their second house of finances, the third house from that person's Ascendant becomes their third house of siblings, and so on.

For example, the fourth house represents the father. The second house from the radical fourth house is the radical fifth house. However, when viewed from the perspective of the father, it is the derived second house of the father's finances. Therefore, if I want to inquire into the wealth of my father, my radical fifth house would be where I would investigate. If I wanted to find out about my father's sister, I wouldn't go to my radical third house for that information. This is because the radical third house refers to my siblings, whereas the third house from my father refers to his siblings. The third house from my father is the radical sixth house. Therefore, to find out about my father's sister, I would go to the radical sixth house for answers.

FIGURE 4: *Derived Houses*

At first, this may seem like a bizarre expectation to have of a chart. The thought that our chart doesn't just represent us, but also represents people in our lives, may seem preposterous. However, this has been a staple in both Jyotish and traditional Western astrology for thousands of years. Jyotish astrologers are famed for being able to speak about multiple family members from the chart of one person, using their own Eastern system of derived houses. This is very possible for Western astrologers as well. On the topic of derived houses, Bonatti writes:

> *And you should know that each of them is its own 1ˢᵗ (house), and has its own 2ⁿᵈ, 3ʳᵈ, 4ᵗʰ, 5ᵗʰ, 6ᵗʰ, 7ᵗʰ, 8ᵗʰ, 9ᵗʰ, 10ᵗʰ, 11ᵗʰ, and 12ᵗʰ. And it has, following each of them, its own other eleven houses apart from itself from which it receives its significations.*

444

There are some house derivations that are already built into how we view astrology. We already think of the eighth house as the house of our joint resources from marriage. However, the eighth house has far more to do with the money of our marriage partner, than our "joint" resources. This is because it is the second house from the seventh house of marriage. As such, it represents our spouse's money. Many people learn quite early on that the eleventh house is the house of the money we make from our career. However, this is only because the eleventh house is the second house from our tenth house of career. The second house from any house represents the money belonging to whoever the previous house represented. The second house from the first house represents our money. However, the fourth house is the second house from the third house, and represents the money of our siblings. The fifth house is the second house from the fourth house, and represents the money of our fathers. The sixth house is the second house of our fifth house, and represents the money of our children – and so on around the chart.

Other possibilities that we find through house derivation can be very strange. For example, my sister's best friend's dog would take me down a path to first find my sister, then find her best friend, and then find her best friend's dog. My sister is represented by my radical third house. In my search to find her best friend's dog, the third house will be my starting place because this is symbolically my sister's Ascendant. From there, I will locate her best friend, who will be represented by the eleventh house from my sister's derived Ascendant. Eleven houses from the third house takes us to the radical first house. This now becomes the Ascendant of my sister's best friend. In order to find the best friend's dog, I now have to count forward six houses away from the radical Ascendant. This will take me to the radical sixth house. Therefore, my sister's best friend's dog will be represented by the radical sixth house.

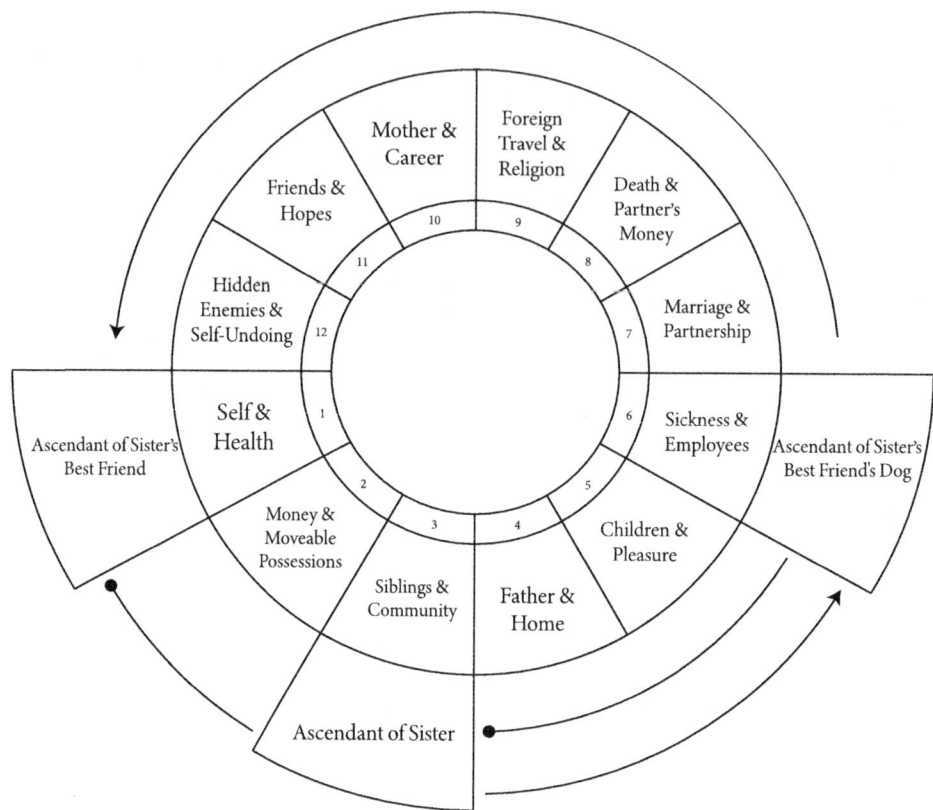

FIGURE 5: *Derived Houses Example*

I use derived houses quite frequently in my astrological investigations into family dynamics within the natal chart. I tend to stick with the first level of house derivations in order to see the chart from the perspective of parents, spouses, children, and siblings. I wouldn't use derived houses to investigate my uncle's neighbor's daughter. In the words of Jean-Baptiste Morin, "the light is weakened the more it is bent." Immediate family relations seem to be where derived houses work most effectively – at least in natal astrology. Horary astrology offers more freedom for exploration and experimentation. Though derived houses are a valuable tool in chart delineation, the best way to astrologically learn about someone's life is to study that person's chart. Your chart may tell you a lot about your mother. However, if you really want to understand her and walk a mile in her shoes, her chart will tell you that much more.

STRENGTH OF THE HOUSES

> *The following are the good places in which it is necessary for them [i.e., the planets or zoidia] to be placed. First, the Horoskopos [first house]; second, the Midheaven [tenth house]; third, the Good Divinity [eleventh house]; fourth, the Good Fortune [fifth house]; after these,*

*the Descendant [seventh house]; then, the pivot point under the earth [fourth house]; after all the ninth place, the so-called God [ninth house]. And these are the good places. Evil are the second [house], the third [house] from the Horoskopos, and the eighth [house]; the two remaining, which are the sixth [house] and the twelfth [house], are the worst.* – HEPHAISTIO OF THEBES

In traditional astrology, everything we find in a chart can be characterized as either strong or weak. The twelve houses are no exception. The primary way the strength of a house is judged is based on whether or not those houses are connected to the Ascendant by aspect. In traditional astrology, the Ascendant is thought to be a source of vital life power that feeds all the other houses within a chart. Houses that are connected to the Ascendant by aspect are thought to be strong. Houses without an aspect to the Ascendant are weak. These aspects have been pre-determined based on an equal division of the twelve houses into 30° each.

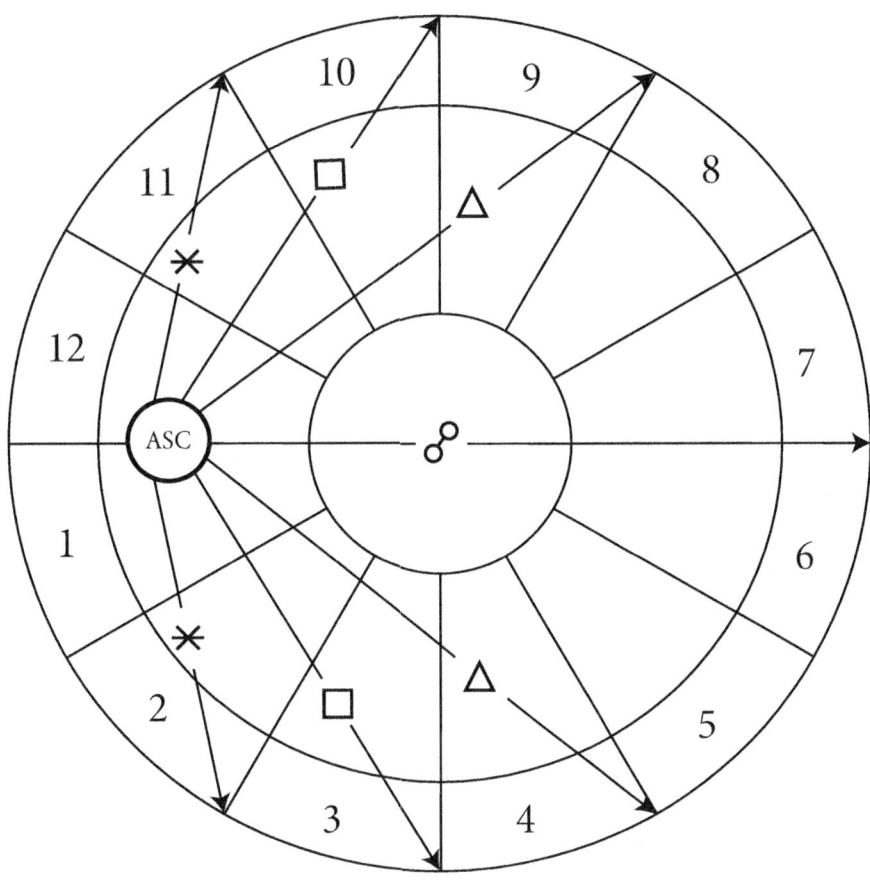

FIGURE 6: *Aspects Between the Ascendant & the Twelve Houses*

447

TABLE 1: *Aspects Between the Ascendant & Other Houses*

| | | | |
|---|---|---|---|
| AVERSION | 2ND, 8TH, 12TH | MALEFIC | DISCORDANT |
| SEMI-SEXTILE | 2ND, 12TH | MALEFIC | DISCORDANT |
| QUINCUNX | 6TH, 8TH | MALEFIC | DISCORDANT |
| SQUARE | 4TH, 10TH | MALEFIC | FORCEFUL |
| OPPOSITION | 7TH | MALEFIC | STRONG |
| SEXTILE | 3RD, 11TH | BENEFIC | GENTLE |
| TRINE | 5TH, 9TH | BENEFIC | POWERFUL |

The symbolic significations of the houses are based on these preset aspect relationships to the Ascendant. This remains the case whether or not the cusps of the houses in a given chart have a direct degree-based aspect to the Ascendant. For example, if 21° Sagittarius was on the Ascendant, 08° Taurus may be on the fifth house cusp. We know that these degrees do not have any traditional aspect relationship with each other. We couldn't say that, in this example, that the fifth house has a trine aspect to the Ascendant. In this example, it doesn't. However, the "symbolic" trine aspect from the fifth house to the Ascendant has been predetermined. It will always carry the imprint of having a trine to the Ascendant even if the degree-based relationship between the cusps of these houses doesn't form one.

FOUR QUADRANTS OF THE TERRESTRIAL HOUSES

> *Nor must you rest content with observing each cardinal point [the angular houses]; you must note with a retentive mind the spaces between them, which extend over a larger range and possess special powers.* – MARCUS MANILIUS

The ancients divided the houses into four quadrants. These quadrants are based on primary motion. Thus, the first quadrant contains houses twelve, eleven, and ten. The second quadrant contain houses nine, eight, and seven. The third quadrant contain houses six, five, and four. The fourth quadrant contain houses three, two, and the Ascendant.

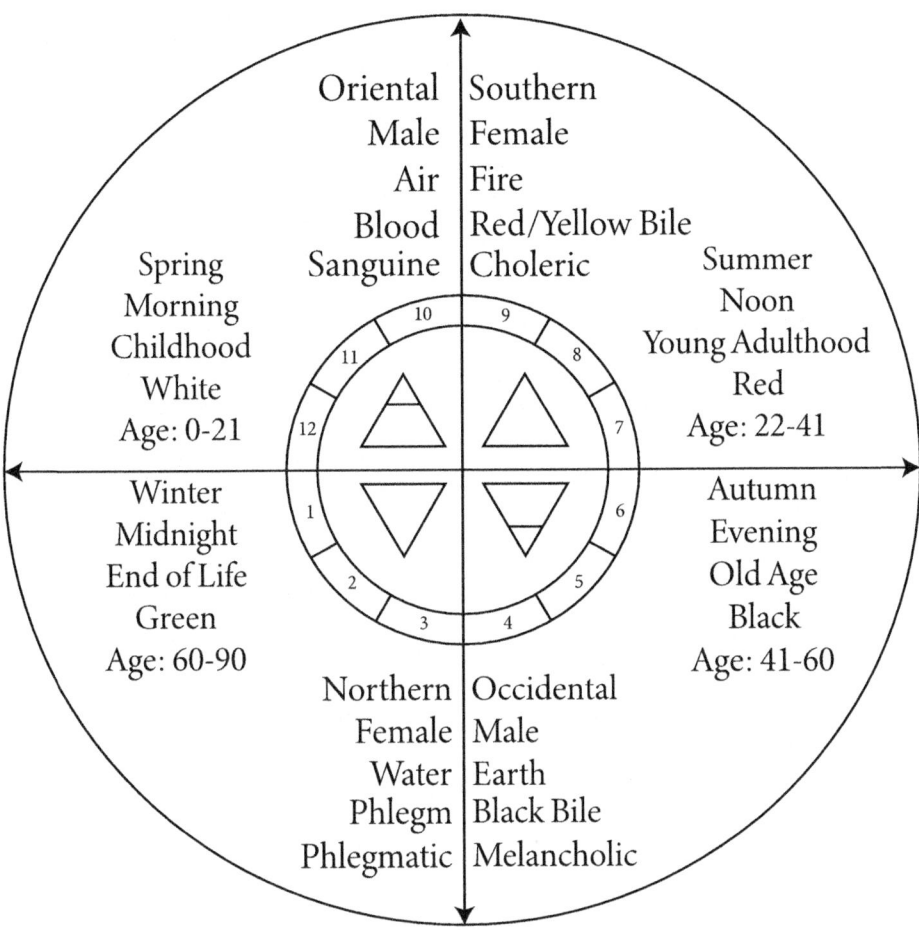

Oriental | Southern
Male | Female
Air | Fire
Blood | Red/Yellow Bile
Sanguine | Choleric

Spring
Morning
Childhood
White
Age: 0-21

Summer
Noon
Young Adulthood
Red
Age: 22-41

Winter
Midnight
End of Life
Green
Age: 60-90

Autumn
Evening
Old Age
Black
Age: 41-60

Northern | Occidental
Female | Male
Water | Earth
Phlegm | Black Bile
Phlegmatic | Melancholic

FIGURE 7: *Four Quadrants of the Houses*

*The curve which stretches from the orient to the topmost point of the circle claims the earliest age and infant years.* – MARCUS MANILIUS

According to Abraham Ibn Ezra, the first quadrant corresponds with the air element. It is oriental, masculine, and symbolizes childhood in the human life cycle. It is hot and wet, and therefore, sanguine in temperament, corresponding with the vital substance (or humour) of blood. Within the wheel of the year, the qualities of hot and wet correspond with the Springtime. Thus, William Lilly calls this quadrant "vernal," from the Latin "vernalis" meaning "of the Spring." Ibn Ezra states that the color of this quadrant is white.

*The slope which sinks down from the summit of the sky till it reaches the occident succeeds to the years of childhood and includes in its province control of tender youth.* – MARCUS MANILIUS

The second quadrant corresponds with the fire element. It is Southern, feminine, and symbolizes young adulthood in the human life cycle. It is hot and dry, and therefore, choleric in temperament, corresponding with the humour of red (or yellow) bile. Within the wheel of the year, the qualities of hot and dry are analogous with the Summertime. Thus, William Lilly calls this quadrant "estival," from the Latin "aestivalis" meaning "of the Summer." Ibn Ezra states that the color of this quadrant is red.

> *The portion which appropriates the setting heaven and descends to the bottom of the circle rules the period of adult life, a period tested by incessant change and chequered fortunes.* – MARCUS MANILIUS

The third quadrant corresponds with the earth element. It is occidental, masculine, and symbolizes adulthood in the human life cycle. It is cold and dry, and therefore, melancholic in temperament, corresponding with the humour of black bile. Within the wheel of the year, the qualities of cold and dry are analogous with the Autumntime. Thus, William Lilly calls this quadrant "Autumnal," from the Latin "autumnus" which denotes the passing of the year. Ibn Ezra states that the color of this quadrant is black.

> *But the part by whose return to the orient heaven's course is done and which with enfeebled strength slowly ascends the backbent arc, this part embraces the final years, life's fading twilight, and palsied age.* – MARCUS MANILIUS

The fourth quadrant corresponds with the water element. It is Northern, feminine, and symbolizes old age within the human life cycle. It is cold and wet, and therefore, phlegmatic in temperament, corresponding with the humour of phlegm. Within the wheel of the year, the qualities of cold and wet are analogous with the Wintertime. Thus, William Lilly calls this quadrant "of the Winter." Ibn Ezra states that the color of this quadrant is green.

There is great harmony in the doctrine of the qualities of the seasons that have been attributed to these four quadrants of terrestrial houses. In Spring, the heat is young, and the residual wetness from the Winter is old and dying. This heat and moisture create the sanguine temperament. In the Summer, the heat is mature. However, the dryness that has replaced the dead moisture of the Springtime is young and vital. This heat and dryness create the choleric temperament. In Autumn, the old heat of Summer dies and is replaced by the young coldness that will usher in the end of the year. The dryness of the Summer is now mature, and coupled with the quality of coldness creates the melancholic temperament. In Winter, the coldness is mature. The dryness dies and is replaced by the newly born wetness. Cold and wet create the phlegmatic temperament.

Al-Biruni writes:

> *For air corresponds to spring, summer to fire, autumn to earth, and winter to water.*

TABLE 2: *Seasons, Qualities, Elements, & the Houses*

| SEASON | QUALITIES | ELEMENT | TERRESTRIAL HOUSES |
|---|---|---|---|
| SPRING | YOUNG HEAT + OLD WETNESS | △ | 1ˢᵀ QUADRANT (HOUSES 12, 11, 10) |
| SUMMER | OLD HEAT + YOUNG DRYNESS | △ | 2ᴺᴰ QUADRANT (HOUSES 9, 8, 7) |
| AUTUMN | YOUNG COLD + OLD DRYNESS | ▽ | 3ᴿᴰ QUADRANT (HOUSES 6, 5, 4) |
| WINTER | OLD COLD + YOUNG WETNESS | ▽ | 4ᵀᴴ QUADRANT (HOUSES 3, 2, 1) |

The ancients also superimposed this process on the four major phases of the Moon. Ptolemy writes:

> *The Moon, during her increase, from her first emerging to her first quarter, produces chiefly moisture; on continuing her increase from her first quarter to her full state of illumination, she causes heat; from her full state to her third quarter, she causes dryness; and from her third quarter to her occultation, she causes cold.*

Though not explicitly stated in Ptolemy's *Tetrabiblos*, by the seventeenth century, this characterization of the Moon was understood to mean that from her conjunction with the Sun at the New Moon to her first quarter, she was hot and moist, and therefore, sanguine. From there towards the Full Moon, she was hot and dry, and choleric. From the Full Moon to her last quarter, she was cold and dry, and melancholic. From her last quarter to the New Moon, she was cold and moist, and phlegmatic.

TABLE 3: *Lunar Phases & the Four Elements*

| LUNAR PHASE | QUALITIES | TEMPERAMENT | ELEMENT |
|---|---|---|---|
| NEW MOON TO FIRST QUARTER | HOT & MOIST | SANGUINE | △ |
| FIRST QUARTER TO FULL MOON | HOT & DRY | CHOLERIC | △ |
| FULL MOON TO LAST QUARTER | COLD & DRY | MELANCHOLIC | ▽ |
| LAST QUARTER TO NEW MOON | COLD & MOIST | PHLEGMATIC | ▽ |

From the houses to the seasons to the phases of the Moon, we see a continuous thread of unity that existed in how the ancients perceived their cosmos.

ANGULAR, SUCCEDENT, AND CADENT HOUSES

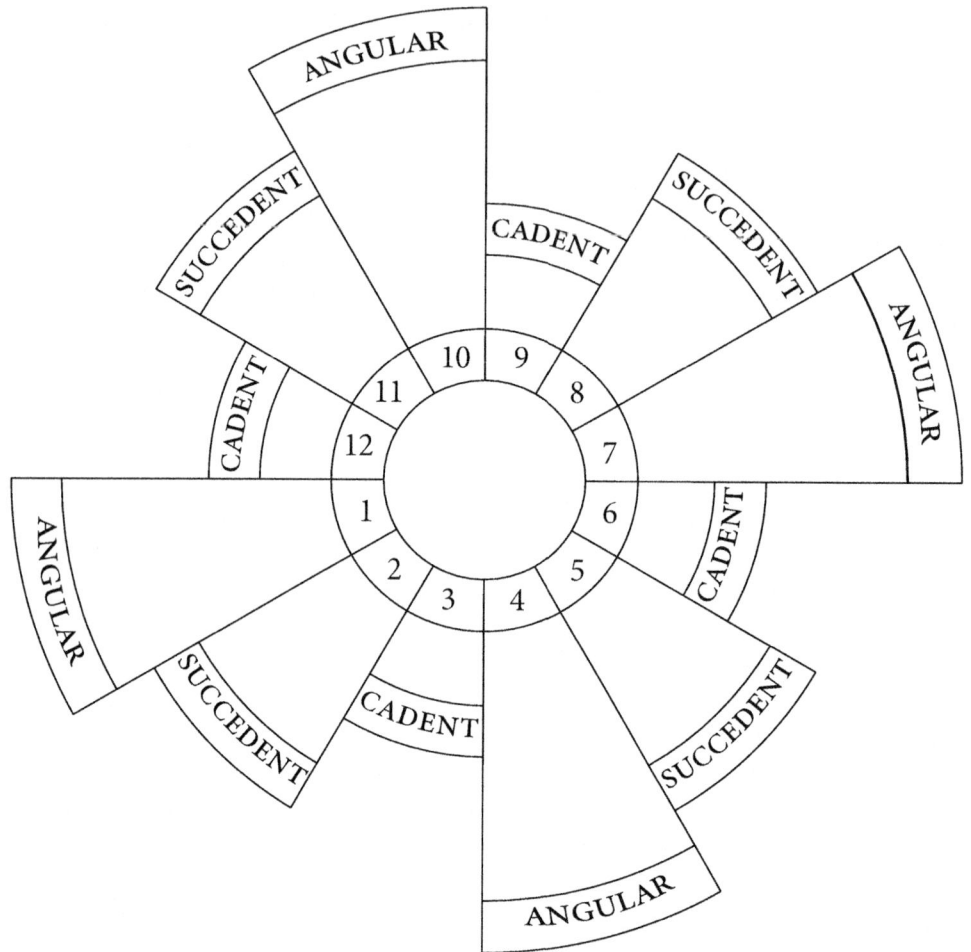

FIGURE 8: *Angular, Succedent, & Cadent Houses*

Another way houses are classified is based on whether or not they are angular, succedent, or cadent. The angular houses are the most powerful houses in traditional astrology. These are the first, tenth, seventh, and fourth houses. These houses are also called the "pivots" or the "cardines." They represent different stations of the Sun throughout the course of a day. The Ascendant is where the Sun rises in the morning. The Medium Coeli ("middle of heaven") is where the Sun attains his highest elevation from the horizon during the daytime. The Descendant is where the Sun sets in the evening. The Imum Coeli ("lower heaven") is where the Sun reaches the lowest point in his twenty-four-hour cycle with respect to the horizon. Manilius writes:

> *Come now, prepare an attentive mind for learning the cardinal points*
> *[angular houses]: four in all, they have positions in the firmament*

*permanently fixed and receive in succession the speeding signs. One looks out from the rising of the heavens as they are born into the world and has the first view of the Earth from the level horizon [Ascendant]; the second faces it from the opposite edge of the sky, the point from which the starry sphere retires and hurtles headlong into Tartarus [Descendant]; a third marks the zenith of high heaven, where wearied Phoebus [the Sun] halts with panting steeds and rests the day and determines the mid-point of shadows [Medium Coeli]; the fourth occupies the nadir, and has the glory of forming the foundation of the sphere [Imum Coeli]; in it the stars complete their descent and commence their return, and at equal distances it beholds their risings and settings.*

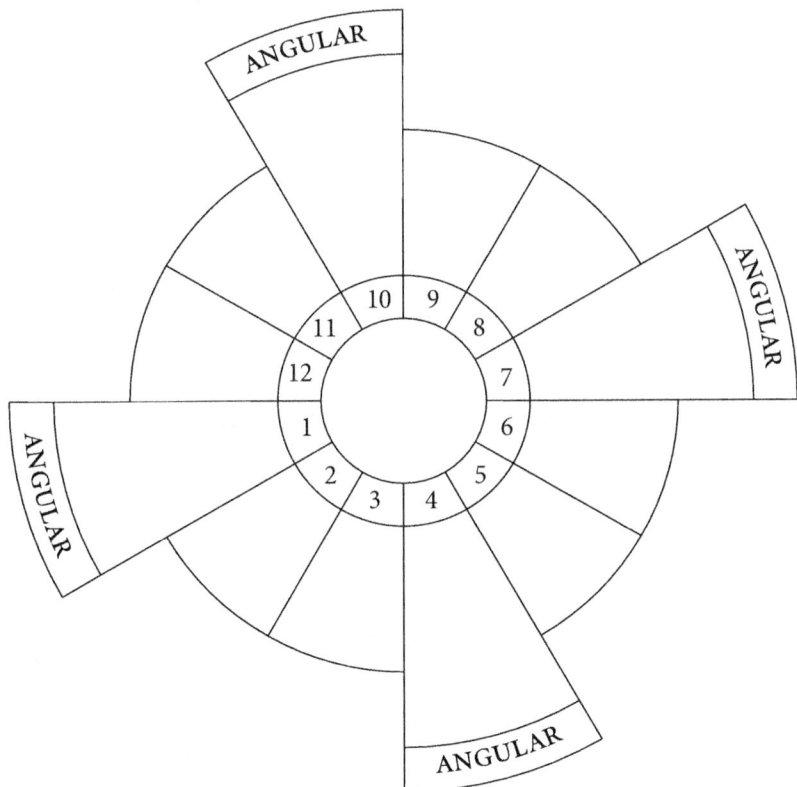

FIGURE 9: *Angular Houses*

The tenth house and fourth house square the Ascendant. The seventh house opposes it. In Uranian astrology, hard aspects are considered to be aspects of material manifestation. This is because of the dramatic ways in which they reflect concrete events that happen within our lives. Conversely, soft aspects facilitate things happening, and do not bear the same creative potency towards action that the hard aspects do. This dichotomy amongst the aspects isn't some unfounded modern astrological invention. What we often find in Uranian astrology is an expansion upon and streamlining of ancient principles. In *The Beginning of Wisdom*, Ibn Ezra writes:

> *The strongest of the aspects is the aspect of the opposition. Next in strength is the quartile [square] aspect, then the trine aspect, and the weakest of all is the sextile aspect.*

Hard aspects reflect concrete events that occur in our material universe in an obvious way. Therefore, these angular houses are houses that are the most important in astrology. They signify the major pivotal areas in our lives. Regarding the importance of these houses, Manilius writes:

> *These points are charged with exceptional powers, and the influence they exert on fate is the greatest known to our science, because the celestial circle is totally held in position by them as by eternal supports; did they not receive the circle, sign after sign in succession, flying in its perpetual revolution, and clamp it with fetters at the two sides and lowest and highest extremities of its compass, heaven would fly apart and its fabric [would] disintegrate and perish.*

On a more microcosmic level, these houses bear a very personal significance within our lives. The first house represents the physical body that serves as our vehicle as we interact with the larger world. The fourth house signifies our ancestral roots to our father, our country, and our family in general. The seventh house represents our primal impulse to reach out to the world around us and form intimate connections. The tenth house symbolizes our mother and the career path we choose to pursue. Much like the heavens, that would "fly apart" and perish should any of these eternal supports be unfastened, it is questionable how well we'd be able to function within our environment should we lose any of these celestial pivots within our lives.

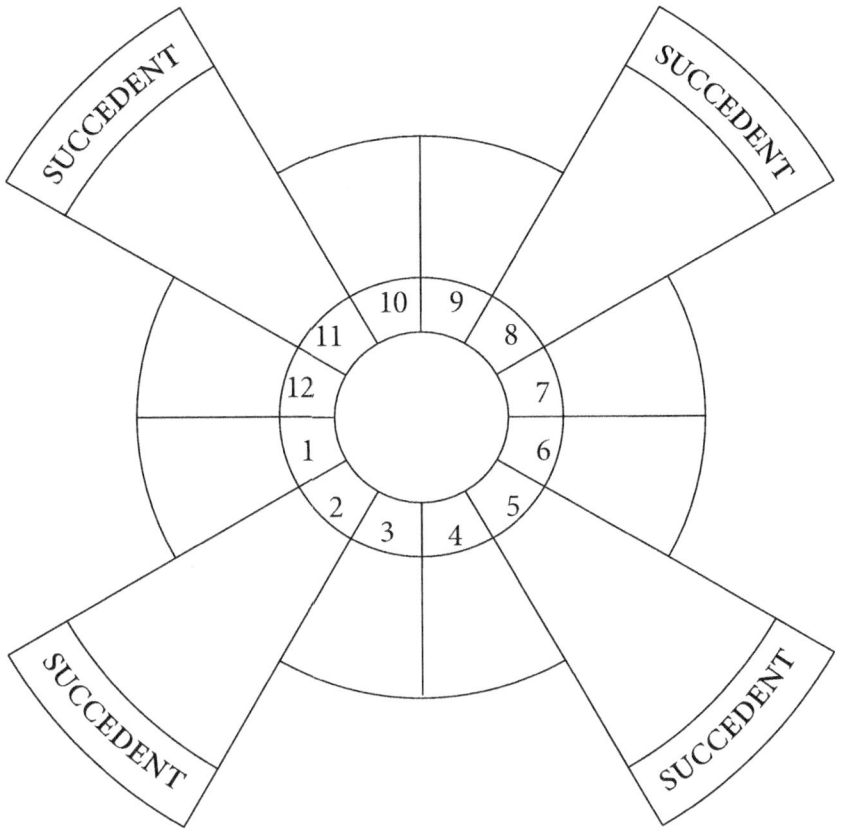

FIGURE 10: *Succedent Houses*

The succedent houses succeed the angular houses. This means, they follow the angles in sequence and inherit some of their power. These are the second, fifth, eighth, and eleventh houses. Of these houses, Ibn Ezra writes:

> *The four houses following the angular ones have average strength, for they shortly become [angular] too. The others [the cadent houses] are falling and have no strength at all.*

The succedent houses are sources of assistance, blessedness, and aid to their adjacent angle. The second house signifies our wealth, and the fifth house represents the wealth of our family. Traditionally, children were symbolic of the fortune of a household, which is why the fifth house is also considered to be a house of children. The eighth house is both the wealth of our spouse as well as the wealth from our ancestors. The eleventh house represents the wealth we gain through our maternal line as well as the wealth we gain from our careers.

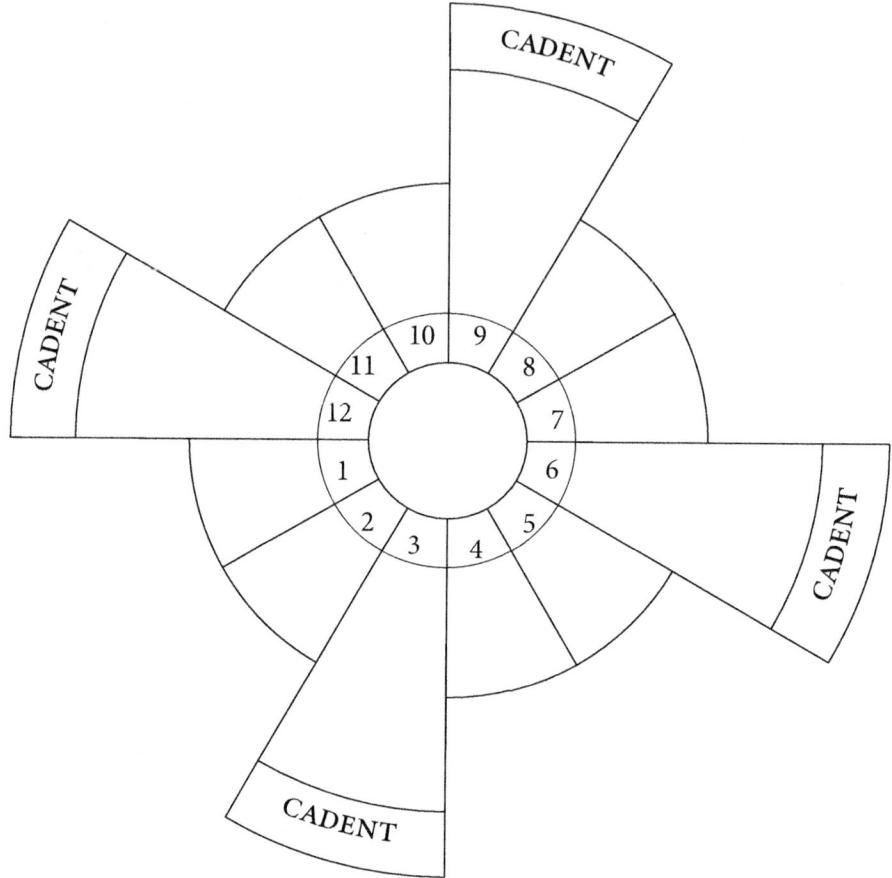

FIGURE 11: *Cadent Houses*

The cadent houses follow the succedent houses. These are the third, sixth, ninth, and twelfth houses. In the writings of Rhetorius the Egyptian, the cadent houses are also referred to as "metacosmic" houses, which can be translated to mean "behind the cosmos." The word "cadent" comes from the Latin infinitive "cadere" which means "to fall." The cadent houses have fallen away from the strength that the angles provide.

Based on diurnal motion, the twelfth house falls away from the Ascendant, the eleventh house builds in power, and the tenth house is where that power reaches its highest expression. The ninth house falls away from the tenth house, the eighth house builds in power, and the seventh house is where this power reaches its highest expression. The sixth house falls away from the seventh house, the fifth house builds in power, and the fourth house is where this power reaches its highest expression. The third house falls away from the fourth house, the second house builds in power, and the first house is where that power reaches its highest expression.

## Three Most Evil Houses of Heaven

*The temple that is immediately above the Horoscope and is the next but one to heaven's zenith [twelfth house] is a temple of ill omen, hostile to future activity and all too fruitful of bane; nor that alone, but like unto it will prove the abode which with confronting star shines below the occident and adjacent to it [sixth house]. And so that this temple should not outdo the former, each alike moves dejected from a cardinal point with the spectacle of ruin before its eyes. Each shall be a portal of toil: in one you are doomed to climb [twelfth house], and in the other to fall [sixth house]. Not more fortunate is the portion of heaven above the occident [eighth house] or that opposite it below the orient [second house]; suspended, the former face downward, the latter on its back, they either fear destruction at the hands of the neighboring cardinal or will fall if cheated of its support. With justice are they [eighth and second houses] held to be the dread abodes of Typhon, whom savage Earth brought forth when she gave birth to war against heaven and sons as massive as their mother appeared. – MARCUS MANILIUS*

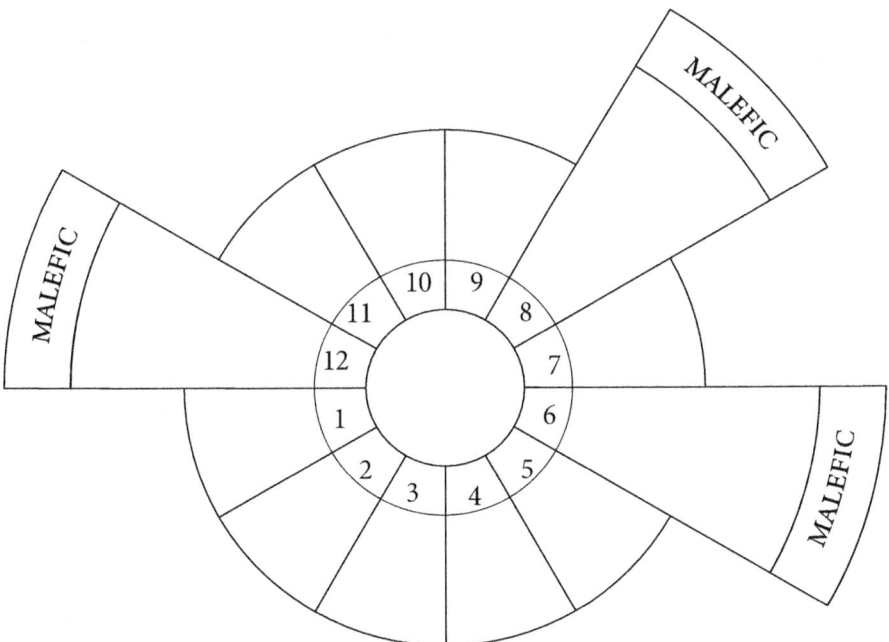

FIGURE 12: *Evil Houses*

The sixth, eighth, and twelfth houses are considered to be the three most evil houses of heaven. This is because these three houses are in aversion to the Ascendant. Though the second house is also in aversion to the Ascendant, it is succedent to it, and inherits the power held there. Also, by diurnal motion, planets within the second house are gifted with the promise of ultimately rising to the Ascendant. Thus, arrival in the second house is a boon for any planet.

The name for the second house is "Anaphora," meaning "Exit from the Gates of Hell." This is in contrast to the name of its counterpart, the eighth house, which is "Epicataphora," meaning "Entry (or falling) into the Gates of Hell." While the second house is thought of as a benefic house, through its existence on the axis of the underworld, it has also been considered an intrinsically evil house within traditional astrology. The overarching point demonstrated here is that all the houses that are in aversion to the Ascendant are considered to be evil houses of heaven. The second house is circumstantially good, even though its essential nature – through its aversion to the Ascendant – should naturally lead it in the direction of causing harm. Interestingly, in Jyotish, the second house is considered to be one of the "maraka" or "killing" houses. Jyotish also considers the seventh house to be a "killing" house. We do not find as many textual references to the seventh house being a house of death in traditional Western astrology as we do in Indian astrology. However, there are a few gems within our literature that indicate that this was a known association in the West as well. Manilius writes:

> *There remains one region, that is the setting heaven [the seventh house]. It speeds the falling sky beneath the Earth and buries the stars. Now it looks forth on the back of the departing Sun, yet it once beheld his face; so wonder not if it is called the portal of somber Pluto and keeps control over the end of life and death's firm-bolted door. Here dies even the very light of day, which the ground beneath steals away from the world and locks up captive in the dungeon of night.*

Abraham Ibn Ezra more bluntly points to this connection between the seventh house and death in his *Book of Reasons*. He writes:

> *Because the seventh house is opposite the first one, the beginning of the seventh pole signifies death, as well as its ruler; but because it is connected with the first house, it does not entirely indicate death. Only the eighth house that conjoins it, and is opposite [the second house] and is not connected with the first will signify death. And because it [the eighth house] is like the second house that signifies money, the eighth signifies inheritance from the dead.*

The opposition aspect the Descendant forms with the Ascendant prevents it from being wholly destructive to the Ascendant. Though in a warlike relationship, the seventh house depends on the Ascendant for its survival.

The twelfth house does not have the circumstantial benevolence we find in the second house – even though it, too, is adjacent to the Ascendant. Not only is it the final house within the sequence of terrestrial houses and, therefore, analogous with endings, death, and sorrow; but, it is also a cadent house.

The cadent houses are collectively thought of as weak and, therefore, potentially malefic, in traditional astrology. Though the third house and the ninth house circumstantially make benefic aspects to the Ascendant, their essential nature as cadent houses is to be weak. Though the ninth house seems to be universally thought of as a "powerful" and benefic house in traditional astrology, there has been some debate as to whether or not the third house should actually be thought of as benefic or malefic. In general, most traditional Western astrologers are of the agreement that the third house is a benefic house, though cadent. The sixth house of sickness, eighth house of death, and twelfth house of suffering, however, are universally thought of as being evil beyond measure.

## Visibility of the Houses

The various houses afford the planets and other celestial factors different qualities of visibility. In traditional astrology, visibility equals power. The more visible something is, the more power that celestial factor has in terms of impacting the overall homeostasis of the chart in general. Bonatti writes:

> And these four houses [the angles] are the strongest and firmer parts of the heaven... indeed the 2$^{nd}$ house, and the 5$^{th}$ and 8$^{th}$ and 11$^{th}$, are called the "succedents" of the angles, because they are immediately next to the angles and are less strong than the angles by half... Indeed the 3$^{rd}$ house, and the 6$^{th}$ and 9$^{th}$ and 12$^{th}$, are called the "cadents" from the angles. And they are very weak houses, and do not promise good nor firmness nor durability nor prolongation of any matter...

If angular houses have 100% visibility, then succedent houses have 50% visibility. Bonatti does not explicitly state what portion of power the cadent houses have in relation to the angular and succedent houses. However, we could safely infer that if the succedent houses have half the power of the angular houses, then the cadent houses have half the power of the succedent houses. Therefore, cadent houses offer planets 25% visibility and power. While these numbers are broad generalizations, they aid us in understanding how dominant a planet can be when in a given house of the horoscope.

## The Houses – Strongest to Weakest

Within William Lilly's *Christian Astrology*, we find the following organization of the houses based on their strength:

1    10    7    4    11    5    9    3    2    8    6    12

The first house is the strongest house. If there were no physical body, there would be no native to experience everything that the other eleven houses represent. However, for Manilius, the first house followed the Midheaven and the Imum Coeli in his organization of the houses by their power. On the power of the first house, he writes:

*The third cardinal [the Ascendant], which on the same level as the Earth holds in position the shining dawn, where the stars first rise, where day returns and divides time into hours, is for this reason in the Greek world called the Horoscope, and it declines a foreign name, taking pleasure in its own. Within its domain lies the arbitrament of life and the formation of character; it will grant success to enterprises, open up the professions, and decide the early years that await men from their birth, the education they receive, and the station to which they are born, according as the planets approve and mingle their influences.*

This notion of the Ascendant following the IC in power isn't something we find as a commonly agreed upon idea within traditional astrology. However, in traditional texts, the first house and the tenth house run very close to having the same amount of strength. Many astrologers have held the belief that the tenth house is stronger than the first. This is because the angular houses represent the dramatic stations of the Sun during his journey through the day. Whereas the Sun in the first house is growing in strength, the Sun in the tenth house is at the height of his power. Also, the Sun in the tenth house is the Sun above the horizon. In traditional astrology, a planet above the horizon has more strength in general than a planet below it. The Sun in the tenth house should technically be stronger than the Sun in the first house, thus making the tenth house a powerful contender for being the strongest of the twelve houses.

On the power of the tenth house, Manilius writes:

*First place goes to the cardinal which holds sway at the summit of the sky and divides heaven into two with imperceptible meridian; enthroned on high this post is occupied by Glory (truly a fit warden for heaven's supreme station), so that she may claim all that is pre-eminent, arrogate all distinction, and reign by awarding honours of every kind. Hence comes applause, splendour, and every form of popular favour; hence the power to dispense justice in the courts, to bring the world under the rule of law, to make alliances with foreign nations on one's own terms, and to win fame relative to one's station.*

I understand the rationale behind viewing the tenth house as more supreme than all the others. However, I still hold the belief that without the vital life represented by the Ascendant, one's rise in life would be completely thwarted. There would be no life to rise in. This is my understanding as to why the first house remains first in the sequence of the strength of the houses according to Lilly.

Though the first house is "strongest," astrologers of antiquity have been willing to view the tenth house as being stronger in matters of career or public prestige. In questions having to do with those topics, the tenth house is stronger than the first house and should be regarded as a more favorable place for planets to inhabit. For example, in the question "Will I get the job I applied for?", while the presence of the ruler of the Ascendant in the first house may be a good omen, the presence of the Ascendant ruler in the tenth house is even better.

Since the angular houses are generally stronger than all the others, the seventh house naturally follows as an angular house. It is stronger than the fourth house because it is above the horizon. In the seventh house, the Sun is still visible, whereas in the fourth house, he is not. The fourth house is the weakest of the four angular houses as far as visibility is concerned. However, in natal astrology, I sometimes wonder whether or not the fourth house is actually the strongest house within the chart. The fourth house represents our father, family, connection to the land, and our heritage. Very often, if someone has a very afflicted fourth house, they have a very afflicted life in general. If a chart could be compared to a building, the fourth house would be the framework upon which that edifice is built. If the foundation is weak, it takes very little for the entire structure to crumble. On the strength and significance of the fourth angle, Manilius writes:

> The next point, though situated in the lowest position, bears the world poised on its eternal base; in outward aspect its influence is less, but is greater in utility. It controls the foundations of things and governs wealth; it examines to what extent desires are accomplished by the mining of metal and what gain can issue from a hidden source.

It is appropriate that the fourth house should correspond with "hidden treasures." The conditions we hold in our fourth house can greatly support or hinder us in finding success in the world later in life.

The eleventh house follows because it has a sextile relationship to the Ascendant, it is a succedent house, and it is above the horizon. Though the ninth house has a stronger aspect to the Ascendant through its trine radiation, the ninth house is cadent. Thus, the eleventh house's succedent sextile to the Ascendant is stronger than the cadent trine from the ninth. For this reason, the fifth house, though below the horizon, follows the eleventh house in the sequence. The fifth house trines the Ascendant. The subterranean succedent trine from the fifth house is stronger than the elevated – but cadent – trine from the ninth house.

The third house comes next. Though it is cadent and technically weaker than the succedent eighth house, the third house aspects the Ascendant by a benefic sextile, whereas the eighth house has no aspect to the Ascendant at all.

The second house follows the third house in power. Out of the houses that have no aspect to the Ascendant, the second house is a succedent house that is conjoined to the Ascendant. Resultantly, the second house receives the power and the blessedness of the Ascendant purely through proximity. Notice that all of the other houses that have an aspect to the Ascendant have come before the second house. Only the houses that do not aspect the Ascendant remain. Of the houses that are in aversion to the Ascendant, the second house is most powerful and benefic.

This leaves the "three worst houses of heaven." The eighth house follows the second house in power. Though it does not aspect the Ascendant, it is still a succedent house and is stronger than the cadent sixth and twelfth houses that follow. The sixth house follows the eighth house because it has no aspect to the Ascendant and is cadent. Technically one would think that the sixth house should come last in this sequence because it is in aversion to the Ascendant, cadent, and below the horizon; whereas the twelfth house has those same conditions but is above the horizon. However, the twelfth house follows the sixth house. I believe this is because the twelfth house comes at the end of the sequence of the houses. Therefore, it has an association with death, destruction, and the annihilation of all things.

## THE FIVE DEGREE RULE

> *And Ptolemy said that the 05° which have crossed over the line dividing one of the houses from the next, is reckoned as, and is said to belong to, the house which is given to that line... For always, the 05° which have crossed the line of a house are reckoned to be in that house...* – GUIDO BONATTI

When a planet is within five degrees of the next house cusp, and in the same sign as that next house cusp, that planet is considered to be in the next house. It has fully given its virtue or power over to the other house, and no longer operates in the house that it is physically in. Lilly writes:

> *... what space is contained between the figure one [first house cusp] to the figure two [second house cusp], is of the first house, or what planet you shall find to be in that space, you shall say he is in the first house; yet if he be within five degrees of the cusp of any house, his virtue shall be assigned to that house to whose cusp he is nearest...*

In general, if several planets are in a house, the planet nearest to the cusp of that house is usually considered to be more powerful within the affairs of that house; that is, unless the domicile ruler of the sign on the cusp of that house is also present there. This can also be altered if there is another planet in that house that is more essentially dignified while in that house, than the planet that is conjunct the cusp. However, it is generally accepted within Medieval and Renaissance astrology that being in a house and nearest to the cusp of that house will give a planet greater impact on what that house signifies. Within a twenty-four-hour cycle, the proximity or distance from a house cusp will be largely based on the primary motion of the sky from a geocentric perspective. We will recall that there are two forms of motion displayed by planets in a chart: primary (or diurnal) motion and secondary (or zodiacal) motion.

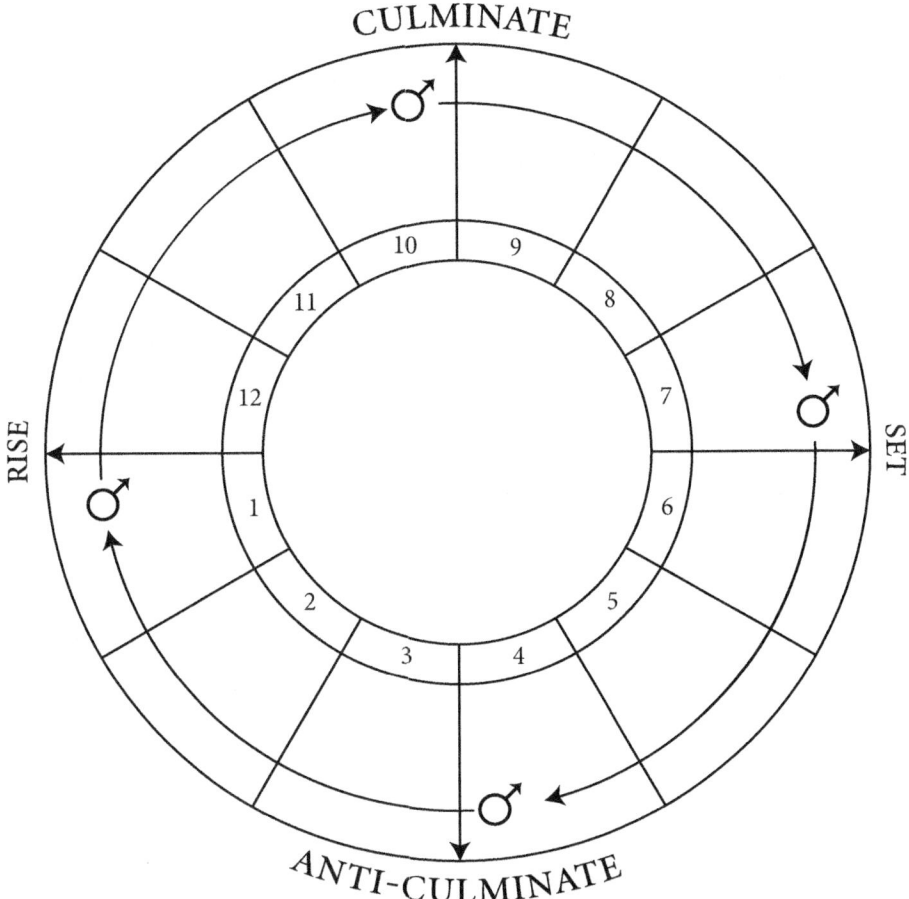

CULMINATE

RISE

SET

ANTI-CULMINATE

FIGURE 13: *Primary Motion*

By primary motion, a planet will leave the first house and enter the twelfth house. This is because by primary motion, planets under the horizon rise "above the Earth" and continue their East to West course in the sky through the MC, the Descendant, the IC, and once again to the Ascendant.

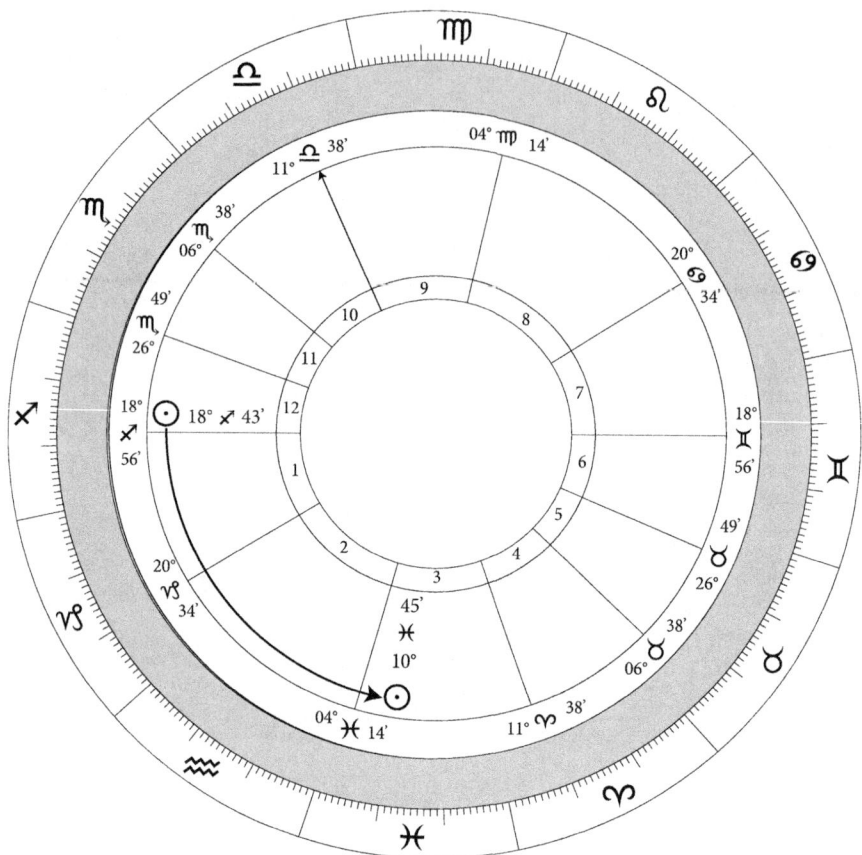

FIGURE 14: *Secondary Motion*

However, by zodiacal motion, planets in the twelfth house move into the first house. This is because the movement of a planet from one degree of zodiacal longitude to another occurs from West to East based on the sequence of the twelve signs.

Put simply, primary motion indicates the swifter, daily motion of the planets that can be observed within a twenty-four-hour period. The Sun at 6:00 AM does not have the same relationship to the horizon at 12:00 PM. However, neither does Saturn, Jupiter, Mars, Venus, Mercury, the Moon, or any other celestial factor we may observe. Secondary motion is the slower motion of the planets that occurs over a longer period of time from one degree of the zodiac to another. It is far less obvious than the more dramatic rising and setting of the heavens. Thus, the Five Degree Rule is based in the zodiacal motion, and not the diurnal motion of the planets.

As a zodiacal motion-based rule, it would seem obvious that the zodiacal sign of both the planet and the house cusp it may potentially enter due to the Five Degree Rule should be the same sign. However, neither Bonatti nor Lilly makes mention of the house cusp needing to be in the same sign as the planet in question. Nevertheless, today it is commonly held that the sign on the house cusp should be a consideration when applying the Five Degree Rule. This seems to be logical from a traditional astrological perspective.

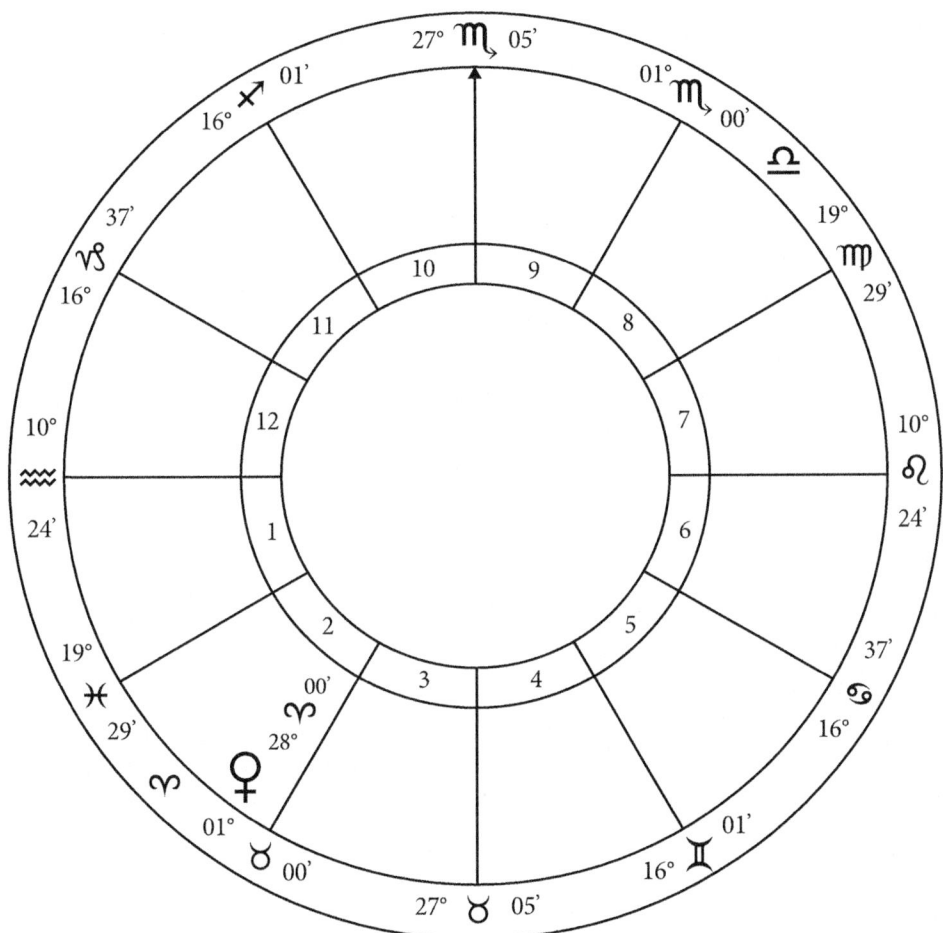

FIGURE 15: *Venus within 5° of Third House Cusp*

If Venus is at 28° Aries, she is not afforded +5 points of essential dignity just because she is within five degrees of her domicile of Taurus. Therefore, if she is at 28° Aries in the second house and the third house cusp is 01° Taurus, it does not seem astrologically sound that she would be able to operate in the third house. The sign on the cusp of the third house bears no relationship to the sign she is currently in. Traditionally speaking, there are fixed boundaries between signs. Though we see multiple aphorisms regarding the weakness of a planet at the end of a sign, it is commonly held within traditional astrology that a sign continues to be that sign throughout its entirety – and that a planet is considered to be in a sign until it leaves that sign completely.

For full disclosure, there is an aphorism in *The Beginning of Wisdom* that completely contradicts what I just said. Ibn Ezra writes:

> *When a planet is at the end of a sign, it loses its strength and all of its power is in the sign it will enter [next]. If the planet is at the 29ᵗʰ degree of the sign, its influence is still in the sign it is in, because within 3° the planet has influence in the degree it is in, one degree before and one degree after.*

There are problems with this aphorism. We do not see overwhelming historical evidence that it was used in a way that would materially alter the essential dignity a planet has at the end of the sign it is occupying. Venus at 29° Aries is an essentially debilitated Venus. Though she is in her face, the overarching reality of Venus at this or any degree of Aries is that she is in her detriment. Her proximity to 00° Taurus does not change her essential debility in Aries. Despite Ibn Ezra's assertion, in concrete astrological practice, Aries is Aries from the beginning to the end of that sign.

There is great symbolic meaning in finding a planet at the end of a sign. None of that meaning is based on the next sign it will enter. Rather, it is fully based on the sign that it is in, and the state of anxiety it experiences there. When a planet is at the final degree of a sign, it is as if that planet is standing on the edge of a cliff. In *Bethem's Centiloquium* we read:

> *A planet in the last degree of a sign, is as one falling from his estate.*

A planet at the end of a sign is frightened about the jump it must take, even if – as in the case of Venus at 29° Aries – it is hopeful about the next sign it will enter.

Regardless of whether you agree with Ibn Ezra's point or not concerning the condition of planets in different parts of a sign, the realities of that sign within itself are unalterable. As we near the final degrees of a sign, that sign doesn't slowly begin to transform into the next sign – an opinion that is commonly held today outside of the traditional astrology community. Aries is Aries throughout its entirety – from 00° 00' 00" of that sign until 29° 59' 59" of that sign. Therefore, by the Five Degree Rule, Venus in our example is still in the second house, even if she isn't strongly impacting the affairs of that house.

Planets are strong or weak within houses based on their proximity to the cusps of those houses. A planet that is conjunct the cusp of a house is considered to be more strongly operative within that house than a planet that is in a house, yet far from that house's cusp. Ibn Ezra writes:

> *Any planet [positioned] at the beginning of the house up to 15° has great power.*

Planets whose influence crosses the boundary of a house cusp based on the Five Degree Rule are more strongly operative within that house than a planet that is physically in that house, but far from its cusp. On the Five Degree Rule, Ibn Ezra writes:

> ... if the planet is away from a house [before the cusp] by less than 5°, then it is considered [with]in the force of the house, but if more [than that], it is falling away from the force of the house.

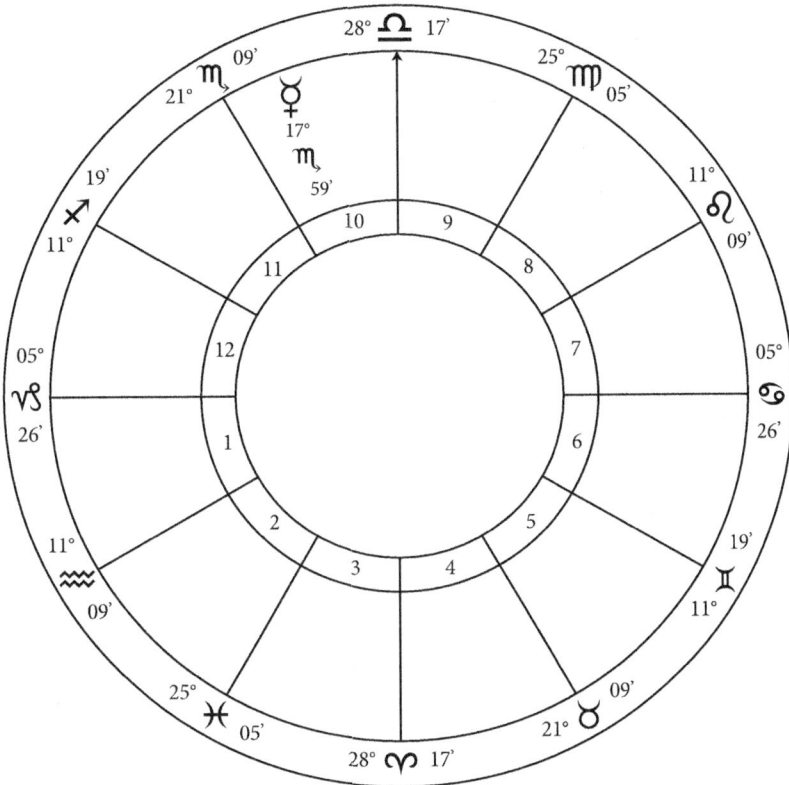

FIGURE 16: *Mercury within 5° of Eleventh House Cusp*

Therefore, if Mercury is at 17° Scorpio in the tenth house, and the eleventh house cusp is 21° Scorpio, though Mercury is physically in the tenth house, his power has already changed over to the eleventh house. He is strongly involved in the affairs of the eleventh house, and is not active in the affairs of the tenth house at all, even though his physical body is in the tenth. This is because Mercury is within five degrees of the next house cusp and in the same sign as the next house cusp. If the eleventh house cusp were 24° Scorpio instead, then Mercury at 17° Scorpio would remain a tenth house planet and would influence the affairs of the tenth house.

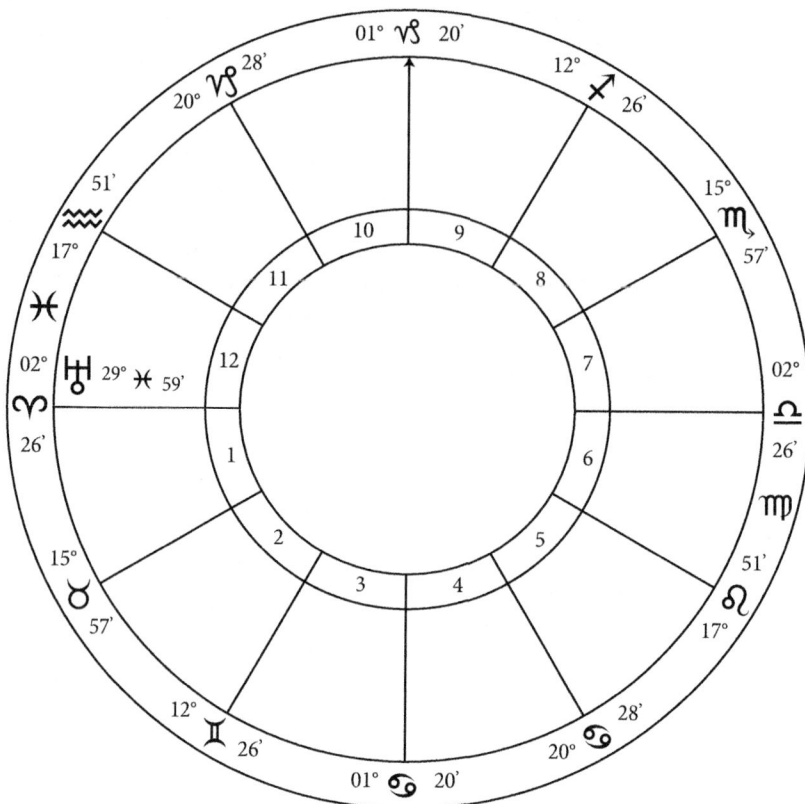

FIGURE 17: *Uranus within 5° of First House Cusp*

If Uranus were at 29° Pisces and the Ascendant were at 02° Aries, then Uranus would remain a twelfth house planet. Even though Uranus is within five degrees of the Ascendant, it is not in the same sign as the Ascendant. Therefore, the Five Degree Rule would not apply to Uranus.

Now that we have established ourselves in a solid introduction to the houses, it is time for us to explore their significations within traditional astrology.

CHAPTER 20 QUESTIONS

1. What is the purpose of the twelve terrestrial houses in traditional astrology?
2. Define the term "interception."
3. What is a derived house?
4. Why are the angular houses considered to be the strongest houses within a chart?
5. Why are the cadent houses considered to be the weakest houses within a chart?
6. Which houses are considered to be the most evil houses of heaven? Why?
7. What is the specific definition of the Five Degree Rule as used within the author?

CHAPTER 21 OBJECTIVES

* Learn the significations of the twelve terrestrial houses.
* Understand the rationale behind the attributions of the twelve houses.
* Discover how the Chaldean Order of the planets correspond with the twelve houses.
* Identify the terrestrial joys of the planets & learn the reason behind their attributions.
* Explore the anatomical correspondences of the houses through the lens of medical astrology.

# CHAPTER 21

## SIGNIFICATIONS OF THE
## TWELVE TERRESTRIAL HOUSES

*These twelve houses are fundamental in the nativity of a person, in inquiries [horary astrology], in elections, and also in judgment for the world in general.* – ABRAHAM IBN EZRA

HAVING A CLEAR UNDERSTANDING of the significations of the twelve terrestrial houses is one of the most important components of a traditional astrology education. In this chapter, we will explore each of the houses and learn how they can be applied to our practice of traditional astrology.

### FIRST HOUSE – ASCENDANT – HELM

*In my opinion, the rising degree is like a newborn coming out of the darkness, and it ascends until it reaches the Midheaven, and then it descends. This is clear from the rising of the Sun in the morning; therefore, the Ascendant signifies life.* – ABRAHAM IBN EZRA

The first house is called the "Ascendant." Anything in the first house will ultimately ascend above the Eastern horizon due to diurnal motion. The Ascendant is also known as the "horoscope" or "hour-marker." It marks the exact hour and moment of the day that a person was born at a particular location on Earth.

The ancient Greeks called the Ascendant "helm." A helm is the steering wheel of a ship. Similarly, the Ascendant is the steering wheel of our lives. It represents the soul, psyche, primary motivation, temperament, thinking, behavior, and habits of the native. Traditionally speaking, the Ascendant symbolizes the person for whom the reading is being given. It is, in a sense, you.

The Ascendant holds the quantum of energy that we all carry in this lifetime by which we flourish in the world. It is a fountainhead of vitality that nourishes everything else within our charts. Houses that are connected by aspect to the Ascendant are considered to be either auspicious or powerful. Houses that have no aspect relationship to the Ascendant, are considered to be debilitated and evil.

The Ascendant is a spatial factor based on the birth location of the native. It is where the local horizon intersects the ecliptic in the East at the exact moment of one's birth. This is why in Uranian astrology, the Ascendant receives the designation of "the environment." It signifies our place in space. It is the immediate environment into which we were born.

The persona that is traditionally ascribed to the Ascendant is a byproduct of our relationship to the environment around us. Seen through this lens, the persona becomes a collection of environmental influences that form our actions and reactions in definite ways. Though representing the persona and how we internally mobilize ourselves within the world, on a more tangible level, the Ascendant signifies our physical bodies. The Ascendant symbolizes the body in its role as the principal vehicle of the soul.

As the first house, the Ascendant corresponds with Saturn, the first planet in the Chaldean Order. The materializing principles of Saturn are analogous with the physical body. The first thing a baby experiences in this lifetime is being in a physical body that is independent of the womb of its mother. Abraham Ibn Ezra writes:

> *In my opinion Saturn was assigned, like the first house, to rule the body because his [organ] is the spleen, from which comes the power to obstruct the body, and [he also rules] the bones which are the foundation of the body.*

Saturn rules the gravity that binds us to the material world. However, he also rules the physical body and the spiritual weight that keeps the soul bound to it for the course of its lifetime. The Ascendant represents the place where this soul-binding occurs. In Jyotish, the Ascendant is known as "lagna." My traditional Jyotish teachers defined this word as "that which ties the soul down." Whether viewed astrologically or philosophically, this enslavement of the soul to matter posed an existential dilemma for ancient philosophers.

The ancients struggled with their understanding of where to place the body within the hierarchy of spiritual evolution. Their qualm was less with the body itself, and more with the Saturnian imposition placed upon the embodied soul; dulling our spiritual perception, and causing us to see the world "through a glass, darkly" from the moment we stepped into physical incarnation. In the *Corpus Hermeticum*, Hermes emphatically outlines his views on the spiritual burden of physical embodiment. He writes:

> *But first thou must tear off from thee this cloak which thou wearest, this cloak of ignorance, origin of every evil, chain of corruption, tangle of darkness, living death, sensation's corpse, the tomb that thou draggest along with thee, the robber in thine own home who through the things he loveth, hateth thee, and through the things he hateth bears thee malice.*

For the followers of Hermes, Saturn's governance over the body sullied the soul, burdened the mind, and made it that much harder for humanity to remember its stellar origins. Herein lies the alchemical imperative to transform ourselves from purely physical, Saturn-ruled creatures, by letting more of the spiritual essence within us shine through the thick garments of our flesh. In *De Signatura Rerum* (*The Signature of All Things*, published 1651), seventeenth century alchemist Jacob Böhme (1575-1624) writes:

> *Paradise is still in this world, but man is very far from it, so long as he*
> *fails to regenerate himself. And this is the Gold hidden in Saturn.*

Böhme's "gold" carries a deeply metaphysical and alchemical connotation. On a more mundane level, we can view this "gold" as the health and structural integrity of our soul, mind, and body within this lifetime, which is astrologically held in our Ascendant. The Ascendant is a cosmic barometer of our overall wellbeing. This is why in medical astrology the Ascendant is one of the most important houses to examine.

The Ascendant is the terrestrial house of joy of Mercury. Mercury rules the soul, intellect, and communication. Who we are, what we know, and how we say it are the pillars around which we organize our very existence in the world.

Mercury also represents the dichotomy of being human. The *Corpus Hermeticum* tells us that man is dual in nature: immortal because he is the brother of God, and mortal because he has a physical body. Mercury alone amongst the planets represents this complete marriage of contradictions. The Ascendant, representative of the merging of the soul with the material world, is the most appropriate house for Mercury to have as his terrestrial joy. Furthermore, the Ascendant – and the horizon in general – represents a space of twilight, of *in-between-ness*, of standing in the gap that bridges two worlds – all of which are functions of Mercury. Abraham Ibn Ezra writes:

> *The Joy of Mercury is in the first house, for he signifies the soul. Wisdom*
> *is also under Mercury, for the Moon signifies the body and he does the*
> *soul, and he is above the Moon and near us.*

Saturn rules the principle of physicality which is expressed throughout the material world of which the body is a part. However, the Moon universally signifies the body itself. This is because the Moon governs the principles of growth and diminution – principles which are expressed through the human life cycle. Mercury being "above the Moon and near us" is symbolic of the reality that the soul (Mercury) is superior to the body (Moon), yet always near and within our reach.

Mercury rules both the mind and how we express the mind in the world through the vehicle of speech. People with Mercury rising or with Mercury in aspect to the Ascendant are considered to be gifted in debating, oratory, and all matters of intelligent communication.

In the physical body, the Ascendant corresponds with the head as the seat of the brain, the mind, and the intellect.

Core Significations of the First House:

Body, mind, vitality, health, intellect, behavior; the querent in horary astrology, the native in natal astrology, the person for whom an electional chart is being erected, and the people of a nation (along with the Moon) in mundane astrology. As the "ship that we sail in," the Ascendant also represents the vehicle we are driving in when asking a horary question about the condition of our means of travel (car, boat, train, etc.).

## Second House – Anaphora (Exit from the Gates of Hades)

> *The second house is called livelihood and Gates of Hades and idle house.* – Rhetorius the Egyptian

The second house is traditionally called "Anaphora" or "Exit from the Gates of Hades." Hades was both the name of the Greek underworld and of the god who ruled it. Though many people think that "Pluto" was the Roman name for Hades, the name Pluto is also Greek in origin. With the second house being the Exit from the Gates of Hades, it represents a place of blessedness, and the promise of an improvement of one's circumstances through wealth, nourishment, and other means of physical support. It is the house of our liquid wealth, moveable possessions that we can lift up and carry, and all the things that are taken into the body for the purpose of supporting life. The second house, along with the fifth house, is the house of food within the chart.

Anything in the second house has the promise of rising to the light of the Ascendant through the diurnal motion of the sky. As a nexus of the underworld, it also represents that which is held in the underworld. Hades was both a place for the dead, and also a place containing all the gems, minerals, precious metals, and hidden treasures of the Earth. In natal astrology, the second house shows our natal promise regarding our wealth and financial wellbeing in this lifetime.

The second house is associated with Jupiter in the Chaldean Order. The ancients considered nourishment to be the second occurrence that a newborn baby experiences in life. A baby may not understand the concept of money and material riches. However, it does understand the value of external material sustenance from the warm and vitalizing milk it receives from its mother. Therefore, the second house plays an important role in how we are nourished and fed. Ibn Ezra writes:

> *Jupiter is like the second house therefore he signifies wealth… Because it [the second house] is close to the influence of the first house, it signifies money, which is the sustenance of life.*

The second house was also traditionally thought to be the house of our closest support systems, our allies, and best advisors. It is the house that represents the person who will pick up our sword and defend our honor if we fall in battle. Though this was a traditional signification of the second house, today we consider all forms of friends and loyal associates to come from the eleventh house.

In the physical body, the second house represents the neck, throat, and all that goes into it in the form of food.

Though the second house is in aversion to the Ascendant, it directly follows the Ascendant and inherits some of its strength. All of the succedent houses – with the exception of the eighth house – inherit the strength and power of the house that went before it. All of the succedent houses, including the eighth house, have a natural relationship with wealth, abundance, and material possessions.

Core Significations of the Second House:

Money, moveable possessions, food, jewelry.

Third House – Dea (Goddess)

> *The third house is called [the house] of the Moon Goddess.... Overshadowed, authoritative, [and] metacosmic. It signifies the topic of foreign [things] and that of dreams and religious observance and banking and friends and brothers and the queen.* – Rhetorius the Egyptian

The third house represents the siblings, kinsmen, community, and our early childhood environment. Everything that is close, familiar, and immediately present within our native community is represented here. It represents our formative environmental contacts with our siblings, young cousins, and neighbors.

The third house is our home away from home, and our familiar surroundings within the world. It signifies short journeys within the community or the immediate environment. All travelling that does not include going into unfamiliar places pertains to the third house.

The third house signifies formative education. It symbolizes acquiring the foundational learning necessary to pursue higher paths of learning and mastery later in life. Coupled with the ninth house, the third house is a part of the axis of how we learn and gather information. It represents reading, writing, speaking, books, and how we view the process of communicating.

As the house of the Moon Goddess, it signifies Earth-based spirituality, such as: paganism, shamanism, Santeria, Vodoun, and other forms of indigenous religion.

In the Chaldean Order, the third house corresponds with Mars. Mars symbolizes our siblings and other blood relations. He also signifies our desire to be in motion and to travel – even if that travel doesn't take us far from home.

The third house is the terrestrial house of joy of the Moon. It represents the formative roots we have within the immediate environment. It refers to all the places in the world where we are suckled and supported as if by our own family. The quick revolution of the Moon also corresponds with the idea of short journeys, one of the principal associations of the third house. Ibn Ezra writes:

> *The Joy of the Moon is in the third house, for her nature signifies short journeys and talk and common intelligence.*

Interestingly, in writing about the joy of the Moon in the third house, Ibn Ezra has this to say about the Moon and her relationship to the ninth house:

> *The Ninth house is the Gloom of The Moon because it is the seventh from her house of joy.*

475

He does not write about this "house of Gloom" in relation to other planets and the opposite houses from their terrestrial joys. This may be because of the relationship the luminaries have to each other. If we place the Sun in the ninth house, his terrestrial house of joy, then the Moon in the third house would be a Full Moon. Therefore, if she is in the ninth house with the Sun, she would be a dark New Moon, making the ninth house the house of her "gloom."

In the human body, the third house corresponds with the shoulders, arms, hands, and fingers.

The third house has a sextile relationship to the Ascendant and is, therefore, seen as being a benefic house.

CORE SIGNIFICATIONS OF THE THIRD HOUSE:

Siblings, our local community, early childhood education, writing (as opposed to publishing), short journeys.

FOURTH HOUSE – IMUM COELI (LOWER HEAVENS)

> *The fourth house is called the Under-earth angle and the time of old age. It signifies the topic of parents and property and hidden matters and the house in which one is born and foundations and the things happening after death.* – RHETORIUS THE EGYPTIAN

The fourth house represents our physical home – the house into which we were born, the stake that we hold in the Earth, and the immoveable plot of land that we own. It symbolizes property, real estate, farm land, and orchards. Paulus Alexandrinus called it "the cave of the planets." Anything that is in the fourth house is completely invisible to us. As the pillar upon which the entire chart stands, it signifies where we come from, our strongest root, our heritage, ancestry, and family.

This subterranean house is the weakest of the four angular houses. However, what it lacks in visibility it makes up for in impact. It reveals how our family environment has either nurtured or inhibited us in becoming well-adjusted human beings. If our fourth house renders us incapable of doing something, it requires an extraordinary amount of personal power to shift those circumstances. As the basement of the chart, the conditions we find in our fourth house tend to be fixed factors in our lives. A wound in the fourth house requires a long time to heal. However, only through healing the wounds of the fourth house can we live happily in the world.

The fourth house is a house of fixed assets and immoveable property. It is a house of buried treasures and of things that have been hidden or mislaid. Through its association with the depths of the Earth, it can represent a wide variety of subterranean things such as graves, basements, and cellars.

Though the fourth house generally represents the family, it specifically represents the father. The father was seen as being the guardian and the provider of the household. He was entrusted to create a stable environment in which other members of the family could flourish. Today, as in ancient times, the fourth house continues to represent the father, regardless of the assertions of modern astrology.

In the Chaldean Order, the fourth house is associated with the Sun. The Sun is the natural significator of the father. The fourth house represents both the father and things that come to us through our father's lineage. Ibn Ezra writes:

> ... and the Sun signifies the father, like the fourth house.

This is one of the primary reasons why, in traditional astrology, the fourth house corresponds specifically with the father and not the mother. Modern astrology, which asserts that the mother corresponds with the fourth house, comes with no comparable logical basis for that assertion.

In the human body, the fourth house represents the breasts, the chest, and the lungs.

The fourth house has a square relationship to the Ascendant, making it a powerful house within the horoscope.

### CORE SIGNIFICATIONS OF THE FOURTH HOUSE:

Father, family, real estate, farm land, immoveable assets, buried treasure. Some classical sources also associate the fourth house with imprisonment and death. However, I have never seen these more dire significations bear fruit in actual practice.

### FIFTH HOUSE (BONA FORTUNA OR GOOD FORTUNE)

> The fifth house from the ASC is called Good Fortune and Course. It is the house of Venus, for she rejoices there. – RHETORIUS THE EGYPTIAN

The fifth house is the house of children and pleasure. Medieval astrologers thought children represented the wealth of the father, in whom he found pleasure. Ibn Ezra writes:

> The fifth house is always in harmonious aspect with the first house and its element, and it signifies children, since there is no love for a man more complete than theirs. Not so the ninth [house] for it is cadent. Because food agrees with the nature of man this house was assigned to [signify] food and drink and pleasure.

As the second house from the fourth house, it represents the money of the father.

The fifth house is important to assess in matters of fertility and pregnancy. It can greatly assist in telling the story of a person's fertility potential.

As a house of children, it also represents all the things that give us the opportunity to feel childlike. It is a house of sports, games, entertainment, parties, theatres, clubs, and all the places in which we find pleasure. As a house of pleasure, it can also be the house where we overdo pleasure. This includes gambling and overindulgence. It is a house of eating and drinking. However, the second house is also a house of food. I believe the second house represents the food we consume for our survival. The fifth house, on the other hand, represents the joy of eating, overeating, and pleasuring ourselves through food.

As a house of pleasure, it has been referred to as the house of "love toys" in the Renaissance. While I would consider a "love toy" to be a second house moveable object, I am not convinced that I entirely know what a "love toy" would refer to in this context. I leave this task of discovery to you.

When I studied Jyotish, I was taught that the seventh house was the house of legally arranged marriages, whereas the fifth house was the house of love marriages. This distinction does not exist in traditional Western astrology. Our boyfriends and husbands are both found in our seventh house, as well as our sweethearts, and the people we have infrequent sexual relations with. German occultist and physician Henry Cornelius Agrippa (1486-1585) in his *Fourth Book of Occult Philosophy*, wrote:

> *The seventh house signifies wedlock, whoredom, and fornication...*

As we can see, the seventh house covers the entire spectrum of intimate connection. Any carnal adventure we can have with another person falls under the dominion of the seventh house in Western astrology. While the fifth house may tell us whether or not the native views romance as a source of pleasure, it is not a house that has a bearing on our romantic life in general. Strictly speaking, our children are the only people our fifth house consistently represents.

Traditionally, the fifth house also represents ambassadors, agents, and people who serve as intermediaries with other parties on our behalf. The fifth house signifies people who represent our personal affairs in the world and help us maintain a good reputation.

The fifth house corresponds with Venus in the Chaldean Order. It is also her terrestrial house of joy. Venus represents the abundance, mirth, merriment, and joyful exchanges that are signified by the fifth house. Ibn Ezra writes:

> *Venus signifies pleasure for she is like the fifth house... The Joy of Venus is in the fifth house because the nature of Venus is rejoicing and pleasure.*

Venus represents the pleasure derived from engaging with the public, entertainment, and the great fortune of having a comfortable life.

The fifth house signifies the heart within the human body.

The fifth house has a trine relationship to the Ascendant. Therefore, it is a benefic house.

### Core Significations of the Fifth House:

Children, pleasure, games, gambling, ambassadors, clubs, bars, restaurants, parties, banquets, eating, and drinking for pleasure.

## Sixth House (Mala Fortuna or Bad Fortune)

> *The sixth house is called evil, cadent, and "pre-DSC," and "first to fall,"*
> *and metacosmic and Bad Fortune. It has signification of injuries and*
> *slaves and enemies and quadrupeds, sometimes also of actions because*
> *it is in right trine to the MC, but it is also the house of the feet and of*
> *sickness involving the feet.* – RHETORIUS THE EGYPTIAN

The sixth house traditionally is the house of sickness and slavery. Whereas the first house symbolizes health, the sixth house signifies anything harmful to health in the form of illness and disease. It is called the "Mala Fortuna" or "Bad Fortune." For the ancients, fortune was not just the state of our material wealth. Fortune represented all the conditions necessary for us to live happily. Illness naturally corresponded with evil fortune in the ancient mind.

Traditionally, the sixth house has nothing whatsoever to do with our career or vocation. In modern astrology, many astrologers try to distinguish between the tenth house representing our "career" and the sixth house representing our "job." Personally, this has always felt like a forced distinction between synonyms; one that proves to be woefully inadequate. When we find the ruler of the Ascendant or the ruler of the MC in the sixth house, it can represent engaging in work that is overly stressful and has no prestige. However, this is purely circumstantial. This is not because the sixth house itself represents our "job."

As far as work is concerned, if we do find the ruler of the Ascendant or the MC in the sixth house, it may represent an inclination towards medical or helping professions that involve working with the sick. This does not mean that the sixth house signifies the medical profession. Wherever we find the ruler of the Ascendant terrestrially placed within our charts, is a place that greatly interests us. Where we find the ruler of the natal MC, is an area that we may be drawn to vocationally. Therefore, having either of those factors in the sixth house can represent a highly stressful career that may or may not involve working with the sick.

Another modern astrology assumption about the sixth house is that it signifies our personal hygiene. It does not.

While we don't consider the sixth house to still represent "slavery" in the traditional sense, it does represent our hired employees. It has more to do with the people who work for us than it has to do with the type of work we do. It represents people who the ancients viewed as being of a lesser status in life. Traditionally, these people included tenants, employees, and slaves. Today, when people rent from us, they tend to do so as our equals and not as our inferiors. Therefore, the relationship between tenant and landlord is now more appropriately viewed as a first and seventh house topic, like all other transactional relationships. The sixth house is no longer relevant in that sort of query. Similarly, if we hire someone to engage in short-term contractual work, then that person is not technically our employee. That person is a partner helping us to facilitate a common vision. If on the other hand, that person is someone we pay a weekly salary to, and who we have more of a relationship with as a "boss," then that person is an employee and rightfully would be signified by the sixth house.

To frame the sixth house of "sickness and slaves" in a less diabolic light, I have chosen to call it the sixth house of "sickness and stress" when I work with clients. The sixth house is a house of anxiety, external pressure that becomes internal pressure, and overworking. It often shows how these factors have the effect of weakening the defenses of the body through too much work and too little recuperation.

Traditionally, the sixth house also signifies small animals such as pets. The standard that defined whether an animal was small or not was its relative size in relation to a goat. If an animal was smaller than a goat, it was considered small and, therefore, a sixth house creature. If it was larger than a goat, it was considered large and, therefore, a twelfth house creature. Small animals were assigned to the sixth because they could more easily be domesticated and made subordinate than beasts of burden could. People who live with many animals, large or small, can have a very emphasized sixth house within their charts.

In the Chaldean order, Mercury is the sixth planet from Saturn. Thus, Mercury has a natural relationship with the sixth house. Mercury was the messenger and the servant of the gods. His role corresponds with the notion of employees in general. Ibn Ezra writes:

> ...and Mercury signifies the slaves for he is like the sixth house.

The sixth house is the terrestrial house of joy of Mars. Mars represents things that poison or sting the body, weakening our physical health, in the same way that sickness diminishes our vital force. Mars is a spoiler of fortune and a danger to the physical body. Ibn Ezra writes:

> ...Mars rejoices in the sixth house, for it is the house of sickness and wounds, as is the nature of Mars.

In the human body, the sixth house represents the small and large intestines.

The sixth house is an evil house because of its quincunx to the Ascendant. Ibn Ezra writes:

> ... the sixth house does not connect with the first house and it is evil, for it is cadent and below the earth, it signifies diseases, for they are like secret enemies.

CORE SIGNIFICATIONS OF THE SIXTH HOUSE:

Sickness, employees, slavery, servitude, and pets; domestic or wild animals smaller than a goat.

## Seventh House – the Setting Degree

*The seventh house is called Descending Angle. It signifies old age and marriage, sometimes too the matter of inheritance and that of injury... And it makes travel abroad.* – RHETORIUS THE EGYPTIAN

The seventh house represents marriage and partnership. In every natal chart it represents the person who we are destined to marry, if we are destined to marry, and what the nature of that relationship will be like. It is an indication for how we interact with love and intimate partnerships in general. Who we date, who we are sexually intimate with, and all other romantic pursuits, are represented by the seventh house. It signifies all aspects of the spectrum of love and intimacy.

Ironically, it is also the house of war, contention, and open enemies. It represents our visible opponent or adversary in the world. It is the house of our legal rivals in court. Though highly uncomfortable, the people we may be in a legal battle with represent another type of intimate partnership. In the *Book of Reasons*, Ibn Ezra writes:

*Because the degrees of the seventh house are equal [to those of the first house] it indicates partners... It is also the house of quarrels and fighting, because of the nature of the opposition.*

In horary astrology more than natal astrology, the seventh house can indicate our business partners and people with whom we have contractual agreements. If a person isn't employed by anyone, but does freelance work, the seventh house will signify their clients. If a person is the employee of someone else, then their employer will be represented by the tenth house. The people whom we engage with in business transactions such as buying and selling will be represented by our seventh house. If we interact with someone who does not already have a designated house in the chart, that person, too, will be represented by our seventh house. For example, our siblings are represented by the third house. However, the stranger we met at the grocery store will be a seventh house character.

In questions of moving from one part of the world to the next, the seventh house represents the place to which we are relocating. Rhetorius states that the seventh house "makes travel abroad." The ninth house is the house of international travel, and more readily answers questions such as "Should I make this trip to Ecuador?". However, the seventh house is the house that we consider in all topics that have to do with relocation. Traditionally, relocation questions were collectively known as questions of "removal." In the seventeenth century, when a querent asked "shall I remove?" what they meant was whether or not they should relocate from one abode to another. If the first house is where we are, the seventh house is where we would like to live instead.

The Moon is the seventh planet in the Chaldean Order. Reflecting the larger patriarchal attitude of his time, Ibn Ezra writes:

*The Moon signifies women for she is like the seventh house.*

This implies that in a love question in which a man is the querent or the native, the seventh house would represent the woman he is asking about. More broadly, the seventh house refers to the people we traffic with in the world at large. The Moon is the universal significator for the voice of the people and the general public in mundane astrology. Therefore, she is naturally symbolic of our daily encounters.

In the human body, the seventh house represents the loins (lower back) and the reins (kidneys).

The seventh house has an oppositional aspect with the Ascendant. This gives the seventh house great power and visibility.

### Core Significations of the Seventh House:

Marriage, business partners, open enemies in a legal battle, people hired to do a short-term contract-based project who are not actually our employees; tenants, transactional relationships. Where we would like to relocate in all questions of removal.

### Eighth House – Idle Place or Epicataphora

### (Entrance into the Gates of Hades)

> *The eighth house is called idle and Epicataphora of the ASC and epikatadysis and dimming. It is the sign that is turned away from the ASC; because of this, and because of its meaning of death, it signifies the turning away of life.* – RHETORIUS THE EGYPTIAN

The eighth house is the house of death and debt. It is considered to be one of the darkest and most abject houses of heaven because of its lack of relationship to the Ascendant. It is a house of decay, misery, and misfortune. The planet that rules the eighth house is called the "Anareta." Anareta comes from the ancient Greek word meaning "destroyer." The planet ruling the eighth house is, therefore, entrusted with the promise of death within the natal chart.

As the first of the two Gates of Hades, it represents the descent into the underworld. The word "Epicataphora" means "to fall into hell." When in the eighth house, we are forced into a crucible of change that feels comparable to death, one that challenges our very right to exist. It is the "valley of the shadow of death" that we find in the book of *Psalms*.

While it is generally the house of "other people's money," it is more specifically the house of our spouse's money. In more traditional times, it represented the size of our spouse's dowry – the money and resources that our partner enters the marriage with from their family. It is also the house of debt and taxes.

It represents all the wealth the dead cannot take with them into the afterlife. It signifies inheritances, wills, and money from our ancestors. Paulus Alexandrinus writes:

> [The eighth house] signifies the completion of life. This place is established as dysfunctional, and when benefics happen to be upon this place, they make for profits from deaths; for they give inheritances...

On a psychological level, it is the house of fear. It indicates anxiety, nightmares, and anguish of the mind. Medieval astrologers considered it to be the house of poisoning, deception, and cunning. It is the house of accidents and unexpected misfortunes. It signifies occultation, or making things invisible.

In the Chaldean Order, Saturn corresponds with the eighth house. As a house of poison, restriction, fear, and the unknown that comes through the dying process, the eighth house bears a natural analogy with Saturn. Abraham Ibn Ezra writes:

> The eighth house returns to Saturn, which signifies death, just like the eighth house, and as he signifies the beginning, so does he signify the end of man['s life].

The same Saturn that gave us a human body in the first house, brings about the destruction of that body through the agency of time. Thus, Saturn is both a god of life and death.

In the human body, the eighth house represents the genitals and the anus as organs of excretion.

The eighth house has a quincunx relationship with the Ascendant. It does not receive any of the life-giving properties of the Ascendant. Therefore, it is a malefic house.

CORE SIGNIFICATIONS OF THE EIGHTH HOUSE:

Death, debt, the money of our partner or spouse. Poisoning, fear, anguish of the mind. Inheritances, gifts we receive from our ancestors, old and ruinous buildings or things.

NINTH HOUSE (DEOS – GOD)

> The ninth house is called God. It is the house of the Sun. it signifies all things concerning the gods and kings and foreigners and dreams and religious observance. It is the astronomical sign and the metacosmic. –
> RHETORIUS THE EGYPTIAN

The ninth house is the house of travel and religion. It represents all the life experiences that take us into parts unknown. It is the house of philosophy and higher education. It signifies any expansive learning we partake in that goes far beyond the familiarity of what we learn in our childhood and adolescence.

As the house of travel, it represents our interactions with the wider world beyond the immediate surroundings of our native environment. It signifies our foreign travels and the people we meet in far, distant places. According to Ibn Ezra:

*When the Sun is at the Midheaven and moves over to the west, it travels from [one] side [of the Midheaven] to [the other] side. Therefore, the ninth was assigned as the house of long journeys, for it is above the earth. The third house is for short journeys for it is weaker.*

The ninth house is a house of religion and spirituality. I have once heard a distinction made between Earth-based spirituality in the third house and organized patriarchal religion in the ninth house. While this may indeed be the case, many people who have spiritual practices that go beyond the sphere of orthodox religion also have heavily emphasized ninth houses. I think it's fair to say that both the third and the ninth house exist on the axis of religious and spiritual experience. The ninth house may represent more systemic approaches to religious and spiritual experience, since it is the house of "God." The third house may represent more natural, animistic forms of spirituality, since it is the house of "Goddess." However, this may ultimately be an arbitrary and unnecessary distinction.

The ninth house signifies astrologers, magicians, doctors, lawyers, writers, spiritual teachers, and educators in general. It is the house of the eternal student. The desire to attain knowledge purely for the sake of knowledge is a ninth house pursuit. Learning foreign languages to continue expanding our world is also a ninth house endeavor. It represents the ability to translate foreign information into more accessible language so that other people can benefit from our journeys into the unknown. Ibn Ezra writes:

*Because wisdom is like a journey of the soul in the quest for knowledge, the ninth [house] was made the house of great wisdom. It is also the house of dreams, because in a dream the soul travels to different places.*

The ninth house corresponds with dreams and dream interpretation, prophecy, divine wisdom, alchemy, and magic.

In the Chaldean Order, we return to Jupiter. The ninth house represents philosophy, learning, and being able to see our lives from a broadened spiritual perspective. These are under the dominion of Jupiter. According to Ibn Ezra:

*Jupiter indicates science and arts, like the ninth house.*

The ninth house is the terrestrial house of joy of the Sun. Though the Sun may reach his highest elevation at the Midheaven, he settles into the fullness of his power when he enters the ninth house. Ibn Ezra writes:

*The house of Joy for the Sun is in the ninth [house], for he signifies art, learning and wisdom and so does the ninth.*

The Sun has a relationship with divination, prophecy, and things of the spirit, all of which have a natural analogy with the ninth house.

In the human body, the ninth house represents the hips and thighs, parts of the body that govern how we mobilize ourselves in the world.

The ninth house has a trine relationship to the Ascendant. Therefore, it is one of the benefic houses. Paulus Alexandrinus called it the "Good Decline." As a cadent house, it represents lethargy and lack of visibility. However, as a house above the horizon that trines the Ascendant, it is a positive house nonetheless.

CORE SIGNIFICATIONS OF THE NINTH HOUSE:

Travel, higher education, religion, spirituality, highly intelligent people. The ninth house also signifies astrology, divination, magic, dream interpretation, alchemy, and one's proficiency in these arts.

TENTH HOUSE – MEDIUM COELI OR MIDHEAVEN (THE CULMINATING DEGREE)

> *The tenth house is called angle, midheaven, and quadrant of the ASC. It signifies youth and action and marriage and children and the substance of the parents. In this house the rulers of the sect rejoice, and they give actions that are good and useful.* – RHETORIUS THE EGYPTIAN

The tenth house is the house of the mother and career.

As a house of career, it represents how we are known in the world and where we find our greatest, most visible success. It represents our "magistry," or the things that we do masterfully. It is both our profession and who we are called to become in order to fulfill our destiny. The tenth house signifies our material purpose, and what we will be known for when we leave this world. It is the power of our presence and the lastingness of our name. Ibn Ezra writes:

> *The tenth house is the most elevated in the wheel, and this is borne out by the Sun and all the planets when positioned in this place. It is said to be the house of kingdom and honor, and also man's trade, which is like his kingship.*

For those of us under the employ of another, it represents our boss, the CEO, or the head of any organization of which we are a part.

The fourth house represents the father, and the tenth house represents the mother. The archetypal father figure gives us the stability we need in order to understand our role in society and our physical responsibilities to the world. However, the archetypal mother figure gives us the internal, non-tangible support necessary for us to flourish within this lifetime. Of the relationship that the parents have to the MC/IC axis, Ibn Ezra writes:

> *We know that the motion of the Midheaven at all locations is in the way of the superior wheel that moves everything equally. The lower pole has the same degree, and it is as if they both generated the Ascendant and the Descendant; therefore, they signify the parents that beget the child.*

In Uranian astrology, the Midheaven is associated with the "moment." Whereas the Ascendant relates to the location where we were born, the Midheaven relates to when we were born. Through our Midheaven we all ask the question: in this continuous and unending river of time, when did my specific being become crystalized? For this reason, it is considered to be the most personal point within the entire horoscope within that system of astrology. Aspects to the Midheaven directly speak to who we are within ourselves and within the world. Whether a planet is conjunct the MC or simply the highest elevated planet in our chart, it has the tendency of spreading its influence over the affairs of the entire horoscope. This gives the life of the person a distinct flavor and tone that conforms to the nature of that planet. Naturally, these attributes also become potent indicators of the career path we will take in life. Very often, we strive to become more of what we already feel we are deep within ourselves.

In the Chaldean Order, we return to Mars. Mars, representing power, self-confidence, and the desire for victory, is analogous to the tenth house as the place where we step boldly forward into life. Ibn Ezra writes:

> *Mars indicates domination like the tenth house.*

The tenth house represents the muscular effort we put behind our career as well as the sense of pride we feel when those efforts bring us public recognition.

In the human body, the tenth house corresponds with our knees. Our knees help us climb upward and onward towards the summit of success. They also allow us to kneel and find humility even amidst our victories.

The Midheaven has a square relationship to the Ascendant. The aspirations we hold within our tenth house represent powerful opportunities for us to grow into who we were destined to become.

CORE SIGNIFICATIONS OF THE TENTH HOUSE:

Mother, career, the boss or manager in an organization, the head of state, the ruler. Public recognition; our ability to gain fame and success within the world at large.

ELEVENTH HOUSE – THE GOOD DAEMON (GOOD SPIRIT)

> *The eleventh house is called Good Daemon and epanaphora of the MC. Consequently, the benefic stars chancing to be in this house in their own faces or domiciles or exaltation or terms signify great wealth and illustrious actions.* – RHETORIUS THE EGYPTIAN

The eleventh house is the house of the fulfillment of our desires. It signifies our hopes, wishes, and friends. Though an auspicious house, it tends to factor less frequently into an overall reading than other more prominent houses, such as the angles and the second house.

As the second house from the tenth house, it can represent the money we make from our career, and the earning potential we have within our chosen field. It is the money that our business makes; which may be quite different from the money represented by our second house. In asking the question "Will this business idea make money?" the eleventh house would be a significant house to assess.

The eleventh house also represents our mother's money since it is the second house from the tenth house of the mother. Often in judging a person's early family dynamic, the fifth house would represent the father's share of the family wealth, whereas the eleventh house would represent the wealth of the mother.

The eleventh house signifies the loyalty of our friends and the people we rely on. It represents support that we receive from others, and the quality of friends we consistently attract into our lives. The eleventh house can show whether we have many friends or few friends. It describes overall themes in terms of our ability to socially engage with others.

The eleventh house is called the Good Daemon or Good Spirit by the ancients. It is the house of our holy guardian angel in a sense; the higher self within us that seeks to guide our path towards truth and victory in this lifetime.

In the Chaldean Order, the eleventh house corresponds with the Sun. The Sun offers us guidance, light, and clarity as we chart a course towards our destiny. The support we find in the eleventh house is meant to provide us with the same. Ibn Ezra writes:

> *The Sun indicates grace, like the eleventh house...*

The eleventh house is the terrestrial house of joy of Jupiter. Just as Jupiter brings us abundance, blessings, and spiritual aid as we navigate the ocean of life, the eleventh house signifies how likely we are to be aided by others should we ever find ourselves in need of support. According to Ibn Ezra:

> *The Joy of Jupiter is in the eleventh house because he signifies gain, favor, wealth, and good fortune, and so does the eleventh house.*

In the human body the eleventh house represents the shins and the ankles.

The eleventh house has a sextile relationship to the Ascendant. However, it is more powerful than the sextile between the third house and the Ascendant. The eleventh house is above the horizon and succedent; whereas, the third house is below the horizon and cadent.

Core Significations of the Eleventh House:

Friends, the loyalty of our friends, the money we receive from our careers, the fulfilment of our desires, hopes, and wishes.

## TWELFTH HOUSE (THE EVIL DAEMON OR EVIL SPIRIT)

> *The twelfth house is called Bad Daemon and "rising before the ASC"
> and metacosmic. It signifies things that transpire before the hour of
> birth, both to the mother and to the one that is about to be born, since
> this sign rises before the expulsion of the fetus. And it is chosen as the
> house of Saturn, inasmuch as through the pouring out of the waters
> the fetus is expelled, and because the new-born is placed in the midst
> of life and death, being beheld by Saturn and Mars by opposition.* –
> RHETORIUS THE EGYPTIAN

The twelfth house is the house of self-undoing, hidden enemies, and silent suffering.

As a house of self-undoing, it represents the negative habit patterns that prevent us from living a life of complete happiness and joy. It can signify a feeling of being stuck, isolated, and unable to tap into the fullness of our personal power. At the same time, it can symbolize habit patterns of self-sabotage and negative reactivity.

The twelfth house signifies the consequences of unbridled craving and living purely on impulse. It represents getting stuck within a desire-based cycle of unconscious action to the point of forgetting that there are other options available. It is the place where the momentum of our earthly lives causes us to forget that we are also divine. It is where we lose sight of our ability to choose a higher path than the one that has been carved out for us by habit and impulse.

The twelfth house is where we find people who support us publicly, but rejoice at our suffering behind our backs. This is why the ancients also considered it to be a house of witchcraft. The witchcraft alluded to here isn't the same as the benevolent, earth-based spirituality that we find in the third house. Twelfth house witchcraft is the witchcraft of cursing, hexing, malicious gossiping, and intentionally doing evil things to others in secret. The ancients considered a person who poisoned a water supply to also be a twelfth house character. The twelfth house signifies people who secretly damage things that have to support the wellbeing of the community.

The twelfth house corresponds with imprisonment, agony, pain, fear, and the threat of death. It signifies places of involuntary confinement such as prisons or asylums. It is a house of sorrow and silent suffering.

In contrast to the sixth house, the twelfth house represents large animals. Large animals have been defined classically as beasts of burden, or animals larger than a goat. In Ibn Ezra's *Book of Reasons*, he writes:

> *Because the twelfth house is cadent and does not aspect the first, it is
> the house of enemies and disgrace, and because it is adjacent to the
> rising degree, it is the house of man's riding [animals].*

In the Chaldean Order, the twelfth house corresponds with Venus, but of a darker nature. Very often, the desires that take us down the paths of pleasure are the same desires that take us down the path of suffering. Venus can represent gluttony and overindulgence. What we consume too much of in our fifth house of pleasure can become an addiction that we hide in our twelfth house of self-undoing. Ibn Ezra writes:

> *Venus indicates quarrel and disgrace, for they are the end of all pleasure.*

The twelfth house is the terrestrial house of joy of Saturn. Saturn, like the twelfth house, also symbolizes beasts of burden. Saturn represents isolation, confinement, death, sorrow, and suffering. Resultantly, he revels heartily in the twelfth house. Ibn Ezra writes:

> *The Joy of Saturn is in the twelfth [house] because he signifies disgrace, discord, and prison, and so does the twelfth house.*

In the human body, the twelfth house corresponds with the feet. The feet are our daily beasts of burden that carry the full weight of our constitution.

The twelfth house is in aversion to the first house and is also cadent. It is one of the most malefic houses of heaven, rivalled only by the eighth house of death.

Core Significations of the Twelfth House:

Self-undoing, hidden enemies, large animals, gossip, slander; negative forms of witchcraft such as cursing, hexing, and wishing someone harm.

CHAPTER 21 QUESTIONS

1. Why is the Ascendant such an important house within traditional astrology?
2. Based on the Chaldean Order, what is one reason why the fourth house is considered to be the house of the father in traditional astrology?
3. Why is the sixth house considered to be the house of servants?
4. Based on the Chaldean Order, what does the first house of Life and the eighth house of Death have in common with each other?
5. Why is the ninth house considered to be the Gloom of the Moon?
6. In the Chaldean Order, the twelfth house is associated with Venus. However, it is the terrestrial joy of Saturn. What similarities do Venus and Saturn share that would make both of them be associated with one of the most evil houses of heaven?

CHAPTER 22 OBJECTIVES

* Differentiate between the terms "dignity" and "fortitude" in relation to planetary strength.
* Discuss the nuances that can occur when applying both essential dignity and debility, and accidental fortitude and debility to the planets.
* Provide a detailed treatment of the accidental fortitudes and debilities that were utilized in seventeenth century astrology.

# Chapter 22

## Accidental Fortitudes & Debilities

*Besides those things which are already spoken of, there happeneth*
*unto the Planets diverse accidents, as well [as] among themselves as*
*in themselves... –* CLAUDE DARIOT

Though the most important planetary strength comes from the planet's zodiacal placement, other environmental factors greatly impact how that planet will function within a chart. These include: the house placement of a planet, the aspects it receives from other planets, and whether that planet is direct or retrograde. Other important considerations are the speed of the planet, the relationship that planet has to the Sun, and its conjunction with surrounding fixed stars. These environmental influences are collectively known as the "accidental fortitudes" and "debilities" of the planets. They are integral in evaluating the condition of any planet within a chart. After judging the essential dignity or debility of a planet, the next assessment to make is of its accidental fortitudes or debilities.

### A Clarification of Concepts

Certain concepts often become conflated in astrology. An example of this is in the use of the words "dignity" and "fortitude." Strictly speaking, there is no such thing as an "accidental dignity." Dignity cannot be accidental. You're either the Queen of England or you are not. There is no proxy queenship that can be bestowed upon you that bears any value in the real world. A dignity is something that is intrinsic. It is not something that can happen to a planet because of house placement, aspect, or conjunction to a fixed star. Thus, we speak of a planet being "essentially dignified" when it has found itself within a degree of the zodiac where it has power. Essential dignity gives a planet health, vitality, and authority that radiates from within. There are essential dignities and accidental fortitudes. However, there are no "accidental dignities."

Accidental fortitudes are environmental factors that bolster a planet's ability to carry out its duties within a chart. The word "fortification" can be defined as "a defensive wall or other reinforcement built to strengthen a place against attack." Who a planet is internally can only be represented by its state of essential dignity or debility. Anything that externally supports a planet is an accidental fortitude.

Unlike the word "dignity" which only refers to the essential state of a planet, the word "debility" serves a dual purpose. There are both essential debilities and accidental debilities. A planet is essentially debilitated when it is in its detriment, fall, or peregrine. The essential debilities collectively serve as a mortal wound that prevents the planets from performing powerfully within a chart. An accidental debility is anything that environmentally weakens a planet. This includes combustion, location in a malefic house, retrogradation, being in hard aspect with malefic planets, and other considerations which we will explore in this chapter. Depending on the strength of an accidental debility, a planet can either be hindered minimally or greatly in delivering on a positive outcome within a chart.

A planet that is strongly essentially dignified, but severely accidentally debilitated is a planet that has a great deal of internal power. However, due to its accidental debility, it is hindered and blocked in expressing that power externally. Traditional astrology is a pragmatic practice. It doesn't matter how strong a planet is on the inside if it cannot utilize that power to perform its duties within the larger ecosystem of the chart.

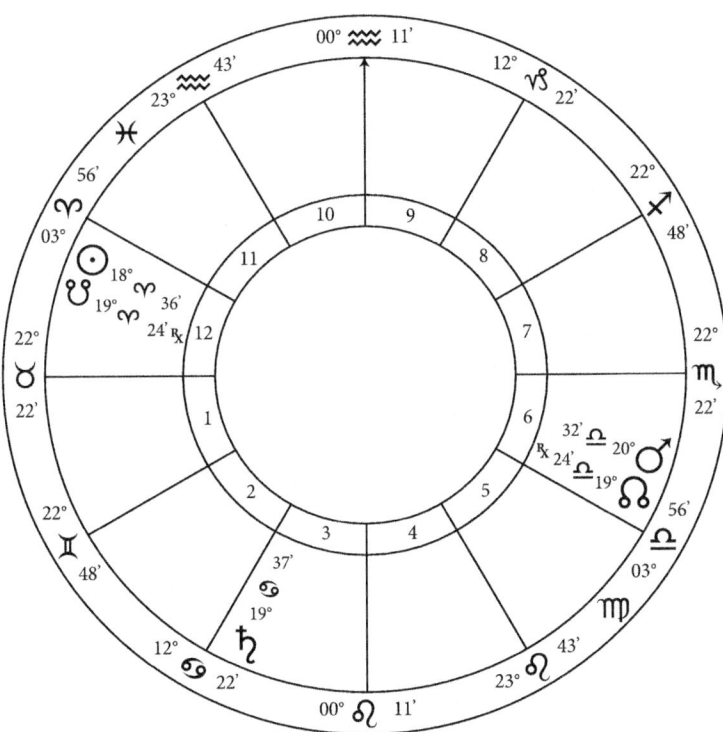

FIGURE 1: *Sun Essentially Dignified, but Accidentally Weak*

The Sun at 18° ARI 36' in the cadent and malefic twelfth house, is a Sun that has no ability whatsoever to express its strength or power regarding the things it signifies in the chart. This would be worsened if that Sun were also conjunct the South Node, squaring Saturn, and applying to the opposition of Mars. The accidental debilities of a planet can be significant to the point of preventing the essential power of that planet from being expressed at all.

A planet that is badly essentially debilitated, but strongly accidentally fortified is one that may be supported by enough environmental compensating factors to make up for its essential deficits.

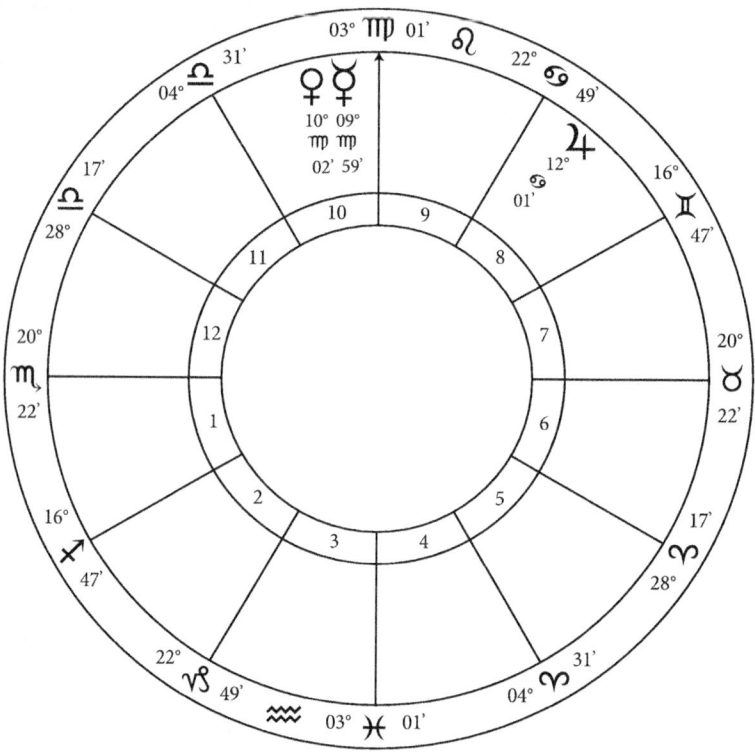

FIGURE 2: *Venus Essentially Debilitated, but Accidentally Strong*

If Venus were at 10° VIR 02' in the angular tenth house, the angularity of the MC would greatly support Venus in functioning within the chart. She would be able to carry out her duties with some modicum of strength. She would further be supported if she were applying to Jupiter at 12° CAN 01' and if her dispositor – Mercury – were also in Virgo and applying to her from 09° VIR 59'. Here, Venus would be supported by being in a sextile relationship with essentially dignified and benefic Jupiter, as well as being received by her dispositor, which, as we recall, is a form of essential dignity. Though nothing may change the fact that Venus is in the sign of her fall, by her surrounding fortitudes of forming a positive aspect with a benefic and being in an angular house, Venus will find the support she needs to do her duties well. Her being received by her dispositor would amplify this tremendously.

Accidental fortification may bolster the benevolence or visibility of a planet. If an extremely essentially debilitated planet is bolstered in terms of visibility, but not in terms of benevolence, that planet will use that visibility to produce damage within the life of the native. Mars at 28° CAN 52', RX., in the angular tenth house will likely inflict havoc on the native in their career.

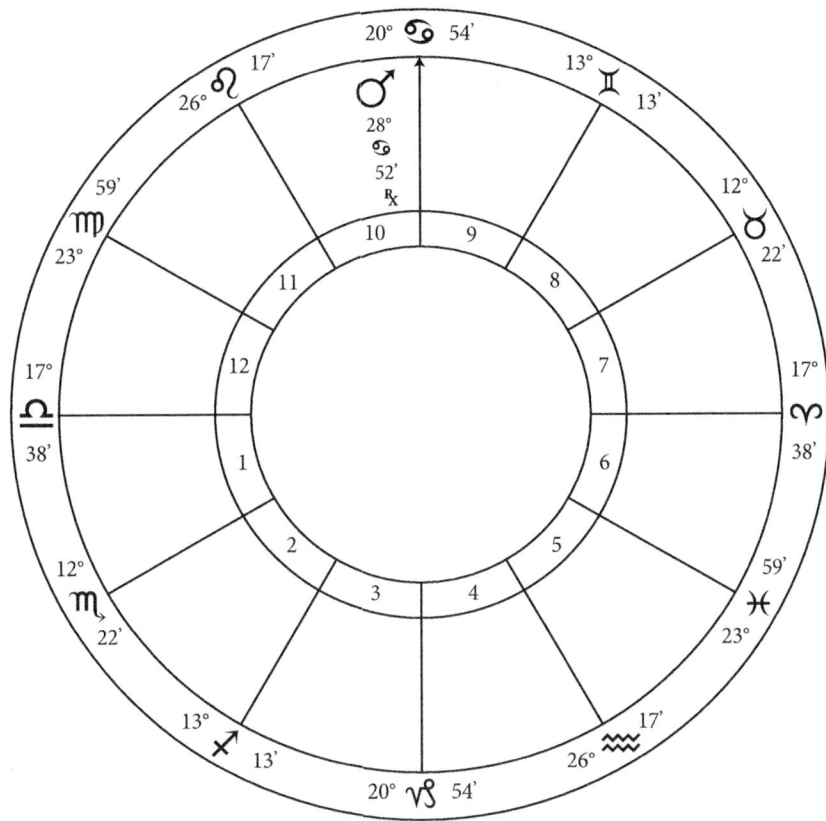

FIGURE 3: *Mars Essentially Debilitated, but Accidentally Strong*

If a planet is essentially debilitated, and yet accidentally fortified in a benevolent and highly visible way, that planet will deliver on some version of its promise, even if it struggles in the process. Planets frequently fall somewhere in the middle of this spectrum of strength and debility. Deciphering the multiple ways a planet may be dignified, fortified, and debilitated requires a nuanced understanding of traditional astrology.

Remember: there is no such thing as an "accidental dignity" or an "essential fortitude." A dignity cannot be accidental. If you are the Queen of England, you are the Queen because that dignity is imprinted within your essence. If you are the

Queen of England in the slums of New York City, your environment may accidentally debilitate you, but you are still essentially dignified. If you are the Queen of England in Buckingham Palace, then you are both essentially dignified as well as accidentally fortified. Your external environment will then support your visibility and your ability to express your essential dignity in the world.

The complexities of this doctrine are vast. Planets aren't just kings or queens in the slums or in their palaces. A planet can be the Queen of England in Buckingham Palace – altogether happy, though missing a leg; or it can be a beggar in the palace, but locked in the basement without hopes of liberty. The combination of essential dignities and debilities and accidental fortitudes and debilities are meant to clarify our understanding of who a planet is and how it will function.

Below is the list of accidental fortitudes and debilities that was most common in the seventeenth century. The following table was taken from John Gadbury's *Doctrine of Nativities and Horary Questions* (1658). I have provided definitions of each fortitude and debility based on my practice and research. It is my hope that after reading this chapter you will have a depth of understanding of not just what rules to apply within your chart delineation, but also why to apply them.

TABLE 1: *Accidental Fortitudes*

| | |
|---|---|
| IN MC OR ASC | +5 |
| IN 7ᵀᴴ, 4ᵀᴴ, & 11ᵀᴴ | +4 |
| IN 2ᴺᴰ & 5ᵀᴴ | +3 |
| IN 9ᵀᴴ | +2 |
| IN 3ᴿᴰ | +1 |
| DIRECT | +4 |
| SWIFT IN MOTION | +2 |
| ♄ ♃ OR ♂ ORIENTAL | +2 |
| ☿ OR ♀ OCCIDENTAL | +2 |
| ☽ INCREASING LIGHT | +2 |
| NOT COMBUST | +5 |
| CAZIMI | +5 |
| PARTILE CONJ WITH ♃ & ♀ | +5 |
| PARTILE CONJ WITH ☊ | +4 |
| PARTILE TRINE TO ♃ & ♀ | +4 |
| WITH REGULUS OR SPICA | +5 |

## ACCIDENTAL FORTITUDES

### IN THE MC OR ASCENDANT (+5)

The angles are the most powerful houses in traditional astrology. However, the MC and the Ascendant are the strongest angles. The Ascendant is the source of the power in the Ascendant/Descendant axis. The MC is the source of the power in the Medium Coeli/Imum Coeli axis. When a planet is in the MC or the Ascendant, it is considered to have an extraordinary amount of strength to influence the overall landscape of the chart.

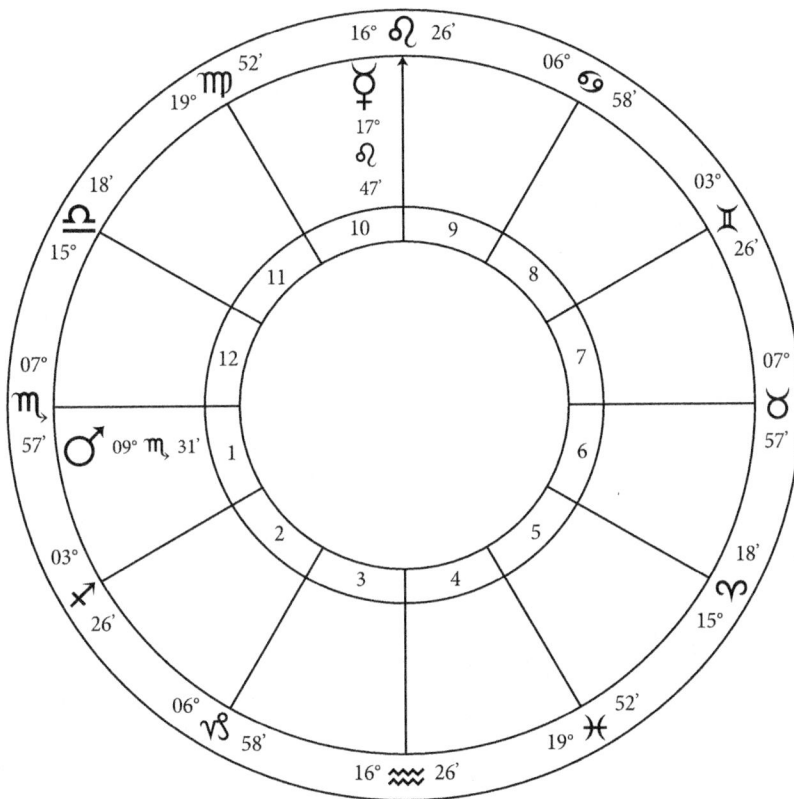

FIGURE 4: *Planets in the MC & the ASC*

Within traditional astrology, there has always been some debate as to which of these angles, the ASC or the MC, is the strongest. As we have previously learnt, in the diurnal cycle of the Sun, the ASC is where the Sun is born, whereas the MC is where the Sun attains his maximum power. It is for this reason why these two houses have always been considered near equals in the allocation of accidental fortitudes. Regarding the Ascendant, Ibn Ezra writes:

*A planet in the rising sign is like the newborn that has come out of its mother's womb or the matter of the moment.*

However, of the Midheaven, he writes:

*A planet in the tenth house is like a person in his authority, dignity, and profession.*

Thus, in questions pertaining to career or public recognition, the MC will be a stronger house for significators to inhabit. In all other questions that do not have to do with the career of the querent or native, the Ascendant should be viewed as stronger than the MC.

IN THE 7ᵀᴴ, 4ᵀᴴ, AND 11ᵀᴴ HOUSES (+4)

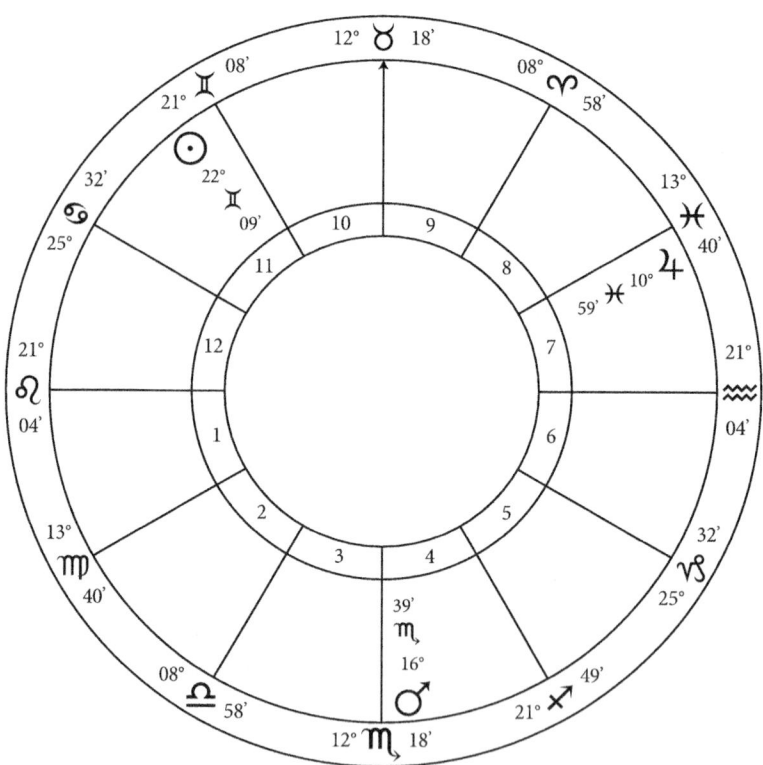

FIGURE 5: *Planets in the Seventh, Fourth, & Eleventh House*

When a planet is placed in any of the angles, it has 100% power to express itself. All angular houses give visibility or great power to the planets. The DSC and the IC are products of the ASC and the MC. Thus, they also share in the power of those primary angles. However, from the perspective of the Sun, his setting at the DSC and anti-culmination at the IC represent the weakest points in his diurnal journey. Planets located in either of these two houses have less power than if they were terrestrially located in the Ascendant or the Midheaven.

Based on Gadbury's table, terrestrial placement in the eleventh house is equal in accidental power to terrestrial placement in the seventh and the fourth houses. I believe this is because the eleventh house is a succedent house above the horizon that positively aspects the Ascendant. By primary motion, the eleventh house is also in its ascent towards the MC, thus making it a powerful house. From the perspective of the daily journey of the Sun, houses above the horizon will always be more powerful than houses below the horizon. In traditional astrology, visibility equals power. Therefore, visibility – along with positively aspecting the Ascendant – is most important insofar as the houses are concerned.

IN THE 2^{ND} AND 5^{TH} (+3)

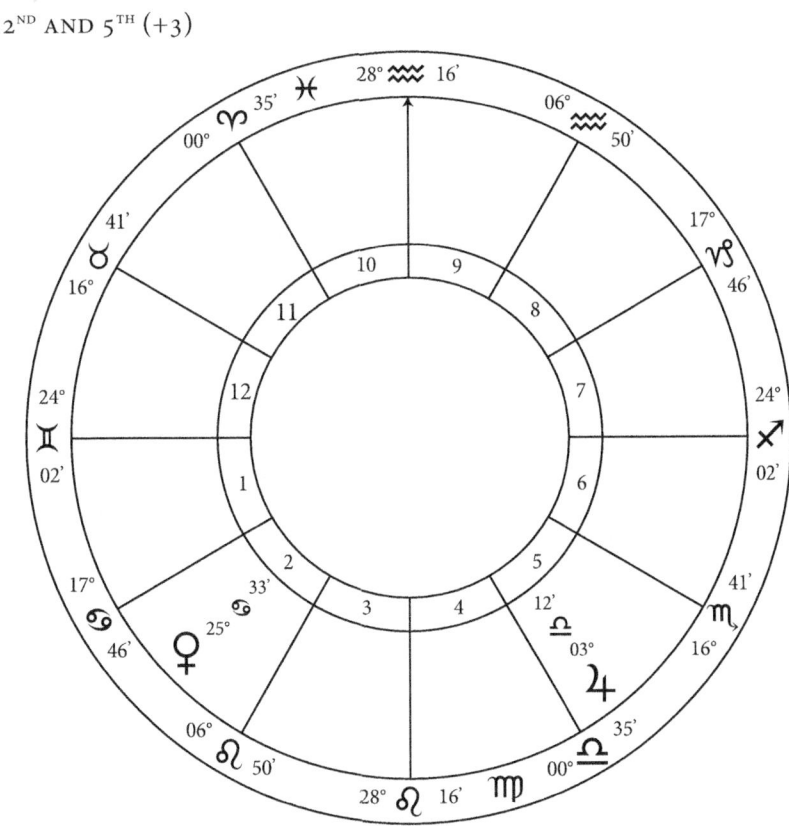

FIGURE 6: *Planets in the Second & the Fifth House*

Though it is directly adjacent to the Ascendant, and therefore, in aversion to the Ascendant, the second house is still a fortunate house. This is because by diurnal motion, anything within the second house has the promise of ultimately rising at the Ascendant. This makes it a positive house of hope and assurance. It is also a house of food and money, serving as a crucial support for the native within this lifetime. In *The Beginning of Wisdom*, we read:

> *A planet in the second house is like a person in the house of his assistants.*

The location of a planet in the fifth house is benefic because the fifth house has a symbolic trine relationship to the Ascendant. I say "symbolic" because, depending on which house system we use, this may or may not be the case. However, in every house system the fifth house carries its positive interpretations of symbolizing children and pleasure. Ibn Ezra writes:

> *A planet in the fifth house is like a person in his business and his pleasure.*

These interpretations are based on this symbolic, idealized trine relationship between the fifth house and the Ascendant. The trine is an aspect of perfect love and friendship. Therefore, even though the fifth house is below the horizon and not an angular house, it is still a blessing for a planet to be located there.

IN THE 9ᵀᴴ (+2 POINTS)

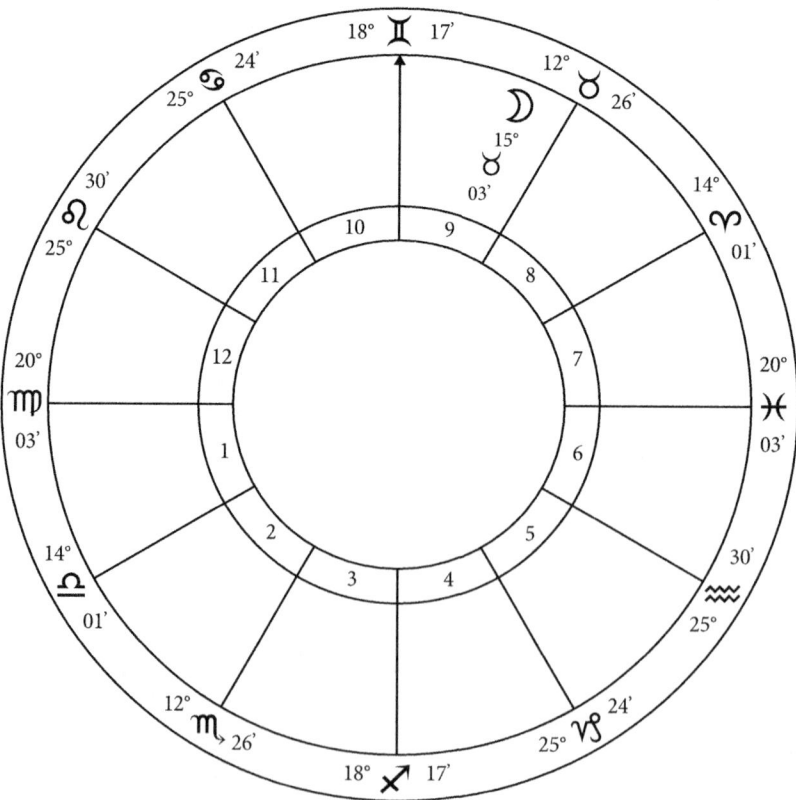

FIGURE 7: *Planet in the Ninth House*

Though the ninth house is cadent, it has a trine relationship to the Ascendant. Since the trine is a benefic aspect of perfect love and friendship, the cadent ninth house is a benefic house. However, I do believe this concept needs to be refined.

Firstly, I feel the degree-to-degree relationship between a ninth house planet and the Ascendant has to be noted. In horary astrology, if the ruler of the Ascendant is in the ninth house and in a square relationship to the Ascendant, this can often represent a person who is embattled within themselves about a decision they are making. Though placement in the ninth house in this context may be circumstantially good for the planet, it may not necessarily be good for the querent.

Secondly, I believe that a planet in the ninth house can only be given accidental strength for being there if that planet is first strongly essentially dignified. The ninth house is essentially weak because it is cadent. It is accidentally strong because it trines the Ascendant. Much of our astrology is built on analogies. A weak planet in the essentially weak ninth house only magnifies the weakness of that house. Therefore, I would consider a planet that is in its detriment, fall, peregrine, retrograde, or combust in the ninth house to be accidentally debilitated through its ninth house placement.

Conversely, if that planet is in radiant health due to it being in its domicile or exaltation, then I would consider that planet to be accidentally fortified through its ninth house placement. Regardless of the aspect that planet makes to the Ascendant, an essentially dignified planet in the ninth house is a powerful planet within the chart.

I believe it will always be wiser to assess the essential condition of a planet first before ascribing strength to it because of arbitrary rules. These classical instructions serve as a guideline. However, they do not represent the applied practice of concrete astrology.

IN THE THIRD (+1)

A planet in the third house has the lowest number of accidental fortitudes based on house placement. This is because the third house is a cadent house below the horizon. Its beneficence comes from the sextile aspect it makes to the Ascendant. Since it positively aspects the Ascendant, it is a benefic house. However, it is weak in every other regard.

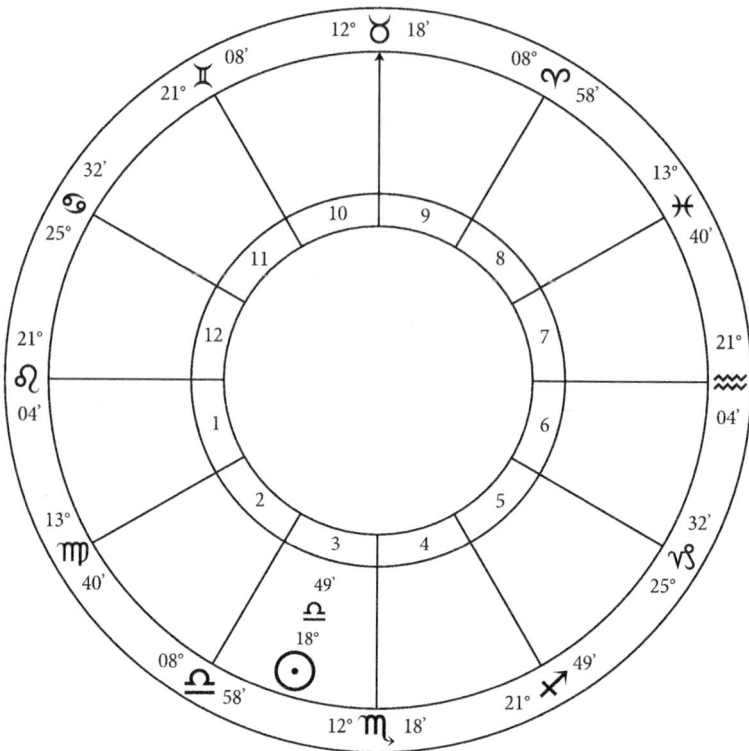

FIGURE 8: *Planet in the Third House*

My thoughts about planets in the cadent ninth house also apply to planets in the cadent third house. If a planet is essentially weak, its placement in the third house is not a fortitude. Astrology is a system based on the analogies that exist between things. Weak planets further highlight the weakness of cadent houses. Strong planets have their strength bolstered by the third and ninth houses because those houses positively aspect the Ascendant, despite their cadency. A weak planet cannot bring out the strength of a cadent house, even if that house positively aspects the Ascendant. A strong planet will not be subdued by the cadency of a house if that house positively aspects the Ascendant.

DIRECT IN MOTION (+4)

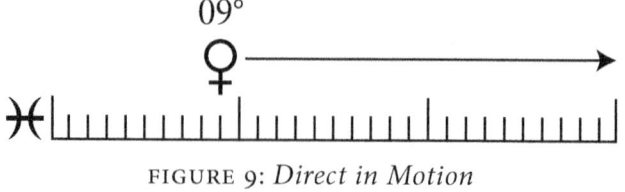

FIGURE 9: *Direct in Motion*

Planets are strong when they are direct. However, giving planets points of accidental fortitude just for being direct has always seemed a bit absurd to me. This means that a planet is accidentally fortified just for being who it naturally is. This makes no sense. Being "normal" is far less noteworthy than being peculiar. The peculiarities of the planets are most notable when attributing points of accidental strength or weakness. However, if you desire to practice astrology fully within a classical framework, then +4 points of accidental fortitude should be given to all Ptolemaic planets when they are direct – bearing in mind that the Sun and the Moon are never retrograde.

## SWIFT IN MOTION (+2)

When a planet is swift in motion, it indicates that the planet is eager to deliver on the promise with which it has been entrusted. Ibn Ezra writes:

*A planet swift in its motion is like a young man running.*

A swift planet is one that is moving at a rate that exceeds its average daily motion. The approximate daily motion of each planet is:

TABLE 2: *Average Daily Speed of the Planets*

| | |
|---|---|
| ☉ | 00° 59' 08" |
| ☽ | 13° 10' 35" |
| ☿ | 01° 23' 00" |
| ♀ | 01° 12' 00" |
| ♂ | 00° 31' 27" |
| ♃ | 00° 04' 59" |
| ♄ | 00° 02' 01" |
| ♅ | 00° 00' 42" |
| ♆ | 00° 00' 24" |
| ♇ | 00° 00' 15" |

Even within our neo-classical astrology, it goes without saying that this traditional consideration regarding the speed of the planets does not apply to Uranus, Neptune, or Pluto. In general, the majority of our classical astrological rules concerning planetary strength and weakness do not apply to the modern planets.

## SATURN, JUPITER, OR MARS ORIENTAL (+2)

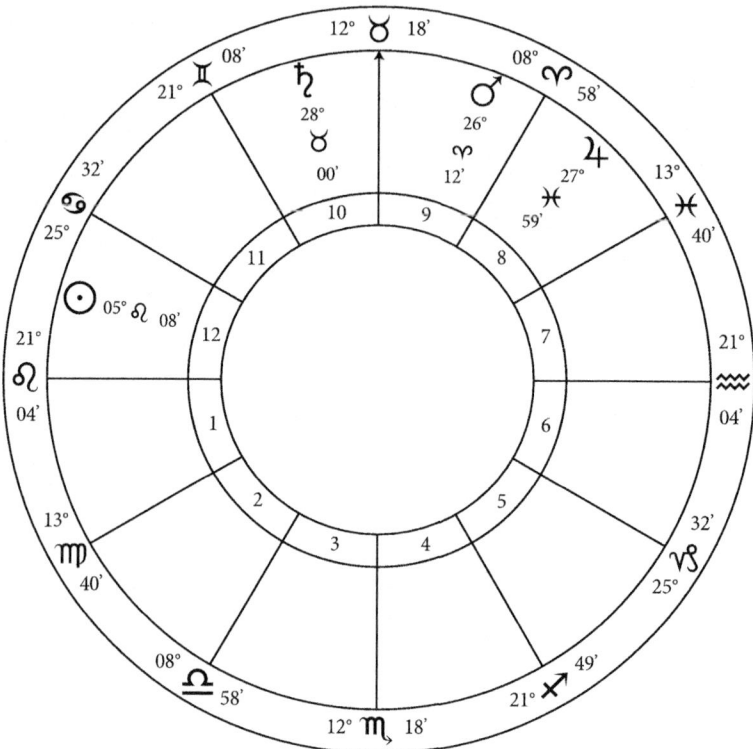

FIGURE 10: *Saturn, Jupiter, & Mars Oriental*

Saturn, Jupiter, and Mars are the superior planets within traditional astrology. This is because in the Chaldean Order, their orbital spheres are above the sphere of the Sun. Therefore, the ancients considered these planets to function better when they were oriental to (or in front of) the Sun. This is why Saturn, Jupiter, and Mars are given points of accidental fortitude when any of them are oriental. Ibn Ezra writes:

> When a malefic is oriental of the Sun, in its power, in a sign where it has dominion, and not aspected by another malefic, it is better than a benefic planet that is combust or retrograde.

If in a chart, Saturn, Jupiter, or Mars rises before the Sun, they are oriental. They would be stronger than if they were to rise occidentally, or after the Sun. This has never been an important consideration in my practice.

## MERCURY OR VENUS OCCIDENTAL (+2)

Mercury, Venus, and the Moon are the inferior planets within traditional astrology. This is because in the Chaldean Order, their orbital spheres are below the sphere of the Sun. Therefore, the ancients considered these planets to function better when they were occidental to (or behind) the Sun. Their natural disposition is to follow the Sun, whereas the natural disposition of Saturn, Jupiter, and Mars is to lead. Thus, Venus and Mercury are stronger if they rise after the Sun in the morning. This is not a major consideration within my client work.

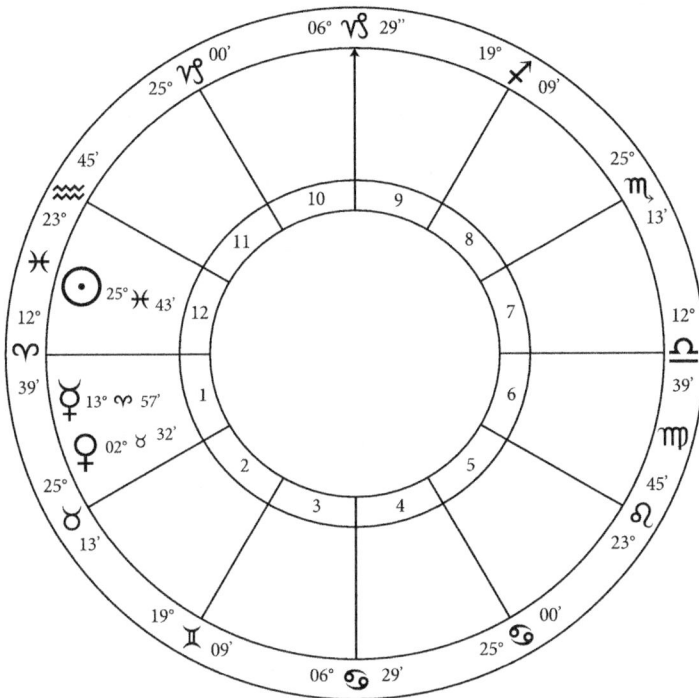

FIGURE 11: *Mercury & Venus Occidental*

## MOON INCREASING IN LIGHT (+2)

Traditionally, the Moon is considered more benefic and life-giving when increasing in light, than when she is decreasing in light. Some would even consider her to be a functional benefic when she is waxing, and a functional malefic when she is waning. The New Moon in particular is considered to be malefic. This is because the New Moon is a combust Moon – conjunct the Sun and, therefore, destroyed in her significations. Under that condition, she will not be able to deliver on whatever promise she has been entrusted with within the chart. According to Ibn Ezra, combustion is one of the worst things that can happen to a planet. English astrologer, botanist, herbalist, and physician Nicholas Culpeper (1616-1654) in *Opus Astrologicum, or An Astrological Work Left to Posterity* (1654), writes:

> *There is no greater affliction to the Moon as her combustion [New Moon].*

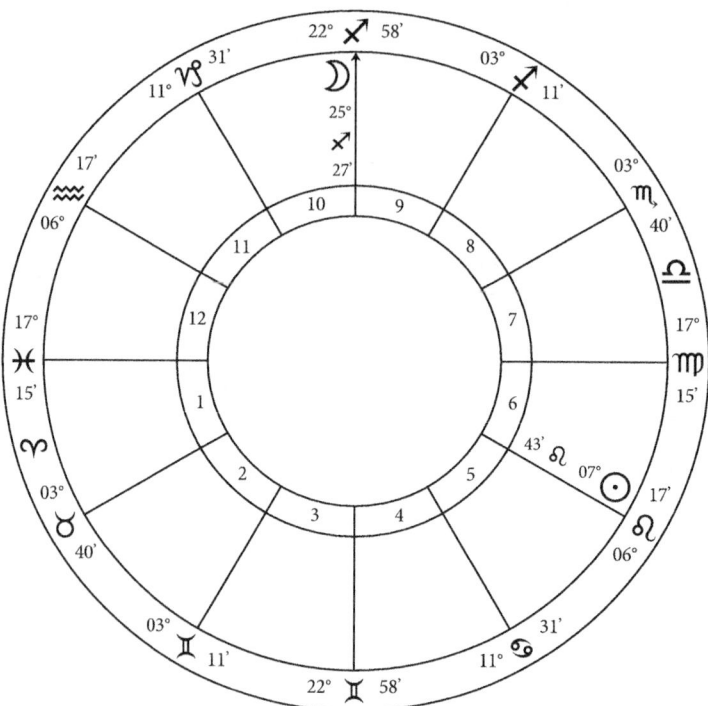

FIGURE 12: *Moon Increasing in Light*

William Lilly writes:

> *In all Questions, know there's not so great an affliction to the Moon as when she is in Conjunction with the Sun; the ill aspect of the infortunes [the malefics] doth afflict her, but none so powerful as her combustion.*

We will learn more about combustion in the following section.

Traditional astrologers tend to be on the fence about the benevolence or malevolence of the Full Moon. While some view the Full Moon as a positive omen, some astrologers view her opposition to the Sun to be a most malefic condition. Culpeper held that any significator in opposition to the Sun would be harmful to the things it signified. He writes:

> *When a planet promising any good in a Question is either in combustion with or opposition to the Sun, he never bringeth the good to pass.*

I believe the waxing Moon indicates a universally benefic period. I place a stronger emphasis on the phases of the Moon within my electional astrology work, than in horary or natal astrology.

NOT COMBUST (+5)

To be combust is to be burnt up by the rays of the Sun. This happens when a planet is within 00° 17' to 08° 30' of a conjunction with the Sun. The planet that falls within this range is destroyed, annihilated, and unable to perform any of its functions. Bethem, in his *Centiloquium*, tells us that a combust planet:

> *...is like a man in prison without hopes of liberty.*

Abraham Ibn Ezra tells us that combustion is one of the three worst things that can happen to a planet – the other two being retrogradation and cadency.

I find it unnecessary for a planet to be awarded points for not being combust. The peculiarity of a planet – the degree with which it deviates from nature – is what makes it noteworthy. A planet receiving five points for being in its normal state is unwarranted.

IN CAZIMI (+5)

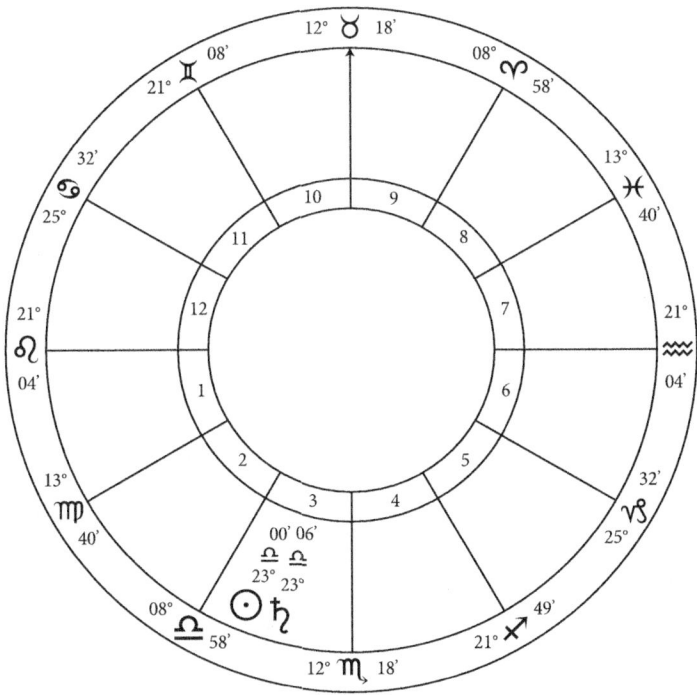

FIGURE 13: *Cazimi*

When a planet is in a corporal conjunction with the Sun it has one of three possibilities: it can be combust, under the beams, or cazimi. Combustion is when a planet is within 00° 17' to 08° 30' of a conjunction with the Sun. A planet is under the beams when it is within 08° 30' to 17° 00' of the Sun. This is considered to be a planetary affliction, which we will discuss later within this chapter. Cazimi is when a planet is between 00° 00' to 00° 17' of a conjunction with the Sun. This means that combustion technically starts when a planet is within 00° 17' 01" of the Sun.

To be in cazimi is one of the greatest things that can occur to a planet. That planet is in the "heart of the Sun." It is protected by the benevolence of the king. In *The Beginning of Wisdom*, Ibn Ezra writes:

> *A planet joined with the Sun is like a person sitting with the king in one chair.*

Within the heart of the Sun, much like in the eye of a storm, there is a lacuna of peace and serenity where the more harmful influences of the Sun are not felt. Culpeper writes:

> *A Planet within sixteen minutes of the Sun is in Cazimi, and exceedingly strong.*

While classically, we don't find much reference to different categories of cazimi, I'm sure that a planet that is in cazimi when the Sun is in domicile or exaltation is much different than when the Sun is in detriment or fall. Similarly, one would imagine that a planet in cazimi in its own domicile or exaltation would be different than if that planet were in cazimi while in detriment, fall, or peregrine.

IN PARTILE CONJUNCTION WITH JUPITER AND VENUS (+5)

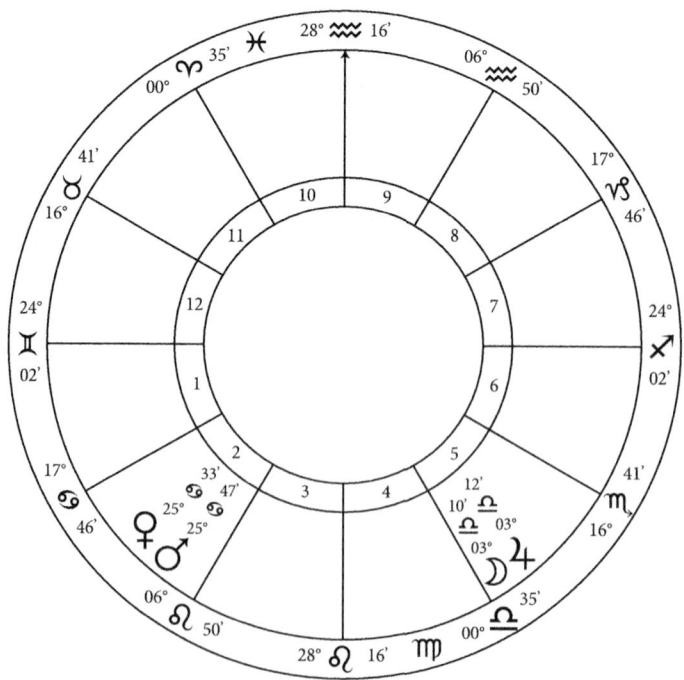

FIGURE 14: *Venus Conjunct Mars, Moon Conjunct Jupiter*

Jupiter and Venus are supporters of life in general. They specifically support the agenda of whichever planet with whom they may be corporally conjoined.

I believe this should be refined. If a planet has a partile conjunction to Jupiter in Sagittarius, Pisces, or Cancer, this would be a powerfully supportive connection for that planet. The same would be true for a planet in a corporal conjunction with Venus while she is in Taurus, Libra, or Pisces. However, if either Jupiter or Venus were essentially debilitated, retrograde, combust, or afflicted by hard aspects from the malefics, this would harm the benefics and weaken their ability to do good. Ibn Ezra writes:

> When the benefics are [in a place] opposite to their nature, or in their houses of detriment, or in their houses of fall, or in cadent houses that have no aspect between them and the rising sign, then they do not bring benefit at all.

While Jupiter does seem to have the quality of trying to be a benefic at all times, a planet conjunct a severely weakened Jupiter may only be supported minimally by Jupiter's natural loving-kindness. Instead of supporting others around him, Jupiter – like all weakened planets – will be focused more on sustaining his own survival. Everything in nature is fundamentally driven by self-preservation. Jupiter and Venus are no exceptions.

This brings us to another important consideration. In classical astrology, planets have universal significations that will never change, and accidental significations based on the chart we find them in. Venus, for example, is the universal significator of love. If, however, she is the ruler of the twelfth house in a chart, she will be the specific significator of hidden enemies, self-undoing, and silent suffering. Jupiter is the universal significator for wealth and abundance. If, however, he is the ruler of the sixth house in a chart, he will be the specific significator of sickness and stress. This would make both Venus and Jupiter functional malefics. Though they are benefic by nature, their rulership over malefic houses charges them with the responsibility of carrying out a malefic function within the chart in question. Therefore, a conjunction to Jupiter or Venus may not be a good thing for a planet if the benefics are specifically determined to the production of evil in a chart.

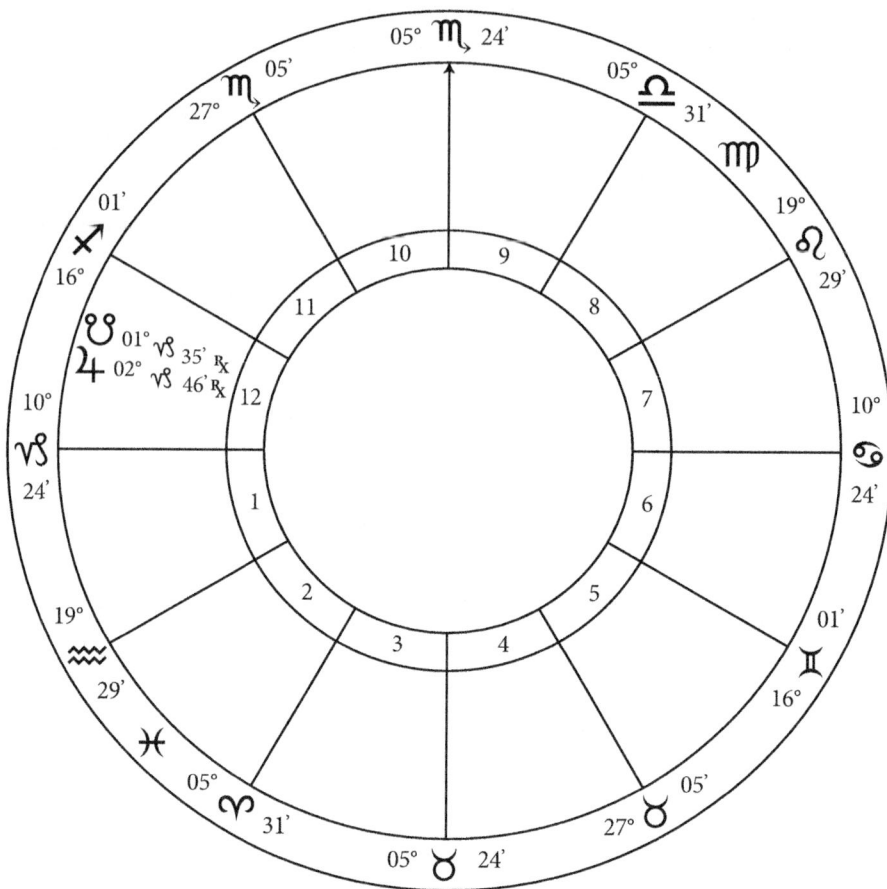

FIGURE 15: *Jupiter as a Functional Malefic*

This would naturally be worsened if Jupiter and Venus were also essentially de-bilitated. A conjunction with Jupiter in Capricorn, retrograde, conjunct the South Node, in the twelfth house, and ruling the twelfth house cannot be thought of as an accidental fortification for a planet. Jupiter, in this example, is determined to the production of evil. The same would be true for a majorly debilitated Venus.

As in all things astrological, we have to thoroughly assess the condition of the planets before making a final judgment. A conjunction to Jupiter in Sagittarius, ruling the twelfth and in the twelfth house may save a person from the perils of the twelfth house. It may even create blessings from twelfth house topics. Howev-er, this will be based on Jupiter's essential dignity, rather than him always being a source of good.

IN PARTILE CONJUNCTION WITH THE NORTH NODE (+4)

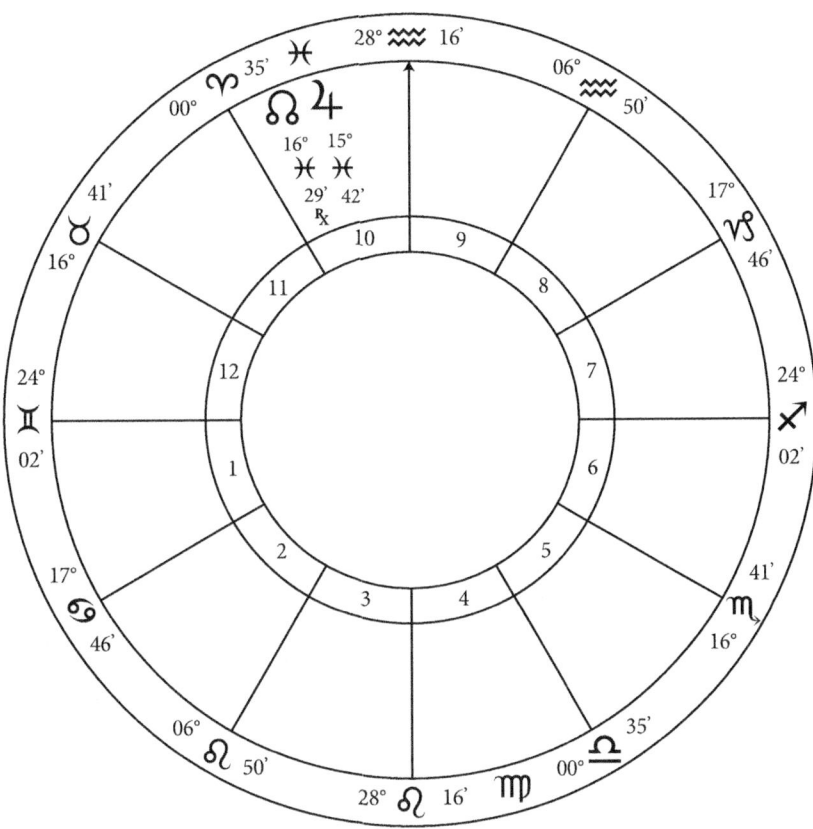

FIGURE 16: *Partile Conjunction to the North Node*

In the Medieval period, the North Node was said to be of the benefic nature of Jupiter and Venus. When a planet has a partile conjunction to the North Node, it is as if that planet has been elevated in its ability to express itself and do good. Benefic planets conjunct the North Node are thought to increase in their benevolence. Malefic planets conjunct the North Node are thought to decrease their destructiveness.

However, I don't quite agree with this last statement. I view the North Node as being similar to the placement of a planet in an angular house. Being conjunct the North Node gives a planet increased visibility. If Saturn is at 29° ARI 32', RX., and conjunct the North Node, it is doubtful whether or not his conjunction to the North Node would stave off his evil or simply make it more visible. The essential state of the planet in question has to be considered always.

Nicholas Culpeper – engaging in the singularly jaw-dropping and unapologetic style of plagiarism that characterizes much of seventeenth century astrology – echoes a peculiar idea about the North Node that William Lilly wrote about seven years prior. In his *Opus Astrologicum*, Culpeper writes:

> *If the Lord of the Ascendant or the Moon be with the Head or Tail of the Dragon, it brings damage to the Question propounded. Look in what house they are in and from the signification of that house you may know whence the damage will come.*

The North Node has been considered to be of extraordinary benevolence throughout two thousand years of Western astrological practice. Thus, the damage spoken of by Culpeper seems to be uncharacteristic of our overarching Western lore regarding this celestial factor. Perhaps, it is this node's relationship to eclipses – which have long been held to be a malefic occurrence within traditional astrology – that gives the North Node this destructive undercurrent. Both Culpeper and Lilly specify that this is something to bear in mind in horary astrology. They do not indicate that this concept is applicable in other branches of astrological practice. I do not regard this aphorism within my client work and teaching. My practical understanding of the North Node is based on what I have outlined at the beginning of this section.

Should a planet be in its minor dignities of triplicity, term, and face, and not occupying any of its major essential debilities, then I do believe the conjunction to the North Node can be helpful. The conjunction to the North Node can bolster the effect of that planet and assist it in performing in a beneficial way. This is one of the few places where I feel a combination of minor dignities really can be helpful in the absence of a major dignity.

## In Partile Trine to Jupiter and Venus (+4)

Jupiter and Venus strongly correspond with their benefic nature only when they are essentially dignified. If they are not essentially dignified, they do not have the ability to deliver a majorly beneficial outcome. If they are functional malefics through their rulership of the evil sixth, eighth, or twelfth houses, this also diminishes their ability to do good. It will actively predispose them towards evil.

Yet, some good may emerge from the trine aspect of these planets. The trine is an aspect of perfect love and friendship. This aspect will always carry the nature of the greater benefic, and will always work towards the fulfillment of a positive outcome. This is especially the case if one of the planets forming the trine is a naturally benefic planet. If Jupiter and Venus are functional malefics, but in a trine aspect to another significator, they may produce good from the evil houses they rule. This is further supported when Jupiter and Venus are strongly essentially dignified.

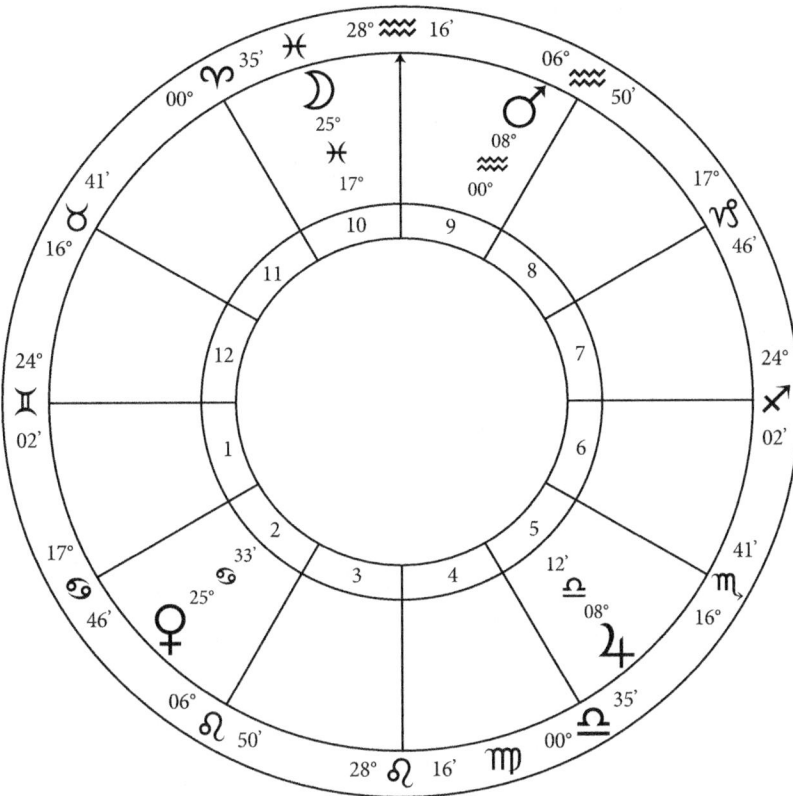

FIGURE 17: *Partile Trine to Jupiter & Venus*

If a strongly essentially dignified Jupiter is the ruler of the eighth house and in a trine relationship with the ruler of the Ascendant, the native or querent may benefit from an inheritance from their ancestors. If a strongly essentially dignified Venus is the ruler of the sixth house and in a trine relationship with the ruler of the Ascendant, the native may benefit from having good employees. As good planets, the nature of Jupiter and Venus is reinforced when they are making good aspects and in a good essential state. In Medieval astrology, the positive aspect of either Jupiter or Venus was thought to mitigate some of the malevolence of Saturn and Mars. Ibn Ezra writes:

> When the benefic planets aspect the malefic ones, they will diminish their harm.

For Ibn Ezra and other astrologers of his time, the greater benefic mitigated the evil of the greater malefic, and the lesser benefic mitigated the evil of the lesser malefic. He continues:

> When Jupiter aspects the malefic, it changes its nature into benefit, yet Venus cannot change the nature of Saturn, except with the help

*of Jupiter. Therefore, Jupiter removes the harm of Saturn, and Venus removes the harm of Mars [even] more than Jupiter [does].*

If Jupiter and Venus are strongly essentially dignified and not ruling malefic houses then the trine from either of them will be a great fortune for the other planet in question. I would also apply this consideration to the sextile of a strongly essentially dignified Jupiter or Venus, even though the sextile has half the power of the trine.

### WITH COR LEONIS OR SPICA VIRGINIS (+5)

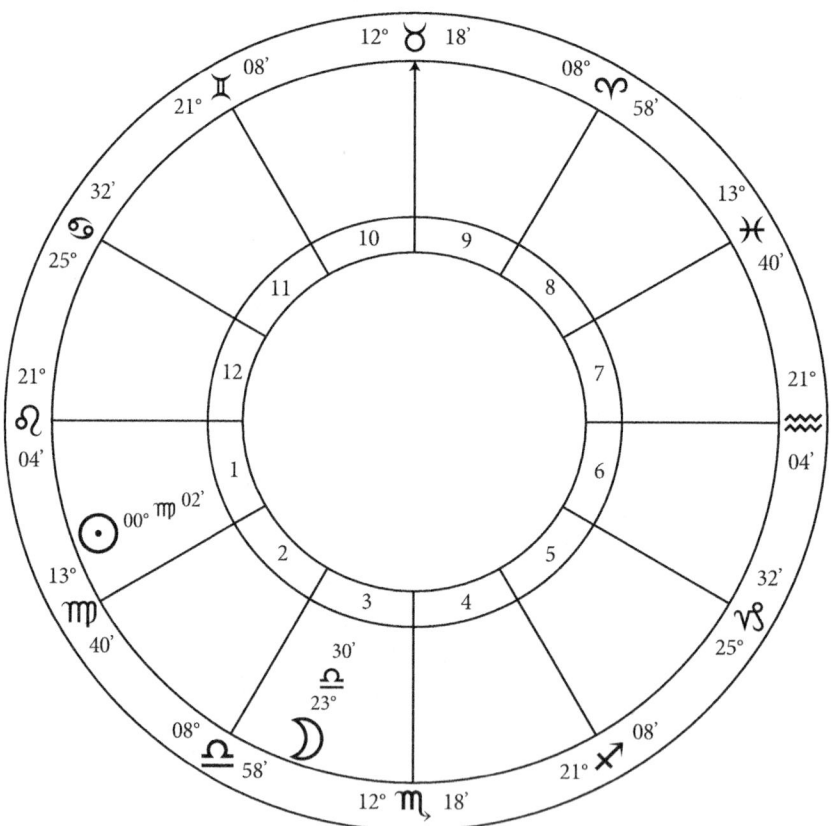

FIGURE 18: *Conjunct Regulus & Spica*

The fixed stars played a major interpretive role in traditional astrology. They continue to be powerful augmenting factors in our chart delineation. The fixed stars in traditional astrology all bear a combination of the influences of the seven classical planets.

Two of the most benefic fixed stars are *Cor Leonis* and *Spica Virginis*. Today, we commonly refer to these stars as "Regulus" and "Spica" (SPIKE-uh), respectively.

While they are not the only benefic fixed stars, the ancients paid great attention to them due to the magnitude of their light. In the *Tetrabiblos*, Ptolemy writes:

> *The bright one in the heart (of the Lion constellation), called Regulus, agrees with Mars and Jupiter.*

In *The Combination of Stellar Influences*, author Reinhold Ebertin tells us that the combination of Mars/Jupiter produces "successful creative activity, a fortunate decision." When a planet is in conjunction with the combination of Mars/Jupiter, Ebertin describes it as:

> *The power to concentrate upon a particular aim or objective, energy, ambition, urge for activity, ability to quickly make decisions and to cope with every situation.*

Thus, Mars/Jupiter is a combination of absolute success (Jupiter) in one's physical activities (Mars).

Of Spica, Ptolemy writes:

> *Spica Virginis is like Venus and partly Mars.*

Ebertin tells us that Venus/Mars in combination represents "the impulse to love. Passion." Therefore, Venus and Mars in combination also signify creative potency. Spica, embodying this combination, can serve as a driving force towards a fertile and successful end.

Due to the precession of the equinoxes, the projected location of Regulus no longer corresponds with the "heart of the Lion." It now resides at approximately 00° Virgo in the tropical zodiac. The projected location of Spica is now approximately 24° Libra in the tropical zodiac. The conjunction of the Ascendant, Midheaven, or any of the chief significators to these degrees is a significant and auspicious omen. However, an entire judgement should not be based purely on the conjunction of a significator with a fixed star. No single testimony should ever prevent us from carrying out a full chart delineation. In practicing astrology in a responsible way, a full analysis of all the relevant factors will always guide us towards a more intelligent interpretation.

## ACCIDENTAL DEBILITIES

TABLE 3: *Accidental Debilities*

| | |
|---|---|
| IN 12ᵀᴴ | -5 |
| IN 8ᵀᴴ OR 6ᵀᴴ | -2 |
| RETROGRADE | -5 |
| SLOW IN MOTION | -2 |
| ♄ ♃ OR ♂ OCCIDENTAL | -2 |
| ☿ & ♀ ORIENTAL | -2 |
| ☽ DECREASING LIGHT | -2 |
| COMBUST OF ☉ | -5 |
| PARTILE CONJUNCTION OF ♄ OR ♂ | -5 |
| PARTILE CONJUNCTION TO ☋ | -4 |
| BESIEGED OF BY ♄ OR ♂ | -5 |
| PARTILE OPPOSITION OF ♄ & ♂ | -4 |
| PARTILE SQUARE OF ♄ OR ♂ | -3 |
| CONJUNCT ALGOL OR WITHIN 05° | -5 |

IN THE 12ᵀᴴ HOUSE (-5)

The twelfth house has no aspectual relationship to the Ascendant. It is amongst the four terrestrial houses that bear this misfortune, including the two Gates of Hades (the second and the eighth houses), and the sixth house of sickness and slaves. Ibn Ezra writes:

> When a planet is not in one of its places of rulership and it is in the sixth house or the twelfth, it does no good.

With the exception of the second house, these houses are dark, abject, and cut off from the life-giving power that flows from the Ascendant. These houses signify sickness, slavery, death, and suffering.

Though the twelfth house and the second house are on either side of the Ascendant, they differ tremendously in strength. The second house is a succedent house that derives its power from its proximity to the Ascendant. The twelfth house is a cadent house that ends the sequence of the houses. It is analogous to endings, suffering, darkness, and things that actively debilitate life. When a planet is in the twelfth house, it does not have the ability to fulfill its promise. Ibn Ezra writes:

> A planet in the twelfth house is like a person in prison.

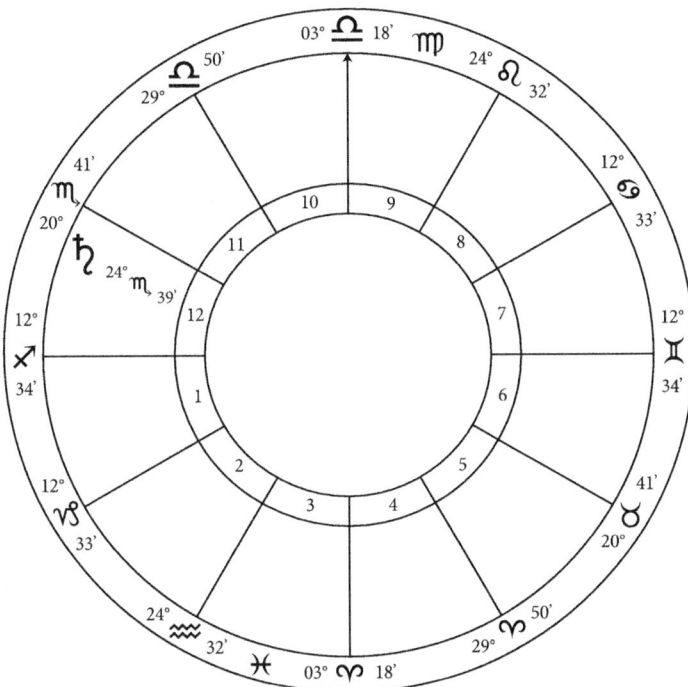

FIGURE 19: *In the Twelfth House*

Any action that twelfth house planets take may be indirectly harmful to the greater strength and vitality of the chart in general, since the twelfth house signifies self-undoing.

## IN THE 8ᵀᴴ OR 6ᵀᴴ HOUSES (-2)

Planets in the eighth house are specifically determined towards death and debt, both of which are harmful to the larger vitality of the chart and the person for whom it was erected. Of the eighth house, Ibn Ezra writes:

> *A planet in the eighth house is like a person stricken with horror and fear.*

Planets in the sixth house are specifically determined towards sickness, slavery, and stress – all of which also bring damage to the native.

An essentially dignified planet like Jupiter in Sagittarius trine the Ascendant from the eighth house can bring out some of the good things that the eighth house represents, such as an inheritance from one's ancestors. However, the goodness from this Jupiter has more to do with its essential dignity and trine to the Ascendant than its placement in the eighth house. Ibn Ezra writes:

> *When a benefic planet is in the eighth house, it indicates neither good nor bad, but if it is one of the malefics, it indicates complete harm.*

517

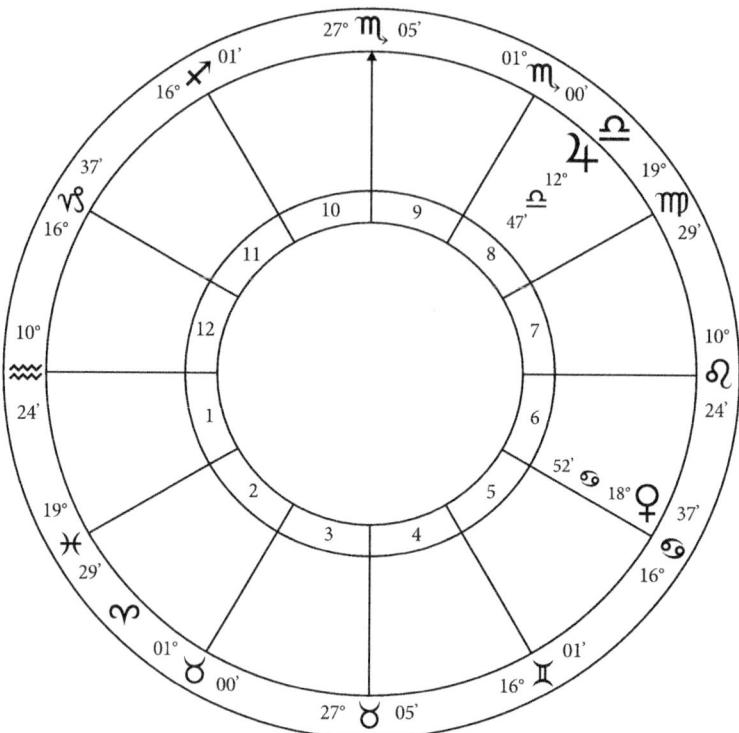

FIGURE 20: *In the Eighth & Sixth House*

Though he doesn't take into consideration what the condition of a benefic planet in the eighth house may be, he does point out that malefics in the eighth house increase in their ability to produce evil. When we place a malefic planet in an environment that is naturally malefic, it amplifies the ability of that planet to cause harm. Conversely, if we place a benefic planet in an environment that is naturally benefic, it amplifies the ability of that planet to produce a positive outcome in terms of the topics signified by that house.

The cadency of the sixth house – as well as the quincunx it forms with the Ascendant – makes it weak. Ibn Ezra writes:

*A planet in the sixth house is like a weak man running.*

Ibn Ezra held that cadency was amongst the worst things that could occur to a planet. On the topic of cadent planets, Bethem writes:

*If cadent, he is as a man dead, having no motion.*

This is particularly true for the sixth and twelfth houses.

Though cadent, the third and the ninth houses are benefic because of the harmonious aspects they make to the Ascendant. However, the sixth and the twelfth houses are in aversion to the Ascendant. Though placement in the sixth house is less malefic than placement in the twelfth, both placements are harmful.

## RETROGRADE (-5)

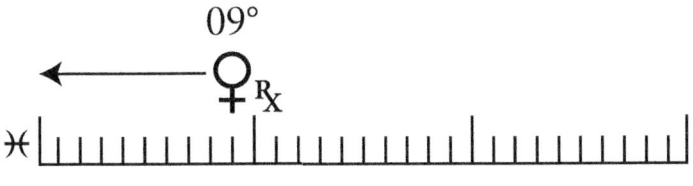

FIGURE 21: *Retrograde Planet*

According to Abraham Ibn Ezra, retrogradation is one of the worst afflictions that can happen to a planet. It is as if the planet is self-sabotaging, going in the wrong direction, and unable to deliver on a positive outcome. The retrograde planet does not have a sense of direction or an intelligent trajectory. Bethem writes:

> When a planet is retrograde, he is as a man infirm, stupefied, and solicitous.

A retrograde planet cannot deliver on its promise. If it does somehow find a way to function, it ultimately destroys any promise that it fulfills. This is truer in horary and electional astrology than it is in natal astrology. Ibn Ezra writes:

> A retrograde planet indicates antagonism and the destruction of anything that is contemplated.

It is doubtful that reception, mutual reception, or positive aspects from benefics could assist a retrograde planet. The retrograde planet, so burdened by the weight of retrogradation, would return any blessing it receives back to the planet that was bestowing it. Retrogradation, along with cadency and combustion, constitute Ibn Ezra's list of the three worst things that can happen to a planet.

## SLOW IN MOTION (-2)

A planet is slow in motion when it is moving slower than its daily average rate. When a planet is slow, it is not able to swiftly deliver on the promise of the things it signifies. Ibn Ezra writes:

> A planet slowing down is like a person who is exhausted and has no strength to walk.

If a slow planet represents the completion of something, the outcome may be delayed due to the lethargic state of the planet in question. I do not pay much attention to this consideration within my practice.

SATURN, JUPITER, OR MARS OCCIDENTAL (-2)

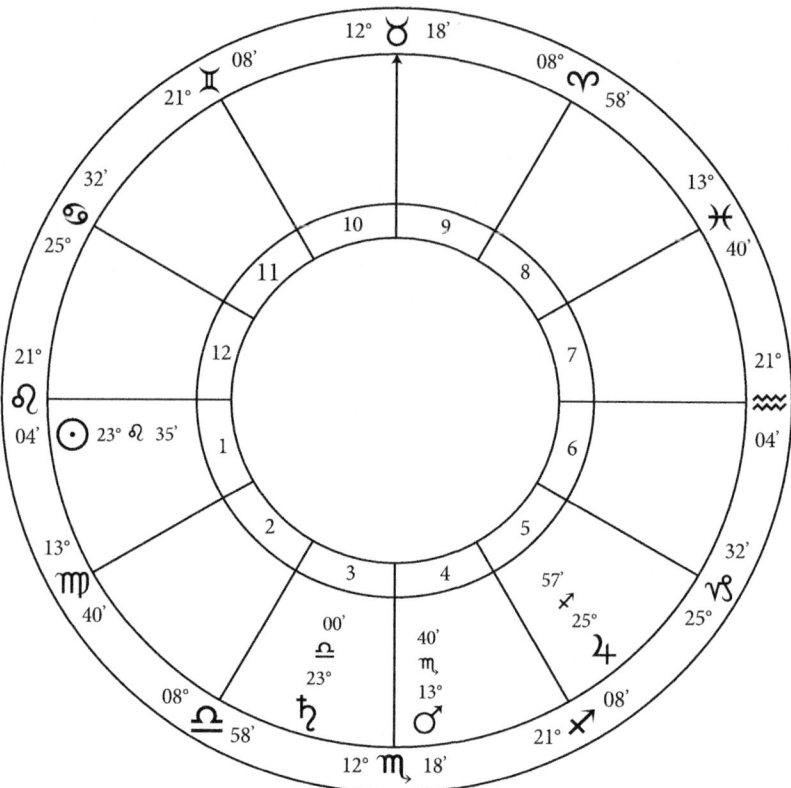

FIGURE 22: *Saturn, Jupiter, & Mars Occidental*

In the Chaldean Order, Saturn, Jupiter, and Mars are superior to the Sun. Therefore, it is their natural inclination to rise before the Sun diurnally. When they rise after the Sun, they are in the position that would normally be allotted to the inferior planets. This is why their occidental rising is an accidentally debility. This does not hold major weight in my chart delineation.

MERCURY AND VENUS ORIENTAL (-2)

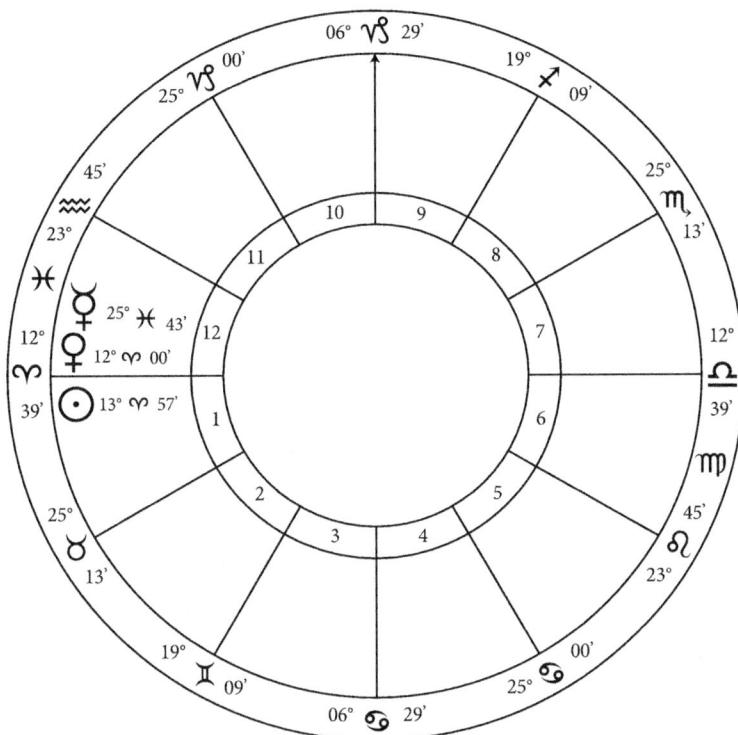

FIGURE 23: *Mercury & Venus Oriental*

In the Chaldean Order, Mercury and Venus are inferior to the Sun. Therefore, it is their natural inclination to rise after the Sun. When they rise before the Sun, they are in the position that would normally be allotted to the superior planets. This is why their oriental rising is an accidental debility.

The ancients considered Venus to be particularly malefic if she rose before the Sun. Her name as a morning star is *Lucifer* – a name that later became associated with the devil in Christianity.

While this placement is thought to be a debility for both Mercury and Venus, I have never seen this make an appreciable difference in chart delineation.

MOON DECREASING IN LIGHT (-2)

Though the waning Moon is malefic for the Moon specifically, it generally is considered to be a bad omen for the entire chart. This is especially the case if the question being asked is regarding the topic of increase, fertility, or growth.

The Moon is the psychic root and cosmic undercurrent of every operation. In every birth, she is the celestial link through which the cosmic influx of the planets makes their impression upon the newborn babe. Therefore, a strong Moon, increasing in the power of her light, is an auspicious omen in general. An old Moon, decreasing in the fullness of her light and returning to the Sun where she will be burnt up and destroyed, is a malefic omen.

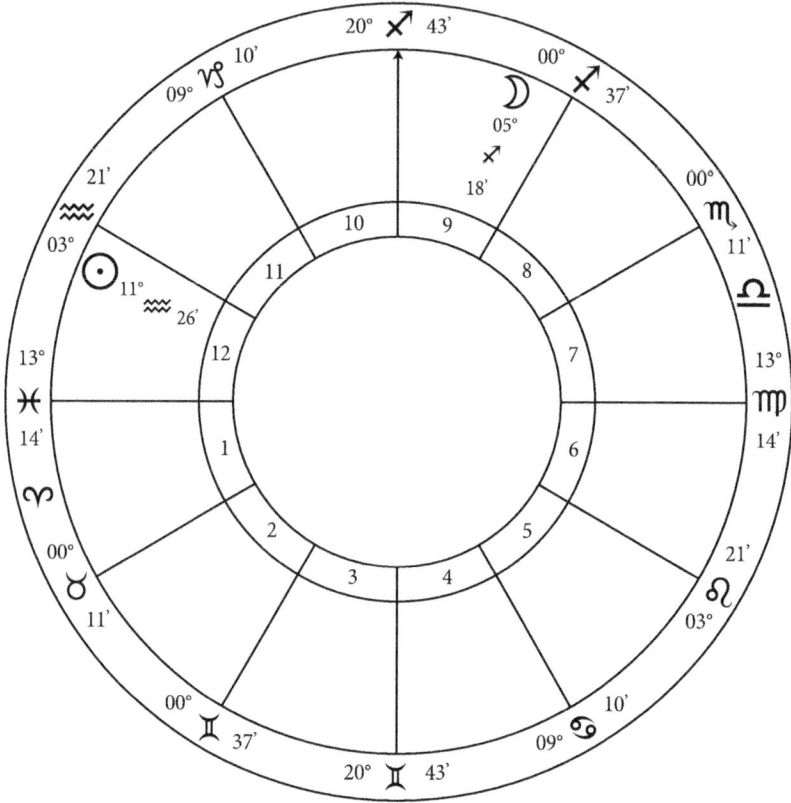

FIGURE 24: *Moon Decreasing in Light*

Things requiring momentum and growth are more auspiciously aligned with the waxing Moon. Things of an internal nature, that require the conservation of energy, releasing attachments, soul-searching, and reflection are more appropriately aligned with the waning Moon.

COMBUST OF THE SUN (-5)

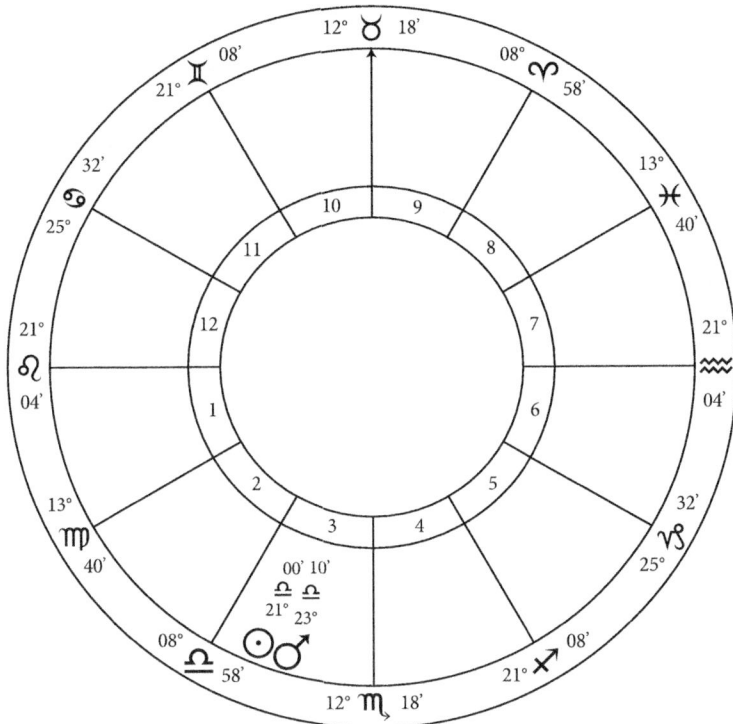

FIGURE 25: *Combust Planet*

Combustion is one of the worst things that can happen to a planet. This is rivalled only by cadency and retrogradation. Within Renaissance astrology, when significators of sick people are combust, this is one sign that the person in question will not be restored to health. Many classical texts even consider this to be a sign of death in medical astrology horary charts (or "decumbitures").

Combustion represents the annihilation of the planet in question. It also signifies the destruction of everything the planet specifically rules within the chart. Ibn Ezra writes:

*A combust planet is like a dying person.*

Whenever a planet is within 00° 17' 01" and 08° 30' of the Sun, the planet is within the range of combustion. It does not matter whether the planet is in the same sign as the Sun or not. Combustion is an astronomical event, not an astrological one. Sign boundaries are of no relevance. When a planet is combust, it is completely destroyed by the rays of the Sun. It can no longer perform or deliver on the promise it has been entrusted with within the chart. Even a planet in mutual reception with its ruler doesn't have the ability to hold onto that gift because of how burdened it is by the weight of combustion.

There is a third solar condition that holds interpretive value in classical astrology. When a planet is beyond 08° 30' of the Sun, but still within a range of 17° 00' of the Sun, that planet is considered to be "under the beams." The ancients were of the opinion that if a planet were under the beams of the Sun, it was still invisible and debilitated, though not combust. Therefore, it would not be able to carry out its functions within a chart. Ibn Ezra writes:

*A planet under the light of the Sun is like a person in prison.*

Within the sphere of my practice, the three solar conditions of cazimi, combustion, and being "under the beams" are worthwhile considerations when assessing the condition of a planet. However, they seem to be of greater value in horary and electional astrology, than they are in natal or mundane astrology.

PARTILE CONJUNCTION OF SATURN OR MARS (-5)

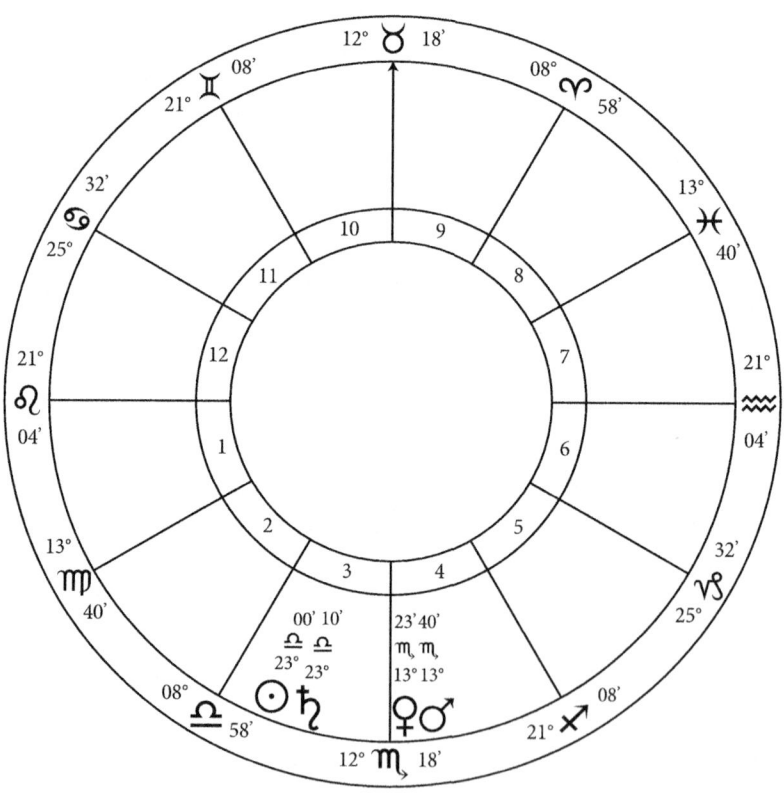

FIGURE 26: *Partile Conjunction of Saturn & Mars*

The conjunction of a significator to either Saturn or Mars is destructive to the planet in question. Both of the malefics harm, destroy, or negatively alter any planet with whom they make contact.

This would clearly be the case if Saturn or Mars were in a state of deep essential debility. However, if Saturn is in Aquarius, direct, oriental, swift and otherwise well-fortified, then Saturn would be in a positive internal and external state. Culpeper writes:

> *Saturn and Mars peregrine are malicious beyond measure: they are not so bad when they are in essential dignities; for then they are like noble enemies that have got their enemy in their hands and scorn to hurt him.*

Any planet that is strongly essentially dignified is benefic in a general sense – even the malefics. Any planet that is strongly essentially debilitated is malefic for the entire world – even the benefics. Planets can only act positively or negatively insofar as their essential dignity augments their performance.

If Saturn and Mars do not rule the sixth, eighth, or twelfth houses and are otherwise strongly essentially dignified, they may actually carry the promise of good within the chart. A conjunction to either of them would be far less evil than if they were essentially debilitated and ruling evil houses. It would also be far less evil than a conjunction to essentially debilitated benefics ruling malefic houses. A thorough analysis of the planets is necessary to understand what their determination is within a given chart.

PARTILE CONJUNCTION TO THE SOUTH NODE (-4)

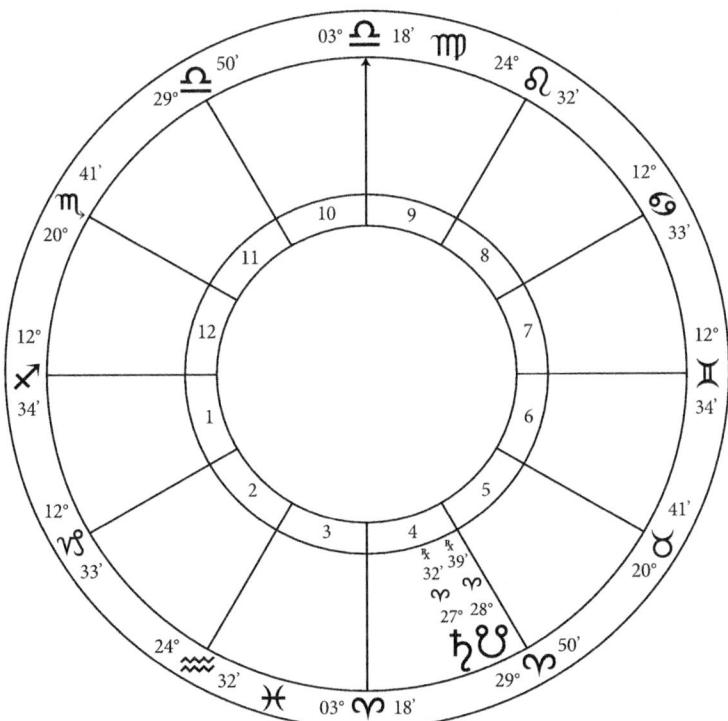

FIGURE 27: *Partile Conjunction to the South Node*

In my astrology, the South Node is one of several "toilet bowls" in the universe. The contact of a planet with the South Node is akin to its power being flushed away. While the North Node is of the nature of Jupiter and Venus, the South Node is of the nature of Saturn and Mars.

It was largely accepted amongst ancient Western astrologers that the conjunction of a benefic planet to the South Node diminishes its ability to do good. However, there is no similar consensus regarding the conjunction of malefic planets with the South Node.

Some astrologers have argued that when a malefic planet is conjunct the South Node, it increases the malevolence of that planet. Others have argued that the evil of the malefic is reduced because of this contact. I believe that if Saturn were at 27° ARI 32', RX., conjunct the South Node and ruling the second house, the South nodal contact would further destroy Saturn's ability to grant financial abundance to the person in question.

## BESIEGED OF BY SATURN OR MARS (-5)

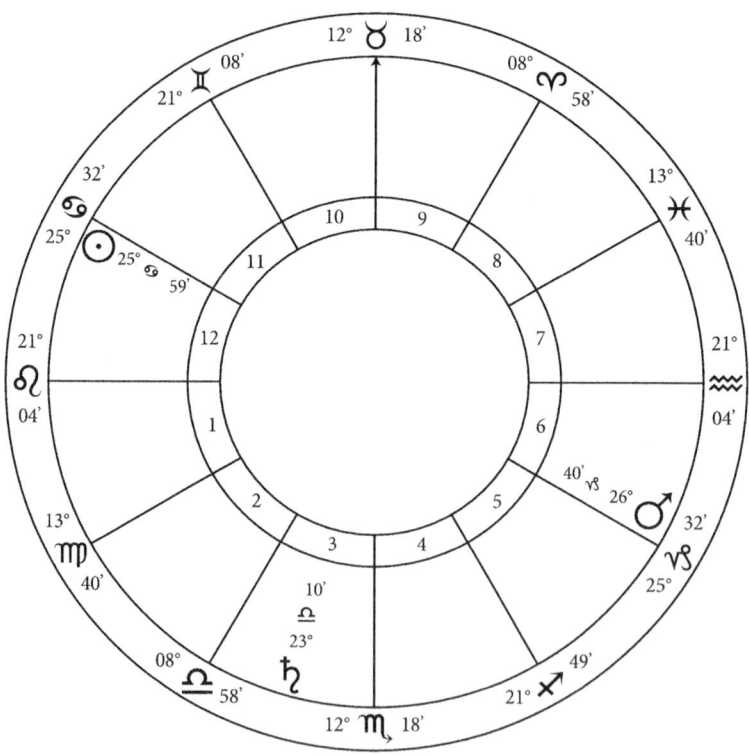

FIGURE 28: *Besieged of by Saturn & Mars*

The dictionary defines "besieged" as "(of a place) surrounded by armed forces aiming to capture it or force surrender." Within traditional astrology, a planet is besieged when it is separating from the hard aspect of one malefic and applying to the hard aspect of another malefic. Examples of this can be: Venus separating from her conjunction to Saturn and applying to the square of Mars; Mercury separating from the opposition of Saturn and applying to the conjunction of Mars; the Moon separating from the square of Mars and applying to the opposition of Saturn. In all cases, we have the proverbial condition of a planet being "between a rock and a hard place." Ibn Ezra writes:

> *The testimony of the significator, if in the evil middle position [besiegement], indicates prison and torture...*

A besieged planet is challenged in terms of its ability to be successful in its endeavors. Its efforts are destroyed by the violent rays of the malefics.

## PARTILE OPPOSITION OF SATURN AND MARS (-4)

The opposition has always been seen as an aspect of enmity. Within the Thema Mundi philosophy, its nature is similar to that of Saturn. Therefore, the opposition between any two or more planets has a malefic effect, since the oppositional rays of the planets are all considered to be warlike and inimical. Ibn Ezra writes:

> *When planets are in opposition aspect, they are like two people fiercely fighting with each other.*

Due to the natural evil of the malefics, their oppositional rays are even more destructive. If given the opportunity to act malevolently, the malefic planets will do the greatest harm. Evil is within their nature.

The planets function best when aspecting other planets in a way that is in harmony with their identity. Jupiter and Venus greatly enjoy being in trine or sextile aspects with other planets. Trines and sextiles are of the same benefic nature as the benefics. Saturn and Mars enjoy being in square or oppositional aspects with other planets. Squares and oppositions are of the same malefic nature as the malefics.

Regardless of which houses Saturn and Mars rule within a chart, their oppositional rays have a twofold impact. The opposing planet is afflicted universally because of its negative aspect to the malefic. However, the topics the malefic and the opposing planet specifically represent within the chart will be at war with each other within the life of the native.

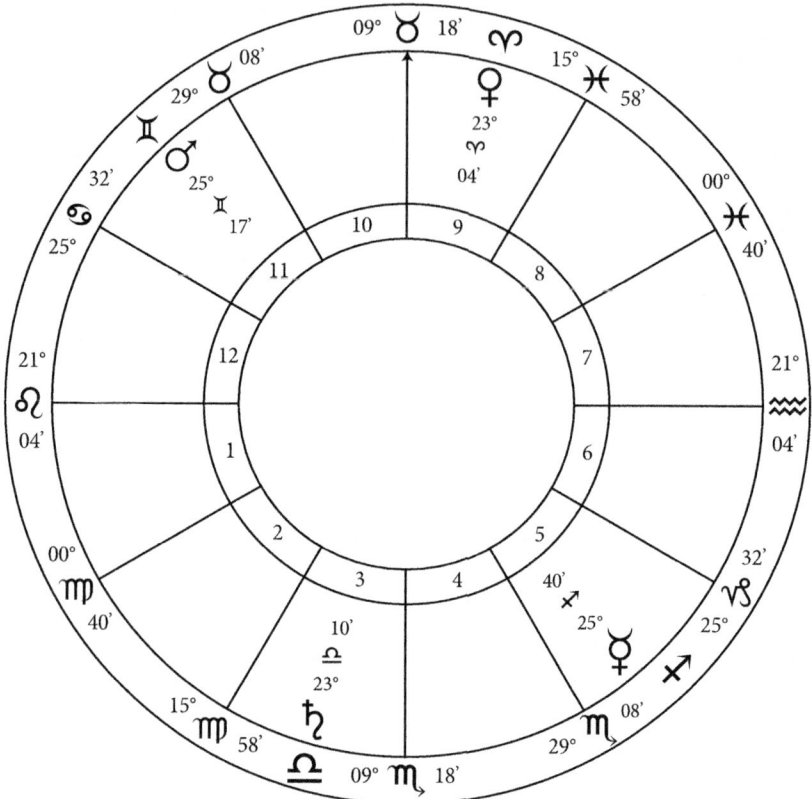

FIGURE 29: *Partile Opposition of Saturn & Mars*

For example, if Venus was in opposition to Saturn in a natal chart, this could universally be interpreted as "suffering or separation in love." This is because, universally, Venus signifies love and Saturn signifies suffering or separation. However, if Venus was the ruler of the tenth house and Saturn was the ruler of the seventh house, their opposition could indicate that the marriage of that person was in direct conflict with that person's career aspirations.

If Mercury opposed Mars, this could indicate that the native spoke in a coarse and violent manner. This is because, universally, Mercury rules speech and Mars represents a lack of social graces, abrasiveness, and violence. However, if Mercury ruled the third house and was in opposition to Mars, ruler of the fifth house, this could indicate constant disagreement between the native's children – represented by the fifth house – and the native's siblings – represented by the third house.

PARTILE SQUARE OF SATURN OR MARS (-3)

While the square between two planets is harmful, the square between a planet and a malefic is even more damaging to the affairs of that planet. Regarding the square aspect, Ibn Ezra writes:

*When planets are in quartile aspect, they are like two people, each one seeking authority for himself.*

Even if Saturn and Mars are strongly essentially dignified, their square aspect will bring out their intrinsic malevolence. Planets will always prefer to express their intrinsic natures, whether good or evil. Good aspects bring out the good within good planets. Evil aspects bring out the evil in evil planets.

Saturn and Mars are the destroyers of life in traditional astrology. They prefer to be in conditions that amplify their ability to destroy. The square provides them that opportunity. If we recall the Thema Mundi, the square aspects to the luminaries come from the domiciles of Mars. As Martian aspects, squares are aspects of war. Both the square and the opposition can represent blockages, delays, contention, and conflict. Ibn Ezra writes:

*If the malefic beholds the benefic by a quartile [square] aspect or an opposition, it decreases from its goodness.*

Nevertheless, the square is weaker in impact than the opposition.

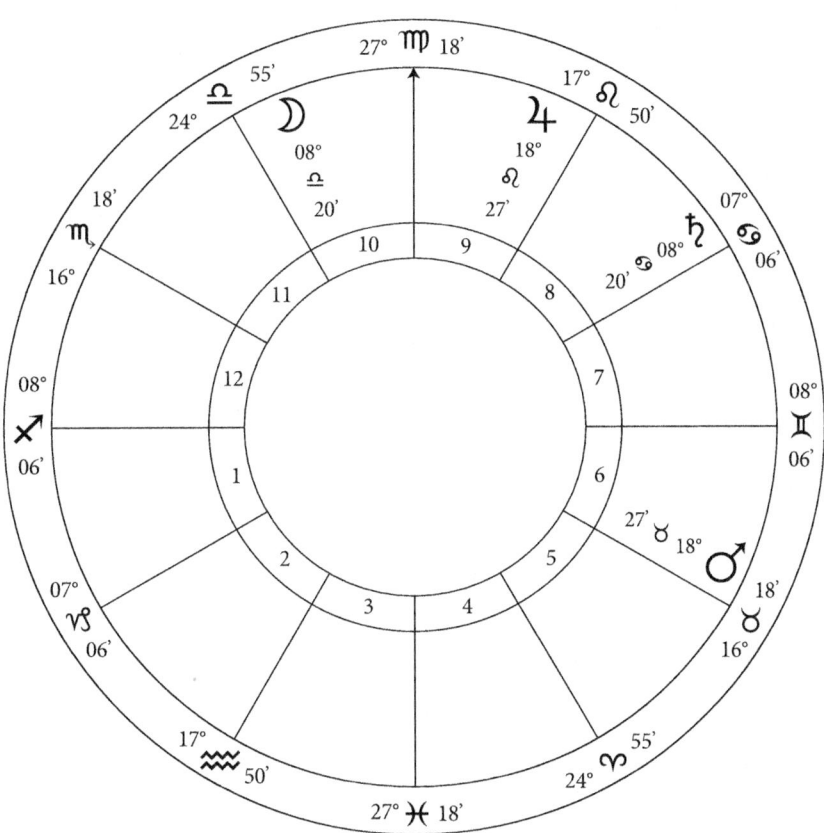

FIGURE 30: *Partile Square of Saturn & Mars*

When Saturn or Mars are in a square relationship with another significator, it shows a harsh confrontation between the topics the two planets signify. If Mars ruled the fifth house and squared Jupiter, ruler of the Ascendant, it can show a parent who is in constant war with their children. If the Sun ruled the Ascendant and squared Saturn, ruler of the Descendant, it could indicate a person who is in constant war with their spouse.

The square between a planet and a malefic would be worsened if both those planets were essentially weak. However, no planets are quite as vicious as Saturn and Mars when they are essentially debilitated. It is within their nature to be causers of harm. Their essential debility would only amplify their inherent evil.

IN CONJUNCTION WITH CAPUT ALGOL OR IN 05° THEREOF (-5)

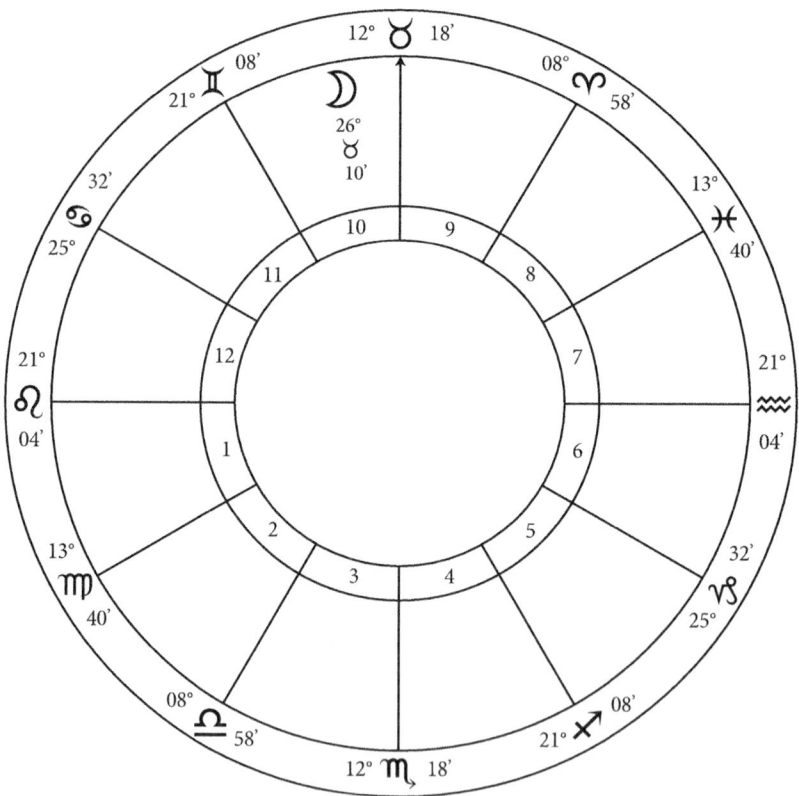

FIGURE 31: *Moon Conjunct Algol*

Algol is one of the most malefic fixed stars in traditional astrology. It currently resides at approximately 26° Taurus within the tropical zodiac. It is called "the Demon's Head," "the Medusa's Head," and "the Demon star." It is classically associated with decapitation, madness, great pain, and suffering. When a significator is conjunct Algol, it is an evil indication. This conjunction represents the doom that lay dormant within the heart of whatever is being asked about.

Though I do believe that being conjunct Algol is a great source of harm for the celestial factor in question, I do not believe that Algol or any fixed star should have a five-degree orb. I only allow for a one-degree orb before and after the corporal conjunction with a fixed star within my practice. Many of the fixed stars that we use in astrology are not on the ecliptic; even less so than the planets, which we know frequently deviate North or South of the ecliptic plane. Since the location of many fixed stars is often an extreme projection from where that star actually resides in relation to the ecliptic, my tendency is to give these projected values an extremely tight orb. For most orb considerations in astrology, the tighter the orb, the stronger the influence – with fixed stars, planets, and with everything else.

## CHAPTER 22 QUESTIONS

1. What is the difference between an essential dignity and an accidental fortitude?
2. What happens to an essentially dignified planet if it is accidentally debilitated?
3. According to Abraham Ibn Ezra, what are the three worst things that can happen to a planet?
4. What is the difference between a planet being cazimi versus combust?
5. Why do the superior planets prefer to be oriental?
6. Why do the inferior planets prefer to be occidental?
7. Why should we use a tighter orb when referring to the locations of the fixed stars in zodiacal longitude?

# PART 4

*We cannot grasp easily with the mind's eye anything for which we are not prepared by earlier learning.*

FIRMICUS MATERNUS

CHAPTER 23 OBJECTIVES

✳ Provide a systematic method for horary astrology analysis.
✳ Demonstrate how the various topics covered in this text work to-
  gether in chart delineation.
✳ Describe the function of the Moon in horary astrology.
✳ Show how the same interpretation rubric can be applied to a variety
  of horary questions.

# CHAPTER 23

## PRACTICE OF
## CONCRETE ASTROLOGY

*... and yet we find there are two things which confound the wisest, the greatest, and proudest of them all, in the very summit of their glory: these are* TIME *and* CHANCE *– two mighty lords upon earth, which bring to pass many strange and marvelous events.*
– ELLEN H. BENNETT

THE OUTCOME OF OUR astrological studies must be the acquisition of demonstrable skills. These skills represent the fruits of our labours in learning this ancient art.

In this final chapter, I have included example horary charts and their delineations. These will enable you to follow my interpretive process, so that you can see how this book has aided your own clear understanding of traditional astrology.

The next book in this series will be exclusively on horary astrology. In it, we will explore more of the technical concepts that directly have a bearing on that specific branch of astrological practice. You'll find in these examples only the terminology that you've learnt within this book.

May these example charts serve as a light for you. I hope that the thread of my logic is both clear and obvious after having read this text. It is my sincerest desire that you feel as if you have been furthered in your journey toward mastering traditional astrology.

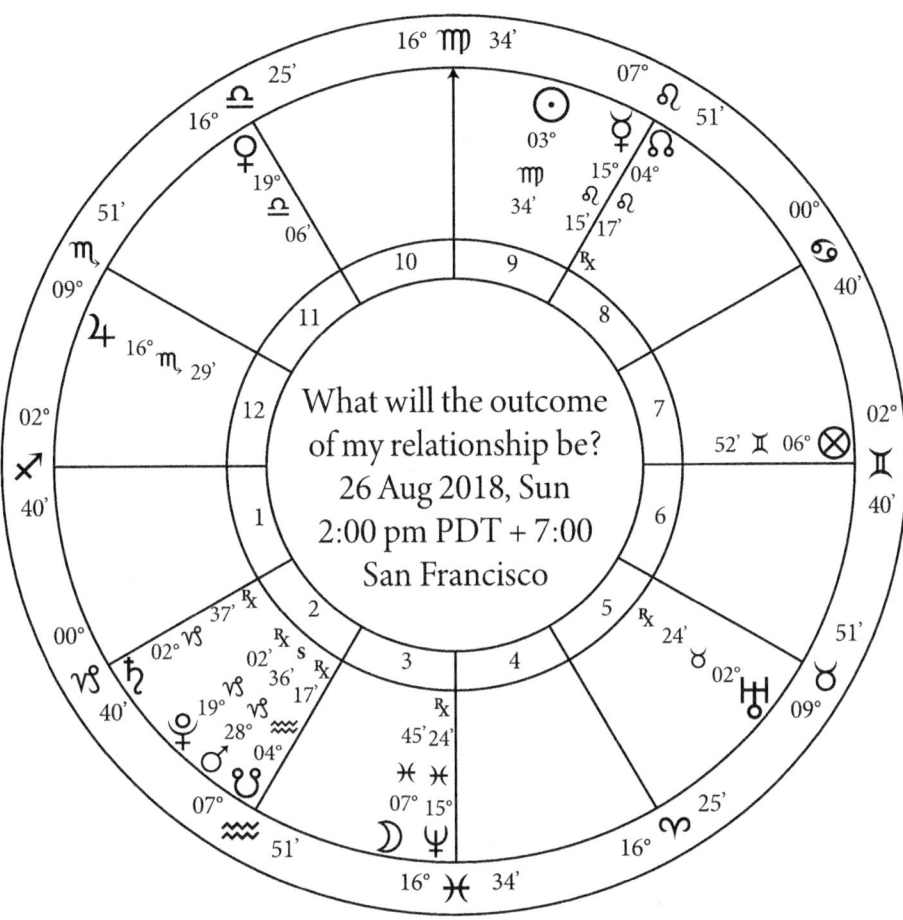

FIGURE 1. *Relationship Horary*

## CASE STUDY 1:
### WHAT WILL THE OUTCOME OF MY RELATIONSHIP BE?

> *This question was asked by someone who was undergoing a period of intense difficulty in his relationship. He wanted to know what the outcome of his relationship with his boyfriend would be. Traditionally, all love horaries are answered through an assessment of the first house for the Querent and the seventh house for the Quesited, and that is how I went about answering this question.*

## Step 1: Identify the Querent

Since we have 02° sag 40' rising, the Querent is represented by the ruler of the asc: Jupiter. Jupiter in this chart is at 16° sco 29' in the twelfth house of self-undoing and hidden enemies.

## Step 1a: Assess the Essential Dignity or Debility of the Querent

Jupiter is in the domicile of Mars, the exaltation of no one, the triplicity of Venus, the term of Venus, and the face of the Sun. Jupiter is not in his detriment or fall. This is an essentially debilitated, peregrine Jupiter.

A peregrine planet is like a person who is lost and confused in the world. It signifies someone who doesn't know how to function within his environment. He is a roving, disembodied soul, without a sense of direction. The client feels like he doesn't know where to turn next in this situation.

## Step 1b: Assess the Accidental Fortitude or Debility of the Querent

At this stage, my preference is to make my assessment based on the strength of the planet's house location. Everything else such as aspects, retrogradation, etc. will be assessed later.

Essentially debilitated Jupiter is further accidentally debilitated in the malefic, cadent twelfth house. Cadent houses have 25% power to support the significations of the planets within them. However, the twelfth house is the worst cadent house of them all.

The Querent feels powerless both internally and externally. He cannot do anything to improve his current circumstances. He may feel as if this situation is actively working against his wellbeing.

## Step 2: Identify the Quesited

The ruler of the seventh house of love and partnership represents the Quesited. The Quesited is Mercury at 15° leo 15' in the ninth house of foreign travel and higher education.

## Step 2a: Assess the Essential Dignity or Debility of the Quesited

Mercury is in the domicile of the Sun, the exaltation of no one, the triplicity of the Sun, the term of Venus, and the face of Jupiter. Mercury is not in his detriment or fall. This is an essentially debilitated, peregrine Mercury.

Though essentially debilitated, Mercury is in the domicile of the Sun and the Sun is in the domicile of Mercury. There is no traditional aspect between these two planets which means they are not in reception or mutual reception with each other. However, since they occupy each other's domiciles and are not in an aspect relationship, they are in each other's generosity. This means they are inclined to offer support to one another. Our peregrine Mercury has a greater level of strength and support than our peregrine Jupiter.

STEP 2b: ASSESS THE ACCIDENTAL FORTITUDE OR DEBILITY OF THE QUESITED

Essentially debilitated Mercury is accidentally fortified in the benefic, yet cadent ninth house. While it would be true in general that planets in the ninth house are accidentally fortified for being there, I sincerely believe this rule only is applicable when the planets in question are essentially dignified. In the case of our Mercury, he is peregrine, and therefore cannot really benefit from the accidental strength the ninth house provides. Nonetheless, he is far more supported in the ninth house than our Jupiter is in the twelfth house. All in all, Mercury seems to have the upper hand as far as this relationship is concerned.

STEP 3: LOCATE THE MOON

The Moon is at 07° PIS 45' in the cadent third house of siblings and community.

STEP 3a.: ASSESS THE ESSENTIAL DIGNITY OR DEBILITY OF THE MOON

The Moon represents the psychic undercurrent that runs beneath the matter. She can indicate the true reason for the Querent asking the question. She symbolizes the energetic atmosphere in which the question is being asked. She gives a general sense of the circumstances that the Querent is in.

The Moon is in the domicile of Jupiter, the exaltation of Venus, the triplicity of Venus, the term of Venus, and the face of Saturn. The Moon is the participating triplicity ruler of all water signs in diurnal or nocturnal charts. Therefore, the Moon is essentially dignified by triplicity.

As far as strength is concerned, the Moon is middling in power. She is neither in a great nor terrible condition. She is alive, but not necessarily thriving. This can represent how the Querent feels within the current condition he finds himself in with his boyfriend.

STEP 3b: ASSESS THE ACCIDENTAL FORTITUDE OR DEBILITY OF THE MOON

The Moon is in the benefic, cadent third house. As an essentially dignified planet, she has the ability to access the goodness that the third house represents. The third house also happens to be her terrestrial house of joy. I have often found that when planets are in their terrestrial house of joy, it signifies a state of comfort more than it represents a condition that empowers the significations of the planet. Planets in their terrestrial houses of joy are planets that are at ease within those houses, whether those houses are good for them or not.

This may indicate that the Querent has made himself comfortable in his present circumstances. However, his present circumstances are uncomfortable at best, and actively represent a real problem within his life. He may have grown comfortable and complacent within the toxic environment of his relationship.

STEP 4: OTHER NOTEWORTHY CONSIDERATIONS

I always include this section in the event that there are factors occurring within the chart that move my opinion more or less strongly in a particular direction.

One noteworthy factor is that Neptune is conjunct the IC. This doesn't have anything to do directly with the question per se. Nevertheless, from an omen-based perspective, it does seem to be indicating that the very basis upon which this question is built is confusion, disillusionment, and possibly deception.

The Quesited in an exact quincunx with Neptune. This can indicate that the love the Quesited is representing will ultimately lead to disappointment for the Querent.

Though it is wide, there is a quincunx between Venus, the universal significator of love, and Neptune. Alfred Witte's *Rules for Planetary Pictures* defines the combination of Venus/Neptune as "false or unhappy love." Venus has also just separated from the exact sinister square to Pluto. Reinhold Ebertin defines this combination as "fanatic love."

These considerations may not fit within a more traditional horary interpretation. However, from a larger divinatory perspective, I find great value in the assessment of universal omens that may be active at the moment of divination. As universal omens, none of these considerations seem to be very encouraging. Furthermore, they corroborate our initial assessment of the Querent's debilitated condition as a peregrine planet in his twelfth house.

### STEP 5: ASPECTS BETWEEN THE SIGNIFICATORS

Mercury is applying to a sinister square with Jupiter. This indicates a very difficult and contentious love relationship between the Querent and the Quesited. Furthermore, by declination, Mercury and Jupiter are in an almost exact contra-parallel with each other. This aspect carries the same significance of an opposition.

There is no reception between the significators that alleviates some of the struggle between them. Mercury is only in the face of Jupiter, while Jupiter is occupying none of the dignities of Mercury. Therefore, they are in a sinister applying square without reception. In *Bonatti on Horary* – translated by Dr. Benjamin Dykes, PhD – Guido Bonatti writes:

> However, those [things] which come to be with striving and effort and obstacles and labor, and great trouble, are when the significators of the querent is joined with the significator of the quaesited matter by opposition, or by a square aspect without reception.

The last aspect the Moon made was her opposition to the Sun in the ninth house, ruling the ninth house. This can indicate that the last thing that occurred between the Querent and the Quesited was a contentious fight regarding foreign travel. This was indeed the case.

The Moon will next form a conjunction with Neptune. If we doubted the significance of the Neptune earlier – through the quincunx to Neptune from both the Quesited and Venus – the Neptune is now being brought fully into the analysis. This indicates that the next thing to happen in the relationship will be disappointment, disillusionment, and possibly deception. This proved to be the case.

STEP 6: FINAL JUDGMENT

The outcome of this relationship will be contention and suffering, particularly on the part of the Querent. He may find himself in a constantly combative partnership with his lover, in which the lover may seem to always have the upper hand.

CONCLUSION:

It was a very volatile relationship. They broke up.

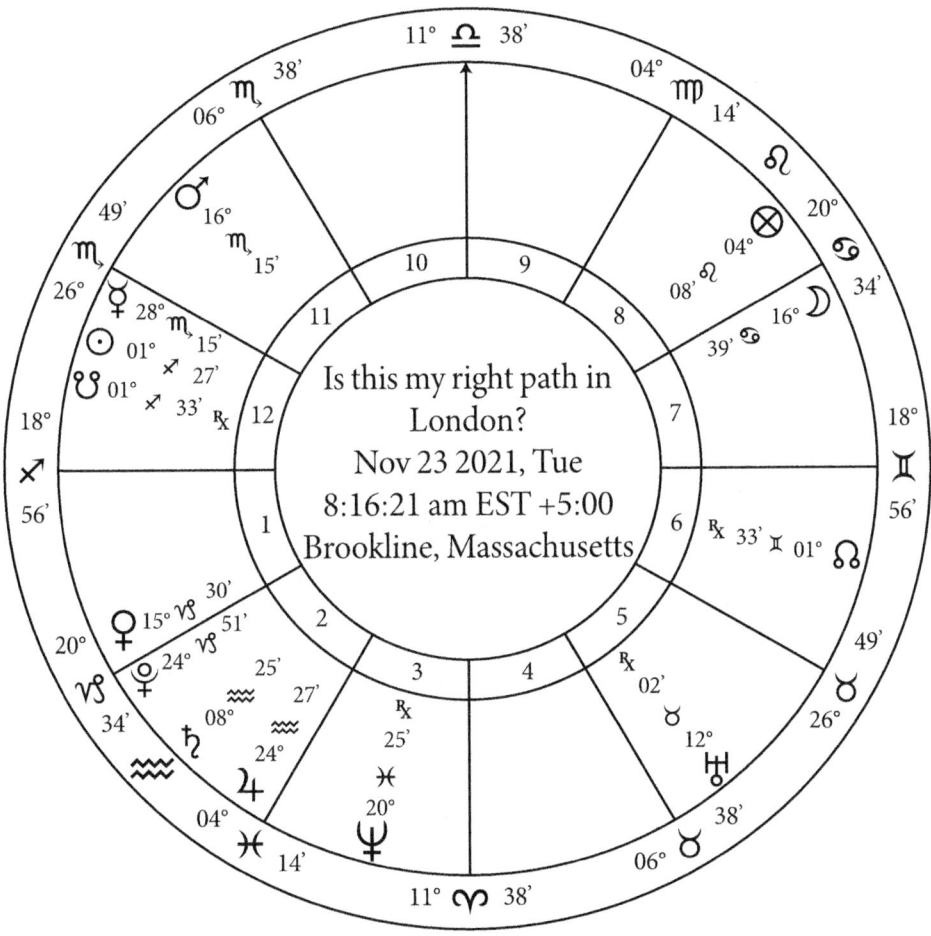

FIGURE 2. *Relocation Horary*

CASE STUDY 2:

HAVE I FOLLOWED MY RIGHT PATH IN MIGRATING TO LONDON?

*In this question, the Querent had already moved to London from Miami. She was experiencing an extraordinary amount of difficulty in that foreign country and wanted to know whether or not moving there was truly in alignment with her destiny. Traditionally, questions that pertain to moving fall under the category of "removals." In traditional Renaissance texts we find "Shall I remove?" being the general way in which this question is framed. In the seventeenth century to "remove" meant to relocate from one place to another. Traditionally, we also find these questions being answered through an assessment of the first house as the place where the Querent is, the fourth house representing the condition of their current location, the seventh house representing where the person is desiring to remove to, and the tenth house which would indicate the benefit they might receive from relocating. The Querent framed the question as her being in a foreign country. She had already removed and wanted to know whether that foreign country was the right place for her to be. Thus, I chose to interpret this question based on the relationship between the ruler of the first house of the Querent and the ruler of the ninth house of foreign travel. Notice that conveniently, the ruler of the seventh house is also the ruler of the ninth house. Therefore, even if we did choose to use the ruler of the seventh house to indicate the foreign place where she desired to relocate, our judgment would still be the same. Since she had already relocated and was feeling quite alien in a foreign land, I chose to use the ruler of the ninth house as the significator of the Quesited.*

STEP 1: IDENTIFY THE QUERENT

Since we have 18° SAG 56' rising, the Querent is represented by the ruler of the ASC: Jupiter. Jupiter in this chart is at 24° AQU 27' in the second house of personal finances and moveable resources.

STEP 1a.: ASSESS THE ESSENTIAL DIGNITY OR DEBILITY OF THE QUERENT

Jupiter is in the domicile of Saturn, the exaltation of no one, the triplicity of Saturn, the term of Jupiter, and the face of the Moon. Jupiter is not in his detriment or fall. This is an essentially dignified Jupiter since he is in his own term. Since Jupiter is in an air sign, he is also a participating triplicity ruler, and is more essentially dignified because of it.

When a planet is in its own term, its essential power is not necessarily increased. That planet simply receives permission to act in a way that is more conformable with its nature. Thus, Jupiter has the permission to be more Jupiterian. The Querent may be optimistic, hopeful, and very certain about the success of her outcome, even if there is no evidence of that on the horizon. In true Jupiterian fashion, the Querent may be stretching herself too thin in this situation. She may also be overcommitting her time and energy in the process. Since the Querent is also in her own triplicity, she may feel as if her circumstances in London have her in a middling state. She may not be completely destitute. However, she doesn't actually feel very strong because of her location.

STEP 1b: ASSESS THE ACCIDENTAL FORTITUDE OR DEBILITY OF THE QUERENT

Essentially dignified Jupiter is accidentally fortified in the benefic, succedent second house of money and moveable possessions. Succedent houses have 50% power to support the significations of the planets within them. Therefore, the Querent in her second house may be an indication that she feels at least marginally strong in terms of shifting the tides of her current circumstances. However, our Querent in her second house may find herself having to spend a great deal of her personal finances in order to support her current living circumstances. Her financial affairs may be her primary concern at this moment. Though she may have the autonomy to change these circumstances since she is in a succedent house, it doesn't alter the fact that her finances are high on her personal list of concerns.

STEP 2: IDENTIFY THE QUESITED

I have chosen to use the ninth house of foreign travel to represent the Quesited. The Quesited is Mercury at 28° SCO 15' in the twelfth house of self-undoing and hidden enemies.

STEP 2a: ASSESS THE ESSENTIAL DIGNITY OR DEBILITY OF THE QUESITED

The Quesited is in the domicile of Mars, the exaltation of no one, the triplicity of Venus, the term of Saturn, and the face of Venus. The Quesited is not in his detriment or fall. The Quesited is peregrine.

A peregrine planet is like a person lost and powerless. London, which is the place the Querent is inquiring about, doesn't have the ability to do many good things for the her at this moment. It also doesn't seem to be able to support her dreams or ambitions. Though Mercury is in Scorpio along with the domicile ruler of that sign, Mercury has long since separated from Mars and is not being received by Mars. There is no reception occurring from Mars to Mercury.

STEP 2b: ASSESS THE ACCIDENTAL FORTITUDE OR DEBILITY OF THE QUESITED

Essentially debilitated Mercury is accidentally debilitated in the malefic, cadent twelfth house. This says that London may actively be working against the Querent. It can also indicate that her decision to migrate there may lead to her suffering. In no way does it seem like a positive place for her to be. Based on the condition of Mercury, migrating to London could make her life extraordinarily difficult.

### STEP 3: LOCATE THE MOON

The Moon is at 16° CAN 39' in the eighth house of debt and other people's money.

### STEP 3a: ASSESS THE ESSENTIAL DIGNITY OR DEBILITY OF THE MOON

The Moon is in her own domicile, the exaltation of Jupiter, the triplicity of Venus, the term of Mercury, and the face of Mercury. The Moon is essentially dignified because she is in her own domicile. She is the participating triplicity ruler in water signs diurnally or nocturnally. Therefore, she also gets points of essential dignity for triplicity rulership. This can indicate that her decision to be in London is something the Querent feels strongly about. She may be very comfortable with the thought of living there, despite the realities facing her.

### STEP 3b: ASSESS THE ACCIDENTAL FORTITUDE OR DEBILITY OF THE MOON

The Moon is in the malefic, succedent eighth house of death and debt. Regardless of how good the Querent may feel in London, it is still something that may be costing her far too much money to realistically sustain. With the Moon in the house of debt and the Querent in the house of her money, there is major pressure being placed on her pocket at the moment. This may not be the most financially comfortable chapter in her life.

### STEP 4: OTHER NOTEWORTHY CONSIDERATIONS

Venus, the ruler of the fifth, sixth, and tenth houses is rising. This can indicate that her pleasures (fifth house) and her career aspirations (tenth house) can be connected to the things that are currently creating stress in her life (sixth house) in terms of her moving to London.

The Moon also opposes Venus. This could indicate that she is currently working against herself in terms of what she thought would represent a good time (Venus ruling the fifth house). This ultimately ended up being the reality of her experience.

Pluto conjunct her second house cusp can represent major demands being placed on her money at this time. She may be spending a lot of money in order to maintain this new life. Resultantly, she may be financially overwhelmed and unable to enjoy the city she is in.

Saturn, ruler of the second house, is opposite the Part of Fortune. This can indicate her money working against itself. This can ultimately lead her into a state of debt. Saturn is also applying to the sinister square of Uranus in her fifth house. This indicates that financial instability will occur within her life as a result of her pursuit of pleasure.

### STEP 5: ASPECTS BETWEEN THE SIGNIFICATORS

Mercury (L9) is separating from a sinister square with Jupiter (L1). This indicates that there is a contentious relationship between the Querent and the Quesited. Furthermore, L9 is in the twelfth house, which already indicates that the desire to move to London is something that isn't going to work out in her best interest.

STEP 6: FINAL JUDGMENT
    She shouldn't move to London.
CONCLUSION:
She had already moved to London before asking this question and was having an awful time there. Unexpected bills kept landing on her from all directions. She was quickly running out of money. She wasn't in a set of circumstances that allowed her to recuperate all the money she was losing.

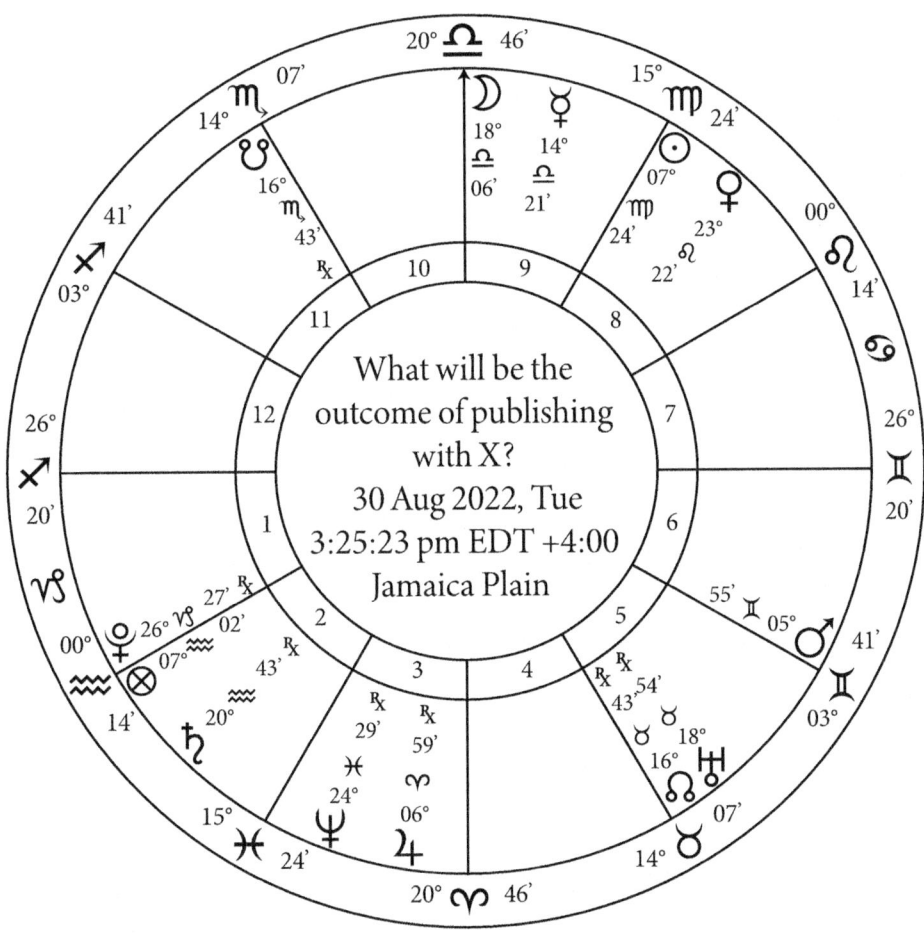

FIGURE 3. *Business Partnership Horary*

545

CASE STUDY 3:

WHAT WILL BE THE OUTCOME OF HIRING THIS COMPANY TO PUBLISH MY BOOK?

*The Querent was concerned about publishing his first book through a particular publishing house. Since this was a relatively simple transactional business agreement, I used the first house to represent the Querent and the seventh house to represent the person/publishing house with whom he was seeking to establish a working relationship.*

STEP 1: IDENTIFY THE QUERENT.

Since we have 26° SAG 20' rising, the Querent is represented by the ruler of the ASC: Jupiter. Jupiter in this chart is 06° ARI 59', RX, in the third house of siblings and community. The third house also signifies publishing and writing from a mundane astrology perspective. It is an appropriate place to find the Querent within this chart.

STEP 1a: ASSESS THE ESSENTIAL DIGNITY OR DEBILITY OF THE QUERENT

Jupiter is in the domicile of Mars, the exaltation of the Sun, the triplicity of the Sun, the term of Venus, and the face of Mars. Jupiter is not in his detriment or fall. This is an essentially debilitated, peregrine Jupiter. Note that even though Jupiter is the out-of-sect triplicity ruler, that does not give him essential dignity.

A peregrine planet is like a person who is out of all hopes of manifesting a successful outcome. It signifies a person lost and confused. He may be "in over his head" and in a realm where people are speaking a language that he doesn't quite understand. He is in need of help because he isn't in a position where he can realistically help himself.

STEP 1b: ASSESS THE ACCIDENTAL FORTITUDE OR DEBILITY OF THE QUERENT

Essentially debilitated Jupiter is further accidentally debilitated by being in the cadent third house. Though location in the third house is an accidental fortitude for the planets, I personally believe that this is only effective when the planets in question are essentially dignified. Since Jupiter is essentially debilitated, the cadency of the third house is emphasized more than its sextile to the Ascendant. Planets in cadent houses only have 25% power to express themselves. *Bethem's Centiloquim* tells us that:

*A planet in a cadent house is like a man dead – having no motion.*

Therefore, Jupiter is in a poor condition both internally and externally. The Querent is also retrograde. On retrogradation, Bethem writes:

*A planet retrograde is like a man infirm; stupefied and solicitous.*

The Querent may feel as if his efforts are in vain. He may be unable to do much to assist himself in a practical sense. The outcome of his working relationship with this publisher may cause him to feel as if he is taking one step forward and two steps back.

## STEP 2: IDENTIFY THE QUESITED

The Quesited is Mercury at 04° LIB 21' in the ninth house of foreign travel and higher education. It is noteworthy that the ninth house is also a house of mass communication and publication within mundane astrology.

## STEP 2a.: ASSESS THE ESSENTIAL DIGNITY OR DEBILITY OF THE QUESITED

The Quesited is in the domicile of Venus, the exaltation of Saturn, the triplicity of Saturn, the term of Saturn, and the face of the Moon. Mercury is not in his detriment or fall. This is an essentially debilitated, peregrine Mercury. Note that even though Mercury is the out-of-sect triplicity ruler, Mercury does not receive points of essential dignity.

The peregrine Quesited may be an indication that the publisher was also in a state of confusion. The publisher could have been navigating circumstances that left them feeling quite lost. A peregrine planet is one that finds itself in an overwhelming set of circumstances that aren't its normal, familiar territory. Both of these peregrine planets do not seem very capable of doing much for each other.

## STEP 2b: ASSESS THE ACCIDENTAL FORTITUDE OR DEBILITY OF THE QUESITED

Essentially debilitated Mercury is accidentally debilitated in the cadent ninth house. Being in the ninth house is technically an accidental fortitude. However, as stated previously, I prefer to only consider this a fortification for planets that are already essentially dignified. Mercury is peregrine; one of the worst conditions of essential debility that exist. It is not being received by its ruler, Venus, and it has no power of its own. Mercury can't take advantage of the bounty that the ninth house has to offer. The state of his condition doesn't correspond with that bounty. Therefore, he amplifies the quality of the ninth house that is most correspondent with his own weak state: the cadency of the ninth house. The Quesited isn't in a strong condition at all.

## STEP 3: LOCATE THE MOON

The Moon is at 18° LIB 06' in the tenth house of mother and career.

## STEP 3a.: ASSESS THE ESSENTIAL DIGNITY OR DEBILITY OF THE MOON

The Moon is in the domicile of Venus, the exaltation of Saturn, the triplicity of Saturn, the term of Jupiter, and the face of Saturn. The Moon is not in her detriment or fall. This is an essentially debilitated, peregrine Moon.

At this point, we see a theme emerging. The Querent is peregrine, the Quesited is peregrine, and the Moon is peregrine. Everyone in this situation seems lost and confused. None of them seem equipped to do any amount of good for each other. The peregrine Moon indicates that the very psychic undercurrent upon which this situation is built is confusing, overwhelming, and unlikely to end well for the parties concerned.

### STEP 3b: ASSESS THE ACCIDENTAL FORTITUDE OR DEBILITY OF THE MOON

The Moon is in the benefic, angular tenth house. The Querent was eager to know how working with this particular publisher would impact his career. Since this was his first book, he was concerned with how working with any publisher at all would further the recognition of his work within the world. Therefore, the Moon in the tenth was a very appropriate indication that represented what truly was most present within his heart.

### STEP 4: OTHER NOTEWORTHY CONSIDERATIONS

One thing worth noting is that Neptune is squaring the Ascendant. This can indicate that this entire situation is one that will lead to disillusionment and disappointment for the Querent in the end. Neptune in the third house afflicting the Ascendant corresponded with the fact that the world of publishing was completely foreign and confusing to him. It felt like he was moving through a fog. He didn't have the opportunity to see clearly based on his inexperience in this field.

Jupiter rules the first, third, and twelfth houses. The Querent's desire to get this third house writing and publishing finalized, may lead to twelfth house regret and silent suffering if he chose to continue with this particular publisher.

The publisher also ruled their own third house (the radical ninth house) and their own twelfth house (the radical sixth house). The publisher might also find themselves regretting their decision to work with this author in the end. Maybe it represented one project too many. Maybe they were pushing themselves beyond their realistic edge, which is a very twelfth house thing to do.

Pluto in the first house could represent the Querent experiencing a great amount of pressure to make a decision. He may have been running out of realistic options quickly. Pluto was also parallel the Ascendant. This amplifies the level of pressure he was under to make a decision.

The Quesited is parallel Neptune. This may indicate that the Querent would be wise not to rely too heavily on this publisher. The publisher may be trying to navigate their own Neptunian confusion while simultaneous attempting to publish this book for the Querent.

The Moon is in the Via Combusta. The most commonly accepted range for the Via Combusta is 15° LIB to 15° Scorpio. When the Moon is in the Via Combusta, she is in a highly challenging state. It is a universally negative omen regarding whatever the Querent is asking about. The Via Combusta is associated with pain, hardship, suffering, and destruction. From an omen-based perspective, this does not bode well for the relationship the Querent is seeking to establish with the Quesited.

STEP 5: ASPECTS BETWEEN THE SIGNIFICATORS

Mercury is applying to the opposition of Jupiter within 02° of arc. Jupiter, by retrograde motion, is equally applying to the opposition of Mercury. This represents a very difficult relationship between the two of them. There isn't the opportunity for either of them to feel truly satisfied. Furthermore, there is no reception between these significators to ease the challenges that will manifest through their working relationship. Guido Bonatti writes:

> *Those things which come to be with the greatest labor, and obstacles, and striving and effort and distress, likewise sadness, and as though after the desperation of friends and blood relations, and yet hardly or never perfect (and if they were perfected their effect will be slow for a long time, even then with expenses) – are those in which the Lord of the Ascendant (or the Moon) and the Lord of the quaesited matter, are joined by opposition without reception.*

It does not look as if they would have had a happy union.

STEP 6: FINAL JUDGMENT

The author and this particular publisher should not work together.

CONCLUSION:

Clearly this is my own horary chart. This represents one of several professional relationships along the path of publishing this book that did not work out in the end. Upon delineating this chart, it was probably for the best.

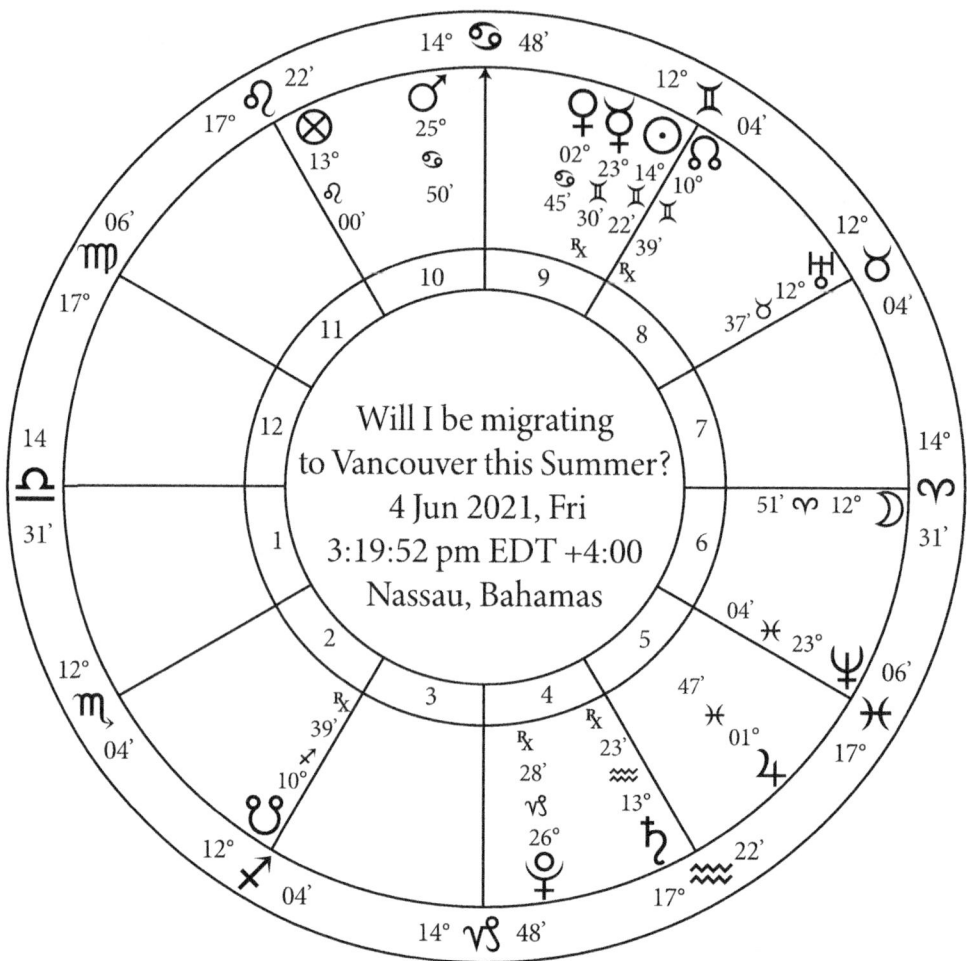

FIGURE 4. *Migration Horary*

## Case Study 4:
### Will I be moving to Vancouver this Summer?

*This is another removal-style horary. In it, I also deviated from the traditional method of assessing the seventh house as the place to which the Querent desired to remove. This is because his question wasn't "Shall I remove?". He was very convinced that he was relocating to Vancouver, and wanted to know whether or not it would be happening in the Summer. Therefore, I looked for the answer to this question through an assessment of the first house of the Querent and the ninth house of foreign travel.*

STEP 1: IDENTIFY THE QUERENT.

Since we have 14° LIB 31' rising, the Querent is represented by the ruler of the ASC: Venus. Venus in this chart is 02° CAN 45' in the ninth house of foreign travel and higher education.

STEP 1a.: ASSESS THE ESSENTIAL DIGNITY OR DEBILITY OF THE QUERENT

Venus is in the domicile of the Moon, the exaltation of Jupiter, the triplicity of Venus, the term of Mars, and the face of Venus. Venus is not in her detriment or fall. This is an essentially dignified Venus.

Venus in her own triplicity means that the Querent is relatively comfortable in his current situation. He could possibly be doing better. However, he feels at ease in the decision he currently wants to make regarding moving to Vancouver.

Venus is also in her own face. Usually, a planet being in their own face represents that planet operating from a state of desperation. However, the combined dignities of triplicity and face rulership could indicate the Querent feeling strongly about his decision to migrate.

STEP 1b: ASSESS THE ACCIDENTAL FORTITUDE OR DEBILITY OF THE QUERENT

Essentially dignified Venus is accidentally fortified in the ninth house. Though the ninth house is a cadent house, it is benefic because of its trine relationship to the Ascendant. It also corresponds with the thing the Querent is asking about: his possible migration to a foreign country. Environmentally, this Querent is supported in his decision to move abroad.

STEP 2: IDENTIFY THE QUESITED

The Quesited is Mercury 23° GEM 30', RX, in the ninth house of foreign travel and higher education.

STEP 2a.: ASSESS THE ESSENTIAL DIGNITY OR DEBILITY OF THE QUESITED

The Quesited is in his domicile, the exaltation of no one, the triplicity of Saturn, the term of Saturn, and the face of the Sun. Mercury is not in his detriment or fall. This is an essentially dignified Mercury.

Usually, this would be very good news. It frames this foreign city in a very positive light. A planet in his own domicile typically can support himself as well as other people who depend on him. However, there are other things occurring with this Mercury that are preventing him from being able to host our Querent any time soon.

STEP 2b: ASSESS THE ACCIDENTAL FORTITUDE OR DEBILITY OF THE QUESITED

Essentially dignified Mercury is accidentally fortified in the benefic, cadent ninth house. However, he is retrograde. This denies him the ability to take advantage of the strength he receives by being in the ninth. In *Bethem's Centilo-quium*, we read:

*A planet retrograde is like a man infirm, stupefied and solicitous.*

Vancouver seems to be doing great on the surface due to the essential dignity of Mercury. Nevertheless, the retrogradation may represent blockages or delays that the Querent is not anticipating. These blockages may be timely, especially if they give him the opportunity to think through his decision more carefully. He may need more time to see whether or not he is in a place to actually make this transition.

### Step 3: Locate the Moon

The Moon is at 12° ARI 51' in the seventh house of marriage and partnership.

### Step 3a.: Assess the Essential Dignity or Debility of the Moon

The Moon is in the domicile of Mars, the exaltation of the Sun, the triplicity of the Sun, the term of Venus, and the face of the Sun. The Moon is not in her detriment or fall. This is an essentially debilitated, peregrine Moon.

Though the Querent may already be "in" Vancouver energetically, his heart may be elsewhere. He may be navigating a period of confusion in his life where he doesn't have the greatest sense of direction. This is symbolized by the peregrine Moon. Therefore, the decision to move to Vancouver may be born out of that confused and directionless state. He may be looking for his place elsewhere because he feels particularly lost in his current location.

### Step 3b: Assess the Accidental Fortitude or Debility of the Moon

The Moon is in the powerful, angular seventh house. An underlying part of his desire to migrate may be his longing for romantic partnership. He may be considering the romantic prospects that he can encounter should he follow through with this move.

### Step 4: Other Noteworthy Considerations

In thinking about a migration, one would imagine that money would be a major factor to consider. The Querent's money is represented by essentially debilitated Mars 25° CAN 50' in fall in the angular tenth house. He may not be in the best financial condition to migrate. Perhaps he needs to take a close look at his personal finances before choosing to follow through with this decision.

Mars is applying to the exact opposition of Pluto in the fourth house. There may be larger things that are making demands on his personal finances. These may need to be attended to first before he can decide whether or not a move is the correct course of action.

Mercury, representing Vancouver, is in an exact dexter square to Neptune in the sixth house. His Vancouver dream may be falling apart right before his eyes because of forces unknown to him. This can represent an oncoming disappointment or a complete dissolving of his Vancouver goal because of confusing circumstances he didn't anticipate. While the city will always be there, his ability to reach out and grasp it may be greatly weakened or diminished.

STEP 5: ASPECTS BETWEEN THE SIGNIFICATORS

There is no aspect between the Querent and the Quesited.

STEP 6: FINAL JUDGMENT

Though the Querent has the desire to move to Vancouver, it does not seem likely for him this Summer.

CONCLUSION:

Once again, the Querent was me. I did not move to Vancouver at all. I moved to Boston.

## CHAPTER 23 QUESTIONS

1. Which house do we customarily begin our delineation from in horary astrology?
3. What do we call the person who is asking a horary question?
4. What does the essential dignity or debility of a significator tell us about that planet?
5. What does the accidental fortitude or debility of a significator tell us about that planet?
6. Why is the Moon considered to be important in horary astrology?

# AFTERWORD

*The object of your quest is God: you are seeking to scale the skies and, though born beneath the rule of fate, to gain knowledge of that fate; you are seeking to pass beyond your understanding and make yourself master of the universe. The toil involved matches the reward to be won, nor are such high attainments secured without a price; so wonder not at the winding route and the intricacy of things. It is enough that we have been given power to make the search: let the rest be left to us... What then shall we give to heaven? How great is the price with which we may purchase all? Man must expend his very self before God can dwell in him. – MARCUS MANILIUS*

IN WRITING A BOOK LIKE THIS, ONE SETS OUT with the intention of putting "first things first." The problem with that goal is that there is a multiplicity of "first things" that one faces in deciding where and how to begin teaching the foundations of classical astrology. It is a far greater task to teach a beginner correctly than it is to teach someone already seasoned within a field. Similar in magnitude is properly teaching traditional astrology to someone who has elected themselves as a beginner, after them having spent years studying and practicing in a purely modern way. Though these may be formidable assessments of one's prowess as a teacher, constructing a book by which beginners can thoroughly teach themselves is the greatest challenge of them all.

As a teacher, I cannot imagine any larger karmic burden than choosing to write an introductory text. The outcome of your experience as the reader of this book is bifurcated. Your reward should be no less than the flowering of a fertile garden of astrological understanding rooted in your grasp of what I have tried to convey within these pages. Mine, however, will be the thorns you have experienced along the way, and the doubts that you may still have – even at the end of us sharing this journey together. While your successes and the achievements you gain from studying this text will be yours and yours alone, I take your misunderstandings as my personal responsibility. Should I have made a mistake, or gone wrong in some way in the organization of this textbook, not only will your uncertainties be mine to bear, but also the doubts of the students of your students. I have considered this within each page of this volume, and to this end, I hope I have done a service to you.

I now extend the question to you, that I ask each of my students at the end of every class: *did you learn something?* Has your understanding been expanded? Do you feel closer to the planetary gods? Do you feel more grounded for having shared this voyage with me? If your answer is "yes" to all of those questions, then my work here will not have been wasted.

Yet still, this is not sufficient. From here, you are meant to seize the sky under which you have been born, which is your divine birthright as a child of that same cosmos. As Manilius tells us, yours is the destiny of becoming master of the universe. However, the mastery you will gain must not be thought of as a dominance over the world around you. Rather, it is a stewardship – a keeping and a caring for the cosmos and every form of life you encounter within it. Your ability to be a celestial steward can only come through divesting yourself of all that gets in the way of God, the infinite, and the light of the cosmos dwelling in you. And there is so much that gets in its way. Pride, covetousness, envy, hatred, racism, war – forgetting how to love each other – all of these things shrink our world and sully our perception of the people within it. These ways of being are all rooted in clinging to the transient states of our material existence as if this tiny world of matter were actually real. Fear of the death that awaits all of us causes many to grasp ferociously onto life and the material symbols of power that we have attained. It is a flawed mode of survival, one that prevents us from living joyfully within the world; one that prevents us from seeing people as they truly are. Locked in a constant survival state, we cannot realize that the light of life, the true celestial splendour of the stars, shines in the eyes and the faces of everyone we meet. Nature takes no shortcuts, and neither will she allow us that privilege. We cannot gain the ability to see the celestial fire of God within others if we cannot first see their humanity. Every woman, every man, every child, every person, every entity within this world is made of the stars. It is only by remembering this that we can begin to see the world as it truly is: radiant and beautiful, wholly composed of light.

As in all things, astrology lights the way. While the next steps you take upon this path may not seem as lofty as "mastering the cosmos," they will most certainly pave the way for that attainment. At the end of this book, you must now take up "your practiced powers and stretch them out" through the practice of concrete astrology. You must take the skills that you have acquired into the actual delineation of charts, a dream I wish to help you attain in the next volume of this series, which will be on horary astrology. From there, we will expand those skills further through natal astrology, and from there into a world of extraordinary practice and discovery. Needless to say, I plan to walk with you for a very long time.

While outlining the steps of our future progress may bring some sense of direction, I do not arrogantly believe it will give you a center of gravity, a reason to keep on going, or the desire to pursue astrology as a professional path. Today, many of us still say that we practice astrology only in our most intimate circles; and even then, it may come with the blush of insecurity and self-doubt. We never truly know how those words will land. We never know whether we will be embraced or ridiculed. Even in being accepted by others, it is highly unlikely that our revelation will register within their minds as us having spent thousands of hours studying and practicing to become proficient at a comprehensive set of skills. Most people who will enthusiastically laud us for our astrological efforts, will have a boundless misunderstanding of what those efforts represent. They may expect us to tell them on the spot what their Sun, Moon, and Rising sign says about their personality. They may say that they, too, are astrologers after having read such-and-such a person's book on Love Signs. Even worse, they may say that after having no astrology practice or genuine education, they teach astrology to others – and supplement that teaching by reading such-and-such a person's book on Love Signs. It would seem as if even amongst likeminded people, we travel very divergent paths. What, then, is the relevance of a skill such as this? In a world that considers astrology to be everything from a fool's errand to a pop cultural moment, to nothing less than the devil's work itself, why should we keep on keeping on?

Astrology continues to be of great importance within an evolving global culture because it is the only real discipline that can help us make sense of our relationship to time. This must be of utmost importance to us since all of our lives are measured in time. Time marks our beginning, and the impact of time upon our bodies will determine our end. Time shows the path of our evolution through the ages as a human race upon this Earth, and time determines how next we might evolve. Time is the only thing that truly impacts our material world. Every war is ripened through time, every love has increased and diminished through time, the callousness that causes us to treat our world as a dead piece of rock has hardened through time, and time will ultimately fashion the final shape of our collective destiny. Understanding time is the only resource we have in order to navigate the tides of futurity.

While not everyone will be called to the service of being a Seer of Time within this world, hopefully you, as a student of astrology, will not turn your back on the task. As an astrologer, your station in life is far greater than reading your best friend's horoscope. The history of our entire species is recorded in the stars. Ours is the job of learning how to decode that stellar history and pass it on to those who come after us, so that the truth of who we are as Star People in a material world will never be lost.

As an astrologer, yours is one of the most important roles that exists in civilization. Every astrologer is charged with the task of studying how the Changeless brings about change within our three-dimensional world, so that we may all grow, evolve, and become wise. I shared this passage with you at the very beginning of this book, yet it seems appropriate to share it with you once more.

> *O that you could grow wings and fly up into the air, and that, poised between earth and heaven, you might see the firmness of the earth, the liquidity of the sea, the course of the rivers and the free flow of the air, the piercing fire, the revolution of the stars, the swiftness of*

*the heavenly movement encircling all these things. What most blessed vision, O son, to behold all that in one moment; the unmoving being moved, the unmanifest being made manifest through what it creates! This is the very order of the universe and this is the beauty of that order.*

The gift of our astrology is no less than the vision described in this passage of Hermes.

Here, at the end of having read and studied this book, you have learnt all of the foundational skills necessary to begin a lifetime of astrological practice and study. May the sky open for you, and may you always drink your fill of the ambrosia of the planetary gods. We can only aspire upward from here, until we find ourselves face-to-face with the source of all beginnings: the Divine Architect that lay behind the veil of matter. I hope to be there by your side.

I look forward to seeing you again on this path, as a friend and as a guide.

May our astrology provide you a road towards finding ultimate freedom. May the stars always hold you in their embrace. May your feet never touch the ground.

# Otzar ha-Milim

## A Treasury of Words

**ANTISCIA**
Antiscia refers to reflection points on either side of the 00 degree Cancer/00 degree Capricorn axis. When a faster moving planet comes to the antiscion of a slower moving planet, those planets are thought to operate just as strongly together as if they were in a conjunction with each other.

**ANAPHORA**
The traditional name of the second house; means "exit from the gates of Hades."

**AFFLICTION**
Any of the conditions that weaken a planet, whether they are celestial (based on sign placement and aspect) or terrestrial (based on house placement).

**ACCIDENTAL FORTITUDE**
Any of the environmental factors that strengthen a planet in its significations and its ability to fulfil its promise within a chart.

**ACCIDENTAL DEBILITY**
Any of the environmental factors that weaken a planet in its significations and in its ability to fulfil its promise within a chart.

**ALMUTEN**
A planet that is strongest within a chart to represent a specific topic, based on weighing that planet against other possible contenders for that role. The almuten of a degree is the planet that has the most points of essential dignity in a particular degree of the zodiac. An almuten of a topic is the planet that is stronger than all the other planets that could represent that topic based on a particular formula. The Almuten of a chart is usually the planet that has the highest points of essential dignity in the chart in general.

**AZIMUTH**
Refers to measurement along the plane of the local horizon. The starting point of this measurement is 00 North.

**ALTITUDE**
Refers to measurement North or South of the Local horizon.

**ASTROLOGY**
The study of time, destiny, and the cosmos. Astrology is the study of how planetary influences in each moment both reflect and describe correspondent events that occur on Earth.

**ASPECT**
The angular relationship between two planets. There are 4 aspects in Traditional Astrology: the 60 degree sextile, the 90 degree square, the 120 degree trine, and the 180 degree opposition.

**ARC OPENING**
An Arc opening usually refers to the specific distance between two planets when we measure that distance on the ecliptic. For example, a planet at 01 degree Taurus and another at 10 degrees Taurus have a 09 degree arc opening between them. Every aspect represents a specific arc opening between two or more planets.

**BENEFIC**
A benefic is a planet that is inherently predisposed to doing good. In Traditional Astrology, Jupiter is the Greater Benefic and Venus is the Lesser Benefic. They are both considered to be benefic because their internal constitution is hot and wet, or sanguine. Since these qualities are also considered to be the fundamental qualities of Earth, our bodies, and of life in general, these planets were thought to be supporters of life. The Moon is also considered to be benefic for this same reason in the philosophy of Claudius Ptolemy.

**BESIEGEMENT**
This refers to when a planet is either between the hard aspect or the bodies of two malefic planets. For example if one planet separates from the conjunction of one malefic planet and applies to the square of another malefic planet, this is besiegement. If one planet has separated from the square of a malefic and applies to the square of another malefic, this is besiegement. Another example could be if one planet separates from the conjunction of one malefic planet and applies to the conjunction of another malefic planet. In all of these examples, the besieged planet is considered to be between "a rock and a hard place", trapped between two evils.

**COMBUST**
This refers to when a planet is within 00° 17' 01" to 08° 30' of the Sun, on both sides. This is considered to be one of the greatest afflictions that can occur to a

planet and literally means that the planet is "burnt up" or destroyed by the rays of the Sun.

## CAZIMI

This refers to when a planet is within 00-17 minutes of the Sun on either side. This is considered to be one of the greatest blessings that can occur to a planet. It is similar to "sitting in the lap of the king" and therefore being under his protection.

## CONJUNCTION

A planetary relationship in which two or more planets occupy the same degree of the zodiac. This is mistakenly thought of as an aspect, though it is not. In an aspect there is an angular distance between two or more planets. In a conjunction there is no distance, therefore there is no angular relationship. A conjunction is technically not an aspect. However, for convenience, it is usually counted amongst the other four aspects in Traditional Astrology.

## CONTRARIETY OF HAYZ

This refers to when a planet is completely unsupported by sect. An example of this would be if a nocturnal planet were in a diurnal chart, in a diurnal sign, above the horizon.

## DEXTER

Means "from the right". This refers to when a faster moving planet is aspecting a slower moving planet that is "behind" it in the zodiac. In other words, the faster moving planet has to send its aspect rays "backward" in the zodiac in order to make the aspect. For example, if Mars were at 09 Cancer and Saturn were at 10 Aries, Mars would be in an applying dexter square with Saturn. See Sinister.

## DOMICILE

This refers to signs of the zodiac that are the property or unconditional homes of certain planets. The domiciles of Saturn are Capricorn and Aquarius; Jupiter, Sagittarius and Pisces; Mars, Aries and Scorpio; Sun, Leo; Venus, Taurus and Libra; Mercury, Gemini and Virgo; and Moon, Cancer.

## DETRIMENT

Refers to signs that are opposite the domiciles of the planets. When a planet is in the sign that is opposite to its domicile, that planet is said to be in its detriment.

## DETERMINATION

This refers to the specific purpose a planet is meant to fulfil within a given chart. A planet may have a universal determination to produce good or evil. Saturn and Mars have a universal determination to produce evil, however, if either of them is the ruler of the third house, their specific determination will be to signify the siblings of the person to whom the chart belongs.

## DEBILITY
Refers to anything that weakens a planet. An essential debility refers to a planet being weakened because it is in a sign of the zodiac that is harmful to it. When a planet is essentially debilitated it is either in its detriment, fall, or peregrine. Accidental debility refers to any number of things that can cause a planet to be harmed, including evil aspects from evil planets, being in bad houses, retrogradation, etc.

## EXALTATION
One of the five levels of essential dignity, that also happens to be one of the strongest. When a planet is exalted, it is elevated, strong, and capable of delivering on its role within a chart.

## ECLIPTIC
The apparent path of the Sun around the Earth from our geocentric perspective. In fact, it is the path of the Earth around the Sun from an objective, heliocentric perspective.

## ECLIPTIC LATITUDE
Refers to measurement North or South of the Ecliptic.

## ECLIPTIC POLES
Either point at the end of an imaginary line that is perpendicular to the plane of the ecliptic, not to be mistaken with the equatorial poles of the Earth that are perpendicular to the Equator.

## EQUATOR
The Great Circle that divides the Earth into the North and South terrestrial hemispheres. It is exactly perpendicular to the North and South Poles.

## EQUINOX
Refers to the first moment of Spring and Autumn, when the day and the night are equal. This occurs when the Sun ingresses into the signs Aries and Libra, respectively.

## FACE
The three 10 degree divisions of the signs of the zodiac, ruled over by the planets in the Chaldean Order starting with Mars ruling the first face of Aries. This represents the lowest level of essential dignity. When a planet only has dignity by face, it is hanging on by threads in order to find power in the particular zodiac sign in which it is located.

**FORTITUDE**

Any of the environmental factors that strengthen or bolster the power and support that a planet has in order to fulfil its promise. These can include angularity, positive aspects from benefic planets, being conjunct benefic fixed stars, being swift in motion, etc.

**HAYZ**

This refers to when a planet is completely supported by sect. An example of this would be if a diurnal planet were in a diurnal chart, in a diurnal sign, above the horizon. See Contrariety of hayz.

**INGRESS**

Refers to the entrance of any planet into a sign. Usually, this term is specifically used for the entrance of the Sun into any of the four moveable/Cardinal signs: Aries, Cancer, Libra, and Capricorn.

**JUDGEMENT**

The most astrologically sound conclusion an Astrologer can come to about the outcome of something indicated by a chart after a complete analysis of all the factors involved.

**MALEFIC**

A planet that is inherently predisposed to the creation of harm or evil within the world. Saturn and Mars are considered to be the Greater and the Lesser Malefics specifically because of the intemperate qualities that make up their constitution. Saturn is intemperately cold and dry. Mars is intemperately hot and dry. Neither of these planets are supports of human life. Because of the Sun's quality of burning things, he was thought to be malefic by bodily conjunction, but benefic by positive aspect. The Moon was considered to be malefic in her waning, but benefic in her waxing. And Mercury could go in either direction, being good with good planets or bad with bad planets.

**MOIETY**

Refers to half of a planet's orb.

**ORB**

Refers to the full circumference of influence that a planet has both in front and behind it in the zodiac.

**OBLIQUITY**

Refers to the 23.5 degree tilt of the Earth on its axis.

**OUT-OF-BOUNDS**
When a planet is out-of-bounds, it is either north of south of the Equator and beyond the 23.5 degree boundary established by the ecliptic in relation to the Equator.

**PEREGRINE**
Refers to when a planet has absolutely no form of essential dignity in the sign of the zodiac in which it finds itself. It is one of the worst forms of essential debility.

**QUERENT**
A person who asks a question that they intend to be answered by a divinatory means. The specific title of the questioner in Horary Astrology.

**QUESITED**
The specific title of the thing that a person is asking about in Horary Astrology.

**QUADRUPLICITY**
A division of the signs of the zodiac based on the portion of the 4 seasons that those signs correspond with, beginning, middle, or end. Moveable or Cardinal signs correspond with the beginning of the season, Immoveable or Fixed signs correspond with the middle of the season, and Common/Double-Bodied/Mutable signs correspond with the end of a season.

**RETROGRADE**
Refers to when a planet appears to be moving backward in the zodiac. This is considered to be one of the worst afflictions of a planet from a traditional perspective.

**STATION RETROGRADE**
The apparent standstill that a planet comes to before it begins its retrograde motion.

**STATION DIRECT**
The apparent standstill that a planet comes to before it begins its direct motion after having been retrograde.

**VOID-OF-COURSE**
When a planet has made the final aspect it will make in a sign before it ingresses into another sign. This frequently happens to the Moon.

**VERNAL EQUINOX**
The first day (and moment) of Spring when the Sun ingresses into Aries, roughly around March 21 each year.

## WINTER SOLSTICE
The first day (and moment) of Winter when the Sun ingresses into Capricorn, roughly around December 21 each year.

## TRADITIONAL ASTROLOGY
A body of astrological teachings that correspond with how the ancients practiced at least 2,000 years ago. Some of its distinguishing factors are: the use of only the seven classical planets as the rulers of the signs of the zodiac, the distinction between sign meanings and house meanings, and giving planets (as opposed to aspects) an orb of influence.

## PLANET
One of the ten celestial bodies that are used within Astrology. These include the seven classical planets: Saturn, Jupiter, Mars, Sun, Venus, Mercury, and the Moon. In our Neo-Classical Astrology we also include the three modern planets: Uranus, Neptune, and Pluto.

## SIGNIFICATOR
A celestial body/factor that represents a terrestrial concept such as a person, place, or thing. Saturn for example is a universal significator for elderly men (people), graveyards (place), and the metal lead (thing).

## GEOCOSMIC
Our subjective perspective of the cosmos from Earth. This point of view places Earth in the center of the cosmos. In a geocentric model, the planets revolve around the Earth.

## HELIOCENTRIC
An objective perspective of the cosmos from the Sun. This point of view places the Sun in the center of the cosmos. In a heliocentric model, the planets revolve around the Sun.

## RULERSHIP
One of five ways in which a planet can have dominion in a sign of the zodiac. The five levels of rulership are: domicile rulership, exaltation rulership, triplicity rulership, term/bound rulership, and face rulership. Refers to any number of ways a planet can be the primary ruler (domicile ruler) over an entire sign of the zodiac, or a partial ruler overt a specific segment of a sign, or of a sign at a particular time of day. For example, Mars is the domicile ruler of Aries unconditionally. However, Venus specifically rules the last 10 degrees of Aries, and Jupiter is thought to rule all fire signs, including Aries in the night. This doesn't change the fact that Mars is still the primary ruler of Aries. However, in Traditional Astrology, there are multiple levels of rulership. See Essential Dignity.

## Essential Dignity

This refers to the level of intrinsic power a planet has to express itself and carry out its promised tasks within a specific chart. Planets are considered to be intrinsically strong or weak based on where we find them in the zodiac. If a planet has rulership in a particular sign of the zodiac in which we find it, that planet is considered to be strong, based on how much power is allotted to the level of rulership it has. A planet in its own domicile receives +5 points of dignity/power; exaltation receives +4 points of dignity/power, triplicity receives +3 points of dignity/power; term receives +2 points of dignity/power; and face receives +1 point of dignity/power. See Rulership.

## Zodiac

The band of twelve signs that serve as the backdrop upon which we project the Suns orbital path. In Tropical Astrology, we can also view the zodiac as being a twelvefold division of the ecliptic itself, that allows us to make sense of where the planets are in reference to the path and speed of the Sun.

# BIBLIOGRAPHY

ADAMS, EVANGELINE. *Astrology: Your Place in the Sun.* New York: Dodd, Mead & Company, 1928.

AGRIPPA, HENRY CORNELIUS. *Fourth Book of Occult Philosophy.* Translated by Robert Turner. London: Askin Publishers, 1978.

ALEXANDRINUS, PAULUS. *Late Classical Astrology: Paulus Alexandrinus and Olympiodorus.* Translated by Dorian Gieseler Greenbaum, (M. A.). ARHAT Publications.

ALLEN, REGINALD E. *Greek Philosophy: Thales to Aristotle.* New York: Simon & Schuster,1991.

APIANUS, PETER. *Cosmographia.* Paris, France: *væneunt apud Viuantium Gaultherot, via Iacobea: sub intersignio D. Martini.* 1553.

BISHR, SAHL IBN. *The Astrology of Sahl b. Bishr: Volume I: Principles, Elections, Questions, Nativities.* Translated by Benjamin N. Dykes. Minneapolis: Cazimi Press, 2019.

BISHR, SAHL IBN, MASHA'ALLAH. *Works of Sahl & Masha'allah.* Translated by Benjamin N. Dykes. Minneapolis: Cazimi Press, 2008.

BÖHME, JACOB. *De Signatura Rerum (The Signature of All Things).* London: John Maycock, 1652.

BONATTI, GUIDO. Liber Astronomiae Part I. Translated by Robert Zoller, edited by Robert Hand. Berkeley Springs, WV: The Golden Hind Press, 1994.

BONATTI, GUIDO. *On Basic Astrology.* Translated by Dr. Benjamin N. Dykes, PhD. Minneapolis, MN: Cazimi Press, 2010.

BURNET, JOHN. *Early Greek Philosophy.* London: A. & C. Black, 1920.

568

CARTER, CHARLES E. O. *An Introduction to Political Astrology.* London, UK: L.N. Fowler & Co Ltd, 1951.

CASE, PAUL FOSTER. *Hermetic Alchemy: Science and Practice.* Boston, MA: The School of Ageless Wisdom, 1931.

COELHO, PAULO. *O Alquimista.* Rio de Janeiro, Brazil: Editora Rocco Ltd., 1988.

COLEY, HENRY. *Clavis Astrologiae Elimata: or a Key to the whole Art of Astrology.* London: 1676.

CULPEPER, NICHOLAS. *Opus Astrologicum, or An Astrological Work Left to Posterity.* London, J. Cottrel, 1654.

DARIOT, CLAUDIUS. *A Briefe and Most Easie Introduction to the Astrologicall Judgement of the Starres.* London: Printed by Thomas Purfoot, 1598.

EBERTIN, REINHOLD. The Combination of Stellar Influences. Translated by Alfred G. Roosedale and Linda Kratzch. Tempe, Arizona: American Federation of Astrologers, Inc., 1972.

EVOLA, JULIUS. *The Hermetic Tradition: Symbols and Teachings of the Royal Art.* Rochester, VT: Inner Traditions, 1995.

EPSTEIN, MEIRA. *Sefer Yetzirah: Translation, Transliteration and Commentary, with Special Attention to the Underlying Philosophical Origins, Ancient Jewish Mysticism, Cosmology and Astrology.* New York, NY: 2018.

IBN EZRA, ABRAHAM. *The Beginning of Wisdom.* Translated by Meira Epstein. ARHAT Publications, 1998.

GADBURY, JOHN. *The Doctrine of Nativities, Together with The Doctrine of Horarie Questions.* London: Printed by Ja. Cottrel, 1658.

HOLDEN, JAMES HERSCHEL. *A History of Horoscopic Astrology.* Tempe, AZ: American Federation of Astrologers, 2006.

HOLDEN, JAMES HERSCHEL. *Six Astrological Treatises by Masha'allah.* Tempe, AZ: American Federation of Astrologers, 2009.

HONE, MARGARET C. *Textbook of Modern Astrology.* London, UK: L.N. Fowler & Co Ltd, 1954.

JANSKY, ROBERT CARL. *Interpreting the Eclipses.* First published 1979. Bel Air, MD: Astrology Classics, 2013.

LILLY, WILLIAM. *Christian Astrology, Second Edition.* Originally printed in 1647. John Macock, London: 1659.

MANILIUS, MARCUS. *Astronomica.* Translated by G. P. Goold. Great Britain: 1977.

MAʿŠAR, ABŪ. *The Great Introduction to Astrology: Volume I, The Arabic Original and English Translation.* Edited and translated by Keiji Yamamoto and Charles Burnett. Boston, MA: Brill, 2019.

MAʿŠAR, ABŪ, AL-QABISI. *Introductions to Traditional Astrology.* Translated by Benjamin N. Dykes. Minneapolis: Cazimi Press, 2010.

OMAR OF TIBERIAS. *Three Books on Nativities.* Translated by Robert Hand. Berkeley Springs, WV: The Golden Hind Press, 1997.

PANNEKOEK, ANTON. *A History of Astronomy.* New York: Dover Publications, 1961.

PARACELSUS. *The Hermetic and Alchemical Writings of Paracelsus.* Translated by Arthur Edward Waite. London: James Elliot & Co., 1910.

PRABHUPADA, ABHAY C. *Bhagavad Gita.* Mumbai: Bhaktivedanta Book Trust, 1997.

PTOLEMY, CLAUDIUS. *Tetrabiblos or Quadripartite being Four Books of the Influence of the Stars.* Translated by J. M. Ashmand. 1822.

PYTHAGORAS. *The Golden Verses of Pythagoras: And Other Pythagorean Fragments.* Forgotten Books, 2007.

RAPHAEL. *Raphael's Mundane Astrology or The Effects of the Planets and Signs Upon the Nations and Countries of the World.* Marlow, UK: W. Foulsham, 1910.

RAMESEY, WILLIAM. *Astrologia Restaurata; or Astrologie Restored: Being an Introduction to the General and Chief part of the Language of the Stars.* London: 1653.

RHETORIUS. *Rhetorius the Egyptian.* Translated by James Herschel Holden. Tempe, AZ: American Federation of Astrologers, 2009.

SALAMAN, C., VAN OYEN, D., Wharton W. D., Mahe, J. *The Way of Hermes, New Translations of The Corpus Hermeticum and the Definitions of Hermes Trismegis-*

*tus to Asclepius.* Rochester, Vermont: Inner Traditions, 2000.

SAUNDERS, RICHARD. *The Astrological Judgment and Practice of Physick.* London: 1677.

SCHÖNER, JOHANNES. *On the Judgments of Nativities.* Translated by Robert Hand. ARHAT Publications.

SIBLY, EBENEZER. *A New and Complete Illustration of the Celestial Science of Astrology; or the Art of foretelling future Events and Contingencies, by the Aspects, Positions, and Influences, of the Heavenly Bodies.* London, 1826.

SIDON, DOROTHEUS OF. *Carmen Astrologicum: The 'Umar al-Tabari Translation.* Translated by Benjamin N. Dykes. Minneapolis: Cazimi Press, 2017.

STROHMEIER, JOHN; WESTBROOK, PETER. *Divine Harmony: The Life and Teachings of Pythagoras.* Harmonia Books, 2012.

WATTERS, BARBARA H. *Horary Astrology and the Judgment of Events.* Valhalla Paperbacks, Ltd., 1973.

# INDEX

motion: primary
- retrograde. *See* planetary
motion: retrograde
- secondary. *See* planetary
motion: secondary
- zodiacal. *See* planetary
motion: zodiacal
moveable signs. *See under* zodiac:
quadruplicities
Müller von Königsberg, Johann, 93
mundane astrology, 47-48, **55**, 56,
131, 473, 482, 524, 570; houses in,
437, 546-547
mundane chart, 10, 14
mutable signs. *See under* zodiac:
quadruplicities
mutual reception. *See*
reception: mutual
mystic rectangle. *See under*
aspect patterns
mythology: ancient. *See* god(s);
goddess(es); Greek mythology;
Roman mythology; *and under names
of individual planets*

**N**

nadir, 104-105, 108, 131-132, 453
natal astrology, xxiii, 47-51, 53-56,
178, 200, 203-204, 208, 238, 259, 276,
349, 387, 390; houses in, 437, 446,
461, 473-474, 481, 506, 519, 556
natal chart. *See* nativity or nativities
nativity or nativities, 1, 7, 11, 14, 34,
43-45, 47, 50, 52-54, 131, 179, 201,
208, 214, 274, 297, 388, 390, 442-443,
446, 481, 482, 496, 528, 568-571;
houses in, 437, 471
Neptune, 3, 23, 80, 82, 151-153, 179,
**182-184**, 201, 566
    absence of domicile rulership, 89
    anatomical correspondences, 182
    ancient mythology, 189

as factor of depletion, 176, 183
discovery, 82
glyph, xvi, 82
house placement: example, 548
in conjunction: examples, 540-541
in hard aspect: example, 399
in horary astrology: examples,
540-541, 548, 552-553
in quincunx: example, 540
in parallel: example, 548
in square: examples, 540, 548,
552-553
orb, 244
orbital period, 182
professions, 182, 184
psychology, 183-184
retrograde motion, 23
sign placement, 389
significations, 151, 183
speed of motion, 182, 249, 503
wet, 183
New Moon. *See under* Moon Phases
newspaper horoscopes, 1
Noah, 43
nocturnal:
    chart, 22-23, 178, 195, 284, 286-
    287, 329, 331-336, 340-341, 346,
    420-422, 424-430, 432, 539
    elements. *See under* zodiac:
    elements or triplicities
    planets. *See under* planets: types
    and terminology
    sect. *See under* dignities: types
    and terminology
    signs. *See under* zodiac signs:
    types and terminology
    triplicity rulers. *See under*
    dignities: types and terminology
nodes, Moon's: *See* Moon's Nodes
*and* planetary nodes
nonagon. *See* novile *under* aspects:
types and terminology
Northern Bending. *See*

# T

Printed in Great Britain
by Amazon

25551247R10357